THE HATCH AND BROOD OF TIME

Documentary evidence supporting this study
appears in a separate volume, published in 1985.

THE HATCH
AND
BROOD OF TIME

A study of the first generation
of native-born white Australians
1788-1828

Volume One

Portia Robinson

Melbourne
OXFORD UNIVERSITY PRESS
Oxford Auckland New York

OXFORD UNIVERSITY PRESS

Oxford London New York Toronto Delhi
Bombay Calcutta Madras Karachi
Kuala Lumpur Singapore Hong Kong
Tokyo Nairobi Dar es Salaam Cape Town
Melbourne Auckland
and associates in
Beirut Berlin Ibadan Mexico City Nicosia

National Library of Australia
Cataloguing-in-Publication data:

Robinson, Portia.
    The hatch and brood of time. A study of the first
    generation of native-born white Australians 1788–1828.

    Bibliography.
    Includes index.
    ISBN 0 19 554497 8.
    ISBN 0 19 554569 9. (set).

    1. Australia—Social conditions—1788–1851.
    I. Title.   II. Title: A study of the first generation of
    native-born white Australians 1788–1828.

994.02

Typeset by Asco Trade Typesetting Ltd, Hong Kong
Printed in Hong Kong
Published by Oxford University Press,
7 Bowen Crescent, Melbourne

CONTENTS

Contemporary terms and expressions   vii
Conversion table   viii
Abbreviations used in the text   ix
Acknowledgements   xi
Preface   xiii

INTRODUCTION   'The Hatch and Brood of Time'   1

CHAPTER ONE   'The seeds and weak beginnings'   21
The Australian children at Botany Bay; origins and parentage of the colony's children, New South Wales, 1788–1813.

CHAPTER TWO   'The observ'd'   39
British parents, colonial children; contemporary assumptions; the nature of penal society at Botany Bay.

CHAPTER THREE   'I am not for marrying'   63
British mothers and colonial children; family influence and example, New South Wales, 1788–1813; the contemporary assumptions.
The nature and structure of female society in New South Wales, the role and contribution of the 'convict' mothers.

CHAPTER FOUR   'The nature of the times deceas'd'   97
British fathers, colonial sons: the rural families, New South Wales, 1788–1813.

CHAPTER FIVE   'The hope and staff of the colony'   119
British parents, colonial children: the 'town' children; colonial attitudes towards child labour; the nature and origins of colonial apprenticeships; the colonial apprentices.

CHAPTER SIX   The first Matildas   145
The currency lasses: daughters, wives and working women; female society and family life, New South Wales, 1788–1828.

CHAPTER SEVEN   'The lads of industrious habits'   177
The native-born farmers and landholders; contemporary assumptions, attitudes, opinions; parentage—the sons of the fathers; the native-born landholders, New South Wales, 1828.

CHAPTER EIGHT   'Artisans ... that useful class of persons'   205
The native-born tradesmen; colonial mechanics and skilled workmen; the nature of skilled labour in New South Wales.

CHAPTER NINE   The stout lads   235
The native-born seafarers; contemporary assumptions; the 'landlubbers'.

CHAPTER TEN   'The art or trade of the worker'   257
The native-born; the unskilled land-workers, labourers, servants.
The 'literate' and government-employed schoolteachers, clerks, constables.
The self-employed; 'professionals', publicans.

EPILOGUE   'To be a Pilgrim'   281

References   283
Bibliography   315
Index A: Select list of Memorials and Petitions   347
Index B: Persons mentioned in the text   350
Index C: Occupations in New South Wales   361
Index D: General subject   364

Note:

Appendixes cited in the text appear in a separate volume of documentary evidence, published in 1985.

CONTEMPORARY TERMS AND EXPRESSION

Native-born (B.C.)	Born in the Colony of New South Wales.
Colonial born (C.B.)	Born in the Colony.
Came free (C.F.)	Arrived in the colony unconvicted; either free settler or official.
Convict (C.)	Man or woman convicted in Britain of a major statutory offence and transported to New South Wales or Van Diemen's Land for a term of penal servitude. Note that a few convicts were convicted in India and other parts of the Empire. A convict was one under the sentence of the law.
Government Servant (G.S.)	A convict assigned either to Government or a private master/mistress.
Ticket-of-leave (T.L.)	A convict permitted, under certain conditions, to work for and support himself/herself while under sentence of the law.
Free by servitude (F.S.)	Man or woman who had served their sentence. Technically free, they could leave the Colony.
Absolute Pardon (A.P.)	Man or woman, pardoned absolutely. Could leave the Colony at any time.
Conditional Pardon (C.P.)	Man or woman, pardoned and technically free, but unable to leave the colony until the expiration of the original sentence.
Free (F.)	This could mean free by pardon or servitude, or free by birth. Occasionally used by those who had arrived free, sometimes as soldiers.
Assigned Servant (A.S.)	Man or woman convict whose services were assigned to a private individual or to Government.
Emancipist	Man or woman convict who had been emancipated, i.e., pardoned, either conditionally or absolutely. Note that this term was used loosely to describe an ex-convict. In this book, emancipist denotes a pardoned convict. Convict at all times refers to those under sentence.
Government	Contemporaries referred to 'Government', i.e., the colonial administrative authority; also Government, the employer of labour. ('He was employed by Government'.) It is used in this form in this book.

'Rising Generation'	The native-born as described by Samuel Marsden, Governors Hunter and King and others.
Concubine	The term used by Marsden to describe the female partner in de facto or other common law 'marriages'. Marsden referred to these as 'Unblessed Unions'.
Loss of character	To be dismissed for criminal or immoral acts. Pregnancy out of wedlock led to 'loss of character'.
'Of the first water'	Men and woman considered to be from the highest social level.
Climbing Boys	Chimney-sweeps.

Note: Variant spelling of surnames was common. As contemporaries were inconsistent, spellings of proper nouns in this book are taken from the immediate reference. Contemporary words and expressions are used throughout this book. Those who arrived unconvicted are described as 'came free'.

CONVERSION TABLE

Imperial measurements have been retained in the text in the interests of historical accuracy and common sense. The following are approximate conversions.

1 inch	2.5 centimetres
1 foot	0.3 metre
1 yard	0.9 metre
1 mile	1.6 kilometres
1 acre	0.4 hectare
£1	$2
1s	10¢
1d	.8¢
1 gallon	4.5 litres
1 ounce	28 grams
1 pound	450 grams
1 ton	1 tonne

ABBREVIATIONS USED IN THE TEXT

CIVIL CONDITION

B.C.	Native-born
B.C.	Born in the Colony
C.B.	Colonial Born
C.F.	Came Free
F.S.	Free by Servitude
A.P.	Absolute Pardon
C.P.	Conditional Pardon
G.S.	Government Servant
C.	Convict
Ex-C.	Ex-Convict
T.L.	Ticket-of-Leave
F.	Free

ABBREVIATIONS IN TABLES

b.	born
bapt.	baptized
dau.	daughter
m.	married
d.	died
w.	widow/widower
bro.	brother
sis.	sister

RELIGION

P. or Prot.	Protestant
C. or Cat.	Catholic
Presby.	Presbyterian
J.	Jew

SOURCES

Col. Sec.	Colonial Secretary
C.S.I.L	Colonial Secretary In-Letters
P.M.S.	Petition in Mitigation of Sentence
Mem. or M.	Memorial
W.O.	War Office
H.O.	Home Office
H.R.A.	Historical Records of Australia
H.R.N.S.W.	Historical Records of New South Wales
M.L.	Mitchell Library, Sydney
A.O.N.S.W.	Archives Office of New South Wales
N.L.A.	National Library of Australia

Note that abbreviations for names of persons are as used in the contemporary source.

N.R.	indicates No Response.

For R.W.R.

ACKNOWLEDGEMENTS

The Hatch and Brood of Time is the first volume in a planned series of investigations into the nature of colonial society. I am grateful for the generosity of the University of Sydney, whose offer of a Studentship for Ph.D. research enabled this work on the first Australians to be completed. It was accepted by that University for the degree of Doctor of Philosophy in 1982. I am grateful for the patience, support and encouragement of the University of Sydney and of my thesis supervisor, Associate-Professor B.H. Fletcher, during the many years it took to reach this present stage.

I alone am responsible for the way in which I have researched the first forty years of white settlement. I am responsible for the assumptions I have made, the conclusions I have drawn. I am very conscious of the contribution of colleagues, family and friends, who have listened to my ideas, commented—not always favourably, but sympathetically—and encouraged the continuance of a task which seemed without end. My debt to Professor Manning Clark is great. Professor B.E. Mansfield, who first showed me the fascination of the past, and Professor J.M. Ward have encouraged my interest in 'the seeds and weak beginnings' of our society. Dr F.G. Clarke has given unstintingly of time, encouragement and advice. Dr J. Waldersee introduced me to the 1828 Census; Dr L.L. Robson shared 'his' convicts and Brigadier M. Austin 'his' Marines and New South Wales Corps. Monica Perrott contributed her own wide knowledge of colonial women and helped to collate and proofread the manuscript. Associate-Professor A.T. Yarwood, Dr A. Frost, Dr J. Walmsley and Associate-Professor R. Mortley have listened sympathetically and commented from their own viewpoints.

It is a pleasant duty to acknowledge the assistance and guidance of 'the professionals', the archivists and librarians: Mr John Cross and his staff at the Archives Office of New South Wales; the staff of the Mitchell and Dixson Libraries, Sydney, and of the National Library, Canberra; Mr H.J. Gibbney of the *Australian Dictionary of Biography*, Australian National University; Tim Robinson, archivist of the Society of Australian Genealogists; Miss Rusden of the Leeper Library, Trinity College, University of Melbourne; and Monsignor Duffey of the Sydney Archdiocesan Archives, St Mary's Cathedral, Sydney.

Family and friends have not only given support and comfort but practical advice and help: Harry and Edith Ferguson, Clara Stagg, Malcolm Stening, Dymphna Clark, Belle Low and Margit Svensson. Gloria Webb has cheerfully helped type the manuscript.

Finally, I acknowledge the help and forbearance of those who have lived with 'my' native-born for so long: Ron Robinson and 'our' native-born, Tim, Leigh and Sarah.

Portia Robinson, Macquarie University

PREFACE

During the last twenty years a major change has occurred in the writing of Australian history. Historians contributed to the quest for an Australian identity. Historians have also contributed to the shift of interest from the great men in the past to the men and women of the people.

Australians wanted their historians to tell them who they were, and why they are as they are. Australians wanted their historians to tell them about the Aborigines, about women, about people, and not about the Governors and Secretaries of State for the Colonies, and all the other people in high places.

In this book Portia Robinson has made a major contribution to this 'new look' Australian history. She has gone back to the invasion of the country by the Europeans in 1788. She has ploughed the first furrow in the field marked 'Australian People'. She has confined her attention to the Europeans. Wisely eschewing the somewhat extravagant generalizations of some of her predecessors who scratched the surface of the field in which she was to labour for so long, she brought to her work the gifts both of the poet and the statistician, the gifts of the historian as artist and the talents of the social science measurer. She has reaped a very rich harvest. Her work has a chance to become one of the works, like the works of Keith Hancock and Brian Fitzpatrick, which all future historians will ignore at their peril. Her work has a chance to become part of a select company. Posterity will almost certainly ask: what did Portia Robinson say about the early Europeans in Australia?

Manning Clark
1983

There is a history in all men's lives,
Figuring the nature of the times deceas'd;
The which observ'd, a man may prophesy,
With a near aim, of the main chance of things
As yet not come to life, which in their seeds
And weak beginnings lie intreasured.
Such things become the hatch and brood of time.

William Shakespeare, *Henry IV, Part 2*

INTRODUCTION

THE HATCH AND BROOD OF TIME

'To create a time, a place, a people.'

Manning Clark.

Some thirty years after the first white settlers arrived at Botany Bay, Sydney Smith, writing in the *Edinburgh Review*, described England's convict colony as 'a sink of wickedness'. In that year, 1819, there were almost 23,000 men, women and children on the mainland of New South Wales. Their society, said Smith, was one in which 'the majority of the convicts of both sexes become infinitely more depraved than at the period of their arrival'. He was echoing the opinions of respectable British society that a colony inhabited primarily by men and women transported for major criminal offences must equate with Sodom and Gomorrah. This assumption was based firmly on the connotations of the word 'convict'. Debased and degraded characteristics were associated with conviction of criminal offences. Man or woman, boy or girl, a convicted felon was expected to be not only criminally inclined, but immoral, drunken, dissolute and debauched.

That familiar term used by Englishman, 'Botany Bay', summed up the expectations and assumptions in Britain as to the nature of colonial society long after it had ceased to refer to a geographic location. In January 1827 an English visitor to the colony expressed this view in a letter to the editor of the *Australian*:

> A person arriving here under the impression that he is landing amongst a people chiefly composed of the off-scourings of society, in a land of pickpockets, *in short, in Botany Bay*, would be astonished to find himself in such a town as Sydney and himself and his property as safe as at home.[1] (Italics mine.)

It was on the basis of the known life-styles of the convicted men and women in Britain, combined with the attitudes and expectations of 'respectable' society towards convicted felons, that Botany Bay first earned its reputation. To Britishers, throughout the period of transportation it remained a land inhabited almost exclusively by depraved and vicious criminals and their offspring. That colonial society was tainted by criminality was accepted without question. That it was complex and diverse in its structure and composition was not. It was, and continued to be, 'Botany Bay . . . the land of convicts and kangaroos'.

Between the arrival of the first fleet and the publication of the first editions of the *Australian* in 1824, a new 'race' had emerged in New South Wales.[2] This was the first generation of colonial-born men and women. They had grown to adulthood with their native land, seeing it develop from that struggling penal camp on the shores of Port Jackson to the thriving community that was New South Wales in the 1820s. This development, familiar to the native-born, was completely unexpected by new arrivals in the colony. In 1827 a 'British Tar' described his impressions in a letter published in the *Australian*:

> ... where I looked for bark huts and weather board hovels, I have found streets as long as Oxford Street, and mansions that might do credit to Hanover Square. Such a metamorphosis as the town of Sydney has presented in little more than thirty years, is certainly without parallel in ancient or modern times—the crowded streets—the elegant shops—the London carriages—the stage coaches, with the guard blowing the horn —the street drays—markets—the women crying fish—the numerous boats and vessels—with everybody speaking English, and no foreigners, black or brown ... have so bothered me at times, as scarcely to be sensible that I was not in England.[3]

This unexpectedly literate 'British Tar' showed clearly that the progress and development of a respectable and delightful town was, once again, measured by British standards. Botany Bay had so impressed him because he had found an unexpected similarity with the towns of England. There were only three differences which 'jogged [his] recollection'. Two of these were favourable: the blue skies and the lack of beggars in the streets. The third, he found 'un-English' and difficult to accept:

> ... the long string of Government convict gangs proceeding to work along George Street ... is among the most melancholy sights in the world; half-a-mile an hour is about their small pace, and their half-clothed almost naked ... emaciated appearance prove that they are half-starved. This, in a land of plenty, is un-English, cruel and unwise.[4]

It was this penal aspect of the colony which was regarded as typically colonial and un-English. The colony's children, however, had been born into this environment. Most had close links with convicted men and women, for most of the mothers and many of the fathers had arrived as convicts sentenced to terms of transportation. As settlement had spread slowly beyond Sydney, beyond Parramatta, British authorities had instructed the colonial governors that provision was to be made for the future erection of churches and schools in the new settlements. These were the outward signs of English civilization. The colonial authorities made provision for symbols of that other side of English civilization to accompany the settlers. The triangles, the lash, the gallows, those punitive enforcers of obedience, industry and order among the assigned convict servants, spread through the Australian bush as each new township was settled. Many of the convict labourers, sentenced as punishment for crimes committed against British society, were employed on the farms or in the households of the parents of the native-born. Punitive labour, and the punishment which could follow idleness or insubordination, were the features of British civilization most familiar to the children of the penal colony. These existed because of the unique nature of New South Wales as a colony of settlement. They accentuated the awareness among the native-born of the necessity to be of proven good character. These 'Australians' were, from infancy, familiar with the indulgences which could be obtained freely from the governor by men and women of industrious habits and 'respectable' character. To the native-born, the words respectability, freedom, liberty, took on entirely different connotations from those accepted by their contemporaries in Britain. All three terms were affected by the associations with criminality inherent in the origins of most of the first settlers. Respectability was equated with lack of criminal conviction; freedom was for those not 'under the sentence of the law'; liberty was neither an accepted constitutional nor an inherited right. In most cases it was earned by penal servitude and the proof was a certificate of freedom, to be carried at all times. To the British-born, these characteristics of colonial society were symbolic of the convict colony of Botany Bay. To the native-born, they were a familiar and natural part of their homeland, Australia.

The first generation, therefore, did not see their own country and its inhabitants with British eyes. Nor did they judge by the same standards as did the British visitors, officials and settlers. They did not call themselves 'the children of Botany Bay'. They were 'the free-born white subjects of Australia'. The British, however, continued to see the colony as primarily a convict one. Its society was convict, its children were the sons and daughters of convicts. In short, it was Botany Bay. There was, therefore, a wide gulf between the ideas of the British-born as to the nature of Botany Bay and the characteristics of the inhabitants and the actual experiences of the colonials living in New South Wales itself. Contemporary assumptions, opinions and comments which supported this view, which highlighted the depravity and viciousness of the convicted felons, were accepted in Britain without question or comment. They confirmed the belief that the colony was simply 'a land of convicts and kangaroos'. This being so, in accordance with the accepted view regarding the nature of criminals, it was also accepted without question that the children born in the colony had no alternative other than a childhood characterized by parental neglect. Their 'home' environment was coloured by 'hourly witnessing' scenes of debauchery, drunkenness, viciousness and crime.

DISTORTING ASSUMPTIONS

Until now, the first generation of Australian-born has remained as William Charles Wentworth described it in the 1820s: 'a long neglected race of men and women'. Assumptions as to their characteristics and life-styles have been based almost entirely on the remaining opinions of a handful of 'respectable' contemporary observers. These commentators, almost without exception, described the colony's children as 'the children of the convicts'. From this assumption stemmed the expectation that they could only 'imbibe vice with their mothers' milk', for were they not the unfortunate sons and daughters of 'the most degenerate set of villains and whores on the face of the globe'? This emphasis on their depraved convict parentage has distorted not only the experiences of the native-born themselves but the characteristics of the whole of colonial society during this formative period.

Contemporary comment describing the native-born has been almost the only readily available source of evidence. This comment falls into two periods: that of their childhood and that of their maturity. In both periods the distorting influence of the 'convict' assumptions is clearly evident. During the childhood of the native-born, from the first settlement to the early years of the administration of Governor Lachlan Macquarie, the emphasis was on the uniformity of the experiences of the colony's children. They were seen as a homogeneous 'class', the children of the convicts. There was no recognition that the children of colonial officials, seamen, marines, soldiers, free settlers, or ex-convicts were equally as native-born as were the sons and daughters of those transported men and women still under the sentence of the law for crimes committed in Britain; James and John Macarthur were as legitimate a part of the first generation as were James and George Bloodsworth, the sons of convicted felons.The future prospects of the 'Rising Generation', therefore, were seen to be disastrous. It was believed that they were either abandoned by their 'unnatural parents' or dragged up amid scenes of indescribable vice, daily witness to the depravity of their parents. Governor William Bligh expressed the fears held by his respectable contemporaries: '. . . not until the next or after generations can be expected any considerable advance to morality or virtue'.

By the 1820s the native-born were emerging as a remarkably honest, sober, industrious and law-abiding group of men and women. To observers, this was clearly the direct result of the triumph of natural morality over the degradation of convict parentage, convict society. The expected and laudable characteristics of the first generation were believed to stem from an instinctive and commendable revulsion against convictism and all its traits, a rejection of parental example and vice. This was evident in the characteristics contemporaries attributed to them. They were described as a distinct and distinctive race of men and women, fiercely proud and independent, scorning all associations with convictism, preferring the isolation of 'the distant hills' or a life at sea to the confining occupations of the towns and townships. It was believed that they were antagonistic to all forms of authority, that they had severed all contact with their convict parents. That these admirable young men and women were the children of the convicts was not questioned by contemporaries. There was instead a smug complacency that these 'convicts' children' had thrown off the evil influences of.a penal environment and had become a credit to their British stock.

It was not only contemporaries who failed to question the assumptions made concerning the life-styles and characteristics of the children born in New South Wales. Historians were to accept these contemporary views as indicative of the nature of the first-born white Australians. Yet, until now, no one has known who these boys and girls actually were. Their individual identities, their varied experiences, have been cloaked under the general description 'the children of the convicts'. Most importantly, both contemporary opinions and later historical interpretations and explanations have been based on British views, not from the standpoint of the *colonial* experience. The convicts themselves were judged on their British backgrounds, their British crimes. Very little interest was shown in their achievements or failures as colonial settlers once they ceased to be actual convicts. Later generations followed the same convention as most of the 'respectable' contemporaries; a convict remained a convict and retained his or her convict identity and characteristics after sentence was served or after pardon. Lachlan Macquarie, one of the few willing to recognize the achievements and potential of the ex-convict settlers, was to tarnish his own reputation among 'respectable' settlers and British officials. Macquarie steadfastly pursued a policy which was abhorrent and unacceptable to the 'pure merinos'. Well might convicted society lament when Macquarie left the colony that they had 'lost a friend'.

A NEGLECTED GENERATION

The contemporary emphasis on the convict parentage of the native-born, on the derogatory influence of the parents, the rejection of the life-styles and values believed to be typical of the convict society of Botany Bay, has continued until the present day. It has influenced interpretations as to the nature of Australian society in its origins. Most importantly, it has limited investigations into the social and economic development of the colony by neglecting the contribution of a whole generation of men and women, and of their parents. The lives of the native-born were inextricably linked with the development of their native land, for they and their colony grew together, sharing a common, and at times conflicting, bond of experiences, disappointments, achievements. It is to these formative years that present-day Australians should look for the emergence of those distinctive characteristics which were to become recurring and typical, to shape the ethos, tradition, mystique, of a future nation. No account of the origins of a people can be accepted if an entire generation is overlooked, if a society's values and characteristics are misinterpreted or distorted. It is imperative that the historical neglect of the native-born be remedied, that their real place in the development of a unique Australian society be established.

Existing sources of evidence describing the native-born and their society have, until now, been inadequate for such a study. The lives and influence of a whole generation cannot be interpreted on hearsay evidence, on the opinions and observations of a handful of literate contemporaries. Whether these contemporaries were officials, visitors, temporary or permanent residents, British or colonial newspaper and journal commentators, their evidence was limited, partial and biased. It is not suggested that the accuracy of their reports is questionable, or that there was deliberate falsification. Most of the officials were acute observers of colonial conditions. It is argued that their observations were limited to certain aspects of colonial life and that they were influenced by preconceived expectations and assumptions as to the characteristics of a convict society. Official reports, private letters and published journals reflect a preoccupation with criminality and immorality, with the drunken, and depraved behaviour of convicted felons. There was little occasion to comment on the life-styles of those men and women which did not conform to the expectations of vice and infamy in the convict colony of Botany Bay. Expectations were based on British experiences, on conviction for major statutory offences committed in Britain. Scant attention was given to the actual colonial life-style, especially after sentences were served and these British convicts became Australian settlers. Nor was any distinction made between a convict and an ex-convict, nor any recognition of the disparity of experiences and opportunities of a man or woman under sentence and a technically free, self-supporting ex-convict. It was on this basis that the colony's children were accepted as 'the children of the convicts' and their expected life-styles based on the assumed characteristics of their convicted parents.

This contemporary British emphasis on the infamous conduct expected of convicts in a convict colony has clouded accounts of the nature and origins of white society in Australia. It has led to an almost complete neglect of the influence and contribution of a whole generation of men and women, the native-born Australians. The contemporary assumption, which has been perpetuated to the present day, that the first generation of Australian-born were simply the 'children of the convicts' has completely distorted the role this unique race of men and women played in the development of a characteristically Australian society.

THE 'NEW' EVIDENCE

This interpretation is now challenged on 'new' evidence, both quantitative and qualitative. It is only by the presentation of a body of evidence which will stand firm as a rock that the first native-born Australians may take their rightful place in the history of their country. This evidence is the re-creation of the first generation of men and women born in New South Wales. The individual and collective biographies of these first white Australians, placed within the context of their society, show clearly the misconceptions, inaccuracies and distortions implicit in the acceptance of contemporary assumptions and opinions.

The evidence on which this present interpretation of the origins and nature of Australian society rests began with the identification of the individual boys and girls born in New South Wales during the first twenty-five years of white settlement. Statistical biographies were first compiled from sources such as Musters, Victualling Lists, the 1828 Census, Convict Indents, Ships' Musters, Governors' Returns, Criminal and Civil Court Records, Parish Registers of Baptism, Marriage and Burial. To this framework—the bones, as it were, of the individuals—was added qualitative evidence which supplied the flesh, bringing to life again the hopes, the ambitions, the disappointments, the achievements, of the native-born and of their parents. A significant source was one rarely used: the Memorials to the Governors, where the Memorialist not only applied for an indulgence for land or stock, or for an apprenticeship for a son, but for assistance in every conceivable human situation arising from misadventure, accident or misfortune. The Memorialist identified himself or herself, describing background, experiences and achievements, and future plans. From the Memorials of the native-born and their parents, this past generation speaks to the present, outlining its own attitudes, its own responses to colonial life. There were other rarely used sources for this more personal biographical data, difficult to obtain where so few of the parents were literate. These included Petitions in Mitigation of Sentence and Applications to Marry, for Tickets-of-Leave, for Pardons, for Permission to Leave the Colony. From a combination of these two forms of evidence, quantitative and qualitative, the native-born and their parents emerged as a distinct group, and as individuals. Their role within, and their response to, colonial society could then be assessed both individually and collectively.

A generation, however, cannot be considered in isolation. It was essential that contemporaries in their own age group be identified and classified as came-free or as ex-convict. It was only by a comparison of the life-styles and experiences of these differing groups within colonial society that the unique characteristics of the native-born could be established. Basic biographical data were therefore gathered for those men and women living in New South Wales in 1828, who had been born in the same period as the native-born, 1788–1813, but who had come to the colony as free persons or as convicts. All three groups, the native-born, the came-free and the ex-convicts, were then placed within the social and economic framework of 'convict' society, with particular emphasis on the family relationships, parental influence, and the nature and structure of the whole colonial society in the forty-year period 1788–1828.

The re-creation of the first generation of white Australians, therefore, is part of the re-creation of the whole of Australian society. It is a re-creation based on people, on individual and collective responses to the colonial experience. In this sense it is the beginning of a history of the Australian people, not as others have seen them but as they themselves saw their own lives, their own achievements and failures. Most of these men and women could not record their lives; many left little trace of their part in building a new society. The myths, legends and ballads of those who arrived as convicts stress the deprivation, inhumanity and barbarity of a convict system which forcibly uprooted them from their homes. The comments of their respectable contemporaries have detracted from the very real part they played in the development of a new society. In Britain they were 'the scum, the sweepings of the gaols, hulks and prisons'. In Australia they were a very large part of a new society, but not the whole society. It was with the children of the colony that the colonial experiences of the parents became evident, that 'Australian' society began at Botany Bay. That those native-born children were to be found at every rank and level of colonial society, convict and free, was determinative in their influence on the emerging Australian society. Now that this 'long neglected race of men and women' has been identified, their life-styles and experiences re-created, the native-born and their parents may take their rightful place in the history of their native land. It is this re-created generation of native-born Australian men and women who now challenge both contemporary opinion and modern assumptions.

There are still areas in which the attitude and influence of the native-born and their parents cannot be determined for the evidence is scant, incomplete or non-existent. Their reactions and responses to the black Aboriginal peoples remain unknown; the evidence is negative. Neither is it possible to determine with accuracy the extent of religious influences on the native-born, except perhaps on the children of the Irish Catholics. Almost the only remaining evidence is related to church ceremonies: baptism, marriage and burial. The extent of actual religious worship or church attendance is unknown. It is known that the sons and daughters of colonial Catholics declared themselves to be Catholics in the 1828 Census. Whether this was a statement of identity or an indication of religious observance cannot be known. When it is considered that these children grew up in a colony without priest or visible signs of their religion, with the exception of the short ministry of Father Dixson, it would suggest parental influence and example as the only sources of their faith.

STABLE FAMILY LIFE

The oversimplification of the description, children of the convicts, completely distorts the experiences of children within colonial society and their influence on the way in which it developed. It is now known that, individually, they were not the children of the convicts. Admittedly, most had a mother who had arrived as a convict. That period spent 'under sentence of the law' was limited. The 1806 Muster shows that the rural families were mostly ex-convicts, ex-soldiers. The children in these families grew to maturity in the households of men and women who were technically free, who were self-supporting and supported their children. The Musters show that this was also the case with the children of tradesmen, publicans, shopkeepers, and even unskilled workers, the labourers, servants, carters, washerwomen and laundresses. When it is considered that the children of farmers and tradesmen alone accounted for almost two-thirds of the male native-born in 1828 it becomes increasingly apparent that the childhood experiences were not coloured by life with a parent or parents who were convicts serving sentences.

It can now be shown that the native-born did not share a common life-style as children. They can no longer be described as children from the lowest orders of colonial society; there were children at every social and economic level in New South Wales. This diversity meant that their influence was not confined to the convict section; their parents were from all civil conditions. Nor was it confined to the poorer sections of the community. Most of the parents had come from the lowest levels of British society. Most were unskilled. Most lacked capital assets of any kind. Most had experienced poverty, unemployment, lack of opportunities to improve their standard of living or to gain any measure of economic independence or security. In the colony, however, once sentence was served or once a soldier completed his tour of duty, and sometimes before, there were opportunities far beyond any that could have been imagined by these same men and women in Britain.

These opportunities were not limited to those from the lowest orders. John Macarthur and his sons owed their colonial wealth, social position, power and influence to the fortune amassed by that impoverished second lieutenant who had come to Botany Bay with the avowed intention of making his fortune. So firmly did Macarthur establish himself as being 'of the first water' of colonial society that he could reject the relative of an earl as a suitor for his native-born daughter. This former English draper had become too great a colonial gentleman to ally his family with the illegitimate son of D'arcy Wentworth and his former convict mistress.

It was most important for the way in which colonial society was to develop that, in its origins, its structure was so complex and diverse, that it was not a static society, that there was continual movement and change within the various levels of that society. It was even more important that the children of the colony shared these changing experiences, at all levels, among the convicted as well as the free, among the successful as well as the failures. They were, in this sense, the children of pioneers, for their material welfare was mainly determined by the enterprise, ambition, industry and luck of their parents. They saw and were a part of the changes in life-styles of their parents. At the same time they were unaware of the British background of experience those parents brought with them to New South Wales, their 'invisible luggage'. It was not these British attitudes and responses which influenced the native-born but the immediate nature of their colonial family life. Until now, the existence and stability of this family life within penal society has been unrecognized. It has been overshadowed by the effect of opinions on the detrimental influence of convict parents. There has been almost no comment about, or recognition of, the concern and the care for their children shown by family men and women from every social and economic level of colonial society.

For the first time a substantial body of evidence has been presented to substantiate the extent of this concern, to show the actual relationships which did exist among the native-born and their parents. This evidence is based on individuals. Every native-born girl and boy who remained living with a parent or parents in 1828, after reaching 'years of maturity', has been identified and the family background investigated. Every native-born landholder has been traced, the parentage of most established, the districts in which they spent their childhood and youth recorded, and the districts and occupations of the parents compared with those of the adult sons. Those native-born women who married farmers and landholders are now known as individual identities; their parentage and backgrounds have been traced and compared with those of their husbands. There has been similar detailed research into all occupational and family groups. Every native-born tradesman has been identified as an individual, every apprentice lad, the land-workers, the seamen, the labourers and the servants. Wherever possible, these men and women have been placed within the context of their own individual experiences as sons and daughters, as wives and husbands, as working men and women, as family men and women. This new interpretation of the nature of colonial society in its origins rests on the collation of all these individual experiences.

CONCERNED PARENTS

This new evidence, presented for the first time, includes an analysis of the Memorials, Petitions and Letters sent to the various governors. Until now there has been no detailed appraisal of these contemporary sources as evidence for the nature of colonial life, yet they express the hopes, expectations, ambitions, failures, sorrows and disappointments of the colonists themselves. They are very personal documents, giving life, substance and reality to the bare biographical and statistical details.

By 1828 almost one-third of the adult native-born males owned land. Almost all of these had written to the governor as Memorialists, asking for a grant of land. Most of those still living at home were the sons of landholders. These fathers, too, had applied for land grants in the same way. Many of the fathers had also applied for land for their sons. Every one of the Memorials which remains in the Archives Office of New South Wales has been read. The concern of the parents that their sons should receive grants to ensure their future security is irrefutable. In addition, the native-born applicants almost invariably stress three points: first, they were the children of respectable parents; second, they had been raised 'in agricultural pursuits', usually by 'a tender and loving father'; third, they themselves were 'honest, sober and industrious'. Their fathers, and the sons, were known to the local magistrates and chaplains, who gave the obligatory testimonials. The most usual phrases for the father were 'he is a deserving and honest man', 'supports his children in an honest way'. Frequently, in the character testimonials for the sons, the magistrate would add that 'he is the son of a deserving man'; 'he is of respectable parents'. Even when allowance is made for the formalized style of the Memorials— and the flourishes of the paid letter-writer—the concern of the fathers to establish their sons 'in a settled way of life' becomes increasingly obvious. The reactions of the sons may be seen in the number of requests for land near their father or in the same district. There is, too, the occasional note of pride, that the father is one of the first inhabitants, was the first tradesman or was the first constable in the colony. In their own words the native-born and their fathers refute the assumption of parental abandonment and neglect.

Parental support, encouragement and continued concern were also found among the native-born who became apprentices and tradesmen. From the experiences of this occupational group it was established that the nature of the colonial work-force and the subsequent attitudes to, and opportunities for, child labour in the penal colony resulted in a distinctive form of apprenticeship. It was also established that the childhood of those native-born who were not reared on farms was entirely different from that of contemporaries in British towns and cities. The chief characteristic of the childhood of these children was the lack of any need to exploit child labour. Following from this was the concern shown by parents, both tradesmen themselves and unskilled workers, that their sons should learn a craft, trade or skill. The evidence for this concern was reinforced by the numbers of native-born tradesmen who continued to work with, or near, their tradesman fathers and brothers. As with the rural native-born, the family links among these skilled workers were strengthened by the marriage of sons and daughters of men who had been convicted together in Britain, or had arrived on the same ships, had served in the Royal Marines or New South Wales Corps together or who had worked at similar or allied trades in Sydney or Parramatta.

OPPORTUNITIES FOR THE YOUNG

The most significant feature of the childhood of these 'trade children', and the one which was to shape their own attitudes to the nature of labour, was the difference between their experiences and those of their contemporaries in Britain. Until now this has been neither investigated nor commented on. Colonial society was composed mostly of men and women who had formerly lived within the lowest orders of British society. As children themselves in Britain they were familiar with the expectation, and necessity, that the children from this social and economic level should begin to work for wages almost as soon as they could walk. The middle and upper classes found this highly desirable and commendable. Not only did it keep 'idle hands' from mischief and crime but it supplied cheap labour. Those orphans, abandoned and destitute children who became the responsibility of a parish, were 'apprenticed' to farmers, tradesmen, shopkeepers, house-holders, sea captains, to anyone who would agree to provide subsistence and some form of training. In return, the master or mistress gained the labour of that child for periods of from seven to fourteen years, or until death. This was the form of labour that Blackstone likened to that of slavery. Child exploitation, starvation and ill-treatment were notorious, both among the apprentices and among the mine, mill and factory children and the climbing boys and girls. Long hours and deplorable conditions were the norm.

In the penal colony the reverse was found to be the case. There were two main reasons for this. First, there was a readily available, and cheap, adult work-force in the men and women transported to serve a term of penal servitude. Second, the nature of the work available was, in most cases, unsuited to child labour. There were no mines, mills or factories. What, then, was to be done with these children? Those accustomed to the British standards lamented that the colonial boys and girls spent their days in idleness; they 'played' on the public wharfs, on the roads and in the gardens. The *Sydney Gazette* castigated the neglectful parents who allowed their sons and daughters to spend their childhood in this fashion when they should be employed, or learning a trade or skill. This parental indulgence strengthened the opinion that the parents were neglectful of their duty to their children.

As in Britain, the opportunities for employment of these children centered around apprenticeships. Contrary to British practice, however, these colonial apprenticeships were for boys to learn a craft or trade under skilled masters. In most cases the parents had originated in the lower classes of British society, but had not remained the unemployed, the unskilled, in colonial society. They actively sought apprenticeships for their sons. The first master was government. Lads were taught their trades at the Dock Yards and Lumber Yard, and their teachers were mainly convict or ex-convict tradesmen. From about the early 1800s opportunities to be apprenticed to private masters grew. Firms such as Kable and Underwood, Simeon Lord, Robert Campbell, began to train colonial youth. The boys they trained were not the poor parish apprentices but boys whose parents paid indentures and kept a watchful eye on the progress of their sons. Apprenticeship in the colony, therefore, had none of the connotations of exploited child labour. They retained the original emphasis on skilled training in a craft or trade. The advantages of gaining these skills were heightened by the continual shortage of mechanics in New South Wales during this period. The native-born, especially those who were themselves the sons of tradesmen, even 'of the indifferent sort', were well aware of the benefits and security of constant employment available for the skilled workers of the colony.

Apprenticeships similar to those of the British parish system were almost non-existent. What, then, were the opportunities for the orphaned and destitute lads of New Wouth Wales? The answer lies in evidence which shows how few *were* abandoned. This may be seen in the very few who became the unskilled workers of their generation, among the fewer who became seamen. In addition, there is evidence from the Memorials, first of concern of a surviving parent for the welfare of children and, second, from the evidence of guardians, both ex-soldiers and ex-convicts, even one or two ladies of dubious profession, who applied for land and indulgences for their adopted children.

RELUCTANT SEAFARERS

One of the traditional ways of 'disposing' of the parish orphans in England, was by indenting them as ships' boys or ships' apprentices. Lads from eight years old sailed on British merchantmen, coastal and river vessels and in the Royal Navy. In New South Wales, this would have appeared the ideal occupation for children in a land without industries, mines or mills. Until now it has been accepted that the native-born were 'naturally inclined to a seafaring way of life'. It is now evident that this was not so. Whatever may have been the opinions of Commissioner Bigge, of ex-convict Edward Eagar, of ship's surgeon Peter Cunningham, New South Wales was not to be a convenient nursery for 'British' seamen. The Australian-born, as a generation, showed little inclination for leaving the shores of their native land. New evidence supports this conclusion. For the first time the Ships' Musters have been analysed, every native-born ship's apprentice, ship's boy, ship's tradesman, has been identified for the period 1816–25. Wherever evidence remains, their parental backgrounds have been investigated. Every voyage made by every individual native-born seafarer has been listed. Those among them who eventually settled in New South Wales have been listed. The collation of this evidence showed clearly how few native-born sailed out of Port Jackson during this period, how few voyages were made by individual seamen. It was found that many who completed apprenticeships as shipwrights, carpenters or coopers sailed on one or two voyages, in all probability as part of their training. It was found that a small group sailed as the sons of ship owners or as the sons of seafaring fathers. It was found that another group appeared to come from those sections of colonial society in which no other form of employment was available. There was a small, indeterminate group who may have sailed from a sense of adventure. Among all groups very few remained to become professional seafarers.

HONEST AND RESPECTABLE

Another assumption made by contemporaries was that the native-born were fiercely independent, scorning all authority and refusing to 'go soldier' or help enforce the law. This belief appeared to be consistent with the experiences of a generation who had witnessed the degradation, punishment and despair of convicted men and women. It was not consistent with the experiences of that generation which had grown to maturity in the stability and security of family backgrounds, aware of the benefits which could be conferred for proven honesty, respectability and industry. It was a British-based, not colonial-based, assumption. From the occupations chosen by the male native-born, from the marriages of the female native-born, from the Memorials of both, the unreliability of this assumption is evident. There were native-born constables at all levels, from the Sydney constables to the District and Chief constables. Some were themselves the sons of constables and stressed in their Memorials that a father was one 'of the first constables of New South Wales'. There were the native-born who actively upheld the law, as private persons, caring for the security of their neighbourhoods. They apprehended bushrangers and burglars, and were officially rewarded. They offered voluntarily to serve as law-enforcement officers in the districts where they lived. They offered to join a colonial militia or locally-raised cavalry, if either were established, to 'serve their country in an honest way'. They stressed in the Memorials where their fathers had been members of the Loyal Associations or were Veterans who had served the king in the army or the navy. There were a few who had voluntarily followed their fathers into the New South Wales Corps and served in His Majesty's wars. One of these was the first Australian volunteer to be killed on active service overseas, at the Battle of Corunna. Others, returning from active service or with military fathers who had been posted overseas, wrote to the governor that they, and frequently their fathers, had returned to their native land to settle, and requested a grant of land. They were few in number but their existence and their experiences added to the characteristics of the first generation. They showed once again the distortion implicit in the general description 'the children of the convicts'.

One contemporary assumption was correct, although the reasoning was mistaken. This was that the native-born, as a generation, were a remarkably honest and law-abiding group of men and women. The contrast with the 'criminality' of their parents was based on the British crimes of the convicted fathers and mothers, not on their colonial life-styles after sentences imposed in Britain had been served in New South Wales. On those rare occasions when a native-born was charged with a colonial offence the parents immediately supported the boy or girl. Their Petitions to the governor, asking for mitigation of sentence, all show clearly the concern and distress of the parents, ex-convict, ex-soldier or free settler. They ask for clemency for a 'misguided girl', a 'mistaken lad', guilty, perhaps, of protecting a friend, of a 'boyish prank', of 'high spirits'. This same concern was evident in the occasional case where a master, newly arrived in the colony, mistreated an apprentice lad. An ex-convict mother did not hesitate to bring charges of cruelty before the magistrates. Again, where a young son was prevailed upon by a ship's captain to sign indentures without the permission of his parents, the ex-convict mother immediately applied to the magistrates to have him released. These and similar cases strengthen the picture which has emerged of the parent–child relationships. The existence of this family life throughout colonial society is now established for the first time.

THE ROLE OF WOMEN

One significant result of the childhood experiences of the native-born was the distinctive nature of female society which emerged in New South Wales. This, too, has been unrecognized until now. This 'new' form of society was firmly based on the experiences of the native-born women as daughters in the households of men and women from all civil conditions and occupational groups. A detailed investigation into the life-styles of the mothers of the native-born and the nature and structure of female society during the first forty years of white settlement shows clearly the extent and influence of these women on their children. Until now, the actual influence of these women, in particular those who arrived convicted, has been misinterpreted. The misinterpretations have resulted from the unquestioned acceptance of contemporary opinions. There has been no investigation into the accuracy or general applicability of these opinions or the 'evidence' on which they were based. The emphasis placed by contemporary commentators on the immorality and depravity of these 'wanton' women, these 'vile baggages', has not been seen as British-based. The actual role of these women in the development of colonial society has been obliterated by accepting opinions formed very largely on the British background and characteristics of many of the convicted women. When their *colonial* lives, that is, after sentences were served, were examined a different picture emerged. In an investigation of this kind it is essential that the words and descriptions used by contemporaries are clearly defined according to the attitudes and opinions of the commentator. When Samuel Marsden 'proved' the immorality of the women of Botany Bay by designating every one a wife or a 'concubine', his definitions were not questioned. They were not, however, indicative either of the standards of the women themselves, of their life-style or their morality. Marsden's definition of marriage was limited to those legally wed by a clergyman of the Church of England. No allowance was made for those of other persuasions who lived together as man and wife, having no priest, minister or rabbi to marry them according to their beliefs. No allowance was made for the traditional custom of common-law marriages. Yet most of these women were from that level of British society where common-law marriages were the norm. By their own standards, many of the women designated as concubines, harlots, whores and prostitutes were family women. This in itself shows colonial society in an entirely new perspective. The normal unit of that society was not the abandoned convict woman.

DIFFERENT STANDARDS

As with the sons, the way of life of the daughters depended on the social and economic levels of the parents. As with the sons, the main influence on the life-style of the daughters was the influence and example of their parents. Definite patterns of family life emerged with the native-born, patterns which differed in characteristics and emphasis from those in contemporary British society, particularly among the rural and urban employed, and unemployed, working classes.

The daughters of the farmers and landholders normally remained at home with their parents until they married. Few sought outside employment. Usually, they married young, frequently choosing a farming husband from the same district. They then either joined the family of their husband or, with him, established their own farms. There were very few cases in which one of these women worked for wages after marriage. They were brought up as 'family women', working within the family, and they continued this pattern after marriage. The exceptions occurred when a child was orphaned or a woman, after marriage, widowed. In these cases the young child almost invariably worked as a domestic servant in the same district; the widow either continued to live on her land or took employment as dressmaker, washerwoman or housekeeper to support herself and her children. Normally, she remarried within one or two years and again became a family woman.

A different but consistent pattern emerged among the daughters of tradesmen and among those whose fathers were unskilled. These girls frequently worked as domestic servants from about the age of fourteen until marriage, which was usually by the age of twenty. They then ceased to be working women. Like their rural sisters, they became family women, working within the households of their husbands or joining his parents. The exceptions were again confined to the widows. This was an entirely different work pattern from that in Britain, where the wives continued to be employed women, if employment were available, after marriage. It was also a different pattern from that followed by the same age group of colonial women who had arrived as convicts or free settlers. These women normally continued to be employed after marriage. The role of the native-born women in colonial society, therefore, was not as working women, employed women, but as family women. It was particularly significant that this role was widespread throughout all levels of society and not confined to the 'ladies' of the colony. This family pattern was the direct result of experiences as children in colonial families. This is now established for the first time.

These first Matildas played another role in shaping colonial society. This, too, has been unrecognized until now. By their marriages they helped to prevent the continuance of rigid social barriers based on civil conditions. To a far more marked extent than their brothers these native-born girls showed little discrimination against prospective marriage partners who were or had been convicts. They did show an acute awareness of the value of material assets and the possession of skills. Their standards of judgement which influenced their choice of husbands were not based on the British past of a prospective bridegroom but on his colonial achievements or potential. This was very clearly a reflection of their own attitudes towards their parents and towards colonial society. This was not only evident among the daughters of the men and women who had arrived as convicts; it was also found among the daughters of the free settlers and ex-soldiers. Most of the colonial-born, with the single exception of the small group who were the children of the self-styled 'pure merinos', were uninfluenced by the British connotations and associations of the word 'convict'. They measured by their own familiar colonial standards. The existence of these standards, the influence of these attitudes, has not until now been acknowledged.

Only a handful of the native-born became known beyond the limits of their native land. Few travelled beyond its shores. Those who did, who were not the sons of soldiers, were the children of those wealthy settlers who wished to give their children the benefits of an English education. These few boys and girls were not typical of their generation for they grew up in both worlds, their loyalties divided. Although they saw New South Wales as their native land their attitudes to the colony and its inhabitants were influenced by their lives in England. Their education in the mother country had misted their colonial childhood experiences.

AUSTRALIA FROM THE COLONIALS' VIEWPOINT

William Charles Wentworth, so typical of colonial society in his parentage, in his inheritance of a convict mother and a free father, was atypical of the native-born. He interpreted their dreams, their ambitions, their goals by the standards he had learned in England. He was a patriot but he saw his native-land with British, not Australian, eyes. The name of his newspaper, the *Australian*, challenged recognition for this new race of men and women. To Wentworth, their roots were in England and they lived in 'Another Britannia'. It was not this native son who was to typify the characteristics of a native Australian society. It was those men and women who had lived all their lives in New South Wales. They were the first white Australians, the men and women of this new society.

No myth or legend surrounds the Currency Lads and Lasses. The ballads, songs and folklore of early Australia do not enshrine them. In accounts of the origins of Australian society the emphasis has been on the British influences, on the misery and degradation brought by the transportation system, on the cruelty and suffering inherent in the convict years. Contemporary records, too, show this emphasis on the penal nature of the colony, on the inhabitants as the scum and sweepings of British society, bringing with them to this new land all the criminality, immorality, vice and wickedness of their British experiences. These men and women, and their children, became colonial society. The native-born were themselves as much a part of that society as were their parents. Their influence spread beyond the 'convict' society of Botany Bay to the whole of New South Wales. Misjudged by their contemporaries, neglected by historians and by posterity, this first generation has been re-created. Now that the individual native-born are known, their life-styles and experiences investigated, the distortion implicit in accounts of colonial society in its origins becomes clear. It is now possible to study the origins of a unique Australian society from the viewpoint of the colonials themselves and not on the basis of British observations. The native-born cease to be 'the children of the convicts' and take their rightful place as the first free-born natives of a new society, Australia.

CHAPTER ONE

THE SEEDS AND
WEAK BEGINNINGS

New South Wales, 'an extraordinary place for children . . .'

W.P. Crook, 31 December 1804.

Forty-one children under the age of twelve years landed with the first fleet at Camp Cove in February 1788.[1] By the arrival of the second fleet, in mid-1790, there were just over one hundred children in the colony. Within five years the number of children had almost doubled and within ten years there were slightly more than eight hundred children in the total population of almost five thousand. Numbers of children continued to increase sharply. After fifteen years there were almost one thousand children and after twenty-five years more than one quarter of the population was under the age of twelve years.[2] With this rapid increase, it is not surprising that residents, visitors and officials considered the colony of New South Wales 'an extraordinary place for children'.[3] To contemporaries, both in Britain and in New South Wales, such a high proportion of children was not in accordance with their experiences of the population structure of England and Ireland. Nor did this abundance of children agree with their ideas and expectations as to the nature and structure of society in a penal colony.

Contemporaries referred to the colony's children as 'the children of the convicts'. A distinction was sometimes made in official papers, which listed the children of the military and civil departments, children of the free settlers and children of the convicts. These distinctions were confined almost exclusively to population returns and lists of persons victualled or not. No indication was given of the birthplaces of the children, nor were they listed under their own civil condition, such as native-born. In Musters and on Victualling Lists in this early period they were entered in the same category as their parents.[4] Some of these children were British-born, some were born in the colony and a few had arrived as juvenile convicts. To contemporary observers, there was no way of determining to which civil category the colonial children belonged. The general description 'children of the convicts' was equated with colonial born. This contemporary assumption, based on the parentage of the children rather than on their condition as denoted by their place of birth, has continued in historical accounts of New South Wales.

It is essential that the first generation of native-born be identified and distinguished from those children who arrived with their families as immigrants. There are two main contemporary records which could identify the place of birth but both sources are limited, suspect and unacceptable as definitive indication of the number of colonial births or the identity of the native-born. These sources are the population returns of the governors of New South Wales and the parish registers compiled by the chaplains of the Church of England.

The efficient administration of the penal colony of Botany Bay required reliable population statistics. This was recognized by the governors and required by the British government. In 1793 Henry Dundas had instructed Lieutenant-Governor Grose that a yearly return of all births and deaths was 'highly necessary'.[5] Grose, Paterson, and Governors Hunter and King found this to be impractical. There was no reliable method by which all births and deaths could be recorded. King explained that this was a direct result of the unique colonial conditions of settlement: 'Births are uncertain and not easily collected from the scattered state of the settlers allotments, and the children born of Catholic parents are not baptised'.[6] The surgeons were responsible for compiling the returns of the known sick, the deaths and the births. Surgeon William Balmain prefaced his report with an apology for their incompleteness: '... the state of Births and Deaths in this Report is as accurate as far as it comes to our knowledge, but people die and children are born without our being made acquainted therewith'.[7]

There was no legal obligation to register the birth or death of a child or any free person in New South Wales during this period. There was no compulsion to inform the surgeons or any authority. There was no general lying-in hospital and surgeons did not normally attend women in childbirth. Their services were requested by the 'respectable' wives of the officials and wealthier free settlers but rarely by the majority of the colonial women. In the outer districts, unless the mother journeyed to a township or to Sydney or Parramatta, there was seldom a midwife available.[8] Any reports, therefore, which relied on the records of surgeons and midwives were extremely limited.

Colonial conditions were too hazardous and distances too great to encourage women to leave their homes in the outer settlements to seek medical assistance for the birth of their children. Nor was such assistance a normal practice for the women from the lower orders of British society. When an infant or child died neither parent was obliged to report the death or the cause of death, whether sickness, accident or misadventure. The number of children and settlers privately buried on rural properties during this period cannot be determined. One of the few such burials reported was that of ex-convict Eliner Magee and her 'beloved infant Ian Magee', both of whom were drowned when returning to the Hawkesbury from Sydney in January 1793. Her husband buried them both at the door of their hut and was castigated by Judge-Advocate David Collins as 'that rascally Williams'. This description, however, was not because of the method of burial but because the 'affectionate husband and father' would sit on his doorstep every evening with one drink for himself and another which he poured on the grave of his dead wife, for 'she loved it so much in life'.[9]

The population figures supplied to the British government by the colonial governors during this period are not a reliable guide to the number of colonial births or deaths. Nor do they give any indication of the identity of the boys and girls born in the colony. The only 'official' records which do indicate the names and parentage of some of the native-born were the parish registers kept by the chaplains of the Church of England. These were at St. Phillip's, Sydney, St. John's, Parramatta, St. Matthew's, Windsor (from 1810), and St. Luke's, Liverpool (from 1811).[10] When a child was baptized by a chaplain from one of these parishes, the names of the parents were usually given. Frequently the date of birth was also recorded. These baptisms represent only a selective group of the colony's children and were not indicative of the numbers of children actually born in the colony. This is evident by comparing the number of recorded baptisms over a given period with the number of children included in the governors' returns. By 1800, for example, less than half the children listed as resident in the colony in that year had been baptized at either St. Phillip's or St. John's. These were the only two parish registers at that time.[11]

The explanations for this discrepancy highlight the partial nature of the evidence based on parish registers. The Church of England had a monopoly of all religious services from the time the first fleet sailed for Botany Bay. This immediately excluded from baptism all those children whose parents did not choose to have them christened by a minister of the Church of England. This applied particularly to Roman Catholics, Jews, and those who were opposed to any form of Christian baptism. Furthermore, in addition to any probable religious prejudice, many of the parents were part of the lower orders of English society. These men and women traditionally did not regard baptism of their children as necessary, customary, or even desirable. Finally, there were parents who may have wished to have their children baptized but were prevented by distance, by the inconvenience of journeying to either Sydney or Parramatta.[12]

Governor King, concerned at the incomplete nature of population statistics, did attempt to remedy the problem, at least with regard to the children of the Roman Catholics. It is even probable that this need for more accurate records had some influence on his decision to allow limited toleration of the Roman Catholic religion. When the Governor gave Father Dixson official permission to perform certain Roman Catholic ceremonies he gave him explicit instructions to keep careful record of the numbers of Roman Catholic marriages, funerals and baptisms he performed. By placing the priest on the government payroll, King, in effect, made him responsible to the governor for his activities.

Catholic historian P.F. Moran interpreted King's actions in granting Dixson a conditional pardon and permission to exercise some of his pastoral duties as the result of 'frequent remonstrances' which had been made to 'the authorities at home':

> ... on the cruelty and injustice of depriving the Catholic convicts of the consolation of religion, and, as a result, instructions were sent to the Governor in 1802 to authorise one of the convict priests to exercise his sacred functions and administer the sacraments to his co-religionists.[13]

This view is not supported by James Waldersee who argues that 'tolerance rested on expediency'.[14] There is no direct evidence to support the assumption that this 'expediency' was linked with the need for more accurate population statistics. It does, however, appear plausible, particularly as Father Dixson, an emancipated convict, received a salary from the government and was allowed to continue his ministry for at least five months after the Castle Hill rising of the Irish convicts.[15] It also appears unlikely that any 'frequent remonstrances' of convicted persons for the indulgence of a priest in a penal colony would have been acceded to by the British government. Not only was there a close link between Irish Catholicism and rebellion (the 1798 Rebellion in Ireland was a very recent event) but religious toleration in England itself was extremely limited. The official view of the British authorities was far more likely to be in agreement with Samuel Marsden, who wrote, 'I am apprehensive this toleration will be productive of some serious evils'.[16]

After the departure of Father Dixson no official records were kept of the births and deaths of the Catholic settlers. The parish registers, therefore, were not sufficiently comprehensive to be an acceptable source for determining the number of children born in the colony or their parentage. Neither were they a reliable guide to the number of annual births, for the ceremony of baptism was not necessarily performed in the same year as the birth. Elizabeth Dell, for example, was born on 16 November 1796 and baptized on 1 June 1800; Enoch Weavers was born on 13 July 1796 and baptized on 16 June 1800. An extreme, but by no means isolated, case was the ceremony held on 16 May 1807, at which the four children of Daniel Cubbitt and Maria Cook were baptized together at St. Phillip's. These children had been born in 1800, 1803, 1805 and 1807.[17]

In December 1810 Macquarie attempted to ensure greater accuracy in the compilation of population statistics by issuing the following Government and General Order:

> As an Act of Reciprocal Benefit to All Classes of Society ... exact Registers of all Marriages, Christenings, Churching of Women and Funerals they may in future perform and make a correct return thereof once in every Quarter ... all Convicts, Prisoners and Free....[18]

Earlier in that same year, Macquarie had issued another order addressed to the chaplains, which gave them strict instructions that all deaths were to be reported immediately by the clergyman to the Commissary.[19] This was not only a step towards ensuring greater accuracy of the victualling lists but also a method of detecting fraud where rations may have continued to be drawn for a deceased person.[20]

Until the notification of births and deaths became compulsory figures could not be exact. During the years of birth of the first generation, the returns of the governors could only supply an approximate indication of the numbers of colonial children but not the numbers of the native-born. The church registers could supply date and parentage for those children whose parents had had them baptized but this was only a selective proportion of the colonial children. Neither source could identify the individual boys and girls who were the first generation.

THE EVIDENCE

It was the 1828 Census which supplied the basic list of names of the men and women who had been born in the colony during the first twenty-five years of settlement and had continued to live in New South Wales. It also provided identification of those children, born during the same period, who had come to the colony with their parents or parent. Additionally, basic biographical information was recorded in the Census. Not only were the year of birth, religion, occupation, district of residence, and ownership of land and stock recorded, but family groupings and the civil condition of wife/husband and children. These data helped verify the claim to native birth.

Accuracy of civil condition was essential and the record of every individual claiming to be native-born was checked against every existing source. When a child had been baptized, the parish registers provided corroborative evidence and helped establish parentage. Where there was no record of baptism, evidence could be obtained from marriage certificates, burial registers of parents, baptisms of children of the native-born, and from the Musters of Population and Stock. A vital source of verification came from the Colonial Secretary's correspondence, the Memorials, Applications for Permission to Marry, Applications for Tickets-of-leave, Petitions in Mitigation of Sentence. Other sources which provided biographical material were Reports of Inquests—and Depositions of Witnesses, Ships' Musters and notices and advertisements in the *Sydney Gazette*.[21] These and similar sources not only served as a check on the authenticity of the Census entries, but added to the biographical information for all the men and women born between 1788 and 1813 and resident in New South Wales in 1828.

The Memorials to the Governor were a particularly important source, not only for civil condition, but for the biographical information they contained relating to parentage and date and place of birth. In some instances, an individual who had arrived in the colony with his parents claimed to be native-born when petitioning the governor for an indulgence. In the Census entry, however, he described himself correctly as 'Came Free', giving the name of the ship and date of arrival.[22] George Pitt Wood had arrived in the colony with his parents, John and Lucy, when he was two years old. As a young boy, he was apprenticed to a builder in Sydney and, when he had partly completed his indentures, he wrote a Memorial to the governor stating that he had been born in the colony, intended to remain, and requested a land grant on which to run his twenty-two cattle. As there were several similar claims to native birth, it may have been that the colonial youth believed that to be native-born increased the likelihood of being granted an indulgence by the governor. All claimants, however, gave their correct civil condition in the Census.

Checking the accuracy of native birth for married women was a particular difficulty. Marriage registers were helpful but, before the 1820s, this only applied to those who had married within the Church of England. Where a record was available, the maiden name and often the parentage were recorded on the marriage certificate. This was also found in applications for tickets-of-leave from intending bridegrooms. In the latter case, there were often Memorials from the native-born girl for land or indulgences because her husband was ineligible to own land until he was pardoned or had served his sentence.[23]

If the native-born girl had been widowed and had remarried it was extremely difficult to find evidence of native birth. In these cases it was necessary to trace both marriages to obtain the maiden name, then trace the parents. Marriage registers did not invariably describe the native-born as born in the colony. Frequently the description 'free' was used, which could also refer to a time-expired or pardoned convict. Native-born Ann Baylis, for example, was listed in the Census as the wife of Joseph Baylis, native-born sawyer, living with her husband and two children at Richmond. The authenticity of the claim to native birth was checked against the marriage register at St. Matthew's, Windsor. It read as follows:

Joseph, aged 22, son of John Bayliss of Castlereagh District and Miss Ann Croft, of Windsor, daughter of Samuel Croft, settler. Married by licence, June 20 1814 at Windsor ... Joseph Baylis, 21 Free, of Castlereagh and Ann Craft [sic] 20, Free, of Windsor.

Ann Croft had been baptized at St. John's, Parramatta. Her baptismal certificate gave her date of birth as 5 September 1795 and verified her claim to be born in the colony. Had she not been baptized, verification would have been necessary from such contemporary documents as applications for marriage licences, Memorials from her father or applications for land grants from her prospective husband.

When a colonial woman applied to the governor for permission to marry a convict or to have a convicted husband assigned to her as a ticket-of-leave holder it was essential that she state her own civil condition. Sarah Podmore, for example, applied to the governor for permission to marry convict Joseph Spencer. Spencer had arrived in the colony in 1815, sentenced to transportation for life, and in January the following year he had married Hannah Gromes. After the death of this wife, he married Sarah Podmore, born in the colony the daughter of Richard Podmore, a shoe-maker who had arrived free in 1792. In the 1828 Census Sarah Spencer is listed as native-born and her ticket-of-leave husband was assigned to her. Sarah's claim to be native-born was beyond dispute.

The general inaccuracies which were detected in the Census entries were usually related to the convicted men and women and concerned a mistaken date of arrival, a few deliberate falsifications of civil condition on arrival or lack of information resulting from incorrect completion of Census schedules. Ex-convict Charles Wright, for example, claimed to have arrived in New South Wales in 1781, seven years before settlement. 1781 was the year in which he had been convicted.

After detailed cross-checking to ensure that all who claimed in the Census to have been born in the colony between 1788 and 1813 were native born, a list of 1167 men and 1161 women was compiled. It was then possible to check these numbers against remaining population statistics for 1788–1813 and to establish what percentage of the colony's children had been native-born. The unreliability of the population figures meant that they could be an approximate indication only, so the list of native-born had to be checked against all sources of information relating to children who had arrived in the colony with a parent or parents, or as convicts themselves. When this information was compared with the probable numbers of children who left the colony and the number who had died, the civil conditions and identity of the children in the colony could be established.

THE MIGRANT CHILDREN: THE CAME FREE

It was particularly important to distinguish between the children born in the colony and the children who had arrived as part of a family group. The native-born could not be considered in isolation but needed to be placed firmly within the context of colonial society, and especially the society of their own age group. In this way characteristics of the native-born could be compared with those of the children from other groups and their origins traced to parentage, childhood experiences or the unique nature of the penal colony itself.

In the first year of settlement, twenty-two of the children who arrived with the first fleet were the children of the marines, nineteen were the children of convicts.[24] In 1790 a few children arrived with the families of the New South Wales Corps. The first recorded arrival of children belonging to free settlers was on 16 January 1793, when four children arrived with their immigrant parents. These children, all from one family, were aged between three and thirteen years. From this date details of immigrant children are found infrequently: they are usually listed as part of a family group and rarely by name.[25] The difficulties in obtaining details are increased by the incomplete nature of remaining records.[26] Ships' Musters and passenger lists, for example, are only available for a proportion of the ships arriving in the colony during this period, and all vary as to the details included.[27] The figures compiled by R.B. Madgwick for the six years of King's administration are a general indication of the small proportion of children 'of free persons' who arrived in the colony. Between April 1800 and August 1806 the total number of free persons, other than officials and military, who arrived in New South Wales was 290, and 130 of them were described as children.[28] These 130 arrivals in six years may be compared with the 1176 children recorded as resident in the colony in mid-1806.[29] It is reasonable to assume that the number of free children arriving prior to 1800 was considerably smaller than during the administration of Governor King, for little encouragement or assistance had been given to intending free settlers by the British government.[30] There was a slight increase in free arrivals from 1807 to 1813 but it was not until towards the closing years of Macquarie's administration that the actual numbers of free immigrants ceased to be insignificant.

The reluctance of the British government to encourage migration to New South Wales was partly the result of the assumption that the nature and function of the colony was purely penal. It was also partly the result of the prevailing British theories regarding colonization and emigration and of the specific conditions caused by the Napoleonic Wars, which increased Britain's need for recruits for her army and navy.

From the beginning of settlement, however, when the petition of a group of free tradesmen to accompany the first fleet was refused, the prevailing attitude towards emigration to New South Wales appears to have been based on the assumed nature and purpose of the colony; that is, that it was primarily a place of punishment and reform for British felons, not a colony of settlement. Its administration, therefore, its social structure and its developing economy were all determined by the needs of those for whom it was intended, the convicts. Macquarie himself held the view that New South Wales was a convict colony. He emphasized this by warning those free settlers who '. . . were too proud or too delicate in their feelings to associate with the population of the Country . . . [to] bend their Courses to some other Country . . .'[31]

In addition to this lack of encouragement from the British government, it is probable that there were relatively few free settlers who were attracted to the idea of migrating to New South Wales. It may have been that the expense of the voyage and the distance of the colony from Britain, when compared with the North American colonies, were not such important considerations as the emphasis on the penal nature of Botany Bay. The contemporary attitude that emigration itself was not for 'respectable' citizens was heightened by the knowledge of the social origins of most of the settlers in the colony. This, too, was reflected in the official attitude to New South Wales as a place to which not only British criminals but the unwanted and the destitute could be removed, to the advantage of the mother country. During the 1820s, the emphasis on 'official' emigration was still centred on the removal of paupers, the destitute and the unemployed; that is, those persons whose continued presence in Britain was considered a problem to the authorities and an expense to the local parishes and the British government.

It was not until increasing numbers of families among the 'respectable' orders of British society were persuaded to seek greater opportunities in the Australian colonies, as shown in the writings by, or attributed to, Edward Gibbon Wakefield, that detailed consideration may have been given to the length of the voyage to Australia compared with that to Canada or the United States of America. It was at this time that the advantages of family settlement in the Australian colonies were considered widely among Britain's prospective emigrants, although the districts favoured were South Australia and, to a lesser degree, Western Australia. However, this was not until at least forty years after the first settlement at Botany Bay and it may be concluded with reasonable certainty that, during the period 1788–1813, there was comparatively little interest in, incentive for or encouragement of free migration to New South Wales. This position supports the conclusion that few of the colonial children had arrived in New South Wales as immigrants.[32]

Table 1/1 is a cautious estimate of the number of children who arrived in New South Wales with free settler parents during the first twenty-five years of settlement.[33]

TABLE 1/1

Year of arrival	Number of children indicated in existent records	Number remaining in 1828 Census*
1792	4 children	1
1794	2 'men and their families'	4
1796–99	8 'married men and their families'	24
1800–1806	130 'children'	132
1811	299 'children of free persons'	223
1813	275 'children of free persons'	282

*The Census figures included all children who had arrived free; that is, children of officials and the military as well as children of free settlers.

THE MIGRANT CHILDREN: MILITARY AND OFFICIAL

The difficulties in establishing how many migrant children arrived in New South Wales during this period are repeated in attempting to determine how many official and military families arrived with children. The only civil condition given for these children is that of their fathers.[34] Most of the military children, both those who accompanied their parents and those who were born in the colony, returned to Britain when their fathers' tours of duty were completed. Most of the marine families who had accompanied Phillip, and were the first free families to live in New South Wales, returned to England when the marines were recalled in 1791.[35] In 1810, when the New South Wales Corps was replaced by Macquarie's own regiment, many of the wives, de facto wives and children of the soldiers and non-commissioned officers returned to Britain with their husbands and fathers. Some of the men of the New South Wales Corps had had long-standing relationships with convict and ex-convict women and had assumed responsibility for the children they bore. Macquarie, on compassionate grounds, permitted most of these 'wives' to accompany their 'husbands', granting the petitions of those who needed pardons in order to return legally to Britain. Macquarie's humane gesture also solved the problem of maintaining women and children who would have been left destitute after the departure of the Corps.[36]

The most important feature in relation to the numbers of 'official' and military children is the decreasing percentage they represented among the colonial children. In 1791 more than half of the colonial children were the sons and daughters of the marines and their wives, and a further unspecified number the children of officials and their convict mistresses. By 1801 the total percentage of officials' children had dropped to less than 25 per cent of all the children in the colony. By 1813 these children represented less than 10 per cent of the total.[37] This supports the conclusion that few of the children classed as the children of free persons had arrived with officials or military parents. Had all the immigrant children belonged to the 'civil–military department', they would still have formed a very small group when compared with the number born in the colony.

THE MIGRANT CHILDREN: THE CHILDREN OF THE CONVICTS

The number of boys and girls who arrived with a convicted parent was also small. Accuracy in assessing exact numbers is not possible for the indents of the convict ships did not always carry information relating to child passengers, whether accompanying parents or born on the voyage. Neither do there appear to have been any government or shipping regulations defining the circumstances under which an infant or child could obtain permission to accompany a convicted mother or father to Botany Bay. Permission was given infrequently, even if the alternative were to leave the infant or child destitute.

Mary Talbot was a young Irishwoman married to a stonemason. Her husband had been crippled when a stone fell on his leg and crushed it, making it impossible for him to work at his trade. With their baby and young daughter they left Ireland in search of some form of work in England. Shortly after their arrival Mary was charged with a theft which, she claimed at her trial, was the result of poverty, want and despair. Although a first offender, she was sentenced to the statutory punishment of death by hanging. At the end of the sessions she was offered a reprieve in the form of transportation for life. Neither her husband nor her children were permitted to accompany her to Botany Bay so she at first refused to accept the reprieve and was sent to Newgate prison, where 'her shrieks resounded throughout the gaol'. The *Dublin Chronicle* publicized her case and, on the understanding that her children would follow her, she was finally transported. Several years later she petitioned the governor for a pardon 'for the sake of my motherless children, they are the only cause of my anxiety and unhappiness'. There is no record of whether or not Mary Talbot and her children were ever reunited.[38]

It was not only the convicted women who had difficulties in obtaining official permission for their children to accompany them to Botany Bay. Convict James Lacey did get permission for his wife to sail with him on the same transport but their young son had to remain in England. In a letter to a friend he described his wife's anguish for her child. 'We could be very comfortable but for the uncertainitu [*sic*] of the Child's situation keeps her Continyally [*sic*] fretting ... her health has been greatly impaired thro' extreme anxiety for her child'.[39]

There is no accurate way by which the number of convict women who did bring a child or children with them may be determined. Nor is it possible to establish the number of children who accompanied a free wife rejoining a convicted husband in New South Wales. The incomplete and contradictory nature of the evidence is shown in the conflicting contemporary accounts of children on board the *Lady Juliana*, which arrived at Sydney Cove in mid-1790. According to David Collins, two children had died on the passage; according to the ship's surgeon, seven infants were born between England and New South Wales. Six children were reported as landing and they were described as 'the children of the convicts'.[40]

It is difficult to establish the civil condition of those women who arrived in New South Wales accompanied by their children. Eighty-seven women aboard the *Neptune* in the second fleet were officially listed as 'convict women'. W.H. Grenville, who succeeded Lord Sydney at the Home Department, had sent the following instructions to Lieutenant Shapcote shortly before the fleet left England:

> As it is probable that some of the male convicts put on board the ships ... may be desirous that their wives should accompany them, it has been thought advisable that so many of them shall be allowed to embark, as can be conveniently accommodated. If the number of convicts who may apply to you ... should not be sufficient ... you will in such case acquaint the rest of the convicts that women who may have cohabited with them will also be received on board.[41]

It was therefore extremely probable that there were both free wives and de facto wives; that is, free, unconvicted women among the eighty-seven listed as 'convict women'. It is also likely that children were born to some of these women on the passage or that some were accompanied by children born in England. No children were recorded as landing from the *Neptune* and only two child deaths were reported on the voyage.[42]

The *Queen* was the first convict transport to sail directly from Ireland, arriving in Sydney in April 1791. Twenty-two of the women listed on this ship were convicted women, one of whom died on the journey, and about seven, the wives or mistresses of convicts, were travelling on the same ship as their husbands. Thirteen children were recorded on board the *Queen*; one died before arriving at Sydney Cove. There is no indication of the civil condition of the mothers of these children. The next year, 1792, five children arrived on the *Pitt*. They may have been the children of convict women but, again, no details were recorded by the authorities. Throughout the first twenty-five years of settlement, there is no consistent or reliable record of how many children arrived with a convicted parent or joined a convicted father in New South Wales. It is not possible, therefore, to estimate with any degree of accuracy how many of the immigrant children were the sons and daughters of convict parents.[43]

Records are also too incomplete to establish how many children travelled to New South Wales with a free parent to join one already serving sentence in the colony. There are documented individual cases but these are too few on which to base a reliable estimate. Despite Grenville's original plan to reunite convict families in the colony, permission continued to be difficult to obtain, even if the convicted father were in a position to pay for the expenses of the voyage. In 1812, the *Report of the Select Committee on Transportation* suggested that more assistance be given to reuniting families separated by the transportation of the father. It was felt by the Committee that this would be both compassionate and humane. In addition, it had the added advantage of helping to reduce the immoral practices believed to be so prevalent in the colony. In the view of the Committee, this immorality, and a great deal of the colony's depravity and licentiousness, were caused by the low ratio of women to men. By encouraging wives and families to rejoin their husbands and fathers, this deplorable standard of conduct could be improved. There is no evidence that this 'compassionate' recommendation was implemented by the British authorities.[44]

To determine the proportion of immigrants among the colonial children, therefore, it is necessary to go beyond existing immigration and shipping records, colonial despatches and official reports. The greatest asset is a clear appreciation of the nature and extent of free immigration during this period, and the attitudes both of colonial and British officials and of the intending migrants. Within this framework it becomes clear that most of the colony's children were native-born. It is also clear that the native-born were not the only group of children in the colony during this first twenty-five years. There were the immigrant children and the children who had arrived as convicts. Any investigation into colonial society must take into account the differing backgrounds, experiences and life-styles of these three groups of children. The predominant group, however, was the native-born. The 'extraordinary' and rapid increase in the numbers of children at Botany Bay, commented on by contemporaries, was a natural one. A cautious estimate would suggest that at least 84–85 per cent of the children living in New South Wales between 1788 and 1813 were native-born; about 15 per cent or even less, had arrived with a parent or parents who were military or civil officials, free settlers, or convicts. The proportion of juvenile convicts—that is, convicted felons under the age of twelve years on arrival at Botany Bay— is impossible to estimate. They would have been no more than 1 per cent of the total child population and all were in the upper age bracket of nine to twelve years. Their importance is greater during the adolescence of the native-born, when a higher proportion of juvenile convicts was in the colony.

CHILD MORTALITY AT BOTANY BAY

One characteristic peculiar to the nature of the society of New South Wales contributed directly to the large proportion of children in the colony's population. This was the comparatively low infant and child mortality rate. Contemporary death records are incomplete and unreliable so direct evidence is unavailable. There were, however, several known local conditions peculiar to the colony and the structure of its population, which lowered the incidence of child mortality. Most significant of these were the environment, the climate, the diet, general living and working conditions, the virtual absence of child immigration during this period, and the age structure of the immigrants, both free and convict.

The chief causes of child death differed markedly in New South Wales from those in contemporary Britain. The differences highlight both the peculiar nature of the colonial experience and the contrast between the life-styles of the colony's children and those of their contemporaries in England and in Ireland. In New South Wales the causes of death were sometimes, but not invariably, recorded on death certificates in the parish registers. Coroners' Inquests, newspaper reports, letters, journals and diaries are further sources of information. The main cause of death during the first thirty years was accident, such as scaldings, burnings, drownings, or wandering away from settled areas and becoming lost in the surrounding bush. In some respects this was a similar pattern to that which had existed in colonial America. Death from these accidental causes was a more or less normal incidence of frontier life, although household accidents were frequent. The infant daughter of John Warby, a settler at Prospect Hill in 1810, was 'so severely scalded as to leave little hope of the unfortunate child's recovery'. The little girl died within a few days of the accident, which had been 'the result of upsetting a large pot of boiling water'. Thomas Peyton, the two-year-old son of a Wilberforce settler, 'died instantaneously ... in consequence of a knife, upon which the child had unhappily fallen, entering the roof of his mouth'.[45]

The comparatively low incidence of infant and child death from infectious diseases, the most common cause in contemporary Britain, was linked directly with the geographic isolation of the colony and the nature of immigration. Prior to white settlement in 1788 there had been no known contact with the infectious diseases of Europe. Neither were there any known indigenous diseases among the Aboriginal population. It was this complete lack of immunity by exposure which caused the smallpox 'to rage with fatal violence' among the Aborigines in 1789. The same lack of immunity existed among almost all of the colonial children. The risk of the infectious child-killers—measles, scarlet fever and whooping cough—being introduced into the isolated colony was greatly reduced because of the age of the immigrants and because there was very little 'family' immigration.[46] The average age of the convict settlers was mid-twenties, by which time they had been exposed to, and had survived, these diseases.

The lack of immunity among colonial children is evidenced by the result of the first prolonged contact of native-born children and English children.[47] George Suttor described the experiences of the wives and children of the men of the New South Wales Corps after they had arrived in England in 1811:

> ... their sufferings in the severe English winter of 1811 were very great ... sickness too attended them; the measles acted like a plague; sixty of the children, born in the colony, and many women, died in one fortnight.[48]

Among these women were native-born girls who had married men from the Corps and were in England for the first time.

Not only were the childhood experiences of the native-born, and the hazards they faced, different from those of their contemporaries in England and Ireland, but they differed also from those of the children of the North American colonies. Both groups of colonial children did share, in a general way, frontier experiences. The specific nature of those experiences, however, emphasizes the differences in life-styles. This is particularly marked in patterns of child mortality. Colonial children, and their British counterparts, all experienced the normal childhood sicknesses, such as teething and convulsions. The children of North America were also subject to death from the summer flux (dysentery) and marasmus (wasting away), both linked with diet. Neither of these ailments contributed significantly to the death rate in New South Wales. The pattern of immigration and settlement in the North American colonies placed heavier emphasis on family migration, family settlement, so that there were children constantly arriving from Britain. This increased the spread of infectious diseases, again in contrast to New South Wales. The evidence suggests that, during this first twenty-five years of white settlement, New South Wales was not only 'an extraordinary place for children' but an extremely healthy one.[49]

INFANTICIDE

A final aspect of this low incidence of child mortality in the penal colony highlights the unique nature of colonial society. The crime of infanticide was not only extremely rare but unnecessary. In eighteenth century England infanticide was a fairly common occurrence. It was closely linked with the problems caused by unwanted pregnancies and mainly practised by the girls and women from the domestic servant 'class', but it was also found among families from the lower orders of society, who considered it a form of birth control.[50] Among serving girls, obvious pregnancy led to instant dismissal and loss of character. This in turn frequently led to inability to obtain any 'respectable' situation and subsequent poverty, destitution and crime. It was therefore essential for the future security of the mother that the physical signs of pregnancy be hidden and, at the time of childbirth, that the child be born in the shortest possible time, in utmost secrecy. Noticeable absence from normal domestic duties had to be avoided. This led to all manner of ruses and deceptions by the 'unfortunate girl'. In Yorkshire, for example, when the mistress commented pointedly on her maid's increasing size, the maid replied that, alas, she took after her family, all of whom were 'pot-bellied'—and 'a shame it was to be so'.[51]

The immediate problem after the birth of an unwanted child was to prevent its being seen or heard by any person. The infant was therefore usually stifled at birth. Its body could be disposed of later at a convenient time. R.W. Malcolmson, in 'Infanticide in the Eighteenth Century', cites the case of a servant-girl in Nottingham. The girl gave birth to her baby at night in the bed she shared with two other maids. Neither of her companions was aware of the birth and the baby was stifled instantly. It was not until the mistress found the body in the privy that the girl was arrested and charged with infanticide.[52]

Although prevalent, the crime did not feature largely in English court cases. There were enormous difficulties in gathering sufficient evidence to gain a conviction, especially as 'some sort of presumptive evidence that the child was born alive' was required by the court before the acceptance of 'the other constrained presumption (that is, that the child whose death was concealed was therefore killed by its parents)'. It was open to the accused mother to plead that her child was stillborn or had been accidentally dropped at birth, sustaining fatal injuries.[53] In unassisted deliveries, who could contradict such a plea?

Most of the women who came to New South Wales during the first twenty-five years of settlement described themselves as 'in service'. They may be accepted as belonging to that 'class' of British women, the domestic servants, who were most familiar with the practice of infanticide, and some may have had first-hand knowledge of this crime. The criminal records of the colony during this period, however, contain few reports of infanticide or attempted infant murder.

The evidence suggests, therefore, that there was little necessity for the women of early Australia to resort to infanticide, for either economic or social reasons. Contemporary opinions indicate strongly that the abundance of children was the 'unwanted offspring' of the colony's abandoned convict women. That these children were not 'unwanted' is itself reflected in the absence of infant murders. At Botany Bay the birth of an illegitimate child, or two, did not carry the same social stigma as did similar births in contemporary Britain. Illegitimacy may not have been condoned by the colonial authorities—indeed, it was continually deplored—but it did not carry the penalty of loss of character which led to the inability of the mother to obtain secure employment.[54]

For the convict women of New South Wales pregnancy meant a reduction in hours of work and an increase in indulgences. This alone counteracted any tendency to resort to infanticide. Governor King complained that the women were useless to the colony for they were unable to work, being fully occupied tending their children, 'charming' as these children were.

DEPARTURE FROM NEW SOUTH WALES

There is one final consideration concerning the proportions of children in the varying civil condition categories in New South Wales during the first twenty-five years: the number who left the colony with their parents. There are few contemporary statistics but colonial conditions do suggest that the number of departing children was negligible and that the greater proportion of those who did leave with their settler parents went to Van Diemen's Land.[55] There was no official encouragement for ex-convicts to return to Britain; indeed the reverse was true, every inducement being offered to encourage both male and female ex-prisoners to settle in the colony after pardon or the expiration of their sentences.

It was extremely difficult to leave the colony. It was necessary to earn passage money, although there were some opportunities for males to obtain berths on returning vessels as ships' crew, ships' carpenters or coopers. Until about 1800 it was also possible for a 'deserving' ex-convict male to leave the colony by enlisting locally in the Indian Army.[56] Before departure, however, permission had to be obtained from the governor. This permission was only forthcoming if the applicant could show that he was not leaving 'encumbrances' in the colony; that is, a wife and/or children. It was almost impossible for a woman to leave the colony unless she accompanied her husband, had sufficient money to pay for her own passage or secured one of the very few positions available as a child's nurse or lady's maid. This was recognized by the Select Committee on Transportation in its Report of 1812.[57] For a woman with children, there were virtually no opportunities of leaving the colony.

New South Wales was, therefore, an extraordinary place for children. Most of those children, born in this English colony between 1788 and 1813, were native-born and few of them left their homeland. There were, however, small groups of children who had come to the colony as family children; that is, accompanying their parents and living in the colony as part of an immigrant family group. Neither the immigrant children nor the native-born were part of a homogeneous social 'class', sharing similar parentage, life-styles, experiences. The childhood of the colony's children reflected all the expectations, attitudes, achievements and failures of all levels of the social hierarchy, bond and free. In particular, these children were influenced directly by the immediate example of the life-styles of their own fathers and mothers. This was central to their responses to the 'new' Australian society which was slowly taking shape in this English colony at Botany Bay.

Contemporaries continued to view colonial society from the standpoint of the British background of its first settlers. Their emphasis remained on the presumed criminality and depravity of the convict men and women. The colony's children, however, were mostly unaware of this background. To the observers, these 'children of the convicts' were fathered by felons of the lowest description, by itinerant seamen, by the dregs of the soldiers of the British Army. Their mothers were tainted with the accepted image of whoredom and prostitution. The childhood of these bastard children, therefore, was assumed to be characterized by their constant exposure to wickedness and vice.

The distortion implicit in these assumptions becomes clear when colonial society is examined, not on the basis of assumptions, observations and opinions, but from the viewpoint of the settlers themselves. It is in the *colonial* experiences of these British parents, in their response to their new society, that their influence on their children, the first generation of Australian-born, may be found.

CHAPTER TWO

THE OBSERV'D

'The children . . . exposed to ruin on all hands.'

Rowland Hassall, 8 August 1801.

THE ASSUMPTIONS

Contemporary observers both in England and in New South Wales would have agreed that the characteristics of the native-born were determined by their relationships with their parents and by the structure of the society within which they were raised. These observers, however, saw these influences as detrimental. The native-born, they believed, rejected the degradation and vice of their parents and, despite their upbringing, became law-abiding, sober and industrious men and women.

The basic error underlying the assumptions was the belief that the native-born were a homogeneous class, the children of the convicts, and that they shared experiences common to a convict background. The predominant characteristics of the first generation, however, were the direct result of acceptance, not rejection, of parental example. They were the result of the complexity and diversity of colonial experiences, not of a common response to a degraded convict experience.

That the native-born were to be found at all levels of the social hierarchy, both bond and free, was not recognized by contemporaries. They were simply 'the children of the convicts' of Botany Bay. In 1810 Macquarie wrote to Bathurst, describing colonial society:

> ... This is, at present, a Convict Country, Originally established for their punishment and Reformation; that at least Nine-tenths of its present Population Consist either of Convicts, Persons who have been Convicts, or the Offspring of Convicts.[1]

J.H. Bent, giving evidence before the Select Committee on Gaols in 1819, described the native-born: '... when I say native youths, I mean those who are born in the Colony, the descendants of persons sent there ...'.[2]

Contemporary observers based their opinions very largely on the accepted assumptions of respectable British classes as to the nature, definition and expectations of convicts living in a penal colony. When Joseph Gerrald, a 'Scottish Martyr', was sentenced to fourteen years' transportation his friend and former teacher, Samuel Parr, wrote to him. His letter stressed the revulsion against the punishment of transportation, the horror that Gerrald had become a convicted felon sentenced to transportation to Botany Bay. 'I hear with indignation and horror that the severe sentence passed upon you in Scotland (i.e. Transportation), will shortly be carried into execution ...'.[3] The following year, 1796, Richard Johnson described the convicts in a letter to the Society for the Propagation of the Gospel. Johnson did not differentiate among the convicts. He described them all as 'The miserable wretches sent out ... being lost to all sense of virtue and religion . . .'.[4] Their infamy was clearly linked with their criminality.

It was this conviction for a major statutory offence which was sufficient to make a man or woman instantly infamous, without virtue, without honour, without any of the attributes expected from respectable members of society. Contemporary descriptions of the lives of convicted felons enhanced these beliefs. In 1803, for example, James Hardy Vaux, himself a convict under sentence of transportation at this time, described those felons whom he joined in the hulks:

> I soon met with many of my old Botany Bay acquaintances, who were all eager to offer me their friendship and services—that is with a view to rob me of what little I had; for in this place there is no other motive or subject for ingenuity.
> All former friendships or connections are dissolved, and a man will rob his best benefactor, or even mess-mate, of an article worth one halfpenny.[5]

When accepted contemporary assumptions as to the depravity of the convicts are examined, and the reasons for their acceptance considered, it becomes apparent that the generality of their application has distorted both the actual nature of Australian society in its origins and the relationship among the British parents and their colonial children.

According to recorded opinions and comments, the native-born of New South Wales were clearly recognized by their contemporaries as a distinct and distinctive group within colonial society, possessing qualities and characteristics peculiar to, and derived from, their 'convict' background and 'penal' experiences. Bigge, for example, reported, 'That class of inhabitants who have been born in the colony affords a remarkable exception to the moral and physical character of their parents . . .'.[6]

Surgeon Peter Cunningham described this distinction: 'Our colonial-born brethren are best known here by the name of *Currency*, in contra-distinction to *Sterling*, or those born in the Mother-country'. Cunningham, an avid supporter of New South Wales and its native-born, added, 'Our *Currency* lads and lasses are a fine and interesting race and do honour to the country whence they originated'. Cunningham's reports influenced the opinions of Sir Sydney Smith, who wrote in the *Edinburgh Review* that the 'Currency' were a very meritorious race.[7] William Charles Wentworth stressed the existence of this 'distinctive race' in the Address of Welcome to Governor Darling.[8] All opinions share the one distorting assumption: that this 'race' was a homogeneous one, with similarity of background and parentage and a common response to colonial conditions. Not only were these boys and girls described as the children of the convicts but as subject to all the influences the connotations of that word implied. It was believed by the commentators that the parents came from the lowest orders of Britain's criminal poor and, in New South Wales, led lives of indescribable vice, dissipation and criminality, neglecting or abandoning their unwanted children and making no attempts to provide for them even the basic necessities of life. So it was assumed that these children were daily witnesses to the debauchery, drunkenness, vice and iniquity of their parents; it was assumed and reported that they lacked all parental care, guidance, protection or restraint.

Governor King held these opinions and made constant reference in his letters and despatches to the neglected state of the children and the need to remove them from the evil influences of their parents. In May 1800 King wrote to Lieutenant Kent concerning 'the distressing prospect of the Rising Generation' unless there were some way in which they could be prevented from 'becoming the inheritors of their abandonded parents' profligate infamy'. Three months later King repeated these fears in even stronger terms in a despatch to the Treasury Commissioners:

> Finding the greater part of the children of this colony so much abandoned to every kind of wretchedness and vice, I perceived the absolute necessity of something being attempted to withdraw them from the vicious examples of their abandoned parents.[9]

The following month he wrote in a similar vein to Richard Johnson that he had 'frequent opportunities of observing numerous children of both sexes going about the streets in a most neglected manner'. King again attributed this to 'the destructive connections and examples of their dissolute parents in whom no reform can be expected'.[10] This was also the tenor of a despatch to Portland the following year, in which King stressed the 'necessity of some immediate steps being taken to save the youth of this colony from the destructive examples of their abandoned parents'.[11]

The widespread publicity King gave these opinions helped to establish this description of the native-born as the children of profligate convicts. King's opinions were echoed by Samuel Marsden. Hassall, writing to Burder in 1801, commented on a sermon preached by Marsden at the opening of the Orphan School attended by the 'orphans' themselves. Hassall reported that 'In the body of his sermon the Revd. Mr. Marsden gave a true description of the children of this colony ... the children's exposedness to ruin on all hands ...'.[12]

When, in the 1820s, the same children emerged as remarkably honest, law-abiding, industrious, and even sober, young men and women, contemporaries saw this as an admirable, if unexpected, revulsion against the life-style of their parents.[13] Parental influence and early social environment were seen by contemporaries as negative influences in that they led to a total rejection by the native-born of the standards, mores and attitudes of convicts and convictism, the direct result of which was the severing of parental connections. The 'convict slate', as it were, was wiped clean by this rejection and Australia's first-born could establish their own independent and respectable family patterns and social standards.

This contemporary picture would have been eminently satisfying as an antidote to the contemporary fear of a continued convict taint pre-dominating in the developing society of New South Wales. This fear was increased by the belief that this taint could be transferred from generation to generation. As late as 1832, during debate in the House of Commons concerning the extension of colonial constitutional liberties, Howick declared that 'emancipists and their descendants were tainted with criminality'.[14] This belief in the hereditary taint of convictism had been condemned by William Wentworth a decade earlier. Discussing those who attempted to restrict constitutional liberties in the colony, Wentworth wrote:

> The covert aim of these men is to convert the ignominy of the great body of the people (i.e. in the colony) into a hereditary deformity. They would hand it down from father to son, and raise an eternal barrier of separation between their offspring and the offspring of the unfortunate convicts ... although none among them dares publicly avow that future generations should be punished for the crimes of their progenitors, yet such are their private sentiments. ...[15]

There is no remaining evidence to suggest that the honesty of the first generation and their apparent rejection of convictism and the 'vices of their parents' was directly used as a counter to the 'hereditary taint' theory. As children, the native-born had been recognized as 'vital to the future of the colony'[16] and, as adults in the 1820s, their commendable characteristics added to the arguments for recognition of New South Wales as a respectable colony no longer deserving the description of a colony of thieves.

The remarkable honesty of the native-born as a group is the one assumption which is supported by both impressionistic and quantitative evidence. As with all other contemporary assumptions, the conclusions were based on false premises. This is illustrated by a consideration of the sources and context of contemporary observations concerning parents and children and convict society. With a few exceptions, these were personal opinions, frequently based on a limited familiarity with the colony and with its inhabitants as a whole. The bias, partiality and generally impressionistic nature of many of these recorded comments may be indicated by dividing the sources of this contemporary evidence into five categories, all with varying degrees of acceptability.

THE COMMENTATORS

The first, and probably the most important category, was the official view. This comprised the opinions of governors, chaplains, missionaries and men such as Commissioner J.T. Bigge and Chief Justice Burton.[17] A similarity of approach towards convicts and convictism is evident in their observations. Both were literate and respectable men and, as with other observers in this category, they were strongly influenced by standards of morality and respectability.

The observations on Botany Bay and its society which these respectable observers have left for future generations were mainly in connection with criminality, immorality and convict behaviour. The establishment and maintenance of order, regularity and respectability in the convict colony were closely linked with the enforcement of decent, moral and honest behaviour. These standards were assumed to be completely foreign to the majority of the colonists. Little mention was made of those who outwardly conformed to respectable social standards. The emphasis was on the problems caused by those who were openly irreligious, immoral, drunken, dissolute and criminal. These opinions reflected the expected behaviour of convicted felons in a penal colony and, although the condemnations were frequently accurate observations on the standards and behaviour of a section of colonial society, they did not reflect the standards of the whole community.

The second category consists of the various published accounts of the colony and its society, and these accounts very naturally reflected the various attitudes to, and expectations of, the writers. This is evident in the extreme differences found in two conflicting accounts, *The Felonry of New South Wales* by James Mudie and *Settlers and Convicts* by Alexander Harris.[18] Many such works were intended primarily for publication and thus may have overstressed those aspects of colonial life in which the reading public showed greatest interest, for they portrayed a life-style which was compatible with preconceived ideas concerning convicts and penal colonies. An example of this selective writing may be found in the convict novels, with the emphasis on barbarity and degradation, although here no mention is made of the convicts' children. Works which were actual accounts of visits to the colony, most notably Peter Cunningham's *Two Years in New South Wales*, or works which purported to be based on first-hand information, such as Edward Gibbon Wakefield's *Letter from Sydney*, reflected the underlying attitudes and prejudices of their authors. Where these accounts do comment on the native-born, their parents and the convict system these opinions are personal ones. This selectivity lessens their degree of acceptability as accurate reflections of the characteristics of the society of New South Wales.

The opinions of both permanent and temporary residents of New South Wales, which are to be found in letters, diaries, journals and private papers, form the third category.[19] These opinions vary in acceptability according to the position and background of the writer and the degree of familiarity with the colony. It is probable that temporary residents such as Elizabeth Paterson and Anna Josepha King were strongly influenced by the official positions of their husbands. Their observations were based on daily familiarity with conditions of life in both Sydney and Parramatta but they would have had little experience of the conditions of children living in smaller settlements or in outer areas. There is strong evidence of Mrs King's charity and philanthropy: her journal of the voyage to New South Wales shows the humanity of her attitude towards the convict women and their children.[20] Her main charitable interest in the colony was providing care for destitute children and thus her comments centre on the abandoned and neglected, with little reference to those who lived with, and were supported by, their parents. Mrs King's attitude and interest was in strong contrast to that of Mrs Macarthur, who appeared to be unconcerned with the problems of 'lower class' women and their children. Although her own children were native-born, there was no awareness that they, too, were part of this new 'race'. Elizabeth Macarthur, together with Elizabeth Marsden, had a far greater degree of familiarity with the colony than did Anna King or Elizabeth Paterson, but the accepted attitudes of respectable 'gentry' towards convicts and convictism appear to have coloured her view of society in New South Wales.[21]

The fourth category consists of the published accounts of casual visitors to the colony, visitors who usually saw little more than the sea-port of Sydney and whose stay was brief.[22] Despite the limited knowledge of the colony on which observations were based, these reports coloured subsequent attitudes towards the colony's inhabitants. The first of these accounts was most probably that of the visiting Spanish expedition in 1793. Their report was damaging to the reputation of the colonial women, some of whom were the mothers of the first generation:

> ... the conduct of our men ashore had not been so orderly as formerly, not because we believed it was difficult for them to resist the continuous seductive advances of the women prisoners—who were degraded by vice, or rather greed, and who were so uninhibited in their conduct that the women of Teneriffe ... would seem chaste by comparison—but because they led them on into drinking some concoctions solely for the purpose of doping them and afterwards robbing them ... There was one crewman ... who failed to show up for roll-call for four consecutive days.[23]

Sea captains were usually the authors of these accounts. Although their opinions were based on their own observations, they were generally limited to Sydney and its immediate surroundings and coloured to varying degrees by expectations of life in a penal colony. The comments of Captain Turnbull were typical of those who assumed that convictism had tainted the inhabitants of Botany Bay:

> The circumstances under which the colony was settled, and the very purpose of the settlement, has had a very visible effect upon the general manners, or what may be called the national character, of Botany Bay....[24]

The last category are the reports and comments found in colonial newspapers, in particular the *Sydney Gazette*, the *Australian* and the *Monitor*. Editorials, articles and letters relating to the native-born and their parents in both the *Australian* and the *Monitor* need to be considered in the light of the attitudes and policies of the editors, for both W.C. Wentworth and E.S. Hall linked the position of the native-born to current preoccupations with changing land and immigration policies. A more satisfactory source, and one as yet little used by historians, is the indirect evidence available from advertisements for work and from descriptions of events in the colony, reported in the *Sydney Gazette*, particularly during that period in which it was the only local newspaper in New South Wales. As a government publication it was relatively uninvolved in debatable issues.

By classifying the observers of colonial life on the basis of their own social and economic backgrounds, it is evident that contemporary observations concerning the native-born and their parents were made by men from the same level of society. The attitudes expressed in these observations and the assumptions on which they were based reflected clearly the standards, mores and expectations of a literate, 'respectable' British middle class. They could, and did, share similar attitudes and assumptions concerning the standard of behaviour of convicts exiled in a penal colony. They could, and did, share similar views on the nature of crime and punishment and the criminal propensities of the lower orders. One main result of this was that certain 'class' attitudes, based on British experiences and life in Britain, shaped expectations as to the nature of life in a convict colony. It also prejudged the nature of the convict inhabitants, endowing these men and women with the characteristics and standards expected of British felons.

CONNOTATIONS OF 'CONVICT'

Chief among the attitudes of these 'respectable' men and women was the definition of the word 'convict'. The connotations of convict extended to the ex-convict, so that assumptions of convict depravity coloured observations of ex-convict behaviour. This was adequately summed up by that eminently respectable Mr Macarthur in his evidence to Commissioner Bigge:

Question: From living in the Neighbourhood of the Town of Parramatta, you must have had opportunities of observing the general Character and habits of the people of that Town. Do you conceive that they are more depraved or less than might be expected of them?

Answer: I seldom go into the Town, and I avoid all unnecessary intercourse with the inhabitants. The lower classes are reported to be disorderly—and they always were so—but I cannot think that they are worse than might be expected under the system of indulgence to Convicts upon which this Colony has been established. And when their past lives and long confirmed habits are considered, it is a Matter of surprise to me that they behave so well. There are a few of the Inhabitants, who have been prisoners, that I am told, live decently....[25]

When asked if he considered emancipated convicts capable of managing convicts assigned to them, Macarthur replied that he thought 'very few of them are deserving such trust'. This low opinion was echoed by fellow landowner Gregory Blaxland, who told Bigge that he considered 'indulgence had been too liberally bestowed', for 'so few of the emancipated convicts had become reformed in their moral and religious habits'.[26] John Oxley concurred:

Question: Are you acquainted with the habits and characters of the small emancipated convict settlers and what do you conceive them to be?

Answer: I have a general knowledge of them; they are far from Industrious; addicted to drunkenness and prefer licentious and unsettled life to the attention requisite for the proper cultivation of their lands.[27]

Generally speaking, guilt had no degree to contemporaries, nor was the nature of the crime considered in relation to the criminality of the offender. It was not the crime itself but the single fact of conviction for a major felony which made the convicted man, woman or child infamous to society. It is important to consider the crimes of those transported to Australia within this contemporary definition. The statutory punishment for most major felonies was death.[28] So the men and women whose sentences were commuted or who were sentenced to terms of transportation were, to their contemporaries, criminals 'of the darkest complexion'. It was the conviction for a major statutory offence, not the crime, which made the convict infamous, repugnant to 'respectable' society. On this basis expectations were formed and assumptions were made as to their behaviour in the penal colony. To their respectable contemporaries they were infamous, and with this infamy was associated a whole range of expected characteristics: convicted felons were assumed to be lacking in decency, morality, honesty, to be devoid of any of the expected social virtues. Phillip wrote to Lord Sydney in 1788, 'Numbers of them (the convicts) have been brought up from their infancy in such indolence that they would starve if left to themselves'.[29] Watkin Tench expressed the practical view that 'To have expected sudden and complete reformation of conduct were romantic and chimerical'.[30] Hassall, in 1807, found the colony 'a sink of iniquity'[31] and Bligh argued against indiscriminate granting of 'Emancipations and Free Pardons' for he believed that

> . . . even those who have been raised to some degree of wealth by such means, if happily they leave off thieving, their habits of cheating and knavery seem to be increased by the giving up the other Vice; fair and honourable principle they cannot admit in competition to their habitual reasonings. . . .[32]

It is probable that these attitudes were reinforced by the belief that only the 'incorrigible offenders' were sent to Botany Bay. In 1791 Pitt told the House of Commons:

> [it is] necessary and essential . . . to send some of the most incorrigible criminals out of the kingdom . . . a worst policy of state to keep offenders of that description home to corrupt others, and contaminate the less guilty, by communicating their own depravity.[33]

In its Report, the Select Committee on Transportation of 1812 emphasized that those men transported were 'the most unruly in the hulks, or are convicted of the most atrocious crimes'.[34]

The major importance of these attitudes towards convicted felons is that they directly, if unconsciously, affected the expectations of both officials, visitors and 'respectable' settlers in New South Wales.

To a certain extent, the acceptance by respectable men and women that conviction of a felony was equated with everlasting infamy has been overlooked by historians as a contributing cause of the unfavourable opinions expressed by contemporaries. This is particularly evident in modern historical accounts of the female convicts. Both Miriam Dixon, in *The Real Matilda*, and Anne Summers, in *Damned Whores and God's Police*, accept contemporary assumptions as to the immoral character of the female convicts. They fail to question the sources on which this unsavoury reputation has been based and concentrate instead on explaining why the women were immoral.[35] It is essential that the attitudes on which contemporary assumptions were based be examined critically before any assessment may be made as to the validity of those assumptions. The connotations of convictism must be central to any attempt to recreate penal society. However harsh the social background of the convicts may have been, whatever may have been the motivation for their crimes, the convict settlers of Australia were convicted felons and, to contemporaries, completely unacceptable to 'respectable' society.

THE DEFINITION OF 'CONVICT'

A second contemporary characteristic which distorted the role and nature of the convicted settlers in early New South Wales was the common failure to distinguish between time-serving convicts and those who had served their sentences or had been pardoned and were technically free men and women. To respectable society, a convict retained the stigma of convictism for life and was frequently referred to as a convict, despite pardon or completed sentence. When Governor King attempted to include 'emancipated convicts' in his own bodyguard, Major Johnston expressed this entrenched attitude. Despite his long-standing relationship with a convict woman, Johnston wrote to King:

I cannot suppose that His Majesty ever intends that prisoners should be considered among that class of persons 'residing within this territory'. Respectable inhabitants, as Lord Hobart remarks are, in my opinion, that description of persons. . . .[36]

Bathurst wrote to Sydney of 'Convicts, after the expiration of their sentences . . .', while both Bigge and Cunningham favoured the expression 'emancipated convicts'.[37] The ex-convicts were themselves aware of this perpetuation of convict status. In a petition to the King in 1821 they complained that:

. . . your Petitioners, retrospectively and prospectively, are to be considered as Convicts attaint, without Personal Liberty, without Property, without Character or Credit, without any one Right or Privilege belonging to Free Subjects. . . .[38]

This description was in accordance with the attitudes of 'respectable' society, typified in the statement of Lieutenant Archibald Bell. When asked by Bigge if he had any 'objection to the admission of Convicts into Society', Bell replied, 'I consider them as having once been tainted, unfit to associate with afterwards ...'. [39]

This broad use of the word 'convict' had important results: the expected characteristics of the convicts became the expected characteristics of the ex-convicts—completion of sentence did not imply reformation of manners; the native-born were directly affected in that they were indiscriminately described as the children of the convicts, regardless of the actual civil condition of their parents. It is therefore necessary to accept with extreme caution contemporary observations based very largely on these assumptions. It is essential to balance this presumptive evidence with some form of unemotive and statistical evidence relating to the parents and their children if the actual characteristics and life-styles of the early settlers of New South Wales are to be determined.

'THE CHILDREN OF THE CONVICTS'

Contemporary opinions as to the actual nature, structure and characteristics of 'convict' society directly affected attitudes to the colony's children, the 'children of the convicts'. A detailed investigation into the parentage of the native-born, however, shows clearly that they were to be found at all levels of colonial society, that they came from both the main groups, the convicted and the unconvicted, and, most importantly, that they were more likely to be the children of ex-convicts than of those who were still under sentence. There were native-born children at the highest levels of society as there were at the lowest levels. Most had parental links with convictism in that they had a mother who had arrived convicted but this does not imply that they were 'the children of the convicts', nor does it imply that their background was a common one of neglect and criminality.[40] This is of even greater importance when considered in relation to the prevailing social attitudes of 'respectable' classes, which attempted to erect rigid class barriers based on civil condition at the time of arrival in the colony. Wentworth claimed that this 'would establish divisions which may serve hereafter to divide colonists into castes'. He added: 'Shall a vile faction be allowed to inflict on the unfortunate convict a punishment infinitely greater than that to which he had been sentenced by the violated majesty of the law?'[41] This division was prevented very largely by the native-born who, far from being a homogeneous class, permeated and linked all classes and orders of colonial society, both in their parentage and by their marriages.

The contemporary assumption that the native-born were the children of the convicts must be questioned on three main grounds: first, the definition, nature and connotations of the word 'convict' as used by both contemporaries and later historians; second, the failure of contemporaries and later observers to distinguish clearly between convicts and ex-convicts, and the failure to recognize that both groups had peculiar and distinctive characteristics, rights and obligations; third, that children were born at all levels of society and that to be colonial-born did not equate with convict parentage.

Quantitative evidence from the 1828 Census alone indicates that more children were born to ex-convicts than to actual convicts under sentences. Although the proportion was comparatively small, children were born to free settlers, civilian and military officials, seamen, marines and soldiers.[42] There were obvious differences between the life-styles, experiences and opportunities of children raised in the household of self-supporting ex-convict parents and those living with a mother, or father and mother, who were still convicts. In the same way, there were essential differences between the lives of children of wealthy parents and the lives of children of labourers. This applied whether the father was a successful emancipist or an immigrant servant. The civil condition of the parents, added to their material wealth and social standing, directly affected the manner of upbringing of the child. It was the diversity of these experiences which placed the native-born at all levels of colonial society and which ultimately determined their role within that society. The effect of this role was more widespread and more influential in shaping the nature of Australian society than would have been possible had the first generation been simply the 'children of the convicts'. The diversity of their parentage and the contrasts in the manner of their upbringing are the key to their influence on the development of their homeland.

THE NATURE OF COLONIAL SOCIETY

The nature of colonial society, in particular the structure of the population, shows the diversity of parentage, background, upbringing and experiences of the first generation. Society in eastern Australia had originated within a settlement which was unique in the history of western civilizations. The English colony founded at Botany Bay in January 1788 was an experiment in penology. This may not have been the intention of the British government but it was hoped that this penal colony would result in possible financial benefit to the British government. At the same time, the possibilities for reformation of convicts in New South Wales could serve as a sop to any slumbering social conscience of the upper levels of the English hierarchy. Botany Bay was unique in that it was purely penal in matters administrative, legislative and judicial.[43] It was unique in that its governance was in the hands of one man, who possessed greater powers in New South Wales than did King George in England. Lieutenant Ralph Clark, after hearing the Commission read, wrote in his journal that he 'had never heard of any single person having so great a power invested in him'.[44] It was also unique in its original social composition, most of the first inhabitants being from Britain's lower orders: the marines and soldiers who were to guard the colony and the convicts sentenced to penal servitude.[45] There were few officials to represent the 'respectability' of Britain's middle classes.

Finally, New South Wales was unique in that it lacked any semblance of the civil liberties which were considered the birthright of free-born Englishmen. Gradually, the first pioneers, convicted and free, were joined by settlers from the civilian and military officials, from the marines, soldiers and seamen, and by the few free settlers who were permitted to try their fortunes at Botany Bay. Naturally, social conditions in a penal settlement differed from those in Britain, but colonial society did develop a basic hierarchical structure based on wealth, influence and position. In the colony, however, wealth was to become more important than birth and there was not, in the beginning, any inherited 'aristocracy'.

Social differences were largely the result of the transportation system itself and the effects this had on the structure of the population of New South Wales. Definitions of 'class', for example, had unique connotations in the penal colony. In England, the 'criminal class' was described by a Select Committee on Police as 'those who normally commit crimes, the poor and the indigent'.[46] In New South Wales this definition of criminals was extended by the 'respectable', unconvicted inhabitants and by British officials to include all men and women who had been convicted of a major felony and transported. An entire section of the community was accordingly designated criminal, despite being technically 'free' after pardon or completion of sentence. These convicts were socially unacceptable. As most of the settlers had arrived as convicted felons, this affected attitudes towards the nature and characteristics expected of Botany Bay Society. Sydney Smith, writing in the *Edinburgh Review* in 1819, summed up this view:

New South Wales is a sink of wickedness in which the majority of convicts of both sexes become infinitely more depraved than at the period of their arrival ... A marsh, to be sure, may be drained and cultivated, but no man who has his choice would select it ... as his dwelling place.[47]

Few contemporaries had any understanding of the complexity of the structure of a society which had been condemned as uniformly depraved.

The unrecognized feature of colonial society during this period was that there were in effect two societies, divided by the artificial barrier of civil condition on arrival. Within both divisions there were all the normal hierarchical divisions and these 'classes' were firmly based on economic and material successes in the colony. Within convict society there were men and women who formed a wealthy 'upper class'. They had earned their wealth and position in the colony and many of them rivalled in material possessions the free men and women of the highest ranks. On the other hand, within the free division of society, there were also men and women at the lowest level, the free labourers and servants. Therefore native-born children were to be found at all levels of free and convicted society and could not in any way be described as an homogeneous 'class', sharing similar backgrounds, parentage and life-styles. Their experiences were dependent on the achievements and position of their parents. There was obviously an enormous difference between the lives of orphans in the Orphan Schools or the children of the actual convicts and the lives of the sons and daughters of successful, self-supporting emancipists. In the same way there was a great gulf between the children of 'free' labourers and servants and the children 'of the first water' of respectable free society. To emphasize the experiences of one group, the 'children of the convicts', to imply that these were the typical experiences of the native-born, is to distort the role and influence of these children. Although most had one parent who had arrived as a convicted felon, these parents were to be found at all social and economic levels in New South Wales. The influence of their children permeated the whole fabric of colonial society. This influence, based on the achievements and failures of their parents, was intensified by the marriage patterns of the first generation, which spanned the bond and free societies. The native-born, by their life-styles, by their very existence, prevented the continuation of rigid class barriers in society, class barriers based on civil condition on arrival at Botany Bay.

It is central to an understanding of the role of the native-born within colonial society that the diversity of the social groupings of their parents be appreciated. Existing evidence, although insufficient to suggest the percentages belonging to the various groups, clearly indicates that the parents came from all levels of convicted and unconvicted colonial society and this affected directly the nature of the upbringing of the children. Given the population structure and the preponderance of convicts among immigrants, it was natural that the smallest parental group formed the upper levels of 'respectable' society. This, however, was the most vocal group. Its resultant influence in colonial affairs balanced the smallness of its size. It was composed of the highest officials, military and civil officers, and the wealthiest free settlers, such as the Blaxlands, the Pipers, the Macarthurs, the Marsdens, the Suttors, the Campbells. The children from this group enjoyed all the advantages associated with the security of wealth and social prestige. Frequently their fathers did share a characteristic common to the upper levels of convicted society: their wealth had been accumulated in the colony itself and they were, in effect, self-made men who had taken advantage of the opportunities offered in the colony to raise their own social and economic status to a level which would have been impossible had they remained in their own social class in England. John Macarthur is probably the most outstanding example of this achievement for he arrived in the colony in 1790 as a second lieutenant in the New South Wales Corps, deeply in debt and determined to make his fortune in this penal settlement. King wrote to Under-Secretary King in November 1801, 'He [Macarthur] came here in 1790 more than £500 in debt and is now worth at least £20,000'.[48]

It was to be expected that the children from this wealthy group inherited the attitudes and prejudices of their parents and accepted without question the wide social gulf which they believed to exist between the convicted and the unconvicted. Native-born themselves, they were atypical in that they continued to extend the stigma of convictism to 'the children of the convicts', generally accepting the contemporary connotations of that word. James Macarthur, although avowedly proud of his native land, referred to the native-born as 'the children of the convicts and the emancipists', and his comments on their abilities and potential value to New South Wales appear to have been based on the assumption that 'native-born' was equated with 'lower orders'. When giving evidence before the House of Commons Select Committee on Transportation, 1837, Macarthur was asked 'Are not the greatest portion of the natives of the colony children of convicts?' He replied:

> The greater portion of them probably are; I do not make any exception as to the whole of the children of the convicts; I say that the exceptions of bad character are principally amongst those who are the children of the convicts.[49]

In answer to another question by Sir George Grey, James Macarthur made it plain that he equated native-born with 'lower class'. Sir George asked if it were possible to compare 'the lower classes of the population in Sydney with the lower classes of the population in any seaport in England'. Macarthur replied:

> I should think that the moral character of the native-born inhabitants was quite as good; at least I know many individuals of that class of the highest character, bringing up families in the most reputable manner. . . .[50]

These attitudes were a direct reflection of those of his parents. His father, John Macarthur, had suggested to Bigge that the native-born youth should be taught agricultural skills on a small model plantation-type farm, the inference being that the only opportunities for the native-born were in connection with farming and grazing.

The men and women from the wealthy levels of free society were convinced of the primacy of land ownership and this, together with their belief in the stigma of convictism, coloured their reactions to the children of the colony. To a certain extent, the children from this social group, accustomed to the standards of their parents, denied their own birthright by describing the native-born as 'the children of the convicts'. James Macarthur, when asked by Sir George Grey, 'Are you native-born yourself?' replied, 'Yes, I am'. From the tone and content of his previous evidence to the Select Committee, however, it is clear that he did not class himself with those usually described as the native-born of the colony.[51] This, to Macarthur, was a general term which usually denoted convict-emancipist parentage and membership of the lower orders of society.[52] It would almost appear as if it were subconsciously accepted by this group that a penal society could only produce convict children and that the upper levels of society must, from necessity, come from British roots. This may be seen in Hamilton Hume's comment that he hoped to lead an expedition of exploration 'altho' an Australian'.[53]

The 'middle classes' of free society had closer links with the convicted, links strengthened by occupations and by marriages. This level was composed of the comparatively smaller landholders and farmers, merchants and traders, craftsmen and master tradesmen. There were families such as that of John and Hannah Dight, who had arrived free together in 1801 and by 1828 were farming their 1000 acres at Richmond and living with their native-born children, Ann (1806), George (1810) and Charles (1813).[54] The fathers of many of the families in this group had arrived either as members of the marines or the military or as free settlers.[55] Some arrived as family groups, notably those who chose to come to New South Wales as settlers, and some married convicted women, thus helping to weaken the artificial division of society into the bond and the free.[56] There are, unfortunately, no existing records which show the attitudes of the free wives towards 'convict' wives. Evidence does underline the successes of these 'tainted' women in raising their children, in helping to develop a structure of family life which was peculiar to this colony. In the case of these 'middle classes', the free status of the father, when combined with a degree of material success, was sufficient to establish the family's 'respectability', despite the civil condition of the mother. The status of the convicted wives in this group is sufficient in itself to indicate the distortion implicit in the contemporary assumption that the convicted women were all 'a pack of vile baggage' and 'a wanton lot'. The life-style of the children of this group depended entirely on the material success of the parents.

It is also necessary to remember that there were unconvicted men—and some women—at the lowest order of free society, the labourers and servants, the washerwomen, seamstresses and the nursemaids. Elizabeth Macarthur was one free woman who was accompanied by her servant. She wrote to her mother in March 1791: 'The same woman is with me that had charge of Edward when I visited you from Plymouth'.[57] During this period, 1788–1813, this free 'lower class' of colonial society was a much smaller group in comparison with the lowest orders of convicted society, but its existence underlines the diversity of free society within the colony and the impossibility of describing the parents of the native-born as coming from one section or level. The lower free levels, particularly among the subsistence farmers and small tradesmen from the ranks of the marines and the military, had the closest links with convicted society, for most of the marriages and liaisons here were with convicted women. Given the structure of female society in the first twenty or thirty years, there was little choice in a marriage partner other than a woman who had arrived convicted.

The diversity found among free society was duplicated among those who had arrived convicted. This is more remarkable when it is considered that most of these convicted men and women came from the same level of society in England and Ireland and shared the same disadvantages of poverty, lack of education and opportunity.[58] As with the free settlers, it is not possible to suggest the percentages in various social groups. From an investigation of the land and stock owned by the parents of the native-born, and from a consideration of occupations and districts of residence, it is apparent that, as with the free society, the highest economic level formed the smallest group, followed by the middle order which corresponded in occupations and achievements with that of free society. The largest group were the lower levels.[59] Most of the parents who could be traced, however, were from the self-supporting and industrious middle classes found in both the rural areas and the towns and townships. The wealthiest group of parents was the most vocally ambitious. They were the merchants, traders, boat-builders, 'manufacturers', landowners and farmers with extensive holdings. This was the enterprising group of convicted society, and their achievements may be considered a phenomenon directly resulting from opportunities offered by the peculiar nature of the penal colony.

These men and women had arrived at Botany Bay without capital, most of them illiterate. They had gained their experience in the colony itself, many as agents and dealers for the officers of the New South Wales Corps. Thus the stigma of convictism had been, in effect, their key to success. Henry Kable was an example. He was a twenty-one-year-old illiterate village labourer from Suffolk when he was convicted with his father and sentenced to death for burglary. The father was hanged and Kable junior transported for seven years, arriving in 1788. Immediately after arriving in the colony with their infant son, Kable married Susannah Holmes, who was from the same village and with whom he had lived in prison in England and on the voyage. By 1800 Kable had established himself as a wealthy merchant, trader, dealer and boat-builder. He had first become involved in trade as the agent for Lieutenant Rowley but had gradually branched out on his own. His outstanding success was primarily the result of his own initiative, application and industry. His children were brought up in the household of a comparatively wealthy family. Diana, the eldest·daughter of these two convicted felons, was married at St. Phillip's in Sydney and, on her marriage certificate, her husband was described as a 'gentleman'. Highly successful emancipists such as Kable were in the minority and there is evidence that they considered themselves the 'middle class' of colonial society and initiated and led a great deal of colonial agitation for civil rights and liberties for all free inhabitants of New South Wales. It was a predominantly ex-convict group led by native-born William Charles Wentworth which approved the Address of Welcome to Governor Darling, outlining colonial land grievances.[60] It was the opinion of surgeon Peter Cunningham, 'Our emancipist body ... forms the most useful and enterprising portion of our community; all the distilleries, nearly all the breweries, and the greater portion of the mills and manufactories being owned by them ...'.[61]

The way in which the emancipists defined free differed from the definition of 'respectable' members of society for it naturally included those men and women who had served their sentences of penal servitude or who had been pardoned. Their own definition of success was based on individual material achievements and these were considerable. H. Grey Bennet wrote of this group in 1819:

> The greater share, I believe, of the convertible property of the colony, rests with this class: and they therefore possess in the various transactions of life that degree of indolence, good and bad, which property may be supposed to give them, and which, too frequently, renders them objects of envy and jealousy of certain of the voluntary exiles.[62]

It is significant that this success originated from their own initiative for, despite some little encouragement from Hunter and King,[63] their success was not based on any positive encouragement from the Colonial Office, whose hopes for reformation of the convicts did not exceed the possibility of a change to honest and moral habits of life. It was not until after the arrival of Lachlan Macquarie that a definite policy of encouragement to deserving emancipists to 'better themselves' is evidenced. Macquarie wrote:

It has been My Invariable Opinion, and Upon that Opinion I have Acted ever since I Came to this Colony, that Once a Convict has become a Free Man, either by Servitude, Free Pardon, or Emancipation, he should in All Respects be Considered on a footing with every other Man in the Colony, according to his Rank in Life and Character.[64]

Macquarie's emancipist ideas were revolutionary both to the 'respectable' members of society and to the Colonial Office. Most importantly, they directly affected the way of life of many of the native-born for their adolescent years coincided with the administration of Macquarie.

The native-born children of the wealthiest of the ex-convicts shared the same material advantages as did the children at the corresponding level of free society. Private tutors were available for the sons and the daughters were reared as young ladies of quality, suitable wives for gentlemen, their education by governesses frequently supplemented by attendance at one of the small but genteel establishments existing in Sydney to 'finish' young ladies.[65] A few of these daughters accompanied parents who returned to England for a visit, sometimes in search of a good match, for the wealth of the parent was frequently sufficient to overcome undesirable social origins. Thus, through his or her children, a former convict could hope to gain the social recognition he himself, or she herself, was denied. It was from this group that the few native-born active in colonial affairs emerged, in a similar fashion to the most vocal of the children of the wealthy free parents. Two of Simeon Lord's native-born sons, Francis and George, became members of the Legislative Council. It is therefore entirely misleading to speak of the children of this group of ex-convicts under the blanket term 'children of the convicts' and to assume that their childhood was spent under the degraded circumstances associated with convict parentage.

It is equally misleading to associate these traits with the children whose parents belonged to the next order of convicted society. The parents here were successful and self-supporting, but to a lesser degree than their spectacularly successful contemporaries. From the evidence of the 1828 Census and from the biographies, it is clear that a large percentage of the native-born children belonged to this group. There were almost as many fathers who were tradesmen as those who were farmers, and these men had exploited the acute shortage of skilled labour to establish themselves successfully in the colony. Those without particular skills appeared to have sought and received land grants, the majority increasing the size of their holdings. An example of this is William Smith, who had arrived as a convict in 1788 and formed a lasting liaison with Ann Smith, who had also arrived with the first fleet. Four children were born to them between 1790 and 1797 and they and their family settled at Prospect, remaining there for forty years. In 1828 William and Ann lived on their 200 acre property which was managed by their eldest son and his wife.

Families of native-born children were to be found among all occupational groups: dealers, shopkeepers, small tradesmen, a few clerks and a sprinkling of schoolmasters, minor officials, publicans and innkeepers. The sons in these families almost invariably assisted their fathers from as early an age as possible, while the daughters helped the mothers in occupations ranging from serving in the family shop or inn to tending domestic animals. Once again there is no evidence to support the belief that these children were neglected or abandoned by their dissolute parents. On the contrary, there is firm evidence both as to the respectability of the parents and their concern for the welfare of their children. The colonial honesty of most of the parents is confirmed by the lack of convictions in either the magistrates' courts or the criminal courts.

The obligatory character references attached to the Memorials were supplied by the magistrates and chaplains of the colony. These show the close link between parents and children. The family of Edward Fletcher is an example. Fletcher, an Irishman, arrived, convicted, in 1801 after the Irish rebellion. He received a conditional pardon for good conduct and industry and applied for a land grant. His application was supported by a character reference from William Howe, the local Justice of the Peace: 'I certify that the Petititioner (Fletcher) is an uncommonly respectable and industrious man, with a numerous family well brought up.'[66] By 1828 Fletcher was District Constable for Lower Minto, where he farmed 130 acres. His son, John (born 1810), and his daughters (born 1812) were living with him; his other sons settled in the same district.

The third group of convicted parents were the unskilled who, in many respects, could be equated with the lower orders of Britain but appeared to lack both their poverty and criminality. These were the labourers, the carters, the servants and the very minor officials, such as gaolers and constables, and the poorest and least successful small farmers. These men were sometimes employed by Government when convict labour was insufficient but more often by private settlers, both those who had arrived free and those who had been convicts. It was difficult to trace the parents in this group: there were few baptismal records and even fewer records of marriages in any of the colonial churches. Where families were traced, there was evidence of the characteristic family link both in occupation and in district of residence. In this group there were few fathers of the native-born who petitioned for land, or apprenticeships or other indulgences for their sons. It would appear that these native-born, to a very large extent, remained in the same occupations as their fathers. There were a few exceptions. One was the application of George Wilson, born in New South Wales in 1810. Wilson applied for a land grant, stating that he was '... entirely reliant on his own hands ... and ... was desirous of becoming a farmer ... his Father having a large family, it had not been in his power to provide for them as he would wish'. His character references stated that the lad was 'steady and industrious' and 'very sober and deserving'. There is no actual evidence that his application was refused but this appears to have been so for he was later found to be working as a carpenter in Sydney.

Some indication of the number of children in this group comes from their occupations. Most were labourers and agricultural workers;[67] this group comprised 9 per cent of the total native-born occupations. They appear to have been boys such as James Carter, born in 1810, who was working as a labourer with his father at Patersons Plains in 1828. His ex-convict father had arrived in 1802 and, having completed his seven-year sentence, married an ex-convict woman and continued to be employed as a labourer. A few of these fathers owned small allotments although they described their occupation as that of labourer. Joseph Croft was typical of these men. He had received an absolute pardon for 'meritorious conduct'. He lived with his wife and their children, aged between five and eighteen, at Portland Head, presumably supporting his family by employment as a labourer in the district.

Comparatively few of the parents from this group can be traced so it is necessary to suggest probabilities rather than form definite conclusions as to the nature of the life-style of their children. Some of the boys may have attended the Male Orphan School, learning a basic trade such as tailoring or shoe-making.[68] It was not necessary, in the early years, for a child to be an orphan in the strict sense of the word. Conflicting evidence was given to Bigge as to whether the 'orphans' had one or two parents. William Cowper, who witnessed many Memorials, believed that:

> ... the Greater Part of them had one Parent living & when it was found that this Parent was either very Profligate or very Poor so as not to afford decent maintenance to the Child, it was admitted to all the benefits of the Institution.[69]

Thomas Bowden claimed that the attendance of the boys was irregular, far more so than that of boys in similar circumstances in England. The reason for this, he said, was 'inattention on the part of the parents'.[70] In addition to the children from this group who may have attended the Orphan Schools, some may have formed a part of the 'neglected children' described by contemporaries as roaming Sydney's streets. If, on the other hand, they were the children of labourers and agricultural workers it is more likely that they grew up in the rural areas where their fathers were employed rather than in the town of Sydney itself.

Most of the daughters in this group were placed as domestic servants at an early age. Some native-born and came-free girls of seven and eight described themselves as servants in the 1828 Census. Others may have been cared for in the Female Orphan School, either as orphaned girls or as 'Deserving Objects of Pity'. King described these girls as '... deserted female orphans who are rescued from those scenes of prostitution and iniquity that disgraces the major part of the inhabitants of this colony, many of whom are from nine to fourteen years old ...'.[71] If the girls from this group did attend the Female Orphan School then the probability increases that they became the serving-girls and nursemaids to colonial families. The surprising feature is that, considering that contemporaries believed all the youth of the colony to be abandoned and neglected, this particular group of native-born appears to have been very small.[72] Some indication of this may be found in the list of native-born extracted from the 1806 Muster of New South Wales. One boy and two girls are listed as 'Orphan, Born Here'. They are: Mark Carey, born on 5 February 1792 in Sydney, the son of Mark Munroe and convict Ann Carey; Catherine Ryan, born on 20 January 1799, daughter of convict James Woodham, who was buried on 25 October 1802, and convict Ann Ryan, buried on 21 October 1805; Mary Briant, born on 10 August 1800, daughter of 'Agen' Bryant, who had been in the New South Wales Corps, and ex-convict Mary Bryant.[73]

There was an even smaller group of parents which left so little trace that it is almost impossible to determine how many of the native-born were from this the lowest level of colonial society. It was the group of convict and ex-convict men and women whose life-styles agreed with the descriptions of contemporaries as degraded and dissolute. They were the men and women in whom drink and despair had dulled self-interest and who attempted to find solace for their enforced exile by recreating the familiar and comforting atmosphere of the criminal haunts of urban Britain. Contemporaries saw these as typical of the 'convict' population and their behaviour and standards agreed with contemporary assumptions as to the expected nature of convict society. It was this group whose notorious behaviour received most official attention, based on the need to control and reform this dissolute section of the community. The notorious Rocks area of Sydney, however, was no worse than many similar districts in urban centres of Britain. During this period, St. Giles in London would have surpassed the reputation of the Rocks. It was this group which received such disproportionate notoriety for its abandoned and criminal behaviour, mainly because this was in accord with contemporary assumptions as to the nature of a penal society.

It may only be assumed that the lives of the children born into this group were similar to those of their contemporaries in the criminal haunts of the cities and towns of Britain. Allowance, however, must be made for the differing circumstances of environment and society, for the differing roles of children and social and economic attitudes to them. The results of these differing circumstances and expectations, in colonial society as opposed to British society, became evident when the first generation became adults. That small group of Botany Bay children whose parents were at the lowest levels of society did not necessarily follow their British counterparts and become the colony's criminals. That the assumed habits and characteristics of the parents were neither inherited, nor imitated, nor forced upon the children, is confirmed by the evidence of the 1828 Census relating to occupations and districts of residence of the native-born. There is also evidence from the Memorials that, in many cases, a close relationship existed between these children and their parents. That the number of first generation Australians convicted in any colonial court was negligible shows clearly that honesty, not crime, was the basis of their way of life, as children and as adults.

There is an additional feature of colonial society which affected contemporary assumptions as to the nature of the native-born children. This was the existence in the colony of juvenile British convicts. There are insufficient remaining records to establish the numbers of boys and girls transported to New South Wales. No records exist prior to 1810, although both Hunter and King commented on the problem of these children. Individual references appear in the convict indents.[74] During the three-year period 1812–15, some 369 boys and 109 girls whose ages ranged from eleven years and upwards were recorded as arriving in New South Wales, sentenced, on an average, to seven years' transportation. The young convict girls were either assigned as domestic servants or nursemaids, although a few may have attended the Orphan School after 1802. There was no segregation of the boys from the older convicts. The most promising were selected to be apprentices in the Dock Yards and in the Lumber Yard, where they shared the work with native-born apprentices, eventually becoming carpenters and blacksmiths.[75] There was little to distinguish these children from the colonial children; they were frequently unsupervised and had no specific living quarters or Barracks. It is quite probable that many were among the boys and girls who roamed the streets of Sydney, appearing to be neglected and abandoned. To the casual observer, they would not have appeared as convicts but as a normal part of the colony's child population, thus adding to the belief that the children were abandoned by their parents.[76]

The distortion implicit in contemporary observations and opinions regarding the characteristics of the convict parents and the nature of colonial society becomes apparent when the native-born and their parents are investigated and researched as individuals, not as a homogeneous 'class' of convicts and their children. It becomes increasingly obvious that almost the only shared characteristics of the native-born with regard to their birth and upbringing were, first, the actual fact that they were native-born and, second, that they shared the background of a penal society in a penal colony. They certainly did not share a common experience during their childhood and adolescence; they did not share equal advantages or suffer the same deprivations. They did develop into a commendably honest race of men and women but this was not a direct result of any aversion to or rejection of their parents. Rather does such an investigation emphasize the two most striking features, the two basic characteristics which were to determine the influence of these children on the nature of colonial society and which contributed so greatly to the breakdown of the artifical social barriers created by the gulf existing between convicted and unconvicted society. The first of these characteristics was the close relationship with their parents from all levels of society, the acceptance by the native-born children of the life-styles and achievements of their parents, and the adoption of the attitudes on which they were based. The second was the marked diversity and complexity of their origins and their experiences as children within the structure of colonial society. In their birth, their parentage, their upbringing, these children represented all levels of colonial society, both convicted and free. It was in this way that their influences and standards were to permeate every level of society while, at the same time, their shared characteristics of native birth, their distinction in being the first white Australians, identified them closely with their native land. This identification, however, was not as a class sharing similar opportunities and ambitions, similar backgrounds, experiences, life-styles. The diversity of their parentage, of their colonial experiences, intensified the effects and influence of their position in colonial society as the 'free-born white subjects of Australia'. They were the children of their society. They could not judge or compare with other societies. It is on their own standards, colonial standards, that colonial society must be viewed. In particular, the nature of the female inhabitants who were shaping female society in the colony needs to be reassessed before the influence of these women on their children can be determined with accuracy.

CHAPTER THREE

I AM NOT FOR MARRYING

'. . . and a benignant spirit was abroad
Which might not be withstood, that poverty
Abject as this would in a little time
Be found no more, that we should see the earth
Unthwarted in her wish to recompense
The meek, the lowly, patient child of toil.'

William Wordsworth, 1793.

The convict women of New South Wales were consistently described by officials as 'refractory ... troublesome ... disobedient characters'.[1] Not only did contemporaries believe that, as convicted felons, these women were criminally inclined but that they were morally 'of the worst description ... totally irreclaimable'.[2] As most of the children born in the colony during the first twenty-five years of white settlement had a mother who had arrived as a convict these opinions directly affected contemporary expectations and opinions as to the childhood experiences of the native-born. As modern historians have perpetuated the belief in the immorality and degrading life-styles of these women it is essential to question the accuracy of the evidence on which this picture rests, to investigate the actual nature and structure of female society in New South Wales during this period.

Not only did the life-styles of the colonial women shape and mould the characteristics of their children but their influence was determinative on the nature of the emerging society at Botany Bay. These influences have been clouded and distorted by the continuous emphasis on their presumed 'convict' characteristics, on the degraded life-style forced upon women in a male-dominated society. This, in turn, has perpetuated the myth that family life did not exist during this early period of settlement, that the 'convict' women were simply 'the companions of the men'. A detailed examination of the sources of these assumptions, within the framework of the contrasting experiences of these women in Britain and in the colony, shows the ways in which the origins of a distinctive Australian female society have been misinterpreted and distorted.

According to contemporaries, the picture of colonial women is typified by excesses of criminality and immorality, of convict women who were vicious, drunken, depraved, vile, abandoned. This reputation was very firmly based on their convictions in Britain for major statutory offences, not on their colonial lives. One of the earliest comments of Arthur Phillip concerning his female charges illustrates clearly the expectations of the behaviour of convict women: '. . . neither virtue nor honesty was to be expected from them'.[3] This belief gained substance from the reports of men whose colonial positions enabled them to comment with seeming authority. Men such as Governor Hunter, who, in 1799, described these women as '. . . the disgrace of their sex ... far worse than the men, and are generally found at the bottom of every infamous transaction committed in the Colony'.[4]

In 1809, George Suttor wrote to Governor Bligh:

One of the first causes of our present evils was the officers of the establishment connecting themselves with the convict women ... and these women have a much greater influence over them than a virtuous woman, and instigate them to things which a virtuous woman would be ashamed of.[5]

Governors Hunter and Bligh, and their chaplain Samuel Marsden, expressed concern as to the effects of this immorality and licentiousness on the 'Rising Generation'. Their fears were echoed by gentlemen such as T.W. Plummer, a colonial theorist, who wrote to Lachlan Macquarie shortly after his appointment as Governor of New South Wales, strongly advising that measures should be taken to improve the morals of the females in that unhappy colony. Plummer informed Macquarie that the female convicts were allotted to settlers immediately after arrival. The purpose of this assignment was to provide settlers with housekeepers and servants, but in practice the women became 'paramours ... avowed objects of intercourse' and the whole colony was 'little more than an extensive brothel'. This led to the children being exposed to 'an example that is at once infamous and contagious'.[6]

There has been until now a lack of acceptable sources of evidence relating to the lives of the colonial women of early Australia, and a corresponding lack of interpretations by historians. This paucity of secondary accounts may also be attributed to the recent origins of historical interest in the role of women as a distinct group in any place or time. The major interpretative studies concerned with the nature of female society in colonial Australia, notably those by Miriam Dixson and Anne Summers,[7] have a distinct feminist bias. This has led to a distorted view not only of the characteristics of these women but of the whole society. The feminist writers have accepted the assumptions made by contemporaries as to the standards of behaviour of colonial women and have made no attempt to investigate the reliability, accuracy or general applicability of contemporary comment. Instead of investigating the accuracy of the evidence on which they base their arguments, both Dixson and Summers have commented on and, to a large extent, condoned the 'Damned Whore' stereotype.[8] Their method is excuse–explanation rather than historical questioning.

The general picture presented by the feminist writers on female society in early New South Wales is one in which colonial women lived within a male-dominated society and lacked both social and economic opportunities. They became, therefore, by necessity, the 'victims' of that male society for their role was a purely sexual one; they were the victims of the male frustration–aggression complex, 'The victims of victims'.[9] Summers, in her chapter on colonial women, argues that 'The social and economic conditions of the first fifty years of white colonization of Australia fostered whores rather than wives ...' She continues, 'That many women were *whores* is beyond dispute. What historians have failed to appreciate is the extent to which women had any choice in this ...'[10] Summers' argument is mainly based on an interpretation of contemporary comment, not on the evidence of the life-styles of the individual women concerned. There is no definition of 'whore' within the contemporary context nor discussion of the skills, or lack of skills and capabilities and expectations of these women. Both Summers and Dixson link their explanations very closely with the erroneous assumption that the description 'convict' women equated with 'colonial' women. Thus the picture of society created by both Summers and Dixson has been completely distorted by the absence of a precise definition of colonial women and by the lack of recognition that during this early, or foundation, period there were various categories of women within New South Wales society and that each category was consciously aware of the advantages and disabilities attached to its distinctive group. Dixson, for example, heads one chapter 'Our Founding Mothers, the Convicts'.[11] This broad description of the women who were the founding mothers, the pioneer women of early Australia, creates an erroneous impression of the nature of female society, partly as a result of the connotations of the word 'convict' and partly because pregnancy and childbirth were not the sole prerogative of convict women during this period.

Distortion of the actual role of women in early New South Wales has also resulted from the nature of the only evidence which has been readily available to historians. This evidence is based on the recorded contemporary comment, reports, observations—and lamentations—of governors, chaplains, surgeons, magistrates, civilian and military officials, wealthier free settlers and visitors to the colony. This is the same group which has left recorded comments on the nature and characteristics of the colony in general and on the children, the convicts and the women of early Australia in particular. As all of these contemporary observers came from the same general class origin of European society they shared similar expectations of the nature of life in a penal colony inhabited predominantly by convicts. Most of the commentators were actively concerned with the maintenance of law and order and the promotion of morality so that these were the two aspects of colonial behaviour which were emphasized in their reports. They were, therefore, concerned primarily with the 'causes' of these disturbances, the women convicts.

The opinions on women convicts were influenced by preconceived expectations as to their behaviour and moral standards. These expectations were based very largely on three known characteristics of the convicted women felons who were transported to Botany Bay. First, they were convicted felons, guilty of a major statutory offence for which the punishment was usually death but sentenced instead to a term of transportation with penal servitude.[12] Second, as convicts, they were not only criminally inclined but must necessarily be morally tainted, so that wanton, degraded, dissolute and abandoned behaviour was expected from them. Third, as the illiterate, unskilled girls and women from the lower orders of British society, they formed the lowest rank in the social hierarchy. Contemporary comment, therefore, centering as it did on this one group of women, was firmly based on expectations; that is, on their 'characters' in Britain, not on their behaviour in the colony. There were among these women those whose life-styles and criminal inclinations justified this expectation, and it was the comments of colonial observers on their standards of behaviour which were accepted by respectable contemporaries in Britain and in New South Wales as typifying the conduct of the colonial women of Botany Bay. Modern historians have perpetuated these opinions. No scholarly attempt has been made to determine whether this group of women was representative of all the colonial women of New South Wales. No attempt has been made to determine whether a few opinions expressed by one 'class' were an accurate description of the lives of the women of early Australia, our 'founding mothers'. The main drawback appears to have been a lack of any alternative source of evidence.

There is one reliable way by which 'new' sources of evidence may be the basis for a recreation of the nature, structure and characteristics of female society in New South Wales. This is to identify as many as possible of the individual women who lived in the colony during this period.[13] By collecting and analysing biographical data for these women, it becomes possible to reconstruct their colonial lives and, on this basis, to examine their role in, and influence on, the emerging Australian society. The results of this detailed investigation show clearly the inaccuracy and distortion implicit in currently accepted assumptions. Furthermore, this biographical evidence rejects entirely the feminist excuse–explanation interpretation of the forced degradation of the colonial lives of the women in New South Wales during the first forty or so years of white settlement. Female society emerges as complex and diverse, with a strong emphasis on family life, with a close interrelationship evident among mothers and children and a surprising ability to adapt to colonial conditions, to take advantage of the opportunities offered in the new environment. This refutes the 'whore' stereotype of colonial women, which not only distorts the role of the women themselves but misrepresents the actual nature of the whole community. It was not the abandoned woman prostitute, the whore, who was the normal unit of society but the single man. This feature, unrecognized until now, has affected the nature of Australian society until the present day.

The single most distorting feature in both contemporary and modern accounts of colonial women is this continual emphasis on convict women. This has precluded any attempts to define the structure of female society. Colonial society itself was complex, and the experiences of the women living within that society were as diverse as those of the men. The four distinct civil condition categories into which the women as well as the men were divided all indicated differing life-styles, opportunities, disadvantages, privileges and disabilities. The first category was convict; that is, women under the sentence of the law. The second, the ex-convict, represented those who had served their sentences or had been pardoned and were technically free women. The need to differentiate between convict and freed is not merely a semantic one. Although contemporaries referred to all who had arrived convicted as convicts, the experiences and opportunities available to a freed woman differed greatly from those available to one who was still under sentence. Normally a convict woman had little control over her own life-style: she could be assigned without consultation or she could be returned to government. This convict portion of her life, however, was only one part of her total experience in the colony. It was after sentences, imposed in Britain for British criminal offences, had expired that she could, to a large extent, determine the pattern of her own life. It was then that these women were most influential in shaping the characteristics of their society.

The third category comprised women who had come free, the 'respectable', unconvicted women. They were mainly family women; that is, the wives and daughters of officials, free settlers, marines, soldiers, convicts and ex-convicts. A small minority, probably less than a dozen during the first twenty-five years, had come to New South Wales as single women or as widows with some means for the express purpose of improving their economic position, usually by conducting 'seminaries' for young ladies.[14] Some of these young ladies were to be found in the fourth category, the native-born girls, or currency lasses, as they were called by contemporaries. They were the daughters of women belonging to all categories so they formed a link between the various groups within the female society of Botany Bay.

Contemporaries were acutely aware of the importance of civil condition and its effects upon the lives of those living in the colony. At all official occasions civil condition had to be stated; in all applications to the governor for indulgences, land grants, permission to marry, to leave the colony, to move within the settlement and at Musters. A letter from the convict husband of Mrs Margarot to Under-Secretary King described the indignity felt by this free woman at being mustered with convicted women.

> Governor King thought it necessary to have a general Muster of both men and women. Mrs Margarot you are not unaquainted with, and you may judge from her appearance and behaviour, that such a Muster could no ways be agreeable to her feelings ... No man of but decent education and behaviour could have expected her to attend his levee of female prostitutes and thieves ...

The result, however, was most unexpected and described the convict women in favourable terms.

> Mrs Margarot ... found herself in the midst of nearly two hundred women of the class before mentioned; yet such was the effect of *je ne sais quoi*, which I cannot describe ... from them she experienced nothing but respect—every eye beamed commiseration, every tongue ejaculated indignation at a treatment towards her which they had contentedly submitted to themselves.[15]

It was the intention of Margarot, the Scottish martyr, to reveal Governor King in the most unfavourable light to the British government. The reaction of his wife, however, illustrates the importance to the 'respectable' ladies of the colony that their dignity as free women be maintained. Even a convicted husband did not detract from their belief in their social superiority. Few of the women who arrived convicted managed to evade acceptance of their official civil category and the stigma it emphasized. Esther Abrams, after her belated marriage to Major Johnston, was still described officially as 'Free by Servitude'.[16] Elizabeth Burleigh Dalton, who arrived convicted in 1788, described herself as 'Elizabeth Burleigh, Came Free', possibly with the connivance of her husband, Surgeon Arndell.[17] Mary Reibey, after her visit to England, could and did state with accuracy that she had 'Come Free, 1821', which was her year of return. These and similar attempts by women to escape the stigma of convictism underline the importance of civil classification to contemporaries.

The population statistics are neither sufficiently reliable nor detailed to give more than a cautious estimate of the proportions of women in all four categories during the first forty years of white settlement. An analysis of the returns of the governors, the victualling lists, and the musters of population indicates that most of the women at any period after the first few years of settlement were not convict but ex-convict. In 1804, for example, only 44.3 per cent appear to have been actually serving sentence; in 1820, 16.7 per cent were under sentence, 43.8 per cent were ex-convicts; 24.9 per cent compared with 23 per cent. The main reason for this increase in the late 1820s was the general rise in the number of felons transported from Britain.[18] Table 3/1 indicates the proportions within the various categories between 1788 and 1828.

Proportionately few free women arrived in New South Wales during the first forty years and their significance lies in their existence as family women rather than in their numbers. The first white women to land on Australian soil were free women: the chaplain's bride, Mrs Mary Johnson, and the wives of the marines who were landed at Camp Cove a week before the female convicts.[19] By 1810 few free women had come to Botany Bay; during the six years of Governor King's administration only eighty-three free women (exclusive of soldiers' wives), female children and infants arrived in New South Wales.[20] By 1820 free women represented 16 per cent of the total adult females; by 1824 this proportion had increased to 23 per cent; by 1828, to 25 per cent. The convict wives were an important part of the free section of female society in the colony, partly because they represented all social levels and partly because they formed a link between the convict and the free societies. One of these ladies, Mrs Anne Fulton, was a gentlewoman of good education who came with her convicted husband, Reverend Henry Fulton, in 1800 and lived with him at Norfolk Island during the early years of his transportation. Another free woman, Martha Pennell, described joining her husband:

[She] came out to the Colony agreeable to the Order of the Hon.le the Secretary of State, hoping to render the banishment of her unfortunate husband less irksome than the weight of his years and of his bodily infirmities must necessary [sic] reduce him to.[21]

Martha 'commenced in Trade, having purchased several articles previous to leaving England', and had her husband assigned to her. By 1828 John and Martha, then aged sixty-three and sixty-two, were living in Gloucester Street, Sydney, where John was a dealer.

It was not until 1820 that the adult native-born girls were listed regularly in a separate category in the musters, although as early as 1806 these young women were identified as having been 'Born in the Colony'.[22] By 1820 they formed 23 per cent of the total adult females; their number increased to 25.8 per cent in 1824 and reached 26.1 per cent in 1828. Although their numbers were small in the early years they were an integral part of female

TABLE 3/1

The structure of female society, New South Wales, 1788-1728
Source: Portia Robinson, 'The First Forty Years: Women and the Law', in In Pursuit of Justice,
eds J. Mackinolty and H. Radi, Sydney, 1979.
Note. Figures are approximate; owing to the incomplete nature of contemporary records and the
possibility of inaccuracies, it is only possible to suggest numbers of women in the various civil condition
categories.

Key:

 Govt Servant
(Convict)

 Freed
(Ex-Convict)

 Came Free

 Native-Born

 Free and Freed
(No Differentiation)

Percentages:

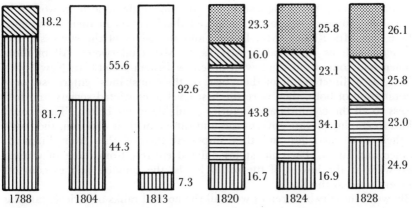

society, particularly after they reached marriageable age. By 1814 they were
listed as wives, daughters, servants and housekeepers.[23]

There were, therefore, definite categories and the description 'convict
woman' could only with accuracy be applied to one of the four divisions of
society. The complexity of colonial society was not limited, however, to this

division into civil categories. It was divided both vertically and horizontally so that the assumption that colonial women, being convict women, were from the lower orders of both British and colonial society increases the inaccuracy of their purported role.

The division most frequently commented on by historians is the artificial vertical division into 'respectable' and 'tainted'; that is, those who had arrived as convicts. When the contemporary terms 'exclusive', 'pure merinos', 'free objects' and 'emancipists' were used they usually referred to colonial males. This may have been because it was possible for women, through marriage, to move outside convicted society, although still carrying the stigma of their civil category.

It is the second division of colonial society which has received little attention from historians. This was the horizontal 'class' grouping, similar to the traditional hierarchical pattern of British society. The distinctive feature was that this economy-based class structure existed within both artificial divisions of colonial society, the bond and the free. Colonial women, therefore, were not confined to the lowest order of the criminal 'class', the convicts. Within respectable society there were the colonial ladies 'of the first water': the wives of the governors, Anna Josepha King, Elizabeth Macquarie, Eliza Darling; the wives of the chaplains, Mary Johnson, Elizabeth Marsden; the wives of the officials and free settlers, Mrs Macarthur, Mrs Blaxland, Mrs Suttor, Mrs Macleay. At the other end of the scale were the free and unconvicted wives who had accompanied or followed marine, soldier or convict husbands. Lastly, there were the free servants, many of whom had come with the wives of civilian or military officials.[24]

The same 'class' pattern was equally evident within the convicted section of female society. At the highest level were some of the wealthiest women in the colony, some of whom had achieved this position in their own right. There was Mrs Reibey, Mrs Driver, and the wives of the successful ex-convicts, such as Mrs Kable, Mrs Lord, Mrs Underwood. All of these women had come from the lowest orders of British society. In New South Wales, as a direct result of their own or their husbands' enterprise, or a combination of both, they were the first level of convicted society and had access to all the comforts and luxuries available in the colony. They could afford to employ private governesses and tutors for their children, they rode in their own carriages and they imported their clothes from England, France and India. Their life-styles differed entirely from those of women who were at the lowest of the social levels: the convicts and ex-convicts who gathered at the Rocks.

Between these two extremes were all the normal ranks of society, ranging from the wives of the smaller landowners and farmers to the traders, dealers, publicans, shopkeepers, tradesmen, labourers and servants.[25] The daughters of all these women could not with any accuracy be described as 'the children of the convicts'. Their life-styles were shaped by the type of household in which they were brought up. This was more influential in determining their responses to and expectations from colonial society than was the British background or colonial civil condition of their parents.

As the evidence for the currently accepted picture of female society is based mainly on the comments of contemporaries, and as these comments are in direct contrast to the picture which emerges from a study of the lives of the individual women concerned, it is therefore necessary to question both the accuracy and the general applicability of these opinions and to explain the assumptions and expectations on which they were based.

Three major characteristics of the convicted women were influential in shaping expectations as to their life-styles. First, they were convict women; second, they were women from the lowest level of British society; third, they had arrived in the colony as single, unprotected women.

As convicts, the image of these women was clothed with all the connotations of that word despite the nature of the crimes for which they had been sentenced. Crime and immorality were close bedfellows and the female felons were expected to be not only vile and degraded but lacking in all moral decency. Samuel Marsden expressed this view in a letter to the Archbishop of Canterbury when he described those 'who still live in scenes of immorality, tho' now they are free of the shackles of the law'.[26] Ralph Clark summed up the contemporary attitude when he exclaimed in despair, 'O my God! Not more of those damned whores!'. Clark was totally unfamiliar with the women on the *Lady Juliana* and had no knowledge of their crimes; he automatically thought of them as whores.

That most of these 'convict' women were from the lower classes,[27] meant that they were not only illiterate and lacking in any skills but were the class from which the serving-girls and the street-walkers came. The virtue of the servant-girls was almost as suspect as that of the women 'on the town'. The house servants were frequently expected to 'oblige' the master and his sons. If the results of this 'obliging' became evident in the shape of pregnancy and the girl was unable to rid herself of the child, either by abortion or by infanticide, she lost her character and after dismissal had little alternative but to become a harlot. This reputation for loose and promiscuous living was increased by the prevalence of common law, rather than legal, marriages among the men and women of this class.

The third characteristic which increased expectations that these women were not only criminal but immoral was that they had arrived in the colony as single women; that is, unprotected by family or husband. The normal role of virtuous women was within the security of the family unit, protected by the head of the household, the father or the husband. These convicted women, therefore, whether widowed or married in Britain, arrived alone and thus technically single, unprotected and outside the normal role of respectable women. They were, as single women, in direct contrast to the pioneer women of the North American colonies and the women of early New Zealand, both of which groups were primarily family women and thus, by definition, respectable.

The expectations of observers, based very largely on these three characteristics, were apparently confirmed by the behaviour of a section of the convicted women. As the reports of the governors and chaplains concentrated on notorious and abandoned behaviour the problems of immorality in the colony were equated with criminality and the criminal 'class', in particular the women. No allowance was made for the existence of a similar 'class' in London itself or in any of the main towns or cities of Great Britain and Western Europe.[28] Prostitution, drunkenness and abandoned female behaviour were not confined to Botany Bay.[29] As the settlement was a penal colony, however, and the majority of the inhabitants were convicted felons, disgraceful behaviour was expected and that group of women who conformed to these expectations was accepted as typical of the colonial women of New South Wales. There was little need for official comment on those women who either married or contracted 'unblessed unions', and lived as family women, at least outwardly respectable, honest, industrious—and sober. This bias is shown clearly in a report on the 1806 Muster by Governor King. Although he has evidence that 'out of the 1412 women in these settlements, 1216 are of no expense to the public, being married or living with free people of all descriptions, and with those who from good behaviour hold tickets-of-leave', King highlights the immorality of these women, in particular those from London and Ireland:

> There are many ... whom no punishment or kindness can ever reclaim. ... Those who behave well bear but a small proportion to the many who from their infancy were thoroughly depraved and abandoned, which is mostly the case with the London females and the greatest part of those from Ireland. Among the comparatively few from the English Counties are some well-behaved women, and soon after their arrival are selected and applied for by the industrious part of the settlers, with whom they either marry or co-habit; nor does a separation often occur....

It would appear that King's previous association with convict Ann Innett had not led to any tolerance or understanding of the convict women. Although he reported that the 1216 women who supported themselves also provided for their 'numerous families of children' so that no government assistance was required, he qualified this statement by stating that the 'greater part of the children assisted their parents in agricultural or domestic labour'. This did not agree with his statement that their children were 'real objects of charity'. As they had suffered from '.. the early abuse they were subject to from the abandoned examples of the greater part of their parents ... [and] from the destructive examples of their dissolute parents, in whom no reform can be expected ...'.[30] These comments show the reluctance to admit that the parents of the children were not uniformly 'bad characters' and that the mothers were not 'incorrigible'.

In addition to official reports, two major contemporary sources have been accepted by modern historians as confirming the accounts of the notorious behaviour of the wanton women of Botany Bay. These are the observations of Chaplain Marsden in his Female Register of 1806 and the Reports of the Female Factory at Parramatta.[31] Both of these sources have been accepted uncritically and without question. Both are not only highly selective and partial, referring only to one category of colonial women, the convicts, but are misleading in relation to contemporary definitions of marriage, morality and prostitution.

The influence of Samuel Marsden's opinions has been almost irreparable in terms of the reputation of the women of New South Wales. It was his Female Register and the terminology - he used which confirmed the suspicions of the British Government that New South Wales was synonymous with Sodom and Gomorrah and that the single cause of this was the flagrant viciousness of its women.[32] In 1806, the year of the Muster, Marsden drew up a list of all the adult female inhabitants in New South Wales, 'A Female Register'. He designated every woman as either 'Married' or 'Concubine'; there were only one or two exceptions, when a woman was described as a widow. He also listed their children, both male and female, designating them as either 'Legitimate' or 'Illegitimate', and describing the latter as 'National children'. His summary of the condition of these women was that, out of a total of 1430 living in New South Wales at that time, 395 were married and the remaining 1035 were 'Concubines'.[33] Governor King supported the implications of this description by noting there were 'very few of the unmarried but who co-habit openly with some man'.[34] Marsden's Register listed only 125 of the convict women as legally married; he also applied the term 'convict' to all women who had arrived convicted, making no allowance for pardons or commutation of sentence. Among the 1832 colonial children listed, Marsden described 807 as legitimate and the remaining 1025 as illegitimate.[35] This was further evidence of the moral corruption of the colony.

Marsden took this Register to England with him in 1807 and it is highly likely that it was a direct influence on the opinions of men like Wilberforce, Plummer and Castlereagh. This helps to explain why Macquarie was given such specific instructions and advice to improve the moral standards of the colony, encourage marriage and abolish prostitution.[36] It is highly probable that, before drawing up these instructions, Castlereagh discussed the morals of the colony and the depravity of its women with William Wilberforce, who was familiar with Marsden's Register. In 1808 Castlereagh wrote to Wilberforce, outlining this intention:

> I have not yet been able to lay my hands upon Mr Marsden's Botany Papers—they are however in perfect Safety, and shall be found as soon as I can get access to my Papers in Town. I shall be happy to confer with you upon the State of that Colony it requires a fundamental Revision and I am now preparing Measures for sending out a New Governor and Garrison.[37]

As Marsden's Register presented such a definite picture of an immoral society, and as this picture was firmly based on detailed and seemingly conclusive statistical 'evidence', it must be accepted that this Report was highly influential in reinforcing official British attitudes towards the colony. In particular, it offered 'proof' that the women of Botany Bay not only lived in concubinage, but openly flaunted their licentiousness. Were not the majority of their children illegitimate? On the other hand, if Marsden's 'evidence' is examined on the basis of the life-styles of the individual women and if the terminology he used is defined according to his own standards and the traditional standards of the women concerned a completely different picture of female society emerges. This picture is supported by the experiences of the children who lived with these 'concubines'.[38]

A close examination of the women listed on Marsden's Register indicates the criteria on which he based his categories of wife and concubine. He accepted as legally married all those women, either convict or free, who were officially described as wives on their arrival in New South Wales and who were accompanied by or rejoined their husbands. The range of women within this description included 'ladies' such as his wife and the wife of John Macarthur, who were listed as Mrs Marsden and Mrs Macarthur, and also the free wives of Catholic convicts, listed as Mary Hayes and Elizabeth Hobbs. These women, married in Ireland by a Catholic priest and accompanied by legal husbands, were accepted by Marsden as wives but were not accorded the title of Mrs. Within the colony itself, however, Marsden did not recognize Catholic marriages: his definition of a legal marriage was confined to one performed by a clergyman of the Church of England. The actual religion of the participants was immaterial to this definition. Susannah Wilkinson, a Jewess, had arrived as a convict in 1791 and had married fellow-convict John Langford in December 1792. On his death two years later, she had married Jewish convict James Larra. Both wedding ceremonies were performed by Chaplain Bain.[39] Marsden listed her as 'Susannah Wilkinson, Married in New South Wales'. Another instance was the marriage of Catholic Sarah Maloney to a fellow-Catholic, convict James Connelly, in 1800; Marsden listed her as 'Sarah Connelly, Married, New South Wales, 3 legitimate children'.

Those colonial women who did not choose to be married by a clergyman of the Church of England had no choice except to remain legally unmarried, a 'Concubine'. With the exception of the brief period of toleration of Roman Catholics granted by Governor King, Catholic women could not be married according to the rites of their own faith. Since most of these women were Irish countrywomen,[40] accustomed to the influence and direction of their parish priest, it is highly probable that many would have considered it a far worse sin to be married by Marsden than to live together 'in the sight of God'. Some of these women did choose marriage according to the precepts of the Church of England, for reasons which may only be surmised. It may have been that the advantages of legal marriage outweighed religious scruples; extra land, for example, was granted to a married man. It may have been that some of these women preferred to have their children recognized as legitimate. This supposition is supported by those who had their Catholic sons and daughters baptized at St. Phillip's or St. John's. Some Catholic convicts such as Edward Macdonald and his first wife, Sarah 'Tillery', had their son Edward baptized at St. John's. However, for Catholic convicts such as James McCarthy and his 'wife', there is no record of a marriage and no record of the baptism of their two sons, James and Owen, or of their daughter, Elizabeth, all of whom were listed in the 1828 Census as born in the colony. Marsden defined these women as concubines and their children as illegitimate, despite evidence of permanent relationships.

Marsden's definition of marriage also excluded those to whom common-law marriage was as acceptable, traditional and binding as a church marriage. This exclusion had more effect than had the lack of recognition of religious scruples, for the majority of those who arrived convicted were from Britain's lower orders and so did not necessarily consider legal marriage customary or desirable. It may have been that the high incidence of single men and women among the convicts[41] who arrived in New South Wales was affected by the numbers who were only married according to common law. In New South Wales, Marsden consistently listed common-law wives as concubines. These women included Sarah Bellamy, a 'concubine' who had lived with James Bloodsworth from 1788 until his death in 1804 and had several children. Mary Marshall and Robert Sidaway had lived together for eighteen years and she, too, was described as a concubine. Esther Abrams, who had lived with Major Johnston since 1788, was also described as a concubine by Marsden.

In addition to the de facto wives, many widows were included in the concubine category. They included Jane Kennedy, the former wife of a marine; Hannah Mullens, the wife of George Best; and Ann George. Ann Innett had gained respectability as a married woman after her marriage to William Robinson. The Register, however, also included a few unlikely concubines: one of these was twelve-year-old Sarah Gout; another was sixty-four-year-old Elizabeth Bird. Another was Margaret Catchpole. When these women are considered as individuals and judged not by Marsden's definition of morality but by their own traditional standards, the distortion implicit in Marsden's Report becomes apparent. That few women were legally married did not necessarily imply that the conduct of the remainder made New South Wales 'a sink of infamy'. It simply meant that the standards of morality and the definitions of marriage familiar to the women concerned did not agree with those imposed on society by Samuel Marsden. Contemporaries accepted his conclusions as to the nature of the women of Botany Bay and modern historians have continued to perpetuate this view, which completely distorts the role, nature and influence of the colonial women.

There is only one official who recorded a differing view of the women convicts, but his evidence to the Select Committee on Transportation, 1812, is seldom cited by historians. This was Commissary John Palmer, who had frequent opportunities for observing both male and female convicts as he was in charge of the government stores issued regularly and personally to the victualled inhabitants of the penal colony. When asked by the Committee if the 'respectable part of society' was increasing, he replied that this was so and that there were a great number of families and children in New South Wales. He was then asked specifically whether he would agree that 'the morals of the women are very dissolute?' His reply: 'I cannot say it is as bad as you might expect; many of them are reformed, and behave extremely well; those of them who have been servants, and get married, have done extremely well'. Palmer's evidence as to the existence of a link between prostitution and assignment would suggest that the assumptions made by the Colonial Office with regard to this were based on Marsden's

Report rather than on any actual evidence of neglect on the part of the governors. Palmer was also asked 'whether the women were not taken for the purposes of prostitution than for servants?' He replied: 'No, in general, for servants; they might be in some instances, but the Governor endeavoured to prevent it as much as he could'.[42]

Although Palmer's partiality for Bligh must be considered, his evidence suggests a different picture of the morals of the Botany Bay women and agrees with that found by a close reading of King's observations on the 1806 Muster.[43] The question remains as to why these few favourable opinions were ignored by contemporaries. It may have been that they deviated so far from expectations that they were simply dismissed as biased and unreliable views; it may have been that it was considered necessary by the British government to show that the men and women transported to Botany Bay were indeed the hardened villains who deserved this punishment, a punishment which, as an alternative to death, was granted by a benevolent sovereign. Whatever may have been the reason, neither contemporary observers nor modern historians have given consideration to this minority view.

Marsden did not waver in his opinion on the morals of the women of Botany Bay. By 1815 he was in direct conflict with Macquarie over many of the Governor's policies, in particular his treatment of 'deserving emancipists'. The condition of the women convicts was one basis for his attempt to discredit Macquarie with the Colonial Office. Marsden reported to London that 'the moral evils increased with the increasing number of female convicts transported from Europe'. His opinion of these 'Unhappy Objects' was that 'their vices have rendered them loathsome to the better part of society'. He illustrated this belief with specific reference to the mismanagement of the Female Factory at Parramatta:

> ... instead of the Government Factory being a House of Correction for abandoned females and a benefit to the Colonists and other inhabitants, as a check upon public vices, it becomes a great source of moral corruption, insubordination, and disease, and spreads its pestilential influence throughout the most remote parts of the Colony.

The way in which Marsden used the Factory to attack and discredit the Governor was by attempting to show that Macquarie had neglected to provide proper and adequate housing for the convicted women. They were thus forced to prostitute themselves to earn sufficient money to pay for their board and lodging in the town of Parramatta.[44] This was despite continual pleas from the Chaplain, who was deeply concerned for the moral wellbeing of these 'Unhappy Objects'.

To the 'respectable' colonists the women from the Factory were notorious. John Macarthur, for example, told Commissioner Bigge that he avoided Parramatta whenever possible.[45] Bigge repeated these opinions with elaborations in his Report:

The women, who had become the most profligate and hardened by habit ... The Factory at Parramatta was not only defective, but very prejudicial. The insufficient accommodation that is afforded those females who might be well disposed, presented an explanation if not an excuse, for their resorting to indiscriminate prostitution.[46]

Bigge's emphasis underlines the accepted assumption that these women were not averse to immorality and that they required strict supervision to maintain their virtue. As single, unprotected women, they were not only vulnerable but easily disposed to immoral habits. These opinions were accepted as indicative of the nature of the colonial women. They represented only a minor proportion of the women living in New South Wales during this period. Figures for 1815 show that there were only 150 women in the Factory that year.

It has often been overlooked, by both contemporaries and modern historians, that all the women in the Factory were not necessarily hardened criminals undergoing punishment. There were three distinct classes of women. First, there were the women who had arrived as convicts from Britain and who had not been assigned immediately; they were sent to the Factory for protection while awaiting assignment. This, incidentally, led to a peculiarly colonial male crime, punishable by flogging, 'Spending four days escorting female prisoners when two days would have sufficed'.[47] (These women were rowed by convicts up the Parramatta River to the Factory.) Second, there were women and girls who had been assigned to private masters and mistresses and had been returned to the Factory as unsatisfactory, pregnant or both. Third, there were women from all civil conditions who had been convicted of a colonial crime. These crimes, which were considered minor, such as a three-month colonial sentence for loose living, were punishable by confinement in the Factory. More serious crimes such as perjury, theft and the passing of counterfeit money, were punished by a term of transportation, usually to Van Diemen's Land or to King George Sound.[48] It could therefore be expected that the most abandoned women in New South Wales were congregated at Parramatta, although those who were confined for punitive purposes were guilty of unsatisfactory behaviour in a moral rather than a criminal sense. The minority who had been confined as a direct result of criminal prosecution were only those guilty of minor crimes. Most importantly, however notorious their behaviour may have been, however immoral, however criminal, these women were representative of a minor and specific group of colonial women. Descriptions of the women of the Factory cannot be accepted as indicating the characteristics of the majority of colonial women, who had no connection whatsoever with the Parramatta Factory.

What, then, were the life-styles of the colonial women? What were the characteristics of the convicted women who settled in New South Wales? Obviously their reactions to the new life in the penal colony were based very largely on their background and experience in Britain. Their average age on arrival was mid-twenties, so they brought with them preformed attitudes and standards as well as occupational skills, or lack of such skills. The only evidence available for their previous lives in England and Ireland is concerned with their crimes and convictions.[49] Although it is not possible to generalize as to the reasons for their crimes, motivation being notoriously difficult to attribute, it is possible to gain an insight into the differing life-styles of groups of these women by dividing their crimes into categories. There is one important major division, and that is between the Irish women, particularly the rural Irish, and the English. The rural Irish women were mainly first offenders: they lived in what could be described as an occupied country, subject to the 'foreign' laws, taxes and tithes of England and the English Church. There is evidence of the disastrous poverty caused by this situation, not only in the amount of emigration by Irish families to Liverpool and Manchester, but in the words of some of these women at their trials. One family woman who had travelled to Liverpool with her husband and children in search of work told the judge who sentenced her for theft that:

> Distress and want, hunger and poverty—nothing else—drove us to this country. It was the will of God—Glory be to His Blessed Name! To fail the taties. To be sure, I couldn't dig one out of the ground fit to be ate![50]

Despite this and similar cases which argue against the Irish women convicts fitting the 'Damned Whore' stereotype, their reputation in the colony remained tarnished. Adverse expectations were the direct result both of their nationality and their religion. As rebels, or potential rebels, against King George and as Roman Catholics, they were suspect. David Collins, writing on the 'proposed insurrection' of Irish convicts on the *Marquis Cornwallis*, described these women as 'of the same complexion as the men', adding:

> ... their ingenuity and cruelty were displayed by the part that they were to take in the proposed insurrection; which was, the preparing of pulverised glass to mix with the flour, of which the seamen were to make their puddings. What an importation![51]

Governor King reported the Irish transported women as 'thoroughly depraved and abandoned'. Marsden had some difficulty in determining which were most damaging to the colony, the evils of drink, the Catholic religion or the Irish women convicts.[52] It is clear that it was the national background of these women which added to their notoriety as lower class female felons.

The background of the English women convicts was more diverse than that of the Irish. Coming from the cities, towns, villages and hamlets scattered throughout England, Scotland and Wales, they brought a multi-plicity of backgrounds and experiences to the small colony of Botany Bay. The single example of speech and dialect illustrates the variety among these women. There were cockney girls from London, milkmaids from Devon, mill-girls from Manchester, serving-girls from Glasgow, housewives from

Cardiff, fishermen's daughters from Penzance, shopgirls from Liverpool, farmers' daughters from Shropshire, country women from Somerset. Scattered among them were those who described themselves as 'on the town' or 'poor unfortunate girls', the street women of Britain. Most of these women had already led adult lives in Britain and their colonial lives became extensions of their past experiences. The voyage to Botany Bay was undoubtedly a significant, possibly traumatic, event but it did not obliterate all memories of past life. Nor did it necessarily alter standards of conduct nor radically change preconceived attitudes towards society, morality, child-bearing and child-raising. It was the background of these British experiences which shaped their responses to the opportunities and disadvantages of life in the penal colony, their adopted homeland.

An understanding of the British experiences of the transported women is essential to an understanding of the ways in which they adapted to colonial conditions. Contemporary records are too incomplete for detailed individual biographies but some indication of the general experiences may be found from an analysis of the types of crimes for which they were sentenced to transportation, or death. These crimes may be divided into five broad categories, each category indicating a possible life-style in Britain. These categories are: crimes linked with prostitution; crimes of violence; professional crimes; casual crimes; and the crimes of the servant girls.[53]

Any acceptance of the 'Damned Whore' stereotype would suggest a high incidence of crimes linked with prostitution but few of the women transported between 1788 and 1813—that is, the period during which the first generation was born—were guilty of these offences. Prostitution itself was not an indictable offence and crimes linked with this 'profession' usually involved some form of theft. For example, a woman would take a customer to a deserted alley. Shortly after, an accomplice would shout 'Watch!' as a warning that the night watch was approaching; the man would be unable to protect himself and the woman made off with whatever valuables she could snatch.[54] Other cases involved the theft of articles belonging to the client. Ann Baker was transported to Botany Bay for theft when she stole the watch and monies of the man with whom she had been in bed.[55] In general, the actual street-walkers escaped prosecution and remained unconvicted in Britain for the reason that a client would often make the complaint at night but, when sober the following morning, would withdraw it because of possible embarrassment at the public proceedings which would follow.[56]

Lloyd Robson has suggested that no more than one woman in five transported during the sixty-year period of transportation to Eastern Australia was, in all probability, a full- or part-time prostitute. This assumption is based on the admission of the woman at her trial that she 'was on the town' or where she was described in court as 'a poor unfortunate girl of the town', or where gaolers recorded that a certain woman earned her livelihood in this manner.[57] During the first thirty years there are few identifiable cases. Of the first fleet only three of the women sentenced to transportation could be identified from their trial papers as prostitutes; one was described as 'a poor unfortunate girl of the town'; the other two were Ann George and Eleanor McCabe, who were convicted of assaulting John Harris in a dwelling-house and taking his monies from his person. Both Eleanor and Ann were to become mothers of first generation children.

Those convict women who were presumed to be prostitutes were tried in the main cities of London, Liverpool, Manchester and Dublin. These cities were notorious in Britain for the numbers of women who earned their living on the streets or in bawdy houses. Patrick Colquhoun estimated that there were at least 50,000 harlots on the streets of London alone. If Robson's estimate of one in five is accepted, it becomes obvious that only a minority of Britain's prostitutes were transported to Eastern Australia as only 2927 convicted women came to New South Wales and Van Diemen's Land between 1787 and 1813.[58] Further evidence that street women in Britain were able to escape prosecution for theft comes from the crime figures for 1811 for England and Wales. In that year, 3859 males and 1478 females were committed for trial; 3163 men and women were convicted, 1234 acquitted and 940, mainly women, were discharged, 'No Bills Found and Not Prosecuted'.[59] There is no evidence as to the nature of the cases dismissed but it is probable that they were concerned with crimes linked with soliciting and prostitution. Phillips found that, when such cases were actually brought to trial, the judge and jury frequently took a moral view of the incident and 'felt that the prosecutors in such cases had by their conduct contributed to their loss'. The case could then be dismissed or a verdict of 'Not Guilty' brought in.[60] In the light of the evidence which is available and within the context of the vast numbers of 'harlots' in Britain, it is reasonable to assume that few of the mothers of the first generation earned their reputation as whores as a direct result of the nature of the occupation they followed in Britain. This is not to misquote Professor Wood and suggest that the abandoned women remained in England and the virtuous were transported to Australia,[61] but it is an attempt to differentiate between moral and criminal behaviour, to distinguish between women called whores because they were convicted felons and women who were whores by profession. There is no evidence to suggest that the British experiences of the convict women were the experiences of street women and prostitutes. Except for a minority of cases, the evidence on which this assumption was based was the expectation that lower-class female felons were morally depraved because of their proven criminality.

Immorality was closely linked with class in British society. A Swiss visitor to London in the late 1770s claimed that the major characteristic of the ladies of quality, the respectable wives and daughters, was their easy virtue. His experiences may not have been typical but he recorded that 'The greatest difficulty is not always to persuade an English woman to suffer you to carry her off, but to find a convenient opportunity for telling her you wish to do it'. The ladies of quality, he recorded, were closely chaperoned by family and servants, but a lady could manage 'to make her appointments at some house either on her return from a walk, from a play, or from a ball ...'.[62] Such conduct would certainly not have met with the approval of Samuel Marsden yet similar occurrences did occur among the ladies of quality of Botany Bay. Elizabeth Macarthur described the conduct, or misconduct, of Mrs Bland in this way:

> Poor Mrs Bland (late Miss Henry) has made a sad break in the marriage bed—which caused Mr Bland to chalenge [*sic*] the man he found in Bed with her and as the man (Captn Brake Brother of the ship *Larkens*) refused to meet him, Bland has entered an action against him at £2500, but when I was at Sydney last week they had not apprehended him.[63]

Had Mrs Bland been a convicted woman it is doubtful if Elizabeth Macarthur would have described her as 'Poor Mrs Bland'.

In England, 'serious liaisons' similar to those between the respectable officials of Botany Bay and their convict mistresses, were openly discussed in the highest circles of society. The alliances were usually between a male aristocrat and the daughter of a lower-class family and, in some cases, these liaisons led to marriage. Parreaux cites three examples of liaisons: the Earl of Sandwich and Martha Roy; Lord Seaforth and Harriet Powell; the Earl of Agremont and Mademoiselle Duthe. These three women, all from working-class backgrounds, appeared in court circles accompanied by their lovers and all three women were renowned for their beauty and charm. The Earl of Coventry eventually married his mistress, Mary Gunning, who was acknowledged as the most beautiful woman at the court of George III depite her lowly origins; the Duke of Hamilton married Mary's sister. Viscount Maynard also married his mistress, Nancy Parsons, who was the daughter of a tailor. Had these women remained within the class into which they had been born and had they formed similar relationships with men from the lower orders, they would have been considered harlots by Colquhoun. It was this behaviour at Botany Bay which led to Marsden's definition of concubine. In London these women were described by their contemporaries as women of 'quality and brilliance'; in Botany Bay, the mistresses of officers were considered, at least by their 'husbands', to be 'women of the better sort'.

In the social circles of London, there was no suggestion that, as women living outside legal marriage, their honesty and morality were suspect. A typical description of one of these women, openly cohabiting in the same manner as many of the convicted women of Botany Bay, clearly emphasizes the contemporary distinction between the standards of the lower and upper classes, between acceptable behaviour in the court circles of London and infamous behaviour in the colony of New South Wales:

> Fanny Temple ... a finer woman in every respect could not be ... Her manners were perfectly correct, nor did I ever once hear a vulgarism or coarse expression pass her lips ... She inhabited an excellent house in Queen Anne, and has besides a neat lodging in the country ... kept her own chariot, with a suitable establishment of servants.[64]

In New South Wales, in 1810 Macquarie issued a General Order to ensure that no woman who cohabited outside lawful marriage could benefit by inheriting the property of the man with whom she lived.[65] This Order was a direct attempt to enforce morality by legislation, without any regard for the circumstances or religion of the woman or the duration of the liaison. The moral standards accepted by the court of George III were completely unacceptable to the governors and chaplains of His Majesty's penal colony.

This class attitude towards morality was also reflected strongly in attitudes towards criminality. Criminals were from poor, illiterate, unemployed classes; gentlemen were rarely convicted; 'ladies' not at all. The first comment by a Select Committee to acknowledge this distinction in law was that of 1828, which included the following comment in its Report:

> The sons of the persons of the highest rank in this country, when at school, often commit offences out of the exuberance of spirits and activity, which the law, if it visited them at all, must visit by sentence of great severity. Offences of a similar kind, passed over as frolic in the sons of the rich, are treated in the children of the poor as crimes of magnitude.

The Lord Chancellor himself, Lord Eldon, told the assembled House of Lords that as a boy he 'had stolen fruit and gone poaching'.[66] Had His Lordship been a member of the lower orders and had he been apprehended in this 'frolic' he would have been transported—or possibly hanged, as this was the statutory punishment for poaching.[67] When an eleven-year-old apprentice stole from her master, the judge trying the case saw it as a 'heinous offence' and sentenced her to be hanged; when young Mary Reibey 'borrowed' a neighbour's horse the offence was a capital one; when two teenagers, Elizabeth Cole and Mary Johnson, stole a pair of men's worsted stockings the sentence was death. All four of these young girls were reprieved and transported to Botany Bay, to become a part of that society considered infamous and abandoned.

Although crimes linked with prostitution were not prevalent among the transported women the stigma of immorality remained. A study of the second category of crimes, crimes of violence, shows how few of the women were guilty of crimes causing bodily harm, which would suggest that few were vicious criminals. Phillips has defined violence as 'offences against the person or against property in the commission of which some element of force was involved'.[68] The majority of the women were convicted of crimes against property[69] but there is little record of robbery with violence. Robson found that 1 per cent of his female sample had been transported for violent offences; that is, murder, manslaughter, assault, aiding and abetting rape. This figure was for the entire period of transportation. Between 1788 and 1813 slightly less than 3000 women were transported; this was 12 per cent of the total women convicts. The crimes of this group have been accepted as less violent, of 'a lesser complexion', by their contemporaries when compared with the offences which were committed after the Napoleonic Wars.[70] The only crimes which could be considered to have an element of violence during this period, committed by a minority of the transported women, were those connected with highway robbery or the results of a brawl, usually following disputes over the division of the proceeds of a robbery or theft. Two of these women, Charlotte Sprigmore and Mary Harrison, future mothers of children in the first generation, were transported after conviction of assaulting a third woman. In the words of their indictment, they:

> ... unlawfully, wilfully, maliciously and feloniously did make an assault upon Sussannah Edhouse, with intent to burn, spoil and destroy her clothes ... and did spoil, burn and deface, a certain garment ... one cotton gown ... which she had on her person.[71]

In the case of highway robbery the wording of the indictment presupposed violence in the commission of the crime. Mary Braund, who married William Bryant shortly after her arrival in New South Wales and escaped with him and their infant children by rowing to Java, was convicted with Catherine Fryer, who became the de facto wife of marine Matthew Prior, and Mary Haydon, who married William Eaton. Their crime was:

> ... feloniously assulting Agnes Lakeman, Spinster, in the King's Highway ... feloniously putting her in corporal fear and danger of her life ... and feloniously taking from her person and against her will ... one Silk Bonnet valued at 12d. and other goods value 11sh. her property.[72]

Children were born to all of these women in the colony and the only woman to be convicted of a subsequent crime was Mary Bryant, accused of escaping unlawfully from Botany Bay.

The lack of violent offenders among the transported women may have been a reflection of the nature of crime in contemporary Britain as well as an indication of the social circumstances of the criminals. Crime generally, among both male and female offenders, was of a non-violent nature. Crime was directed at the acquisition of property which had a ready resale; this would suggest a necessity based on need. It was not until 1828, however, that any official pronouncement was made as to the non-violent nature of contemporary British crime. In that year, the Select Committee on Criminal Commitments and Convictions, while acknowledging the high incidence of crime in Britain, reported that these crimes were mainly offences against property rather than offences against persons:

> Without pretending to any great exactness on this subject, it may be inferred that the whole quality of crime is greater in proportion to the population in England than in France; but that offences against the person are more, both in proportion to the whole number of offences and to the population, in France than in England. The general conclusion from this and other facts seems to be that crowded towns and flourishing manufactures tend to increase depredations upon property, and to diminish acts of violence against the person.[73]

This comment would appear to argue against the contemporary belief that crimes of violence increased after the Napoleonic Wars, largely as a result of the unemployment and poverty of the lower classes. It could, however, be suggested that this increase, when considered in relation to the nature of crime in neighbouring European countries, reinforced the assumption that violent crime in England before the Napoleonic Wars was minimal. The convicted women who were transported to Australia between 1788 and 1813, therefore, could not be described as criminal in the sense of vicious or violent women who committed physical abuse on fellow citizens. Following from this, the degree of their criminality would not suggest that they were social misfits, women without scruples who did not hesitate to commit violent offences for their own advantage.

There were, of course, women living in Britain during this period who committed the crimes of murder and manslaughter, and were convicted of these offences. It was very likely that these women suffered the capital punishment to which they were sentenced and that it was exceptional for any person convicted of these crimes to have their sentences commuted to transportation. This is not to argue that there was a conscious recognition by the legislators that these crimes were far less reprehensible than crimes against property, such as larceny. In 1819 Sir James Mackintosh, then a member of the House of Commons, expressed the opinion commonly held by the upper classes that crimes against property were as serious as crimes against the person. This idea may have been influenced by the fact that the majority of criminal assaults which led to death or serious injury were committed by members of the lower orders and inflicted on members of their own class of society, whereas crimes against property affected the respectable middle and upper classes. Sir James was speaking in the House in a debate which concerned alterations and modifications to the existing penal code. He argued that '... whatever attacks the life or the dwelling of a man ought to be punished with death ... it would be unsafe to propose any alteration to this'.[74] This opinion sums up the attitude of the legislation; that is, that violations of their property must be punished with the utmost severity of the law, for such offences were equal to the most violent of crimes against human life. The results of this belief are apparent in the sentences received by criminals in Britain during the first forty years of settlement in eastern Australia.

In New South Wales this lack of violent crime continued to be characteristic of the women convicts, particularly after sentences were served; very few of these women were reconvicted. It was rare for a woman to receive a capital sentence in the colony. The first woman to be hanged was Judith Jones, alias Ann Davis. In England she had been convicted and sentenced for the theft of six pairs of silk stockings. She was a married woman, the wife of William Davis, and was accompanied by her eight-year-old daughter, Jenny. Her subsequent conviction in the colony was based on circumstantial evidence that she had stolen goods from a fellow convict. Despite her attempt to save her life by 'pleading her belly', she was hanged in 1789 as an example to her fellow convicts.[75] Throughout the first twenty-five years of settlement few women were charged with major criminal offences which could be described as violent. The records of the Court of Criminal Jurisdiction and the magistrates' courts of the period show that those women who were convicted of colonial crimes were usually guilty of minor thefts and were almost exclusively those who were still serving original sentences which had been imposed in Britain. These colonial crimes were similar to the 'casual' category of crime in Britain.

Crimes in Britain which could be described as casual, in Patrick Colquhoun's use of the word, were mainly small thefts in which the articles stolen could easily be sold to a fence, or receiver, and the proceeds would provide sustenance for a few days, after which, presumably, another small theft was committed. Pickpocketing and shoplifting appeared to have been a way of life to many of the unemployed women of Britain. Given the contemporary standards of detection and the methods of apprehension, prosecution and conviction, it is probable that the risk to the individual of being apprehended, brought to court, found guilty and sentenced to death was so slight that the incidence of casual thieving was far greater than contemporary records of convictions would suggest.[76]

Although these casual crimes were most likely to have been the direct result of poverty and destitution caused by lack of employment opportunities[77] and an inadequate system of poor relief,[78] few of the offences involved the theft of food; stealing the traditional loaf of bread appears to have occurred more in fiction than in fact. Only three of the women convicts on the first fleet had been convicted for thefts of foodstuffs and only two of these offences may have been construed as theft for personal use. Elizabeth Evans, a serving-girl, had stolen three pounds of tea from her master. It may have been that this was one of a succession of small thefts which led to prosecution by her employer, conviction and transportation, or it may have been that the tea was stolen for her own use. Elizabeth Powley, on the other hand, of 'no trade', had broken into a dwelling-house and stolen the following articles: '. . . ten pounds weight of Cheese . . . three pounds weight of Bacon . . . twenty-four ounces of Butter . . . three pounds weight of Raisins . . . seven pounds weight of Flour `. . . two rolls of Worsted'. This could not be classed as a 'casual' crime although the food may have been taken for personal use and the theft of the worsted an afterthought. Elizabeth Beckford, the third first fleet woman guilty of the theft of food, had stolen twelve pounds of Gloucester cheese; she was seventy years old at the time of her conviction. These three women did not commit further offences in New South Wales.

The most frequently committed casual crime was shoplifting. At least seventeen of the first fleet women convicts had been indicted specifically for stealing 'privily from the shop'. The articles stolen were usually small and easily concealed about the person, handkerchiefs being the most common items taken in this way. The following cases were typical: at the age of eighteen Mary Martin stole fourteen handkerchiefs; Sarah Davies, aged twenty-two, stole four; Elizabeth Dalton, aged nineteen, also stole four linen handkerchiefs. These women described themselves as 'in service' and, from their trial papers, these were their first known offences. None were reconvicted in the colony. Handkerchiefs were the simplest of stolen articles to sell and it is unlikely that they were stolen for any reason other than to gain money. Clothing, on the other hand, often appeared to be stolen for personal use, particularly when the thief was of 'no trade' or a servant. Elizabeth Fitzgerald was a former domestic servant who was convicted at the Old Bailey of shoplifting a cotton gown; Jane Marriott, who described herself at her trial as 'in service', was sentenced to seven years' transportation for shoplifting a woman's black silk coat.[79] These and similar casual thefts by pickpockets indicated a way of life. Although few of these women were second offenders it was more probable that this was the first offence detected rather than the first committed. That few of these women were reconvicted in the colony suggests that when employment opportunities existed the motivation for crime was removed. Transported felons such as Mary Morton, who became the de facto wife of Assistant Commissary Zachariah Clark; or Elizabeth Powley, who married fellow-convict Anthony Rope and remained living with him and their children at Evan for at least forty years. Sarah Davis married Thomas Restill Crowder and her only colonial offence was being charged with her husband for making 'a disturbance at half-past ten at night'; her husband was reprimanded and Sarah was sentenced to 'work for one month'.[80] Elizabeth Fitzgerald married Thomas Biggers, who received absolute pardon from Governor Hunter. They settled at Petersham and, although Biggers was frequently charged with drunkenness, there is no record of any colonial offence by Elizabeth.[81]

Crimes described as professional were those which could be presumed to yield a large profit, sufficient to provide an 'income' for a considerable period. It is among this group of women convicts that the chief criminals should be found; that is, not those who stole to relieve an immediate want but those who planned and carried out large thefts and robberies for major gain. Most of these 'professional' offences were burglaries and, in most cases, carried out with the aid of male accomplices, who were not always apprehended. One case was that of Elizabeth Lee, who was twenty-three when she described herself as a cook at her trial at the Old Bailey. If she were in fact a cook she may have been taking her occupation seriously: the theft for which she was convicted included the following:

> . . . thirty gallons of wine, called red port . . . twelve gallons of other wine, called Malmsey Maderia . . . three gallons of white port . . . three gallons of claret . . . three gallons of rasin wine . . . three gallons of orange wine . . . three gallons of rum . . . one gallon of arrack . . .

As she also stole 124 bottles, it may be presumed that the liquor was for resale.

Women who acted as receivers of stolen goods were professional criminals and this was recognized in law, longer sentences being imposed on receivers. Ann Lynch of Bristol was sentenced to transportation for fourteen years for receiving stolen goods, Mary M'Cormack of Liverpool was twenty-one when she was transported for fourteen years for 'divers felonies, and receiving and buying stolen goods, knowing the same to be stolen . . .'

Mary Wickham from Wiltshire received fourteen years' transportation for receiving 'one silk handkerchief ... 2 silk handkerchiefs ... one lawn apron ...one cambric apron, one sheet and other things'.[82] The nature of the goods sold to these female receivers supports the suggestion that the small thefts which were committed by casual thieves were for the specific purpose of sale to a fence. The shoplifter or pickpocket was usually sentenced to seven years' transportation. If the value of the goods exceeded one shilling for pickpockets or five shillings for shoplifters the statutory punishment was death.[83]

If there were a criminal class among the women convicts at Botany Bay it would, presumably, be formed from the professional thieves. This, however, was not the case. Few of these professionals were reconvicted, fewer appeared before a magistrates' court on any charge at all and the most notorious in Britain became the most respectable 'wives' and mothers in the colony. Former cook Elizabeth Lee was chosen by Lieutenant King as a woman of good character to accompany him to Norfolk Island in February 1788. Ann Lynch became the common-law wife of marine Private Thomas Cottrell and the mother of his son, Thomas. Mary M'Cormack married William Parr—they were both from Liverpool—immediately on arrival at Sydney Cove. Mary Wickham married John Silverthorn—they were both from New Sarum. She died in childbirth some eighteen months later and their son died at the age of two weeks. Margaret Dawson, who had been sentenced to death at the age of fifteen, became the de facto and recognized 'wife' of Surgeon William Balmain and the mother of his children. Their son, John Henderson, became the first native-born surgeon although his qualifications appeared to have been self-given. These women had all been convicted of crimes which were professional rather than casual yet their lives in the colony bore no resemblance to the criminality of their lives in Britain.

The most notorious 'criminals' among British women were the servant-girls. The description 'servant' or 'in service' could apply to both domestic and farm servants but, from the places of origin given for these women at their trials, most of those who were transported to Botany Bay were domestic servants. The reputation for dishonesty may have been influenced by the relative ease with which household thefts were discovered and the wrongdoer arrested as compared with the difficulties of apprehending pickpockets and shoplifters.

Lloyd Robson's investigation showed that 'nearly all the female convicts were domestic servants of one sort or another'.[84] A few were specialized servants, such as nursemaids, cooks, laundresses and washerwomen. Allowance must also be made for those who gave their occupation as 'in service' rather than describe themselves as 'of no trade' or 'on the town'. It is possible that such women believed they may have had greater opportunity of escaping or reducing their punishment if they could establish the respectable background of employment.

Although most of the female convicts were, or claimed to be, servants this did not indicate that most stole from their masters or mistresses. That several of these serving-girls were convicted of highway robbery, burglary or breaking and entering, all crimes which involved prolonged absence from any place of regular employment, suggests that if they were servants then they were not employed at the time of their arrest for professional crimes. That they described themselves in this way also added to the criminal reputation of their 'class' as a whole.

It is clear from an analysis of the crimes and given occupations of these women that they shared similar class origins and a similar background in Britain of poverty, deprivation and, at times, desperate want. It is also clear that most lacked any occupational skills which could be used to advantage either in Britain or in New South Wales. Their only hope for honest employment in Britain was as domestic or rural servants. This, or prostitution, was the limit of their opportunities. The occupational skills they brought with them to New South Wales were extremely limited. Accordingly, most were employed as domestic servants or housekeepers during their term of penal servitude in New South Wales.[85] Contrary to their British reputation, few of these colonial servants were charged with theft during their assignment period.[86] There was a wide discrepancy between their infamous record for thievery in Britain and their apparent honesty as servants in New South Wales. There are three probable reasons for this although there is little substantive evidence apart from the record of their individual life-styles in New South Wales. It is possible that the motives for thefts in Britain had been linked with need or despair, particularly in those cases where a servant was dismissed for pregnancy— Esther Abrams, for example.[87] It was also possible that, when the need to obtain money or goods for subsistence by thievery was removed, the impetus for crime did not exist. There were, of course, exceptions. In 1804 an ex-convict and former servant, Mary Tirley, was charged with theft from her dead employer. Mary had been the housekeeper and after the master's death had 'put a bag (containing) soap, nails and sundry other articles' into the possession of another servant and asked him to hide it carefully from the constable. She was convicted of theft.[88]

Another possible factor contributing to the honesty of these colonial servants was the relationship often established between master and servant, a relationship which frequently led to legal or common-law marriages. When this was the case, to steal from the master was, in a sense, to steal from oneself. In the colony it was more likely that the assigned woman worked in a household where she was virtual mistress, which was the reverse of the domestic situation in Britain. This left less need to improve one's position by theft. In one London case, for example, the desire to improve her situation was very obviously the main reason for theft from her master: Jane Dundas stole the household linen and attempted to pawn it; she wanted to obtain sufficient money with which to buy a lottery ticket. After her conviction and arrival in Sydney, she became the Commissary's housekeeper and gained respectability by the honesty and sobriety of her life.[89]

One of the rare occasions when a colonial woman stole from her 'protector' was the case of Elizabeth Leonard. In January 1804 Elizabeth, who had married Kelyhorn in 1788, was accused by him in the Criminal

Court with 'in his absence, making away with every moveable' although she had 'long partook of the fruits of . . . her protector's industry'. From the report of the trial proceedings it appeared evident that Elizabeth's actions were provoked, the result of a domestic quarrel rather than the result of a wish for personal monetary gain. She was, however, found guilty and sentenced to labour for the Crown for two years. This was the only case of this nature reported before 1813 in the *Sydney Gazette*. There were, however, reports of one or two cases which, although not typical of the experiences of the assigned women, did suggest an element of provocation from their masters. The *Sydney Gazette* reported in April 1804 that an assigned woman, Mary Carrol, was beaten violently and inhumanely by her de facto husband. In 1805, the murder of two assigned women was reported. Both were recently arrived Irish convict women who were murdered by their masters and in both cases death had been caused by a beating after the man had been drinking. For Bridget Kean, there was no evidence of remorse but with Bridget Horan remorse was almost immediate, the man seeking assistance and crying, 'I fear I have killed poor Biddy'.[90] Poor Biddy and Bridget had been unfortunate in their assignment, experiencing the worst hazards of a system described as a lottery.

The reputation of the convict women had been formed on the basis of their lives and crimes in Britain, not on their colonial experiences, but they were unable to avoid the stigma of the immoral and criminal associations linked with their civil condition. There is abundant evidence of their life-styles in the colony to show that their reactions to the colonial environment, varied as they were, did not fit the pattern ascribed to them and expected from them. In addition to the biographical evidence from Musters, and the 1828 Census, which detailed their occupations, residence, and legal or de facto relationships, there is evidence from many of these women themselves, describing their lives in the colony, their hopes and ambitions, their achievements and their failures. This evidence, in which these women speak for themselves, is found among the Memorials to the Governors, Petitions in Mitigation of Sentence, Applications for Permission to Marry, and in the evidence given to coroners' morgues and inquests. When this evidence is combined with reports relating to women in the *Sydney Gazette* and with biographical data concerning their lives as family women, employed women and 'business women', who were as enterprising as the male ex-convicts, an entirely different picture of the nature of female society and the characteristics of the mothers of the first generation emerges.

It is possible, on the basis of this new evidence, to see clearly the vast differences which existed between the lives of these women before conviction in Britain and after their sentences were served in New South Wales. Among the Petitions in Mitigation of Sentence there is a testimonial for a former 'professional' criminal, Charlotte Holland, requesting a pardon. Her Petition was written by Henry Lane, who wrote that she had been well recommended to him by Mrs Anna King, the later Governor's Lady, and was now employed by his family as a housekeeper. A Petition from Eleanor Lennard described how she had been sentenced to seven years' transportation in Limerick, Ireland, in 1804. She had married sergeant

Thomas Hudson of the 102nd Regiment which was preparing to depart for England. She petitioned for permission to accompany her husband and their children. Her character testimonial showed that there was no suggestion that she was one of the 'depraved and infamous refuse from Ireland'.[91] Judith Kelly had been sentenced to fourteen years' transportation for receiving stolen goods—she, too, was a 'professional' criminal. She was married with three children when she was convicted and her husband and one child came to New South Wales with her; her remaining two children stayed in England with her parents. Judith had been granted an Absolute Pardon and she wrote to Macquarie asking that this be confirmed, showing evidence that, since her arrival, 'she had conducted herself in a becoming manner, steadily and prudently as a wife and mother'. Her life-style in the colony bore no resemblance whatsoever to that assumed to be typical of convicted women.

Among other Petitions for Confirmation of Pardons which were received from women who had arrived as convicts were a number who wished to return to England for 'family' reasons: Catherine Osborn explained in her Memorial that she was now a widow and 'planned to return to England to see her numerous family'. Ann Sidgwick 'had been in the Colony ten years and had behaved very well'. She was the wife of a soldier in the New South Wales Corps and he wished to take her and their three children back to England with him. Judith Quinland 'had lived with David McKin, the late gaoler, for many years and had had many children by him'. She had received a Conditional Pardon for good behaviour but, as 'Her children still need her care' and McKin wished to return to England, she requested an Absolute Pardon. These were typical of the requests from former convict women who had lived as family women in the colony after their sentences had been served and, in accordance with contemporary standards, had followed their husbands' decisions to leave New South Wales with their regiment.

There were Petitions from women which described their occupations. Ann Rolph was one of the few skilled women, a cambric worker; she had been transported for life and had two small children, for whose sake she requested that Governor Macquarie confirm the Pardon which Paterson had granted her. Another reference to the need to care for children came from Sarah Townson, a former Irish convict who had been in the colony for ten years and had lived with soldier William Neal for the whole of that time, bearing him five children. She requested a Pardon so that she and Neal could marry because she was 'bringing up the children'. Margaret Connolly, another Irish woman, had married ex-convict Thomas O'Brien and lived with him on their farm. She requested a ticket-of-leave as she 'has a small child and a large number of stock to mind'. One dubious request came from Ann Kennedy and was granted by Macquarie. Ann wrote that she had arrived on the *Experiment* sentenced to seven years' transportation:

The Lieutenant-Governor gave her leave to obtain her livelihood on her own which she has done with Thomas O'Neale in an honest industrious way at 103 Pitt Street Sydney. She has a child and is now on a small farm two miles from Sydney. She requests a Ticket-of-Leave.

These and similar Petitions showed that these women, whether legally married or living in de facto relationships, were family women who had maintained stable relationships with one partner for many years, and whose chief responsibilities in the colony were the care of their children, the management of their households, and assisting their husbands. As former convict Elizabeth Sidebottom wrote, her time 'could not be better employed than in looking after her husband, her family and their business'. These Petitions were, of course, written to obtain indulgences so the writers would wish to appear in the most favourable light. It was, however, obligatory that every petitioner included two character testimonials from a magistrate or a clergyman. William Cowper testified that Elizabeth Sidebottom was 'an industrious wife and attentive to her family'. Samuel Marsden attested to the 'good character' of Martha Morris, the wife of a private in the 73rd Regiment and the mother of his three children. The Chaplain recommended her for a pardon, which was granted.

Among these Petitions were several from women wishing to change their occupation. Ann Thompson requested the Governor to grant her a separation from her husband 'who has left her for another woman'. She explained that she wanted 'to get into service and be independent'. It would have been quite proper for this woman to ask assistance from Government Stores, as did Hannah Cole after the death of her husband, the former Superintendent of the Lighthouse at South Head. Hannah successfully petitioned that she, her son and her government servant be put on stores as her husband's 'premature death had involved her in the greatest distress'. Other women showed considerable enterprise in petitioning on behalf of their husbands. One of these was Sarah Wells, an ex-convict who had been in the colony 'upwards of twenty-five years'. She wrote that her husband was a wheelwright, and requested permission to employ a blacksmith 'for whom they now have enough work, owing to a great increase in stock'. Hannah Morley wrote to the Governor for assistance in securing a liquor licence which, she said:

> ... had been refused by D'Arcy Wentworth on the grounds that her husband was a drunkard. She stated that she was in debt, as she had just erected a house suitable for a Public House and if her licence was not granted she would become poverty-stricken and she could not repay the debt and she had six small children.

There were Petitions which showed the desires of a number of these women to rejoin husbands, even if they were confined at penal settlements. Mary Bay, for example, requested permission to join her convict husband at Port Macquarie, where he had a further five years to serve. Maria McKone petitioned for a ticket-of-leave for her husband, who was a prisoner for life, as 'she needs him to support the family of two children'. There were corresponding Petitions from convict and ex-convict husbands for permission for their wives to join them. The husband of Parramatta prisoner, Mary Bosworth, was serving his sentence at Newcastle. He successfully petitioned that his wife 'be forwarded' to him. Caleb Wilson requested permission for Catherine Ferrier to leave the Parramatta Factory where she was confined so that they could be married. There were also occasional examples of hardship in which a wife was prevented from rejoining her husband because of her usefulness to her master. One such case concerned John Blaxland, who requested that the Petition of the husband of his servant, Mary King, be refused. Mary's husband had been transported to the Derwent and he wanted his wife to join him there. Blaxland wrote: 'I have four daughters who she is now instructing in music and the difficulty of getting the female part of a young family educated in this Colony must be obvious to Your Excellency'. Mary remained where Blaxland considered it was her duty to be, as governess to his daughters. It was not only the respectable free settlers who considered the welfare of their daughters. John Tarlton, a settler at Prospect, married Mary Duggen 'to be a mother to his daughter'; the marriage was in 1812 and Tarlton was twenty years older than Mary. In 1828 the couple were still living on their farm at Prospect with their son, William. Mary had received an Absolute Pardon for good conduct.

The Petitions and Memorials from the convicted women, their husbands and their masters, show the strong attachments of family life, with or without benefit of clergy, and a strong sense of maternal responsibility. This is also shown in their relationships with those children when they reached maturity. Naturally, all the evidence is not uniformly favourable. The Public Notices which appeared from time to time in the *Sydney Gazette*, warning that a husband would not be responsible for the debts of his absconded wife, show another side of the picture.[92] Nor did these women lead an idyllic or easy life, as was shown in extreme cases by suicide, or by the problems resulting from bushfires, droughts and floods.[93] Nor were they without the many cares and problems associated with the raising of children, with the family life, as is seen in reports of accidents to children, such as burnings, drownings, falling in wells, snake bites, scaldings and wandering away from the settlement.[94] There are reports, too, of problems with adolescent children. A mother and father, for example, complained to the magistrates that their son, Thomas Jones, had been 'seduced' from his home by an infamous woman, Ann Harris;[95] another parent complained that his daughter 'was of a fretful temper'. The Petitions and Memorials written to the governors, and the newspaper reports, reveal the many facets of family life in the penal colony. Most importantly, they show clearly that family life did exist in the colony from the earliest days of settlement and that colonial parents from all civil condition categories were concerned with the problems and difficulties of raising children.

There were, of course, women in the colony whose actions and life-styles justified the descriptions of the governors and chaplains, the complaints of the respectable settlers. Women who were drunken, criminal, immoral; women from whom no sense of maternal responsibility or concern would be expected. Women such as those who cohabited with visiting seamen and later complained to the Bench of Magistrates for maintenance for their bastard children. In some of these cases, the 'fathers' denied that there was any proof that the child was theirs.[96]

A Petition to the governor from a settler, V. Jacobs, complained about the character and behaviour of his assigned female servants: 'Catherine Bryan ... arrived drunk and does not appear to be a fit person to be received into a respectable family ... of the other three, only evil could be expected and one was a vicious prostitute'. These women, however, were the exceptions. Most of them had arrived in the colony shortly before comment was made on their behaviour, so this comment reflected their British life-styles, not their response to colonial opportunities and experiences. Those who, like Catherine Bryan and her friends, were assigned almost immediately on arrival in New South Wales, were continuing the type of life to which they had been accustomed in England. Their standards of behaviour, therefore, were similar in 'class' to women of the same social and economic backgrounds in all the towns and cities of western Europe. Their behaviour in the colony differed from that in Britain only in one respect: in Britain this way of life was frequently the result of economic necessity; in the colony it was from choice and inclination. To group these women in the same category as those who cohabited in more or less stable relationships is to distort the role, nature and contribution of the convicted women to colonial society.

In 1806 Samuel Marsden divided colonial women into two distinct groups: 'wives and concubines'. In 1972 Anne Summers continued this view by discussing colonial women as *Damned Whores and God's Police*. This strict division makes no allowance for the vast divergence among the life-styles, experiences and expectations of the women living in the penal colony. Neither does it allow for the completely different opportunities which were available to the women in the colony, in contrast with their former lives in Britain, nor for the individual responses of the convicted women to the colonial situation. Contemporaries formed their opinions on the lives and conduct of the women of Botany Bay very largely on the basis of their experiences in Britain. Modern historians, such as Summers and Dixson, have tended to ignore the effect of this 'invisible luggage' which these women brought with them to New South Wales. They have continued to interpret their responses to colonial life on the basis of their *British* experiences and standards. Admittedly, their crimes in Britain did indicate certain life-styles, with the emphasis clearly on the effects of poverty, poor working conditions and wages, and lack of opportunities to obtain an acceptable standard of living in an honest way within the limitations and expectations of their class origins. On the other hand, the comparative lack of crime by these women in the colony indicated either a complete behavioural change or a lack of motivation for criminal activities in their new homeland.

That some of these women retained their previous 'degraded' life-styles showed clearly that colonial women should not be divided into two groups, good and bad, or wives and concubines. It is essential to define 'degraded' and 'immoral' within the contemporary context of the attitudes and standards of these women themselves. Criminality must be separated from immorality in order to avoid perpetuating the misconceptions of 'respect-able' contemporary observers. Obviously, all of Britain's criminal class had not turned to crime from sheer necessity. To many it was a traditional way of life, a normal livelihood for the receivers, the counterfeiters, the 'professional' criminals. These men and women, however, were more skilled at evading detection, more cunning in the ways of avoiding apprehension and conviction. It was the amateur criminals, the Mary Talbots, who stole from necessity, from poverty, from want, from desperation. The almost insoluble problem is to distinguish between those women who were criminally inclined and continued to be so in the colony and those who were, quite simply, the girls and women from Britain's lower orders, without skills, without opportunity, without hope of becoming either family women or working women. The only way in which such a distinction may be attempted is by a consideration of the responses of these women to the entirely new society which was taking shape at Botany Bay. The only way by which these responses may be determined and analysed is by studying the individual lives of these women, by recreating their colonial life-styles on the basis of their own individual achievements and failures, by taking their own descriptions of what they themselves believed they had achieved, and by tracing their influence on their own children. It was this influence which was their greatest contribution to the nature of colonial society, for it was the responses of their children, both to their family backgrounds and to the society created by their parents, which determined the nature and characteristics of the first generation.

CHAPTER FOUR

THE NATURE OF THE TIMES DECEAS'D

'... having strenuously endeavoured ... to instruct his children ... to comport themselves to the full satisfaction of their superiors, and in good fellowship with all mankind, having led his family from their juvenile years into the Path of Industry ... feels it is a duty incumbent on him as a Parent to endeavour to behold them settled in life ...'.

John Turnball, 'an honest and deserving man'.

During the first twenty-five years of white settlement the parents of the first generation lacked any awareness of an extending arable frontier in New South Wales. To them, and to their children, the colony was simply a narrow coastal strip, hemmed in to the west by seemingly impassable mountains beyond which in all probability there lay nothing but a vast desert. In 1790 Phillip had described the way in which these mountains were a barrier to the spread of settlement to the west: '... after the first day's journey ... such a constant succession of deep ravines, the sides of which were frequently inaccessible ... [they] returned ... not having been able to proceed more than fifteen miles in one day ...'.[1] It was not until 1813 that there was any real possibility of settlement beyond the Blue Mountains, and even then the handful of settlers who sought and received land grants were mainly in search of pasture.[2] It was not until after about 1819, when these western lands were named the County of Westmoreland, that general settlement beyond the mountains was encouraged.[3]

To the south, it was 1819 before land was freely available in the Jervis Bay–Illawarra area,[4] and few native-born or their parents appear to have ventured farther south than Liverpool before that date. In 1814, for example, the total population of Liverpool was 627, the total population of New South Wales 12,173. According to the Muster for that year, taken for Liverpool, Airds, Appin and Places Adjacent, there were twenty-one adult native-born listed as resident in this district.[5] Of these, fourteen were married women, all of whose husbands were ticket-of-leave men or ex-convicts, and four were described as 'single women' who appear to have been living with their parents. Of the three native-born males living in the district, one was Thomas Acres who lived with his ex-convict landowner parents; the second was landowner Hamilton Hume; and the third, John Neal(e), was a seventeen-year-old labourer.[6]

Although the Hunter River had been discovered in 1798 the spread of settlement to the north was similar to that in the south in regard to the slow development of the settled areas. Some limited occupancy was available from about 1813 but it was 1822 before the land on both sides of the Hunter River was available for settlement. Settlement was permitted at Patersons Plains from about 1813 and in that year native-born John Tucker, his wife and his ex-convict father received land 'to cultivate and reside on' but not to own. Tucker was an exception among the native-born for, by 1820, there were only twelve farms at Patersons Plains and another eleven at Wallis Plains.[7] These farms were held under a regulation published in the General Order of March 1818:

> ... they are not to regard the land so given them as their own Property, the right being exclusively vested in the Governor, and that

they are only allowed to cultivate and reside on their Farms so granted during their good conduct and the pleasure of His Excellency the Governor ....[8]

During the childhood of the native-born, 1788–1813, none of their parents had settled in the Hunter Valley area and, during their adolescence, fewer of the parents and their families ventured north than did those who took up land in the south-western districts. In general, the parents remained within the settled areas of the Cumberland Plain. It was within this 'compact area'[9] that those of the parents who were farmers or graziers obtained their lands. By 1813 settlement was clustered mainly around Sydney and Parramatta, and around Richmond, Windsor, Pitt Town and Wilberforce. The population of the rural districts was estimated at 6,439; that of Sydney and its vicinity, 5,356.[10] These figures indicate the nature of the settlement during the childhood of the native-born, and this compactness affected not only the children of those who owned lands but the tradesmen and labourers of the towns and townships.

It was to be most important to the development of the children born in the colony, to their attitudes towards the colony in general and towards land ownership and farming in particular that, during their childhood, neither they nor their parents had any realization of the existence of the fertile lands which lay beyond the Cumberland Plain. It was equally important that, during their adolescence, when exploration had opened the north, west and south, there was still little inclination among the parents to move beyond the already established areas of settlement. Between 1788 and 1813 these known and settled areas stretched a bare forty miles from Windsor to Appin, a bare twenty miles from Parramatta to Nepean. To the young native-born, New South Wales was, in effect, the narrow Cumberland Plain.

The youthful experiences of the native-born were directly affected by the location of their parents' land. The actual granting of land in any specific area was, from the time of Phillip, a somewhat haphazard process, although the general principles on which it was alienated from the Crown remained virtually unaltered until after the arrival of Governor Brisbane.[11] During this period, the granting of land was mainly dependent on the attitudes of the various governors, and the two lieutenant-governors, Grose and Paterson.[12] Their attitudes were influenced by the nature of their instructions, Grenville had first written to Phillip concerning the size of land grants in 1789:

... to every non-commissioned officer one hundred acres, and to every private man fifty acres, over and above the quantity directed by Our General Instructions to you, to be granted to such convicts as may hereafter be emancipated or discharged from their servitude, free of all fees, taxes, quit rents, and other acknowledgements for the space of ten years; but after that time to be liable to an annual quit rent of one shilling for every ten acres. ....[13]

Grants did not follow an orderly pattern. Governors' instructions did not specify the maximum number of acres which could be granted, although an intending marine or ex-soldier settler usually received a larger grant than an ex-convict, and allowance was made in both cases for additional land for a wife and children. Grants to free immigrants and to the higher civil and military officials were generally influenced by the amount of capital the grantee possessed. The general nature of the instructions, and the leeway left to the decisions of the individual governors, may be seen from the instructions sent to Hunter in 1794: '... any meritorious settler or well-deserving emancipated convict becoming a settler could be granted an unspecified quality of land'.[14]

To a certain extent, the alienation of land and the size of grants was governed by the belief among the officials that the availability of suitable farming land was limited. This belief prevailed even after the discovery of the lands to the north, west and south. As early as 1804 King had believed that the supply of arable land within the Cumberland Plain itself was exhausted.[15] Botanist George Caley had advised that 'greater care should be taken in the disposal of land', for the supply of arable land 'was not so extensive as was generally imagined'.[16] In 1817 Macquarie wrote to Bathurst, 'Disposable lands are now getting Very Scarce in this part of the Colony, as far as Forty Miles in every Direction from the Seat of Government'.[17] John Oxley, in his evidence to Bigge, reported that '... the scarcity of grantable land within a reasonable distance of the markets now [is] so great as to render it impossible for the Governor to place any settlers of respectability'.[18]

The actual choice of areas in which land was to be granted was normally made by the governor. The successive governors were influenced by the reports of the explorers, the use to which the land could be put, the ease of access to markets for perishable products and any problems which might arise from the need to control and protect the settlers.[19] For example, the settlements at the Hawkesbury favoured small-scale farming, allotments of thirty to fifty acres being considered suitable for self-sufficiency.[20] This accorded with the intentions of the British government to encourage ex-convicts, ex-marines and ex-soldiers to remain in New South Wales as small farmers after the completion of their sentences or their tours of duty.[21] By 1799, 54.9 per cent of the cultivated land in the colony was in the Hawkesbury, 36.6 per cent at Parramatta and 13.8 per cent at Sydney.[22] These figures indicate the major areas in which the 'rural' native-born were raised and the types of farms on which they lived: small crop-producing agricultural and pastoral lands. In addition to this, these areas indicate that the native-born, generally speaking, were not raised in isolated areas, for the Parramatta–Hawkesbury districts had access to rivers both for the transportation of perishable goods and as a means of communication. Whether the settlers themselves had had any choice in the location of their grants is doubtful. The report of Lieutenant-Governor Grose to Dundas in 1794 suggested that the final choice remained with the Governor: 'I have settled on the banks of the Hawkesbury twenty-two settlers who seem very much pleased with their farms'.[23] At least six of

TABLE 4/1

The first Hawkesbury farmers: native-born children

Settler/father	Civil condition	Children, year of birth	Children, 1828
Barnett, Daniel	ex-convict	Daniel 1798	labourer, 30 acres Pitt Town
Butler, Joseph	ex-convict	James 1802	farmer, 60 acres Lower Portland Head
		Sylvester 1804	farmer, 60 acres Lower Portland Head
		Walter 1807	carpenter Sydney
		Elizabeth 1813	with father Windsor
Acres, Joseph	ex-convict	Thomas 1798	settler, 10 acres Airds
Saunders, Thomas	ex-convict	Thomas 1800	farmer, 135 acres Pitt Town
		Elizabeth 1800	with father, Prospect 110 acres
		Virginia 1806	as above
		Sarah 1808	as above
		Mary 1810	as above

these settlers were the fathers of rural native-born who were resident in New South Wales in 1828. Table 4/1 indicates the civil condition of the father, year of birth of the son and occupation of the son in 1828.

It was most important for the native-born that there was no attempt to persist with what appears to have been a practice of Phillip—the segregation of ex-convict settlers from those who had arrived as marines, soldiers, officials or free settlers. An examination of the grants made by Phillip shows that ex-convicts were given grants in separate areas unless needed as labourers for free settlers. A probable reason for this may have been Phillip's firm belief in the differences between settlers of convict origin and free settlers. In 1792 eight of the Royal Marines received grants averaging eighty acres at the appropriately named Field of Mars, while twelve ex-convicts received grants averaging thirty acres at Eastern Farms, just above the village of Ryde. In January 1793 the first free settlers received grants at Liberty Plains.[24] One freed convict, Walter Rouse, received a smaller grant in the same area, the grant being set apart from those of the free settlers, all of which were adjoining. This ex-convict was a brick-maker by trade and so possessed occupational skills which were needed by the settlers. That they themselves were conscious of the distinction of being free is shown by the description of the naming of the settlement: 'Being all free people—one convict excepted who was allowed to settle with them—they gave the appelation Liberty Plains to the district in which their farms were situated . . .'.[25]

This practice, although nowhere stated as a definite policy, was followed by Grose in 1794 when land was granted at Concord to six non-commissioned officers of the New South Wales Corps, four free men and one ex-convict.[26] The ex-convict was Eleanor Frazier, who had arrived on the *Prince of Wales* in 1788. By 1800 only one other ex-convict, Isaac Nichols, had obtained a land grant at Concord. It was not until 1796 that Hunter was granting land in the same areas to free settlers, ex-soldiers and ex-convicts, and he continued this practice throughout his administration. Hunter's grants at Mulgrave Place between 1797 and 1800 illustrate this. Fifty-nine were to ex-convicts, fifty-seven were to marines, privates, drummers, non-commissioned officers and officers of the New South Wales Corps; the remainder were to marines, two free settlers and the free wife of a convict.[27]

England sent no official directive to segregate the lands granted to those who came free from the grants of those who had arrived convicted. The native-born children of these settlers, therefore, did not grow up in an area settled exclusively by ex-convicts, by free settlers or by ex-officials. Although aware of the civil condition of their parents and the privileges or limitations this imposed, they were not accustomed to the geographic isolation of those who had arrived convicted. This is evidenced clearly by the varying civil conditions of the settlers at Mulgrave Place by the end of the administration of Governor Hunter.

Table 4/2 is not intended as an exhaustive list nor does it include all the children of any particular family; its purpose is to illustrate the diversity of the civil conditions of the settler-families in a particular district. There are occasional exceptions to this pattern, but these are so few as not to affect the placement together of settlers of diverse civil conditions from the time of Hunter's administration. One early exception was Governor Hunter's settlement of eight marines on allotments on the banks of the Georges River in 1798, 'where the land promises well'.[28]

The importance of children of ex-convicts, ex-officials and free settlers growing up in the same district becomes particularly apparent when these same children reached marriageable age; proximity encouraged inter-marriage of sons and daughters of parents who were from differing civil conditions. In a number of cases, particularly among the female native-born, this proximity led to marriage with ex-convicts and free settlers as well as to marriage among the native-born. It was in this way that the lack of any policy of segregation among those receiving land grants helped to prevent the permanent division of colonial society into a rigid hierarchy of bond and free.

TABLE 4/2

Examples of differing civil conditions of parents of native-born who received grants at Mulgrave Place, near the Hawkesbury, from Governor Hunter; also showing occupation and residence of native-born children in 1828

Father	Civil condition at time of grant	Children/ year of birth	1828
Bowman, John	free settler		
McManus, James	ex-marine	James 1793	farmer, Bathurst 113 acres B.C. wife, 3 children
		John 1798	wheelwright, Parramatta 50 acres B.C. wife, 2 children
Merrick, Edward	ex-convict	John 1798	farmer, North Richmond 120 acres
		Richard 1805	farmer with above
		Thomas 1805	farmer with above
		William 1802	Constable, Bathurst B.C. wife, 2 children
		Susanna 1812	with parents, Edward F.S. and Mary F.S., farmer, Richmond 140 acres
Ezzy/Ezzey/Ezzoy, Jane	free wife of convict	John 1795	District Constable, North Richmond 70 acres B.C. wife Rebecca Lamb, 5 children
		Louisa 1797	married William Bayliss B.C. 1794 farmer, Cornwallis 32 acres
		Mary 1798	killed by lightning 4 days before her wedding, 17 October 1816
		Sophia 1807	married James Dargen, B.C. 1803, landholder, Bathurst 200 acres
Bates, Thomas	drummer, New South Wales Corps		father of at least 6 B.C. children

Father	Civil condition at time of grant	Children/ year of birth	1828
Nash, William	private, New South Wales Corps	George 1796	farmer, Evan 60 acres
		William 1798	N.R., Illawarra
Reynolds, Edward (Edwin)	ex-convict	Edwin 1794	farmer, Lower Portland Head 20 acres widower, 4 children
Howell, John	private, New South Wales Corps	Henry 1794	householder, Sydney B.C. wife, six children
Ryan, John	ex-convict	John 1793	overseer, Luskentye B.C. wife Elizabeth Cooper
Cunningham, James	ex-convict	John 1800	landholder, Wilberforce 90 acres B.C. wife, 2 children
Connolly, Andrew	private, New South Wales Corps	James 1804	farmer, N.R. 100 acres B.C. wife
Eather/Ether, Thomas	ex-convict	Charles 1799	farmer, Cornwallis 15 acres widower, 1 child
		Thomas 1800	overseer, Patricks Plains C.F. wife, 3 children
		John 1807	F.S., Windsor with widowed mother
Cobcroft, John	ex-convict	Richard 1792	farmer, Wilberforce 215 acres widower, 7 children
		John 1797	farmer, Wilberforce 140 acres B.C. wife Mary Crew 'of the Hawkesbury', 4 children
		Sarah 1799	married William Blackmen, C.F. 1801, innkeeper, Wilberforce
Balmain, William	surgeon, C.F.	John Henderson 1800	'surgeon', Sydney (mother ex-convict Margaret Dawson)

A typical instance of this proximity leading to marriage is that of Mary Martin, the daughter of two ex-convicts, Edward Merrick (one of the first settlers at Mulgrave Place) and Mary Russel. She was their second child, born in March 1795. In 1809 Merrick received a grant of eighty acres at Richmond Hill and moved there with his family. Mary married Robert Martin, whose free settler parents had received 100 acres at Mulgrave Place as a land grant from Governor King and who had later moved to Richmond. Mary, her husband and their two children lived with her parents-in-law at Richmond in 1828. The marriage certificate stated that both Mary and John 'came from the same district'. To the native-born, civil condition was not necessarily considered a bar to marriage. Eliza Lydia Griffiths was born in Sydney in March 1794, the daughter of New South Wales private Michael Griffiths/Griffen and his ex-convict wife. Her father received 25 acres at Petersham Hill in March 1795, and later moved to Pitt Town, where they received another grant. Lydia married John Benn, native-born settler of Pitt Town whose ex-convict parents had received a grant of thirty acres at Mulgrave Place in 1800, an additional grant of sixty acres at the same place in 1803 and had finally settled at Pitt Town. After the death of her husband, Lydia married an ex-convict farmer at Pitt Town, John Macdonald, and remained living in the district.

Although there was no apparent discrimination as to the location of grants, there was a distinction with regard to the amount of land granted to those of convict origin as distinct from those who had arrived freely. By 1800, 70.7 per cent of those settlers who had received grants had arrived convicted, the remaining 29.3 per cent had arrived free. This smaller group held 64.5 per cent of the total land granted. Table 4/3 shows the number of grants and the totals and percentages held by the various groups of grantees.

TABLE 4/3

Civil condition of landholders and amounts of land held in New South Wales, from 22 February 1792 — 25 September 1800

Source: 1802 Muster, B.T. Box 88, Series 1, Bigge Appendix [29]

	Total to receive land grants	Percentage	Total acres held	Percentage
Civil and Military Officers, Shopkeepers, Superintendents (King not included)	44	9.7	20806	49.9
Free Settlers from England (No Order by Govt)	23	5.0	422 (approx)	1.0
Free Settlers from England (Sent by Order of Govt)	37	8.1	4226	10.1
Free Settlers, Discharged Marines	29	6.4	1517	3.6
Free Settlers, Free from Convicts	320	70.64	14671	35.23

As Table 4/3 shows, the minority of landholders who had arrived in the colony as officers held almost half the amount of land granted. Few of these men were the fathers of the native-born and most had received their grants during the administration of their commanding officers, Grose and Paterson. Initially, the size of grants to officers had not been stipulated for they were considered temporary settlers.[30] Grose granted 12,885 acres in two years, Paterson 8340 in nine months, and neither included the residential clause which was attached to the smaller grants to ex-convicts.[31] The usual practice of both Grose and Paterson was to issue a slip of paper which gave written permission to settle to anyone favoured by the military.[32] From the point of view of the smaller settlers a more equitable system was practised by Hunter and continued by King.[33] The scale of grants was not rigid but a time-expired or emancipated convict usually received about thirty acres with an additional twenty if he were married and a further ten acres for every child resident with the family at the time of the grant.[34]

The size of grants to marines and soldiers could vary. Those marines who had chosen to settle at Norfolk Island in 1792 instead of returning to England received sixty acres. Four of these marine settlers—Daniel Stanfield, John Barrisford, John Munday and Lawrence Richards—had wives and children but they received the same grant as the single men. A number of these ex-marine settlers who returned to Sydney during the following two years and enlisted in the New South Wales Corps for a period of five years were eligible to a double portion of land. Some of these received 100 acres or more on their re-enlistment.[35] William Mitchell had arrived in 1788 as a marine and had married convict Jane Fitzgerald. They first settled at Norfolk Island then returned to Sydney and, after his enlistment in the New South Wales Corps, Mitchell received 100 acres at Bankstown. Another former marine, Private John Ryan, received 110 acres opposite Sydney for the same reason. By 1796 the usual allotment for a serving private in the New South Wales Corps was 25 acres, this having been the practice of Grose which was continued by Paterson. In general, military rank below that of sergeant did not appear to influence the size of the grant. Drummer Thomas Bates received twenty-five acres, as did Sergeants Day, Radford, Prosser and West. Most of the privates who were granted land at Mulgrave Place received twenty-five acres each; most of the ex-convicts received thirty acres. The grants to non-commissioned officers were rarely below 100 acres each. Lieutenant Edward Abbott received 100 acres on the Hawkesbury River on 22 July 1795, and Lieutenant Thomas Hobby 100 acres at Mulgrave Place.[36] By the arrival of Governor King, the average size of grants to officers and to other ranks had settled at a much lower scale than that first envisaged by the British government. In 1789 Grenville had written to Phillip:

> To every non-commissioned officer one hundred acres, and to every privateman fifty acres over and above the quantity directed by Our General Instructions to you to be granted to such convicts who shall be emancipated or discharged from their servitude.[37]

The reasons for the reduction in size of the actual grants were partly the result of the belief by the officials in the limited extent of arable land available and partly the difficulties experienced by those who explored beyond the Cumberland Plain.

The extent of land granted to free settlers sometimes depended on the private wealth of the applicant, or on the amount of patronage and influence possessed either in Britain or in the colony.[38] James Badgery was indebted for his extensive grants on the Nepean partly to the influence and recommendation of his patron, Sir Joseph Banks.[39] John and Gregory Blaxland had the support of Lord Castlereagh, who wrote to King that the brothers were 'fit and proper persons to whose authority convicts may be entrusted'.[40] George Suttor had the wealth and social position in England to help him receive large land grants from both King and Macquarie.[41] Less wealthy free settlers who arrived with or without the permission of the British government usually received an initial grant of 100 acres but their allotments were sometimes considerably larger. In 1814, for example, Macquarie wrote to Bathurst concerning three free settlers, Sir John Jamison, Mr Horseley and Mr Williams:

> Having ... Good Reason to think favourably of the two ... Gentlemen, I have promised Sir John a Grant of 1,500 Acres, and Mr Horsley one of 1,000 acres, and in consideration of some respectable Testimonials produced by Mr Williams of his Good Character ... I have promised him also a Grant of 500 acres.[42]

By 1813 only a handful of wealthy migrants, influential officials and ex-officials held large areas of land. The average landholder was the small farmer, the typical allotment being less than 100 acres.[43]

The experiences of the rural children were diverse for there were native-born children living on holdings which ranged from half an acre to upwards of 2,000 acres. Farmer Richard Cheers, an ex-convict who had received a grant of 30 acres at Eastern Farms in 1792, was leasing half an acre 'on the west wide of the Cove in the town of Sydney' in 1797 and, in 1806, was resident there with his wife, ex-convict Esther Weaver, and three native-born children.[44] At the other end of the scale were the three native-born sons of Gregory Blaxland, who had been granted 2,000 acres. An analysis of the landholders listed in the 1806 Muster indicates the proportion of children living on the properties of varying sizes.[45] In this Muster, landholders in the colony, holding land by grant, purchase, lease or rent, are categorized according to the size of the holding. With these divisions, the names of all landholders are given and details recorded as to whether married or not, number of children if any, victualled or not, number of convict servants and number of free men employed, and number victualled. The location is not invariably given nor are the names of the wives and children. Tables 4/4 and 4/5 indicate the number of children in New South Wales in 1806 and the distribution of rural children among the various farm categories.

From Table 4/5 it becomes apparent that the majority of rural children

TABLE 4/4

Children in New South Wales, 1806[46]
Source: Muster of 1806
          (Note: these figures are approximate only)

Total children of landholders	845
Total children of members of the New South Wales Corps	61
Total	906
Total children in New South Wales	1579
Percentage of children of landowners, farmers (rural children)	57.3%
Note: Native-born listed individually in Muster (over the age of twelve)	33
Native-born members of the New South Wales Corps	12

TABLE 4/5

Children of landholders, 1806
Source: Muster of 1806. See also Appendix 4
          List of children resident on farms; list of landholders.

Size of holding	Number of families	Percentage of total children	Number of children	Percentage of rural children	Average families (children)
30 acres and under	90	16.5	262	28.9	2.9
30–50 acres	19	3.4	54	5.9	2.8
50–100 acres	75	15.5	245	27.0	3.2
100–200 acres	56	11.8	187	20.6	3.3
200–300 acres	15	4.4	71	7.8	4.7
over 300 acres	10	1.6	26	2.8	2.3

were not necessarily from the smallest holdings. Although 31 per cent of the children lived on farms of thirty acres or less almost as many lived on farms of between fifty and 100 acres, while more children lived on farms of 200–300 acres than did children on the various-sized holdings. This reinforces the argument that the native-born were not a homogeneous class but came from varying backgrounds. A detailed analysis of the civil condition of the landholder fathers adds to this argument.

There is evidence among all groups of landholders that families remained together until at least 1828 and that those sons who secured land of their own usually did so in the same districts in which their parents lived. The following examples are typical of the patterns of families in the various levels. These examples also show the complexity of the structure of colonial society, there being unconvicted and convicted settlers in all groups.

In the 1806 Muster the smallest properties were grouped as 'thirty acres and under'. Of the 330 proprietors who held 5,660½ acres there were eighty-nine families with children and ninety-three without.[47] One of the smaller settlers was ex-convict William Burgin who rented four acres at the Hawkesbury. Burgin lived with ex-convict Sarah Tandy (he later married ex-convict Mary West) and their three children. By 1828 Burgin had received a conditional pardon, was a publican at Parramatta, where he owned 80 acres and lived with his wife and son, William junior. His eldest son, Henry, was a blacksmith at Parramatta, married to a native-born. Burgin was not exceptional in his success. Other ex-convict fathers of the native-born in this group who increased their holdings included Isaac Cornwell, Samuel Garside, John Martin, Richard Norris and John Small. The sons of these men remained mainly as farmers in the same districts.

A number of men who had been marines, members of the New South Wales Corps or who had arrived free also held land in the under thirty acres category. This land was in the same districts as that of the ex-convict settlers. Typical of these was Richard Allcorn, who had arrived in New South Wales in 1803 with his wife and two sons. In 1806 he was renting sixteen acres at Green Hills (Windsor). Although Richard died in 1812 his family remained in the same area. By 1828 his widow, Sarah, lived with her youngest son, John, on sixty acres at Pitt Town. The two sons who came to the colony with their parents, Edward and Richard, had married native-born girls from the Hawkesbury district and had become farmers, Edward with thirty-four acres at Pitt Town and Richard with sixty acres at Falbrook. Richard's wife, Charlotte, was the daughter of Thomas Gulledge who had arrived as a convict on the *Neptune* in 1790 and had settled at Windsor, where he was a constable in 1828. His two sons, Thomas and Isaac, worked on the property of their brother-in-law.

Several free families in this group increased both their land holdings and their social level. Chief among these were the families of Thomas Eather, George Loder and Richard Tuckwell. The same pattern of family relationships is evident among this group.

The second category in the 1806 Muster was from thirty to fifty acres. It was calculated that a total of 1268 acres was held by this group, with a total of thirty-six proprietors; there were twenty families with children and sixteen without.[48] Both free and unconvicted men owned land in this category and they were situated in neighbouring areas. An ex-convict settler, Anthony Rope, had arrived on the first fleet and in 1788 married convict Elizabeth Pullen. Rope received a land grant in 1792 at the expiration of his sentence; by 1803 he held thirty acres and, in 1806, had purchased forty acres in the Nepean from Andrew Badgery. In 1828 he and his wife were living at Evan on eleven acres with their son, William. A second son, John, was a farmer nearby with eighty-five acres. Another family which remained in Evan was that of George Collis, born in 1771, who had arrived in New South Wales in 1791 and settled with his ex-convict wife, Mary, on forty acres he rented at the Nepean. By 1828 George owned 190 acres at Richmond, where he lived with his wife, two sons and two daughters.

An unconvicted family in this category was that of Francis Oakes, who had arrived as a missionary from Tahiti in 1798. He married the native-born daughter of convicts John Small and his wife, Mary Parker. In 1806

Oakes leased fifty acres at Parramatta. He had one child, Elizabeth. In 1828 he owned 1250 acres at Parramatta and lived with his wife and their nine children, aged between twenty years and five months.

Thomas Bates came to New South Wales as a drummer in the New South Wales Corps. By 1806 he had settled with his free wife on fifty acres at Parramatta. Bates was a boat-builder by trade and in 1828 was living in Sydney, working as a boat-builder, with no land holdings listed. His wife and six children were living with him.

The third category was fifty to 100 acres. The total acreage was 11,178 acres held by 147 proprietors; of these, ninety-one families had children, forty-five had none. Ex-convict families in this group included the Goodwins, Nowlands, Herberts, Larras, Colletts. Edward Goodwin was an ex-convict who had arrived on the first fleet, served his sentence and had married a convict woman who had arrived in 1796. By 1806 they had received sixty acres at Kissing Point and had five children. In 1828, Goodwin and his wife still farmed their original sixty acres and four of their children were still with them. Their eldest son was a wheelwright at Parramatta; another son was an apprentice in Sydney. Two of the Nowland children became farmers: William with 160 acres at Patricks Plains; Henry with 320 acres at Wilberforce, where he also kept a public house. Another son, Michael, became a constable and the youngest, Peter, a labourer at Darling Harbour.

John Herbert, a first fleet convict, had settled on sixty acres at Prospect Hill at the expiration of his sentence in 1792; he had married Deborah Ellam, a convict, in the first week of settlement in 1788. In 1792 he received an additional grant of seventy acres. In 1806 he was described as having 100 acres in the Hawkesbury area; in 1828 he described himself as a dealer, with seventy acres and living in the same area with his son and a second wife. One son was a carter in Parramatta and had sixteen acres; three other sons were farmers: James with 16 acres at Evan, Charles with 16 acres at Evan and Thomas with 100 acres at Minto. Pierce Colletts, an Irish convict who had arrived with his free wife in 1801, had 70 acres in the Nepean district in 1806. In 1828 he was an innkeeper at Bathurst, had 200 acres and was living with his wife and youngest daughter. One son was a blacksmith with twenty acres at Evan and another an overseer at Mount Pleasant.

Free settler families included in this group were the Blackmans, the Bowmans and the Badgerys. James Blackman and his wife had arrived in 1801 and by 1806 had a grant of 100 acres at Richmond Hill where they lived with their seven children, four of whom had been born in England. In 1828 Blackman was a constable at Bathurst (no land holdings were listed in the 1828 Census); he and his wife lived with two of their sons and a daughter. Three other sons were landholders, one at Cooke, one at Evan and one at Bathurst. Other free settlers were the Bowmans, the Badgerys and the Palmers. The sons of John Bowman became extensive landholders: George, who had arrived in the colony as an infant, owned 7,500 acres at Richmond in 1828 and had a large number of stock; James settled at Patricks Plains with 11,000 acres. The four sons of James Badgery, who was originally granted 100 acres at Evan in 1803, all became landholders. In

1828 Henry had 800 acres at Sutton Forest; Andrew had 160 acres at Cabramatta; and William and James lived with their widowed mother on 1900 acres at Bringelly.

In this category, there were settlers such as Owen Cavanagh, an ex-sailor, and Edward Field, an ex-soldier of the New South Wales Corps. Cavanagh, whom Governor King later described as 'Industrious', had arrived on the *Sirius* in 1788 and had married a convict woman, Margaret Dowling. He received his first land grant in 1792, sixty acres at Norfolk Island, where he had remained after the wreck of the *Sirius*. He received a further sixty acres at Norfolk Island in 1797 and, after his return with his family to New South Wales, received 100 acres at Mulgrave Place in 1803. In 1828 Cavanagh was a farmer at Lower Portland Head with his wife and son: he owned sixty acres. Two sons farmed at Lower Portland Head and another at Argyle.

Edward Field, who had arrived with the New South Wales Corps and married a convict woman, was settled at Evan on eighty acres in 1806. Edward and his wife had six children at this time. In 1828, his wife, who had remained on their grant at Evan after his death in 1826, lived with one of their sons on thirty-two acres. Two other sons owned land in the same area.

The fourth category was 100–200 acres: a total of 11,170 acres and eighty-one proprietors, fifty of whom had children and seventeen no children. In this category there were settlers from ex-convicts, convicts, mariners and free settlers. John Dight and his wife Hannah, for example, had come free to Richmond, where he eventually became the coroner and owned 997 acres. In 1828 four of his children were still living with him and another son was a millwright in Sydney. Edward Powell had first come to the colony as a seaman on the *Lady Juliana* in 1790 and had returned as a free settler in 1793. He married Elizabeth Fish, one of this group of first free settlers, and received grants at Liberty Plains and at Concord. In 1828 his son, Edward, was a farmer at Richmond and another son, John, a farmer at Patersons Plains.

There were several ex-convict families in the 100–200 acre category. These included the Cobcrofts, Freebodys, Dunstons/Dunsams, and Smallwoods. The Cobcrofts were typical. John Cobcroft, described by King as an industrious farmer, and his 'wife', who had arrived as a convict on the *Lady Juliana*, owned 120 acres at Mulgrave Place in 1806. At that time they had five children. In 1828 both John and his wife had received conditional pardons and were living at Wilberforce on 485 acres with two of their sons and two daughters. Another son, Richard, who was a widower with six children, farmed 215 acres at Wilberforce, and a fourth son, John, was also a farmer, with 140 acres at Wilberforce.

The fifth category was 200–300 acres. Here a total of 5,266 acres was divided between twenty-three proprietors, fifteen of whom had children. There were three families without children. Most of the settlers in this group were men who had come free, like Rowland Hassall. There were, however, some ex-convict settlers, such as Thomas Dargin and his ex-convict wife, Mary Loveridge. The sons of both these settlers became landholders. Hassall's son, Thomas, settled at Cooke, where he had almost 3,000 acres; his son James was with his widowed mother in 1828, having 400 acres at Parramatta. One of Dargin's sons settled on 200 acres at Bathurst; another went to Patricks Plains, with 100 acres; a third became an inn-keeper at Cornwallis and owned seventy acres; the fourth remained with his mother and younger sisters at Windsor.

The highest category was upwards of 300 acres; 12,599 acres of this land were held by twelve men. Ex-convicts Simeon Lord, Andrew Thompson, James Squire and Isaac Nicholls were included here with free settlers Robert Campbell, Gregory Blaxland, Garnham Blaxcell, and Hannibal Macarthur. The children in this wealthier category were more likely to live in the towns of Sydney or Parramatta rather than on the rural properties of their parents. Tracing the quantities of land held by these parents from their first grant, purchase or lease until 1828 (or until their death, if this occurred before the Census of 1828) underlines the successes of many of those who began with a small portion of purchased or leased land. In addition to this, it also underlines the ability of many ex-convict families to compete with and, in many cases, to exceed the material attainments of those who had arrived unconvicted.

When all children living on all farms in 1806 are listed according to district and parentage and then compared with their occupations and districts of residence in 1828 two important features emerge: first, the extent to which these children remained in the district of their youth; second, the extent to which the sons of farmers became farmers themselves, usually with or near their parents. Both of these features are particularly marked in the cases of children of ex-convict families. These trends, furthermore, are supported by evidence from two other sources: the Memorials to the governors from the native-born and their parents requesting land grants[49] and from an analysis of the parentage of the native-born who were listed by Darling in 1827.[50] This list gives the dates and locations of land grants to native-born from the arrival of Macquarie until 1827. It contains inaccuracies, where emancipists and those who came free were included as native-born, and over 120 omissions. (Edward Allcorn, who had arrived free in 1803; James Bean, arrived free 1814; William Bowman, arrived free in 1801; George Bowman, arrived free in 1798; John and James Davidson, arrived free in 1802: all are listed as native-born.) After these errors and omissions were removed and the parents of the remainder traced, it was found that more than half were ex-convicts, the remainder ex-soldiers, ex-marines, free settlers and ex-officials. The ex-convict families were the largest single group among the 76 per cent of parents who could be traced, and almost all of these held their land either by grant, lease or pur-chase during the childhood of their children.

The children living on farms, in particular the smaller farms, were expected to help their parents from as early an age as possible, so they grew up accustomed to rural life. This is evident in the Memorials from the sons who applied for land of their own. Native-born James Collis of Evan, for example, wrote that he 'had been bred to agriculture under his father'. Archibald Bell, the second son of Lieutenant Archibald Bell, wrote that he had been 'bred in the colony actively and wholly to agriculture pursuits'. The boys worked at tilling, hoeing, harvesting, felling trees and clearing the land. The girls helped with household tasks and with the care and supervision of domestic animals. In August 1806, the *Sydney Gazette* reported that the young farm children drove the pigs into the woods to pasture each day.[51] Earlier that year, a Government and General Order had stated that 'labour of women and children can be usefully employed' in sowing the wheat.[52] Alexander Harris described the rural family: '. . . a miller . . . an old man who had come to the colony a prisoner in early life . . . his lads were working the adjacent block, felling and cutting up an iron bark into fire logs . . .'.[53]

The life-style of the farm children changed little in the first forty or so years. In February 1824 the *Sydney Gazette* described the occupations of young rural children: 'On a farm at the Hawkesbury, the young son minded the pigs, while his still younger sister kept the cockatoos away from the maize at the same time as minding her baby sister'.[54] James Tucker, in the convict novel *Ralph Rashleigh*, described the life of Big Mick's daughters, who 'worked from infancy at tasks as great as their strength would permit'.[55]

Most of the landholding parents in 1806 had an assigned convict servant who, at least among the smaller landholders, lived with the family. This led to daily contact between native-born and convict servants. In the case of the females, it resulted in a number of marriages. The daughter of ex-convict farmer George Best married a government servant assigned to her father. Best gave evidence to Bigge:

> One [daughter] is married to a servant of mine, a Prisoner. They live on my son's Farm the young man was attached to my Daughter & she to him, & I was induced to consent to their marriage. He has behaved very well, & is now living on a small piece of land belonging to my eldest son. I built him a house & found him in provisions at first & now he finds himself. I have let him have one of my Government men. . . .[56]

Assigned servants were not limited to the owners of larger properties. Thomas Leeson, for example, with twenty-five acres at the Hawkesbury, had two convict servants; Thomas Jones, with thirty acres at Eastern Farms, had one; Daniel McKay, with thirty acres at Parramatta, had five assigned servants. On the basis of the numbers of property owners who had convict servants in 1806 it may be assumed that the majority of rural children during this period had daily familiarity with convict labour.

From the analysis of the Muster, it would appear that the parents of those 260 children living on farms of thirty acres or less grew wheat as their main crop on a third of their land and used another quarter of the land to graze hogs, goats and sheep. The parents of the forty-eight living on farms between thirty and fifty acres used almost half of their land for pasture of sheep, goats and hogs although, in total, this group owned far less livestock than those holding smaller farms. The main crops were wheat, 18.8 per cent, and maize, 12.8 per cent. There were 223 children living on farms between fifty and 100 acres. Two thirds of this land was used for pasture and owners in this group possessed the most livestock. The main crops were wheat, 8.8 per cent and maize, 8.8 per cent. On the farms of 100–200 acres, there were one hundred children. Two thirds of this land was used for grazing sheep, goats and pigs; 11.8 per cent for the growing of wheat. Seventy children lived on properties of 200–300 acres. Here, too, two thirds of the land was used for grazing, the main animals being sheep, hogs and a few goats. On properties larger than 300 acres there were only nineteen children and here 87.1 per cent of the land was used for grazing, mainly sheep, followed by hogs then goats. Only 2 per cent of the land was used for wheat growing.

The majority of these rural children, therefore, were more familiar with the care and maintenance of animals than with the growing of crops. Very small portions of the land were used for the growing of vegetables (peas, beans and potatoes); on an average, less than 1 per cent of the total land held. This was also the case with gardens and orchards. The amount of land allowed to lie fallow averaged about 10 per cent although for fifty 100 acre owners it was as low as 0.9 per cent. These youthful experiences were not similar to those on the farms of the adult native-born, where the animals were horned cattle and the main use of the land agricultural.

Although the majority of the fathers of the native-born had been granted land, and therefore had, presumably, little choice in its location, there was a proportion who, according to the 1806 Muster, had purchased their land. A few of these may have had a previous grant which they had sold. Where there is evidence of a former grant, this was usually added to by purchase. It would appear that the majority of those who purchased their land had earned sufficient to purchase or barter for their land. This would suggest that they were not among those settlers so despised by Phillip,[57] Hunter and King[58] as idle, worthless and dissolute but were, on the contrary,

TABLE 4/6

Numbers of properties purchased by parents of native-born, 1806
Source: Muster of 1806

	Number of proprietors	Number of purchases	Evidence of previous grants
Under 30 acres	340	31	9*
30–50 acres	36	7	9
50–100 acres	144	12	9
100–200 acres	82	14	11
200–300 acres	23	10	8
over 300 acres	12	4	1

Note: Not all grants or purchases are specified; where land is held by grant and purchase this is included as purchase.

**Allotments in the towns of Sydney and Parramatta not included.*

industrious and successful workers. This becomes more significant when it is understood that the majority of those who purchased their land were the settlers holding less than thirty acres in 1806. Table 4/6 shows the number of families who had purchased their land.

It is not possible to suggest why these purchasers did not hold land grants. During the childhood and adolescence of the native-born, that is, until the departure of Macquarie, there were few conditions attached to the granting of land. It was necessary to produce testimonials as to good character and there was the stipulation that the grantee must reside on and cultivate the land granted. This latter regulation was copied from those attached to the land grants which had been made in Canada.[59] Under Grose and Paterson this regulation had not been strictly adhered to, particularly in the case of the military settlers.[60] There is also evidence that, at least during the administration of Hunter, little scrutiny had been made of the characters of intending settlers. In 1797 Hunter commented:

> ... the worthless and abandoned characters who have been permitted in such numbers to become settlers in different parts of this country, do not make the most of it, and give me such trouble; those sent as free settlers from England are many of them impositions upon the Government. They have no turn for farming in this Country, where much labour and diligence is required. They amuse themselves at speculations of some other kind not of any benefit to this Colony and are a Dead Weight on the Shoulders of Government. My task has been most arduous and difficult I ever engaged upon.[61]

That most of the land-holding parents of the native-born were not in this category, not a 'Dead Weight upon the Shoulders of Government', is evident from the analysis of the parents listed in the 1806 Muster. There had been difficulty in enforcing the stipulation ordered by Dundas in 1793 that all grantees must reside upon and cultivate their grants for a period of five years and were strictly forbidden to sell their grants within that period.[62] This regulation was neither adhered to nor enforced by the governors; few grants were actually cancelled for this reason before the administration of Governor Darling.[63] The sale of granted land was almost a common practice. The first examples were among the free settlers at Liberty Plains: Joseph Webb sold his allotment to Captain Rowley, while Simeon Lord bought the grants allotted to Edward Powell and Webb's brother, Thomas. During the administrations of Hunter and King land was sold by smaller settlers when they became impoverished by drought, flood, debt or drink.[64] The sale of these small allotments made it possible for the wealthier settlers to consolidate their holdings, as did Simeon Lord in the case of Powell and Webb. The importance of the ability to sell granted land is that it reflects the early governors' overall lax attitude to conditions surrounding the alienation of land from the Crown, and the lack of any apparent means to enforce those few conditions which were attached to land grants. J.D. Lang believed that this was very much the case during the administration of Governor Macquarie. It was Lang's opinion that

Macquarie was 'indiscriminate' in his grants and many he made were 'never taken possession of by the grantee but were sold immediately and generally for rum'.[65] In defence of Macquarie, he did insist on applications for land being supported by character testimonials from magistrates or chaplains who had personal knowledge of the applicants. If land were sold within five years of the grant it was probably possible because of the lack of efficient administrative machinery.

The general smallness of the grants when compared with the size of grants in other British colonies, such as the Canadas, the Bahamas and Dominica, has been linked with the belief of the early governors in the necessity to avoid too rapid a use of the available arable land. It could also be linked with the civil condition and class origins of the majority to whom it was granted and with the proposed development of the colony as envisaged by the British government. Until the time of Macquarie, and throughout his administration, most grantees were emancipated and time-expired convicts or ex-soldiers. It was the hope of the British government that the offer of small farms would encourage these men to settle and remain permanently in the colony rather than return to Britain. Grenville had written to Phillip of the desire of the Crown to 'encourage ex-convicts to remain in the Colony by the offer of indulgences'.[66] In Phillip's Second Commission it had been specifically stated that, '... whereas many of our subjects employed on military service at the said settlement, and others who may resort thither ... be desirous of proceeding to the cultivation and improvement of the land ...'.[67] At no time was there any intention that ex-convicts, private marines or soldiers be given sufficient resources to improve their material standing to such an extent that they became wealthy landholders. Thus the size of the initial grant was considered sufficient, on the one hand, to be an inducement to a better material standard of living and to remaining in the colony rather than attempting to return to Britain and, on the other hand, to be just large enough to enable the ex-convict to be self-supporting.[68]

The smallness of the grants was not only tied to this belief that the amount of land was limited. This is apparent by comparing the size of those grants within the Cumberland Plain made to free settlers and officials and ex-officials with those made to the ex-convicts (average thirty acres), ex-marines and ex-soldiers (average twenty-five acres). Within the area of Sydney itself, Surgeon Harris received 1500 acres at Concord, almost half the total amount of land granted in this area up to 1813. Thomas Moore, master boat-builder, had holdings of 470 acres and 700 acres at Bulnaming, almost half the total area granted in this district before 1813. The granting of comparatively large areas to selected individuals, despite a known scarcity of land, is shown more clearly by a consideration of the size of grants and the civil condition of grantees in one area, Petersham. By 1813 ex-convicts Henry Kable and Thomas Biggers, both of whom were fathers of large native-born families, had each received thirty acres; privates in the New South Wales Corps, such as John Brown, Thomas Bolton and William Adams, had received twenty-five acres; Lieutenant Nicholas Bayly had received 450 acres; Surgeon Belmain [sic] 550 acres; Chaplain Richard

Johnson, two grants, of 260 and 100 acres. This pattern of grants scaled to civil condition, occupation and social rank, is evident throughout the various districts settled between 1788 and 1813.[69]

During the first twenty-five years, approximately 180,000 acres were alienated in New South Wales by approximately 1355 grants to individuals.[70] Other land was obtained by purchase or by lease. B.H. Fletcher has estimated that 45,299 acres were alienated before 1800 and, between 1788 and 1810, a total of 198,462 acres. Fletcher has estimated that, in 1792, 80.1 per cent of the landowners were former convicts; in 1801, 69.2 per cent; in 1806, 72.1 per cent; and, in 1810, approximately 75 per cent.[71] That the majority of the parents of the rural native-born were former convicts appears indisputable. It is, however, equally important to stress that these ex-convict parents were to be found in all categories of landholders, from those with less than thirty acres to those with upwards of 300 acres. Although the native-born children who were raised on farms and grazing properties shared many similar experiences, there was no common experience, for the type of life they led was linked with the material standing of their parents, not solely with their civil condition. Had these native-born children been aware of any 'policy' guiding the granting of land to their parents, it would have appeared a very flexible one, with little emphasis on ability or experience to cultivate the lands granted. To the native-born, the two most important features were the need to produce testimonials to honesty, industry and good character and that, when land was granted, it was freely given and frequently accompanied by indulgences such as seed, stock and assigned labour. The emphasis on the need to substantiate an honest and industrious character in order to receive indulgences from the governor was an accepted part of the background of the colony's children. It was based on the evidence of the colonial experiences of their parents. When the native-born were themselves of an age to apply for their own land grants, they not only stressed that they were, one and all, 'lads of industrious habits' but that they had been raised in the 'respectable' households of parents who were 'sober and deserving'.

The emphasis on the character of the parents was closely linked with their colonial experiences. The son of first fleet convicts Anthony Rope and Elizabeth Pullen applied to the governor for a land grant and stressed that his father '... had arrived in the First Fleet ... since arrival his character has been honest and upright and his demeanour such as to merit the approbation of his superiors'. The native-born accepted their parents on their colonial achievements, respecting the standards which had gained for them varying levels of independence and material prosperity. For the 'rural' native-born these achievements were inextricably linked with the cultivation of the land. For their counterparts who lived with artisan and tradesmen fathers or with unskilled labourers, material success at all levels was equally linked with the 'respectable' endeavours of their parents. In their case, however, the ownership of land played a lesser part both in shaping their family life as children and influencing their ambitions as young Australians.

CHAPTER FIVE

THE HOPE AND STAFF
OF THE COLONY

'On useful labour alone depends their future welfare.'

The *Sydney Gazette*, 1 November 1804.

CHAPTER FIVE

THE HOPE AND STAFF OF THE COLONY

During the childhood and adolescence of the first generation the nature of apprenticeships in Eastern Australia was linked directly with the lack of exploitation of child labour. This was the result of the distinctive population structure, the ready availability of free convict labour and the absence of the traditional English Parish system of apprenticeships for the children of the poor. The experiences of the colonial children of New South Wales differed entirely from those of their contemporaries in England and Ireland. It was their unique upbringing in the penal colony, combined with the influence and example of their parents, which shaped their attitudes towards the nature of and the rewards for labour. As these youths were to become the first free native labour force, their attitudes formed an integral part of the origins of the Australian working tradition.

By the mid-1820s commentators such as William Charles Wentworth and E.S. Hall were asserting that it was the aspiration of the young men of the colony to obtain land grants and to 'cultivate . . . the soil . . . of their native clime'.[1] A leading article in the *Australian* in 1826 argued forcibly that 'Every young man in the Colony ought to be able to look forward with certainty to the prospect of having his own farm'. In January 1829 Hall, the editor of the *Monitor*, expressed this belief in a letter to Sir George Murray:

A few indeed native-born were originally apprenticed as mechanics, but generally, they prefer to indulge their independence in the wilds of their native forests, where they can brood over their discontents without restraint or contradiction.[2]

These words and the sentiment they contained were an almost exact echo of Wentworth's description of the landless native-born in the speech of welcome to Governor Darling in 1826, in which he described these same young men as 'brooding in the distant hills'.[3]

The reason behind this presumed discontent of the native-born had been summed up as early as 1819 by the ex-convict Edward Eagar in his evidence to Commissioner Bigge:

. . . the Native Colonists have been overlooked, and the respectable Children of respectable Settlers are either refused Land, or when Granted it had been in such small portions and with such restrictions, as to render it not worth their acceptance.

Eagar had implied that this discrimination was the result of a 'degree of Neglect' by the colonial authorities, for he was of the opinion that 'the standing Instructions to the Governors showed that His Majesty particularly intended that they should be assigned both Land and Cattle'.

Eagar described the native-born as 'the Hope and Staff of the Colony',[4] an opinion repeated by the *Australian* seven years later:

> ... they settle in general with much more fixed and steady industry to their pursuits than the wandering emigrant ... The people who are Born in the Colony are the people who will beautify and improve the Colony. It is to them we look for the neat farm-house, the fenced paddock, the yeoman's dwelling, and the squire's mansion with parks and plantations, and all the beauties which delight the travellers in England.[5]

This article emphasized the view that the colony should develop as the idealized Arcady nostalgically believed to have existed in England before the Industrial Revolution. This opinion was based on the agricultural nature of colonial society and the future potential of wool and the pastoral industry. It assumed that the native-born, having grown to 'years of maturity' in a rural environment, would automatically wish for no other life than that of farmer, yeoman or, possibly, squire.

Neither Eagar nor Wentworth made any allowance for the numbers of native-born who had been raised in the towns of Sydney and Parramatta, whose fathers were tradesmen and who chose to follow a trade by becoming an apprentice at an age far younger than that at which it would have been possible to apply for a grant of land. These apprentices, therefore, had not turned to trade as an occupation because of rejected applications for land grants. On the contrary, it would appear that their natural inclination, based on their parentage, background and upbringing in the colony, inclined them towards being the builders of the cottages and mansions rather than the yeomen and farmers who inhabited them. According to the Census of 1828 almost 30 per cent of the native-born males who stated an occupation were tradesmen and apprentices. This was only slightly less than the percentage who described themselves as farmers and landholders.[6] Furthermore, it appeared that the native-born youth were more likely to become apprenticed to a trade than were the free immigrants in the same age group. A comparison of all the free and freed males in the colony aged between fifteen and forty years showed that the highest proportion of apprentices was among the native-born: 22 per cent of the native-born under twenty years of age in 1828 who stated an occupation were apprentices. Among the came-free, 11 per cent of the same age group as the native-born were apprentices.[7] There are no accurate figures for the convict boys who were traditionally apprenticed in the Dock Yards or in the Lumber Yards nor for those who were apprenticed from the Male Orphan Schools. 'Deserving' boys were 'put to a trade', which was usually limited to the basic trades of carpenter, shoemaker, tailor and, occasionally, blacksmith.[8] The small numbers at the Orphan Schools made it unlikely that the percentage of orphan apprentices significantly affected the high proportion of native-born among the colony's apprentices.[9] An investigation into the parentage of the apprentices and tradesmen and the occupations followed by the fathers suggests two major findings: first, that a native-born tradesman was frequently the son of a colonial tradesman; and, second, that many were the sons of privates from the New South Wales Corps who had settled in the colony and resumed the trade they had practised before their enlistment.[10] John Dell had been a stonemason before he enlisted in the New South Wales Corps. His son, also John Dell, was born at Sydney in 1802, his mother being Elizabeth Robinson, a convict woman. In 1828 John Dell junior was employed as a stonecutter in Sydney, working with William Lane, the fourteen-year-old native-born son of his employer, George Lane, an ex-convict.[11] Other native-born sons of soldiers and ex-soldiers who became tradesmen included George Anderson, born 1812, the son of Private Robert Anderson and his free wife, Mary Franklin; John Evans, born 1813, a weaver at Botany with Simeon Lord, was the son of ex-private William Evans and his free wife, Mary Anne; James Brackenbrig, born 1797, was a carpenter at Parramatta. He was the son of Private James Brackenbreg and his wife; James Connor, born 1807, a shoe-maker in Sydney, was the son of Private James Harris and his ex-convict wife, Elizabeth Phillips; George Donnelly, born 1806, was the son of Private Simon Garrett, who died that same year. It is probable that George learned his trade at the Male Orphan School.[12]

Among the ex-convict 'trade' families, sons frequently followed the same or an allied trade as that of their fathers. James Evans, born in the colony in 1801, was a carpenter who worked with his father in 1828 in Princes Street, Sydney. His father was a carpenter by trade and had arrived as a convict in 1792. John and Joseph Flood, born in 1797 and 1799 respectively, were carpenters in Sydney; carpentry was the trade of their deceased father, John, after whom John junior named his own son. William Byrnes, born in Parramatta in 1809, became an apprentice saddler; he continued to live with his ex-convict father David, a tailor, and his freed-by-servitude mother. Thomas Cosier junior, born 1810, worked as a blacksmith with his ex-convict father at Parramatta, where his elder brother, William, was also a blacksmith. It is most likely that both sons learned their trade from their father. George Howe, born in 1807, followed the trade of his ex-convict father who had been a printer. There is no evidence to indicate whether Howe junior was formally apprenticed or whether he simply worked in the family offices of the *Sydney Gazette*.

The native born did not necessarily follow the same trade as their fathers. It is perhaps more remarkable that some of the native-born sons of the unskilled, such as carters and labourers, became apprenticed than it is that the sons of mechanics followed their fathers in their choice of occupation. Thomas Cook was an ex-convict labourer at Newcastle; he lived with his apprentice son, Thomas Cook junior, born in 1810. Joseph Butler was an ex-convict labourer in Sydney, living with his wife and son, Walter, who was a carpenter. It was, however, more frequent for the son to follow a similar or allied trade to that of the father. Henry Hough, born in New South Wales in 1804, became a millwright; he was the son of two ex-convicts, his father's trade being that of baker.

The colonial boys who sought apprenticeships during the first thirty or so years of white settlement were limited in their choice of trades. In the *Sydney Gazette* of 1805, for example, there were only two advertisements for

apprentices, one for a ship's apprentice,[13] the other for journeyman smiths:
'. . . one or two apprentices from 12 to 14 or 15 years of age, who will be
taught their business thoroughly'.[14] Despite this lack of advertisements for
apprentices the *Sydney Gazette* commented in August of that same year that
the colonial youth appeared reluctant to apply for apprenticeships:

> Frequent invitations have been given to parents by reputable tradesmen
> to give their children the advantage of a profession; but from what motive
> the backwardness proceeds, nobody knows, and yet a single male
> apprentice is scarcely to be found in Sydney. It is remarkable at the same
> time that every avenue at every period of the day abounds with well-
> grown boys indolently squandering the season in which they might be
> initiated into useful branches of profession, and become profitable instead
> of remaining burthersome to parents.[15]

This opinion was at a variance with the assumption that the children of
the colony were abandoned and neglected by their parents: it indicated that
the children, at least of Sydney Town, were supported in idleness by
parents who might have been considered indulgent in that they did not
insist that their children follow the normal pattern for children of the lower
orders of Britain and begin work at as early an age as possible. The
opinions of the *Sydney Gazette* clearly echoed this traditional attitude, that
laziness among the children of the poor led to the adoption of criminal and
vicious habits. This attitude was expressed long before the settlement of
Botany Bay and the emergence of the problems associated with children
growing up in a penal environment in what was described as a colony of
thieves. In mid-eighteenth century London, Sir Josiah Child warned that:

> . . . the children of the poor, bred up in beggary and laziness do by that
> means become not only of unhealthy bodies and more than ordinarily
> subject to many loathsome diseases . . . but . . . are, by their vile habits,
> rendered for evermore indisposed to labour, and serve only to stock the
> kingdom with beggars and thieves.[16]

When these children were in a penal colony, and their parents believed to
be the convicted scum of British society, how much more dangerous for the
future of Botany Bay if its children were permitted to 'indolently squander'
their childhood without the discipline and training of an occupation.
Despite the assertion of the *Sydney Gazette*, apprenticeships were advertised
infrequently. The question then arises whether, within the peculiar labour
situation which existed in New South Wales, there were other conditions
which led to the lack of opportunities for the colonial youth to train as
future tradesmen and mechanics.

In 1804 the *Sydney Gazette* had written more optimistically of advantages
for the colonial youth as they approached maturity: 'The inclination to
train the juvenile orders of society in laudable pursuits beggars encomium,
and claims the wreath of universal acquiescence'. Although it was a
government publication the introduction of a colonial newspaper made it

possible for private masters to seek apprentices by advertising. Few, however, did so. The *Sydney Gazette* praised in particular the firm of Kable and Underwood for:

> ... receiving under their protection a number of Boys of different ages ... which it was hoped would promote industry, and secure youth from fatar [*sic*] indolence ... On useful labour depends alone their future welfare; and who would deny the patriotic aid necessary to promote so genuine and excellent an object?[17]

Henry Kable and James Underwood, both of whom had arrived as convicts in the first fleet, continued to advertise for apprentices. There is no evidence to support the assumption that these two men were the first colonial traders to become interested in offering apprenticeships to the colonial youth because of their own backgrounds and experiences; that is, from patriotic reasons. Considering that there was no lack of cheap convict labour in the colony, however, it may have been partly the result of having been sentenced to death as 'Youths of no Trade'.[18] If this were so, their motivation may have been the patriotic aid of providing for the future welfare of some of the colony's children. This would suggest a possible sense of gratitude, or even obligation, to their adopted homeland and an interest in its future growth and development by encouraging the Rising Generation to train for a 'profession'.

Until the first years of Macquarie's administration, apprenticeships in the colony were restricted almost entirely to the basic trades of carpenter, blacksmith, boat and ship-builder, tailor, shoemaker and seaman on colonial vessels. There were few exceptions. Potter Samuel Skinner advertised for apprentices early in 1804 but, as his business failed the next month it is unlikely that any of the first generation received training in the specialized craft of pottery making.[19] It is probable that Skinner advertised for apprentices in preference to employing convict labour because he had some interest in the future development of New South Wales. He was, for example, a consistent supporter of the Loyal Association, having volunteered as a member of the Sydney Company, formed to protect the colony after the abortive Irish rising in 1804.[20]

The few apprenticeships were limited to offers from blacksmiths such as Thomas Storer, ship owners such as Garnham Blaxcell, merchants such as Robert Campbell, traders such as Isaac Nichols, Henry Kable and James Underwood.[21] All of these men were prominent in activities whose prosperity rested on the future growth and development of the colony. There is no sound evidence to support the assumption that it was the interest in their adopted homeland which prompted these men to offer apprenticeships to the colonial youth. As these were the first men to advertise for apprentices, however, and as assigned labour, some of it skilled, was readily available and more economical than training an inexperienced boy, it would appear that at least part of the motivation was concern for the welfare of the youth of the colony. It may have been that the initial interest of the successful ex-convicts, such as Kable, Lord and Underwood, led to the free merchants and traders encouraging the Rising Generation. The background to the successful ex-convicts was a childhood which experienced the conditions familiar to the lower orders of England, in particular the lack of opportunities for material security. The background of the free merchants was one which had accepted the traditional assumptions regarding the need to train the children of the poor in the habits of productive labour to insure against inherent depravity, vice and criminality. In New South Wales the successful ex-convict could rival the wealth and achievements of the free immigrants. The influence of these differing backgrounds, experiences and assumptions resulted in the encouragement of the colonial children to take advantage of the opportunities offered by applying themselves to the demands of an apprenticeship. This could secure their future security and, at the same time, help to ensure the future stability of the colony.

By 1813 there was some variety in the nature of apprenticeships offered as small 'manufactories' commenced. Opportunities, however, were still strictly limited. In April of that year, the first advertisement appeared in the *Sydney Gazette* which could be likened to the type of apprenticeships which were being offered by masters in contemporary England:

WANTED 20 Apprentices for the following trades: viz
Twelve for Weavers and Spinners
Six for Pottery
Two for Dyers
When the number is indentured, a Sunday School will be opened from 7 in the morning until 9 and from 2 in the afternoon to 3 for the Instruction of the said Apprentices in Reading and Writing.[22]

This advertisement was unsigned but it was probably placed by the ex-convict Simeon Lord, who at this time was commencing various business ventures loosely described as 'manufactories'. That same year Reuben Uther, a free man who had been indentured to Simeon Lord, advertised for two apprentices to the 'Hat Manufactory'. Another advertisement in that year would suggest that the offer to instruct apprentices in reading and writing was not obligatory but more of an inducement to prospective apprentices or their parents:

EVENING SCHOOL
Mr W.P. Crook begs leave to inform Parents and Masters, that for the benefit of such Boys and Apprentices who have not the opportunity of receiving Instruction in the Daytime, an Evening School is now open at his schoolroom No.12 Bligh Street. Terms moderate.[23]

The small demand for apprentices in the colony was in direct contrast to the numbers of children from the lower orders who were apprenticed in contemporary Britain, where this was the normal and inexpensive way to provide for the destitute children of the poor. Between 1802 and 1811, for example, out of a total of 5815 parish children 'in or near London', 3789 were 'bound to trades, sea-service, or household employments'. A further

2026 were 'bound to persons in the country'.[24] The settlers of New South Wales, both convict and free, were accustomed to this system of apprenticeship where child labour was exploited in exchange for board, lodging, clothing and token training. The comparatively small demand for apprentices of this sort in New South Wales may be explained by the ready availability of free convict labour in the form of assigned servants. The exploitation of child labour was, therefore, both unnecessary and uneconomical. This was the direct result of conditions in the colony differing from those in England; poverty as experienced by the lower orders of Britain did not exist and opportunities for work removed any necessity to steal to live. Food and clothing were available to the children and their parents from the government store. The colonial youth, whether indentured or working with their parents, became accustomed to an entirely different work situation from that of their contemporaries in Britain. This affected the definitions and connotations of an apprenticeship.[25]

Traditionally, there were three levels of apprenticeships in England. The highest was where the apprentice shared the same social background as his master, paid a high premium and lived as part of the family. On occasions he would marry the daughter of the house.[26] The second level was where a lad of lower social level was indentured by his parents or guardians with the intention of gaining sufficient skills to obtain qualifications as a trades-man or craftsman.[27] The lowest level of apprenticeship, the parish system, was almost synonomous with cheap labour, exploitation and drudgery.[28] M. Buer described this third form of apprenticeship as 'little better than a form of slavery ... children of the poor were bound to years of illtreatment and drudgery'. Dorothy George cites the example of William Hutton who was apprenticed at the age of seven years in a Derby silk mill. George also describes the impressions of an American loyalist who visited a factory in Halifax and saw fifteen small children making wire cards for wool winding. His comment was '... this employment not only keeps their little minds from vice but ... takes a heavy burden from their poor parents'. Daniel Defoe summed up this general attitude of the British middle and upper classes towards the children of the poor. Defoe and his counterparts believed that these children should work almost as soon as they could walk. Defoe commented favourably on the widespread employment of young children throughout the whole Island of Great Britain: 'hardly anything above four-year-old but its hands are sufficient to itself'. This attitude was accepted without question by the respectable classes of British society, in particular by those considered to have been the most humane, the clergy. This is evidenced by the comment of an English clergyman who was renowned for his sympathetic attitude towards the poor of his parish: '... no poor relief should be given on behalf of any child over six who could not knit, or of any child over nine who could not spin linen or wool'.[29]

Thompson saw this attitude as morally based. He described the benefits in 'the eyes of the rich' which resulted from keeping the factory children, for example, 'busy ... industrious ... useful', as keeping them 'out of their parks and orchards'. Thompson argued that the whole period between 1780 and 1830 in Britain was one of 'drastic increase in the intensity of exploitation of child labour'.[30] It is therefore understandable that these traditional attitudes towards the occupations of children were brought with the colonists to New South Wales. It is more difficult to explain the differing attitudes of the parents of Botany Bay as compared with those of the parents in England. It is possible that the 'neglect' of their children, which was attributed to the convict and ex-convict parents by respectable contemporaries, was neglect in a moral rather than in a physical sense; that is, 'neglect' in ensuring that their children were gainfully employed from as early an age as possible, thus 'keeping their little minds from vice'.[31] The *Sydney Gazette* in 1804 for example, commented on the evils which would befall children who had leisure to seek amusement. Colonial parents, it was argued, were too indulgent, '... suffering their children to seek amusement at the wharfs, to the manifest danger of their lives and the total destruction of their morals'. This comment followed the report of the death of a child who had been 'playing' on the Hospital Wharf; the inference was that the misadventure had been caused by undisciplined idleness but a far greater evil would have resulted to the moral character of these children.

A similar attitude was expressed more fully in May of that same year, 1804, in a report of 'numbers of youngsters' fighting in gangs, 'to the terror and annoyance of every accidental passenger', watched by their parents. These parents were admonished by the *Sydney Gazette*, for 'it was their duty ... to check this spirit of unnecessary hostility ... and ... its dangerous consequences'. Rather than spend their time 'indolently squabbling', it would be better, advised the *Sydney Gazette*, that these children become apprenticed and thus 'profitable ... to their parents'.[32]

Considering the traditional attitude towards the activities of the children of the lower orders, it would have been difficult for the respectable colonists, that is, those who had arrived unconvicted, to have accepted that the colonial youth could spend their time in idleness and play without disastrous effects on their characters. When observance of this unprecedented style of upbringing was combined with the assumptions as to the social and moral characteristics of the parents, the concern expressed for the future of this Rising Generation was understandable. Furthermore, that the parents permitted, or appeared to permit, this 'undisciplined idleness' reinforced the acceptance of the belief in the lack of parental concern for the welfare of their children. The extra dimension of lack of interest in shaping the moral characters of their offspring was added to the expected physical neglect of the children of the convicts. There existed, therefore, a discrepancy between the expectations of the respectable observers and the actual life-styles of the colonial children. There was no appreciation that this may have been caused by the nature of the work-force in the colony. The neglect of the children was seen simply as the direct result of a deplorable lack of parental care and guidance. What other behaviour could be expected from parents who were convicted felons?

In England parental neglect was also seen as a major cause of juvenile delinquency. In 1828, for example, the Select Committee on Police in the Metropolis reported that children and young people were in the habit of gathering in parks, particularly on Sundays, and indulging in the 'vice of gaming'. The Committee saw this 'neglect of children ... as a primary source of mischief'. The mischief was attributed to the parents:

And Your Committee have heard with deep regret, that instances are not unfrequent, of parents so wanting in duty and affection, as to view with indifference the degradation and expulsion of their children for misconduct from those charitable institutions, which some parents ought to have considered as affording the best hope of rescuing their children from the dangers of temptation.[33]

In the colony this neglect was linked with the 'abandoned parents' profligate infamy'[34] and this, in turn, led to the belief that the Rising Generation could only be saved from infamy by work and education.[35]

Although the basic attitudes towards employment and pursuits of children were similar among the respectable classes in England and in New South Wales the actual experiences of the children had little in common, especially with regard to apprenticeships. One of the most extreme differences was in relation to the apprenticeship of children being accepted by parents as a legitimate source of income, as in the case of child chimney-sweeps in England.[36] Dorothy George cites David Porter, a master chimney-sweep who was an active campaigner for government protection of apprentices. Porter described the system:

It was the common practice for parents to carry their children to the master chimney-sweepers and dispose of them to the best bidder as they cannot put them to any other master at so early an age.[37]

In 1798 a London witness had told the Society for the Bettering the Condition of the Poor that 'half the climbing boys are now purchased from needy and illiterate parents'[38] The need to sell children as apprentices in this manner did not exist in the colony because the peculiar nature of the government-administered penal colony did not reproduce the conditions familiar to Britain's 'needy and illiterate' men and women.

A major difference between colonial society and British society, which affected directly the childhood experiences of the colonial children, was the absence in New South Wales of the traditional system of parish apprenticeships. From the time of the introduction of the Elizabethan Poor Laws, those children whose parents could not support them were placed by their parish as farm or household apprentices with the ratepayers of the district or, preferably, in another parish so that the burden of their support would be removed. As children became an increasingly important part of industrial labour in English mills and factories large numbers of these boys and girls were apprenticed in the industrial areas.[39] This practice continued to operate in parts of England until the 1840s. It was not until 1788 that the initial term of indenture for these children was reduced so that they could leave their masters or mistresses at the age of twenty-one instead of remaining apprentices until they had reached the age of twenty-four years. It was accepted by contemporaries that the terms of an apprenticeship bound a child as a slave. Blackstone, when discussing the rights to the labour of a Negro slave brought to England by his master, compared the condition of the slave with the experiences, duties and obligations of an apprentice to his master: '... the slave will remain in the same state of subjection for life, which every apprentice submits to for the space of seven years and sometimes for a longer period'.[40] The natural analogy in New South Wales would have been between the apprenticed child and the assigned labour of the convicts. There is, however, no evidence to suggest that such a comparison was made by contemporaries.[41] The main reason for this difference was that the normal apprenticeship in New South Wales was not aimed at securing board and lodging for a destitute child, but to teach a craft or skill. Cheap labour being available removed the need to exploit the labour of children.

In New South Wales there was an almost complete lack of advertisements for children to be apprenticed in the manner customary for the children of the poor in England. There were no institutions similar to the British Parish Workhouses and those men and women who wished for inexpensive labour, in particular for farm or domestic purposes, could apply to the government for assigned convict labour. Macquarie had been instructed that:

> ... whereas such persons as are or may become settlers ... may be desirous of availing themselves of the labour of part of the convicts who are or may be sent there ... it is our will and pleasure in case there should be a prospect of their employing any of the said convicts to advantage, that you assign to each grantee the service of any number of them that you may judge sufficient to answer their purpose.[42]

The first advertisement to appear in the *Sydney Gazette* which could be placed in the workhouse or parish category was in 1806:

> Any Person having an Orphan Boy under his protection whom they can spare conveniently, may be assured of his being taken care of and of his receiving every proper encouragement in a family at the Green Hills; for whom application may be made at the Gazette Office.

There was another advertisement of this nature in 1809: 'WANTED A Youth from 12 to 15 years of age as Apprentice at a Farm House. An Orphan would be preferred. Apply to Mr Driver'. John Driver was an extensive landholder at Parramatta; he also had a family of young native-born children. It is unlikely that Driver would have been seeking inexpensive labour, so it may have been humane motives which prompted him to advertise for an orphan farm apprentice. This may also have been the case with Gregory Blaxland, a wealthy free settler who advertised in 1806 for apprentices but did not specify the trade. 'Wanted. Several apprentices, whose treatment will be liberal. Boys from 10 to 14 years will be accepted'.[43] Blaxland, too, had a young family, so there is the possibility that neither Driver nor Blaxland wished to employ convict labour exclusively, preferring an unconvicted native youth.

The advertisements by Driver and Blaxland were representative of the scant half dozen which appeared in the *Sydney Gazette* between 1802 and 1811, and they appeared to be similar in intent to those applications in Britain which sought child apprentices for labour purposes. It was not until 1811, when the Male Orphan School was opened, that an institutional source of non-convict orphan labour existed in the colony. The purpose of this refuge for destitute colonial boys, however, differed from that of the Parish Workhouses in Britain, which was primarily to relieve the authorities of the expense in the care of these children by transferring responsibility for their welfare and upkeep to private masters. The purpose of the Orphan School, as described by Bigge, was '. . . to relieve, protect and provide with lodging, clothing, food and a suitable degree of plain education, and instruction in some mechanical art, poor, unprotected male orphan children'.[44] The care of the children placed in the Orphan School was carefully organized and was in complete contrast to the conditions experienced by their British counterparts. Thomas Bowden, then Master of the Male Orphan School, described to Commissioner Bigge the hours of schooling and exercise, diet and general care of the young inmates:

> They work in the garden from rising till 8. They go into school from 9 to 12. Till 2 they dine and play—from 2 till 5 they work at their trades of Taylor and shoemaker and some in the garden.[45]

The contrast of these conditions, even allowing for some partiality in a description given by the Master, may be seen in the First Factory Act, passed by the British Parliament in 1802 at the instigation of Sir Robert Peel senior for the benefits of apprentices employed in mills and factories:

> Section IV: That no Apprentice . . . shall be employed for more than twelve Hours in any One Day (reckoning from six of the Clock in the Morning to Nine of the Clock at Night), exclusively of the Time that may be occupied in eating the necessary meals.[46]

This contrast between the conditions of colonial orphans in the Male Orphan School and the children of the poor in Britain is emphasized further by the description of the lives of the children employed in the mills which was given by Sir John Hobhouse in the course of a debate in the House of Commons in 1825. Hobhouse unsuccessfully attempted to have a Bill passed which would regulate the working conditions of the mill children. In a House of Commons Debate, Hobhouse argued that:

> In the best regulated mills, the children . . . work twelve hours and a half a day, and for three or four days in the week were not allowed out of the mills to get their meals, which they were obliged to take off the floor of the mill, mingled with the dust and down of the cotton . . . They scarcely bore any resemblance to their fellow-creatures . . . Their skins were literally the colour of parchment. . . .[47]

It is also important to note that not all the child mill and factory workers were apprenticed from the parish in England but were frequently 'let out to hire, the wages they earn being received by their parents and guardians'.[48] When it is considered that these children were known to suffer 'permanent deterioration of the physical constitution' as the direct result of the nature of their employment in mills and factories,[49] a different interpretation may be placed on the contemporary condemnation of the 'unnatural' parents of Botany Bay, who were reported as neglecting and abandoning their children. A defence of the English parents could perhaps be based on dread of the workhouse, an institution which did not exist in New South Wales during this period. This dread was so great that it may have resulted in a situation in which the exploitation of their children was preferable to having to apply to the parish for assistance. A ballad of 1810 described graphically 'the pauper palace' which could be the only refuge for the destitute poor and unemployed:

> That giant building, that high-bounding wall
> Those bare-worn walks, that lofty thund'ring hall!
> That large loud clock, which tolls each dreaded hour,
> Those gates and locks, and all those signs of power;
> It is a prison, with a milder name,
> Which few inhabit without dread or shame.[50]

In New South Wales there was another source of child labour which does not appear to have been exploited by the authorities. This was the juvenile convict. Within the context of the assignment system in New South Wales combined with the parish apprenticeship system in England, it would appear probable that boy convicts transported to Botany Bay would be apprenticed to a master or mistress in the colony in the same manner as the traditional workhouse child-servant; this would reduce the government's expense of maintenance and help to alleviate those moral problems associated with the confinement of men and boys. There were, however, few instances of juvenile convicts being apprenticed for the specific purpose of learning an individual trade; these apprenticeships were the result of unsolicited requests from the prospective masters and not the result of government instigation. George Clew, for example, had arrived in New South Wales as a convict; he had served his seven-year sentence, married a native-born girl and established himself as a nailor in Sydney. Clew petitioned Governor Darling for a convict boy to serve as an apprentice. He requested that the governor:

> . . . allow a lad to be assigned . . . as a Government Servant and learn the trade . . . he had heard well of one, William Baxter, although he had no previous knowledge of but Representation he would be willing to work and become a Tradesman and thereby serve me and make himself a mechanic.[51]

Clew gave no reason for his application. There were both native-born and immigrant lads whom he could have chosen as an apprentice and, in this case, most likely demanded an indentures fee, so it is possible that Clew's motivation was humane and a genuine attempt to help a boy whose circumstances were similar to those he himself had experienced. The date of Clew's arrival in the colony is not known; he had served his seven-year sentence by 1828 and in that year was twenty-five years old. It is most likely that he had arrived in New South Wales in his mid-teens and thus it is probable that he had learned his trade as a nailor while serving as a 'Government 'Prentice', probably in the Lumber Yards.

There are no remaining records which indicate the actual number of juvenile convicts who may have been transported to New South Wales during the first thirty years. Neither are there reliable estimates of the number of convict boys who were apprenticed at the Dock Yards or the Lumber Yards. One of the earliest references to juvenile convicts was made by Governor King when, in 1803, he wrote to Lord Hobart that the funds were insufficient to open a Male Orphan Institution but he intended

> . . . to lessen the evil as much as possible the convict boys that arrive (of which I am sorry to say there are a great number) are put 'Prentices to the boat-builders or carpenters and several have made themselves very usefull. [sic].[52]

King appeared to follow the traditional belief among members of his social class, that the discipline and training associated with learning a trade or craft was beneficial to the character of a young boy. His sentiments were similar to those expressed by the *Sydney Gazette* in the following year, with reference to the colonial youth: that such training would 'promote industry and secure youth from indolence'.[53]

An indication of the number of convict boys in New South Wales during the administration of Governor Macquarie may be found in the evidence of Major Druitt to Bigge in 1819. Druitt, the colony's chief engineer, was asked by Bigge to describe the principles upon which the male convicts were classified in the sleeping rooms. Druitt replied that there was only one specific classification, apart from the general 'male convicts', and this was 'the Boys, who are kept in a room to themselves from the age of 14 to 19 to the amount of fifty'.[54] Bigge was also informed by the ex-convict carpenter Thomas Messling that the boys who were prisoners, or who had been prisoners, were taught the trade of carpentry at the carpenters' shop in the Government Yard. Messling claimed that during the unspecified period in which he had himself worked at the Yard there were upwards of thirteen or fourteen convict boys apprenticed '. . . and some of them did very well'.[55] It is difficult to explain Messling's reference to 'those who had been prisoners' and who were apprenticed at the yard unless it implied that these convict boys had begun an apprenticeship with Government and had completed their sentences before their indentures had expired, so that they remained in government employ although technically freed.

From all remaining evidence, it would appear that no direct attempts were made by officials in Britain or New South Wales to attempt to apprentice convict boys to private masters. These boys, therefore, were not in competition with the native-born for the available apprenticeships. It may have been that the lack of any need on the part of prospective master to employ apprentices was the underlying motivation for the colonial authorities' assuming the responsibility of training juvenile convicts. Such a practice would have been completely opposed to any contemporary policies or practices in British gaols. It was not until the opening of the Parkhurst Gaol on the Isle of Wight in 1838 that direct government attempts were made to train English juvenile prisoners in a 'particular kind of craft or occupation'.[56]

Those children who did become apprentices in New South Wales during the first thirty years of settlement were mainly taught their trades as 'Government 'Prentices'.[57] It was the governor who selected applicants and determined the wages and conditions of colonial apprenticeships during this period. The normal way in which an apprenticeship was obtained was by a Memorial to the governor from the father or guardian of the boy. This Memorial described the boy's parentage, upbringing and family background. That of George William Board, who applied for an apprenticeship for his son Gregory, was typical:

> Your Petitioner is a free man, resident in this Colony for nearly seventeen years, and possessed of a large Family and is desirous and with the anxious wish of his son, Gregory, now fourteen years of age—who has received a liberal, Colonial Education, to apprentice him to Government in His Majesty's Dock Yard and to learn the art and trade and avocation of a shipwright. He is a youth of docile temper and good morals.

The father had arrived in the colony as a prisoner for life in 1805 but had received a conditional pardon and worked as a bricklayer in Sydney.

Apprenticeships served with Government were as binding as those with private masters; this may be seen from the reluctance of officials to allow an apprentice to break his indentures. The case of William Chapman is an illustration of this, and it is also an indication of the regulations and conditions which governed the life of a 'Government 'Prentice'. William Chapman was born in the colony in 1802, the son of Henry Chapman and his wife, and was apprenticed to Government in 1817 at the age of fifteen. In 1822, having completed five of his seven years' indentures, William decided to leave his trade and become a missionary; he had the opportunity of accompanying the Reverend W. Lawry to Tongataboo. Chapman applied to the Colonial Secretary for permission to be released from his indentures for this reason and was informed that the indentures could only be cancelled if Chapman reimbursed Government for the expenses involved in maintaining and training him for the previous five years. The sum suggested by the Colonial Secretary was far in excess of any that Chapman could afford, even with some assistance from the Reverend Lawry. Chapman wrote again, asking for his case to be reconsidered. To strengthen his application, Chapman described how he had helped to build both the gig used by His Excellency and a government lifeboat. In reply he received an itemized list of the expenses which had been incurred on his behalf over the previous five years and the curt information that he could be released from his indentures when the amount claimed by Government was paid in full.

The estimated cost of training an apprentice is of interest because it suggests the expense involved in training convict boys. For the first two years of his apprenticeship, the Colonial Secretary claimed that the boy's financial value was barely equal to the cost of his provisions and did not cover the added expenses of clothing, lodging and training. In his third year, his value was estimated at 2 shillings a day; this was the average wage at that time for an unskilled labourer. In his fourth year, his labour was worth 3 shillings and sixpence a day. From the total monies earned the cost of slop clothing and provisions had to be deducted. This left a deficit of £57.12.8 which 'must be paid immediately and in full'. There is no record of this amount having been paid to the Colonial Secretary's office nor of any alternative agreement having been made, but some agreement must have been reached for Chapman's name appeared on the passenger list for Tongataboo in that same year. In 1828, six years after Chapman had requested that his indentures be cancelled, he was living with his wife and children at Darling Harbour and described his occupation as that of master shipwright; his younger brother, James, was apprenticed to him. From the estimated cost of his training and upkeep, according to the Colonial Secretary, it would appear than an apprentice was not an economical asset, at least during the first five years of his indentures. This strengthens the suggestion that few private masters offered apprenticeships because the alternative form of labour, assigned convicts, was more profitable and did not involve the necessity of training in a skill.

In New South Wales the formal terms and conditions of apprenticeships followed closely those which had existed in England towards the end of the eighteenth century. There is some evidence to suggest that this was not always the case, however. In 1822 the Committee of the Male Orphan Institution was told that Mr Uther 'the hat maker' had expressed a wish to have one of the boys as an apprentice but 'had declined on account of a clause inserted in the Indentures for nullifying the apprenticeship by the marriage of the Boy with the sanction of the Committee'. The Committee then resolved that:

It appears to Members expedient that the children should be apprenticed precisely on the same conditions as Boys are apprenticed to trades in England—and that the Secretary be directed to submit the same for the consideration of His Excellency, Governor Sir Thomas Brisbane, the Patron.[58]

These conditions were those which in all probability had applied to both private and government apprentices in the colony. The apprentice undertook to serve his master faithfully for a stipulated period, which could be for up to seven years. During this period he could never marry, nor enter into any illicit connection, nor should he play cards, nor dice, nor 'games' nor indulge himself in spirituous liquors. He was bound to apply himself solely with learning his trade. These were the standard conditions imposed in England on trade or craft apprentices.[59] The exact extent to which they were enforced in New South Wales cannot be determined. By the 1820s, when more private apprenticeships were available, there were occasional reports in the newspapers of Sydney apprentices being whipped for alleged neglect of duty, drunkenness or immoral habits. Cases of unjustified cruelty were exceptional and the master, in these cases, was usually a newly-arrived immigrant from Britain, familiar with the conditions of English apprentices. In 1826 the *Australian* reported a court case in which Mrs Reynolds, a Sydney shopkeeper who had arrived as a convict, charged Mr Bell, an upholsterer, with 'ill-usage towards Francis the complainant's son, a youth who it appeared was articled to Mr Bell for a number of years'. The report continued:

> The lad had been absent on Friday last from his employment, his master stated without leave ... received corporal punishment for his offence ... evidence was given of the horse-whipping and the extent of the punishment ... Bell was reprimanded by the Bench although reserving the Master's right to chastise an apprentice was indisputable but the law did not authorise punishment to so severe an extent. The master promised not to correct the lad in future, was dismissed and the boy returned to his master.[60]

Bell was a young free immigrant married to a native-born girl. The boy's mother, Mary Reynolds, had arrived in the colony in 1803, sentenced to seven years' transportation. At the time of the complaint she was a shopkeeper and lived with her younger daughter, Elizabeth. She had been sufficiently successful in the colony to obtain a private apprenticeship for her son and to afford the indentures fee. She also showed sufficient interest in his welfare to charge his master before the magistrates with ill-treatment of her boy. By 1828 Francis had completed his apprenticeship and was working as a carpenter at Parramatta.

The case of Francis Reynolds is not only an example of the continuing interest of an ex-convict parent in the welfare of a son. It also indicates the attitudes of the colonial magistrates towards the rights of masters to punish disobedient apprentices. No fine or remonstrance other than an oral reprimand was imposed for this severe horse-whipping of a child. The verdict in the next case, heard by the same magistrate, shows the influence of British attitudes in the colonial courts. An assigned servant convicted of cruelty to his master's horse was sentenced to fifty lashes.[61] Compared with cases of ill-treatment of apprentices in contemporary England, however, those in New South Wales were negligible. The following case, described by Dorothy George, was reported in *The Times*:

> An apprentice ... was brought by his friend to Bow Street to shew one of

the modes of punishment adopted by the master, when one of the boys commited any fault. It consisted of an iron collar, fastened round the neck with a padlock. The lad said he had worn it above a month, and that he understood it was his master's intention that he should wear it until he was out of his time.[62]

In the colony such punishment was inflicted from time to time on women convicts convicted of colonial crimes. The lack of widespread exploitation or abuse of apprentices in New South Wales could be linked with the comparative smallness of the population and the size of the towns. This made for ease of contact between parent or guardian and child even if the child lodged with the master, which he usually did.

It was not until early in the administration of Governor Darling that there was any government attempt to regulate or control relations between masters and apprentices.[63] Those colonial apprentices who had been indentured to private masters were protected, to a certain extent, by the terms of the indentures and by the payment of an indentures fee, which could be reclaimed if it were proved that the master had neglected his obligations. Parental consent in writing was a prerequisite for the legality of the indentures. As it was the parent or guardian who paid the indentures fee, it could be assumed that concern for the welfare and progress of the boy would continue. This could be particularly pertinent where the apprentice was employed near to his parental home, as in the case of Francis and Mrs Reynolds. It is probable that proximity, combined with continuing parental interest, helped to make it more likely that the master fulfilled his obligations for any abuse or ill-treatment of the lad could be noticed and reported.

The indentures could be broken legally if the boy absconded; the master was then entitled to retain the indentures fee. They could be broken by mutual agreement, although this involved the apprentice in expense because he was obliged to reimburse his master for out-of-pocket expenses for food, clothing, lodging and training. If the indentures were cancelled at the request of the apprentice the master was entitled to retain the indentures fee.[64] It is probable that the knowledge of the expense and difficulties involved in cancelling apprenticeships when the apprentice was legally indentured prompted dissatisfied apprentices to abscond. It is indicative, however, of the conditions under which colonial boys served their time, as compared with those of boys in England, that so few of the native-born did abscond from their master. Among those who did, a high proportion were ships' apprentices who experienced differing conditions from those on land. Although a few notices relating to absconding apprentices appeared in the *Sydney Gazette* from time to time before the arrival of Macquarie, it was not until the latter part of the 1820s that such notices appeared in the colonial press with any degree of regularity. In January 1828 a boot-maker, R. Bogg, advertised that his fourteen-year-old apprentice, George Gregory, had absconded. Gregory, 'of dark hair and sallow complexion', had been apprenticed to Bogg from the Male Orphan School.[65] He had arrived in the colony as an infant in 1814 with his mother,

possibly his father and his elder brother, Edward. In the Census of 1828
both George and his brother described themselves as shoemakers but did
not indicate by whom they were employed or where they lived. In
November of that same year, an advertisement appeared for a 'Runaway
Apprentice', Lawrence Butler, who had left his master, Mr Hill of Sydney,
and absconded to Argyle in the neighbourhood of Lake George.[66] Butler,
who was apprenticed to the printing trade, was sixteen years old. Two of
his brothers farmed at Portland Head; the third was a carpenter in Sydney.
His father, an ex-convict, worked as a brick-maker at Windsor. In the
Census, taken shortly before he absconded, Butler was described as a
printer working for Catherine Clarkson, a publican and printer who had
arrived free in the colony in 1805.

   In the early period almost all reports of absconding apprentices were
concerned with ships' apprentices. Absconding seamen were not limited to
these boys; almost every issue of the *Sydney Gazette* reported the desertion of
sailors. It may have been that one voyage was sufficient to cure a would-be
colonial seaman from any desire to make seafaring his career. Desertion
was so prevalent during the administrations of King, Bligh and Macquarie
that the authority of Government and General Orders was used in an
attempt to deter any assistance being given to deserters, whether
apprentices or seamen. In September 1804, for example, Governor King
proclaimed that a punishment of six months' hard labour would follow the
conviction of any person for 'Inveigling, Harbouring, or Secreting a *Deserter*
or *Apprentice* from any of His Majesty's ships or vessels or from merchant
ships of any Nation'. In the same issue in which this order was published
the front page of the *Sydney Gazette* carried an advertisement which offered
'Five Pounds Reward ... for the apprehension and lodging in Gaol ... of
Michael Mansfield, Seaman ... Deserted from the ship '*Ocean*' ... aged
about twenty-five years, dark complexion and five feet six inches tall'.[67] In
the following year, 1805, an advertisement appeared, headed 'A Caution':

> All Masters and Owners of Vessels, and the Public in general are hereby
> particularly cautioned against harbouring, or employing John Chandler
> ... A boy of about 15 years of age, eloped from his servitude to Captain
> Lucas, to whom he is indentured as an Apprentice....

Similar notices continued to appear. Captain Wilkinson cautioned all
inhabitants against 'sheltering or harbouring' four youths, legally bound to
him by articles of apprenticeship. These four had been apprenticed in
England and had jumped ship at Sydney Cove. They were apprehended
and taken back to England by their master. In 1806 Kable and Underwood warned that the 'Law would be rigidly enforced against ... any
Person harbouring or encouraging' their absconder apprentice, George
Mowbray.[68]

   Advertisements for ships' apprentices usually stated that 'Stout Lads'
were required for a colonial vessel. Occasionally inducements were offered,
such as that which appeared in the *Sydney Gazette* of October 1808:

Wanted for the ship *Elizabeth*, three Apprentices from twelve to fifteen years old, to be bound for the Term of Five Years, on the same terms as if bound in England; and for further Encouragement, when ever the Vessel is in Port, they will have the advantage of Evening School.[69]

There are insufficient records to estimate the number of colonial boys who were bound to the sea. Contemporary accounts of the lives of seamen both in the Royal Navy and on merchant ships would suggest that few would remain sailors from choice—and this might be linked with the high rate of desertion. A contemporary description was that of a seventeen-year-old boy from Liverpool, C.R. Pemberton, who was pressed into the navy after running away from home. He described his life and his companions:

I was now one of themselves, to toil as they toiled washing and holy-stoning the decks—to come at a whistle and run at a blow—to scramble as best I could through that congregated mass, some of them the most depraved and abandoned characters, thieves and pickpockets too—to wallow in degradation and misery—to watch continually in avoidance of abuse and beating and to watch in vain—to be scourged with ropes by brutes who were charmed with delight at the sound of the heavy dense blows which they dealt around in sheer wantonness, who rejoiced in their muscular arms, for strength was proved only because it enabled them to smite with greater energy; whose best sport was watching and smiting at and prolonging the suppressed cries and writhings of their victims. I do not exaggerate . . .[70]

When the discipline of contemporary ship life and the nature of the work are considered in comparison with the lives of the native-born who grew up at Botany Bay it could be suggested that the 'independent' spirit of the colonial boy was unsuited to the occupation of a mariner, and it is probable that few who became ships' apprentices completed their indentures.[71]

It was a peculiarly colonial characteristic, and one which would affect the nature of colonial society, that native-born and free immigrant government apprentices worked in close association with convict labourers, convict apprentices and convict masters. Private masters could be ex-convicts who frequently employed government-assigned servants in addition to an apprentice. The colonial labour conditions were such that it would not have been possible for an apprentice to shun contacts with convict and ex-convict workers. That skilled ex-convicts remained in New South Wales after their sentences had expired and worked at their trades resulted in a social difference in the standing of skilled workers from that which existed in Britain. The master craftsman in England was conscious of the added social prestige attached to his skill. In his workshop there was a traditional 'class' distinction between the master and his labourer, the apprentice and the labourer. The master blacksmith, for example, was higher socially and economically than his striker; the bricklayer belonged to a higher social level than his labourer.[72] In New South Wales, in addition to these traditional levels based on skill, there was the social division based on civil condition. The rigidity of this division of society into respectable and tainted was lessened by the work situation where the skilled convict or the ex-convict could be in the position of the master, possessing the skills which entitled him to a higher level within the working 'class'. At the same time he was rejected as socially inferior by the unconvicted sections of colonial society because of his conviction of a major felony. The free immigrant or the native-born, wishing to learn a trade, frequently had no alternative but to work for a convict or ex-convict master. Those who were apprenticed to government, and this was the majority, had no other alternative. Unintentionally, within the context of colonial society and the structure of the skilled level of the work-force, the barrier between convicted and unconvicted labour was lowered by the need for skilled tradesmen to teach their crafts to colonial youths. This need was caused by the lack of free masters in the colony and by the dependence on the skills of convict and ex-convict mechanics.

An analysis of the male apprenticeships in New South Wales in 1828 reveals that most of the colonial boys were apprenticed to convict and ex-convict masters and that the trades of these masters differed very little from those who had advertised for apprentices since the administration of Governor King. Forty years after white settlement the skilled work-force still relied heavily on those who had arrived as convicts and the skills required in the colony were still essentially limited to the basic and subsistence trades.

TABLE 5/1

Years of arrival of came-free apprentices, New South Wales, 1828
Source: 1828 Census

Year of arrival in New South Wales	Number of apprentices
1828	*1*
1827	*2*
1826	*3*
1825	*1*
1824	*1*
1823	*3*
1822	*1*
1821	*1*
1816	*2*
1814	*1*
1813	*3*
1812	*1*
N.R.	*5*

Note: This is a summary only. See Appendix 5

In 1828 there were 106 male apprentices whose ages ranged from eleven to twenty-four years. Of these, eighty were native-born, twenty-five had come free and one was a convict boy. This boy, John Yeates, had arrived in 1827 at the age of sixteen, sentenced to transportation for life. He was apprenticed to John Champley, an ex-convict shoe-maker in Pitt Street, Sydney. There were no discernible differences between the trades to which the native-born and the came-free were apprenticed or in the civil condition of the master. There was, however, one characteristic of the came-free apprentices which is difficult to explain. This was that few of those who had come free had parents or relatives in the colony in 1828: only seven of the twenty-five had a relative who could be traced in 1828. George Green had arrived in the colony with his father in 1822 at the age of twelve and was apprenticed to boat-builder Thomas Day. His father was a labourer in Sydney. Edward McCabe had arrived with his family in 1826 at the age of eleven. He was apprenticed to George Ross and Company; his mother and younger sister, both of whom had come free, lived in Sydney. James Johnson had arrived at the age of twelve in 1824 with his free mother, Sarah. In 1828 James was apprenticed to a freed-by-servitude Sydney carpenter and his mother worked in Sydney as a servant. Sixteen-year-old Mazzegara [sic] junior had arrived with his family in 1816 and was apprenticed to a free cabinet-maker. His father, John, who was 'a dealer in curiosities', had accompanied his convict wife, Mary, to Sydney in 1816, together with their two sons. James Tindall, who had arrived with his family in 1814 at the age of five, was apprenticed to a ticket-of-leave carpenter at Parramatta. His elder brother, Daniel, who had arrived in the colony with him, was a carpenter at Liverpool, where he lived with his wife and four children. There is no trace of any colonial family or relatives for the remaining eighteen came-free apprentices. A few of these apprentices had arrived in New South Wales as infants and it is possible that their parents had died; James Deacy had arrived in 1814 and Henry Logan in 1816. Most of these apprentices, however, were recent arrivals. James Bicknell was sixteen years old and had arrived in 1828. In that year he was apprenticed to an immigrant ship-builder. Henry Reid had arrived in 1827 at the age of fourteen, as had John Bradley. Table 5/1 indicates the years of arrival of the came-free apprentices.

Table 5/1 shows how few of the British-born colonial apprentices had arrived in the colony as infants or young children. Few, therefore, had shared the same colonial experiences as the native-born. Those young children who did arrive with parents during the first twenty-five or so years of white settlement did not seek apprenticeships; the majority stayed with their parents on family land or became landowners themselves. That those lads who arrived late in the 1820s, possibly without parents or family connections, became apprenticed shortly after arrival may be an indication of concern on the part of colonial authorities for the welfare of orphan boys. There is, however, no evidence in the correspondence of the Colonial Secretary for this period which would support this assumption.

Both the native-born and the came-free were apprenticed to masters from all civil conditions. There appeared to be no reluctance for a boy of free parents to be apprenticed to a master who had arrived as a convict or one who

TABLE 5/2

Colonial apprentices: civil condition of masters
Source: 1828 Census. See Appendix 5

Civil condition of master	Native-born		Came free	
	Number of masters	Number of apprentices	Number of masters	Number of apprentices
Came free	16	22	8	8
Native-born	10	14	2	2
Free by servitude	15	20	6	7
Absolute pardon	nil			
Conditional pardon	5	11		
Ticket-of-leave	5	5	3	3
Government servant	2	2	1	2
N.R.	5	5	3	3
Dockyard		1		

held a ticket-of-leave. Table 5/2 shows the civil conditions of the masters of the colonial apprentices in 1828.

As Table 5/2 shows, twenty-six of the masters of the native-born apprentices were free by birth or by arrival and twenty-two had arrived convicted. Ten of the masters of the came-free apprentices had arrived as convicts and ten were free. There is no indication on the part of the masters that they preferred British-born to colonial-born apprentices and in a number of cases lads from both civil conditions trained together.

The trades followed by both the native-born and the came-free were similar and were mainly confined to the basic subsistence trades, neither group being apprenticed to 'luxury' trades such as jeweller, silversmith, gunsmith or carver.

These trades were similar to those followed by most of the fathers of the native-born apprentices. William Regan and his native-born son were both carpenters and had petitioned Governor Brisbane for permission to go to 'an outlying settlement, as carpenters', but possibly with the hope of securing a grant of land. Both came-free and colonial-born apprentices applied for land grants. George Pitt Wood, who had been two years old when he arrived in the colony with his parents in 1802, wrote to the governor that:

> ... [he was] the son of Mrs Lucy Wood, widow of the late Mr John Wood, was born in the Colony ... bound apprentice to Mr James Smith, Builder, for the term of four years ... and has now two years and five months to serve and intends to remain in the colony ... has 22 horned cattle and no land or farm ... lost his father at an early age ... his mother a most respectable woman ... maiden name Pitt ... sober and industrious....

Wood received his land grant and settled as a farmer at Richmond. A native-born, Nathaniel Payten, who had worked with his father, Issac, as one of the contractors who built the new Factory at Parramatta, also applied for land and received 60 acres. It was, however, unusual for a native-born apprentice to apply for a land grant. Some of the fathers were farmers but they usually had small holdings, averaging forty to sixty acres. A few of these had been 'labouring men of no trade' who had arrived as convicts and remained as settlers when their sentences had expired. The families of these men, had they remained in Britain, would have had entirely different opportunities from those which were available in the colony. James Lane, for example, petitioned for and received a land grant 'to cultivate for the support of his family'. Patrick Kirk, who had four children, wrote to the governor for an additional grant as he was 'anxious to improve his farm for his family's future'. That future did not necessarily lie on the land. These fathers put at least one of their sons to a trade. Lane apprenticed his son to a rope-maker, a skilled trade and one in great demand in the colony. Kirk's son, Thomas, was apprenticed to a carpenter in nearby Parramatta.

There are no remaining records to indicate which of the native-born were apprenticed from the Orphan Institution. Some apprenticed boys had lost a parent at any early age but most of the lads remained with the surviving mother or father. James Chapman's father died when he was two months old; his mother, the former Ann Marsh, who had arrived as a convict on the *Lady Juliana*, took over his father's business. Young James was apprenticed as a shipwright. Thomas Cook, who was apprenticed to a carpenter, remained with his father, a labourer at Newcastle, after the death of his mother. James Euther remained with his mother and younger brother at Windsor, where he was apprenticed to a wheelwright. His mother had arrived as a convict in 1790. Thomas Kinsall [*sic*] had lost his father when he was one year old; he remained with his mother who apprenticed him to an upholsterer. Stephen Murphy, a clerk in the Dock Yard, was left a widower with two young children when his wife, Alice Schofield, died in 1810. His son, Richard, who was less than a year old when his mother died, remained with his father, eventually being apprenticed in Sydney. The only native-born apprentice who may have come from the Orphan Institution was John Fry. Born in 1810, the son of Richard and Margaret Fry, John Fry was in the Orphan Institution in 1824 and by 1826 was apprenticed to a tailor, William Pendray. Pendray had two other native-born apprentices, Phillip Fitzpatrick and James Foster. Neither Fitzpatrick nor Foster had been baptized nor had their parents living in 1828. As tailoring and boot-making were the two trades to which orphans and poor children were traditionally apprenticed it is probable that Pendray, a conditionally pardoned convict who had arrived in the colony in 1818, accepted apprentices from the Orphan Institution.

The family link between apprentices and parents was as strong as that between the rural, or landowning, parents and sons. This was evident not only among the established trade families but at all economic levels. Pensioners, for example, arranged apprenticeships for their sons. James Pithers, born in 1811, was the son of a 'soldier for twenty-six years and three months', an out-pensioner of the Chelsea Hospital who had a family of six native-born children. He received a land grant of 100 acres and he apprenticed his younger son to a tailor. William Osburn had been a sergeant in the Royal Veteran Company; he apprenticed his son, George, to boat-builder Thomas Day. Thomas Colebrook, was a pensioner who had arrived as a convict in 1790 and had received an Absolute Pardon. He had married ex-convict 'Betty' Wade in 1810 and worked as a constable in Sydney. He apprenticed his son, Thomas junior, to a ticket-of-leave carpenter in Sydney.

The experiences and prospects, therefore, of the 'Stout Colonial Lads' who became apprentices differed in almost all respects from those of their contemporaries in Britain. Not only were they assured of lucrative and constant employment on the completion of their indentures but very few, if any, were apprenticed as destitute Parish boys and very few masters accepted an apprentice primarily as a source of cheap labour. The experiences of these lads, as working boys, were directly affected by the nature of the colony in which they lived. On the one hand, there was the link between work and punishment, with the major labour force being convict. On the other, there was the link between work and reward, evident in the achievements of their parents. The children of the colony during this period were completely unfamiliar with the poverty, misery and destitution which resulted from lack of employment, lack of opportunity, even lack of incentive to work. Misery, degradation and punishment were linked with criminality. This was evident in the chain gangs that worked on the streets of Sydney. Their own parents had no need to exploit the labour of their children so both sons and daughters were more accustomed to 'family work' than to employment at an early age. The family links continued when the boy was apprenticed. The master chosen was usually in the same neighbourhood in which the parent or parents lived. As with Mrs Reynolds, the parent continued to watch the progress of the son. When the parents were living the apprenticed lad continued to be a family lad. In these respects the native-born apprentices fulfilled the description of Edward Eagar,[73] for they were the 'Hope and Staff of the Colony', a colony which, as Hunter had foreseen in 1798, would continue to depend on 'the useful labour' of its artisans.[74]

CHAPTER SIX

THE FIRST MATILDAS

'thy blue ey'd daughters with the flaxen hair,
And taper ankle, do they bloom less fair
Than those of Europe?'

William Charles Wentworth,
'Australasia: A Poem', 1823.

Almost half of the children born in the colony during the first twenty-five years were females. By 1828, 1161 of these 'Currency Lasses' were still resident in New South Wales. They represented almost one quarter of the adult female population at that time, slightly more than the number of women who had come free and slightly less than the number who were still under sentence of the law. By 1828 one woman in two in the colony was free, either by birth or by arrival, while among those who had been convicted one in two had served her sentence or had been pardoned and so was technically free. This was a far higher proportion of free and freed than existed among the colonial men, most of whom were still under sentence.[1] The structure of female society, with regard to the ratio of free to bond, was basically different from the structure of male society. This characteristic was reflected in the marriage patterns of the native-born women and in their choices of occupation and districts of residence.

The native-born girls had shared similar backgrounds with the native-born boys, with the exception that graver doubts were expressed concerning their future moral welfare. They, too, were described as the children of the convicts and all the connotations of that description were attributed to their parents, in particular their mothers. Chaplain Marsden wrote to William Wilberforce that the moral dangers to which these young girls were exposed were solely attributable to the 'infamous characters of their unnatural mothers'.[2] The problem of protecting the virtue of these young girls was seen as far more pressing than the problem of what to do with the young boys who played idly on the wharves and streets of Sydney Town. The solution was to establish a place of refuge and instruction so that these girls could be 'snatch'd from scenes impure', 'entirely secluded from other people and brought up in habits of religion and industry'.[3]

The establishment of the Female Orphan School, however, did not have the proposed corrective effect on the females of the Rising Generation because only a minority of the Currency Lasses became inmates. The School began in 1801, with a total of thirty-one girls from Sydney Town. It was under the auspices of a committee headed by those two charitably inclined ladies, Mrs Anna King and Mrs Elizabeth Paterson.[4] The committee reported in 1803 that the original thirty-one had grown to fifty-four children who '. . . appear to have made considerable improvements both in their morals and education, considering the situations from whence they have been taken'.[5] By August 1820 fewer than 217 'orphan' girls had been cared for at this institution. These girls had not necessarily stayed for long periods, nor were they all 'orphans' or neglected children.[6] One father, Thomas Hughes, wrote to the governor for assistance in reclaiming his daughter, Amelia, from the Female Orphan School, claiming that she was put there 'some little time ago contrary to the wishes of the Memorialist'. Hughes added that he was 'in every way capable of supporting his said daughter'.[7] Why she was placed in the Orphan School, and by whom, is unknown.

In January 1810 Macquarie found it necessary to issue a General Order forbidding the admission to the school of children whose parents were still living.[8] An Order issued some two weeks later suggested that one of the reasons parents sent their daughters to the School was not solely for care, protection and maintenance but to obtain education and instruction. In his General Order of 24 February 1810 Macquarie, 'being extremely desirous that the Rising Generation ... should receive Instruction which alone can render them dutiful and obedient to their Parents and Superiors', announced that 'A Public Charity School will be established at Sydney, for the Education of Poor Children ...'[9]. Samuel Marsden, who was treasurer of the school, supported the order that only orphans were to be admitted. Characteristically, his reason was fear of the moral danger to the girls from any form of contact with their 'abandoned' parents:

> The admission of children into the Female Orphan School who have parents in this Colony, being a deviation from the spirit of the original institution, and the bad example set by those girls when restored to their parents being productive of very serious evils.[10]

'Serious evils' had also resulted from lack of proper supervision of the Orphan School before the arrival of Macquarie. It was described in 1809 as 'a bawdy house', supervised by 'a notorious street-walking strumpet and a prisoner for life'.[11] Shortly after his arrival, Macquarie found that 'very unfair and improper means were used to seduce [the girls] from the paths of virtue and to entice them to quit that asylum'. Macquarie announced his intention of prosecuting any person:

> ... of whatever rank, class or denomination, to the utmost rigor of the law, who shall dare to attempt to seduce or entice away any of the girls of the Orphan School from that Institution, besides exposing their names publicly in the *Sydney Gazette*.[12]

The wording of the General Order, and the threat of publicity to the seducers, would suggest that it was not the 'convict parents' who were leading these girls from 'the paths of virtue' but persons of 'respectable' rank.

That so few native-born girls found refuge in the Female Orphan School was not primarily the result of specific and deliberate limitations on numbers of girls admitted. Few girls were anxious to be confined at the School, fewer parents willing to have their daughters taken from them, and fewer still were in such distressed circumstances that they were forced to relinquish their children. From the Memorials and Petitions to the governor from widows who were in need of assistance, there is no evidence that these women considered sending their 'orphan' daughters to the School. The petitioners asked instead for grants of land, or to be placed on stores, or both, so that they would be able to support their 'fatherless daughters'.[13] The Memorial of Nancy Davis, 'relict of Joseph of Sydney', showed that, even in

circumstances of extreme distress, the mother did not attempt to put her
daughters in the Orphan School:

> [she was] left with a large and helpless family of six children . . . depends
> solely upon the exertions of her eldest son, who is as yet but fifteen . . .
> That Memorialist, finding that in consequence of his Youth and trusting it
> may be an apology for his neglect . . . his application to business is what
> cannot be called close thereby rendering his earnings inadequate to the
> support of the family . . . so allow two boys, five and seven, to be placed in
> the Male Orphan School.

The boys were received into the Male Orphan School; the two daughters and
a younger boy remained with their mother.

During that period between the establishment of the Female Orphan
School and the arrival of Macquarie, despite the admission of children who
were not orphans, a very small percentage of the native-born girls were
placed there to be brought up 'in the habits of religion and industry'.[14] Most
of the Currency Lasses grew to maturity with their parents. Actual orphans
were frequently cared for by friends or, on some occasions, charitable
neighbours. One case reported in the *Sydney Gazette* concerned a 'little girl of
four', who had been found sleeping and playing alone in the Rocks area.
Asked why her pinafore was torn, she replied that she must 'mend it myself
. . . my Mammy's dead'. This child was not placed in the Orphan School but
taken home by a bystander.[15]

The belief that the native-born girls were in need of some form of asylum to
rescue them from the wretchedness of their homes and to protect them from
the vile examples of their degraded parents was firmly held by
contemporaries such as Governor King, his wife Anna, Samuel Marsden and
Mrs Paterson. This belief was based on the assumption that these children
were the daughters of the convicts, lower-class girls who would have to
support themselves by their own skills and industry. It was, therefore,
essential that they be segregated from the immoral practices of their parents.
Chaplain Richard Johnson had expressed the need for this as early as 1796.
In a letter to the Society for the Propagation of the Gospel he lamented that
'The miserable wretches sent out . . . being lost to all sense of virtue and
religion, as long as this offspring continue with them . . . every means used for
their instruction will be ineffectual'.[16]

It was also essential that these young girls be taught a trade suitable to
their class origins and prospects. These trades were the same as those
available to girls in comparable situations in Britain; that is, some form of
domestic work, laundering or plain sewing. The Currency Lasses were
expected to become the servants for the 'respectable' settlers at Botany Bay.
What contemporaries did not realize, however, was that the girls born in the
colony came from a wide range of social and economic backgrounds. Even
among the daughters of the labourers and unskilled workers there were close
family relationships which differed entirely from the commonly accepted,
degraded picture of convict households.

The family backgrounds of the Currency Lasses were as diverse as those of the Currency Lads. These children formed a natural link between the two divisions of society, the free and the convicted. Although most of the mothers had arrived in New South Wales as convicts there were some who were free and respectable family women, the wives of settlers and officials or free wives who had joined convicted husbands. Many of the convicted women married or formed liaisons with free men. These unconvicted fathers were from all levels of the colonial social and economic hierarchy. Since it was the material well-being of the family which directly affected the nature of the children's upbringing, there was a wide disparity between the life-styles, for example, of the four daughters of Major Johnston and ex-convict Esther Abrams and the daughters of former soldier Thomas Dargin and his ex-convict wife, Mary Warren. That Dargin and Mary Warren were legally married and Major Johnston and Esther were not did not affect the social standing of the children in the families.[17] It cannot be argued, therefore, that the native-born girls were from the lower order of colonial society because they were the children of the convicts or, more specifically, the daughters of convict mothers.

The nature and structure of colonial society itself affected the connotations and definitions of 'class'. Most of the fathers had arrived as convicts, soldiers or seamen. In Britain they belonged to the lower orders of society who would normally expect to be employed as labourers, servants, unskilled workers, and a minority of tradesmen. Almost all of these men and women arrived in New South Wales with no material assets yet many became farmers, landowners, self-employed tradesmen, shopkeepers and publicans. Many employed workers of their own or were assigned government servants. They were thus able to support their children far more comfortably than would have been possible had they remained as the lower orders of British society. The daughters of these men and women grew to maturity in an entirely different environment from that familiar to their contemporaries in Britain, particularly with regard to employment. These girls became accustomed to working in their own homes, helping with the family trade, business or farm.[18] They did not face the necessity common to the daughters of the British working class of finding whatever work they could at as early an age as possible. It was not necessary for them to go out to work as young children in order to help their parents financially. Nor was it necessary, when they did seek work outside the family, to travel far from their native place in search of employment. In Britain work was frequently of a seasonal nature and this meant that young girls lived away from the care and protection of their parents.[19] The colonial daughters, therefore, were unfamiliar with the poverty and destitution, the search for work necessary for survival, which characterized the youth of many of their mothers. In these circumstances it was most unlikely that the colonial girls would have any economic necessity to 'deviate from the paths of virtue'. It is clear that the fears expressed by officials for their future moral welfare were based on the British characteristics of their mothers, not on the colonial life-styles of mothers and daughters.[20]

There were only exceptional cases in which the daughter of a convicted parent was herself charged with a criminal offence and, almost without exception, these cases had resulted from 'unhappy associations'. In every recorded case, one or both parents applied to the governor for mitigation of sentence. Mary Partridge was a bonded servant who wrote on behalf of her daughter, Ellen, who had been sentenced to transportation to Van Diemen's Land for perjury. She wrote that she and her daughter 'were anxious to be together again (and was certain that His Excellency) would be desirous of aiding so natural a wish'. Ellen was reunited with her mother and served her sentence as an assigned servant in the same household. A plea to Governor Brisbane from John Leighton, on behalf of his 'unfortunate child', expressed the reactions of a former convict to the transgressions of his daughter:

> Under circumstances the most afflicting and heart-rending ... Mary (the eldest of five children and *she* just attained her fifteenth year) has been tried at the Criminal Court now sitting, for forging and uttering an Order, purporting to be signed by William Heynes [writing illegible] Esquire and on conviction was sentenced to be Transported to a Period which terminated with her Life ... [her father] bows with most profound respect to the Decision and is therefore left without Hope, but in the application to the Fountain Head of Mercy prays ... allow the Unfortunate Exile to be considered a Government Servant to her afflicted Parents ... [this will] arrest Vice and promote Virtue ... long to see his Daughter a living example to the Rising Generation.

In this case the Judge-Advocate intervened and had the girl assigned to his own household.[21]

In childhood, the lives of the native-born girls were determined by the occupations and civil conditions of their parents. Very few were employed at an early age at work outside their family interests.[22] Some of the daughters of the more affluent settlers had private governesses. John Macarthur's daughter, Elizabeth, 'was too delicate to be left at school in England and returned with her father, accompanied by her governess, Miss Penelope Lucas'.[23] The daughters of John Blaxland were instructed in music by a convict governess who had been assigned to him. Other young ladies, the daughters of parents who had arrived convicted as well as those who had arrived free, attended one of the 'seminaries' which were advertised in the *Sydney Gazette*. These were conducted by genteel ladies prepared to 'instruct young members of [their] own sex in matters pertaining to morals, deportment, manners and education'. That these schools existed in the colony from at least as early as 1806 and increased in number[24] indicated that there was a need for such establishments. There is no remaining record of which young ladies received the benefits of this education but, from the Muster of 1806, it is evident that most of the colony's families were of convict origin, that some ex-convicts were among the wealthiest settlers, that there were insufficient young ladies from the families which had arrived free to support these schools. It is likely that the pupils included colonial-born, such as Diana Kable, Lucy Day, Elizabeth Dring, Jane Huxley, Elizabeth Pearce and Isabella Hume. Native-born girls from all social and economic classes, despite the convict origins of one or both parents, remained 'at home' until they married.

There were opportunities for the daughters of poorer settlers to receive at least the rudiments of an education.[25] This was the result of concern on the part of the early governors, in particular Phillip, Hunter and King. These men had not received specific Instructions from England regarding the education of colonial children, although all governors had been instructed to set land aside for the support of a schoolmaster. The Instructions to Governor Hunter specified that:

> ... a particular spot, in or near each [proposed] town be set aside for the building of a church, and 400 acres adjacent thereto allotted for the maintenance of a minister, and 200 for a schoolmaster.[26]

The reason for this reservation of land was to make certain that a conveniently located site for a future church and school would be available, despite spread of settlement. Lack of direction from the British government to establish schools and employ schoolmasters was in accordance with current practices in England, where the education of the children of the poor was in no way considered to be the responsibility of the British government, especially under the Tory ministry of William Pitt. On the contrary, it was believed by officials and by members of the middle and upper classes that the education of the children of the lower orders could not only lead to social turmoil but even to the possible breaking down or questioning of the existing hierarchy of class structure and privilege. Despite the theories of a minority, such as Adam Smith and his following who argued that the instruction of the poor, 'that inferior class of people', would help lessen the possibility of rebellion,[27] those in power in parliament agreed wholeheartedly with the opinions of such men as the Bishop of London that '. . . it was safest for both the Government and the religion of the country to let the lower classes remain in that state of ignorance in which nature had already placed them'. The House of Commons cheered the speech of Davies Giddy, a Tory member who warned the government that:

> However specious in theory the project might be, of giving education to the labouring classes of the poor, it would in effect, be found to be prejudicial to their morals and happiness; it would teach them to despise their lot in life ... it would render them factious and refractory ... it would enable them to read seditious pamphlets ... it would render them insolent to their superiors; and, in a few years, the result would be that the legislature would find it necessary to direct the strong arm of power towards them. . . .[28]

When it is considered that these opinions were representative of the governing class in Britain it is difficult to explain why the official British attitude towards the education of poor children in the colony changed. By 1806 Bligh was given specific instructions regarding the education of colonial children. He was the first governor of the colony to be instructed in this way.

I am to draw your particular attention towards forming some plan for the Education, and particularly the Religious Education of the Colony ... As considerable difficulty may occur in finding proper Persons within the Colony capable of instructing the Children of the Settlers, I have directed enquiries to be made and shall hold out encouragement to a few correct and intelligent Persons to proceed to the Colony for this Purpose.[29]

This plan was for the 'Children of the Settlers'. There are no means of determining whether this included ex-convict families although it is highly probable that this was the intention, considering the small number of free settlers in New South Wales at this time. There is no direct evidence but these Instructions, contrasting as they did with the theories and practice of the Tory government towards the children of the lower classes in contemporary England, may very possibly have resulted from the care and interest in the Rising Generation shown by King in his despatches and by the introduction of the Female Orphan School.[30] King's own Instructions had not mentioned education, although the need to enforce 'a due observance of religion' was emphasized.[31] This interest may also have been caused by the increasingly high proportion of children in the colony's population, an increase so great as to make official responsibility for the care and welfare of the colonial children an integral part of those measures necessary for the regulation and good order of the colony. This reflected the peculiar conditions of the early penal colony which necessitated the direct intervention of the governor in a number of spheres normally outside the scope of government.

Whatever may have been the reasoning behind the changing attitude of the British government towards the education of the children of Botany Bay, as indicated in Bligh's Instructions, the earlier disregard may not be interpreted as neglect. It was compatible both with Tory sentiments and with British assumptions as to the nature and purpose of the colony and of the structure of its population. If the education of the poor in England were regarded as dangerous for peaceful government it was of even greater importance in a penal colony that no policies be initiated which might lead to dissatisfaction, civil disorder or even open rebellion. In addition to this, most of the inhabitants of New South Wales, both convicted and free, came from the 'inferior' ranks of British society and their social rank in Britain was directly linked with lack of education. Education was an outward sign of social status and helped to preserve the status quo by ensuring a docile and obedient deference from the illiterate lower orders towards their literate betters. It is very likely that the question of the education of the children of Botany Bay simply did not occur to Pitt's ministers, nor to those subordinates who were responsible for the planning and maintenance of Botany Bay during its earliest years.

There were opportunities, however, for native-born girls as well as boys to receive at least the rudiments of an education. It was a characteristic peculiar to the colony that this was not confined to higher social and economic levels. Most importantly, had the families of these girls remained in Britain very few would have had even limited opportunities for any form of the most basic schooling. In the colony brothers and sisters attended local schools together. Parents were prepared to pay a small sum for the schooling of their daughters as well as for their sons. At the Newcastle School in 1816 one of the day pupils was six-year-old Catherine Hector, the daughter of a ticket-of-leave labourer and his convict wife; Catherine's two younger brothers, Henry and Timothy, later joined their sister at this school.[32]

Daughters from families which could be described as 'working class' sometimes took employment as domestic servants, usually from about the age of fourteen years until about the age of twenty, when most of them married and ceased to be employed.[33] 'Going into service', however, was not an invariable pattern, even among the daughters of labourers. In families where both parents were still alive, it was more usual for the daughters to remain at home in the rural families and to become employed if their parents were not landowners. Presumably, the rural daughters were needed to help with the farm. Sarah Chandler, who was aged nineteen in 1828, was the eldest daughter of William Chandler, a conditionally pardoned stonemason, and his wife who was freed by servitude. The Chandlers lived and worked in Cumberland Street, Sydney, with their two younger children, Samuel and Thomas; Sarah was employed as a servant in Market Street. Elizabeth Gorman, fifteen, and her young sister Catherine were both employed as servants at Parramatta, where their father Thomas, a conditionally pardoned wheelwright, lived with their mother, freed by servitude, and the two younger children. Colonial girls who remained with their parents on farming properties included Elizabeth Quinn, who lived with her father, a farmer who had arrived free, her mother, an ex-convict, and a younger brother on their farm at North Richmond. Seventeen-year-old Susan Galvin lived with her parents, both of whom had arrived as convicts, on their farm at Lower Minto; there were six younger children. Girls such as this had no experience of being 'employed women'. Normally, they remained on the parents' farm until marriage, which was usually with a son of a neighbouring landowner.[34] Jane Lyons of Wilberforce was the daughter of two former convicts and lived on her parents' farm with the four younger children until her marriage to Edward Robinson, also of Wilberforce and the son of ex-convict farmers. Jane and Edward settled on a grant of sixty acres at Wilberforce near their families.

In families where the mother had died or, less frequently, where the mother was widowed the eldest daughter remained at home. This was common among both rural and town families. Nineteen-year-old Elizabeth McCarthy lived with her ex-convict father and her two elder brothers on their farm at Evan. Mary Turnbull, aged seventeen, remained on the farm of her widowed father, Ralph, caring for her four younger brothers and sisters; sixteen-year-old Sarah Thornton, whose parents had arrived as free settlers, lived with her father, a publican in George Street, Sydney, after the death of her mother. Eighteen-year-old Sarah Pawley remained with her widowed mother, an ex-convict woman who ran a public house in Harrington Street, Sydney, with the help of her eldest son.

Most of the native-born girls who became employed as servants were orphans and had presumably sought employment as a means of livelihood. Some may have come from the Female Orphan Institution but there are no records to identify these girls. An analysis of all the native-born female servants of all ages listed in the 1828 Census showed that orphan girls were employed as servants from the age of six or seven years. Seven-year-old Clara McGowan was a servant at Parramatta while her nine-year-old brother, Alfred, was in the Male Orphan School at Cabramatta. Their widowed father, who had arrived in 1822 for fourteen years, was an assigned servant also at Parramatta. Six-year-old Mary Herring was an orphan employed by Anne Burrel, a landholder at Seven Hills who had arrived free in 1821. There were very few of these exceptionally young servants among the native-born and none under the age of eleven among those who had come free. In general the servant women who had come to the colony as free girls or women were far older than the native-born.[35] For the came-free women domestic service was employment which could continue after marriage; for the native-born it was an occupation for that period between marriage and leaving a parent's home. Employment as a way of life was not customary for the Currency Lasses. Had they been asked to define work it would, in most cases, have been seen as a natural part of the life of a daughter, wife or mother, working within a family group for the benefit of that family. In this way the life-styles of the native-born girls from the poorer families differed from those of the wealthier families in degree rather than in nature.

In 1828 only 148 of the 1161 native-born women aged between fifteen and forty years were employed women. Almost 80 per cent described themselves as servants, a further 16.8 per cent were housekeepers. There were three nursemaids, five laundresses, a cook, eight seamstresses, a mantua maker, a governess and an innkeeper. Thirteen were landholders, farmers or settlers, one was a dairywoman and another a stock-keeper. This compared with just over 200 came-free women in the same age group who were employed at a far wider variety of occupations: shopkeepers (five), school mistresses (two), pipe maker (one), office keeper (one), milliner (two). These women were, on an average, five to ten years older than the native-born. Among the came-free servants most were over, not under, twenty years of age.

The employment pattern of the native-born women and girls differed from that of those who had arrived as convicts. Among the same age group of ex-convict women approximately 216 were employed at paid occupations. The average age of these women was mid-thirties; few had received pardons and most had served their full sentences. Slightly more than one quarter of these women were employed as servants, a further 31 per cent described themselves as housekeepers and there were five house-servants and two housemaids. Most of the ex-convict women whose occupation was listed as housekeeper in the 1828 Census were considerably older than the native-born women. Mary Smith was eighty years old. Mary was a housekeeper for William Prosser, a seventy-year-old ex-convict miller who had arrived in New South Wales as a convict in 1790, a year before Mary Smith. Martha Blower was seventy-eight. An ex-convict woman who had arrived in 1806, she was a housekeeper at Prospect. There were three seventy-year-old ex-convict housekeepers and all of these women worked for men of approximately their own age who had arrived in the colony at approximately the same time. Elizabeth Hyland of Sydney had arrived on the *Neptune* and was housekeeper for John Limeburner, a first fleet convict. Elizabeth Griffiths had arrived in 1806 and was housekeeper at Lower Portland Head for Henry Hale, a seventy-two-year-old farmer who had arrived as a convict in 1791. Mary Jones of Pitt Town had arrived in 1790 and was housekeeper for William Walker, a labourer who had arrived as a convict in 1793. Considering the ages, civil condition and length of residence of the colony, it is more likely that these women were de facto wives rather than housekeepers and had continued to describe themselves in the terminology current in the early years of settlement.

In general, the occupations of the ex-convict working women reflected the backgrounds of these women in Britain. They also emphasized the differing experiences of the native-born women. In the colony there were far more laundresses and washerwomen among the ex-convict group than among the native-born. Those native-born women who followed this occupation usually did so to help support their children after the death of their husbands. Few native-born girls were employed as dairymaids, possibly because the rural native-born worked on their parents' properties until marriage. Ex-convict women, however, were employed as dairywomen or dairymaids. There was more similarity between the occupations followed by the ex-convict women and those who had come free.

The ticket-of-leave women were mainly unemployed, being assigned to their husbands. In this age group, the only employed ones were three servants, a shopkeeper and a housemaid. There was no difference between the occupations of the employed ex-convict women and the women still under sentence, although the latter were considerably younger. Of the 456 who were employed, almost 60 per cent were servants and a further 16 per cent were housemaids and house-servants, with eighteen described as house-keepers. The remainder were cooks (five), dairywomen (two), labourers (ten), washerwomen (four), laundresses (sixteen), mantua makers (two), needlewomen (four), nurses and nursemaids (fifteen), seamstresses (two), and one charwoman, a pastrycook, a shepherd, a shoe-binder and a shoe-maker.

Most of the occupations for working women in the colony, therefore, were filled by convict and ex-convict labour and women who worked to support themselves and, in a number of cases, their children. The convict women had no choice but to work; this was an integral part of their sentence, penal servitude. Both the came-free women and the ex-convict women who were employed worked for a far longer period than did the native-born. Work, to these British-born women, was a natural part of their lives, so many continued to be employed after marriage. Convict Esther Park was a nurse to James Lamb of the Hunter River, where her ex-convict husband was employed as a dairyman. Mary Ann Shillito, who had arrived as a convict in 1824, was cook to Sir J. Jamison at Evan, where her ex-convict husband was the butler. Anne Walker, free by servitude and a widow aged forty-nine, was employed as a servant by James Greenwood of Petersham; her fifteen-year-old native-born daughter, Sarah, was a servant in the same household. Mary

Spolin, who had arrived to serve a seven-year sentence in 1800, was a dairywoman to Dr Moran of Ravensfield, Wallis Plains, where her husband Brian, also an ex-convict, was overseer. Andrew and Agnes Cowen had come to the colony as free settlers in 1825; both were employed by John Dickson of Cooke as his overseer and dairywoman. Charles and Mary Beal had also come free in 1825, with their five children aged from three years to eleven; both Charles and Mary were employed as servants by the Australian Agricultural Company at Port Stephens. Elizabeth and John Creamer were both free by servitude and both worked for Peter Howell, of Sydney; Elizabeth was a servant and John a labourer.

The different attitudes of the native-born girls toward employment were the direct result of their upbringing in the colonial families, with employment being within the family and for the benefit of the family in most cases. Whatever their social origins were, few native-born women were employed for wages except during the brief period before early marriage or if they were widowed and thus became the supporters of the household. When this occurred those native-born women whose husbands had been farmers or landowners usually remained on the land. Those who needed to work for wages became employed as housekeepers, laundresses/washerwomen or seamstresses/dressmakers. The native-born who followed these occupations almost invariably had children to support. Sarah Crane, aged twenty-five, was one of the very few exceptions and may have been influenced by her husband who had come free to the colony as a shoe-maker. Sarah, despite having three small children, was a laundress. Elizabeth Johnstone was a more typical example. Aged thirty, Elizabeth was a widow with five children whose ages ranged from thirteen years to three. She supported her family by working as a laundress for Bridget Nowlan, an ex-convict dealer of Gloucester Street, Sydney. Sarah Byfield, aged thirty, worked as a dressmaker in Sydney to support two young children while her husband, Mark, was in Sydney Gaol. It was only when there was no alternative, when the native-born mother found herself the sole support of her family, usually owing to the death or imprisonment of her husband, that she became a working woman. Table 6/1 shows the occupations followed by these working women.

The fourteen native-born women who were landholders in their own right were mainly the wives of ticket-of-leave men who were ineligible to become landholders until their sentences were served or they were pardoned, or they were widows or, in one case, waiting for a husband to be released from imprisonment. At Lower Portland Head in 1828, twenty-five-year-old Mary Morris was the landholder, her husband, Price, twenty years her senior, was a ticket-of-leave man. They had five children aged nine years and under and lived on their thirty acres, twenty-five of which were cleared and cultivated. Ann Young, also of Lower Portland Head, was married to a government servant who had arrived in 1819 sentenced to fourteen years transportation. Ann's husband was assigned to her and they lived on her 100 acres. Sarah Harrex, aged thirty-nine, was a widow of Parramatta who had been left almost 2000 acres; she had five children, ranging in age from nineteen to one year. Ann Poer was a seventeen-year-old wife with a baby, who had been left

TABLE 6/1

Occupations of the native-born working women, 1828
Source: 1828 Census

Occupation	Total	Percentage of total employed
Servant	*88*	*59.4*
Housekeeper	*25*	*16.8*
Nursemaid	*3*	*2.2*
Laundress/washerwoman	*5*	*3.3*
Cook	*1*	*0.6*
Seamstress/dressmaker	*8*	*5.4*
Mantua maker	*1*	*0.6*
Governess	*1*	*0.6*
Innkeeper	*1*	*0.6*
Landholder	*9*	*6.6*
Farmer	*3*	*2.2*
Settler	*1*	*0.6*
Dairywoman	*1*	*0.6*
Stock-keeper	*1*	*0.6*
TOTAL	*148*	*12.7 (of B.C. females)*

Note: This is a summary only. See Appendix 6, Table 6.
For comparative analysis of 1814, see Appendix 6

to look after 500 acres at Seven Hills when her young native-born husband had been sentenced to Norfolk Island for two years for perjury. Her brother-in-law had tried unsuccessfully to have the sentence reduced, claiming the boy had perjured himself unknowingly to help a family friend.

Slightly less than 1000 of the native-born women were not employed women in 1828. Seven-hundred and six of the women were married, 205 were living with their parents, another thirteen with a brother or sister. Thirteen described themselves as householders—one of these was an eighteen-year-old married dressmaker—twenty-four simply stated they were 'living with' or 'at' and thirty-three were lodgers. Table 6/2 shows the age groups of those who were living with parents.

TABLE 6/2

Native-born women resident with parents, 1828
Source: 1828 Census

Age group 15–20	21–25	26–30	31–35	36–40	N.R.	Total
168	*26*	*4*			*7*	*205*

Note: This is a summary only. See Appendix 2

That more than half of the unmarried native-born females between the ages of fifteen and twenty years were living with their parents was quite contrary to the predictions of Samuel Marsden and Governor King. Almost 65 per cent of the fathers with whom the native-born women and girls were living had arrived in the colony as convicts. This alone would indicate that convict families were at least as stable and permanent as those of the 'free objects'.

The main occupation of these fathers was concerned with the land. Most were farmers. William Eaton and his wife Jane, both of whom were free by servitude, farmed at North Richmond, where they had 117 acres. Their three children lived with them: Ann, fifteen; George, nineteen; and John, seventeen. Other fathers were employed at a variety of occupations. The father of sixteen-year-old Eliza Fletcher was an ex-convict constable at Minto, where he lived with one of his sons, eighteen-year-old John, Eliza, and five-year-old Blanche. Eighteen-year-old Susannah Hughes and her sixteen-year-old sister, Margaret, were two of the nine children living with their parents at Richmond. The father, Matthew Hughes, had received an absolute pardon; his wife was born in the colony in 1791 and his occupation was schoolmaster. The father of Ann McGlin, nineteen, and Mary, eighteen, was an ex-convict labourer at Bringelly. Six of their children lived with their parents, both of whom were ex-convicts. John Yeoman had arrived in the colony in 1791 and his wife in 1792; four of their children were still with them in 1828. Their eldest son Robert, born in 1792, was a shoemaker at Wilberforce and his brother George, born in 1803, was a publican and farmer at Wallis Plains, living with another brother Richard, born in 1804. The Yeoman convict family, therefore, had been living in the colony with at least three of their children during that period when King and Marsden were lamenting the neglect of children by 'abandoned' convict parents. That the children in these and similar families remained living and working together clearly contradicts the contemporary view that these parents were worthless and indifferent to their children.

Although there was approximately the same number of boys as girls among the first generation, more sons than daughters remained with their parents. Compared with the 205 women, there were 340 men resident with one or both parents in 1828.[36] This larger proportion was influenced by the lower marriage rate among the native-born males and, compared with the native-born girls, the later age at which they generally married.[37] The civil condition of the mothers and fathers with whom the native-born males were living is shown in Table 6/3.

Table 6/3 shows that most of the native-born who remained with their parents were the sons of ex-convicts. Although a considerably larger proportion of the sons remained with their parents the same characteristic was evident among the native-born daughters. Most of the boys and girls who did remain at home were aged between fifteen and twenty. As a group, there were more native-born older than twenty-one living with parents in 1828 than there were among the same age group of came-free men and women. Table 6/4 compares the age groups for both came-free and native-born.

The occupations of the parents of the male native-born were similar to

TABLE 6/3

Native-born males resident with parents, 1828
Civil condition of parents

Source: *1828 Census*

Civil condition	Fathers	Mothers
Free by servitude	134 (39.4%)	137 (50.3%)
Conditional pardon	56 (16.4%)	4 (1.4%)
Absolute pardon	31 (9.1%)	1 (0.3%)
Ticket-of-leave	15 (4.4%)	5 (1.8%)
Government servant	4 (1.1%)	3 (1.1%)
Came free	83 (24.4%)	66 (24.2%)
Born in the colony	3 (0.8%)	27 (9.9%)
Free	4 (0.1%)	1 (0.3%)
N.R.	10 (2.9%)	28 (10.2%)
TOTAL	340	272

those of the parents of the females although there were more tradesmen
fathers among the males, suggesting that the father and son worked together.
There were, however, several differences between the occupations of the
fathers of the native-born, both boys and girls, and the fathers of the came-
free in the same age group. Although there were labourers and gardeners
among the came-free parents most were tradesmen and professionals, as well
as landholders. There was the Colonial Treasurer, clergymen, merchants,
millers, clerks, a ship's chandler, a distiller and a mathematical-instruments
maker. More than half of the fathers resident with native-born sons were
farmers or landholders but their occupations ranged from labourer (two),
scourger (one), to tradesman (thirty), dealer (one), shopkeeper (two),
coroner (one), publican (ten) and pensioner (three). The nature of the
fathers' occupations indicated that the native-born son sometimes remained
after marriage, his wife joining the parents' household. When this wife was
native-born she simply continued the family life she had lived with her own
parents, as in the case of Lucy Day, who had grown up on her parents' farm.
She had been born in 1802, the daughter of Samuel Day and his wife, Mary
Bishop. She married Thomas Acres, the son of Thomas and Ann Acres, and

TABLE 6/4

Comparative age groups for native-born and came free males resident with parents, 1828
Source: *1828 Census*

Civil condition	15–20	21–25	Age groups 26–30	31–35	36–40	N.R.	Total
Native-born	242	74	8	5		11	340
Came free	86	29	9	2			126

settled on their farm at Airds. Ann Acres continued to live with her son and daughter-in-law after the death of her husband. Lucy's own mother, who had arrived in the colony in 1790, lived in Sydney with her eldest son, Thomas, who was a boat-builder as his father had been, and his native-born wife and five children. William Rope, born in the colony in 1804, lived with his parents, both of whom had arrived in the colony as convicts in 1788, on their farm at Evan; he and his three small children remained there after the death of his wife. His elder brother John, born 1806, lived on a nearby farm with his native-born wife and four children. William's youngest daughter was called Elizabeth after her grandmother, who had been Elizabeth Powley, described by Ralph Clark in his *Journal* as one of the abandoned convict women who, on the voyage to Botany Bay, 'went through the bulkhead to the seaman' and became 'with child'. Clark had suggested that the seaman responsible be punished by being forced to marry Elizabeth and remain at Botany Bay. Three months after arrival, in May 1788, Elizabeth married Anthony Rope, having a wedding feast which featured 'sea-pie'. As this coincided with the disappearance of a goat belonging to Major Ross she and her husband were charged with its theft. They were found innocent, however, and this was the last appearance of Elizabeth Rope before any colonial court. However 'notorious' her ship-board conduct may have appeared to Lieutenant Clark, she remained a family woman in the colony, raising her own children and then those of her widowed son.

There were married native-born who took their wives to live with widowed fathers. Native-born Sarah Parsons was eighteen when she married cabinet-maker Edward Parsons, born in the colony in 1803, and went to live with him and his father in Castlereagh Street, Sydney. The father had come free in the New South Wales Corps and had remained when the Corps returned to England after the arrival of Macquarie. Parsons senior was a baker. Joseph Inch, on the other hand, left his family with his parents while he organized his property at Argyle. Joseph, a grazier and the native-born son of convict parents who had arrived in the colony in 1790, left his daughter, who had been called Jane Ann, the names of his mother and grandmother, at his father's house in Pitt Street, Sydney. Inch showed a strong sense of family for, in 1820, he arranged for his father's elderly mother to join the family in Sydney. She arrived in 1821, aged eighty-eight, and was still living with her son, grandson and great-grand-daughter in 1828, aged ninety-five. Although Inch was an exception there were a sufficient number of both native-born males and females who, after marriage, lived with or near parents and parents-in-law to show continuing family ties, especially among those families where parents had arrived as convicts.[38]

There were 706 married native-born females in 1828; that is, approximately 65 per cent of the first-generation females. This was far in excess of the number of married native-born males, 282, or barely 25 per cent. Few of the native-born males had married at an early age whereas the majority of the females were married by the age of twenty-five years. Table 6/5 shows the comparative ages of the married native-born.

A higher percentage of came-free males in the same age group was married in 1828 (35.7 per cent); most of these men were over thirty years old,

TABLE 6/5

Age groups of married native-born males and females, 1828
Source: 1828 Census

Native–born	Age groups						
	15–20	*21–25*	*26–30*	*31–35*	*36–40*	*N.R.*	*Total*
Females							
Percentage of age group	40.6	78.2	79.8	80.9	86.2	49.9	60.8
Males							
Percentage of age group	3	24	49	64	53	8	24.6

although 4.8 per cent under twenty were married, as compared with 3 per cent of the native-born.[39] The higher marriage rate among the came-free is very largely explained by the numbers who arrived with their wives and families, particularly in the mid to late 1820s. John Hallam and his wife Valetta, aged twenty-eight and twenty-two respectively, arrived in the colony early in 1828 with their infant son; both husband and wife were indentured servants to the Australian Agricultural Company.[40] Manuel Despraedo and his wife Ellen arrived together in 1816; in 1828 he was a servant and they lived in Sydney with their seven native-born children. John and Eliza Brogan arrived in 1823 with their daughter Jane; he was twenty-nine and Eliza was twenty-five. Brogan became a publican in King Street, where they lived with their six children.

Among the same age group of ex-convicts 19 per cent married, just under 5 per cent less than the native-born and 15 per cent less than the came-free. This figure does not allow for those ex-convicts who may have been widowed or married in Britain. Only two of the married ex-convicts were under the age of twenty; thirty-four were between the ages of twenty-one and twenty-five. More than half of the married ex-convicts were over thirty years old and represented approximately one quarter of the ex-convicts in this age group.

The marriage patterns of the native-born women showed, first, that the majority of these girls married men who had arrived as convicts and almost one third of whom were still serving sentences or were ticket-of-leave men; second, there was no recognizable pattern regarding the civil condition of parents and the civil condition of husbands; third, there was evidence of the influence of religion in the choice of a partner, particularly among those who described themselves as Roman Catholics and also among the daughters of clergymen, missionaries and chaplains; fourth, the choice of the native-born women appeared to be influenced by the occupation of the future husband. They preferred to marry a man with either property or skill, or both. Less than 10 per cent, for example, married unskilled workers; included in this category were the ticket-of-leave husbands. Many of the wives of these men held land in their own right.[41]

The marriage patterns of the native-born males bore little resemblance to those of their sisters. Almost three quarters of the Currency Lads married native-born girls; just under 14 per cent married girls who had come free, while only 8.1 per cent married girls who had arrived as convicts. Table 6/6 compares the civil condition of the husbands and wives of the native-born.

There are at least three explanations for the high percentage of native-born girls who married men who had arrived as convicts. First, those girls who were employed as domestic servants in colonial households worked with male assigned servants and labourers and this sometimes led to marriage. Mary Ann Wood was the daughter of Benjamin Crew and his 'wife', Sarah Wood. After the death of the father, Mary Ann's mother settled at Pitt Town and Mary Ann was employed as a servant at Campbelltown, where she met and married assigned servant, Thomas Avery, who had arrived in the colony in 1825. Avery secured a ticket-of-leave and they were married at St. Peter's, Campbelltown. By 1828 they had settled at Minto, where Thomas worked for himself as a saddler, supporting his wife and their five children. Richard Podmore was a shoemaker who had come with the New South Wales Corps in 1792 and remained to work at his trade when the Corps was recalled. In 1828 he was working for an ex-convict shoemaker, Alexander Hamilton, in York Street, Sydney. His wife had died; one son was a servant to Jame Mudie at Petersham, another was a tanner to William Cox at Windsor. His daughter, Sarah, was a servant employed at Liverpool, where she met her future husband, convict Joseph Spencer. Spencer had arrived in New South Wales in 1815, sentenced to transportation for life. Sarah, eleven years his junior, applied to the governor for permission to marry Spencer in 1825. When this was granted they settled at Liverpool. Spencer worked as a butcher for his wife, to whom he was assigned.

TABLE 6/6

Civil condition of wives and husbands of native-born, 1828

Source: 1828 Census

Civil condition of husband/wife	Wives of B.C. males	Husbands of B.C. females
Born in the colony	220	233
Came free	39	126
Free by servitude	12	155
Government servant	7	54
Ticket-of-leave	1	51
Absolute pardon		27
Conditional pardon	1	37
N.R.	2	11
TOTAL	282	694
TOTAL, convict origin	21	278

Note: the discrepancy between the number of native-born husbands and wives is caused by the absence of thirteen husbands from the Census: one, a prisoner at Norfolk Island, two 'at sea'; absences from the colony, in Van Diemen's Land and in England, were temporary.

Another way in which the native-born girls met convicts whom they later married was when these men were assigned to their parents. George Best, for example, was a wealthy sheep farmer who had arrived in the colony as a convict at the age of twenty-seven in 1791; he received an Absolute Pardon, married a convict woman, Martha Chamberlain, who had been sentenced to seven years transportation, and settled on his land grant at Seven Hills. While giving evidence to Bigge, Best told the Commissioner that one of his daughters had married his assigned servant, who was 'one of the better sort', and he and his sons had given them land and helped with the building of their house.[42]

When the prospective convict son-in-law was not assigned to the future father-in-law there is evidence of parental approval both from the written permission necessary for the wedding to take place and from attendance of parents at the wedding. Parents in these cases were not necessarily convicts themselves. Matthew Pearce, a soldier in the New South Wales Corps, had arrived in the colony with his free wife Martha in 1790. They had at least four native-born children, three of whom were still living with them on their farm at Seven Hills in 1828. Their eldest daughter, Elizabeth Sophia, married with their permission a prisoner of the Crown, James Bates. By 1828 James was freed by servitude and working for himself as a nailor at Parramatta, supporting his wife and four children.

The third way in which native-born girls met future convict husbands was the way in which most of the husbands of all civil conditions were met; that is, by proximity of residence. Maria Everingham was living at Sackville Reach with her widowed ex-convict mother when she applied to the governor for permission to marry government servant Thomas Cotton, a prisoner for life who had arrived in the colony in 1818. Her application described Cotton as a schoolmaster at Sackville Reach, 'of strictly correct character'. When they were married with the permission of her mother Cotton was thirty-eight and Maria seventeen. By 1828 Cotton described himself as 'free' and was employed as a schoolmaster at Portland Head, where Maria's brothers were farmers. Another case in which a native-born girl had married a convict older than herself was Catherine Soar, whose parents had a farm at Pitt Town. Catherine, with their permission, married neighbouring farmer John Bootle, an ex-convict more than twenty years her senior. They remained at Pitt Town where, by 1828, they owned a total of 521 acres. They had seven children who lived with them as did Catherine's brother John, whom her husband employed as a labourer.

Not all the marriages between convicts and native-born girls were successful. One such case was that of Charlotte Cubitt, daughter of Daniel Cubitt, the Master of the Guard of the Row Boat, and Mary Ann Cook, both of whom had arrived convicted. Charlotte was one of a large family. She was nineteen years old in 1820 when she married Thomas Currey, a 'gardiner' aged twenty-eight who was serving a fourteen-year sentence; he had arrived in the colony in 1815. Charlotte was married at St. Phillip's with the consent of her parents; her brother John was her witness. Two years later Charlotte sent the following Memorial to Governor Brisbane:

Born in the Colony, daughter of Daniel Cubitt, Master of the Row Guard Boat, wife of the unhappy Thomas Currey ... under sentence of death for his offence ... asks for clemency ... this awful warning will reform him from evil-doing ... restore him to society and his two infant babes. ...[43]

There is no record of a reprieve. One of the two infants, George, born in 1822, died at eight weeks of age; Charlotte later appeared on a Ship's Muster as a passenger to Van Diemen's Land but had returned to Sydney by 1828 and was living near her parents as Charlotte Cubitt.[44]

The problems were not always caused by the convict partners. The convict husband of native-born Mary Onslow found it necessary to petition Governor Brisbane to prevent the continual interference of Mary's parents in their marriage. George Onslow, a comb-maker, had arrived as a convict in 1821 and two years later married sixteen-year-old Mary McEvoy. That same year Onslow wrote to Brisbane:

> ... [he and his wife] had lived together for two months, occupying a house in Pitt Street belonging to Mrs Laycock ... about six weeks ago, his wife left him without any provocation ... Memorialist believes she is led astray by the advice of some ill-informed persons ... Onslow procures an honest livelihood by his trade.

An unsigned document from an official in the Colonial Secretary's Office had added that 'the father and mother were sent for and desired to settle the family differences which they promised to do'. Mary, however, died less than three years later and the coroner's verdict on her death, 'Died from a Visitation of God', implied that she was intoxicated at the time.[45] Four months later Onslow, undeterred, married another sixteen-year-old native-born girl, Eliza Davis, again with the consent of her parents. There is no record of the success or failure of that marriage; the last reference to George Onslow is in the 1828 Census; he described himself as a landholder at Botany, where he lived with his wife, Eliza.

David Foley was a ticket-of-leave wheelwright when he wrote to the governor 'on the subject of my enlargement [sic]'. He informed the governor that, if he were not to be permitted to leave the colony, he would marry 'but will not if the contrary be the case'. Six years later he was still a ticket-of-leave man, married to a native-born girl; they had three children and owned 700 acres of land. It would appear that Foley, sentenced to transportation for life, had determined to make the best of the colonial situation. Serving his sentence as a landholder among his own family must have appeared preferable to the alternative which he would have faced in England had he not been transported.

There was no recognizable pattern which could be established regarding the civil condition of the parents and the civil condition of the husbands of the native-born.[46] Discrimination against the daughters of the convicts did, of course, exist among the higher levels of free society and was, at times, apparent in unexpected places. The Reverend Henry Fulton, despite his own trial and conviction for felony, did not appear to regard himself in the same category as the convicts of Botany Bay.[47] In February 1809 Fulton wrote to Castlereagh concerning the insurrection during the administration of Governor Bligh. He included a charge against Doctor Harris and Major Johnston of 'encouraging a Lieutenant of His Majesty's Ship, *Porpoise*, to marry a lady whose mother was a convict, and were present at the marriage, though they would not suffer an officer of the New South Wales Corps to do the same'.[48] The explanation for Fulton's attitude towards those of convict descent was based on his educated and 'respectable' background, family and upbringing. On this basis he shared the respectable contemporary view that the description 'convict' was equated with infamous characteristics. In this particular instance it would appear that Fulton considered the lady in question a highly improper match for one of His Majesty's naval lieutenants.

Not all the officers and gentlemen in the colony shared Fulton's concern for convict parentage in their wives. Captain John Piper had showed little reluctance in marrying a convict's daughter. John Henry Black, Esq., the son of a master mariner, was an accountant to Simeon Lord; he married Louisa Skinner, the daughter of a widowed convict woman Louisa Skinner and Charles Armitage. Francis Oakes married Rebecca Small, the daughter of two convicts. There were, too, colonial gentlemen who themselves married convict women and saw their daughters marry 'gentlemen'. Andrew Hamilton Hume, for example, married convict Elizabeth More Kennedy and their daughter, Isabella, married George Barber 'of the same District', who was later described as a 'gentleman'. Surgeon Arndell married convict Elizabeth Dalton and their daughters were brought up in a manner befitting the daughters of a wealthy and respectable land-owning family. In these and similar cases there were no apparent drawbacks to being the daughters of women who had been transported to New South Wales as punishment for major crimes committed in Britain.

In a colony with such a relatively small population as New South Wales it was not surprising that friendships endured among those men and women who had come from the same British towns or parishes, who had been convicted together or who had arrived on the same ship. This was especially noticeable during that period when settlement was confined to the Cumberland Plain; that is, during the childhood of the native-born. The sons and daughters of these early settlers, both those who had arrived as convicts and those who had arrived free, frequently intermarried and then remained living in the same district as their parents, thus giving more stability to the emerging family patterns in the colony. These marriages, resulting from parental friendships, were not confined to the rural or land-owning native-born families.[49] There were frequent examples of marriages between the children of parents who were employed together or who worked at similar or allied trades.[50] Most of these marriages, both in the towns and the rural areas, were between boys and girls who had grown up together, sharing the same experiences during the first years of settlement. They could, therefore, be described as the first 'Australian' families for neither native-born partner had any experience of life-styles other than those in the penal colony nor any first-hand knowledge of society or of family values and attitudes other than those with which they themselves had grown to maturity.

These first native families extended beyond those in which the partners had been brought up. In the case of the first generation few of the children had relatives in the colony other than their own parents and brothers and sisters. Their own children, however, grew up in the extended family of grandparents, uncles, aunts and cousins. The patterns of family life, begun with the first generation and their parents, continued with the second generation of children so that the attitudes of the convict and free parents during the first forty years of white settlement influenced the characteristics of the Australian family.

Examples of marriages such as those previously mentioned may be found in almost all of the marriages between native-born girls and boys during the first forty years.[51] The Beckett and Best families were typical. James Beckett had arrived in the colony in 1790, the year before George Best; both had married convict women and both had become successful settlers after sentence was served. Mary Beckett, born in 1801, had lived with her parents at Seven Hills; she married Thomas Best of Castle Hill, born in 1798. Elizabeth Powell was the daughter of free parents, ex-seaman settler Edward Powell and his wife, the former Elizabeth Fish; she married Richard Driver, the son of free landholder John Driver. Ann Everingham, born in 1802, was the daughter of convict settlers at Sackville Reach; her father, Matthew, had held land there since 1806. Ann married John Chaceling, whose convict parents had owned thirty acres at Portland Head in 1806. Ann and John settled on a fifty-five acre farm at Lower Portland Head after their marriage. Two of Ann's sisters-in-law married her brothers and these two families also settled on farms in the Portland Head district. A third Everingham daughter, Louisa, married George Turnball, a son of an ex-New South Wales Corps settler. The father had arrived in 1791, three years after Everingham senior. Louisa and George also settled at Portland Head, where George farmed 100 acres.

Other examples include Ann Bloodsworth, born 1798, the daughter of convicts James Bloodsworth and Sarah Bellamy, who had both arrived in 1788. Ann married Thomas Bray, whose father had arrived with the New South Wales Corps; he had eventually settled at Concord with his ex-convict wife and their family. Native-born Ann and Thomas Bray were living on the family property at Concord in 1828. Maria Field, also the daughter of an ex-New South Wales Corps private, grew up on her parents' farm at Evan and married the son of ex-convict settlers Elizabeth and Anthony Rope, also of Evan. Rope's eldest daughter Mary, born in 1791, had married a convict who had been assigned to her father. When her husband received a conditional pardon they settled on a farm at Evan. The father of Esther Smallwood was an ex-convict settler at Pitt Town. Esther married William Grono, the son of free settlers and also of Pitt Town; Esther and William remained as farmers in the district in which they had been raised. Elizabeth Nowland, the daughter of ex-convicts who had settled at Windsor, married the son of neighbouring settlers and remained with her husband, who was a wheelwright and landowner at Windsor.

These marriage patterns, particularly evident among the sons and daughters of the rural families, show stability among the early colonial settlers. This was especially marked among the earliest families, both convict and free, who settled within the Cumberland Plain. This stability began with the marriage or partnership of the parents and was reinforced by the inter-marriage of children from the same districts. One of the chief results was the reluctance of the first generation to leave home and journey to new lands as they were opened for settlement.[52] Although the extension of settlement north to the Hunter, south to Jervis Bay and west beyond the mountains began at a time when the native-born were of an age to apply for land, they showed a marked preference for remaining in the familiar districts where many of their parents still lived. The group most likely to move away from family land holdings were those native-born girls who married ex-convicts or recently arrived free settlers. These women frequently went with their husbands to the outer settlements although even here the tendency was to remain within the Cumberland Plain. Typical were the native-born wives of landholders at Goulburn Plains in 1828; they were the wives of men who had come to the colony as free settlers, not the native-born.

The marriage patterns for the native-born men were similar to those of their sisters. Most of the native-born landholders had their properties in the districts of Portland and Lower Portland Head, at Parramatta, Richmond, Windsor, Wilberforce, Cornwallis, Evan and Pitt Town. Native-born land-holders as a group included more married men than any other occupational group in 1828. In Windsor all the native-born landholders were married; 83 per cent of those in Portland Head and Lower Portland Head, 80 per cent at Even and approximately 60 per cent of those at Wilberforce, Pitt Town and Cornwallis.[53] Twenty-three of the twenty-six wives at Portland Head and Lower Portland Head were native-born, ten of the fourteen at Richmond, six of the eight at Windsor, all fifteen at Wilberforce, eight of the ten at Pitt Town, and eleven of the twelve at Cornwallis. Seven male native-born owned land at the Upper Hunter River District but none of these were married; four were landholders at Argyle and two of these were married, one to a woman who had come free and the other to an ex-convict. At Patricks Plains, three of the seven landholders were married, two to a native-born and one to a came-free woman. Those who had married native-born women were Joseph Dargon, born in 1802, and Philip Thorley, born in 1800. Thorley's father, William, had been a landholder with 100 acres at Richmond in 1806 and Dargon was also the son of a free landholder.

Those native-born sons who sought land in the newer settlements were the exceptions among the first generation. They were also less likely to be married and their wives, when they did marry, were more often women who had come free to the colony rather than native-born women. The expected attitude of the Currency Lasses to 'the Bush' was expressed in a letter by Betsey Bandicoot, published in the *Australian* in 1827. This was an answer to unfavourable comments published in the *Sydney Gazette* in a letter to the editor, purportedly written by a recently arrived immigrant, Miss Fanny Flirt. Betsey wrote of the joys of galloping without a saddle, of running barefoot, of swimming, of caring for her Bill.[54] There were few of Betsey's sisters, however, who showed such enthusiasm for the pioneering life. On the basis of the districts in which they chose to reside in 1828 and the occupations of the men they chose as husbands, the first generation of Currency Lasses showed a marked preference for the familiarity of family surroundings rather than any desire to venture to the outer settlements. An analysis of the parentage of the native-born women and the districts in which they had spent their childhood shows clearly that there was little movement away from their familiar surroundings.

This preference was shared by most of the women who lived in New South Wales. A comparison of the places of residence of all colonial women in 1820, before there was any significant settlement beyond the Cumberland Plain, with the places of residence in 1828 showed that most of the came-free and freed women in New South Wales remained living in Sydney and the surrounding districts or at Parramatta and its environs.[55] By 1828 almost half of all the women who had come free, a third of all the native-born, slightly less than a third of the ex-convicts, and approximately the same proportion of convicts, lived in Sydney and the neighbouring districts.[56] The second largest concentration of women in the colony was at Parramatta. This was influenced by the location of the Female Factory and the numbers of convict women who were sent there to await assignment after their arrival in New South Wales.[57] At Windsor there were more native-born women than women from any other civil condition, which reflected the influence of parental landholdings.[58] The highest number of came-free women was at Hunters River and Port Stephens, where many were indentured with their husbands to the Australian Agricultural Company, having travelled from England for this specific purpose.[59] At Airds and Appin native-born women were in the majority,[60] while at Liverpool, ex-convict women predominated.[61] In the outer settlements there were comparatively few women from any civil condition and the native-born were invariably fewer than any other free group. In Bathurst, for example, where there was the largest number of women outside the Cumberland Plain: fifty-one had come free, thirty-one were native-born. At Argyle and St. Vincent, there were thirty-six who had come free, thirty-one native-born, thirty-two ex-convicts and twenty-five convicts. The reasons for settlement in these outer areas were linked directly with the occupations of the husbands of the free women, with assigned service for the convicts.[62]

As James Waldersee noted in his study, *Catholic Society in New South Wales*, there was a relatively high proportion of Irish Catholics in the Airds–Appin–Campbelltown region in 1828 and, consequently, a higher proportion of colonial born.[63] In this district, and among the daughters of Catholic settlers throughout New South Wales, religion played some part in their choice of husbands but this was not invariably so.[64] By 1828 there were 189 first-generation women and 185 men who described themselves as Catholic in the 1828 Census. This was despite the lack of priest or church during their childhood and adolescence, with the exception of the brief ministry of Father Dixson. The only way by which these children could have learned about Catholicism was from their parents. That they called themselves Catholics clearly associated their choice with that of their parents. If this statement of religious persuasion were a means of establishing an identity rather than an affirmation of actual religious beliefs, then that identity was based on their associations with their parents, most of whom had been transported from Ireland or had been convicted in England after journeying there in search of work.

There was some attempt made by the more literate of the transported Irish men and women to teach the younger generation the principles of their faith; this was, however, severely limited. There was Francis Kenny, a transported Irish rebel, who had for a short time conducted a school in the Rocks area of Sydney for the particular benefit of Catholic children. Ambrose Fitzpatrick, who was a child in Sydney at this time, later wrote in his recollections of the efforts to instruct the children of Catholic parents in their own religion.[65] Fitzpatrick's own father had been transported after the Irish Rebellion and his mother, a former schoolmistress from Dublin, had brought young Ambrose and his elder brother from Ireland to join their father at Botany Bay. Fitzpatrick recollected that his mother would not permit either himself or his brother to attend the schools which were run by the government. Her reason was that she recalled the effects on the local children in Ireland when the British Government had attempted to teach their own religious principles in the Government Irish Schools. Fitzpatrick wrote:

> She therefore determined at all and any risks to keep her children where their faith might not be tampered with, and as there were none but Protestant Schools in those days, she was under the necessity of keeping us at home and teaching us herself and as religion was in her opinion of paramount importance, she taught us not only our Catechism and Church services, but also how to sing hymns and vespers.[66]

The social origins of most of the Irish women who were transported to New South Wales as convicts[67] or who rejoined convict husbands made it unlikely that many were as literate as Fitzpatrick's mother or even had the ability to read or write.[68] It is reasonable to assume, however, that these women would have considered it their obligation to instruct their children in their own religion, especially as many were from the rural areas of Ireland and would have associated the religion of the colonial governors and magistrates with that of the English 'usurpers'. An unfortunate result of the illiteracy of most of these women was that there are few written records of their reactions to their exile in a land devoid of any of the outward signs of their religion. One of the few remaining examples of this reaction was a letter to Phillip, signed by a small group of Catholic marines and convicts, including marine's wife Marie MacDonald. They petitioned the governor for permission to have the services of a priest of their own religion, so that their children could be baptized and they could be married and buried according to the rites of their own church. This request was refused.[69]

Another example is to be found in the recollections of Fitzpatrick, who described the reactions of one Catholic woman:

> Shortly after the deportation of Father Flynn, Hannibal Macarthur who was then the great man of Parramatta, met a Catholic man, and asked him why his children did not attend the Sunday School. The man replied that

his wife was a free woman and would not allow him to interfere with the children. 'Very well', said Mr. Macarthur, 'no odds; if your children are not at Sunday School next Sunday, you may expect my severe displeasure.' The man went home and told his wife all that had passed, but she was free, and started off with her children to Sydney, where she reared them all as strict Catholics which they still remain.[70]

Among the native-born females slightly more Catholics than non-Catholics were married: 63.8 per cent compared with 61 per cent. Most of these Catholic marriages had taken place after the arrival of Father Therry. Therry had the official permission of the British government to celebrate marriages between Catholic partners in the colony according to the rites of the Catholic church. Macquarie accepted the legality of these marriages when performed by accredited Catholic chaplains but he did point out to Fathers Therry and Conolly in 1820 that such marriages would not have been legal in contemporary England.[71] Religion, however, did not increase the marriage rate among the first generation. Although slightly more Catholic women married than non-Catholic, almost the same proportion of Catholic and non-Catholic males was married in 1828. One characteristic was that the majority of the Catholic husbands of the native-born females had arrived in the colony as convicts. Although there is no supporting evidence it is probable that these men chose Catholic brides. This characteristic was not repeated among the native-born Catholic men. Here, the Catholic wives were mainly native-born. The explanation for this was that the majority of first-generation men who were married by 1828 were farmers, landholders or worked on family land. All native-born men in these occupational groups, from all religious denominations, tended to marry local girls. Table 6/7 illustrates the proportions among the religious denominations of the wives and husbands of the native-born.

Catherine Kennedy is an example of a native-born girl raised in a Catholic household who married a Catholic convict. Catherine was the daughter of

TABLE 6/7

Marriage partners of the native-born, 1828
Civil condition and religious groups

Source: *1828 Census*

Native-born	Civil condition of marriage partners								
	B.C.	C.F.	F.S.	G.S.	T.L.	C.P.	A.P.	F.	N.R.
Protestants									
Wives	189	113	109	37	36	28	18	12	7
Husbands	174	31	10	4	1	1			1
Catholics									
Wives	38	9	37	13	5	9	8		3
Husbands	38	5	1	3					

Donald Kennedy, a freed-by-servitude farmer at Evan. Kennedy had arrived in 1790. In 1828 he was living with five of his children, including his two eldest sons, born in 1800 and 1804, on his farm at Evan. His daughter Catherine, born in 1794, had married Patrick McCann, who had arrived as a convict five years earlier. They settled on a farm at Evan, near Catherine's parents. By 1828 they had eight children, all described as Catholic in the Census. The eldest daughter was named Ann after Catherine's ex-convict mother, one son was named Donald for the father and another Patrick for the husband. These Catholics had been married by a clergyman of the Church of England at Parramatta. As this was before the arrival of Father Therry, it may have been that they preferred to be 'legally' married.

Another example was the family of William Silk. Sentenced to transportation for life, William was joined in 1791 by his free wife and their infant son, Thomas. They eventually settled on a farm at Prospect, William receiving a ticket-of-leave and being assigned to his wife. By 1828 William, then a widower and still holding a ticket-of-leave, was living on his farm at Prospect. Both his sons, Patrick and Thomas, had married native-born girls, and were farmers, one at Windsor, the other at Richmond. Thomas and his wife Sarah, formerly Sarah Roberts, called their eldest son William after his grandfather, showing no repugnance to the fact that he was a convict.

In cases when there was a marriage between a Catholic and a Protestant, the children of that marriage did not necessarily follow the religion of the father or of the Catholic partner. Hugh O'Donnell and his wife, Mary, had settled near Parramatta. Hugh, native-born, described himself as a Catholic and his wife, who had come free, as a Protestant. All their children were listed in the 1828 Census as Protestants. Native-born Mary Rope, a Protestant, married Catholic convict John Ryan; their seven children were described as Catholics.

As many of the native-born girls who married native-born males moved from the home of their parents to that of their husbands' parents, both religion and occupation could be expected to influence the choice of marriage partner. Occupation, however, rather than religion, dominated the choice of husband and the nature of the life-style of the married Currency Lasses. As has been shown, many married farmers and landholders and were themselves the daughters of farmers; their life-stlyes changed very little with marriage except that, in time, they became the mistresses of their own homes and farms and responsible for the care and upbringing of their children. In the case of those who married tradesmen, and this was the second largest occupational group of the husbands, the girls were frequently the daughters of tradesmen or had been raised in the towns of Sydney and Parramatta. Most of these husbands had arrived as convicts, proportionately fewer of the native-born skilled workers being married men. Out of the 151 native-born women who married within this occupational group only forty-six married colonial-born. In almost all of these cases, a clear link was evident between the occupation of the husband and the occupation of the father or brothers. There was, in addition, evidence from the marriage certificates which indicated the friendships that had developed among the colonial 'trade' families had resulted in intermarriage. A typical case was that of Mary Ann

Stubbs who married native-born Charles James Brackenreg, described on the marriage certificate as a carpenter and joiner. Both Brackenreg and Mary Ann were the children of men who had arrived in the colony during the first four years of settlement, Stubbs as a convict, Brackenreg as a private in the New South Wales Corps. Both settled in the Parramatta distict. The witnesses at the wedding of their children were native-born Thomas Day, boat-builder, and his wife Susannah, the elder daughter of Stubbs. Another example of marriages between the children of men who had arrived at approximately the same time, settled in the same districts and followed similar or allied trades, was that of George Peat, shipwright, born in the colony in 1792, and Frances Ternan, born in 1808. Peat was a widower and married Frances with the consent of her mother Margaret, who had come to the colony in 1790 with her husband, a private in the New South Wales Corps. The mother was a witness at the wedding. The second witness was native-born carpenter George Wilson, who had married Frances' sister the previous year. Hannah Mansfield, born in Sydney, married native-born Sydney carpenter James Wallbourn. Their witnesses were native-born carpenter George Bloodsworth and Eliza Chipp, daughter of a 1788 marine. As Bloodsworth and Wallbourn had both served apprenticeships at about the same time it is probable that their friendship had begun in childhood, both having grown up in Sydney families.

Occupational links were found in marriages among native-born women and seamen or ships' tradesmen. Elizabeth, the daughter of Mrs Ann Williams of Sydney, who had come to the colony in 1800 to rejoin a convicted husband, married a ship's cooper, George Shuker; three years later, Elizabeth was a witness to the marriage of her sister to a mariner, William Howe; in that same year, Ann Howe was witness to the wedding of native-born Hannah Dark to another mariner, Richard Buckle.

There was little pattern which could be traced in the marriages of the native-born girls to men who were convicts and to men who had arrived free. The only recurring characteristics were that most of the husbands were either tradesmen with some skills or, eventually, became farmers and landowners. There was evidence of proximity, the daughters of rural families marrying the came-free men from neighbouring properties or the assigned servants of their fathers, and the daughters who had been raised in Sydney marrying tradesmen or workers who were employed in that town. There were, however, a number of marriages between native-born and unskilled workers although these were in the minority and, in such cases, the husbands were not necessarily convicts or ex-convicts but men who had come free. Elizabeth Sims, who had been born in the colony in 1810, married labourer James Green, who had arrived free in 1822 and was still described as a labourer in 1828. Green may have worked for boat-builder Thomas Day, who was a witness at the wedding. Ann Shannon, born in 1803, was married by Father Therry in 1826 to convict labourer Lawrence Kennedy.

At the other end of the economic scale there were marriages to men with extensive landholdings. Some of these men had arrived as convicted felons, others had come free. Mary Higgins, native-born, had married convict Thomas Seymour who had been assigned to her father, landholder Robert

Higgins. Seymour was granted a ticket-of-leave and by 1828 was farming 570 acres. Elizabeth Huon married extensive landowner William Mitchell. They were married by Father Therry. There was the same variety in economic standing among the tradesman husbands from both civil conditions, convict and free. Charlotte Hutchinson married a skilled craftsman, silversmith Alexander Dick, at the Scots Church, Sydney. Mary Tyrrell married convict mason William Parrott, with her parents as witnesses. Elizabeth Oakes married the surveyor for the Australian Agricultural Company; Dorinda Cozier married came-free ship-owner Thomas Street; Sophia Bishop married a free millwright, Alexander Dykes; Lydia Bates, daughter of a shipwright, married a came-free shoemaker; Mary Elliott married a came-free carpenter. Sarah Rope married a convict constable, as did Elizabeth Alcorn.

Few of the married native-born were identified as orphans, except where the consent of a guardian was given. Louisa Skinner, who was the ward of Simeon Lord, married with Lord's consent John Henry Black, a clerk at the Bank of New South Wales. Caroline Green was an exception. Born in the colony in 1811, she had been cared for in the Female Orphan Institution and was married to Everitt Summons, who had come free in 1825, with 'the Consent of the Committee of the School Corporation of Clergy'. Summons was an indentured servant to the Australian Agricultural Company. In general, the marriage certificates of the native-born women were further evidence of the continuing family ties between the first generation and their parents, both the bond and the free. Men who had arrived as convicts, remained in the colony as settlers and established and supported families gave their consent to the marriage of their daughters. Such men included landowners George Best, Anthony Rope, Matthew Everingham, James Ruse, Robert Higgins; tradesmen William Tyrrell, James Wallbourne, Thomas Pearson, Daniel Cubbitt, James Smallwood; merchants and shipowners Henry Kable, Joseph Underwood, Simeon Lord; publicans Issac Moss, Timothy Lacey, James Dargon; overseer William Morgan; labourer Thomas Murphy. All of these men had arrived convicted before 1800 and had reared families during the administrations of Governors Hunter, King, Bligh and Macquarie.

The native-born women, therefore, were influential in shaping the type of female society which was emerging in New South Wales during the first forty years of white settlement. Their own attitudes towards marriage and family life had been formed by their own experiences as children growing up in a penal colony, inhabited mainly by convicts and ex-convicts. To these girls, however, the peculiar and unique social structure of their homeland was not abnormal for they had no knowledge of any other form of society against which it could be measured. That most of the mothers and many of the fathers had arrived as infamous felons, outcasts of British society, meant little to them because they were accustomed to seeing men and women from all walks of life who had been convicted in Britain. They themselves did not hesitate to marry convicts or former convicts and did so with the consent of their own parents. Their choice was directed not by the British reputation and experiences of their prospective husbands but by colonial standards, attitudes and expectations, linked with the known opportunities which were then available to men from all civil conditions.

These 'First Matildas' were accustomed to being supported in their own homes by their parents. They were unfamiliar with the need which existed in contemporary Britain for girls of their social origins to find employment of any kind from as early an age as possible. They did not, therefore, expect to become 'working women' for the greater part of their adult life. Those who did seek employment outside the home were mainly the 'town' girls whose parents lived and worked in Sydney, Parramatta, Liverpool or Windsor. These girls worked as servants, but only until their marriage. To the colonial women, work was within the family, for the benefit of the family. In the same manner in which they had worked in the homes, shops and farms of their own parents they expected to work with their own husbands or their husbands' families. In this way the colonial family life which took shape with the first generation, first as children, then as wives, differed from that in contemporary Britain among women of the same class origins. The families of the first generation exceeded and reinforced the characteristics of the first white settlers, for the majority of these men and women had arrived as technically single people, without relatives of any kind. Even the first free families, the marines, the soldiers, the officials, the free settlers, were limited to mother, father and children. The native-born girls and boys, however, kept in touch with brothers and sisters and so families expanded. The links were strengthened by the intermarriages of brothers to sisters-in-law, of sisters to brothers-in-law. This stability was further increased by marriages between the children of men and women who had arrived in New South Wales at about the same time, had worked at similar occupations, had lived in the same districts. In this way, a pattern of family life emerged, based on the nature and experiences of the penal colony. It was a pattern which exceeded the nature of family relationships familiar to the first settlers but it was to develop as the basic characteristic of colonial society. Above all, it was a pattern which grew from the experiences and expectations of the 'First Matildas'.

CHAPTER SEVEN

THE LADS OF INDUSTRIOUS HABITS

'In this Colony the best possible description of Setlers [*sic*] would be the white Native-born Children . . .'

Edward Eagar to Commissioner Bigge,
19 October 1819.

In the 1828 Census of New South Wales almost 25 per cent of the adult male native-born listed land they either owned or rented. Three quarters described themselves as farmers, landholders or graziers. A further 17 per cent did not give an occupation directly concerned with the cultivation of their land; 4 per cent gave no occupation and 2 per cent were tenant farmers. The remainder of these landowners simply stated that they did own land but gave no details of the size of the holding or the location.[1] That only about one in four did own land appears to contradict the assumptions of contemporary commentators.

Commissioner Bigge had linked the supposed preference for 'agricultural pursuits' with a reluctance of the colonial born to work at any occupation which was traditionally filled by convict labour. Bigge held the opinion that the native-born were the sons of the convicts, the lower ranks of colonial society. He further believed that they preferred 'a miserable existence upon the land granted to their parents to that of serving as labourers and overseers on the farms of the more opulent inhabitants'.[2] Bigge did not reconcile this characteristic with the current belief that these same young men had been abandoned by their vile and depraved convict parents who, in turn, had been rejected by their children.

William Charles Wentworth expressed forcibly his opinion that the native-born desired no other occupation than that of farmer or landholder. In his 'Address of Welcome to Governor Darling', Wentworth reminded the newly-arrived Governor that this 'race of men' was neglected by both British authorities and the local administration. He claimed that the native-born rightly felt that the free immigrants received preferential treatment when applying for grants of land. Darling was told that:

> ... Grants of Land, which they [the native born] consider their own as it were by natural inheritance ... they have seen of late years, through the recommendation of the late Commissioner of Inquiry, lavishly bestowed upon Strangers ...[3]

It was this discrimination, Wentworth argued, which was causing discontent among the native-born. This opinion may have been coloured by Wentworth's antagonism to Bigge, and accentuated by his support of Governor Macquarie and his administration and the long friendship which had existed between Macquarie and Wentworth and his father D'arcy.[4]

In a leading article published in the *Australian* in 1826 Wentworth again linked this neglect of the rights of the native-born with the contrasting favouritism which he claimed was shown to the immigrant:

Every young man in the Colony ought to be able to look forward with certainty to the prospect of having his own farm; of being able to settle upon it, as soon as he arrives at years of maturity. He can, on leaving his parental roof, commence in the world with much less capital, and yet with a greater prospect of success than the emigrants.[5]

Wentworth's specific accusation was linked with the changed forms of crown land alienation and tenure following the introduction of capital requirements and purchase. He claimed that the native-born were prevented from obtaining their natural inheritance, the ownership of their own land.

This contemporary assumption as to the primacy of land ownership in the ambitions of the native youth is not supported by quantitative evidence from the 1828 Census nor by the qualitative evidence regarding parentage, parents' occupations and child–parent relationships. It is probable that contemporary observers, who were from the wealthier and educated classes, equated land ownership with material success and stability, with social position and prestige, and so assumed it to be the common ambition of all 'industrious young men'. The young Australians held differing views as to the merits of rural occupations. To understand the actual relationship which existed between the native-born and the land it is necessary to go beyond contemporary opinion and to identify those native-born who actually owned land or worked on it. This rural group may then be placed within the context of colonial society during the administrations of Macquarie, Brisbane and Darling. Some comparison is necessary with the other two free social groups of the same age, the came-free and the ex-convicts, and with the native-born who lived and worked mainly in the townships as professionals, apprentices, tradesmen, servants, labourers or other employed unskilled workers. In both

TABLE 7/1

Native-born landholders I

Source: 1828 Census

Occupation	Age group							Percentage of total adult male native-born
	15–20	*21–25*	*26–30*	*31–35*	*36–40*	*N.R.*	*Total*	
Farmer	13	50	53	27	2	3	148	12.6
Landholder	6	17	12	4	2	6	47	4.0
Settler	5	15	11	3	1	2	37	3.1
Grazier	1	3	1				5	0.4
Other major occupation	6	18	15	14	5		58	4.3
No occupation stated	1	2	2	5	1		11	0.9
Tenant	2	2	2	1			7	0.5
TOTAL	34	107	96	54	11	11	313	

Note. The categories are as given in the 1828 Census: farmer, landholder, settler, grazier.

considerations the key to any understanding or explanation of the attitudes of the native-born towards the land and rural occupations is the nature of the relationship which existed between colonial children and their parents.

The native-born landholders were a comparatively youthful group, the youngest being sixteen-year-old George Thompson and the oldest forty-year-old William Davis.[6] Table 7/1 is a summary of the age groups of the native-born landholders.

The occupations of those who owned land but did not describe themselves as farmers, landholders or graziers are shown in Table 7/2.

As may be seen from Table 7/2 the occupation of publican or innkeeper was frequently associated with the ownership of land. Alexander Harris described two inns which were kept by men whom he believed to be native-born: Tommy Parnell and Tom Small, both of whom were also landowners. Of Tommy Parnell, Harris wrote: 'Mr Parnell is a native, and, like all his caste, a free-hearted fellow, very easy to scrape acquaintance with ...'[7] Harris was mistaken for Parnell was not native-born; he had arrived in New South Wales in 1796 as an infant with his convict father and free mother. He had, however, grown up in the colony. In 1828 he was married to a native-born girl and described himself in the Census as a farmer; his public house was a 'second' occupation. As his ex-convict father lived with him, it is probable that he helped the wife with the management of the family inn.

Harris described Tom Small in the following manner: 'A native of the colony, who had very large timber concerns in the bush, and a very good public-house on the river bank.' Small was the son of two fomer convicts and had married a native-born girl. In 1828 he lived with his father and family at Kissing Point, where father and son each owned sixty acres. Small described himself as an innkeèper. If the accuracy of contemporary descriptions such as that of Alexander Harris, the emigrant mechanic, is

TABLE 7/2

Native-born Landholders II

Source: 1828 Census

Occupation	Number of native-born
Tradesman	25
Apprentice	1
Publican/innkeeper	11
Constable	8*
Overseer	2
Labourer	4
Clerk	2
Servant	2
Schoolmaster	1
Carter	1

Note. Occupations are stated as described in the 1828 Census.
*These included 2 District Constables and 1 Chief Constable.

accepted, the ownership of rural public houses and the possession of a spirit licence would appear to have been more profitable than working the land, either as the owner of a small farm or an employee:

> On Saturday afternoons and evenings all bushmen come in to the head stations for their next week's rations; and when this happens to be also a place where liquor is sold, it may easily be imagined that many of them do not go out again without those excesses to which bushmen are so universally prone. It is a saying among themselves that they 'earn their money like horses and spend it like asses'.[8]

As a group within colonial society the native-born landholders almost equalled in numbers those from the same age group who had arrived as free settlers. Table 7/3 indicates the numbers and percentages of those colonial landowners who had been born during the same period as the first generation, that is, between 1788 and 1813.

Although almost the same percentage of native-born owned land as those who had arrived as free settlers the native-born were an older group than the British-born. This age difference may have been partly the result of differing economic resources. Most of the senior civil and military officers and many of the free immigrants could purchase land and could afford to make immediate improvements. Few of the native-born had purchased their land, the majority relying on grants as their parents had done.[9] A second contributory reason was linked with the purpose for which the majority of immigrants came to the colony: to secure land. The native-born, on the other hand, showed a greater diversity in their choice of occupations.[10] Additionally, as

TABLE 7/3

Comparative summary of landholders, 1828
Male, aged between 15–40

Source: 1828 Census See Appendix 7

| Civil condition | Age groups | | | | | TOTAL |
	15–20	21–25	26–30	31–35	36–40	
Born in colony	25	85	77	34	5	237 (11 N.R.)
Percentage of age group	4.7	25.5	48.1	41.9	33.3	20.30
Came-free	13	39	49	51	39	191
Percentage of age group	10.4	20.8	19.5	33.0	30.0	22.0
Ex-convict	—	5	66	89	89	249
Percentage of age group	—	1.2	4.6	10.1	8.8	6.6

Note. 'Landholder' is defined in this table as one who described his own occupation in the Census as farmer, settler, landholder, grazier. Those who owned land but listed another occupation are not included.

TABLE 7/4

Occupations of heads of households, 1828
Resident 'rural' sons

Source: *1828 Census*

| Occupation | Head of household | | | | | Native-born |
	Father	Mother	Father & mother	Brother ·	Total	Percentage of total adult male B.C.
Farmer	18		44	6	68	5.8
Landholder	16	6	38	3	63	5.4
Settler	1	1	22	1	25	2.1
Agriculturist			1		1	0.08
TOTAL	35	7	105	10	157	13.4

land was usually only granted after the applicant had 'reached years of maturity', this could also influence the average age of the landholders, many of the free settlers and ex-officials being men of sufficient wealth to purchase land for their children.[11]

The ex-convict landholders were the oldest group; this was directly related to the average age on arrival in the colony, twenty-six.[12] It was only possible for land to be granted after sentence was served or after pardon. The free wife of a prisoner or ticket-of-leave man, however, could apply for a land grant in her own name. Native-born Hannah Mocklan was the daughter of two convicts. Hannah married Richard Webb who had arrived in 1814, transported for life; he had secured a ticket-of-leave as an 'honest and industrious man' and settled as a shopkeeper at Parramatta.[13]

The number of native-born who, although not technically landowners themselves, lived and worked on family land must be taken into account in any estimation of the actual numbers who owned land. Slightly more than half of the native-born males were described in the 1828 Census as living with relatives; no occupation was recorded and they lived on family land; that is, land owned by a parent or brother. Table 7/4 shows the occupations listed for the heads of these households in the Census. The percentages indicate the proportion of these native-born in comparison with the total adult males born in the colony.

The position of these rural native-born leads to difficulties in establishing a definitive list of landholders, especially where it appears probable that the titular owner of the land was not the one who worked on it or supervised its cultivation. Seventy-nine-year-old William Smith, who had arrived as a convict in 1788, owned 250 acres at Prospect in 1828. Smith described himself as a landholder. He lived with his wife, his thirty-eight-year-old son, his son's wife and their two children. In this and similar cases, the father was the titular holder of the land which was worked by the son. The size of Smith's property and those of many other parents, aged or widowed, contradicts Bigge's assertion that the native-born simply remained on poor farms which had been granted to their parents, preferring this 'miserable existence' to working for wages.

That the sons of parents with both moderate and large holdings remained on the family land is additional evidence of the link which existed between the native-born sons and their parents. This family link is emphasized further in the applications by fathers requesting portions of land and other indulgences for their sons. Applications such as that of James Orr show parental concern for the welfare of the sons. Orr was an assistant storekeeper who applied to the governor for land for his four sons, stating that he himself did not have the means to support the boys on their own land. William Holmes, a farmer at Richmond, applied for land for his eldest son who was 'twenty-one years of age and has been devoid of reason from his infancy'. The father hoped that a grant of land would 'secure a maintenance for his afflicted son who is a freeborn subject of this Colony'. Holmes and his wife were both ex-convicts, had raised their son despite his disabilities and were concerned for his welfare after their deaths.

Applications from the native-born themselves frequently contain the phrase that they were applying for a land grant 'in compliance with the wishes of their Parents'. Peter Moore, aged nineteen, wrote that his parents were 'inclined to assist him with every assistance necessary for agricultural pursuits'. Richard Cheers wrote that he wished to become an agriculturist 'through laudable and industrious motives' and he stressed that he had the support of his parents. He wrote that '. . . [the] Petitioner's father, being possessed of considerable property and being willing to establish your Petitioner in life. . . .'

James and Thomas Owens wished to earn their livelihood 'without becoming an encumbrance on their indigent parents'. However, poverty or misfortune did not necessarily lead to family disintegration. John Kerighran who, with his brothers Thomas and Patrick, was the son of ex-convicts Patrick and Catherine Kerighran, all of the District of Airds, wrote to the governor: '. . . due to unforeseen incidents [Patrick] was involved in debt, to discharge which his [father's] farm was sold . . . the family in great distress . . . it afflicted his [father's] health and brought him to his death'. At the time of writing John and his brothers were 'under the care and protection of Hamilton Hume', who supplied John's character testimonial: 'a native youth of the Colony, a lad of industrious habits and sober, of a moral disposition'. Parental indigence, examples of which appear in the Memorials, was not confined to the ex-convict families, as is shown by the request for land from native-born John Spears: 'James Spears . . . son of William, late of His Majesty's 73rd. Regiment of Foot . . . [was] anxious to settle apart from his family . . . to find an honest support as well as to relieve his parents'.

The Memorials contain many examples of continuing family relationships, of a sense of obligation to widowed mothers, of the beneficial example of industrious fathers. John McGuigan wrote that on the death of his father, a former Irish rebel, he had lost a 'tender and loving Parent' and did not wish to continue to be a burden to his widowed mother as she had five younger children to support on the family property. Stephen Tuckerman lived with his ex-convict mother, his 'father many years deceased'. John O'Hara had been 'motherless this Eight Years past, under the care of his father', during which time he had 'by Labour and Industry' acquired his own livestock and required land on which to pasture them. Lawrence Hyland had also 'accumulated a small stock of Cattle by honest Industry' while living with his parents.

Most of the Memorials contained conventional sentiments and allowance must be made for the stylized form of expression. The character references supplied for both applicants and parents help to counteract any impression that the sentiments expressed lacked substance. Abraham Herne, for example, was described by the District Magistrate as 'a constable under my charge, honest, industrious'. Herne had written that he was an ex-convict, married to a woman who had been freed by servitude; he was '. . . the Father of Five Children Born in the Colony . . . as a parent wishing to make some Provision or growing Benefit for his offspring . . .'.[15]

Sense of obligation was also evident in the application of Thomas Day, who requested a land grant for his son 'prompted to accomplish the duty of a Father'. This evidence of parental concern is at variance with the accepted assumption of parental neglect. It also suggests an attitude towards the governor as a protector and potential benefactor rather than a punitive enforcer of moral standards. Such an attitude was found in the Memorials of the native-born themselves. When Francis Boxley lost his right arm while felling a tree he applied to the governor for a grant of land which would provide for his future support, as he was unable to continue working at his trade. When Andrew McGuigan asked for help after the death of his father he stressed the known patronage of the governor for the colonial youth. The native-born had been accustomed to their fathers receiving land and indulgence from the governor; they were also aware that it was the governor who granted pardons or tickets-of-leave. In all probability this unquestioning acceptance of this aspect of the governor's power was the basis for their general attitude towards him as the ultimate benefactor.

The Memorials of the native-born and of their parents also suggest attitudes towards land ownership which differed from those which were customary in contemporary Britain. Normally, in Britain, the eldest son inherited the family farm or land and the younger sons of small farmers and yeoman tenants had little opportunity to own their own farms unless they themselves could accumulate sufficient resources for purchase. Prior to 1825 in New South Wales land could be freely granted and so capital for purchase was not a prerequisite for land ownership. This led to a differing pattern of family relationships. First, several sons could, and did, apply for their own grants of land, sometimes simultaneously. The four sons of farmer James Orr, William, Spencer, Ebenezer and James, all applied for land grants at the same time. The three sons of farmer David Danston (Duston, Damsam), Edward, David and Richard, applied together and each received sixty acres, as did John and Joseph Gosport. The second change in family patterns among small farmers was that the younger son remained with the parents after the elder sons had received their own land. In the Cupitt family it was the youngest, George, who remained and worked with his father on the family land. In the Cavanagh family the eldest son, Owen junior, received sixty acres at Lower Portland Head where the family had settled. The next son, Richard, received sixty acres in the same district and the youngest brother remained with the parents. In this way a larger percentage of the sons of small farmers may be assumed to have had the opportunity of obtaining their own farms than would have been the case in Britain, where land ownership depended on inheritance or purchase. Most importantly, the free grant system shaped the expectations of those native-born whose parents had received land from the Crown. Those who wished to remain on the land expected that a grant would be as available to them as it had been to their parents.

It was not until the latter part of the administration of Governor Darling that there were any specific regulations concerning the granting of land to the native-born as a particular group of colonists deserving of separate regulations. There had been no mention of the native-born in the instructions concerning the alienation of land which had been given to Phillip, Hunter, King, Bligh, Macquarie, Brisbane or Darling. Phillip had set aside a portion of land at Norfolk Island for the benefit of two orphaned children but this did not establish a precedent which was adhered to by subsequent governors.[16] There is some evidence to suggest that King, as Governor, might have believed that the children who had been born in New South Wales had some claim to the land by right of birth. In 1803 he wrote to Hobart: 'The method which I communicated in my Last, settling all additional grants on the Children will at least have the advantage of naturalizing them to the Soil their Fathers have cleared and Cultivated'.[17]

William Wentworth suggested the establishment of a colonial plantation where the native youth could be trained in farming and agricultural pursuits. He argued that this training and experience would result in greater success and more profitable cultivation when they obtained their own farms.[18] This suggestion was in accordance with his belief that it was the major ambition of the colonial born to own their own land.

John Macarthur, in connection with proposals for expanding the colonial flocks of sheep, suggested a similar plan:

> An extensive farm might be established which might be conducted upon approved principles, to the instruction of such Colonial Youths as might be desirous to learn and practice a better system of cultivation than the ruinous one at present carried on by their Fathers.[19]

It is probable that Bigge was influenced by Macarthur's opinion of the capabilities of the colony's small farmers when he reported that the native-born lived in poverty on their parents' farms. The Commissioner had, however, heard evidence from ex-convict Edward Eagar, who had informed him that 'In this Colony the best possible description of Setlers [sic] would be the white Native-born Children a great number of whom have been a long time Men and Women'. Eagar concluded by describing the native-born as 'the Hope and Staff of the Colony'. He added that 'of all others the Native Colonists should be Preferred and Encouraged'.[20] Commissioner Bigge, therefore, was clearly aware of the existence of the native-born; he had heard comments as to their parentage, mode of life, characteristics and capabilities. He was the first official since King to report to the British government that the native-born deserved some consideration as a group who had particular and peculiar claims to the land. At the same time he was sufficiently influenced by the ideas and attitudes of settlers 'of the first water', such as John Macarthur, to assume that being native-born was equated with membership of the lower orders and convict parentage. Bigge reflected this influence in his Report:

> I think it necessary to state that the same principle should generally prevail of previous capital of means [with regard to land grants] yet there is one description of persons, with regard to whom it appears to me that this qualification should not be applied with strictness . . . the individuals to whom I allude consist of the sons of persons who have been convicts and whose parents are alive and settled in the Colony. To them I conceive that land should be granted on their obtaining the age of twenty-four years; and that cattle should be distributed returnable in kind at the expiration of four years.[21]

It was not until 1829 that a policy similar to this recommendation was introduced into the colony. In that year Darling proposed that certain regulations govern the granting of land to the native-born, but the regulation framed and passed by the Executive Council referred to native-born as 'small settlers from the lower orders'.[22] This regulation was aimed primarily at small settlers, not specifically at the native-born.

As there were no specific regulations for the granting of land to the native-born as a distinct group before 1829, the decision to accept or reject applications remained the sole responsibility of the governor. The native-born applied in the same manner as the free immigrant and ex-convict; that is, by Memorial to the governor. These petitions were normally presented in person on a specific day once a year. The significance of the governor's decision, which was usually made immediately after reading the Memorial, may be seen from this description of the procedure: '[the Governor] . . . on perusing the statements and looking at the certificates, wrote in pencil on the margin the initial letters of the indulgence that was to be given, or rejected the petitions altogether'.[23] Macquarie frequently added the notation '60 acres, Lachlan' on the reverse side of the Memorial. To the native-born this was a further example of the powers of the governor and the direct personal link between their applications and his decision.

This would appear to support Bigge's description of the summary manner in which decisions were made by the governor himself. It is probable that Bigge emphasized this summary procedure as further indication of the capricious and disorderly manner in which Macquarie, according to the Commissioner, administered the colony and as an example of the absolute nature of his authority. There may have been some connection between Bigge's report and the establishment of the Land Board in 1826, from which time all applications for indulgences were considered by the Board rather than individually by the Governor.[24] This new procedure was in accordance with the gradual reduction of the powers of the colonial governors by the British government; its unintentional effect on the native-born was to remove effectively the almost paternal relationship between governor and applicant as shown in the wording of the Memorials.

The absolute nature of the governor's power in the matter of granting or withholding indulgences had been described by Eagar: '. . . the distribution of Land and Cattle have been Considered in this Colony rather as the Personal Gift and Favour of the Governor'.[25] Grants to the native-born could therefore be considered to depend largely on the governor's opinion of the colonial youth in general, and of the individual applicant in particular. There is little direct evidence as to the opinions of Macquarie or Brisbane regarding the native-born. The testimonials accompanying the Memorials, however, were invariably favourable. Richard Clee, for example, 'a Colonial Youth aged 16 years, eldest son of Richard Clee', possessed a few sheep and applied to the governor for land on which to pasture them. Broughton testified that he had 'lived with me for upwards of four years' and was 'honest and industrious'. William Brown, justice of the peace and the second character witness, wrote: 'I have no personal knowledge of the Petitioner, but relying on the respectable testimony in his favour, and being of the General Opinion that the Colonial Youth are generally sober and well disposed . . .'. Similar testimonials would suggest that there was no contemporary evidence which would cause the governors to think adversely of the native-born as a group.

There is also the suggestion evident in the Memorials that the native-born themselves expected the patronage of the governor. Alexander McGuigan, for example, wrote: '[he] solicits your Excellency, who is so graciously pleased to patronize the youthful generation of this Colony'. More concrete evidence of the attitudes towards the native-born may be found in the number of grants of land given by the governors, particularly by Macquarie. There were few cases where an application from a colonial youth was refused. One such case was that of Timothy Lacey, who had been imprisoned for sheep stealing—a 'boyish prank' according to his parents. Refusing to grant the land, the governor admonished Lacey for applying: . . . it would be more becoming the modesty of a young man to defer your application . . . until your conviction by a criminal court . . . shall have been effaced from the Public memory'. By 1828 Lacey had still not received a land grant and was living as a publican at Windsor, the district in which he had been born.

There was one characteristic of the Memorials from the native-born which distinguished them from those of the free immigrant youths. This was the stress on the respectability of the parents' own honest character, aptitude for and experience in land cultivation. It may have been that the generally poor reputation of 'convict' parents made it necessary to counteract any unfavourable impressions. It may have been that the applicants thought a grant would be more likely if an industrious background were emphasized. Whatever may have been the reason, the native-born stressed the beneficial influences of their childhood and upbringing,. This was in direct contrast to the contemporary assumptions concerning the parental neglect of the colony's children. There is no evidence that the Memorials of the native-born or the testimonials of their parents caused contemporaries to question the discrepancy between the assumptions and the reality, as described by these 'industrious young men' and their fathers, who 'endeavoured to ... behold them settled in life ...'.

The respectable characters of the parents, as described by the sons, were supported by testimonials from magistrates and chaplains. Thomas Scott lived with his parents; they were described in the accompanying testimonial as 'of good character and industrious'. The testimonial of James Burke stressed the honest reputation of his ex-convict father: 'The father of the Petitioner I have known for many years. He is an honest man and the Petitioner is a fine promising youth'. The father of James and Thomas Owens, an ex-private of the New South Wales Corps, had 'always supported the character becoming a soldier'. The mother was an ex-convict. Thomas Sanders was 'born of respectable parents' both of whom were ex-convicts. James and Joseph Colletts stressed that they were 'bred to the care and management of a farm' by their father, Pierce Colletts, an Irish rebel transported for fourteen years. The sons of another Irish ex-convict, Michael Nowland, stated that they had been 'reared in habits of industry and particularly in a country way of life'. James Mosley lived at Toongabbie 'with his Father and Mother and supported an honest and industrious character'. John Mobbs wrote that '[he was] a free born subject of the Colony, 18 years of age, resides with his parents at Northern Boundary, followed agricultural pursuits and supported an honest and industrious character ...'.

James Foulcher, who lived with his father at Parramatta, owned a few head of cattle and was 'an industrious young man'. The continual emphasis was on the respectability of the parents, the industry of the sons and their experience in 'an agricultural way of life'. Almost invariably the applicants claimed that these skills were the direct result of parental instruction and example. This was frequently supported by their referees. Chaplain Samuel Marsden and Magistrate John Campbell, for example, were the witnesses to the character of Thomas Best, the son of two ex-convicts: '...(he had) always been brought up to farming and was a very industrious young man and will do well on a farm ...'. The applicant himself had also stressed the respectability of his wife's family. She was formerly Mary Beckett, the daughter of ex-convicts James Becket and Ann Calcutt who had married in 1781. Best wrote:

> ... his wife is a native and belongs to a respectable Family. That by honest industry he has acquired a little Property of 20 horned cattle, 4 horses ... only 60 acres from Governor Macquarie ... bred to farming business and having a good knowledge of agriculture in all its branches.

Jonas Bradley, who had arrived unconvicted and married a convict woman, was the father of native-born Thomas and William. He wrote to the governor that his 'family has constantly resided on their little farm and wholly employed themselves in agricultural pursuits'. In 1828 these two sons were still with their father; the three described themselves as farmers and owned 4200 acres at Goulburn Plains.

Although the children of ex-convict parents or from families where the mother was an ex-convict appear to have believed it necessary to establish the respectability of their background, there were also instances where a free settler appeared to have felt a similar need. This, however, is only found among those who were from the lowest social category. John Turnbull, for example, described as 'an honest and deserving man ... [who] has brought up his family with much credit to himself', farmed 7 acres in 1828. He had described the upbringing of his five sons in eloquent manner:

> [Petitioner] having strenuously endeavoured in himself to instruct his children ... Also to comport themselves to the full satisfaction of their superiors, and in good fellowship with all mankind, and having led his family from their juvenile years gradually into the Path of Industry and to a knowledge of Agriculture, and now being himself far advanced in life ... feels it is a duty incumbent on him as a parent to endeavour to behold them settled in life before he may be called from amongst them.

Turnbull added that he was 'desirous to endeavour to establish his sons according to the Hopes and Proposals under which they have been Raised and Instructed'. Only three of his sons appeared in the 1828 Census: George and John were farmers with 80 acres each at Portland Head and William Bligh, born 1806, farmed with his father in the same district.

According to the character testimonials, those native-born who applied for land grants were a group of 'honest, sober and industrious young men' irrespective of the civil condition of their parents. Thomas Frances junior, whose father was an ex-convict settler at Evan, was described as 'a well-disposed youth'; John Wood, also of ex-convict parentage, was 'a fine young man'; William Morgan, whose father had received a conditional pardon and whose mother was freed by servitude, 'bore an honest and industrious character'; John Hannibus at the age of nineteen 'was supporting himself by his own exertions and maintains an honest character'; Joseph Jacklin, the son of ex-convicts, was 'steady, honest and industrious ... his father had been a free man these twenty-six years ... resides on a farm at Portland Head'. Joseph's brother, John, was recommended in the same terms. George Loder, the son of free parents was 'a sober and correct young man'; Thomas Saunders, according to Marsden, was 'very industrious and deserving'; Thomas Day 'was deserving of encouragement'.

These consistently favourable testimonials for these 'industrious lads' added to their reputation as an honest, law-abiding and sober group of young men. It may have been that these character references, in addition to the details supplied in the Memorials, were the base on which the factual evidence of lack of criminal convictions was built, thus establishing their reputation throughout the colony as 'lads of industrious habits'.

As a group, the native-born landholders represented 20.3 per cent of the total male native-born, or 35 per cent of those who gave an occupation in the 1828 Census. This was slightly less than the total percentage of landowners who had come free, 22.7 per cent and considerably more than the ex-convict group, 6.6 per cent. These native-born owned approximately 4.6 per cent of

TABLE 7/5

Approximate guide to the land and stock held by the native-born
Source: 1828 Census

	15–20	21–25	26–30	31–35	36–40	N.R.	Total
				Age groups			
Acres	10683	24015	15549	16620	1196	35053	103146
Horned cattle	3247	6998	5561	4908	506	2890	24110
Horses	141	386	278	291	22	57	1175
Sheep	8628	6177	3645	8029	600	5475	32554

the total amount of land which had been granted in the colony: 284,929 acres by 1828.[26] They owned 9 per cent of the cattle and 6 per cent of the sheep, so were mainly farmers.[27] Table 7/5 is a guide to the land and stock owned by the native-born. A number did not state the extent of their holdings or the numbers of their stock and thus figures are approximate only.

Most of the native-born landholders were small farmers within the County of Cumberland. Few were large sheep or stock holders. By 1828 approximately 271 male native-born owned some stock. Collectively, they owned approximately 9.1 per cent of the cattle in the colony.[28] The majority had obtained their first cattle as indulgences from Government. This could have led to the belief, shared by Bigge and Bathurst, that the native-born were of convict parentage and lacked the resources to purchase stock. Bigge had recommended that 'cattle from Government herds should be distributed to the native-born, returnable in kind . . .'.[29] This recommendation appears to have been followed in the early years of Brisbane's administration but by May 1825 Brisbane reported to Bathurst that the system of 'loans of cattle to the Sons of Persons who have been Convicts and are alive and settled in this Country' had been 'totally abandoned'.[30] This altered policy may have been linked directly with the changes in land alienation from grant to purchase.

There were few native-born sheep owners. Those who did concentrate on sheep breeding rather than on land cultivation were almost exclusively the sons of sheep owners, such as Henry Badgery, George Best, Thomas Hobby, Hamilton Hume, James and William Macarthur, all of whose fathers were pioneers of the sheep industry. The reasons for this were probably the need for capital to purchase flocks and the need for large areas on which to run them. Although the number of sheep in the colony increased yearly there was no corresponding increase in the numbers of native-born sheep farmers. In 1810 it was estimated that there were 25,888 sheep in New South Wales; in 1821, 190,158; by 1828 this had increased to 536,391. The native-born owned slightly less than 6 per cent Among the native-born, five had less than ten sheep, nine had one hundred and under, fifteen had 500 and under, six had 1000 and under, two had 1500 and under, and seven had over 1500 sheep. Those native-born who did own 500 sheep or more also had extensive landholdings. Edward Cox, with 2005 sheep, held 4500 acres at Evan. His parents had been free settlers; in 1828 Cox senior owned over 5000 sheep and almost 11,000 acres.

It is clear that most of the native-born farmers and landholders settled around the Hawkesbury District, at Portland Head, Lower Portland Head, Richmond, Wilberforce, Pitt Town and Cornwallis. These were the areas in which most of them had been born and where most had spent their childhood on the properties of their parents.

The size of the average grant to the native-born was about sixty acres. There were no Instructions to the governors concerning land grants to the native-born; neither were there colonial regulations governing the size of these grants. In 1819, however, Oxley told Bigge '... the average grant to

TABLE 7/6

Size of land grants to the native-born, 1810–1827
Source: Darling's List

Size of grant (acres)	Native-born grantees
17	1
40	4
50	8
60	261
80	15
90	3
100	27
110	1
120	2
140	4
142	2
150	19
180	4
200	11
250	2
300	33
400	1
435	1
500	13
600	5
640	1
700	2
800	1
900	3
1000	4
1110	2
1150	2
1200	1
1280	1
1920	1
2500	1
2560	1

emancipated Convicts was forty acres, and to Youths born in the Colony Sixty. Settlers from England usually had Land in proportion to their means'.[32] An analysis of the size of grants issued to native-born between 1810 and 1827, drawn up by order of Governor Darling, confirms that sixty acres was the usual size of these grants. Almost 60 per cent of the grants to native-born included in this analysis were for sixty acres; 5.8 per cent received grants of 500–1000 acres; 3.2 per cent received in excess of 1000 acres. Table 7/6, based on Darling's List, indicates the size and number of grants to the native-born.[33] Figures are approximate only.

That the average grant to the native-born was for sixty acres is confirmed by the handwritten notations on the Memorials submitted to Governor Macquarie. The fourteen native-born who are listed as receiving grants totalling 1000 acres or more were all the sons of wealthy free settlers, officials or ex-officials and most received their major grants during the administration of Brisbane. William Charles Wentworth, for example, received two grants in 1824, one for 1700 acres and one for 2000 acres; James and William Macarthur both received 3650 acres from Brisbane; John Piper received 2,635 acres, Thomas Jamieson 2500 acres and Charles Marsden 1100 acres. The twenty native-born who received 500-900 acres each were also the sons of well-to-do settlers: applicants such as William Lawson's sons, who received 500 acres each from Brisbane.

Those who received an initial grant of sixty acres—usually from Macquarie—sometimes applied for additional land and the reasons given for these applications indicate the success of the applicants. It is also probable that this concrete evidence of industry and application added to the reputation of the native-born landowners. Edward Kenny, for example, the son of a transported Irish rebel, wrote that he had entirely cleared and cultivated the sixty acres Macquarie had granted him in the district of Airds and had no land on which to graze his increasing number of sheep and cattle. His younger brother, Francis, was also a large stock-holder with 120 acres at Lake George, all of which was cleared; Francis Kenny owned 2795 sheep, 905 horned cattle and thirty horses. John Jenkins Peacock had also received an initial sixty acres from Macquarie and wrote that it was 'totally inadequate'. Hugh Byrne, native-born settler at Airds, wrote that 'the lands hitherto granted to him are not sufficient for the support of his numerous family, flocks, herds . . .'; James Jenkins, another recipient of sixty acres, found that 'his present farm was too confined'. This phrase, 'the lands hitherto granted are insufficient', appears constantly in the requests for additional land. Occasionally there was an undercurrent of complaint that the grantee had found himself 'at considerable expense to obtain extra land on which to pasture his cattle'. Applications of this type showed that the native-born gave no consideration to the idea of purchasing extra land. They expected that the governor would continue to grant additional lands freely, as they were required. This had been the experience of many of the parents of the native-born since the time of King's administration;[34] it may be assumed that the idea of purchasing land was not only outside their expectations but may have been considered a form of imposition.

Most of the first generation Australians who did settle on the land received their land grants during the administration of Macquarie and almost all of these had the experience of land being granted to their parents. When a parent had initially purchased or leased land, as did many of the small farmers in 1806, grants had usually followed successful cultivation.[35] Few of the first generation had been old enough to apply for a land grant before 1813. There was only one native-born landholder listed in the 1806 Muster; the first grants on Darling's List are dated 14 June 1811 and were to William Wentworth, William Laycock and Joshua, Richard and John Rose. The next grants were in 1813. *An Accurate List of Landholders*, 1813, included the following native-born and colonial children.

Thomas Bray, born in the colony in 1792, 30 acres, Concord.
The five children (unnamed) of William Broughton, 500 acres, Evan.
The four children of Nicholas Bayly: Sarah, 264 acres, Cabramatta; Augusta, 200 acres, Cabramatta; Henry, 200 acres, Cabramatta; George, 200 acres, Cabramatta.
George Johnston jun., 500 acres, Bankstown, 100 acres N.R.
William Jamieson jun., 100 acres, Cabramatta.
Other children of John Jamieson, 700 acres held in trust.
Children of Governor King: Maria, 600 acres, Evan; Mary, 280 acres, Evan; Elizabeth, 610 acres, Evan.
Children of James Larra, 300 acres, in trust, Bankstown.
Thomas Reiby, [*sic*] 100 acres, Wilberforce.[36]

It is clear that before the arrival of Macquarie land grants to the native-born were closely related to the wealth or official or social position of the parent. The grant appears to have been more of a provision for future security than an encouragement for the grantee to become a small farmer.

There is no background of applications for small grants which could be considered to have set a pattern of land ownership by the native-born. As so few had applied for land grants before his arrival, Macquarie had no precedent to guide his decisions regarding the size of grants to the native-born applicants. In the 1806 Muster, for example, most of those native-born who were included were tradesmen or apprentices.[37] It would appear that those boys who did not remain on their parents' farms preferred to be apprenticed at either the Dock Yards or the Lumber Yards. The reasons for this were probably varied but a major factor would have been the age of the native-born. An apprenticeship could begin from the age of ten or twelve years but an applicant for a land grant needed to have reached 'the age of maturity'. This helps to explain the steadily increasing number of applications to Macquarie throughout his term as governor. The period of his administration coincided with most of the first generation reaching 'years of maturity'. It is probable that the difficulties following the Bligh Rebellion, with regard to the granting of land, may have affected the opportunities for those native-born wishing to become small farmers.[38] Whatever may have been the reason, the pattern of land grants before Macquarie's administration suggests that land was more likely to be freely given to the sons of wealthier settlers rather than to the sons

TABLE 7/7

Land grants by Macquarie to the native-born, 1810–1821
Source: Darling's List

Size of grant (acres)	Number of grants	Total acres
40	1	40
50	6	300
60	204	12240
80	9	720
100	18	1800
140	2	280
200	6	1200
300	6	1800
500	6	3000
600	2	1200
700	1	700
1500	2	3000

of small farmers who may have been of an age to apply for independent grants. In the first instance, the land was a form of investment in the future; in the second, it was the means of earning a livelihood. As this was similar to the policies which resulted from the changes under Brisbane, it could be suggested that it was only during the administration of Governor Macquarie that those native-born who lacked assets or capital could have the opportunity to become independent farmers.

During his administration Macquarie made approximately 265 land grants to the native-born; 204 of these were for sixty acres. The consistency with which he granted sixty acres to native-born applicants suggests that this was a deliberate decision. It would appear that Macquarie judged the claims of the native-born to be above those of ex-convicts but below those of the free settlers.[39]

Table 7/7 shows the number and size of Macquarie's land grants to the native-born during the period of his administration.

The conditions attached to these grants were the same as those for free settlers and ex-convicts. They were subject to a quit rent, the government reserved the right to roads and timber, and the grant could not be alienated for five years.[40] Between 1788 and 1810, 177,500 acres had been granted to settlers. An individual grant had seldom exceeded 100 acres according to Surveyor-General Oxley. The forms of these grants had been 'very various' and Macquarie had consolidated the differing forms shortly after his arrival. Macquarie had granted a total of 400,000 acres and most of those who had received these grants were 'allowed an almost uncontrolled right of selection'.[41] The native-born, therefore, had received approximately 7 per cent of the land granted and, presumably, had had some choice in its location, unlike many of their fathers. This is important in relation to the numbers of native-born who secured land grants in or near the districts in which they had spent their childhood. It confirms both their reluctance to move to the outer settlements and their continuing links with their parents.

Macquarie's grants to the native-born show that there was seldom any variation in the size of a grant to an applicant with ex-convict parents or to an applicant with free parents. One of the few exceptions was to the sons of John Bowman, both of whom received 140 acres in 1821. There still remained, however, a decided link between the size of the grant and the material status of the parents. For example, the 5 per cent of the native-born grantees who received 500 acres or more from Macquarie were all the sons of well-to-do settlers. One of these was the son of ex-convict clergyman, Henry Fulton, another the son of ex-convict farmer, Richard Fitzgerald.[42] Macquarie's lack of discrimination with regard to the civil condition of the parent when this parent had achieved material success would appear to be in accordance with his general principles of encouraging 'deserving' ex-convicts.[43] It is ironical that Macquarie's largest grants were to James and William Macarthur, the sons of the bitterest critic of his 'policies', John Macarthur.[44]

Bigge estimated that 324,251 acres had been granted in New South Wales.[45] He stated that 83,502 acres were held by 'convicts whose sentences had expired'; 35,309 acres were held by grants and 50,884 acres by purchase.[46] The native-born held approximately 27,000 acres by grant in 1821; that is, 8.3 per cent of the total amount of land which had been granted in New South Wales. By the end of December 1821 there were 23,939 inhabitants of New South Wales according to the Muster of that year. The civil condition of the population is reflected in Table 7/8.

The adult native-born, therefore, represented 6.2 per cent of the population. Assuming that half of the native-born were males, 36 per cent had received land grants during the administration of Macquarie. This is slightly more than the total number of native-born landholders in 1828. This is some indication of the effects of the regulations of 1825 on the native-born as a group.

During the administration of Governor Thomas Brisbane, there was a complete change in the system of land alienation and this affected the native-born. These changes were primarily the result of Commissioner Bigge's Report and recommendations and the degree of influence these had had on the policies and attitudes of the British government towards the colony and its future. Bigge had stated very clearly that:

TABLE 7/8

Civil condition of population of New South Wales, 1821 [47]

Persons who had come free	*1307*
Persons who had been born in the colony	*1495*
Persons holding absolute pardons	*159*
Persons holding conditional pardons	*962*
Persons freed by servitude	*3255*
Persons holding tickets-of-leave	*1422*
Convicts	*9451*
Children (age not stated)	*5668*
Persons on colonial vessels	*220*

It is my opinion, that persons of this class [ex-convicts] have very little chance of success in the cultivation of the land of ordinary quality in New South Wales, without the possession of some pecuniary means to enable them to meet the heavy expenses of clearing and bringing the land into such a state of cultivation as may render it profitable without exhausting it.[48]

Bigge's recommendations formed the basis of Brisbane's Instructions from Bathurst. In September 1822 Bathurst wrote that, 'with respect to the System of Making Grants to Emancipated Convicts ... no Grants beyond ten acres be in future given unless to those possessed of property'.[49]

Bigge had further recommended that land for free settlers be in proportion to the capital they brought to the colony and that additional quantities of land should be sold. Although admitting that the native-born had some claims to favourable treatment, Bigge suggested that small grants be made to them after they had attained the age of twenty-five years. His chief emphasis was on the increase in revenue to the Crown from the sale of lands which had hitherto been granted freely. This, combined with his view that the future of the colony lay in 'pasture rather than tillage', influenced future attitudes of the British government and colonial governors as to the manner by which Crown lands should be alienated.[50] The full effects of this change in policy were felt with the arrival of Governor Darling, the first governor of New South Wales not to be instructed to settle ex-convicts on small allotments.[51] As the rural native-born were in general small farmers their use of the land for cultivation was more in keeping with that of the ex-convict farmers than with the immigrants, who were expected to have the capital necessary to purchase land for pasture.

Brisbane's attitudes towards land alienation, and towards the colony itself, coincided very largely with those which had been expressed by Commissioner Bigge. Shortly after arriving to take up his position as Governor of the penal colony, Brisbane wrote to Bathurst outlining the ways in which the free granting of land was prejudicial to the interests of Britain, to the colonial administration and to the colonists themselves.[52] Unlike Macquarie, Brisbane's main concern was not for the ex-convict settlers but for the free sections of the community. Brisbane expressed his opinion of the convicts in 1825 when he wrote to Bathurst that 'The bad character of the Masses of the Inhabitants must in itself be for many an extreme difficulty to settlers from Europe'.[53]

Brisbane's recommendations for the sale of land previously granted freely may have been associated with his attempts to increase colonial revenue and decrease administrative costs. This appears to have been a part of a general policy of economy. One historian, John Ritchie, has claimed that Brisbane himself regarded the success of economy 'policies' as his greatest achievement as governor.[54] Brisbane did agree with Bigge's recommendation that some small grants should be available to selected settlers and that purchase should be primarily a means of enlarging grants.[55] As this system would restrict those settlers who lacked capital from increasing their holdings, this policy would necessarily favour the wealthier settlers.

Bathurst agreed in essence with Brisbane's proposals but differed as to the extent to which purchase should be introduced. Bathurst saw purchase as a form of tenure equal to that of grant and as a form which could co-exist with the grant system. Purchase was not to be limited entirely to large-scale pastoralists. This was an important decision for the increasing numbers of free settlers who came to the colony during the 1820s. Until 1831 free settlers could obtain land by grant if they had sufficient capital. The minimum grant up to this date was about 320 acres and this was given freely to those with capital to the value of £250.[56] F.G. Clarke describes the suspicion with which spokesmen for the English working classes viewed these regulations:

'When arrived [in Australia] you depend on the public authorities for a grant of land. If you have money to purchase pieces of ground already cleared and cultivated, your servants are convicts, and you are at the joint mercy of them and the murdering natives. Even for the service of the convicts, your sole dependence is on the pleasure of the public authorities.'[57]

Apparently commentators such as Cobbett saw the alienation of the Australian lands as linked with 'class' attitudes and also dependent not so much on policy and regulation as on the decisions of the 'public authorities'. This public authority, during the childhood and adolescence of the native-born, had been the governor himself; from 1826 it was the Land Board, although ultimate authority still rested with the governor.

Most of the native-born did not possess capital equal to that brought to the colony by the immigrants. They were, therefore, disadvantaged by a system dependent on capital resources. One result of this was that, to both colonial and British officials, they appeared to belong to the same category as the ex-convict settlers. Although small grants were still available to them, opportunities for increasing their holdings were limited because the majority lacked the necessary capital. This appeared to reinforce the idea that the native-born, as a group, were from the lower orders and very largely of convict descent. This assumption, and its perpetuation, is evidenced very clearly in debates in the House of Commons concerning the extension of civil rights to the 'convict colony' of New South Wales. Clarke reports the attitude of Howick:

In his parliamentary reply ... Howick was prepared to concede that trial by jury would be introduced as quickly as possible ... but he was adamant that emancipists and their descendants were tainted with criminality and therefore unfit to be given a legislative assembly. In Howick's view, the constitutional conflict between emancipists and exclusives in New South Wales resembled a struggle between the forces of good and the powers of darkness: 'A constant struggle ... was going on between those who had once been convicts, or who were the descendants of convicts, and those who were wholly untainted.'[58]

Thus the native-born continued to be regarded by the British officials and respectable classes as the sons of convicts, tainted with inherited criminality. In these circumstances it is understandable that no general regulations were formed to govern the granting of land to those who had been born in the colony. The only specific regulation was for young men described as 'settlers from the lower orders'. These regulations classed the native-born with the ex-convict applicants.[59]

Although Bathurst's decisions regarding the manner in which land was to be alienated were made several years before Howick's public statement that the native-born of New South Wales were tainted with criminality, Bathurst clearly regarded the native-born as children of the convicts, who therefore belonged to the lowest rungs of the social hierarchy. This may have been a contributing reason for the changed land regulations containing no provision for any inherited 'right by birth'. The emphasis was solely on capital; in particular, capital possessed by newly arrived immigrants. The reasoning behind this demand was primarily that too many previous grantees had possessed insufficient capital to clear and cultivate the lands granted. Land given indiscrimately to applicants, without regard to the grantees' ability or resources to improve or develop it, frequently remained uncultivated or was sold for speculation. Neither of these results were beneficial to the British government or to the colony itself. The Instructions from Bathurst to Brisbane on this point were specific:

> In the event of resident Settlers making application for new Grants, you are authorized to refuse them altogether, if they have neglected to bring the Grants already in their occupation into a due state of cultivation ... [or] if it appears that their present Grants require the applicaton of fresh capital. . . .[60]

If the applicants satisfied the necessary capital requirements Brisbane was instructed 'not to hesitate to make new Grants to them precisely upon the same terms as to new Settlers'.[61] As 'resident Settlers' were not defined and no specific reference was made to the native-born it may be assumed their applications to Brisbane for additional land would be considered in accordance with these conditions.

Bathurst was also of the opinion that the nature of the work-force of New South Wales was an almost insuperable obstacle to the efficient development of the land. Most of the population of New South Wales continued to be convict or ex-convict. In 1828 three out of every four adult males had arrived as a convict. The work-force in general, and the agricultural workers in particular, were mainly assigned government servants or ex-convict labourers. The efficient working of the assignment system was therefore essential to the profitable development of the colony's agricultural and pastoral resources. Most of the convicts who formed this work-force had little experience of farming or agricultural pursuits and they had little inclination to adapt to the isolated routine of bush workers.[62] Thus, although labour was readily available and the cost of maintenance of the labourers comparatively inexpensive, their lack of skill, experience, inclination or incentive resulted in that labour being inefficient and in need of constant supervision. In Bathurst's view the problems of successful land cultivation were aggravated by the lack of awareness on the part of many migrant settlers that the free convict labour readily available would not equate with the expectations of masters accustomed to labour conditions in Britain.[63] Bathurst believed that it was commonly accepted by these prospective settlers that the only resource they needed under the free grant system was their own personal exertion and the labour of as many convicts as could be assigned to them. With the aid of this virtually free labour they assumed that they could rapidly convert 'wild and uncleared Country' into the Profitable Pastures and Arable fields. Bathurst was convinced that the only way to avoid the 'severe consequences' of a settler's dependence on unskilled labour and the effects of a lack of capital was to impose strict conditions governing the alienation of land.[64] The result of this for those native-born who lacked capital resources was that, during the administration of Darling, they found themselves in the same position as the ex-convicts and the poorer settlers and could only obtain free land under the conditions relating specifically to 'Settlers from the Lower Orders'.[65]

The regulations of 1 January 1825 did not only change the ways in which land could be alienated. The introduction of capital requirements altered the way in which society was to develop by introducing what could be termed a class system based on wealth and capital resources. Future settlers were to be divided into two categories: those who could buy land at a 'fair market price' and those who could only become 'Settlers by the Bounty of the Crown', that is, by free grant.[66] Until this time most of the settlers could obtain free grants 'by the Bounty of the Crown', particularly ex-convicts, ex-soldiers and the native-born. From 1825, however, this latter class was strictly limited to those applicants who could prove that they possessed capital or resources sufficient to equal one quarter of the value of the land granted—and that value was to be determined by its improved and cultivated value. In addition to this a quit rent of £5 per year was to be imposed.[67] Although Bathurst stated quite clearly that these regulations were intended to ensure the more profitable development of the colony's rural resources it could also be argued that they prevented the 'lower orders', in particular the ex-convicts and the rural native-born, from becoming independent landowners. This was later reinforced by Darling's regulations allowing small grants of land to the lower orders. The pattern of rural society which was to emerge was no longer that of the yeoman peasantry envisaged by Macquarie, where free land grants were an incentive to convict reformation. Instead the pattern was more in accordance with the recommendations of Bigge: the role of the ex-convict was seen more as labourer than as farmer.[68] Bigge had recommended that no ex-convict settler receive a grant larger than 10 acres. Brisbane reported that he had adhered to this recommendation '... as far as considered expedient to give due encouragement to that class of inhabitants combined with the means they possess of doing justice to a grant of land'.[69]

From the time of the administration of Governor Darling the qualifications for the native-born who wished to become small farmers and landholders were entirely different from those to which they had been accustomed since childhood. A good character as an honest and industrious young man was no longer sufficient to secure free land, nor could the paternal patronage of the governor be relied upon to favour the applications of the colonial-born. These changes are reflected in the decreasing number and increasing size of the grants to the native-born made by Brisbane and Darling.

During his administration Brisbane granted land to approximately 181 native-born applicants, the majority of whom received their grants prior to the mid-1820s. By November 1823 Brisbane had written to Bathurst on the 'huge' increase of applicants for land and complained that:

> ... a large portion of my time, diverted from subjects of much greater importance, is engaged in refusing land. Already had I promised 163000 acres ... [I have] been obliged to refuse more applications than even the ones I granted. ...

He added that 'Not a cow calves in the Colony but her owner applies for an additional grant in consequence of the encrease [sic] of his stock'[70] This would appear to imply that the majority of the applications were for additional grants. It is probable that some of these grants were among the 340,000 acres of 'unexecuted promises' left by Macquarie. Brisbane claimed that a great deal of alienated land in the Colony was 'held by naked Possession without a Shadow of Right'.[71]

Approximately 54 per cent of Brisbane's grants to the native-born were for 60 acres: this compared with 84 per cent by Macquarie. From Brisbane 30.5 per cent received grants of over 300 acres as compared with 7.1 per cent from Macquarie. A contributing reason to the larger size of grants may have been the location. Macquarie's grants were almost all within the Cumberland Plain, where unoccupied arable land was limited. Brisbane granted land in the new settlements at Liverpool Plains, in the Hunter Valley and beyond Bathurst. The land obtained by the native-born from Macquarie was used primarily for agriculture; during Brisbane's administration requests for land for pasture were increasing and pasture required larger holdings. In addition, the changing emphasis on the need for capital favoured the sons of the wealthier settlers of the colony.

Table 7/9 indicates the number and size of grants to the native-born during the administration of Governor Brisbane.

Those native-born who did receive sixty acres from Brisbane were from the same background as those who had received similar grants from Macquarie. They were mainly the sons of small farmers who had arrived in the colony as convicts, marines, sailors or soldiers and had settled within the Cumberland Plain. The two sons of William Spears, for example, each received sixty acres; their father had arrivèd as a private soldier in the New South Wales Corps in 1801. The sons of ex-convicts George Field and William Everingham also received sixty acres each. Although the size of the grant under Brisbane did not appear to be unduly affected by the civil condition of the parents, in the cases of the smaller settlers it did bear a distinct relation to the position and material wealth of the father. The sons of wealthy free settler George Suttor received 300 acres each; both the sons of John Macarthur received grants of 2500 acres

TABLE 7/9

Land grants by Brisbane to the native-born
Source: Darling's List

Size of grant (acres)	Number of grants	Total acres (approximate)
40	1	40
50	1	50
60	72	43200
80	1	80
90	3	270
100	12	1200
110	1	110
120	2	240
140	4	560
150	18	2700
200	7	1400
250	3	750
300	28	8400
366	1	366
400	2	800
435	1	435
500	8	4000
600	3	1800
640	1	64
800	1	800
900	3	2700
1000	3	3000
1100	1	1100
1200	1	1200
2000	1	2000
2500	2	5000

each;[72] the son of Chaplain Marsden received 1100 acres. Despite the size of these grants Brisbane had shown some hesitation in alienating large areas of land to individuals whose fathers had already received 'Munificently of the Royal Bounty':

> I have much difficulty in deciding how far it would accord with Your Lordship's views in giving Grants of Land to the Sons of Settlers whose Fathers have already received Munificently of the Royal Bounty, as in the case of the sons of Mr Macarthur and Mr John Blaxland, who have applied to me for 2000 acres of land; but I have paused in my reply until guided by Your Lordship's Instructions. I cite these Instances merely but my Object is the principle of the Offspring of Settlers generally having claims.

Brisbane's reluctance to grant these large areas may have been connected with Bigge's disapproval of the considerable free grants which had been made to Blaxland and Macarthur: Macarthur's grants had exceeded 3000 acres and Blaxland's were in excess of 6710 acres.[73]

Those native-born who had received their grants at the commencement of Brisbane's administration did so in accordance with the General Order of 20 May 1820 and Brisbane's subsequent amendments.[74] This regulation was simply a statement of the conditions that had existed throughout Macquarie's governorship, that all applicants must submit written proof as to their good character in the form of two testimonials. Proven honesty and sobriety were essential for the success of the applications. These testimonials were to be obtained from the local chaplain and magistrate and the importance of these being genuine character references was stressed.

It was two years after the publication of this Order that Brisbane added an amendment. It did not replace the necessity for character references but added an additional way in which land could be granted. This was that, for every 100 acres granted freely, the grantee must maintain one convict servant for one year free of all expense to the Crown.[75] It was a direct attempt to reduce colonial expenditure by encouraging settlers to maintain their convict servants. As there was no choice by the settler of the convict to be assigned, the chief benefit to the settler was the opportunity to obtain 100 acres: it was most unlikely that the convict would be experienced in agricultural work.

When Governor Darling arrived in the colony there were at least four main ways by which land could be alienated from the Crown. First, there were those grants which had been received from Macquarie and needed confirmation of tenure because the order granting the land had not passed the Great Seal. This had led to considerable anxiety and hardship on the part of those who had cultivated this land although they had no strict legal title. Second, land could be granted in accordance with the regulations of permanently maintaining a certain number of convicts. Third, land could be granted for pasture or grazing only, in which case a yearly quit rent of 15 per cent of the value of each 100 acres could be enforced. Finally, land grants could be made for non-commissioned officers and for private soldiers discharged from the service for the express purpose of settling in the colony.[76]

None of these forms of grant related directly to the native-born as a group. That no regulations had been framed specifically for the granting of land to the colonial youth had not disadvantaged the native-born who had applied to Macquarie nor those who had applied during the earlier years of Brisbane's administration, as the number and size of grants shows. With the arrival of Governor Darling, however, new techniques of organization and method of alienating land were introduced into the colony. The position of the native-born as a group was still almost unrecognized, both in the report prepared by Oxley as Surveyor-General shortly after the new Governor's arrival and in the regulations governing purchase and grant.[77] 'A List of Lands Granted ... 1828' shows the effects of the changes in land alienation policy and the results of the changed emphasis on land use from agricultural to pastoral. Eight native-born grantees and four purchasers received land from Darling, the holdings ranging from 560 acres (one) and 640 acres (nineteen) to 2560 acres (twenty-nine) and 17,813 acres (one, Simeon Lord).[78] Only one of these landholders received land within the Cumberland Plain. The native-born, raised mainly on agricultural farms within the Cumberland Plain and receiving grants which averaged 60 acres, found themselves by the end of the 1820s in a position entirely different from that which they had known since childhood.[79] This was the direct result of the changes in the land alienation policy which had been recommended by Bigge. It was also indicative of the emphasis Great Britain placed on her colony as a place for the punishment of felons and the profit of the mother country. Both views were based on currently accepted views and assumptions in Britain as to the nature of the colony and its inhabitants.

From this investigation into those 'lads of industrious habits' who became the first Australian farmers and landholders a clear picture emerges of the nature and composition of rural society in New South Wales during the first forty years of white settlement. Although it cannot be accepted that land ownership was the ambition of all industrious young men in the colony it is now evident that the native-born landowners were strongly influenced by their parents and by their childhood experiences with those parents. It was rare for a native-born youth who was not the son of a farmer to apply for land for himself. Rural occupations were, in effect, family occupations. Those born on the land normally married 'rural' women and settled near, or with, their own parents or parents-in-law. In this way stability and family life developed in the colony with the first pioneer families. These pioneers, the men and women who opened up the land within the Cumberland Plain during the first thirty or so years of settlement, were mostly the rejected lower orders of Britain's poor. Few had farming experience. Their position in the colony was the result of skills learned there. Their achievements and failures were soundly based on colonial conditions, opportunities and attitudes and their responses to this new environment. The inheritance they gave their native-born children was a colonial one and unconnected with prior lives in Britain.

It was to be significant for the way in which the colony developed that the native-born youth were not all the sons of landholders, that all did not, themselves, aspire to own land. The contemporary assumption that this was so narrowed their influence on colonial society. The added emphasis that they were the sons of settlers 'in miserable circumstances' was as great a distortion as the assumption that they were the children of the convicts. Almost one third of the first-generation men did become landowners. At the same time another third became tradesmen and apprentices. These were as strongly influenced by their parental background and their experiences as children of tradesmen as were the rural native-born. Colonial society was not simply a land-based one. The native-born who had experienced a childhood in the family of skilled or partly skilled tradesmen were acutely aware of the advantages which came from the possession of a skill or craft training. These 'stout lads' were as influential in shaping the development of the colonial work-force as were their rural brothers in influencing the nature of rural society in New South Wales.

CHAPTER EIGHT

ARTISANS ... THAT USEFUL CLASS OF PERSONS

'Work keeps at bay three great evils: boredom, vice, and need.'

Voltaire, *Candide*.

The conditions and opportunities for skilled craftsmen and tradesmen in New South Wales during the first forty years of white settlement differed from those in Britain in almost every respect. There had been a constant and unsatisfied demand for skilled workers for the colony from the time the first fleet had sailed from England. The nature and structure of the population was such that the colony remained heavily dependent on the skills of the convicts and the ex-convicts; the opportunities for a mechanic or skilled craftsman, on completion of his sentence or after pardon, were more immediate if he worked at his trade than if he accepted a land grant. Although one of the first men to be emancipated, James Ruse, was a farmer by occupation Phillip offered incentives to industrious mechanics, recommending to Under-Secretary Nepean that the families of men who proved useful in the colony be given permission to join them in New South Wales.[1] That governors, officials and settlers continued to recognize the value of skilled men was evident at the first state funeral in New South Wales, held in 1804 to honour the ex-convict James Bloodsworth. Bloodsworth was described in his obituary in the *Sydney Gazette* as:

> ... generally lamented, for many years Superintendent of Building in the Employment of Government. He came to the Colony among the first Inhabitants in the year 1788, and obtained the Appointment from his exemplary conduct, shortly after his arrival. ...[2]

Governors continued to ask the Colonial Office for more artificers to be included among those convicts transported to Botany Bay but the supply remained inadequate for the colony's needs. One of Macquarie's conflicts with the wealthier free settlers concerned the assignment of skilled labour. Robert Lowe described to Commissioner Bigge in 1820 the inconveniences caused by the lack of convict carpenters and 'Mechanicks':

> I myself have been compelled when an accident has happened to my Plough or Cart—to send 3 and 4 times to Parramatta and back a Distance of more than 40 miles before I could get it repaired—much more are we inconvenienced when anxious to erect comfortable Houses and other suitable Buildings—We then struggle with almost insurmountable difficulties from the enormously high price of labour demanded by the free Mechanicks. ...

John Macarthur was more cautious in his open criticism of Governor Macquarie. When asked by Bigge if 'Government' had ever refused him a tradesman or 'Mechanic', Macarthur replied, 'I have not applied directly to the Governor for such men, because I have frequently heard him Complain, that there were not a sufficient Number to Carry on the Public Works . . .'.

It may have been that the scarcity of skilled men in the colony and the consequent continual demand for their labour was a main cause for the absence of any formation of colonial trade unions or friendly societies during this period. The demand for labour was so great that even convicts under sentence had opportunities to earn money from the practice of their trades in their spare time. Major Druitt agreed with Bigge that mechanics arriving in the colony as convicts would sometimes conceal their skills in an attempt to avoid employment by the government, for '. . . if they are successful in the Concealment of their Trade & are sent off to a Settler they can exercise their Trade at spare hours & gain a Great Deal of Money . . .'.[3]

With such a favourable labour market, not only the ex-convict but the immigrant and the native-born lacked any incentive to form organized unions to regulate and protect their skills. One important result of this was that the colonial tradesmen did not follow the British pattern of radical agitation which had been a strong feature of the British working classes from the early 1790s and which would have been familiar to both convicts and immigrants from Britain during this period.[4] The native-born, therefore, had no direct experience of worker-organization movements and no background of agitation to encourage them, as a group, to join the debates on constitutional rights in the 1820s. Although the leading spokesman in these issues was a native-born Australian, William Charles Wentworth, he was atypical for he was English-educated and proud of his aristocratic British heritage; had it not been for the circumstances of his birth he might have considered himself as great an exclusive as James Macarthur. The native-born in general had no experiences of any form of 'political' agitation based on labour conditions and played little part in the demand by ex-convicts for legal, constitutional and economic freedoms. This lack of any 'political' experiences was a direct indication of the specific labour situation which had developed in the colony as a result of the population structure with its heavy penal emphasis; the continual flow of convicts into New South Wales was far in excess of the combined total of free immigrants and native-born. By 1828 approximately three in four of all adult males had arrived in the colony as convicts and most of these men were from the lower orders of Britain.[5]

One main difference between the British tradesman and his free or freed colonial counterpart was that the colonial worker had more control over the nature and location of his labour than had the skilled British worker. The choice of 'rural' or 'town' work in New South Wales could be made by the tradesman on the basis of individual choice, not solely on the availability of employment. An influencing factor in this was the lack of industrialization in the colony, which prevented the growth of particular trade areas, such as Manchester or Leeds in England.[6] This, combined with the colonial lack of seasonal skilled labour, such as for weaving or spinning, meant that the practice of regular employment at one trade and in one place over a number of years was common in the colony but infrequent in Britain. Mayhew, for example, estimated that 'about three-fourths or four-fifths of the carpenters working in the Metropolis . . . were from the country'. Thompson also found that 'the skilled or apprenticed man, who owned his own tools and worked for a lifetime in one trade, was in the minority'.[7] The comparative stability of conditions for colonial tradesmen meant that their children were accustomed to living as a family in one district. A direct result of this was that few of the native-born who themselves became tradesmen moved from the district in which they had been born.[8]

The nature of the unskilled work-force in the colony, the convicts, and the assignment system by which their labour was controlled, prevented the growth in the number of colonial-trained tradesmen. A master who could obtain free convict labour had no need or incentive to train apprentices. It was even possible that a master might, in some circumstances, secure a convict mechanic as an assigned servant. Druitt told Bigge that if it did happen that there were more convict mechanics in the Lumber Yard than could be employed they were given 'to any of the respectable Tradesmen in the Town'.[9] Assignment in the town was preferable because skilled men could be recalled easily if needed by government.

The free convict labour market also influenced the nature of apprentice-ships for it removed the need for child labour. Those colonial boys who trained to become tradesmen did so, in most cases, from their own choice or that of their parents and not as a result of poverty, necessity or lack of any alternative employment. This contrast between conditions and opportunities for apprentices and tradesmen in New South Wales and in England was particularly marked during the post-war period of depression and unemployment in Britain following the Napoleonic Wars. This period corresponded to the latter half of Macquarie's administration in New South Wales when the first generation were reaching 'years of maturity' and facing the decisions involved in the choice of occupation. The high proportion of apprentices and skilled tradesmen among the native-born in 1828, which was almost one third of all those who stated an occupation in the Census of that year, and the low proportion of unskilled labourers and servants is a clear indication of the advantages available to the colonial youth.[10] The increasing numbers of juvenile convicts transported to New South Wales during the same period could be seen as an indication of the conditions faced by boys from the working classes of Britain.

The most important results of these differing conditions in Britain and in New South Wales were that the native-born who became skilled tradesmen joined a work-force which was unique, having developed from the peculiarly penal bases of the colonial population. The elite of that work-force, the tradesmen and mechanics, were in constant demand by both government and private settlers so could obtain high returns for their labour. A willingness to work combined with skill led to the security of constant and lucrative employment. It was perhaps significant for the attitudes of the native-born towards convicts and convictism that the largest proportion of these skilled workers were convicts or ex-convicts. There would have been a conscious awareness, therefore, of the advantages, both social and economic, which were attached to skilled labour. Those of the native-born who were themselves the sons of convicts or ex-convicts or who had served their own apprenticeships under ex-convict masters, whether government or private, would have seen by personal experience that the results of skill and industry could, in economic terms, transcend the stigma and connotations of conviction.[11] Native-born John Cubitt, born in Sydney in 1803, was the son of two ex-convicts, Daniel Cubitt and his wife, Maria Cook. John's birth was recorded in the *Sydney Gazette*, an unusual circumstance. His father had become superintendent of the Lumber Yards and, by the early 1820s, was Master of the Guard Boat. The father of another native-born tradesman, Thomas Cozier, had arrived as a convict in 1795 and had eventually become a landholder at Parramatta although he still worked at his trade as a blacksmith; his son, also trained as a blacksmith, worked with him. Another ex-convict tradesmen who worked with his native-born son was James Evans, a carpenter. Evans had arrived in 1803 and by 1828 was freed by servitude and working with his carpenter son in Princes Street, Sydney. John Harper junior lived and worked with his father, John, who had been transported for life. By 1828 Harper senior was a butcher and owned 800 acres.[12]

Some of the fathers, landowners as well as tradesmen, had achieved outstanding success in the colony. This material success far exceeded any possibilities for tradesmen in contemporary England or Ireland. John Town, former convict, was a miller whose son worked with him. Town senior had received a conditional pardon, married an ex-convict woman and worked at his trade at Richmond; by 1828 he owned 1854 acres and ran 221 horned cattle and 206 sheep. At the other end of the scale were those ex-convict tradesmen who appeared to have gained an adequate livelihood for themselves and their families by working at their trades. Such a man was Charles Beales, who supported his family at Airds; his eldest son, Charles, born in 1805, lived and worked with his parents and his two younger brothers. Men such as Beales, who had both security and continuity of employment, differed from their counterparts in Britain where such conditions were rarely available. It is important to note that native-born sons continued to live and work with tradesmen fathers at all levels of economic success.

In accordance with the structure of the colonial population there were, numerically, more ex-convict tradesmen within the fifteen to forty age group than there were either free immigrant or native-born. Proportionately, a higher percentage of the intermediate age groups of the three civil conditions were ex-convict, with the exception of the 36-40 age group where 40 per cent of the male native-born were tradesmen, compared with 21.1 per cent of the convicts in the same age group. The highest percentage of the total males in any of the three groups to become tradesmen was the native-born, 23.5 per cent describing their occupation as working at a skilled trade in 1828 as compared with 18.3 per cent of the came-free males and 21.6 per cent of the ex-convict males.[13]

The trades followed by the native-born were limited almost exclusively to the basic subsistence trades, for there had been little opportunity in the colony for specialized or luxury trade apprenticeships and manufactories were almost non-existent during the adolescence of the native-born. Specialist tradesman Samuel Skinner, the only colonial potter, became bankrupt in 1809. Ferdinand Meurant, transported for life in 1800, had attempted to work at his trade of jeweller but turned instead to farming and 'the culture of the grape'. Meurant wrote to Governor Brisbane in 1822 that he had established a Vineyard ... has three children whom he proposes to interest in the thorough knowledge of the Vineyard'. By 1828 two of his sons, Ferdinand junior and Albert, worked with their father on his 160 acre property at Seven Hills. In the *Sydney Gazette* of 1806 there was one advertisement for a goldsmith, silversmith and jeweller.[14] In the *Sydney Gazette* of 1810 the only tradesmen, other than those practising the subsistence trades, who advertised were J. Yoel, a seal engraver, William Cluer, a pipe-maker, and Joseph Davis and M. Lane, watch-makers. Advertisements were constant for bakers, blacksmiths, bricklayers, butchers, cabinet-makers, millers, 'gardiners', tailors and upholsterers.[15] It was this demand for basic trades which influenced the choice of trade and resulted in the complete lack of speciality or luxury trade training among the native-born.

With the exception of the carpenters, the trades followed by the native-born differed very little from those of their contemporary came-free or ex-convict tradesmen. Table 8/1 indicates the most popular trades among the native-born in 1828, compares the proportionate numbers of tradesmen in the other two civil condition groups and lists those trades which were followed exclusively by the came-free and the ex-convict groups in this age division.

The distribution of these trades among the three civil condition groups is indicative of the shortage of free skilled tradesmen in the colony forty years

TABLE 8/1

Comparative trades, free and freed males aged 15–40, 1828

Trade		Civil condition			
	Native-born		Came-free		Ex-convict
Carpenter	23.0%		2.1%		13.0%
Shoemaker	11.7%		10.3%		17.4%
Blacksmith	8.8%		0.1%		7.8%
Wheelwright	8.2%		1.2%		2.0%
Cabinet-maker	8.2%		3.2%		0.4%
Trades followed by came-free only:					
Engraver	2	Potter	1	Pastrycook	1
Trades followed by ex-convicts only:					
Turner	1	Framework-maker	1	File-cutter	1
Cutler	1	Bookbinder	3	Boot-closer	1
Ironmonger	1	Tinsmith	7	Locksmith	2
Calico-printer	1	Brewer	5	Jeweller	1
Brush-maker	1	Distiller	1	Watch-maker	1
Flax-dresser	1				
Trades followed by ex-convicts and came-free but not by the native-born:					
Barber		Gunsmith		Sail-maker	
Hairdresser		Gun-filer		Silversmith	
Brass-founder					

after settlement and of the continued dependence on those few skilled convicts who settled in the colony after their sentences had expired or after pardon. The nature of the trades followed indicates clearly that most of the colonial tradesmen had been trained in the basic rather than specialized crafts. Among the free immigrant artisans this lack of luxury tradesmen could indicate that there was an insufficient market for their skills or at least a belief that this was so. There was, therefore, little incentive to migrate to New South Wales. It could also suggest that the labour and unemployment situation in Britain may have affected only the subsistence trades, where there was an over-abundance of labour, particularly in the main cities, so that there was no economic incentive or necessity for luxury and specialist tradesmen to leave Britain. Those skilled workers who may have left their homeland at this time did so, in all probability, for reasons other than lack of sufficient employment; they do not appear to have chosen the penal colony of Botany Bay as their future homeland.[16]

The largest group of workers in Britain at this time were the agricultural workers and servants. The largest occupational trades-group of workers were those employed in the building trades; these workers formed the largest single occupational group in Britain. The largest single trade in Britain as opposed to a cluster group of related trades, such as the building trades, was carpentry. Tailoring was the second largest individual trade, with half as many tailors as carpenters. It was on the basis of comparative membership of the differing trade groups that E.P. Thompson concluded that the typical skilled workman in early nineteenth century London was a member of the building trades or a tailor. Thompson found that, after the carpenters and tailors, the largest groups in order of membership size were the shoemakers, the cabinet-makers, printers, clock-makers, jewellers and bakers. These remained the main trade groups in England during the nineteenth century. Eleven years after the 1828 Census in New South Wales Henry Mayhew estimated that there were some '17,000 operative carpenters resident in the metropolis' of London, with 'work sufficient to give employment only to two-thirds'. Mayhew defined carpenters as 'anyone who cuts, fashions, and joins timber for building', and described how most carpenters were forced to 'work many miles away from their homes, and seldom or never take a meal in their own homes, except on a Sunday'.[17] Mayhew's descriptions of the lives of these men, although in a later period, are indicative of the English labour conditions

TABLE 8/2

Numbers of tradesmen in the three categories, building, subsistence and specialist/luxury trades, free and freed males, aged 15–40, New South Wales, 1828

Trade category	Civil condition of tradesmen		
	Native-born	Came-free	Ex-convict
Building	111	71	375
Subsistence	55	43	322
Specialist/luxury	3	13	70

which were familiar to the ex-convict and the immigrant tradesmen, most of whom were carpenters.

Most of the native-born tradesmen were carpenters but the reasons for this reflected the needs and nature of the colony. The conditions for skilled workers in the building trades in the colony contrasted so greatly with those in Britain because these tradesmen did not work in an oversupplied market but where there was a constant demand for their skills; carpentry was essential for the colony's establishment, survival, growth and expansion. There was no corresponding need or demand for luxury goods and those specialized goods which were required were imported rather than made in the colony.[18] Table 8/2 indicates the preponderance of building and subsistence tradesmen in comparison with specialist and luxury tradesmen in New South Wales in 1828.

The recommended scale of payment for work within the various trades is an indication of the economic value of the different tradesmen to the colony and, in most cases, emphasizes the higher wages which could be obtained in

TABLE 8/3

Trades and tradesmen, aged 15–40, New South Wales, 1828
(See Metric Conversion Table)

Trade	Payment	Civil condition of tradesmen		
		Native-born	Came-free	Ex-convict
Boat-builders generally	7/-	3	3	1
Bookbinders	5/6–6/-	0	0	3
Brass-founders	10/-	0	1	10
Bricklayers	8/-	0	0	63
Blacksmiths	6/--7/6	15	8	65
Carpenters, ship or house	7/6	37	39	108
Carpenters, including joiners & cabinet-makers	7/6	14	6	8
Coopers	7/6	3	8	9
Gardiners (sic)	5/-	1	0	0
Harness-makers	5/--7/-		2	8
Iron founders	10/-	0	0	1
Locksmiths	6/--7/6	0	0	2
Millwrights	7/6	8	7	12
Pump borers	10/-	0	0	0
Plasterers	7/6	0	0	19
Painters & glaziers	7/--7/6	0	2	17
Plumbers	7/--7/6	0	0	0
Stonemasons	7/--7/6	5	3	41
Tin men	7/--8/-	0	0	7
Tailors	4/6	7	8	51
Wheelwrights	5/-	14	2	17

New South Wales in comparison with seven shillings and sixpence a day;[19] an 'established' carpenter, 'working for the best prices' in London some twenty years later, reported 'I have always had five shillings a day, and, in busy times and long days, have made thirty-three and thirty-five shillings a week, by working overtime'.[20]

In 1824 Colonial Secretary Goulburn issued a list of 'Prices paid to good Mechanics and Tradesmen . . . in the Town of New South Wales'. Table 8/3 lists these trades with the recommended daily payment, and the numbers of native-born, came-free and ex-convict tradesmen.[21]

As a standard of comparison, laborers received from 2/6 to 5/- per day. Table 8/3 shows clearly the colony's heavy reliance on convicts and ex-convicts to supply skilled tradesmen. Most of these ex-convict tradesmen were from those trades which were oversupplied with labour in Britain and among whom unemployment was common. These were the carpenters, blacksmiths, tailors and bricklayers. That so large a proportion of the

TABLE 8/4

Government demand for convict skilled labour, 1825

Trade	Convicts employed
Carpenters	70
Painters	2
Joiners	5
Turners	1
Wheelwrights	15
Cabinet-makers	5
Blacksmiths	8
Shoemakers	8
Tanners	1
Bricklayers	13
Plasters [sic]	3
Masons	7
Stone-cutters	4
Tailors	6
Watch-makers	1
Bakers	1
Millers	4
Butchers	2
Millwrights	1
Coach-makers	2
Coopers	2
Brick-makers	10
Farriers	2
Nailors	1
Saddlers	1
Tin men	1
Bootmakers	5
Upholsterers	1

transported tradesmen were from these trades is an indication of the conditions for skilled workers in contemporary Britain.

Among the convict tradesmen serving sentences in the mid-1820s, government demand was similar to the demand for free mechanics. The list (Table 8/4) is an extract from Governor Brisbane's report on 'The Present Demand for Convict Labour', dated April 1825.[22]

This list shows that, with the exception of the watch-maker, the government need was for men skilled in the building and subsistence trades. It also indicates that the number of convict tradesmen employed by the government was in the same ratio as the number of native-born, came-free and ex-convicts who were skilled in these particular trades.

THE BUILDING TRADES

An examination of the individual trades and trade groupings followed by the native-born reveals a pattern which was the combined result of the needs and opportunities in the colony, the relationship between the native-born and their parents (in particular, between tradesmen and their sons), the labour situation in the colony and the individual experiences of the native-born during childhood and adolescence. The largest group of native-born tradesmen was made up of those who worked within the building trades: carpenters, cabinet-makers, coach-makers, builders and ship-builders. This group represented almost one third of all the native-born tradesmen and may have been larger, for those ships' carpenters and coopers who were at sea on colonial vessels when the Census was taken were not recorded. Table 8/5 shows the age groups of the native-born in the building trades; the number married is indicated in parentheses.

CARPENTERS

There were thirty-seven native-born carpenters in 1828, most of whom lived and worked at Sydney or Parramatta and usually remained in the town or district where they had been born.[23] George Tyrrell was the son of William Tyrrell and his wife; Tyrrell was one of the very few convict carpenters who

TABLE 8/5

The building trades: native-born tradesmen

	15–20	21–25	26–30	Age group 31–35	36–40	N.R.	Total
Native-born	22	26	6	7	1	1	63
building trades	(1)	(10)	(4)	(7)	(1)	(1)	(24)
Native-born	62	64	20	14	6	4	170
all trades	(3)	(24)	(13)	(13)	(5)	(0)	(58)

had arrived in 1788. Tyrrell senior had married convict Ann Wade the month after landing at Sydney Cove and George, their eldest child, was born the following year. Tyrrell senior received a land grant from Governor Hunter and was active in colonial affairs, to the extent that he was a signatory to the Settlers' Petition of Grievances in 1798 and signed a petition to Governor Bligh from the Hawkesbury settlers in 1807 and another from the Inhabitants of New South Wales in 1808. It was most probable that Tyrrell abandoned farming and returned to his trade as a carpenter after a disaster in 1810. On 14 January of that year the *Sydney Gazette* reported this disaster; it was indicative of the difficulties faced by settlers and may also be seen as a report of some of the childhood experiences which may have influenced the native-born to prefer the life of a tradesman to that of a farmer:

> By the lightning on the evening of yesterday se'nnight a barn belonging to William Tyrrell at Kissing Point was set fire to and totally consumed, together with about 15 bushels of wheat which he had reserved to seed his ground with for next year's crop. In his little dwelling house his wife was unfortunately struck on the left side of her face by the electric fluid, which has severely scorched her face and neck, and much crippled her in her limbs. As this poor man has twice previously had his house and everything he possessed destroyed by fire, he is now reduced to extreme distress, with the severe affliction of having a now helpless wife and three unfortunate children to participate in miseries proceeding not from his own imprudence but from causes against which it is not in the power of mankind to guard.[24]

Tyrrell senior lived and worked with his eldest son until his death in June 1827; his son entered his father's occupation as carpenter on the burial certificate and this was the occupation he gave for himself in the 1828 Census. George Tyrrell's youngest son, called William after his ex-convict grandfather, became an apprentice blacksmith in Sydney.

Approximately twenty per cent of the native-born carpenters worked for landholders on country properties: there were two at Bathurst, one at Evan, one at Wallis Plains, one at Upper Neptune, one at Lower Portland Head, one at Patricks Plains, and one at Goulburn.[25] There is evidence of a link between these 'rural' carpenters and their parents. Native-born John Regan, a carpenter, lived and worked with his carpenter father for a landowner at Goulburn Plains; his mother, Margaret, worked for the same landowner as a servant. The father and mother had both arrived as convicts and were both freed by servitude. Regan senior had petitioned the governor for permission 'to go carpenter to such settlement as his Excellency may choose and with indulgences he may grant to himself and his son'. Regan's second son, William, was a farmer with his family in nearby Sutton Forest. Thomas Raynolds was a carpenter at Patricks Plains; he had been born at Wilberforce where his father still farmed. His elder brother was a carpenter at Parramatta, one younger brother was a harness-maker who lived with the youngest brother, an apprentice harness-maker. It was not unusual for many of the sons of ex-convict tradesmen to become tradesmen themselves and continue working with their father or their brothers.

There were opportunities for native-born carpenters to work for government although not, apparently, at the highest levels. Two native-born carpenters, George Lucas and Thomas Warrington, were employed by government at the Male Orphan School at Cabramatta. Lucas' mother was Olivia Gascoigne who had arrived convicted and later married Nathaniel Lucas, a fellow convict. In 1828 Olivia, then a widow, lived with her eldest son who continued his father's business at Liverpool. All three sons had become tradesmen themselves. One native-born carpenter, Richard Dalton, tried unsuccessfully to obtain the position of Superintendent of the Carters' Barracks in 1825. Richard was the son of Richard Dalton, who had arrived in the colony as 'a free object', was appointed a district constable by Macquarie in 1810 and later became the Master of the Benevolent Asylum. His younger son, William, became a cabinet-maker, married a native-born girl and continued to work at his trade in Sydney. Richard junior had married native-born Rebecca Scrivenson shortly after he had finished his apprenticeship at Carpenters' Barracks but she had died in childbirth and in 1828 Richard was working as a carpenter in Sydney and living near his brother. The successful applicant for the position Richard had attempted to obtain was a Mr Andrew Murray, who had recently arrived from England and who in 1828 was receiving the salary of £128.0.0 per annum. If Richard were not self-employed, his weekly wage at that time would have been approximately £2.0.0, or £104.0.0 per annum. No reason had been given for the rejection of his application for the position of Superintendent.

CABINET-MAKERS

The fourteen native-born who became cabinet-makers were all born after 1803 and had served their apprenticeships during the administration of Macquarie. Before this there had been little opportunity for apprentices to train in this craft. There were few skilled cabinet-makers in the colony and no advertisements for apprentices appeared in the *Sydney Gazette*. All except one of these native-born cabinet-makers lived and worked in Sydney. The exception was a farmer's son, William Hazleen, born in 1803 to two ex-convicts with whom he still lived at Concord. Richard Kellick was a native-born who employed another 'currency' cabinet-maker in his business at Princes Street, Sydney. Few from this trade group owned land. One, nineteen-year-old William Hanks, had applied to the governor for a land grant. The son of two ex-convicts—his father worked as a carter—Hanks junior lived with his parents and two younger sisters. He wrote to the governor that, by laboriously applying himself to his trade, he had been able to amass a considerable sum of money. This was exclusive of the assistance offered by his parents. He requested a land grant from Governor Brisbane as he had 'an inclination to enter into the domestic scene of life ... was desirous of withdrawing into the cultivated part of the country where he might enjoy the sweets of rural retirement'. His application was rejected on the grounds that he did not supply the necessary character references, nor had he given assurances that he did intend to settle the land if it were granted.[26] By 1828 Hanks may have found some of the 'domestic scene of life' he was seeking, although quite probably not that which he had in mind. He was living in Sydney with his two unmarried sisters and was employed as a cabinet-maker.

There were among the native-born tradesmen brothers who lived and worked together or in close proximity. This was in accordance with the usual pattern of occupation evident among the sons of tradesmen. The sons followed the same trade as or one allied to that of their father. William Dalton, a cabinet-maker in Princes Street, was the brother of Richard Dalton, carpenter of Pitt Street. Joseph Miller, cabinet-maker of George Street, lived and worked with his younger brother, John, a blacksmith. Charles Morris, cabinet-maker of George Street had an elder brother who worked as a shoemaker in Pitt Street.

COACH-MAKERS

There were five native-born coach-makers, forming the smallest and youngest group of tradesmen. All worked in Sydney. George Tuckwell had lived at Parramatta with his widowed mother until 1826 and then transferred to Sydney. Not all were the sons of men and women who had arrived as convicts. The father of Gerald Anderson had been a private in the New South Wales Corps and had married and remained as a settler when the Corps was recalled to England in 1810.

BOAT-BUILDERS

From the beginning of settlement, the colonial boat-building trade relied heavily on convict labour. There were few skilled boat-builders in the colony. In 1828 none of the immigrants in the 15–40 age group described themselves as boat-builders and only one of the ex-convicts did. There were three native-born boat-builders and two who used the description 'builder'. All these native-born completed their apprenticeships at His Majesty's Dock Yards. Daniel Egan had served the usual seven-year apprenticeship. When this was completed in 1825 Egan successfully applied for the position of Master Builder of the Dock Yards. He requested that this appointment be publicly gazetted. Thomas Day also served his seven years at the Dock Yards. He was then appointed Boatswain of the Police Row Guard Boat, at a salary of £10 a year.[27] Both Egan and Day were also landowners, as was Thomas Crumpton, who lived and worked with his father at Lower Portland Head. All of the native-born boat-builders were married to native-born girls and some lived with the parents of their husbands.[28]

SHIPWRIGHTS, MILLWRIGHTS, BLACKSMITHS, WHEELWRIGHTS, COOPERS, STONEMASONS

Fifty-two of the native-born became shipwrights, millwrights, blacksmiths, wheelwrights, coopers or stonemasons. Table 8/6 shows the age groups of these native-born tradesmen; the number married is indicated in parentheses.

TABLE 8/6

Native-born tradesmen: shipwrights, millwrights, blacksmiths, wheelwrights, coopers and stonemasons

	15–20	21–25	26–30	Age group 31–35	36–40	N.R.	Total
Native-born these trades	15 (1)	21 (8)	7 (5)	6 (5)	3 (2)	0	52 (20)
Native-born all trades	62 (3)	64 (24)	20 (13)	14 (13)	6 (5)	4 (0)	170 (58)

SHIPWRIGHTS

The shipwrights were among the oldest of the native-born tradesmen, five having been born before 1797. The pattern was the same for both ex-convict and immigrant shipwrights; among the ex-convicts, most were in the older age group. That most of the native-born shipwrights were among the oldest group of the surviving first generation in 1828 meant that they had experienced the changing conditions in the colony. They had seen the changes in regulations governing the building of vessels in the colony and they had watched Sydney Cove emerge as a bustling seaport.[29]

It was not until after 1804, when advertisements for apprentices could be published in the *Sydney Gazette*, that the number of apprentices required indicated both the growth of the colonial boat-building trade and the development of trading interests. In particular, these advertisements showed the success in these ventures by the ex-convict partners, Kable and Underwood. In November 1804 Kable and Underwood advertised for ten boys, a number which exceeded the combined total of all advertisements for apprentices in that year. The wording of the advertisement is evidence of the acceptance by contemporaries wishing to employ apprentices that parents would seek such positions for their sons:

APPRENTICES

Ten Boys, from 10 to 14 years of age, will be received by Messrs. Kable and Underwood as Apprentices to the business of shipwright ... Such persons as have sons whom they wish to be taken on trial, are requested to apply to either of the above co-partners.

Kable and Underwood clearly expected that the fathers of these intending apprentice shipwrights would arrange for the apprenticeships and outlined encouraging terms in the indentures.[30] That this was the assumption made in 1804 by ex-convicts who were both fathers of large families is particularly significant as it was at this time that the Governor, King, and his principal chaplain, Samuel Marsden, were continually deploring the depravity of the unnatural convict parents and the manner in which they neglected and abandoned their offspring. There is no evidence to identify the apprentices chosen by Kable and Underwood, but they may have included William Fielder, born in 1795, John Jones, born in 1796, and William Humphries, born in 1795. Shipwrights also appear to have had more opportunity to train with private masters rather than with government . In addition to Kable and Underwood there were others, such as Garnham Blaxcel, who advertised in the *Sydney Gazette*. One of Blaxcel's advertisements is of particular interest. Not only did it specify 'Three or Four Lads from 13 to 16 years old to work as Apprentices' but it showed the continuing awareness of parental concern. by stipulating the care which would be taken of these apprentices: 'Proper attention will be paid to their diet and lodging, and clothing found them, if required'.[31]

Most of the future colonial tradesmen who trained with Kable, Underwood or Blaxcel were the sons of men and women who had arrived as convicts. William Fielder, born in 1795 and named for his father, convict William Fielder, grew up in a convict household until his father had served his sentence. By 1806, when William junior would have been eleven years old, the father was supporting his family by working as a 'gardiner' in Sydney. In that year he signed the 'New Year's Address of Welcome to Governor Bligh from the Inhabitants of New South Wales' and on 26 January 1808 he signed the address to Major Johnston from John Macarthur and others supporting the deposition of Governor Bligh. Fielder, although he lacked any skills himself, had shown sufficient enterprise and parental interest to obtain an apprenticeship for his son with a private master. In all probability this involved the payment of an indentures fee, which would have been beyond the ability of a carter in similar circumstances in England.

The two oldest shipwrights, Charles Peat, born in 1792, and John Irving, born in 1790, both trained at the Government Dock Yards. Both were the sons of skilled convicts who were employed by government. The third shipwright, William Chapman, born in 1802, was the son of a plumber and glazier who had been employed by government until his death in 1810, 'leaving a widow and nine children to lament his loss'. At this time, William Chapman was eight years-old. He and his numerous brothers and sisters were fortunate that they were not orphaned that year; their mother had accidentally drunk poison in mistake for medicine and it had been necessary for their father to assure an investigation that this had not been the result of negligence at the General Hospital.[32] William junior and his brother, George, born in 1807, both worked as shipwrights at Darling Harbour in 1828 and their youngest brother, James, who had been born shortly after their father's death, was apprenticed to them. Not only is there evidence of these continuing links among the sons of ex-convict tradesmen but there is evidence of intermarriage among trade families. Shipwright William Fielder married native-born Mary Ann Dalton, sister of carpenter Richard Dalton. William Chapman married Ann Chennals, the daughter of a Sydney blacksmith, and shipwright John Irving was a witness at their wedding.

John Irving had served his apprenticeship at the Dock Yards; he was the son of first fleet convict John Irving, who claimed that he had been 'bred to surgery' and had received the first pardon from Governor Phillip, in recognition of his services to New South Wales during the first years of settlement. Irving senior died in 1795. His son eventually married the daughter of Lieutenant Ball and convict Sarah Partridge. Sarah's brother, Richard, continued this link between convict and free by marrying Margaret Perry, who had arrived in the colony as a convict in 1817. Richard Partridge and his wife settled on his father's land grant at the Field of Mars. Irving became a master builder at the Dock Yards. He showed pride in his skills learned there. When applying to the governor for a grant of land, he emphasized that he had, as the Dock Yards' master builder, supervised the building of a 'Lifeboat and Cutter, the latter being admired by all for her capacity and velocity'. When Irving left government employ he worked for himself as a shipwright. He applied successfully for permission to build two vessels to trade between Sydney and Newcastle. His application was strongly supported by William Cowper:

> Irving is an industrious young man with a wife and children and is desirous to facilitate the conveyance of goods to and from Newcastle up the River as well for the convenience of the Colony at large as for his own ends.[33]

That Irving, the son of two convicts, was genuinely 'desirous' of benefitting the colony is supported by his later career in New South Wales. In the early 1830s he became noted for his strong advocacy for the inherent superiority of the Currency, or native-born, over the Sterling, or British born. This was particularly evident in reports and editorial comment in the short-lived nationalistic newspaper, the *Currency Lad*. The following 'Notice' appeared in the first edition, published in September 1832: 'Mr Irving (a Currency Lad) challenged any whale boat in the Colony to run against his boat for fifty guineas'. The wager of fifty guineas, which would have been more than six months' wages for a skilled British tradesman, could be seen as indicative of Irving's material success—or, perhaps, his addiction to gambling. In its seventh issue the *Currency Lad* reported that Irving's challenge had been taken up by William Chapman who, although also native-born, appeared to have less patriotic sentiments than his friend and fellow-shipwright, John Irving. The *Currency Lad* described the race:

> Mr. Irving's boat (manned only by Currency Lads) winning with ease. Mr. Chapman's boat, pulled by a crew of Australians and Europeans ... Mr. Irving himself steered. A second boat of his, steered by C. Bolger, came in second.[34]

More important than the outcome of the race were the sentiments of John Irving, who had lived in the colony since the time of Governor Phillip and had witnessed the growth and expansion of his homeland. Irving would have been consciously aware of the opportunities offered by the colony to the industrious and enterprising ex-convict and his family.

Another native-born shipwright, also the son of first fleet convicts, who became outstandingly successful in his native land was George Peat, born in 1790, the son of Charles Peat and Ann Mullins who had married in 1788. George worked with his father, a former convicted highwayman who had defended himself at his trial at the Old Bailey, where he was charged additionally with being unlawfully at large after sentence of transportation. Ironically, it was the convicted felon Charles Peat who was a leader in the formation of the Night Watch, the first law-enforcement body established in the colony. That his son was proud of his father's colonial career was evident in his first Memorial to the governor; he described himself as 'a native colonist, the son of Charles Peat, the first Chief Constable in the Colony'. George Peat served his apprenticeship in the Dock Yards, probably through the influence of his father, and then settled on the Hawkesbury River, becoming the owner of several of the small vessels which were engaged in the river trade and in the ferrying of passengers between the Hawkesbury settlements and the town of Sydney. Peat worked in partnership with two other native-born, James Webb and John James Peacock. Peacock, born in 1790, was also a landowner and by 1828 had settled with his native-born wife and family at Lower Portland Head. By 1828 Peat and his family had returned to Sydney, where he described himself as a shipwright. He had been influential in building the river trade and a system of ferries which enabled both goods and passengers to travel more freely within the colony.

MILLWRIGHTS

In contrast to the shipwrights, the native-born millwrights were a comparatively younger group of tradesmen and almost all of them had followed their fathers into this trade.[35] The oldest, the only one over twenty years of age, was John Lucas, of Liverpool, the son of two convicts, Olivia Gascoigne and her husband Nathaniel Lucas. Lucas was a carpenter and a miller. John lived and worked as a millwright with his father until his parent's death; he then took over his father's business at Liverpool, where he lived with his own family and his widowed mother. John and his father had erected one of the first mills in the colony and requested that Governor Macquarie himself name their mill.

John Dight, born in 1810, was the son of free settlers John and Hannah Dight, who had arrived in 1801 and settled at Richmond, where Dight senior became Coroner and eventually owned almost 1000 acres. John junior, who had been born at Richmond, worked as a miller in Sydney and then, after marrying a native-born girl from Argyle, moved to Campbelltown. One of his sisters, Elizabeth, married native-born landowner Hamilton Hume, who was from the same district. The millwright trade was the only one not concentrated in Sydney, mills being established in those areas to which grain could be easily and quickly transported. In addition to John Lucas at Liverpool, there were George Howell at Parramatta and James Watson and Henry Hough at Richmond. Watson was the son of an ex-convict who had been sentenced to life transportation and whose free wife had accompanied him to the colony in 1796. Watson junior lived with his parents and his two sisters, one of whom, Elizabeth, was a laundress. Henry Hough's father was an Irish ex-convict who farmed at Richmond, where he lived with his native-born wife and their five younger children. George Howell was also the son of convicts, James Howell and his ex-convict 'wife', Hannah Hill. George had been born at Parramatta in 1805, when his father was still serving his sentence, so had spent his early years in a convict household. Although still a convict, Howell senior had signed a petition to Bligh in 1808. He died in 1811 at the age of forty-seven and his son continued to live with his widowed mother at Parramatta. These three native-born millers, George Howell, Henry Hough and James Watson, were all employed by the same millwright, John Smith, who lived in Sydney.

BLACKSMITHS

The trade of blacksmith had been one of the basic and essential trades from the time of the colony's foundation; however, it is doubtful if any of the native-born blacksmiths served as apprentices at the Government Dock Yards or Lumber Yards. As early as 1804 advertisements for apprentice blacksmiths to private masters began to appear in the *Sydney Gazette*, which might have been indicative of a shortage of trained blacksmiths among the convict labour force. In July of that year ex-convict Thomas Storer advertised for two apprentices to learn the trade of a smith.[36] By 1828 there were fifteen native-born tradesmen who described themselves as black-smiths. Four of these were in Sydney, two at Parramatta and two at Patricks Plains. There was one each at Wilberforce, Pitt Town, Sutton Forest, Evan, Lower Minto, Spring Hill and Bathurst. Few of these blacksmiths had been born in Sydney; the way in which they were scattered through-out the colony indicates the need for smiths both in the townships and on the properties of private masters. Those in Sydney were Henry Hughes, born at Parramatta in 1811, John Miller, born in 1812, and his brother, William, and George Webb, born in 1810. None of these tradesmen were living with their parents and there is no record of the parentage of the Miller boys or George Webb. Among those who lived and worked outside Sydney was William Cosier, who had been born at Parramatta. He was the son of an ex-convict blacksmith, Thomas Cosier, and his wife, ex-convict Ann Sydney. It is probable that William had learned his trade from his father. In 1824 William Cosier had applied to Governor Brisbane for a land grant but he listed no land holdings in the 1828 Census. Three of the native-born blacksmiths were also landholders: Robert Wright had thirteen acres at Pitt Town, James Lavello had five acres at Liverpool and John Sewell had been granted sixty acres at Sutton Forest. Two more owned stock, Henry Burgin at Parramatta and Edward Bailis at Patricks Plains. Few of the parents of these blacksmiths were alive in 1828. Those who were did not live with their sons. In 1828 the blacksmiths among the ex-convicts and the immigrants belonged to older age groups than did those from among the native-born. There were, for example, sixty-five ex-convict blacksmiths in the same age group as the first generation and all were over the age of twenty-five. This is explained by the age of the convicts when they arrived and the length of their sentences.[37]

WHEELWRIGHTS

Among the fourteen native-born wheelwrights, only one was employed by a private landowner; he lived on his master's property together with convict and ex-convict servants. This was James Powell, born in 1806, who worked for William Cox at Clarendon. He was the son of Edward Powell, a former seaman and one of the first group of free settlers.

Two of the wheelwrights lived and worked in Sydney. They were David Hill and William Small, both the sons of ex-convicts. Four were in Parramatta: Charles Blakefield, James Goodin, John McManus and John Walker, three of whom had spent most of their childhood in the district of Parramatta. James Goodin on the other hand had been born on Norfolk Island in 1795, where his ex-convict parents were settlers. When that settlement was abandoned the father received a land grant at Kissing Point, where he was still living with his wife and five younger children in 1828. John McManus was the son of a marine settler who had arrived in 1788. He received a land grant at Mulgrave Place, where his two sons were born. After his death, in April 1798, his widow received 160 acres in trust for their children. John, born shortly after his father's death, remained at Parramatta where, in 1828, he worked for himself as a wheelwright and owned sixty acres. His elder brother, James, born in 1798, was a farmer with 113 acres at Bathurst.

Among the wheelwrights living and working at Windsor was Thomas Freeman, one of four brothers who had been born there and had lived with their ex-convict parents, William Freeman and Elizabeth Chaffrey. In 1828 the four sons, aged between twenty-seven and nineteen, lived together on fifteen acres. James and John described themselves as labourers, George was a shoemaker and Thomas, the youngest, a wheelwright. The Freeman brothers are an example of a 'convict' family in which the parents were not married but the children remained together and continued to live in the district where they had been born. The two other wheelwrights in Windsor were James Powell and Christopher May. Although May described himself as a wheelwright he may have been an apprentice as he was only fifteen years of age. Another wheelwright, James Lavello, was one of the oldest of the first generation, being thirty-nine years old in 1828. He was a widower, living with his two young children at Liverpool.

COOPERS

Only three of the native-born followed the specialized trade of cooper; this compares with eight free immigrant coopers and nine ex-convicts coopers in the same age group. It is probable that the number of coopers may have been higher among both the native-born and the ex-convicts resident in New South Wales as those on coastal vessels were not included in the 1828 Census. Advertisements for coopers, but not for apprentice coopers, were frequent in the *Sydney Gazette*.[38] The native-born coopers were all born between 1803 and 1807; two were in Sydney and one in Pitt Town. The two in Sydney were Peter Brennen and George Green. Brennen and his younger brother, who was an apprentice cabinet-maker, were the sons of an ex-convict. John Wright, of Pitt Town, was the brother of blacksmith Robert Wright, shoemaker Thomas Wright and carpenter Charles Wright. All were sons of ex-convicts Joseph and Eleanor Wright, who had married at St. Phillip's in 1790.

STONEMASONS

It was only among the stonemasons that most of the native-born tradesmen described themselves as Catholics. The most likely reason for this could be found in the country of origin of most of their parents, Ireland. The chief occupation of these fathers in the colony was that of stonemason or stonecutter. Native-born Patrick Byrne was the son of a transported Irish rebel, a stonemason by trade, who was sentenced to life in New South Wales after the 1798 Rebellion. Byrne received an absolute pardon, remained in the colony working at his trade and by 1828 was a widower living in Sydney with five of his children. It is possible that Patrick junior learned his trade by working with his father.

Another native-born stonemason, who in all probability was apprenticed to his father, was Henry Boulton, the son of a former member of the New South Wales Corps, Thomas Boulton, a stonemason by trade. In 1828 Henry lived and worked in Sydney with his father, his native-born step-mother and eight brothers and sisters. John Dell was the son of another former private in the New South Wales Corps, John Dell senior, and his second wife, Sarah Green. After their deaths he was cared for by Mr George Lane, a stonemason of Sydney. Lane wrote to the governor asking for a land grant for his ward and Dell received 60 acres. The Memorial applying for land stated that George Lane was a stonemason of Sydney. The influence of the occupation of the father, whether convict or came-free, and, in the case of John Dell, the guardian, is evident in the choice of trade by the native-born stonemasons. This is reinforced by the size of the families of tradesmen such as Byrne and Boulton senior, and that all children remained with the parents.

SHOEMAKERS, TAILORS, WEAVERS, HARNESS-MAKERS

Native-born shoemakers, tailors, weavers and harness-makers may be considered as a trade group. Table 8/7 indicates the ages of the native-born who followed these trades. Those married are indicated in parentheses.

SHOEMAKERS

After carpentry, boot- and shoemaking was the largest single trade among the native-born, as it was with the free immigrant tradesmen in the same age group. It was also the largest trade followed by the ex-convicts. The reason for the large number of convict and ex-convict shoemakers may have been that this was the largest single trade in London, employing both men and women. It was oversupplied with workers and wages were poor and unemployment common. In the colony the wages of shoemakers were consider-

TABLE 8/7

Native-born shoemakers, tailors, weavers and harness-makers, 1828

	15–20	21–25	26–30	Age group 31–35	36–40	N.R.	Total
Native-born	16	11	3	0	1	0	31
these trades	(1)	(4)	(1)		(1)		(7)
Native-born	61	65	20	14	6	4	170
all trades	(3)	(24)	(13)	(13)	(5)	(0)	(58)

ably less than those for building worker. By 1822 a colonial shoemaker could earn only an average of four shillings to six shillings a week if he were employed by a master shoemaker. This was approximately the wage which could be demanded and obtained by by a good labourer. In London some twenty years later, shoemakers averaged only twenty shillings a week, and that was if they were constantly employed.[39] The trade did not have the prestige of the building trades. In New South Wales, shoemaking and tailoring were the chief trades taught at the Male Orphan School, being considered suitable for destitute children from the lowers orders.[40] Few of the native-born shoemakers and tailors were baptized and there is little record of their parentage. It could be assumed that many were taught their trade as 'deserving orphans' rather than as apprentices either to government or to private masters. This assumption is reinforced by the locality in which these tradesmen were employed and by the common characteristic that they did not work themselves or with brothers but were employed, usually on country properties. George Donnelly was a shoemaker for Mr. Kennedy of Appin; his brother, Garrett, worked as a sawyer at Illawarra for J.H. Spearing, a landholder who had arrived as a free settler with his family in 1825. Samuel Fry was shoemaker to James Hassall at Cooke and his brother, Richard, a boot and shoemaker working for Thomas Williams of Pitt Street, Sydney. His third brother, John, was an apprentice tailor. There is no record of the civil condition, occupation or death of their father, George Fry, except that he signed a Petition to Governor Bligh from the Sydney Settlers and Inhabitants on 22 December 1806.[41]

John Going, born in 1810, was another native-born shoemaker whose parents could not be traced and who was employed by a freed-by-servitude shoemaker in Sydney. Another was James Harris who was employed as a shoemaker by William Hatwood, a nailor who had received a conditional pardon. Three tradesmen whose parents could not be traced were George Morris, shoemaker, living with his family in Pitt Street, and his brothers Thomas and John, both turners who lived nearby. Among those in this occupational group whose fathers were known were William Deane, born in 1807, the son of an ex-convict baker who had been transported from Ireland for his part in the rebellion of 1798. Deane and his father lived together in George Street, Sydney. Another was John McNulty, born in 1811, who lived and worked with his ex-convict father, a shoemaker in Clarence Street, Sydney. George Freeman, shoemaker of Windsor, lived with his three brothers, all of whom had been born in the district. In those cases where parentage could be identified the occupational link between father and son could be established clearly. In many of these cases the first generation tradesmen learned their trade from their fathers; there do not appear to have been any opportunities for securing private apprenticeships. Considering the high proportion of shoemakers and tailors among the convict tradesmen, it is unlikely that government needed to train boys in these skills. All the evidence would suggest that those who were trained by government or by the Male Orphan Schools were orphans or destitute children. After training, they were placed with tradesmen. This would explain the way in which brothers were separated, which was not the normal pattern of trade families.

Shoe manufacturing was one of the early small manufactories begun by private enterprise in the colony. In 1809 there was an advertisement in the *Sydney Gazette* for 'a Person to superintend a Boot and Shoe Factory'. This was placed by a Mr Hayes who, although not identified by the newspaper, was the former Irish convict Michael Hayes. In January of the following year Michael Hayes advertised that at his warehouse he had 'a large assortment of leather ... Morocco and Spanish coloured skins; English tanned foal leather, wax calf skins, seal skins, etc.' Hayes advised the public that he had quantities of:

> Hessian boot legs, shoes and boots, boot top leather, ladies and childrens shoes, colours, russet calf skins for ladies' shoes ...
> N.B. Naval and Military Officers can be furnished with boots and shoes at the shortest notice. Wholesale purchasers will meet encouragement. Contracts will be entered into for any quantity of Boots and Shoes.[42]

From the wording of this advertisement, it would appear that Hayes had a large warehouse and employed a number of skilled tradesmen. He did not, however, advertise for apprentices, nor did the other two boot and shoe-makers who advertised their trade in the *Sydney Gazette*.[43] This may have been the direct result of the ready availability of convict and ex-convict tradesmen skilled in these trades, which made it both unnecessary and uneconomical to train young boys in the mysteries of the craft.

Although the trade of shoemaking was less profitable and more likely to be followed by the poorer sections of the working classes, this did not necessarily mean that the native-born son of a shoemaker who followed his father's trade remained on the same level as his parents. One parent, Thomas Smart, was an ex-convict shoemaker who lived in Sydney with his eighteen-year-old son in 1828. This son later went into partnership with a Sydney draper, Andrew Oliver, and, on Oliver's death, married his widow and thus inherited his late partner's share of the business. Thomas Smart junior eventually became the manager of the Sydney Banking Company and was M.L.A. for Glebe from 1860–65; he then became a member of the Legislative Council and, at his death in the late 1800s, was a director of the A.M.P. Society, a position which would appear to have been beyond the expectations of the son of a convict shoemaker. Such a career would have been exceedingly difficult for a tradesman in the same situation in contemporary England.

TAILORS

Tailors were on the same social level as shoemakers, and were as poorly paid. Most of the seven native-born tailors were the sons of tradesmen and all were under the age of twenty-six. Only one lived outside Sydney. This was Thomas Bogg of Liverpool, the son of an ex-convict bootmaker. Other tradesmen fathers in this group included John Flood, a carpenter. Flood's three sons were tradesmen: Thomas, a tailor, and Joseph and John, carpenters. The three brothers lived near one another in Sydney.

WEAVERS

There were only three native-born weavers, which was in accordance with the lack of opportunity for the colonial youth to learn this trade. The female convicts at Parramatta were employed to weave for government, producing 'Parramatta Cloth' which was used for shirting, towelling and sheeting.[44] In 1798 the first hand looms were imported and by 1804 Governor King was able to inform Sir Joseph Banks that 'our crop of flax gives constant employment to nine looms—half of them making sailcloth'.[45] These nine looms managed to produce 100 yards of cloth a week, giving employment for fifty women convicts and eighteen men. Individual settlers were also encouraged by the governors to spin and weave in their homes; prizes of sheep and cattle were awarded to industrious householders. Wealthier settlers such as John Blaxland set up small 'factories' on their own properties, producing cloth for their own needs and particularly to clothe their assigned servants. Blaxland told Bigge that he employed three persons in this way; they produced thirty yards of cloth a week at a cost of four shillings a yard.[46] In 1811 Simeon Lord began to manufacture hats and a few years later established the first private woollen mill, employing labour and selling cloth by contract to the government. In 1811 Lord moved his mill to the mouth of the Lachlan Swamps at Botany Bay.[47] These mills expanded slowly and in 1828 three of the first generation were employed there. They included Robert Blue and his thirteen-year-old brother, John. Their father was ex-convict William Blue, a landholder at Hunters Hill, where he lived with his eldest son. Simeon Lord also employed the other two native-born weavers, John Evans, fifteen, and James Hoppy, twenty-one. There were few weavers in the colony in the same age group as the first generation in 1828. There were no free immigrants and only twenty-two among the ex-convicts. Most of the ex-convict weavers were employed by Simeon Lord, so that the three native-born weavers would have been accustomed to working with and being instructed by ex-convict tradesmen.

HARNESS-MAKERS

There was only one native-born harness-maker in 1828. This was Richard Reynolds, harness-maker to Richard Keppard, a wheelwright who had been conditionally pardoned. Richard lived and worked with his younger brother, James, who was an apprentice wheelwright to Richard Keppard. Their father, William, free by servitude, had arrived in 1791 with his brother, Richard. In 1828 William was a labourer on Richard's farm at Wilberforce

TABLE 8/8

Native-born bakers, pastrycooks, butchers

	15–20	21–26	26–30	Age group 31–36	36–50	N.R.	Total
Native-born these trades	6 (0)	2 (0)	2 (1)	1 (1)	1 (1)	0	12 (3)
Native-born all trades	63 (3)	64 (24)	20 (13)	14 (13)	6 (5)	4 (0)	171 (58)

and his youngest daughter, Elizabeth, lived with him. Their father had no land of his own and this may have been the reason for his two sons becoming tradesmen.

THE FOOD TRADES

Few of the native-born tradesmen worked in the food trade. Table 8/8 illustrates the age groups of those who became bakers, pastrycooks or butchers. Those who were married are indicated in parentheses.

BAKERS AND PASTRYCOOKS

Baking was a trade stictly regulated by government. Throughout this period there were continual Government and General Orders enforcing regulations to ensure correct weight; standard bread prices were published in the *Sydney Gazette* several times a month.[48] In January 1809 a 'whimsical' paragraph in the *Sydney Gazette* highlighted the need for these regulations:

> The following whimsical remark is contained in a recent British paper: Among the Turks the penalty inflicted on a baker for making bread short of weight is to order him into his Oven.—Query, Were the same dreadful mode of expiating a similar offence resorted to in this country, what size must the oven be?[49]

From 1804 bakers were required to register their names with a magistrate. Failure to do so required a fine of twenty shillings.[50] There was no evidence of any discrimination on the grounds of civil condition nor were women prevented from obtaining baking licences.[51] There were, however, attempts made to identify the bread baked on different premises. In New South Wales by 1810 all bakers were required by government order to stamp their initials on their loaves and so facilitate identification of those bakers who sold underweight or inferior bread. Most of the colonial bakers could be classified as 'small' bakers, such as Mrs Bennett, William Morgan and Hugh Murphy, whose assistants were their immediate family and assigned convict labour. There were also ex-convicts with multiple interests, who erected bakehouses and advertised for skilled labour but not for apprentices. These included Henry Kable, Thomas Rose and William Chapman, all of whom had native-born children, but none of their sons or daughters continued these particular business interests.[52] There were only four native-born bakers in 1828, and one pastrycook. Two of these were the sons of bakers. One was George Phelps, who lived and worked with his ex-convict father, Richard. The other was William Deane, who also worked with his ex-convict father, William senior, in Sydney. Deane had arrived in 1798 and had his bakehouse in George Street. Most of the colonial bakers in this age group were ex-convicts, a total of forty-one as compared with seven free immigrants and the five native-born. The two remaining native-born bakers were the sons of former privates of the New South Wales Corps. Thomas Hancey was a baker in Kent Street, his brother Richard was a sawyer at Kissing Point and their father a settler at Baukham Hills. Edward Parsons, baker, lived in Sydney with his native-born wife and his ex-soldier father, who was a cabinet-maker. The fourth native-born baker was George Williams, a sixteen-year-old who worked at Liverpool. His ex-convict father and native-born mother were farmers at Camden, where they lived with their six younger children.

BUTCHERS

The only similarity between the butchers and the bakers was that they, too, were licensed by government.[53] Mostly, the butchers were a wealthier group than the bakers, and they usually owned cattle and land. In the colonial newspapers there were no advertisements for apprentice butchers; on the contrary, some of the native-born butchers had completed apprenticeships in another trade, such as carpentry, before establishing themselves as colonial butchers. This may indicate a need for capital in this trade. The oldest of the native-born butchers was former shipwright James Bloodsworth. In many ways his career was more typical of those of many of the ex-convicts rather than of the first generation. James was born in the colony in 1789, the first son of James Bloodsworth and Sarah Bellamy, who had arrived convicted on the first fleet. James Bloodsworth claimed that he was 'the first in this colony which served his time in His Majesty's Dock Yard'. After he had completed his apprenticeship, which was most probably seven years, he served on ships sailing between Sydney and Calcutta as a seaman and as ship's carpenter. He then married Maria Lee, or Pantony, who had been born on Norfolk Island, the daughter of a convict woman and a marine. Her brother had an extensive land holding at Bathurst. By 1828 he described himself as a butcher, was living in O'Connell Street and owned 150 acres, 150 cattle and 600 sheep. His younger brother, George, who had also served his apprenticeship at the Dock Yards, became a publican in York Street. Neither of the Bloodsworths continued to maintain family connections with their mother after the death of their father. In this respect they were not typical of the native-born, but more in accordance with the assumption that the first generation rejected their convict parents. In 1824 James and George attempted to deprive their mother of her inheritance from their father, claiming that the house in which she lived belonged to them and requesting assistance in removing her.

Another wealthy native-born butcher was Humphrey Thorn, who lived with his brother, native-born wife and infant child at Parramatta, where he owned 370 acres. His elder brother John, born in 1793, was Chief Constable at Parramatta and owned 1850 acres, 275 horned cattled and 300 sheep. It is most likely that these two brothers worked together, the younger buying his cattle from the elder. The remaining five butchers all lived in Sydney; they were all young men and all employed by master butchers. Peter Curtis, who was fifteen, was employed by ex-convict William Sharp; his brother was a married cabinet-maker who lived in Phillip Street. Edward O'Hara was the son of a former convict who had received an absolute pardon and worked as a ship's chandler in Kent Street. Edward was employed in Pitt Street. John Prentice was employed by a ticket-of-leave blacksmith in Cumberland Street, where his sister Mary was employed as a domestic servant. George Wall was nineteen and employed as a butcher in York Street. He lived with his mother, Mary Ann Wall, an ex-convict woman who was a baker, and his younger brother. It becomes apparent that there was a clear economic distinction among butchers, based on their material possessions. Thorn and the Bloodsworths were comparatively prosperous men. The younger, employed butchers were simply tradesmen working for wages; they do not appear to have needed any prior training or experience in their trade as there is no evidence of apprenticeships being available in the colony during this period. There is, however, evidence of the existence of family trade links and close association in occupation and areas of residence with brothers and parents, with the notable exception of the Bloodsworths.

MISCELLANEOUS TRADES

There were a few miscellaneous trades followed by native-born who were the sons of ex-convicts, ex-soldiers and settlers. These trades were those of turner, tanner, painter, rope-maker, saddler, shingler, cordwainer, nailor and plaisterer [sic]. It has not been possible to trace whether these trades were learned from a parent or by apprenticeship. The rope-maker, for example, was seventeen-year-old James Roberts, whose father was an Argyle landholder. No advertisements for apprentice rope-makers appeared in the *Sydney Gazette* and there were few skilled rope-makers in the colony.[54] In 1828 in the same age group as the first generation there were no free immigrant rope-makers; there were only eight among the ex-convicts. There was a continual need for rope-makers in the colony and this makes it difficult to explain why there were no apprentices taught the trade. In 1806, for example, the *Sydney Gazette* reported that rope was in increasing demand; in May 1806 it was reported that John Jennings had completed a cable made from English cordage; it was 15 inches wide and was to be used on HMS *Buffalo*. The Governor himself had commented on the excellence of the workmanship and was 'pleased to testify the highest approbation at the accomplishment of a work of which in this Colony could scarcely have hoped'. By 1810 Samuel Pugh was offering rope for sale but there is no evidence to indicate who were the colonial rope-makers or whether the rope was imported.[55]

The native-born cordwainer was George Fieldhouse, who in 1828 lived with his wife and children in Upper Hunter Street. His wife had been sentenced to fourteen years' transportation at the age of thirteen and had arrived in the colony to serve her sentence in 1821. George was the son of a settler from the New South Wales Corps and, although his father's trade is not known, there is the possibility that he may have been a cordwainer before enlistment.[56] One tradesman who did follow his father's trade was Charles Prentice, a shingler who lived at Luskentyre with his twenty-three-year-old brother, John, a fencer, and their father, Charles, a shingler. All three were employed by and lived on the property of Alexander McLeod. Charles Prentice senior had arrived in the colony in 1800; he was not convicted. The parentage of Henry Brown is not known. He was employed as a fencer by a free farmer at Sutton Forest. The only native-born saddler was Daniel Knight of Liverpool, whose father was an ex-soldier settler with 100 acres at Georges River; Daniel's brother was a blacksmith at Lower Minto, employed by native-born wheelwright George Graham. The only native-born nailor was the son of a nailor and lived and worked with his father at Windsor. This was John Bayless, born in 1808; his father, Joseph, was an ex-New South Wales Corps private. The tanner, William Pawley, followed a trade which was not allied with that of his father, an ex-convict tailor. Pawley lived with his native-born wife and family in Castlereagh Street, Sydney. His elder brother, John, lived with their widowed mother, who had arrived as a convict in 1796 and in 1828 was a publican in Sydney.

Thomas Morris was one of at least five brothers, all of whom were tradesmen in Sydney in 1828. Their father, James Morris, was an ex-convict who had been involved in a number of business ventures during their childhood. By 1808 Morris was described as a brewer and also held a wine and spirit licence, which was renewed in 1809 and 1810. He owned a shop in Pitts Row, Sydney, and the amount of goods stolen when it was broken into in March 1809 indicates the extent of his trading. In addition to considerable quantities of 'stock of clothing', materials and haberdashery, one of the stolen articles was described as a 'shirt mended on both shoulders', so it is probable that he also conducted a repair service, which would have been a lucrative sideline in a colony where there was a large number of single men.[57] Morris was also a landowner and in 1809 he advertised for a shepherd to care for his flocks. His eldest son, James, born in 1795, was a carpenter and lived with his wife and family of six children in Castlereagh Street, Sydney. William, born in 1797, was a baker and lived with his wife in King Street. Thomas, the turner, born in 1799, lived with his wife, his brother John, born 1807, and John's wife in Pitt Street. John's twin, George, was a shoemaker in Pitt Street, where he lived with his wife. None of the sons appeared to have developed the multiplicity of interests held by their enterprising father. That all the sons were apprenticed and became self-supporting tradesmen is indicative of the parental interest of this ex-convict father and his convict wife. They remained in Sydney where they had been born and continued family relationships; this is characteristic of most of the colonial 'trade' families.

This biographical investigation into the parentage, training and upbringing of the individual native-born tradesmen and their families, superimposed on the unique labour situation and population structure of the colony during the first forty years of white settlement, clearly reveals the erroneous nature of accepted contemporary assumptions that the first generation were the abandoned children of worthless and dissolute convict parents, that they themselves rejected the standards and life-styles of those parents. On the contrary, this investigation shows the close family ties among the trade families and underlines the influence of the parents, whether ex-convict, ex-soldier or free immigrant, in obtaining apprenticeships for their sons, in instructing sons in their own trades or in working in partnership with tradesmen sons. The existence of close family links is evidenced further by the number of brothers who lived together or in close proximity and worked at similar or allied trades, and the number who remained in the districts where they had been raised.

The nature and structure of the penal society, the composition of the work-force, the dependence on the skills and labour of convicts and ex-convicts, the shortage of skilled artisans, the lack of craftsmen from the luxury trades, all produced a situation where a man skilled in a basic trade could become the elite of the work-force and command wages and conditions far in excess of those in contemporary Britain. The aristocrat of the colonial tradesmen was not determined by the nature of his craft, its status and organization but by the economic reward it could command. The privileged section of colonial tradesmen were those who were materially successful and who had sufficient enterprise to work for themselves and employ others. In this way the boat-builders, shipwrights, butchers and carpenters could rank with the traditional trade aristocrat, the miller. The native-born, working within the ordinary building and subsistence trades, experienced conditions which differed entirely from those of their British counterparts. The native-born tradesmen had no experience of a labour situation in which the conditions of their trade needed to be protected and regulated; they were as unfamiliar with unemployment, low wages and poor conditions as they were with sweat-shops and exploited child labour. Those among them who followed the lowest ranking trades, those of tailor or shoemaker, had opportunities and conditions far more favourable than those of skilled artisans in Britain. The evidence suggests that those tailors and shoemakers were colonial orphans or destitute children. It is possible that they were found positions by government on outlying properties although there is no definite evidence to support this assumption. It is clear, however, that the ready availability of work for skilled men made it unnecessary for tradesmen to accept employment on outlying properties unless they wished. Among the few who did, with the exception of the tailors and the shoemakers, it was usually a family move; for example, the Regan father and son applying to the governor to go together as carpenters to 'an outlying settlement' and the Prentice family working together for McLeod at Luskentyre.

A direct result of the dependence on the skills of the transported tradesmen during the early period of colonial development was that the native-born tradesmen became accustomed to working with and for convict and ex-convict masters. Most of the 'elite' work-force in New South Wales had arrived as convicted felons; many of the most successful master tradesmen were ex-convicts, as were most of the superintendents at establishments such as Carters' Barracks, the Dock Yards and the Lumber Yards. This influenced the attitudes of the young native-born apprentices and tradesmen towards the nature and rewards of labour. To be responsible to, and to learn a trade from, a convict master influenced attitudes towards convicts and convictism. It is probable that material achievements, some measure of economic success which could result from the possession of a skill, were seen to outweigh social considerations of class, parentage and inheritance. The standards of material success among the tradesmen of New South Wales were measured by individual enterprise and achievement. The yardstick was not British expectations and conditions but colonial experiences.

When the development of colonial labour patterns is placed within the framework of the nature and structure of the colony it becomes less remarkable that almost as many of the first generation 'Currency Lads' chose to become tradesmen as those who chose to become landholders. The greatest single influence in both cases was the example and interest of their parents. It was the determining factor.

CHAPTER NINE

THE STOUT LADS

'Scott: We find people fond of being sailors.
Johnson: I cannot account for that any more than I
can account of other strange perversions of the
imagination.'

Boswell, *Life of Johnson*.

Contemporaries assumed that the native-born youth were 'naturally inclined' towards a seafaring life, that a 'love of the sea' was a natural part of their birthright.[1] In 1819 Edward Eagar told Commissioner Bigge that 'Our rising Generation is almost naturalised to the Sea, and capable of becoming excellent seamen'.[2] This belief was based partly on the geographic location of the settlement itself, with Sydney as a major seaport and the colony dependent on sea links both for communication and trade. Geographic dependence suggested a natural need for free men and boys in the colony to man colonial boats and ships. This need was evidenced in the frequent advertisements in the *Sydney Gazette* for 'stout lads', particularly in a period during which few apprenticeships of any sort were advertised unless they were directly concerned with seafaring and shipping. These 'stout lads' were required to 'learn the art and craft of mariners' on whaling, sealing and coastal voyages or to work as apprentices in the colony's ship and dockyards. Furthermore, the regular requests which appeared in the *Sydney Gazette* for ships' crew, seamen, mariners, coopers and carpenters[3] suggested that there was a ready availability of employment for experienced colonial seamen or for men and boys prepared to work on colonial vessels. Convicts under sentence were not permitted to sail on boats or ships, so this type of employment was available only to free men and was not linked with the traditional forms of convict labour in the colony.

The assumption that the native-born preferred a seafaring life was based partly on the presumed characteristics of the native-born, in particular their aversion to convicts and to all forms of labour associated with convictism. Both J.T. Bigge and Peter Cunningham stressed this predilection for the sea and gave as the prime reason the reluctance of the native-born to be employed with convicts at convict trades. Peter Cunningham explained that this was from '. . . a sense of pride . . . an unwillingness to mix with convicts so universally employed on farms'.[4]

Despite these assumptions and despite the opportunities for training and employment, the native-born showed a reluctance to go to sea. Few became professional mariners, fewer rose to the rank of officer, chief mate or captain, and there was a high incidence of absconding among ships' apprentices, of desertion by ships' boys, and of 'running' among crew members.[5] Contemporaries continued to accept the exploits of a handful of notable exceptions as indicative of the attitude of the first generation as a whole. Men such as Philip Parker King, James Kelly, George Reibey and Henry Marsh gained fame in their own lifetimes as outstanding seamen and navigators, and all were known as native-born Australians. That these men were exceptions, however, is evidenced by an analysis of the Ships' Musters of 1817–27, which listed details of all crew and passengers who sailed from the port of Sydney during this ten-year period.[6] This analysis showed that the crew members who were described as native-born, sailing on colonial, coastal and overseas ships of all descriptions, made one or two voyages and then did not reappear on crew lists. They did not, therefore, become professional seamen.

Why the lads who had been born in the colony had signed on as crew or ships' boys and made so few voyages is difficult to determine. An analysis of the biographies and backgrounds of these men and boys suggests at least four reasons which influenced their decision not to remain at sea as a career. The first reason explains why a small group who had all recently completed apprenticeships made one or two, or possibly three, voyages, usually as far as Calcutta, and then returned to Sydney where they worked at their trades. As all these lads had been apprenticed in the colony's shipyards, either to Government or to a private master such as the firm of Kable and Underwood or Robert Campbell's company, and usually sailed on their masters' vessels, these voyages were simply a natural culmination to their apprenticeships.

A second group of boys, comprised of both unskilled lads and those who had completed apprenticeships, appears to have been prompted to join a ship for a voyage or two simply from a sense of adventure or desire to 'see the world'. They then returned to settle permanently in their homeland. These adventurous lads included George Chapman, who by 1828 was a shipwright living at Darling Harbour, and William Brozill, himself the son of a sailor, who after one voyage to London settled as a servant at Bringelly. A third group also appears to have found one or two voyages sufficient antidote to any desire for a career at sea. These lads were placed as ships' boys by their fathers, mothers or guardians and it is possible that it was the desire of these parents to ensure that the sons secured a trade, rather than the natural inclination of the boy, which led to their becoming a part of a ship's crew. All these lads were entered in the Ships' Musters with the notation 'with the consent of the father/mother/guardian'. John Munday, for example, the son of a former Marine, was listed as ship's boy on three voyages: to Bass Strait, Port Dalrymple and the River Derwent. Jonathan Bradley, born at Parramatta, made one voyage as a ship's boy with the written consent of his father, a former New South Wales Corps private; Joseph Coffee, who joined the *Jupiter* of Port Jackson, was an orphaned boy supported by his guardian, Martin Coffee. It was his guardian who secured the position on the *Jupiter*. All these and similar cases strongly suggest parental concern with securing a trade for the boy jas the prime motivation.

Finally, there were native-born seafarers who appear to have 'jumped ship', with or without permission, either at Van Diemen's Land, New Zealand, India or Britain and did not return to Sydney.[7] Such appears to be the only reasonable explanation when there is no further trace of a native-born on the Ships' Musters, no record of a death and no record of residence in New South Wales.

This apparent lack of interest in following a permanent career as a seaman may have stemmed from a number of related factors. Chief among these were the effects of colonial attitudes towards child labour and the expectations and attitudes of the native-born themselves towards labour and its rewards. The availability of convict labour meant that the life-styles of the colony's children differed greatly from those of their contemporaries in Britain. The colonial children were not accustomed to the severity of discipline imposed by regular employment from an early age and, to them, corporal punishment was strongly linked with convict labour. On this basis, it could be argued that the severity of life at sea and the incidence of punishment for breaches of discipline would have likened the conditions for seamen to those for convict labourers. Such a life-style would have held little appeal for the children of the penal colony.

The location and nature of the colony made it certain that both desertions and punishments of seamen would have been known by the colony's inhabitants. The high incidence of desertions from colonial and British vessels and the number of apprentices and ships' boys who absconded served to emphasize the severity of shipboard life. Absconders and deserters were reported in the *Sydney Gazette*. A notice which appeared in 1808 is indicative of the extent of desertion, and also the type of deserters. Five seamen had absconded from HMS *Porpoise*; whether they were pressed men or volunteers is unknown. A reward of 'Forty shillings for apprehending each of the said Deserters' was to be paid to any informer after these men were 'safely lodged in His Majesty's Gaols in the Colony'. One of the seamen was thirty-four-year-old John Boure, a cooper 'subject to fits, mostly produced by intoxication'; two were described as having voices 'rather effeminate'; another was twenty-year-old Daniel Cummings, a third, twenty-six-year-old William Mitchell; thirty-year-old Henry Geddes was described as '. . . about 5 feet eight inches high of a dark complexion, black hair large whiskers, several scars on his face, and his voice very hoarse'. The youngest, Richard Westbrook, aged sixteen, could have been undetected among the colonial youth of Sydney. These advertisements were similar to many which appeared in the *Sydney Gazette*. In 1806 Captain Meyrick of the *Auroa*, inserted 'A Caution' in the *Sydney Gazette*, warning against 'harbouring, seducing or concealing from their duty' any of his crew:

> He considers it incumbent on him at the same time positively and unequivocally to declare, that should any Seaman whatever desert the said Vessel, every possible means will be resorted to for apprehending and enforcing The Law against him.[8]

Punishment of deserters was linked closely with the authority of the colonial governor and the enforcement of colonial law by the courts and by the magistrates. The governors supported the authority of ships' masters and officers, with Government and General Orders being issued specifically to warn all inhabitants against harbouring absconders and specifying severe penalties for both absconders and protectors. The link between the authority of the colonial government and the enforcement of discipline at sea on all vessels was emphasized further by the role of the colonial magistrates. These civil officials tried, convicted and ordered punishment for breaches of discipline, disobedience and other offences by seaman on board colonial vessels at sea. The colonial youth, particularly those resident in the port of Sydney, were consciously aware of the severity of the punishments inflicted by colonial magistrates on seamen; they were reported in the press and the punishments administered publicly, as with convicts. One typical case concerned a sailor, already employed on one ship, who obtained an advance of wages from another 'on pretence' of joining that crew. He was sentenced to 200 lashes; the Sydney magistrate hoped that this public punishment would serve as a deterrent to the numerous other seamen who committed this offence.[9] Another case published in the *Sydney Gazette* concerned a seaman on the colonial brig *King George* who was sentenced to twenty-five lashes by magistrate William Lawson for neglect of duty and leaving his ship without permission. These punishments and the nature of their enforcement tightened the links between the life of a convict and the life of a sailor.

The most severe breach of discipline was mutiny, for which no extenuating circumstances could be offered. William Bligh issued a Government and General Order in 1806 that the crews of all colonial vessels should witness the punishment of mutineers.[10] Punishment was not confined to sailors: ships' boys could be involved in mutiny and punished with the mutineers. Native-born William Evans, for example, was ship's boy on Robert Campbell's brig *Venus* when it was taken by the chief mate and others in 1806.[11] It is possible that the boy had no alternative but to join the mutineers but he shared their punishment after capture.

Mutiny was more common than might have been expected on colonial ships and could indicate that conditions were such that even the dread of death or severe corporal punishment, or both, did not deter potential mutineers. There were, for example, three mutinies reported in the colonial press in 1806.[12] Statutory punishment for mutiny on navy, merchant or passenger ships was death but, 'if mercy were extended', the mutineers could be flogged through the fleet at Sydney Cove, tied to triangles in boats especially prepared for this purpose. This had the added advantage of attracting public notice to the crime and its 'aweful' punishment, thus serving as a warning to all potential mutineers. Early in 1806 four mutineers were punished in this manner. The *Sydney Gazette* reported the incident in detail and praised the clemency which had revoked the death sentence, adding that it was 'sincerely hoped' that the severity of the punishment would 'duly operate upon the minds of the offenders, and that their example guard the unwary against the dangers that await intemperance and crime'.[13] The inhabitants of the port of Sydney, particularly the children so frequently described as 'idle',[14] would have been able to witness these punishments. The apparent link between the conditions and experiences of the convicts and those of the sailors and mariners was a strong one. Not only were the punishments similar, but they were enforced by the same magistrates. The major causes of these punishments, particularly those concerned with mutinies and other breaches of discipline, could only create an unfavourable reaction to the severity of life at sea among the colonial children. This reaction was increased and strengthened by the awareness of the high incidence of desertion by ships' crews and absconding by ships' apprentices. Any comparison, therefore, between the conditions which governed the life of a ship's apprentice or a mariner and those applying to occupations connected with trade or land owning made it highly improbable that the 'independent spirit' of the first generation would welcome the opportunity of becoming 'naturalised to the Sea'.[15]

The 1828 Census includes only ten native-born mariners who were in New South Wales when the Census was taken. It is difficult to estimate the exact number of native-born who may have been on colonial vessels at this time, for there is some doubt as to the accuracy of the Colonial Secretary's Returns for 1828 with respect to crews on colonial and overseas vessels. The figures vary so greatly from those on the Ships' Musters for the previous year that they are not sufficiently reliable to indicate the numbers of native-born who were employed as sailors or mariners in 1828. In the Returns of the Colonial Secretary, under the category 'Colonial Marine', 253 native-born are listed and 250 who came free, making a total of 503 men and boys serving in various capacities on colonial vessels. No ex-convicts are listed as ships' crew.[16] There are two discrepancies in these figures when they are compared with other contemporary reports. The first is in relation to the numbers and civil conditions of the seamen when compared with the Ships' Musters for the preceding ten years, which name a far smaller percentage of native-born among colonial seamen and a far higher percentage of ex-convicts who had either served their sentences or received Absolute Pardons. The second discrepancy is in relation to the number of colonial vessels described in the Colonial Secretary's Returns, which stated that in 1828 there were ninety-three vessels with a tonnage of 6409 tons. Not only does this not agree with the number of ships in the Ships' Musters for the previous year but there is further discrepancy with the Returns of the Colonial Secretary for 1826. To take an example: under the Description 'Fisheries' the following Returns were given in 1826:[17]

Men on Vessels Belonging to or Sailing from the Colony

Sperm Whale Fishing	76 men
Sea Elephant Fishing	60 men
Seal Fishing	246 men

These figures indicate that, in 1826, 75 per cent of the colonial seamen were engaged in the Fisheries Trade. As the majority of sealing gangs were composed of ex-convicts, this would suggest that the proportions given to both the native-born and the came-free in 1828 were inaccurate. It is not possible to suggest reasons for this although it may have been simply a clerical error in relation to the allocation of the numbers of civil condition categories. The discrepancy in the number of colonial ships may have been caused by the inclusion of 'boats', possibly the numerous small boats engaged in river trade and ferrying.

As neither the Census Returns nor the Returns of the Colony were sufficiently reliable to indicate the numbers and parentage of the native-born seamen, the Ships' Musters became a principle source. The Musters, recorded from December 1816 until December 1825, were compiled by the ships' captains, who were personally responsible to the Harbour Master for their accuracy; it was on the information they contained that port dues were determined and clearance to sail was given. The master of the vessel was also personally responsible for ensuring that there were no convicts on his ship, either as crew or stowaways, and that all on board had the governor's permission to leave the colony. He was obliged to give the following details of ship, crew and passengers: name of vessel, tonnage, port of registration, name of master, name and civil condition of all passengers and crew, and whether all individuals listed 'came with the ship', were 'free by certificate' in which case the number and date of the certificate had to be supplied, or were 'free by birth in the Colony'. If native-born, the name of parent or guardian had to be stated and, in the case of boys and apprentices, the written consent of the parent or guardian was obligatory. The master had to note that he had seen such permission. William Hanks, for example, had been born in the colony in 1807; he was the son of two ex-convicts, his father being employed as a carter, his mother as a dressmaker. He was mustered on the colonial brig *Campbell Macquarie* on 23 June 1820, at the age of thirteen, and it was entered on the Muster that he had joined the ship with 'the consent and aspiration of his mother, Mrs J. Hanks of Castlereagh Street, Sydney'. William Hanks did not continue as a seaman but returned to Sydney, where he became an apprentice cabinet-maker, completing his indentures by 1828, working as a tradesman and living with his parents and sisters Phoebe and Luisa, who were employed as dressmakers with their mother.

It was also obligatory for the master to enter on the Muster the name of the previous ship for all crew members who joined in Sydney and the reason for transfer, this usually being either 'cleared out' or 'run'. It is thus possible to trace the previous experiences of many of the seamen. Native-born Henry Gulley, for example, was mustered on 23 June 1823, as 'a Native Seaman', with the notation that he had been 'cleared out', that is, discharged from 'His Majesty's Ship, *Bathurst*. Saw his discharge. His mother's consent'. Gulley was one of the very few native-born who enlisted in the Royal Navy and, unlike Philip Parker King, did not make the navy his career. Edward Eagar had assured Bigge that the colony was:

... capable of becoming a Nursery for the supply of strictly British Seamen to our Fleets in India and the Pacific Ocean, a description of Seamen infinitely preferable in the hour of danger, to the feeble and treacherous Malays and Lascars of Asia.[18]

The need for replacing ships' crew, as a result of death or desertion, before returning to England had led to the practice of enlisting the only labour readily available. It is difficult to explain why there were no official incentives to encourage native-born youths to enlist on His Majesty's ships. From the evidence of the Ships' Musters, it must have been extremely difficult to find sufficient inducements to encourage colonial youths to leave the colony and, if they were prepared to do so, to venture further than coastal waters, with an occasional voyage to India or to China. This was the reverse situation in the case of many of the ex-convicts, particularly in the early days of the colony, when a berth on a ship bound for India or England was one of the few ways of returning to England after completion of sentence.

It was noted on the Musters if a seaman had transferred from another ship. For the native-born this indicated any previous experience and also

provided evidence of brothers sailing together. William Hughes, one of the
few native-born listed in the Musters on three voyages, sailed first on the
Little Mary to Hobart Town in July 1822. He was then mustered as steward
on the *Caroline* of London, described as 'came with the ship'. The *Caroline*
sailed to Macquarie Island in February 1824. In July of that year Hughes
was steward on the same ship, sailing to Hobart and Dalyrmple. This is the
last reference to him in the Musters. He may have died, deserted at one of the
ports of call or sailed with the *Caroline* to London and remained there. The
interesting feature is that his brothers made one voyage on the *Little Mary*,
Henry in May 1820, and Jonathan with his brother William in July 1822.
The three boys were the sons of Private John Hughes of the New South
Wales Corps and his wife, former convict Sarah Marlove. There is no remaining record of Henry's later career or that of his brother, Jonathan.

The official Muster form given to masters of vessels contained a column for
physical descriptions. These were normally completed for ex-convicts, frequently for those who had arrived in the colony as free men and signed on at
the port of Sydney, but rarely for the native-born. This may have been because the descriptions were a safeguard against convicts escaping from the
colony as seamen or posing as free men. It was also a safeguard against a
master unwittingly signing on a known deserter from another ship. Descriptions of deserters were published in the *Sydney Gazette* and even a master in
need of crew could not avoid a fine by claiming ignorance if he were obliged
to enter the description of his crew on the Muster. As for the native-born,
they were identified as born in the colony by the regulation that their parents
or guardians must give written consent before they sailed and this, combined
with their comparative youth, made further identification unnecessary. One
rare exception was the description given of Edward Maskey, a seaman born
in the colony in 1803 who was first mustered on the *Fame* of Sydney, bound
for Port Stephens in May 1824, and then on the *Newcastle* of Sydney, bound
for New Zealand. The description given by the Master of the *Newcastle* was:
'5'5½'', hazel eyes, brown hair, ruddy complexion'. This basic description
was in sharp contrast to the details given for ex-convicts, which included
scars, speech impediments, pock marks and length of beards or side-
whiskers. One ex-convict seaman, for example, was described as having a
distinguishing scar on his left leg, which was the result of a wound received at
Waterloo.

An analysis of all individual entries on the Ships' Musters for the eleven-
year period for which they are available showed that there were
approximately 110 native-born recorded as members of ships' crews sailing
from the port of Sydney. There were approximately eighty mustered in
1817–22 and thirty in 1823–27. The discrepancy indicated by these figures
in comparison with those reported by the Colonial Secretary for the year
1828 may have been influenced by the numbers engaged in river trade but
there is no evidence to support this assumption. Had such men and boys
been employed on colonial rivers they would have been obliged to complete
census forms and so would have been included in the returns. As this was
not the case it can only be assumed that the information given to the
Colonial Secretary was incorrect.

The destination for the ships whose crew included colonial-born seamen was usually within coastal waters and to Van Diemen's Land, either to Hobart Town, Port Dalrymple or the River Derwent. There were voyages simply described as 'to the whale fishing' or 'sealing', although only one native-born was described as a sealer. This was Thomas Farmer, born in the colony in January 1799, the son of convict John Farmer, who died the following year, and convict Ann Johnston. In October 1821 Farmer was on board the *Caroline* (*Charlotte*) of London bound to Hobart Town and New Zealand.[19] There were voyages to New Zealand, usually in colonial vessels such as the *Governor Bligh* of the Hawkesbury or the *Active* or the *Elizabeth* of Sydney, so this removes the probability that colonial seamen may have sailed to England after the completion of one voyage and remained there. There were voyages in colonial vessels: to the islands north-west of Australia on the *Glory* of Richmond; to the islands in the South Seas for sandalwood on the *King George* of Sydney; to Port Stephens on the *Fame* of Sydney; to Kangaroo Island on the *Perseverance* of Sydney, and 'to the Eastward' on the *Daphne* of Port Jackson. Voyages of greater distance were on ships registered in London, Calcutta or Java, and it was on these ships that the possibility existed for native-born seamen to be 'cleared out' or to 'run' when the vessel reached its home port. One such voyage was that of the convict transport, the *Fame* of London, whose destination in 1817 was given as 'Batavia and eventually to England'. There was one native-born in the ship's company: John Ramsay, born at Parramatta in 1795, the son of an ex-convict settler John Ramsay and his wife Mary. There is no further record of John Ramsay junior. One native-born who appeared to make a voyage to London and returned to the colony was William Brazell, or Brozill, who sailed on the *Regalia* of London in 1820 and in 1828 described himself as a servant employed at Bringelly. Another, William Chaffey, born at Parramatta in 1797, the son of convicts William Freeman and Elizabeth Chaffey, joined the *Caroline* of London on its voyage to Macquarie Island and then to London in 1824. By 1828 he was a prisoner at Moreton Bay, serving a fourteen-year colonial sentence.

Most of those who sailed on British ships simply disappeared. Richard Cheers, for example, the brother of John Cheers, a publican at Newcastle, sailed with the *Alfred* of London to the South Seas Fisheries in 1824; Frances Duffey was a seaman on the *Emerald* of London, which sailed to Hobart Town and eventually to London in 1821. Ships registered in Calcutta and sailing between their home port and Sydney signed on native-born crew and most of these have left no further record after one, or possibly two, voyages. An exception was George Bloodsworth who, after serving his apprenticeship at His Majesty's Dock Yards in Sydney, was mustered as a carpenter on his first voyage, on the *Lynx* bound for Calcutta in 1820. In February 1822 he was mustered on the *John Bull*, also of Calcutta and bound for Madras. By 1828 he had married native-born Maria Cox and had settled as a publican in Sydney. Among those who sailed for Calcutta and for whom no further record exists were Peter Leadon, who joined the *John Shore* of Calcutta in 1820; Thomas Pugh, a son of ex-convict settlers Samuel Pugh and his wife Ann; and James Rickett, son of settlers Samuel

Rickett and his wife, Mary. Rickett joined the *John Bull* of Calcutta in 1822. Andrew Biggers also joined the *John Bull* and failed to reappear on any Ship's Muster. Four years before Andrew became steward of the *John Bull* he and his brother Thomas had petitioned Governor Macquarie for land, stating that they had been promised a grant and that they had 'an aged father who is desirous of quitting this country'. Andrew was at sea at the time the petition was presented: Thomas explained that his brother was 'under Lieutenant King on discovery' while he himself was in the service of Lieutenant Johnston. Both boys were granted sixty acres. There is, however, no further record of either boy, although their 'aged' father Thomas was entered in the 1828 Census as an overseer at Upper Portland on the Hunter River. Biggers senior was then sixty-five years old and was living with his ex-convict wife Elizabeth, who had arrived in the colony in 1793, on the same ship, the *Boddington*.

From the evidence of the destination of the ships, it could be suggested, therefore, that some of the native-born bound for London or Calcutta remained at those ports. There is, however, no evidence to show what happened to those who returned with their ship from voyages in colonial waters. John Hunter, for example, sailed twice to New Zealand and back on the *Active* of Sydney; Henry James sailed with the consent of his parents, who were ex-convict landholders, to Macquarie Island and back on a sealing voyage. In two or three cases there is evidence of death. At the age of nineteen John McLaughlin sailed to New Zealand (with his mother's consent) on board the *Samuel* of London. He died the following year and was buried at Newcastle. Other deaths could be presumed, particularly in view of the age of some of the native-born seamen. William McDougal, for example, was born in Sydney in 1795 and is last recorded as sailing on the *Asia* of Aberdeen to Batavia in 1822; William Humm was born in 1799 and was last recorded as sailing from Sydney for the South Seas in 1819. In some of these cases the families of the native-born seamen remained in New South Wales, which would increase the expectation that they would return to their native-land. William Humm's father was a sergeant in the New South Wales Corps who had married ex-convict Mary Hook and settled at Parramatta. William was their only son and, after the death of William senior, Mrs Humm and her daughters moved to Sydney. Thomas Ralph was the son of Luke Ralph and his wife Mary, both of whom had arrived free in 1801. Their son was last recorded as sailing from Sydney on the *Little Mary* in 1820, with the consent of his parents. Whatever may have been the reason, few of the native-born appear to have become professional seamen.

There were skilled tradesmen and unskilled labourers among the native-born who made one or two voyages. Among the skilled workers it would appear that one or two voyages followed the completion of apprenticeships as carpenters, coopers, rope-makers or shipwrights. Jonathan Wright, for example, was a cooper who, after two voyages, joined his brothers at Pitt Town; George Chapman settled as a shipwright at Darling Harbour; William Hanks became a Sydney cabinet-maker; Joseph Flood, carpenter, rejoined his brothers in Sydney. The unskilled included Thomas Ambrose, of the *Glory* of Richmond, whose father had died when he was twelve years old. Ambrose made one voyage to the coast of New Zealand and Port Dalrymple in 1824 and returned to Sydney where he was 'cleared out'; he then married the native-born daughter of William Reynolds, a carpenter, who had arrived with his brother in 1791, both sentenced to seven years' transportation. In 1828 Thomas Ambrose and his wife were described as 'living with' his father-in-law who was a labourer to his brother. The elder brother was a farmer at Wilberforce.

Among the native-born who made one or two voyages were those who later applied for land grants, usually at about the time of the second voyage. Their Memorials requesting grants make it quite clear that it was their intention to settle to 'agricultural pursuits'. Whether this was after rejecting the life of a sailor or whether the voyages were made simply in the spirit of adventure is impossible to determine. It is, however, evident that life at sea held no further attractions for this group of native-born seamen. Among these former sailors, who would have formed less than 10 per cent of the entire number mustered between 1817 and 1827, were youths such as William Landres, who had sailed to Calcutta on the *St Michael* 'with his mother's consent'; he was the son of Antoine L'Andre, who had married ex-convict Ann Cook at Parramatta in 1801. In his petition to Macquarie, William Landres described himself as the son of 'Antony Landran, deceased, formerly in the employ of the Government as Superintendent of the Cooperage'. He wrote that he was now twenty years old and wished to become a settler but was unable to buy land. He made no mention of his time at sea. Macquarie granted him sixty acres. Landres was not listed in the 1828 Census.

Land grants were also received by James Davis, John Griffiths, William Hanks, Henry James, Edward Powell, John Roberts and Hugh Scott. The Memorials from these native-born youths made no mention of their current or former occupation as seamen or ships' boys but stressed their parental background and their own aspirations to become settlers on their own land. James Davis, for example, wrote that he was the son of Evan Davis of the Royal Veteran Company, 'who came to the Colony in 1809 as a member of the 73rd. Regiment as a Private'. Evans, who had made one voyage as a seaman on the *Nereus* of Sydney to Port Dalrymple, requested a land grant 'as he wishes to farm'. The obligatory character testimonials were attached to the application. In his reference Samuel Marsden showed the necessity of having a 'respectable' upbringing. 'I know the father of the Memorialist, who is of good character but I do not know him—if he had been bad I should have known him.' If the boy had been at sea it is unlikely that Marsden would have known of him.

John Griffiths was a carpenter on the *Glory* of Richmond when he sailed to Port Dalrymple and the islands north-west of Australia in 1820. The vessel was owned by his father, Jonathan Griffiths, and the crew included a younger son, William. In 1824, John Griffiths requested a land grant, stating in his Memorial that he was native-born, twenty years old, a resident of Evan, and that he was 'bred to agriculture by his father who rents a farm in the district of Evan'. In 1828 John was described as a farmer at Evan, where he held twenty-two acres, all of which was cleared and cultivated. It was most likely that his time as a seaman had been linked with his father's boating and shipping interests and, although he had sailed as a boy, when the time came to choose a permanent occupation Griffiths preferred the land.

James Henry joined the *Midas* of London at the age of fourteen, 'with the consent of his parents'. The voyage was to Macquarie Island and back for the purpose of sealing. At the age of nineteen, he applied to Macquarie for a land grant, stating that he wished 'to enter agricultural pursuits', and received sixty acres. Two years later he wrote to Brisbane stating that he was:

> ... the son of William Henry of Hunter's Hill ... granted by Macquarie 60 acres at Hunter's Hill and other Indulgences ... to be on stores for six months ... but these were not received and he requested that they be granted.

This grant does not appear to have been confirmed. In 1828 Henry was living with his father, who was a watchman, and neither owned land.

Edward Powell's application for land showed the influence of his father's career. Powell senior, having first come to the colony as a seaman in 1790, returned as one of the first free settlers on the *Bellona* in 1792. In his land application of 1824 Powell junior stated that he was 'of free birth in the colony his parents being free', and he stressed that his father was 'the first free settler to apply to come to the Colony'. Powell junior was granted sixty acres and the following year applied for a further 1000 acres '. . . since he has become possessed of some farms and stock from his father which will enable him to support a considerable establishment . . .' He was granted 500 acres. It seems quite clear that Powell left the sea as there were greater opportunities for him on his father's land. He was described as second officer on the *Campbell Macquarie* of Sydney in 1821 so it is evident that his original intention had been to become a professional seaman.

John Roberts, an apprentice on the *Governor Bligh* of Sydney in 1820, applied for land with his younger brother, James, stating they were native-born and the sons of Widow Roberts of Windsor, who had arrived in the *Scarborough* in 1798; they requested 'a land grant for cultivation' and each was granted sixty acres. Their elder brother George had also been a ship's apprentice, on the *Glory* of Richmond. In 1828 James was a District Constable at Bathurst and there is no record of either George or John.

Hugh Scott, who had joined the ship's company of the *Elizabeth Mary* of Sydney for a sealing voyage in 1822, applied for a land grant with his brother Walter, stating that they were the native-born sons of Walter Scott, deceased, and were: '. . . part of a numerous family; their mother had five younger children. They requested each a portion of land adjoining each other for agriculture and to raise stock . . .' Both were granted adjoining blocks of sixty acres. By 1828 there is no record of either boy, although Hugh Scott, came-free, is entered as a mariner in the Census.

From an analysis of the parentage of the native-born seamen, where this could be traced, combined with Memorials presented by the parents it is possible to come to some conclusions concerning the background of the native-born seamen entered in the Ships' Musters and to suggest possible influences on their choice of the sea as a possible career. There are, for example, cases in which the boy was orphaned and cared for by a guardian. In these instances indenting the boy as a ship's apprentice at an early age appeared a satisfactory way of ensuring his future. William Butcher was a ship's boy on the *Alligator* of Java, sailing to Port Dalrymple and Kangaroo Island. A letter to the Colonial Secretary from Hannah Hobson, alias Mary Hobbs, requesting mitigation of sentence described the boy's background:

> ... his mother, Ann Butcher, was killed by natives ... Hannah Hobson has been confined for three years for losing her Ticket-of-Leave. She is a widow and has been in the Colony for 33 years ... she has an orphan son whom she has brought up from 14 weeks and who is now 18. He has been at sea but is now in Sydney and willing and able to support her and continue to when he goes to sea ...

A note from the Colonial Secretary added to this Petition stated that Hannah Hobson/Mary Hobbs, aged fifty-three years, 'has been a prostitute on the Rocks for several years until in 1824 when all women found at large at the General Muster were sent to the Factory'. This was dated 23 April 1826. Hannah Hobson gained her freedom and became a laundress in Gloucester Street, Sydney; there is no further record of her adopted son, William Butcher. On the basis of Hannah Hobson's letter and the Colonial Secretary's comment, William Butcher's experiences as a child were not typical of the native-born in general but they do suggest that it may have been the boys who had no opportunity of following the occupation of their fathers who were more likely to become ships' boys. Hannah Hobson, despite her alleged profession, had reared the boy and maintained sufficient contact with him for William to be willing to support her if necessary. This, too, is contrary to the accepted attitudes of women from her background towards their children.

There are some Memorials which suggest that the parents were not among the most successful of the colony's inhabitants and that their poverty was increased by the need to support a large family. In these instances it is important to note that the family appeared to remain as a group and there was no evidence of the parents, either ex-convict or free, avoiding the responsibilities of rearing their children. It may have been their comparative poverty which led to one or two sons being placed as ships' apprentices. The father of Michael Connor, for example, who was apprenticed on the *Rosella* of Sydney in December 1815 at the age of fourteen, petitioned the governor, writing that '... he was an aged man, Constable of Windsor ... requesting a situation as some help to gain a living ...' He was granted 50 acres; three years later he wrote to Brisbane, complaining that this grant had not yet been measured and requesting that this be done. At this time he was Gaol Constable at Parramatta. William Douglass is another example of this type of parent. In 1820, four years before his son William Douglass junior was listed on the crew of the *Elizabeth* of Sydney, he petitioned for a land grant, stating that he had arrived in the colony in 1802 and '. . . has a large family and requests land continuous to his own at Caddie as his house and barn has been burned'. He was granted 60 acres. Two years later he again petitioned the governor for an additional grant, stating, '. . . he has eight children from sixteen years to eleven months in age. He is District Constable for Windsor and has been there for twelve years'. In 1828 he was District Constable at Pitt Town, where he lived with his native-born wife and six of their children. His son William, the former seaman, was a labourer in the same township.

Where there is no known Memorial from the father, the occupation of the parent who gave written consent to the boy joining the ship's crew is an indication of the nature of the youth's upbringing. Jonathan Bradley, for example, joined the *Queen Charlotte* of Sydney at the age of twelve years, 'with consent of his father' who was a labourer at Kissing Point, where he lived with his wife Sarah. Both were freed by servitude. Jonathan Davis was the son of Abraham Moor, ex-convict labourer, and Mary Davis, whom he had married in 1806; William Hanks was the son of a carter; Thomas Pawley was the son of a tailor; Jonathan Prentice the son of a butcher. On the other hand, there was a minority who came from well-established homes where the father had gained some measure of economic success in the colony. Edward Bolgar, for example, was described as 'the son of Mr Bolgar', a coach-maker who had arrived in the colony as a free man in 1798; William Bray was the son of ex-New South Wales Corps sergeant John Bray, who was a landholder of substance at Concord; George Chapman was the son of shipwright William Chapman; Dan Cubitt was the son of the Master of the Guard Boat, Daniel Cubbitt senior.

Their younger son, Jonathan, was also a seaman; his birth had been announced in the *Sydney Gazette*, which reported that 'Mrs Cupid was safely delivered of a fine boy',[20] Joseph Flood was the son of boatman Joseph Flood senior, who died when the boy was nine, and his common law wife, ex-convict Ann Germaine.[21] Some of these boys obviously followed the profession of their father—Chapman, Cubbitt and Flood, for example—but the remainder did not choose the sea as a profession for lack of an alternative. However, as with the boys from poorer backgrounds, few of them remained for more than two voyages before returning to life on the land.

There is a Memorial from one native-born who remained at sea long enough to become master of the colonial brig the *Elizabeth Henrietta*. His letter to the governor gives some indication of the rigours of shipboard life and probable reasons for abandoning the profession. In 1819 Captain David Smith wrote to Governor Macquarie:

... he has been in the Service of Government in the Maritime for several years and now holds the Command of His Majesty's Brig, *Elizabeth Henrietta* ... That your Petitioner, finding his Health much impaired in undergoing the fatiguouse [*sic*] attending such a situation ... Born in the Colony, married to a young woman also Born in the Colony, he has a young family ... Wishes to retire from the Sea and become a settler at Van Diemen's Land ... seeks permission for a grant of land.[22]

This proposal to settle in Van Diemen's Land may explain why so few of the former seamen were in New South Wales at the time of the 1828 Census. There is evidence for only two others remaining in Van Diemen's Land but this adds to rather than detracts from the probability that a number of the colonial-born seamen, particularly those on voyages to Port Dalrymple, Hobart Town or the Derwent, left their ships, either legitimately or by absconding, with the intention of settling there. One of these was William Griffiths, who had sailed to Port Dalrymple on his father's vessel the *Glory* of Richmond and become a permanent settler at Port Dalrymple. The other was sea captain James Kelly, who lived in Van Diemen's Land until his death in 1856. Captain Smith had received every assistance from Governor Macquarie, being granted 300 acres for himself and his family, two government men victualled by the Crown for twelve months, and being loaned two cows for two years. The reply was prompt: in the August of the year in which he requested the grant Smith and his family appeared as passengers bound for Port Dalrymple. There is no reason to suppose that Macquarie was not equally generous to other legitimate settlers proposing to establish themselves in the smaller colony.

Among the Memorials from the native-born and their parents there was only one which suggested that life at sea may have been idle rather than laborious for the ships' crew. This was from John Marman, who had received a colonial sentence of two years and had been ordered by the Criminal Court to serve his time on board a colonial vessel. As this was not a common practice it may have been that the court considered it a more beneficial form of punishment than confinement at a penal settlement or in a road gang. In 1822, however, Marman petitioned Governor Brisbane, 'humbly begging' that His Excellency would show clemency and change the sentence to one which could be served on land. Marman gave the reason that he would prefer 'labour, rather than leading an idle life of confinement' at sea.[23]

The trend among the native-born to remain at sea for short periods rather than as a career may help to account for the few who could be termed professional seamen in that they became officers, mates or masters. One or two of these owed their advancement in part to the shipping and trading interests of a parent—George Reibey, for example—but others such as James Underwood junior, who became a ship's apprentice in 1825, do not appear to have gained by family connections. The majority of those who became ships' officers, however, had some family links with seafaring through the occupations of their fathers. The officer, or professional, group was confined to a bare half dozen of the native-born. The remainder were ships' boys, apprentices, ships' company, seamen, carpenters, coopers, and an occasional steward. The few who did become officers included two who were very well known to their contemporaries and who so impressed Commissioner Bigge that their careers added to his belief in the natural aptitude of the native-born for life at sea. These were Captains James Kelly and George Reibey. Their exploits, added to those of Philip Parker King in the Royal Navy, emphasized this presumed natural ability of the colonial-born as a group. George Reibey, a son of Captain Thomas Reibey and his ex-convict wife Mary, joined his mother in her successful trading and shipping interests after the death of his father. His main concern was with shipping and he sailed as master of the *John Bull* of Calcutta, which left Sydney for China and Mauritius in November 1824. Reibey included native-born in his crew: his steward, Andrew Biggers, and ship's boy, James Foster. Reibey continued to sail on both coastal and overseas vessels and settled in Van Diemen's Land, where he looked after his mother's business interests until his accidental death, which was reported in *The Australian Almanac*:

> George Reibey, an Australian (and one of the most promising young gentlemen in the two Colonies) met with an early death in Van Diemen's Land, occasioned by a fall from a tree whilst in the act of fowling on his estate.[24]

Reibey, although atypical of his generation in that his interests were primarily concerned with shipping, was representative in his birth, for his mother was convict and his father free. Unlike his compatriot William Charles Wentworth however, it was the enterprise and success of his ex-convict mother, not his free father, which had given Reibey a position of wealth and influence and aided his advance in his chosen career. Despite this, or perhaps because of it, Reibey, like Wentworth, preferred to imitate the customs and life-styles of his free father, as is shown by the manner of his death, 'fowling on his estate'. This estate and the life he led as a gentleman were directly attributable to the enterprise of his mother, the transported horse-thief.

Two of the native-born who attained the rank of ship's officer had fathers whose careers were closely linked with shipping interests. They were Edgar Bolgar and Edward Powell. Bolgar's father, John, had arrived free and married a woman transported for seven years. They had two living sons, the elder of whom, Walter, was an apprentice carpenter at the Government Dock Yards and at the completion of his indentures worked with his father in Sydney. The second son, Edward, was apprenticed as a ship's boy at the age of thirteen, joining the crew of the *Elizabeth and Mary* in December 1818. In November 1820, again with the consent of his parents, Edward transferred to the London brig *Hope*, which was bound for a sealing voyage and then to London. By 1824 Edward was on the brig *Ann*, bound for Mauritius, and he was described as the mate. Edward may have transferred to overseas vessels; there is no further record of him in the colony. His brother remained working as a carpenter and living with his parents in Sydney.

Three of the native-born ships' officers had no apparent parental links with seafaring or shipping. These were George Grinus, James Shannon and John Watson. George Grinus was born in 1800 and by April 1817 was first mate on the *Campbell Macquarie*, bound for Calcutta. It is probable that he began his career as a ship's apprentice on colonial vessels. The last record of Grinus in the Ships' Musters is as third officer on the brig *Lynx* of Calcutta, on a sealing voyage in October 1820.

James Shannon was the son of two convicts, Patrick Shannon and Margaret Holmes; he was born in Sydney in 1799 and baptized at St. Phillip's the following year. He went to sea as an apprentice shortly after his father's death. His widowed mother remarried John Millet and, when widowed a second time, she married Edward Mills. James Shannon, or Holmes, appeared on the first Muster in January 1817 as a seaman on the big *Lynx* of Calcutta, bound for Calcutta. By 1821 he was the third officer on the *Jane* of London, bound for Batavia; in 1824 he was second mate on the *Phoenix* of Calcutta, bound for Calcutta. After this voyage there is no further record of him in New South Wales.

The career of second mate John Watson showed that it was possible for a boy with no parental influence to rise from the lower decks to the position of ship's officer through his own perseverance and industry. Watson had been born in Sydney in 1797 and was the son of two convicts, John and Esther Watson. After Esther's death, the father indentured the boy as ship's apprentice; his name appeared twice in the *Sydney Gazette* of 1808–09 as having the Governor's permission to leave the colony.[25] There is no record of other ships on which Watson sailed as an apprentice. When he was mustered as a seaman on the *Active* in 1817 there was a notation that he had been discharged, again as a seaman, on the *Kangaroo* the previous year, so it may be assumed that he completed his indentures and remained at sea. He was on the *Active*, voyaging between Sydney and New Zealand, from 1817 until 1820. In October of that year he was first described on the Muster, as second officer. Watson remained at sea until his death in 1833. Described on his burial certificate as a seaman, he was one of the very few native-born who fulfilled the expectations of such contemporary observers as Commissioner Bigge and Surgeon Cunningham.

This analysis of all the native-born listed as crew on the Ships' Musters for the period December 1817–December 1825 showed that those native-born who joined colonial or overseas vessels belonged to one of three distinct categories: those whose fathers were directly concerned with shipping or seafaring; those who had recently completed apprenticeships at dockyards; and those who were orphaned, fatherless or from poor families. A consideration of the parentage and class origins of these boys and men, combined with the duration and success of their careers at sea, indicates the most probable explanation for the general rejection of a seafaring life by this first generation.

The smallest group of seafarers was that which would be expected to contain the professional, or career, sailors. The fathers of this group were all directly concerned with ship-building or sea and river trade, or had been sailors or mariners. Edward Powell, William Howe, Charles Dowdle and John Mundy, for example, had all served their time as ships' crew or as marines. James Underwood and William and John Griffiths were ship-builders. Thomas Day and William Chapman were shipwrights. From the evidence of the Musters, the sons in this category made, on an average, more voyages than those from the other two groups but few became permanent seamen and fewer ships' officers.[26] In the same way as the native-born farmers and tradesmen followed the occupations of their fathers, these boys began their careers by following the choice of their fathers. Unlike the farmers and tradesmen, however, the seafarers changed their occupational choice for a career which was based on the land. In some cases this was despite evidence of success at sea. Edward Powell was second mate on the *Campbell Macquarie* when he applied for a land grant from Governor Brisbane in 1824; Captain David Smith was master of his own vessel when he determined to retire and settle with his young family in Van Diemen's Land. It was not only the life-style of a mariner which was rejected but also the possible career opportunities in favour of a life associated with the land. Although this was the group with parental influence and example, it was only the atypical James Kelly and George Reibey who showed any natural inclination to a seafaring way of life.

The second group was made up of those native-born lads who had completed apprenticeships as shipwrights, carpenters or coopers. These boys usually made one or two voyages, probably as a normal and accepted part of their training. There is no remaining evidence to support this assumption but the regularity with which those who had completed apprenticeships joined the crews of colonial and overseas vessels for a short period before settling to their chosen occupation in New South Wales would indicate that this was a normal procedure. It would also explain why these lads made only one or two voyages: there was no intention of remaining at sea. Both Bloodsworth brothers, for example, sailed to Calcutta as ships' carpenters, Jonathan Green sailed as a cooper and William Chapman as a shipwright.

There were other lads in this group who sailed as part of their apprenticeship training, always with the consent of their parents. Edward Bolgar, for example, the 'son of Mr Bolgar', sailed on a sealing voyage 'with the consent of his parents' at the age of twelve years. Henry James, at the age of fourteen, joined a sealing voyage in 1821 'with the consent of his parents'; Thomas Waterhouse, a carpenter in New South Wales in 1828, sailed to Calcutta in 1821 'with the consent of his father'; Thomas Bradley, who eventually settled as a farmer at Goulburn Plains, sailed on a sealing voyage 'with his father's consent'. If this were the normal practice for colonial apprentices in those trades concerned with ship building, maintenance and repair, it would explain why so many of the native-born made only one or two voyages. As with those who had completed their apprenticeships, these apprentices had no intention of remaining at sea.

The class origins and occupational training of the young men in both these categories were not the normal backgrounds for seamen of contemporary Britain.[27] In England, unless they were pressed men, seamen were usually unskilled, with the exception of a handful of carpenters, coopers and shipwrights. The sailors learned their craft at sea and, as long as they remained on the lower decks, they had the same economic and social level and status as an unskilled land worker. The elite of this labour force, that is, below officer rank, were the few skilled tradesmen necessary to maintain the ship. It would therefore be unusual for a boy of 'good' family, or one who had recently completed his apprenticeship, to join a ship's company as a common seaman or a ship's boy. Such lads usually began their career at sea with the rank of midshipman.[28] The occupations of sailor or ship's boy were only suitable for the young men and boys from the unskilled labouring classes. It was in all probability this consideration which prompted Commissioner Bigge to assume that the native-born, being 'the children of the convicts', were eminently suited for the occupation of seafarer. Furthermore, there was the problem of employment for these children of the lower orders of colonial society. With the cessation of free land grants and the changing policies of land use and alienation, it was not the intention of Bigge or his colonial advisers to encourage the children of the convicts to become the owners of large areas of land. Nor were there mills, factories or industries in need of the labour of young men. The obvious alternative, for a colony with the geographic location of New South Wales and its dependence on shipping for supplies, trade and communication, was to encourage the native youth 'to go to sea'. It was the third category of native-born sailors who fitted this description and were most similar to the typical contemporary British 'tar'.

This third group most closely resembled Bigge's expectations of the parentage and class origin of the native-born. Many had lost their fathers at an early age and had 'gone to sea with the consent of the mother'. Richard Fry, for example, had died when his son was seven years old; William Howe had died when his son was twelve; Thomas Ambrose when his son was eleven. All three sons had joined colonial vessels as ships' boys and all with the written consent of their mothers. There were boys who had lost both parents: William Hand, 'whose mother and father are both dead; has no guardian'; and William Kiernon, who sailed with the consent of his guardian. Those whose parents were still living had two characteristics in common: most were the children of unskilled men and most were from large families. The father of Jonathan Bradley was a Sydney labourer; Michael Connor's father was 'a poor and aged man'; James Freeman's father was 'Keeper of the Pound'; William Douglass was a child 'of deserving parents'.

The boys from this group who joined colonial vessels did so as an alternative to a future as an unskilled worker, as a safeguard against employment as a labourer or servant, as a way of relieving a parent or guardian of the expense of their upkeep, or as a combination of all three reasons. This motivation was more typical of English society than of the patterns of colonial employment for the native youths. One characteristic was common and determinative in the occupational choice: the father had no trade to teach the son, no land on which to employ him, no means to pay an indentures fee to a private master. There was no 'family' work available for the lad. With no opportunity to work with his parents or brothers and with no skills, experience or promise of parental assistance, the boy could not substantiate an application for a grant of land. The only employment available to these lads was that of unskilled labourer.

Within the distinctive and unique composition of the labour force in the penal colony, combined with the absence of mining, industrial or factory work, opportunities for unskilled lads were limited in the colony of New South Wales. Opportunities for unskilled labour on river, coastal and overseas vessels, however, were abundant. The shortage of labour to fill ships' crews was accentuated by the prohibition of convict labour on ships and by regulations which prevented the holders of conditional pardons from leaving the colony. Furthermore, the employment of poor parish boys and orphans was traditional in both the British Navy and with the merchantmen. All vessels sailing from England carried boys as part of a ship's complement.

The convict transport *Hillsborough*, had a crew of forty seamen and fifteen boys.[29] If these colonial boys went to sea because there was no alternative form of employment for them this could explain why so many made only one or two voyages before seeking alternative occupations.

Among all three groups there were, undoubtedly, those boys who joined ships' companies from a sense of adventure, that is, 'with their own consent and aspiration'. It may have been that these were the boys who left no trace of their subsequent careers in the colonial records. It may have been that, in search of adventure, they joined the crews of overseas vessels and served on British, American or other foreign ships. It may have been that they settled at a port of call on the east coast of America or in New Zealand, or even in parts of Britain. It may have been that these lads died as ships' boys, from illness, disease or misadventure. Whatever may have become of this elusive group, the evidence of the Ships' Musters shows how few remained as sailors on ships and other seafaring craft sailing from the port of Sydney. The Musters show very clearly how few of the first generation chose the sea as an occupation. The native-born mariners were a minority occupational group and one in which few of the Currency Lads persevered. Those who did could not be seen to represent the independent and adventurous spirit which contemporaries ascribed to the native-born; they may have felt 'naturalised to the sea' and chosen this profession willingly. They were, however, atypical within their generation, for the native-born saw their future linked very firmly with the land of their birth and the opportunities it offered. They did not consider themselves island dwellers nor did they see the sea as their major link with life. The future for the native-born was inextricably linked with the development of their land and with life in the colony itself. It may have been the reason why so few 'stout lads' joined colonial or coastal vessels and made so few voyages away from their native land. The profession of a mariner, with the discipline and rigours of a seafaring life, did not appeal to the native-born. They were, from birth, 'naturalised' to their native-land, not to the sea.

CHAPTER TEN

THE ART OR TRADE OF THE WORKER

'It is partly in the hostile sentiments actively instilled in them by their parents . . .'

The *Australian*, 14 February 1827.

In February 1827 the *Australian* published an editorial concerning 'Our colonial-born brethren—better known here by the familiar name of Currency'. This article claimed that

> The young men are more disposed to embark in the profession of some art or trade as stockmen, than follow the drudgery of common farm labourers. This arises in great measure from their unwillingness to mix with convicts so universally employed in farming, but also in no inconsiderable degree from a sense of pride; for owing to convicts being hitherto almost the only agricultural labourers, they look upon that vocation as a sort of degradation.[1]

According to the Census taken the following year, only 5.4 per cent of the male native-born listed an occupation which could be classified as an agricultural 'art or trade', as defined by the *Australian*. An additional 6.8 per cent described themselves as labourers. On the basis of the location of their employment, these were agricultural labourers. Therefore approximately 12 per cent of the employed currency lads were agricultural workers and most of these were unskilled labourers. As almost one third of the male native-born were landowners and another third were skilled tradesmen and apprentices, the agricultural workers formed a very small occupational group among the first generation. Despite the opinion of the *Australian*, few of these young men were disposed to embark on this 'profession'.[2]

The belief that the native-born were employed as agricultural workers persisted, although the reasons for this differed. Whereas the *Australian* had claimed that it was revulsion against convictism which prevented the native-born from becoming labourers but did not discourage them from becoming skilled land-workers, E.S. Hall, editor of *Monitor*, argued that the native youth had no choice but to become 'humble assistants to our large graziers'. Hall viewed this as the direct result of 'discriminatory' land regulations which favoured the free immigrant and prevented the native-born from ownership of the lands which were their birthright. So few of the native-born were employed as agricultural workers, either skilled or unskilled, that it is necessary to consider whether these opinions were published in support of particular arguments or whether they rested on sound evidence. Were those native-born who worked on the properties of their parents, on 'family' land, considered by contemporaries as agricultural workers'? Did they remain with their parents by choice or had they no alternative? Precedent for the acceptance of these ideas could be found in the report of Commissioner Bigge, who had described these parents as farmers 'in the poorest circumstances'.[3] John Macarthur had suggested a scheme for '. . . the instruction of such Colonial Youths as might be desirous to learn the practise [*sic*] a better system of cultivation than the ruinous one at present carried on by their Fathers ...'.[4] The inference in the observations of both Macarthur and Bigge was that the native-born were suited to agricultural work by the circumstances of their birth and parentage but that they lacked expertise, which was the direct result of the economic conditions of their parents. According to this view, they were no more than agricultural labourers on the farms of their fathers.

In 1828, 12.5 per cent of the male native-born were living with one or two parents who owned land; an additional 0.8 per cent were living with a landowning brother.[5] An analysis of the size of the properties and the civil conditions of the parents shows that they came from all levels of the colonial social hierarchy, both convicted and free. As a group, they could not be described accurately as living 'in the poorest circumstances'. There was, for example, enormous disparity in the acreage of the various properties. Among those who had arrived as convicts, parental holdings varied from fourteen to almost 3000 acres. William Blue lived with his elder son at Hunter's Hill, where he farmed fourteen acres; William and Mary Batman and their son farmed twenty-five acres at Parramatta; John and Mary Town had 2854 acres and lived with their son at Richmond. There was a similar diversity among those parents who had arrived free: William Evans and his wife had 1130 acres at Patricks Plains; Archibald Bell had 2685 acres at Windsor; Owen Cavanagh and Peter Hibbs were both at Lower Portland Head and had sixty acres each.[6] From these few examples the inaccuracy of Bigge's description becomes apparent: colonial children who remained with landowner parents did not necessarily live 'in the poorest circumstances' nor were their parents necessarily unskilled convicts, so that the sons were not, by definition, agricultural labourers.

There were 190 native-born males living with both parents on family land in 1828; an additional seventy-one lived with a father and twenty-seven with a mother.[7] In a number of these cases the parents were of advanced age while in others the father or mother had been widowed. In both these circumstances it is reasonable to assume that, had the son not remained on the property, it would have been necessary for the parent to employ an overseer as well as convict or free labourers. The son was, therefore, in the position of landowner rather than worker. Joseph Trimbley was eighty-one and described as a farmer in the Census; he lived at Wallis Plains with his two native-born sons, Joseph junior, born in 1794, and James, born in 1795. No occupation was listed for either of the resident sons but on the basis of the age of the father, it could be assumed they were farmers on family land.

Where a son lived with a widowed mother it could be assumed that he was occupied with the management of the property rather than simply working on it as a labourer. One of the smallest farms was that of widowed Sarah Millen, who lived on her three acres with her twenty-two-year-old son Edward. All the property was cleared and cultivated. Richard Morgan, also twenty-two, lived with his sixty-four-year-old mother, Eleanor, who had a twenty-acre farm, all of which was cleared and cultivated; Sarah Alcorn lived with her son, John, on sixty acres at Pitt Town; Eliza Broughton, widow, lived with her sons on 2000 acres at Appin. There is ample evidence as to the age, civil condition, size of property and marital status of the land-owning parents to exclude the resident sons from the technical classification of employed agricultural workers. All the evidence indicates that, in the majority of cases, the resident son or sons were working on family land, and that they had remained not so much from necessity but as a result of the age of the parent or the size of the property. In addition to this, there is no evidence that these colonials were refused grants of land.[8]

The native-born who could be classified as agricultural workers, therefore, were limited to those who worked for wages on the properties of farmers and graziers. It is not possible to attribute motivation for this choice of profession but, as many were the sons of parents who did not own land, were orphaned or had lost their fathers at an early age, it is probable that they had no other occupational choice than to work on the land for wages. Unlike the sons of landowners, they could not work on family land; unlike the sons of tradesmen, they had no opportunities to learn a trade; unlike their contemporaries in Britain, they had no opportunities to work at urban occupations, in mills, mines or factories. They showed little inclination to become constables, less inclination to go to sea, and they lacked the literacy to become clerks or schoolteachers.[9] In addition to this, their employment opportunities were limited by the ready availability of free labour in the form of convict assigned servants. With this background, it is understandable that they chose the only available occupations, despite these being filled traditionally by convict labour.

The *Australian* had expressed the opinion that the native youth were the elite of the agricultural work-force rather than the actual labourers.[10] It may have been assumed that, being free, they were preferred by employers to those who had arrived as convicts. Neither opinion nor assumption is correct. During the first forty years there was a heavy reliance on convict labour throughout the colony, particularly for agricultural work, simply because there was no other labour force. The assigned 'rural' convict servants were not necessarily skilled in farming, the majority being former British urban dwellers, but they had two advantages: they were cheap and they were available. The continual shortage of free labour meant that the best workmen had little difficulty in finding employment in the towns and settlements. In 1825 James Atkinson found that the free men 'could not be tempted into the country unless very great wages are offered them'. Atkinson also commented on the increasing numbers of free labourers, in which category he made no mention of native-born and defined 'free' as '... most of them were formerly convicts, but have served their time out or obtained their pardons; there are also a great number who hold tickets of leave ...'[11] These observations are supported by an analysis of the civil conditions of the agricultural workers employed on rural properties in 1828. In that year, among the same age group as the native-born, 13.1 per cent of those who had come free described themselves as landworkers; that is, slightly more than the native-born. Among the ex-convicts, 24.2 per cent were employed on rural properties. Any free-by-birth worker, therefore, employed 'Up Country' would have shared his working and living conditions with free men who had arrived as convicts and with those who were still prisoners. Whether or not this deterred the native-born from seeking these occupations may be determined by an examination of the backgrounds of those who were employed on rural properties compared with the backgrounds of those who had become landowners and tradesmen.[12] It is clear that there were insufficient native-born seeking agricultural employment for them to make any significant impression as a group on the nature of the rural labour force. This is evidenced by the lack of acknowledgement by Atkinson that they were a part of that work-force. That slightly more were employed as unskilled labourers than those who worked at rural occupations which demanded some skills would also suggest that these native-born did not necessarily regard these pursuits as degrading because of their association with the forced punitive labour of the convicts.

The diversity of agricultural occupations demanded various levels of skill and, as with other occupational groups in the colony, there was an accepted 'class' hierarchy based on these skills. This hierarchy had two characteristics which were unique to the conditions in the penal colony and had resulted from the nature and composition of the work-force: first, skill overrode civil condition, so that an unskilled native-born labourer was at a lower 'class' level than a convicted overseer; second, the skills which determined ranking in the rural work-force had been gained in the colony in the majority of cases and were not linked with British background, experiences and training. The native-born rural workers, being familiar with colonial conditions since birth and, in many cases, raised in the settlements where they eventually became employed, should have been preferred to assigned convict labour. This would be expected for positions of responsibility such as that of overseer. This was not the case. Although William Howe had advised Bigge to select 'good and diligent Overseers' to superintend the labour of the convicts, no mention was made of the suitability of the native-born for this role.[13] It may have been that contemporaries, regarding the native youth as 'children of the convicts', did not see them as fitted by parentage or upbringing for positions of responsibility or skill. In 1828 most of the land-workers in the colony were ex-convicts. There were 5.4 per cent of the native-born employed in such positions as overseer, sawyer, fencer, bullock-driver, dairyman, stockman; among the same age group of came-free men there were 7.9 per cent; among the ex-convicts, 24.2 per cent.

The native-born land-workers, both the skilled and the labourers, were a younger group than their ex-convict and came-free counterparts; most of the native-born were under twenty-five years of age; both the came-free and the ex-convicts were over twenty-six years. That the average age of the ex-convicts was higher was to be expected as most had arrived in the colony as adults, sentenced to a minimum of seven years' penal servitude.[14] That their highest age group was between twenty-six and thirty would indicate the influence of the changes in the land regulations. These prevented most of the former convicts from receiving land grants on the completion of their sentences. Before the introduction of these regulations in 1824 many of the younger men in this age group could have applied for and received free grants of land. This had been the common practice during the administration of the earlier governors. After the introduction of the new capital and purchase regulations by Governor Brisbane, however, these former convicts lacked the capital necessary to purchase and develop land. They had little alternative but to become 'the humble assistants' of wealthier landowners and graziers. It was their experience, gained as assigned convict servants, which enabled many to obtain skilled positions, and it was this experience which made them invaluable to their employers.

The new land regulations, described by Hall and Wentworth as discriminating against the native-born,[15] had a far wider effect on the 'class' structure of the colony by reducing the opportunities available to the ex-convicts to raise their economic position by the ownership of land. The chief direct result was to increase the number of ex-convicts who had no alternative but to work for wages as agricultural labourers, servants or skilled land-workers. Many remained employed where they had worked formerly as assigned labour and this contributed to a stability in the rural work-force. The single change in the method of land alienation, from free grant to purchase or grant dependent on capital, effectively altered the class structure of the colony. It virtually ensured that those who had arrived convicted could not, on completion of their sentences, become independent, self-supporting landowners but were dependent for employment on the properties of wealthy, established farmers and graziers. The ex-convict artisan–tradesman group could prosper as their skills were in continual demand; the agricultural workers had little opportunity but to remain as employed labour.

Among the came-free there was a higher percentage of males employed as land-workers in 1828 than there was among the native-born, particularly among those aged between thirty and thirty-five years. In this group, 9.2 per cent of the came-free described a specific agricultural occupation, compared with 4.9 per cent of the native-born. The explanation for this may be linked with the date of arrival of these migrants. In almost all cases it was after the departure of Governor Macquarie. They had not, therefore, shared the same childhood experiences as the native-born and they were not familiar with the practice of obtaining free grants of land nor with the general conditions and opportunities of labour in the colony. It is most unlikely that these men and boys had any expectations of becoming landowners themselves, except by their own accumulation of capital. Most had migrated to New South Wales for the specific purpose of working on the land for wages. This is apparent from the description of the agricultural occupations which they followed. With very few exceptions, they became overseers or superintendents.[16] Without previous familiarity with the cultivation of crops and the care of stock in the colony, it is unlikely that these 'new chums' would have been selected by prospective employers solely on the basis that they were free and unconvicted. Governor Brisbane had commented that '. . . some of the large Stockholders will trust a Convict in preference to the freemen they get here'.[17] The reason for this was that a convict or ex-convict who had been an assigned agricultural servant had more practical experience and knowledge than an immigrant totally unfamiliar with colonial conditions. There was no recognition that the native-born had even greater familiarity with the agricultural peculiarities of the colony and that they were, in addition, of free birth. Neither of these characteristics led to the majority of the native-born land-workers being employed in supervisory positions. The overwhelming majority of men employed as skilled and semi-skilled land-workers were the ex-convicts. Excluding labourers, there were 659 men who had been pardoned or had served their sentence and were the same age as the native-born, who were employed as land-workers; this was almost one quarter of the ex-convicts. Among the came-free, there were sixty-seven, or 8 per cent; among the native-born, fifty-five, or 5.4 per cent. Among the ex-convicts, 15.4 per cent were employed as overseers and superintendents; among the came-free, 44.7 per cent; and among the native born, 24 per cent.[18]

The native-born land-workers who were employed as overseers were mainly the sons of families settled on the land and had grown up accustomed to 'rural pursuits'. Their parentage and background indicated clearly that they had agricultural experience, which would have influenced their selection for positions of responsibility. Their parentage also showed that the fathers were propertied men of some substance in the community. John Collett, for example, had been 'born at the Hawkesbury' and was the son of Pierce Colletts, a transported Irish rebel, and his free wife, Mary, who had accompanied him to New South Wales in 1801. In 1828 John was overseer for Joseph Underwood at Mount Pleasant, Sutton Forest, where he lived with his native-born wife, their four-year old daughter and his sister. The owner of the property lived in Sydney and John Collett was responsible for its care and management. His parents lived at Bathurst with a younger son and daughter; his father was a publican who ran 360 horned cattle and 300 sheep on his 200 acre property. Another son, James, was a stock-holder at Mount York, Bathurst, and a fourth was a married blacksmith at Evan, where he owned twenty acres. Native-born overseers with similar backgrounds included Edgar Kable, William Eggleston, John Neal, Thomas Ether and James Harper. These native-born could be expected to be more experienced land-workers than recently arrived immigrants such as James Cann, who had come to the colony in 1822 at the age of thirty-four. Cann was employed by John Herring of Patersons Plains. John Furner had arrived in 1823 at the age of twenty-three; he was overseer at Newcastle for the pilot, Mr Richard Siddons. John Howell had arrived in 1825 and was superintendent for James Hassall of Bathurst.

Tables 10/1, 10/2 and 10/3 provide summaries of the comparative number of land-workers among native-born, came-free and ex-convict males in New South Wales in 1828.[19]

TABLE 10/1

Comparative summary of colonial land-workers (labourers excluded), New South Wales, 1828

Civil condition	Total	Percentage of total males
Born in the colony	59	4.9
Came-free	67	7.9
Ex-convict	659	24.2

TABLE 10/2

Comparative summary of colonial land-workers (labourers included), New South Wales, 1828

Civil condition	Total	Percentage of total males
Born in the colony	139	11.8
Came free	111	13.1
Ex-convict	2069	53.8

TABLE 10/3

Occupations and age groups of native-born land-workers, New South Wales, 1828

Occupation	15–20	21–25	26–30	Age group 31–35	36–40	N.R.	Total
Sawyer	1	12	4	1	3	2	23
Overseer	1	3	2	3		1	10
Shepherd	2	2	2				6
Stockman/stock-keeper	8	2					10
Fencer	1	2			1	1	5
Dairyman			1				1
Bullock driver		1					1
Timberman		1					1
Gardiner [sic]	1						1
'In Service of Landowner'	1						1
TOTAL	15	23	9	4	4	4	59
Total B.C. males	520	333	160	81	15	53	1167

The numbers and age groups of those native-born who followed rural 'arts and trades' are shown in Table 10/3.[20]

Within the 'class' hierarchy of agricultural workers, the overseers were of the highest rank; their position involved considerable responsibility, particularly when the master was not resident on the property. It was essential that the overseer be not only skilled but trustworthy. Bigge had disapproved of the practice of employing ex-convicts as overseers. He recommended that settlers, in particular those who 'had stations for the feeding of sheep in the interior', should have a free and unconvicted person as overseer.[21] Bigge may have been influenced in forming this opinion by evidence from men like Robert Cartwright. Cartwright claimed that non-attendance at church by free settlers was caused in part by the lack of 'trusty servants' to leave in charge of the farm or household during the absence of the master.[22] Brisbane, however, found that this was not invariably the case, for a great number of the larger stockholders preferred to trust a 'convict' overseer rather than the free men who were available.[23] This preference was linked with colonial experience for in 1828 many of the ex-convict overseers had been in the colony as long as, or longer than, many of the native-born. Thomas Herbert, for example, had arrived in 1792, sentenced to transportation for life; he received an absolute pardon and became overseer for the Macarthurs at Camden. Thomas McKeever had arrived in 1801, also sentenced for life; he, too, received an absolute pardon and became overseer for John Howe, a came-free farmer at Patricks Plains. Neither Bigge nor Brisbane recommended that the native-born were suitable as prospective overseers. This may have been linked with their assumptions as to the parentage and prospects of the Currency Lads.[24]

The occupation which ranked lowest in the hierarchy of colonial agricultural workers was that of shepherd. It was considered by contemporaries as the harshest and most degraded of all 'bush' work.[25] Living in a crude, slab, bark-roofed hut, the shepherd was completely responsible for the safety, care and feeding of his master's flocks. He was usually an assigned servant who had no alternative but to work as directed at this lonely and degraded occupation. In 1828, for example, within the same age group as the native-born there were almost 500 convict shepherds; another 128 were men who had been freed by servitude. This compared with six native-born and seven who had come free. The six native-born represented less than 1 per cent of all the males who had been born in the colony. Few had been baptized and there was little record of the civil condition and occupation of their parents. Where this information was available, it became apparent that the boys who became shepherds were usually the children of men 'of no trade', the majority of whom had arrived in the colony as convicts. The parents had usually died when the boy was a child. The young shepherd showed no reluctance to being employed by an ex-convict sheep owner or to working with ex-convict overseers and assigned convict labourers. Edward Cruise was a typical example. He was born in the colony in 1813, possibly at Parramatta where his two younger sisters were at the Female Orphan School in 1828. He was employed by ex-convict Edward Redmond at Bathurst and worked with an assigned convict labourer and a freed-by-servitude stockman. Another native-born who was employed at Bathurst was Thomas Crowder, the son of a conditionally pardoned settler from Norfolk Island. Crowder was employed by Richard Hall, conditionally pardoned overseer for Samuel Marsden. The household at Bathurst consisted of Hall, Crowder and a fifty-six-year-old assigned convict labourer. The evidence available concerning the native-born shepherds, although admittedly limited, does suggest that, in their parentage, experiences and upbringing, they were the rural counterparts of those 'stout lads' of Sydney who became ships' boys.[26]

The occupation of sawyer was in direct contrast to that of shepherd because sawyers were held in high repute among the bush workers. Alexander Harris commented that he supposed there was no other class of men who entertained 'such brotherly feeling towards one another as sawyers'.[27] These sawyers, working in pairs, and thus dependent on one another, had played an important part in the development of the colony from the time of the first landing at Botany Bay in 1788. Phillip put men ashore on the uninviting marsh area to establish a saw-pit in case he could find no alternative site for the settlement.[28] Sawyers remained in constant demand. In 1804 the *Sydney Gazette* carried no less than eight advertisements for sawyers. Simeon Lord offered constant employment to six men for at least six months; another advertisement was for 'three pairs of sawyers to work for six months at the Government Wharf'.[29] This would suggest that few convicts arriving in New South Wales were skilled sawyers. It was therefore necessary to advertise for those men who had gained this skill in the colony itself. Contemporaries could have assumed that this was a trade familiar to the native-born youth. In 1828, however, most of the colonial sawyers in the same age group as the native-born were ex-convicts. There were 115 sawyers who were free by servitude, fifty-five who were still convicts, five who had come free and twenty-three native-born. That so few of the native-born did follow this occupation supports the finding that the rural native-born preferred to become farmers and landholders or to remain on their parents' land rather than become employed agricultural workers. This was the case even when there were opportunities in a respected and prosperous occupation, such as sawying.

Sawyers could be self-employed or they could be employed by private employers or by government. They could also work in family groups. William Spears had arrived in New South Wales as a private with the New South Wales Corps in 1801. After his tour of duty he had remained as a settler at Hunter's Hill. Spears and his three unmarried sons worked together as sawyers. These sons had applied to Governor Brisbane for land grants in 1824 and had each received sixty acres, although this is not listed in the 1828 Census. James, who was born in 1803, stressed his skill as a sawyer:

> My character as a free-born subject of this Colony remains untarnished and unsullied and I entertain no doubt of its continuance, being by trade a sawyer, in which capacity I am enabled by diligence and sobriety to support myself.[30]

The sawyers and overseers were men with some skills; the labourers, however, were the unskilled workers of the colony. Most of this group had arrived as convicts. There were very few native-born who qualified for the description 'labourers of no trade'. Tables 10/4 and 10/5 show the age groups

TABLE 10/4

Age groups of native-born labourers, New South Wales, 1828 (summary)

Labourers				Age groups			
	15–20	21–25	26–30	31–35	36–40	N.R.	Total
	40	24	13	1		2	80
Total in age group	520	333	160	81	15	53	1167

TABLE 10/5

Comparative age groups for colonial labourers born 1788–1813, resident in New South Wales, 1828 (summary)

Civil condition				Age groups			
	15–20	21–25	26–30	31–35	36–40	N.R.*	Total
Born in the colony	40	24	13	1		2	80
Came-free	15	7	7	8	7		44
Ex-convict	6	152	565	327	360		1410

*The numbers for came-free and ex-convict exclude men who did not state their age specifically in the 1828 Census.

of the native-born labourers and the comparative numbers of labourers in the three civil conditions.

Most of the labourers in New South Wales in 1828 had arrived as convicts. This was understandable and to be expected considering the structure of the colonial population and the occupational backgrounds of the men and women transported. That so small a percentage of the native-born were labourers was not to be expected considering their parentage: most had a mother who had arrived convicted and a father who had been either a convict, a marine, a soldier or a sailor. It would have been reasonable to assume that the children of settlers who had originated in the lowest orders of the British social hierarchy would have emerged as unskilled workers. The contemporary explanation was that their fierce pride prevented them from turning to those occupations normally filled by the punitive labour of transported felons.[31] An analysis of the parentage and background of the first generation showed that this was not the explanation. Contemporaries judged the parents of the native-born on the basis of their British background and British 'class' characteristics. The native-born accepted their parents on colonial standards of occupation and achievement. The parents, in most cases, encouraged their sons to follow in the way of life they had built for themselves and their families in the colony. As has been shown, rural sons followed their fathers on the land, tradesmen's sons and the sons of men who had achieved economic independence in the colony became apprenticed. The children who were left orphans or belonged to the minority group of poor parents and widowed mothers were those who became the unskilled.[32]

Colonial labourers differed from their British counterparts in terms of the connotations of the word, the nature of labour, the opportunities and rewards for labour. The strong convict connotations made exact definition difficult for, when used by officials to denote the labour of assigned servants, 'labourer' referred to a variety of occupations. Convict tradesmen were described as 'convict labourers'; convicts assigned to settlers for a variety of duties were 'labourers'; convicts retained in government service were 'convict labourers'.[33] This lack of precise definition of the word was also found among those ex-convict and free labourers who were employed in the colony during this period. James Waldersee, investigating Catholic society in New South Wales, concluded that in the 1828 Census there were 'undoubtedly many included under the general description of "labourer" whose occupations were far from unskilled'.[34] A convict still under sentence could, and did, describe his occupation as that of 'labourer', implying that he was a 'Government Servant'. In this sense, he was indicating his civil condition rather than his occupation. Daniel Barney was born in the colony in 1798, the son of two ex-convicts. In 1828 he was serving a colonial sentence. He lived at Pitt Town, where he owned thirty acres which he presumably cultivated in spite of his conviction. In the Census, Barney described his civil condition as 'Government Servant, Born in the Colony' and his occupation as 'Labourer'. Another native-born landholder, Patrick Keighran, also described his occupation as 'Labourer' despite his thirty acres. Keighran had never been convicted and there appears to be no explanation for this description.

Colonial labourers, both ex-convict and free, had greater choice and opportunities for labour in the colony than in Britain and received far greater rewards. In Sussex, for example, in 1821 the Select Committee on the Depressed State of Agriculture was told by a farmer that the wages of agricultural labourers were 'distressingly low'. A man, his wife and two children could only expect to receive ten shillings a week.[35] In 1825 William Cobbett described the conditions of a 'young, hearty labouring man' in Sussex:

> Here in this part of Sussex, they give the single man sevenpence a day, that is to say, enough to buy two pounds and a quarter of bread for six days in the week, and as he does not work on Sundays, there is no seven-pence allowed for the Sunday, and of course nothing to eat.[36]

In contrast to this, Bigge was told by Archibald Bell in 1820 that the 'Sum of £10 would be perhaps a fair sum for Convict labourers'.[37] This sum was for a year's work, in addition to rations, clothing and lodging at standards set by the colonial officials; a convict working under sentence could receive sixpence halfpenny seven days a week as a reward for extra labour. Bell also advised Bigge on standard wages in the colony, suggesting that 'Artificers, Stockmen and Shepherds receive £10.0.0. per year, Labourers (Men) £8.0.0, Boys and Women £6.0.0'.[38] Those native-born, therefore, who were employed as labourers by agriculturalists and farmers could reasonably expect a greater return for their labour than that received by their counterparts in contemporary England. Although basically unskilled workers, they were not obliged to live in the 'distressed condition' of the majority of Britain's agricultural labourers.

Almost all the native-born labourers were rural workers. Unlike the labourers in Sydney, Parramatta, Richmond, Windsor and Liverpool, they lived mainly on the properties of their masters, sharing accommodation and working conditions with ex-convicts and assigned servants. In the towns, labourers were more likely to work for hire, as did native-born Thomas Condon, who was a labourer to a publican. Evidence which remains as to the parentage of the native-born labourers[39] combined with that from the few Memorials requesting land grants indicates that most had been born in rural areas, not in Sydney or its environs. The native-born Memorialists stressed that they had been accustomed to rural pursuits since their childhood. Native-born George Fieldhouse described himself as 'bred as a Labourer in Agriculture'. These descriptions were similar to the way in which ex-convicts described their former occupations in Britain. Joseph Clarke, an ex-convict who applied to Governor Brisbane for a land grant, wrote that before his conviction he had 'been bred in early life to the habit of industry in a small village in Bedfordshire as a Farmer's Labourer'. In the colony of New South Wales, prior to the changes in the forms of land alienation, a man who had been 'bred' as a farmer's labourer found this no bar to applying for a free grant of land. This in itself indicates clearly the basic differences between the free or freed colonial labourer and the agricultural labourers of Britain.

The greatest number of native-born labourers was resident in the district of Airds. Here, 20 per cent of the employed native-born were labourers. That five of these working men also described themselves as Catholics may help explain the lack of any record of baptism. In general, the native-born labourers worked in the main agricultural districts, around Pitt Town (17 per cent of the employed native-born), Wilberforce (9.5 per cent), Richmond (7.4 per cent), Windsor (5.8 per cent), and in the outer areas of Prospect, Cornwallis and Illawarra. None of the native-born labourers were employed at Sydney or at Parramatta.[40] These labourers were comparatively young men, almost half being under the age of twenty and 80 per cent being under twenty-five. They were not, therefore, the children whom King had described as 'abandoned' by their worthless parents, for almost half were not born until after the deposition of Bligh. They were more likely to be among that group of children whose later childhood and adolescence coincided with the administration of Macquarie. They could, therefore, be expected to have had more occupational opportunities than those children who had lived in New South Wales during the earliest years of settlement.

The native-born labourers shared with the land-workers the characteristic that they showed no reluctance to be employed by men who had been convicts or to work with assigned convict servants. From the composition of the remaining Householders' Schedules it is possible to reconstruct the types of households in which some of these labourers were employed. In the district of Bathurst in 1828 there was a native-born labourer, James Charlton, who was employed by John Piper, the householder. Charlton was one of six labourers, four of whom were assigned servants and the fifth a ticket-of-leave man.[41] Also at Bathurst was Peter McAlpin, a labourer for a conditionally pardoned landholder, Mr John Nevill, who lived on his Bathurst property and employed McAlpin and assigned servants.

Why these native-born chose the occupation of labourer is difficult to establish mainly because of the paucity of available evidence about their parentage and background. Where such information does exist, from sources such as the Memorials, marriage and burial records and Musters, it does suggest that many were raised by their mothers, after the death of the father or where the mother had not formed a permanent liaison with the father.

These fathers were not necessarily convicts or men who had arrived as convicts. A large proportion had been privates in the New South Wales Corps. The father of native-born labourer John Braddock had been a private in the 102nd Regiment and had died when his son was four years old. James Rixon, another private, had died when his son William was one year old. James Neals, an ex-marine settler, had died when James junior was one year old, as did the ex-marine father of Richard Windsor. John Vardy, a private, was drowned when his second son Thomas was eight years old. All the native-born labourers who remained with their parents and possibly worked with their fathers were the sons of ex-convicts, with the single exception of Isaac Boulton. His father, Thomas Boulton, had arrived as a private in 1801. As well as the six who lived with parents, a further five lived with brothers, suggesting that slightly more than 10 per cent had retained family ties.

In addition to the labourers, there was another occupational group which could be classified as unskilled. This was the servants, who could be either agricultural or domestic. A total of thirty-five native-born described their occupation as 'servant' in the 1828 Census and most of them were domestic servants. They represented less than 3 per cent of the adult male native-born in New South Wales. They were, however, an easier group to trace than the labourers, several of the fathers being established tradesmen or farmers in the same district. William Baylis, for example, had arrived as a private, married ex-convict Ann Price and eventually settled as a nailor at Windsor. Three of his children, William, born 1802, Jane, born 1813, and Maria, born 1814, were employed as house-servants to Thomas Kite, a conditionally pardoned landholder at Bathurst. James Evans was a carpenter who had arrived as a convict, received a conditional pardon and settled at Botany. One son worked with him as a carpenter; a second son, Charles, was servant to the publican and landholder George Onslow, at Evan. Several of the native-born servants were employed in the households of prominent settlers and officials: Francis O'Brien was a servant to Chief Justice Francis Forbes; Andrew Smith was a servant to the Reverend Samuel Marsden; Alexander McDonald was house-servant to the Reverend Henry Fulton; George Podmore was servant to James Mudie of Petersham. All of these employers were concerned with the writing of character testimonials for those native-born who wished to apply for indulgences or land grants from the governor. As their testimonials were all favourable, it may have been that they preferred to employ the native-born young men in preference to the ex-convicts or those who had come free.

Only one of the native-born servants owned land: William Carver, servant to George Howell of Parramatta, owned and cultivated 120 acres. The only evidence of continuing family links was that four of these servants worked in the same households as brothers or sisters. In three cases the children were orphaned. In general the native-born servants were a young group, almost two thirds being under the age of twenty. Table 10/6 shows the age groups and gives the comparative ages for convict and came-free servants.

Table 10/6 shows that most of the colonial servants in this age group were ex-convicts. The servants who had come free to the colony were almost twice as numerous as the native-born, although overall there were more native-

TABLE 10/6

Comparative age groups for colonial servants born 1788–1813, resident in New South Wales, 1828

Civil condition				Age group			
	15–20	21–25	26–30	31–35	36–40	N.R.*	Total
Born in the colony	23	8	2			2	35
Came-free	19	24	17	14	11		85
Ex-convict	4	37	110	75	65		291

*The numbers for came-free and ex-convicts exclude men who did not state their age specifically in the 1828 Census.

born than came-free. The native-born, a far younger group, worked in areas outside Sydney and were usually resident at their employer's house. Their youth, combined with the districts in which they lived, would suggest that they were mainly 'rural' children. Their number was very small and this indicates that their choice of occupation was exceptional. Most of their 'rural' contemporaries remained on family land or applied for land grants. The explanation for this may only be surmised because the evidence is limited but it is certainly probable that, at least in some cases, these were the orphaned rural children. They lacked family support and the most acceptable employment available for them in their own districts was that of servant.

That such a minority of the first generation became land-workers and unskilled labourers and servants was unexpected. It was at a variance with contemporary assumptions concerning their parentage, natural inclinations, occupational abilities and opportunities. That so few became 'professional' workers, in the sense of following occupations which demanded various levels of educational ability, was in accordance with the British class origins and educational standards of most of the parents.[42] Barely 2.5 per cent of the male native-born who listed an occupation in the 1828 Census could be placed in this category. This compared with 0.5 per cent of the ex-convicts in the same age group and 14 per cent of those who had come free. Additionally, William Charles Wentworth, the first native-born barrister, could have been included in this group, either on the basis of his legal qualifications or as the former editor of the *Australian*. Wentworth, however, described himself as a landholder. Accurate as this description was, it did exclude his 'professional' occupations.

The first native-born to qualify at a British university as a surgeon was not included in the Census. This was William Sherwin, himself the son of a surgeon, who was at Melville Island when the Census was taken. Sherwin had been appointed to the government position of Assistant Surgeon at Melville Island, at an annual salary of £385.5.0, and took up his appointment from 1828.[43] John Henderson, the 'surgeon' listed in the Census, lacked Sherwin's undoubted qualifications. It is even possible that his title of 'surgeon' may have been self-bestowed. Henderson was the son of Surgeon William Balmain, who arrived in 1788, and Margaret Dawson, a former servant who was sentenced to death at the age of fifteen at the Old Bailey. On account of her youth and this being her first offence, the sentence was commuted to 'seven years on the eastern coast of New South Wales'. 'Dawson', as Balmain called her, lived with the first fleet surgeon until his death, bearing him two children. She and the children accompanied Balmain to England and returned after his death. Although they did not marry, Balmain left all his property to 'Dawson' and their children.[44] There is no evidence that Henderson received any formal medical training in Britain. It is probable that as a youth he was employed at the Sydney Hospital, assisting D'arcy Wentworth and William Redfern. In 1820 he was a passenger on the *Minstrel* sailing for London, listed on the Ship's Muster as 'Dr Henderson'. In the *Sydney Almanac* of 1828 he was included as 'apothecary and druggist'. By 1830 he was publicly describing himself as 'surgeon and apothecary' in the *Australian:*

> J. Henderson, surgeon and apothecary, begs leave to inform his friends and the public in general that he has moved his residence from Elizabeth Street to no. 58 George Street ... genuine medicines of every description by the latest arrivals. Prescriptions and family recipes accurately prepared ... medical chests made up....[45]

Henderson, like William Charles Wentworth, was the son of a man and a woman whose class origins and British experiences were typical of the division of early colonial society into the bond and the free, the 'respectable' and the 'tainted'. Unlike Wentworth, he was not accepted by his father's British relations; unlike Wentworth, it was his father, not his convict mother, who died before his formative years; unlike Wentworth, who associated himself with his aristocratic relatives, the Earl Fitzwilliam and his family, and received his education at the Middle Temple and at Cambridge, Henderson remained a colonial boy. He was dependent on his mother's colonial connections and on the favour of his late father's colonial associates. Wentworth returned to his native-land with British qualifications for his colonial career. Henderson used his colonial experiences to establish himself as a professional man.[46]

Schoolmasters and clerks belonged in this professional group, despite this being an occupation in which 'gentleman' convicts, and even a convict woman or two, were employed. There was only one native-born schoolmaster in 1828. This was John Edney, born at Parramatta in 1803, the son of John Edney and convict Hannah Johns. His father was a soldier in the New South Wales Corps and, when that Regiment 'retired from Sydney to Ceylon', eight-year-old John (or William) and his mother accompanied Private Edney. Later they went to England, remaining there until Edney senior was invalided out and became a Chelsea Pensioner. Edney and his father then returned 'to his native land', by favour of the Duke of York. Both applied for and received sixty acres from Macquarie in 1820 but this was not measured or confirmed. In 1824 Edney junior wrote to Brisbane, asking that this be done. In his Memorial, Edney wrote that he had kept a school 'to instruct youths ... the Sussex Street Academy ... for a considerable time'. He now wished to retire and 'engage in a situation under Government ... as storekeeper, superintendent, or any other vacancy ... at Moreton Bay or elsewhere ... at some of the new settlements'. Edney, one of the few of the first generation who had lived for a considerable time outside New South Wales, showed quite clearly that he considered himself not an Englishman but, as he told Brisbane, 'a free born subject of Australia'.

Twelve of the native-born were 'Lads who wrote a Fair Hand'[47] and were employed as clerks. This occupation had strong convict associations; from the beginning of white settlement the administration had to depend heavily on the penmanship of convicted felons, 'Gentlemen' convicts such as Michael Massey Robinson, who was called by contemporaries Macquarie's poet-laureate. Another was that likeable rogue James Hardy Vaux.[48] Men who were lesser known acted as clerks for the governors and commissaries and in all branches of the penal administration. That such employment was from necessity and not for the benefit of the felons, was shown by the comment of the Molesworth Committee on this situation, which had existed throughout the period of white settlement.

> ... the employment of convicts as clerks in various departments of Government ... where they have had means of acquiring knowledge, of which the most corrupt and dangerous use has been made; ... the employment of convicts as clerks to attorneys, with free access to the gaols, which has given rise in the colony to an unparalleled system of bribery and connivance at crime; at one time even the clerk of the Attorney-general was a convict, and performed all the legal business of his master. . . .[49]

It is probable that this close connection between the occupation of colonial clerks and the employment of 'gentlemen' convicts prompted Bigge to suggest that the native-born should be employed as clerks in preference to 'Persons who have been convicted'. This, however, did not prove practical as few who had literary abilities found it an enticing occupation. Brisbane commented on Bigge's recommendation cautiously: 'Due attention has been paid to this as far as circumstances will admit'.[50]

The twelve native-born who did follow this occupation could be classified into three groups. The first, although described as clerks, held high positions in the colony, which gave them both economic and social standing in the community. There was John Sherwin, the brother of the native-born surgeon William Sherwin; he was assistant to the Commandant at Moreton Bay. There was Simeon Lord's protegé, John Black, clerk at the Bank of New South Wales; there was James Long, the Parish Clerk for St. James's Church.[51] In the second group were colonial-born sons of established land-owners, such as William Fishburne, clerk to a public official at Baulkham Hills, and William Longford, a commissary's clerk who lived with his father, a landowner with 640 acres. The third group were the young men who were employed as clerks by colonial businessmen or by government. William Lambe, for example, was clerk to merchant Richard Pritchard of Sydney; Thomas Byrne and his brother John were clerks at the Customs Department.

Closely connected with the occupation of the clerks was that of printing, which also demanded literacy and accuracy. There were, however, very few opportunities for any young colonial men to learn and practise this trade. The three who did were George Howe, John Cubitt and Lawrence Butler. All were of convict parentage. Howe continued in the family business; he was the son of George Howe, transported for felony, who began the publication of the *Sydney Gazette*. After his death his elder son, Robert, succeeded him as editor and, when Robert was accidentally drowned in 1829, George Howe took his brother's place. Cubitt and Butler were the sons of convicts who had been transported on the *Neptune* in 1790. Cubbitt senior remained in Sydney, becoming Master of the Row Guard Boat and being continually employed by the government. Butler settled in the Hawkesbury district, where his two elder sons remained as farmers; a third son was a carpenter in Sydney and the youngest a printer. There is no remaining evidence to suggest that the two men continued their association but, as their sons, with the exception of George Howe, were the only two native-born to follow the trade of printer, it is probable that this was the result of a continued friendship.

The group of native-born who could be classified as self-employed was also a small one, made up of three native-born dealers and seventeen publicans. One of the dealers was George Kable, son of ex-convict entrepreneur Henry Kable, who began his colonial career as an agent and dealer. The seventeen native-born publicans were not typical of the other occupational groups. Almost half were also landowners, fifteen were married, two were ex-tradesmen and one had served a colonial sentence. This was Timothy Lacey of Parramatta, who had been gaoled for what his parents described as 'a boyish prank'. The colonial authorities, however, did not share this view of the offence. Shortly after his release Lacey wrote to Governor Brisbane, requesting a grant of land. This was refused with the following admonition:

'It would more become the modesty of a young man to defer your application for indulgence from the Crown ... until your conviction in a criminal court has been effaced from the Public Memory'.

Most of the native-born publicans were the sons of ex-convicts. Their inns and public houses were mainly in the outlying districts. There were only two in Sydney and three in Parramatta. Frequently, it was the wife who saw to the travellers who stayed at the inn, the husband being more concerned with the care of his land and stock. Alexander Harris described the inn of native-born Tom Small and his wife on the banks of the Hawkesbury:

I landed at Tom Small's, a native of the Colony, who had very large timber concerns in the bush and a very good public house on the river bank ... The mistress found me a good bed.[52]

There were almost as many native-born constables as there were publicans. Although so few native-born were employed in positions which were directly connected with the enforcement of the law, evidence does exist of a concern with the maintenance of law and order in their native-land. In 1822 native-born John Frazier wrote to Governor Brisbane:

This neighbourhood of Concord wherein I reside, being much infected with Bushrangers (two of whom I have already taken and brought to justice) and there being no officer appointed to look after such dangerous characters, I have taken the liberty of offering for the situation of Constable of that District should it meet with your approbation. I am witness to the Book and a Free Man Born in the Colony and can be much recommended.

The following year Francis Kenny, native-born son of transported Irish Catholic rebel James Kenny, wrote to Colonial Secretary Goulburn:

As it is the intention of Government to establish in this Colony a Police Corps of Native-Born Youths, and, as I should feel myself Honoured by being in the Service of my Country and this Government; provided I would in some measure follow the Industrious Course of Life I have been bred to and I feel myself confident in saying that several other young men would follow my example.

This request, from the son of a man convicted of treason against the King of England, was an unexpected example of the desire of the native-born to be of service to their country. In 1824 Governor Brisbane did propose to Bathurst that a Colonial Cavalry should be formed to act mainly for the protection of settlers in areas such as Bathurst, where, 'in consequence of violent outrages . . . seven stock-keepers had recently been murdered in a cruel and barbarous manner'. Brisbane suggested that, in the first instance, this troop should consist of thirty-two members.[53] There is no evidence of Bathurst's reactions to this proposal or of the opinions of the native-born regarding this service to the colony, which involved protection from the native black inhabitants, not from the lawlessness of bushrangers. Certainly no such proposal was considered by Brisbane's successor, Governor Darling. Macquarie, however, had suggested to Bathurst in 1819 that the 'establishment of a Horse and Militia Raised in the Colony' should be beneficial as the military establishment was 'of inadequate strength . . . to repel any serious efforts . . . should a Factious Demagogue come forth to Light the Torch of Sedition'. Macquarie suggested that a force might be raised from the Population, among the inhabitants free by arrival or servitude: '. . . 700 men could be found without loss to the Industry of the Colony'. He added:

The young men of the Country who have been born here are of a Sober Steady Disposition, and might be fully Confided in—and I am persuaded that Many of this description would Cheerfully enrol themselves— particularly in the Cavalry, to which their Pride would naturally enough lead them to give Preference, many of them being possessors of Horses and good Horsemen.[54]

At this time, however, there was no colonial militia which the native-born youths could join. In 1826 the Colonial Secretary noted in the Military Returns for that year, under Returns of Local Corps:

There are no militia in the Colony of New South Wales. The only Local Corps raised therein are the Governor's Body Guard and the Mounted Police, both of which are borne upon the strength of the Regiment serving in the Colony.

At that time the Governor's Body Guard consisted of one non-commissioned officer and seven rank and file. The Mounted Police was limited to three officers, fifty non-commissioned officers and fifty-nine rank and file. None of these sixty-six were native-born and none of the Governor's Body Guard were colonial youths.[55] Those native-born who wished to 'go soldier' could follow their fathers into their regiments, as did a few of the native-born who joined the New South Wales Corps before it was recalled in 1810.[56] Those who had fathers from a higher social level than the privates of the New South Wales Corps could enlist in England but records for them are almost non-existent. One who did choose a military career—and was wounded at Waterloo—was Thomas Douglas White, who had returned to England with his father, Surgeon White, and joined the Royal Engineers. White later returned to the colony and rejoined his ex-convict mother who had married a wealthy emancipist.

Those native-born, therefore, whose occupations were concerned with the enforcement of the law were limited to the constables.[57] Colonial constables did not enjoy a high reputation for it was an occupation favoured by convicts, ticket-of-leave men and ex-convicts. Commissioner Bigge was of the opinion that the standard and reputation of colonial constables was directly linked with, and caused by, the prevailing official attitudes towards the rank and file of the constabulary. He cited the opinion of Judge-Advocate Wylde, who wrote to Macquarie that:

> The degree of excellence and service in general protection to the Colony from the System (Police) necessarily seems almost altogether to develop upon the character and independence, to a certain extent, of the officers in charge of it.[58]

The native-born constables were found both among the rank and file and among those in charge. John Thorn, Chief Constable for Parramatta, owned a large area of land and was the son of a wealthy free settler.[59] Frederick Meredith was Chief Constable for Liverpool; his brother William was a Police Officer at Bathurst. Among the rank and file were John and William Small, sons of an ex-convict settler; John Small, born in 1794, was a constable at Kissing Point, where he had seventeen acres; his brother was a constable in Sydney. One characteristic of the native-born constables was that they were an older group than those in other occupations, and almost all were married. Although most had married native-born women, some wives had been convicts or were still serving sentences; a Sydney Constable, Robert Melville, brother-in-law of Constables John and William Small, for example, was married to a woman who still had five years of her original sentence to serve.

An even smaller percentage of the native-born was in that group convicted

for infringements of the law. A total of seven native-born were described as
'Government Servants, under colonial sentence' in the Census. This must be
taken as an approximate number because those who may have been found
guilty of a more serious charge and transported to Van Diemen's Land were
not included.[60] Nor does this number include those who may have served
sentences or who had received pardons. For example, on the Muster of the
schooner *Mary Anne* of Sydney in 1823 William Perkins, native of the colony,
is included. He was described as a 'Government Passenger' and was being
taken to Port Dalrymple, sentenced to transportation for life. He was
emancipated and allowed to return to the main colony and in 1828 was living
with his native-born wife Louisa at Lower Portland Head. Nor is there any
indication in the Census that three young men, listed as publican, farmer and
constable, had served colonial sentences. These were Timothy Lacey,
William Baldwin and John Brown. The parents of these youths wrote to the
Colonial Secretary, both jointly and separately, unsuccessfully requesting
mitigation of their sentences. The parents, former convicts themselves, were
concerned for the welfare of their sons, who had been 'brought up in habits of
honesty, industry and sobriety' and would suffer harmful consequences by
continual association with convicts under sentence of the law. The mother of
William Dargon wrote:

> ... the convicts, with their slothful and hardened habits may probably be
> the future misfortune of my son ... a very young man convicted at the
> Quarter Sessions at Windsor in November 1824, for three years
> transportation. After a considerable time in Sydney Gaol, he was removed
> to Van Diemen's Land ... [She] gratefully acknowledges the humanity
> extended in transporting him to Van Diemen's Land in lieu of a more
> severe penalty ... he has sent letters of sincere contrition ... already
> endured a severe punishment that he has hitherto laboured under a great
> agony of mind.

One native-born who doubtless 'laboured under a great agony of mind'
was Morgan Poor, sentenced to Norfolk Island for perjury and leaving behind a seventeen-year-old wife and an infant son. The native-born, however,
as a group did justify the contemporary assumption that they were both
honest and law-abiding. It cannot be accepted that this was the result of a
natural revulsion against the criminality of their parents.

From this detailed investigation into the individual male native-born who
followed 'the art or trade of the worker' it becomes increasingly apparent that
contemporaries were, once again, mistaken in their assumptions as to the
occupational preferences and opportunities for the native-born in the society
of New South Wales. They were mistaken as to the influence of the parents,
and the nature and consequences of that influence. They were mistaken in
the belief that the native-born viewed the ownership of land as the primary
aim for 'all the young men of the colony'. They were mistaken in assuming
that the repugnance at working with, and for, convicts and ex-convicts
influenced the native-born against becoming labourers and servants. Above

all, they were mistaken in assessing how many of these Currency Lads were 'forced to become . . . humble assistants of our large Graziers'.

That so few native-born did follow the occupations which could be classed as semi-skilled or unskilled clearly reflected the influence of the father's occupation and material standing. It did not reflect the civil condition of either parent. It was most noticeable that most of the unskilled workers appeared to have been without parental guidance or influence. Many fathers had died when the child was young. In a number of other instances there was no record remaining as to parentage. This was confined to this occupational group, with the exception of one section of the seafarers.

That so few native-born became 'professional' workers was in agreement with their parentage, background, educational opportunities and parental influence. Those who did were, in most cases, the sons of the wealthier settlers, both ex-convict and free. This strengthened the influence of the native-born at both levels of colonial society and highlighted the distortion implicit in the description 'children of the convicts'.

The variety in the experiences of the native-born within the various colonial occupational groups meant that their influence extended throughout the work-force in New South Wales. In the same way as the apprentice lads influenced the nature of colonial apprenticeships and were, in turn, directly affected by the unique nature and conditions of the colonial work-force, so did the workers influence the nature of labour and the rewards expected from labour in the colony. This occurred at all levels of the economic hierarchy, from the self-employed, the professionals, soldiers, constables, publicans, dealers, shopkeepers to the unskilled labourers and servants and bush workers. Contemporaries based their assumptions and opinions on British standards, on British opportunities. They failed to appreciate the gulf which existed in the upbringing, experiences and ambitions of the native-born and their counterparts in England and Ireland.

EPILOGUE

TO BE A PILGRIM

Now, Reader, I have told my Dream to thee;
See if thou canst interpret it to me . . .
    Take heed, also, that thou be not extreme,
In playing with the outside of my dream;
Nor let my figure or similitude
Put thee into a laughter or a feud . . .
Do thou the substance of my matter see.
    Put by the curtains, look within my veil,
Turn up my metaphors, and do not fail,
There if thou seekest them, such things to find,
As will be helpful to an honest mind.
    What of my dross thou findest there, be bold
To throw away, but yet preserve the gold;
What if my gold be wrapped up in ore?
None throws away the apple for the core.
But if thou shalt cast all away as vain,
I know not but 'twill make me dream again.

John Bunyan, *The Pilgrim's Progress*

Notes: Appendixes cited in the References appear in a separate volume of documentary evidence, published in 1985.

REFERENCES

INTRODUCTION

1. The *Australian*, 17 January 1827.
2. The word 'race' was used by William Charles Wentworth in the Address of Welcome to Governor Darling ... to describe the native-born Australians.
3. The *Australian*, 3 January 1827.
4. Ibid. There is no proof of the identity of this discerning British 'tar'.

CHAPTER ONE

1. This estimate is based on the children landed at Camp Cove who were included in the 1788 Victualling List, T1/688, M.L. See alphabetical listing by Portia Robinson, *Sydney Morning Herald*, 15, 16, 17 December 1980. See also Appendix 1.
2. See Appendix 1 for percentage of children in the total population of New South Wales, 1788–1813. Note that twelve years of age and under was the contemporary definition of 'children'. See T.A. Coghlan, *General Report on the Eleventh Census of New South Wales*, Sydney, 1894, p. 47.
3. William Pascoe Crook, Letter to a Friend in England, dated 31 December 1804, Parramatta, Missionary Society Papers, Samuel Marsden Private Letters, pp. 537–8, M.L. See also letter from Rev. Richard Johnson to Rev. William Morris, D.D., Secretary to the Society for the Propagation of the Gospel, New South Wales, 21 September 1799, S.P.G. Archives, reprinted in full in *Some Letters of the Rev. Richard Johnson, B.A.*, George Mackaness (ed.), *Australian Historical Monographs*, Dubbo, 1954.
4. See, for example, General Statement of Inhabitants ..., 30 June 1802, *H.R.N.S.W.*, 5, p. 166. Government and General Order, 21 October 1809, ibid., 7, pp. 220 ff. See also 1806 Muster, A4404, M.L.; Muster of the Female Convicts, 1806, M.L. Ms. 18.
5. Dundas to Grose, 15 November 1793, *H.R.N.S.W.*, 2, p. 80.
6. King to Hobart, enclosure 14, 9 May 1803, *H.R.A.*, 1, IV, p. 109.
7. William Balmain, Surgeon, Returns of the Sick, etc., Note, *H.R.N.S.W.*, 4, p. 326.
8. There are no official records available for the use of the Parramatta Female Factory as a lying-in hospital before the Reports of the Board of Management of the Female Factory and Hospital on 12 April 1826, 4/1791, pp. 255–65, A.O.N.S.W. There were weekly medical reports from April to October 1826, 4/1971, p. 6. For conditions in lying-in hospitals in England, see F.B. Smith, *The People's Health, 1830–1910*, Canberra, 1979, ch. V, 'Childbirth', pp. 131ff. For the uses of the Parramatta Factory as a lying-in hospital, see Annette Salt, *These Outcast Women*, vol. 2, *Macquarie Colonial Papers*, Portia Robinson (gen. ed.), Sydney, 1984.
9. David Collins, *An Account of the English Colony in New South Wales*, vol. 1, B.H. Fletcher (ed.), Sydney, 1975, p. 223. Note that references to individuals mentioned in this chapter may be found in Index B.
10. Transcripts of these Registers may be found in M.L.: St. Phillip's, Sydney,

A4372; St. John's, Parramatta, A4381; St. Matthew's, Windsor, A4385; St. Luke's, Liverpool, B1633. See also Registers of Baptism in St. Phillip's Register, 1780–1809, T.D. Mutch's Emended Text, A4370.

11. This estimate is based on *Index to Baptisms in New South Wales, 1787–1800*, H.J. Rumsey (transcr.), M.L.; see Appendix 1. See also K. Macnab's estimate, 'The Currency Lads', B.A. Hons thesis, University of New England, Appendix 11, 'Population: Sex Composition, 1788–1851'.

12. For British background, see C.M.H. Clark, *A History of Australia*, vol. 1, Melbourne, 1961, esp. ch. 4. See also L.L. Robson, *The Convict Settlers of Australia*, Hong Kong, 1970, ch. 4; David Phillips, *Crime and Authority in Victorian England*, London, 1977. Introduction.

13. P.F. Moran, *History of the Catholic Church in Australasia*, Sydney, n.d., p. 37. For conditional pardon of Father Dixson, see King to Hobart, 9 May 1803, *H.R.A.*, 1, IV, pp. 82–3.

14. See J. Waldersee, *Catholic Society and New South Wales 1788–1860*, Sydney, 1974, pp. 7–8.

15. King to Hobart, 14 August 1804, *H.R.A.*, 1, IV, p. 99.

16 Some *Private Correspondence of the Rev. Samuel Marsden and His Family 1794–1824*, George Mackaness (ed.), *Australian Historical Monographs*, vol. XII, pp. 30–31.

17. Index to Baptisms, transcribed by Rumsey, M.L. Ms. Note that references to individual baptisms and parentage may be found in Appendix 1.

18. The *Sydney Gazette*, 22, 29 December 1810.

19. The *Sydney Gazette*, 11 February 1810.

20. See 'Letter from Thomas Milburn to his Father and Mother, Setting Forth Sufferings on the *Neptune*, Botany Bay, 26 August 1790', M.L. Ms.

21. These records are held by M.L., A.O.N.S.W., N.L.A.; Additional biographical data: Bio. Index, A.D.B.

22. For references to Memorials in this chapter, see Index A.

23. For native-born women married to convicts and for parentage of these women, see Appendix 6. For references to marriages in this chapter, see Appendix 1; for references for individuals, see Index B.

24. See Appendix 1. Parentage of colonial children, 'Convict' and free settler parents; ibid. for examples.

25. This family sailed from England in July 1792. Dundas to Phillip, 14 July 1792, *H.R.A.*, 1, I, p. 365. The children were: Thomas Rose, aged 13, Mary Rose, 11, Joshua Rose, 9, Richard Rose, 3. For Thomas Rose senior, see Appendix 2; for Richard Rose and his wife, see Appendix 7.

26. For example, on 9 November 1800, two 'free' children' sailed on the *Porpoise*; on 20 November 1800 five 'free children' were passengers on the *Royal Admiral*. King to Portland, enclosure 1, 10 March 1801, *H.R.A.*, 1, II, pp.3, 18.

27. See *Guide to Records Relating to Ships and Free Passengers*, A.O.N.S.W. Only a few lists of passengers on ships arriving in New South Wales prior to 1826 have survived. See Miscellaneous Early Lists, 1792–1826, esp. *Royal Admiral*, 7 October 1792, P.R.O., Reel 3554 TI/704; *Bellona*, 16 January 1793, ibid., TI/706; TI/707; TI/704.

28. See R.B. Madgwick, *Immigration into Eastern Australia 1788–1851*, Sydney, 1937, esp. p. 19.

29. See Appendix 1, Colonial children of free settlers. See also Came-free males and females, 1828, ibid.

30. See Phillip to Grenville, 17 June 1790, *H.R.A.*, 1, I, pp. 180–1. Hunter to Portland, 28 April 1796, ibid., p. 559. Hunter to King, 30 April 1796, ibid., p. 565. Hunter to Portland, ibid., p. 592. Hobart to King, 17 February 1803,

57. *Report of the Select Committee on Transportation*, House of Commons Papers, 1812, vol. II, Paper no. 341.

CHAPTER TWO

1. Macquarie to Bathurst, 22 February 1810, *H.R.A.*, 1, X, pp. 17–18. See also Hunter to Portland, 1 November 1798, *H.R.A.*, 1, II.
2. Evidence of J.H. Bent to the House of Commons Select Committee on Gaols, *P.P.*, 1819, VII, 575, p. 125.
3. Letter of Samuel Parr to Joseph Gerrald, May 1795, M.L. Doc. 1890. Gerrald died of consumption five months after his arrival in New South Wales.
4. Richard Johnson to the Society for the Propagation of the Gospel in the South Seas, 1 December 1796, *H.R.N.S.W.*, 3, I, p. 184.
5. *The Memoirs of James Hardy Vaux*, N. McLachlan (ed.), Auckland, 1964, p. 200. For biographical details, see also A. Fink, 'James Hardy Vaux, Convict and Fatalist', *J.R.A.H.S.*, vol. 48, part 5, p. 1962.
6. J.T. Bigge, *Report of Commissioner of Inquiry on the State of Agriculture and Trade in New South Wales*, House of Commons, 13 March 1823, facsimile edn., 1966, pp. 81–2.
7. Peter Cunningham, *Two Years in New South Wales*, reprinted Adelaide, 1966, p. 17. Review by Sir Sydney Smith in the *Edinburgh Review*, vol. 47, no. 93, January 1828.
8. William Charles Wentworth, 'Address of Welcome to Governor Darling', Darling to Bathurst, enclosure 1, 1 February 1826, *H.R.A.*, 1, XII, p. 145.
9. P.G. King to Lieutenant Kent, 23 May 1800, *H.R.N.S.W.*, 4, p. 87. P.G. King to J. King, 3 May 1800, *H.R.A.*, 1, II, p. 505: 'the children ... abandoned ... to every vice of their parents'. Lieutenant King to the Commissioners of the Treasury, 7 July 1800, *H.R.N.S.W.*, 4, p. 113. Also King to Portland, 21 August 1800, *H.R.A.*, 1, III, P. 123: the necessity 'to seclude the male youth ... this forlorn class ... from the bad examples they hourly witness ...'.
10. King to Rev. Richard Johnson, 7 August 1800, *H.R.N.S.W.*, 4, p. 135.
11. King to Portland, 9 September 1800, *H.R.N.S.W.*, 4, p. 133; King to Portland, 21 August 1801, *H.R.N.S.W.*, 4, p. 464: rescued from 'scenes of iniquity and prostitution'.
12. Rev. R. Hassall to Rev. G. Burder, 8 August 1801, *H.R.N.S.W.*, 4, p. 447.
13. K. Macnab & R. Ward, 'The Nature and Nurture of the First Generation of Native-Born Australians', *H.S.*, vol. 10, no. 39, Nov. 1962, pp. 298–308. Ward and Macnab discuss this contemporary view in detail, pp. 304–308. See also Bigge, *Report of Commissioner of Inquiry on the State of Agriculture and Trade in New South Wales*, Facsimile edn., 1966, pp. 81–82; Cunningham, *Two Years in New South Wales ...*, p. 47.
14. *Hansard*, 3rd. series, vol. XIII, 28 June 1832, cited by F.G. Clarke, *The Land of Contrarieties* Melbourne, 1977, p. 43.
15. William Charles Wentworth, *A Statistical, Historical and Political Description of New South Wales*, London, 1819, facsimile edn., Adelaide, 1978, pp. 348–9.
16. Marsden to Wilberforce, 1799, B.T., Missionary, Box 49, pp. 74–5. Lieutenant-Governor King to Lieutenant Kent, 23 May 1800, *H.R.N.S.W.*, 4, p. 87. Lieutenant-Governor King, ibid., 25 May 1800, p. 88.
17. See W. Burton, 'State of Society and Crime in New South Wales during Six Years' residence in that Colony', *The Colonial Magazine and Commercial-Maritime Journal*, R.M. Martin (ed.), vol. 1, 1840, p. 437.
18. For details of sources for these opinions, see Bibliography: Contemporary Sources.
19. Ibid.

20. A contrary interpretation of Mrs King's attitudes towards convict women may be found in Helen Heney, *Australia's Founding Mothers*, Melbourne, 1978, p. 152: 'Mrs King, with her limited sympathies saw no pathos in "a prisoner's lot"'. Mrs King's own journal of her voyage to New South Wales on the *Speedy* is evidence of her appreciation of the difficulties of the convict women and their children.

21. See Letters of Elizabeth Macarthur, *The Macarthurs of Camden*, Onslow (ed.), pp. 20–55.

22. For details, see Bibliography.

23. *The Spanish at Port Jackson, the visits of the Corvettes Descubierta and Atrevida, 1793*, facsimile edn, Sydney, 1967, p. 31.

24. John Turnball, *Voyage Around the World in the Years 1800, 1801, 1802, 1803, and 1804*, 3 vols., London, 1805, vol. 3, p. 182.

25. Bigge Appendix, Evidence of John Macarthur to Commissioner Bigge, n.d.

26. Ibid., evidence of Gregory Blaxland to Commissioner Bigge, 22 August 1820.

27. Ibid., evidence of John Oxley to Commissioner Bigge, n.d.

28. For crimes punishable by Deprivation of Life and Crimes Denominated Single Felonies, see P. Colquhoun, *A Treatise on Police of the Metropolis*, London, 1795, pp. 435–6.

29. Phillip to Sydney, 9 July 1788, *H.R.A.*, 1, I. pp. 46–7.

30. Watkin Tench. *Sydney's First Four Years*, L.F. Fitzhardinge (ed.), Sydney, 1961, p. 134.

31. Hassall to Marsden, 30 January 1807, Private Letters of Rev. S. Marsden, B.T. 49, p. 262, M.L.

32. Bligh to Windham, 31 October 1807, *H.R.A*, 1, VI, p. 148.

33. William Pitt, 1791, Parliamentary History, cols. 1223–4, in C.M.H. Clark, *Select Documents in Australian History, 1788–1850*, Sydney, 1975, pp. 69–70.

34. Report of the Select Committee on Transportation, House of Commons Papers, 1812, vol. II, Paper 341.

35. Anne Summers, *Damned Whores and God's Police*, Victoria, 1975; Miriam Dixson, *The Real Matilda*, Victoria, 1976.

36. Major Johnston to Governor King, 18 February 1803, *H.R.N.S.W.*, Vol. 5, pp. 27–8.

37. Bathurst to Sidmouth, 23 April 1817, Note 5, *H.R.A.*, 1, X, pp. 807–8. Bigge, *Report on State of New South Wales . . .*, p. 140; Cunningham, *Two Years in New South Wales . . .*, p. 179.

38. 'The Humble Petition of the Emancipated Colonists of the Territory of New South Wales and Its Dependencies', Macquarie to Bathurst, Enclosure, 22 November 1821, *H.R.A.*, 1, X, pp. 549–56. Note the description 'Emancipated Colonists', not convicts.

39. Bigge Appendix, Evidence of Lieutenant Archibald Bell, 27 November 1819.

40. See Appendix 2, for convict population, 1788–1805; Appendix 2 for native-born children resident with parents, 1828; Appendix 4, for parentage of native-born children, 1806. See also Portia Robinson, 'Women and the Law', *In Pursuit of Justice*, Sydney, 1979, J. Mackinolty and H. Radi (eds), pp. 5ff. See also Government and General Order, 29 August 1797, *H.R.N.S.W.*, 3, p. 193. For native-born whose fathers were serving in the New South Wales Corps, see Appendix 2, also (for daughters). See also Returns of the New South Wales Corps, 1 September 1808, W.O. 10/37.

41. Wentworth, *A Statistical, Historical and Political Description . . .*, p. 350.

42. See Appendix 1, Parentage of Colonial Children: Convict and Came-Free Children; Children of the Civil–Military Departments.

43. See E. Campbell, 'Prerogative Rule in New South Wales 1788–1823', *J.R.A.H.S.*, vol. 50, part 3, 1964.

44. Ralph Clark, Journal, 1787–92, M.L. Ms., entry for 7 February 1788. Text of Phillip's Commissions, *H.R.N.S.W.*, 1, part 2, p. 24.

45. For composition of Sydney Cove in 1788, see the 1788 Victualling List . . . , T/1. 668, A.O.N.S.W.

46. House of Commons Select Committee on Police . . . , *B.P.P.* 1818, v, p. 216.

47. Sydney Smith, the *Edinburgh Review*, vol. 32, no. 36, July 1819, pp. 18–40.

48. Governor King to Under-Secretary King, 8 November 1801, *H.R.A.*, 1, III, pp. 321–2.

49. Evidence of James Macarthur to House of Commons Select Committee on Transportation, 1837/8, *B.P.P.*, vol. xix, p. 175., questions 2653–4.

50. Ibid., question 2649.

51. Bigge Appendix, 'Memorandum Relative to Mr Macarthur's Merino Sheep', John Macarthur to Commissioner Bigge, 4 February 1820. Note that William Charles Wentworth described James Macarthur as 'a complete chip off the old block': Wentworth letter to his father D'Arcy, 13 April 1819, Wentworth Letters, p. 142. M.L.

52. See Appendix 2, Occupations of the male native-born; Appendix 8; Native-born tradesmen; Appendix 5; Native-born apprentices.

53. Hamilton Hume to Bathurst, 20 April 1825, enclosure, Hay to Darling, 22 October 1826, *H.R.A.*, 1, XII, p. 655–6. See C.M.H. Clark, *A History of Australia* . . . , vol. 2, pp. 251–2, 352–5.

54. For references for individuals mentioned in the text of this chapter, see Index B.

55. Hunter to Portland, for example, 20 June 1797, *H.R.A.*, 1, II, p. 24: 'the military have many children . . .'.

56. See Appendix 10.

57. Journal of Elizabeth Macarthur, 8 December 1789: 'my servant was attacked by a fever that raged among the women convicts . . .'. Elizabeth Macarthur, letter, 18 March 1791, *The Macarthurs of Camden* . . . , Onslow (ed.), pp. 8, 41.

58. For comment on number of convicts from places other than England and Ireland, see Robson, *The Convict Settlers* . . . , Table 4 (j), p. 184, and Table 4 (n), p. 186.

59. See, for example, analysis of size of land holdings of parents of the native-born, 1806, in Appendix 4.

60. 'Address of Welcome to Governor Darling', Darling to Bathurst, enclosure 1, 1 February 1826, *H.R.A.*, 1, XII, p. 146.

61. Cunningham, *Two Years in New South Wales* . . . , vol. 2 Letter XXX. p. 143. For comment on Cunningham's opinions, see review in the *Edinburgh Review*, vol. 47, no. 93, January 1828, pp. 92ff.

62. H.G. Bennet, *A Letter to Earl Bathurst, Secretary of State for the Colonial Department, on the Condition of the Colonies of New South Wales and Van Diemen's Land, as set forth in the evidence taken before the Prison Committee in 1819*, London, 1819. Note also Letter to Viscount Sidmouth, 1819. For review, see the *Edinburgh Review*, vol. 38, no. 75, February 1823, pp. 85ff.

63. Hunter to Portland, 15 May 1798, *H.R.A.* 1, II; p. 153. Hunter to Portland, 1 May 1799, ibid., p. 352. Hunter to Under-Secretary King, 4 June 1798, ibid., pp. 154–5. King to Portland, 21 August 1801, ibid., 1, III, p. 122. Hobart to King, 29 August 1802, ibid., p. 564. Major Johnston to Governor King, 18 February 1803, *H.R.N.S.W.*, 5, pp. 27–8.

64. Macquarie to Bathurst, 28 June 1813, 1, VII, pp. 775–6. Note Bathurst's

cautious approval of Macquarie's plans. Bathurst to Macquarie, 3 February 1814, *H.R.A.*, 1, VIII, pp. 134–5.

65.   In 1806 there were eight schools advertised in the *Sydney Gazette*: Jeremiah Cavanaugh, 4 January; Thomas Faber, 12 April; 'a lady', 1 June; Mrs Perfect, 1 July; Mrs Williams, 10 August; Mrs Marchant, 16 August; G. Howe, 9 November; John Mitchell, 28 December. Four of these schools were described as 'suitable for young ladies'. See also Marsden to Wilberforce, Parramatta, 27 July 1810, Marsden, Some Private Correspondence, M.L.

66.   References for Memorials mentioned in this chapter may be found in Index A.

67.   For agricultural workers, see Appendix 10.

68.   Bigge Appendix, evidence of Thomas Bowden to Bigge, 21 January 1821.

69.   Ibid., evidence of Reverend William Cowper to Bigge, 23 January 1821.

70.   Ibid., evidence of Thomas Bowden to Bigge, 22 January 1821.

71.   King to Portland, 21 August 1801, *H.R.N.S.W.*, 4, p. 164.

72.   Muster for New South Wales, 1806, H.O., Criminal, Convicts, New South Wales and Tasmania. Piece numbers 36/37. See also Appendix 2 for native-born included in this Muster.

73.   See Appendix 2 for backgrounds, physical descriptions, etc., of some of the fathers of the native-born who were marines or soldiers; Appendix 2 for children of men serving in the New South Wales Corps.

74.   For estimates of the ages of male and female convicts, see Robson, *The Convict Settlers* . . . , Table 4 (g) Male Samples: Age Groups, p. 182; Table 4 (p) Female Samples: Age Groups, p. 187. For juvenile convicts, see ibid., pp. 14–17. An indication of the extent of juvenile crime in England may be found in the evidence given to the House of Commons Select Committee on the Police of the Metropolis 1817. *B.P.P.*, 1817, vii, esp. pp. 153ff.

75.   See King, Present State of His Majesty's Settlement . . . , 12 August 1806, *H.R.N.S.W.*, 6, p. 151. (Note that the contemporary spellings of Dock and Lumber Yard varied).

76.   The *Sydney Gazette*, 3 May 1804, 3 June 1804, described the children 'idle and at play'.

CHAPTER THREE

1.   Hunter to Portland, 1 May 1799, *H.R.A.*, 1, V, p. 360. See also *The Voyage of Captain Bellinghausen to the Antarctic Seas 1819–1820*, F. Debenham, ed., London, 1945, vol. 2, pp. 329ff.: '. . . the children being since childhood witness of their parents' way of living, they seem to absorb vice, so to speak, with their mothers' milk'.

2.   King to Portland, 1 March 1802, *H.R.A.*, 1, III, p. 434. See also the Bishop of Gloucester's sermon, 15 February 1805, S.P.G. Papers, B.T. 49, p. 243.

3.   'Phillip's Views on the Conduct of the Expedition and the Treatment of the Convicts', *H.R.N.S.W.*, 1, part 2, p. 51.

4.   Hunter to Portland, 3 July 1799, *H.R.A.*, 1, IV, p. 586. See also King, 'Present State of His Majesty's Settlement, 12 August 1806, *H.R.N.S.W.*, 6, pp. 150ff.: 'Those who behave well bear but a small proportion to the many who from infancy were thoroughly depraved and abandoned'.

5.   Suttor to Bligh, 10 February 1809, Bligh Papers, *H.R.N.S.W.*, 7, p. 23.

6.   Plummer to Macquarie, 4 May 1809, *H.R.N.S.W.*, 7, p. 120.

7.   Miriam Dixson, *The Real Matilda* . . . ; Anne Summers, *Damned Whores and God's Police*. . . .

8.   Ralph Clark, Journal, M.L. Ms., on first sighting the *Lady Juliana* in June 1790, first recorded use of this description of the female convicts.

9.   Dixson, *The Real Matilda* . . . , pp. 122–3.

10.   Summers, *Damned Whores and God's Police* . . . , p. 267.

11.   Dixson, *The Real Matilda* . . . , pp. 115ff.

12.   For statutory punishment of crimes, see Colquhoun, *A Treatise on the Police* . . . , pp. 436–45.

13.   See Portia Robinson, 'The First Forty Years'; Portia Robinson, 'Convict Records: to figure the nature of a times deceas'd', in *Papers Given to the Australian Society of Archivists Conference*, Melbourne, 1981; Portia Robinson, 'The Unhappy Objects', paper given to ANZAAS Congress, Adelaide, May 1980; Portia Robinson, 'The Real Story of Sydney's Convict Women', *Sydney Morning Herald*, 3 January 1981; 'Colleen to Matilda, ibid., 17 March 1984.

14.   See, for example, the *Sydney Gazette*, 26 March 1809: 'Mrs S. Perfect will open an Academy . . .'. Ibid., 2 April 1809: 'Mrs Hodges will instruct young ladies . . .'.

15.   Margarot to Under-Secretary King, 1 October 1810, *H.R.N.S.W.*, 4, p. 216.

16.   Levi & Bergman, *Australian Genesis* . . . , pp. 19ff.

17.   For references to individuals mentioned in this chapter, see Index B.

18.   For numbers of felons arriving in New South Wales from England and Ireland for the whole period of transportation to the Australian colonies, see A.G.L. Shaw, *Convicts and the Colonies*, London, 1966 Appendix, pp. 363ff. For arrivals, male and female, 1788–1813, see Appendix 3.

19.   The 1788 Victualling List . . . , T/1 668, M.L. Note that there was one other free woman, Deborah Brookes, who appears to have been the wife of a midshipman who did not return to England when the naval escort left the fleet. She was the first 'illegal immigrant'.

20.   Madgwick, *Immigration* . . . , p. 19.

21.   For references to Memorials and Petitions mentioned in this chapter, see Index A.

22.   1806 Muster . . . See also Appendix 2.

23.   1814 Muster . . . See also Appendix 6.

24.   Letter from Mrs Macarthur to her mother, *The Macarthurs of Camden* . . . , p. 61.

25.   For brief accounts of the life-styles of some of these women, as described by themselves, see Appendix 3.

26.   Samuel Marsden to the Archbishop of Canterbury, Parramatta, 2 May 1810, Samuel Marsden, Some Private Letters, B.T., 49, p. 293, M.L.

27.   See Robson, *The Convict Settlers* . . . See also Appendix 3 for British occupations of the 1788 convict women; for skills, see Memorials, Appendix 3. For detailed account of the skills of colonial women in New South Wales, see Monica Perrott, *A Tolerable Good Success*, vol. 1, *Macquarie Colonial Papers*, Portia Robinson (gen.ed.), Sydney, 1983.

28.   Colquhoun, for example, estimated that there were 50,000 'women of the town' in London in 1803. Cited by A. Parreaux, *Daily Life in England in the Reign of George III*, Carola Congreve trans., London, 1969, p. 134.

29.   See, for example, John Howard, *The State of the Prisons, 1777*, London, 1919, pp. 215–17: an account of the 'licentious intercourse of the sexes . . . shocking to decency and humanity . . .' in the County Gaol of Gloucestershire, England. Note that Howard added the comment: 'many children have been born in this gaol'.

30.   Present State of His Majesty's Settlement . . . , 12 August 1806, *H.R.N.S.W.*, 6, pp. 150–1. Note the similarity of opinion expressed by Colquhoun in 1795

regarding the corruption of morals which followed the criminal and immoral example of parents. Colquhuon, *A Treatise on the Police* ... , p. 355.

31. 'Observations on the Female Convicts ...', attributed to Samuel Marsden, M.L. Ms.

32. See, for example, Macquarie's Proclamation, 24 January 1810, regarding the 'scandalous and pernicious custom ... of shamelessly co-habiting ...', *H.R.N.S.W.*, 7, pp. 292–4.

33. Marsden's Female Register ... , M.L. Ms. For summary, see Appendix 3.

34. 'Present State of His Majesty's Settlement ... , 12 August 1806, *H.R.N.S.W.*, 6, pp. 150ff. Note that these observations were based on the 1806 Muster, indexed in H.O., 10/7, Reel 72, piece 36, as the 1837 Muster of New South Wales.

35. Marsden's Female Register ...

36. See, for example, T.W. Plummer to Colonel Macquarie, 4 May 1809, *H.R.N.S.W.*, 7, p. 145. Wilberforce to Castlereagh, 9 November 1805, ibid., 5, pp. 727–8. For an occasion where Macquarie took a lenient view, see Petitions for Maintenance in Bastardy, p. 436, A.O.N.S.W.

37. Marsden Papers, courtesy of Dr Alan Frost, La Trobe University, Victoria.

38. Appendix 2 lists native-born (male and female) resident with parent/parents, New South Wales 1828.

39. Marsden, Female Register ... See also Levi & Bergman, *Australian Genesis* ... , pp. 44, 46–70.

40. Robson, *The Convict Settlers* ... , Appendix 7, Tables 7 (a–e), pp. 200–1.

41. Ibid., Appendix 6, Table 6 (g), p. 199; Appendix 7, Table 7 (e), p. 101.

42. Evidence of Commissary Palmer to the Select Committee on Transportation ... , 1812, House of Commons Papers, vol. ii, Paper no. 341. Note also that convict woman Margaret Catchpole wrote from New South Wales to her uncle describing 'the fine young man' who was courting her, adding, 'I am not for marrying'. Margaret Catchpole, Letters, M.L. Ms.

43. 'The State of His Majesty's Settlement ...', August 1806, *H.R.N.S.W.*, 6, pp. 135ff. Note that, although King did comment on those female convicts 'who behaved well', he added that they 'bear but a small proportion to the many who, from infancy, were thoroughly depraved and abandoned'. At the same time he stated that 1216 women 'supported themselves ... providing for their families ... 196 were maintained by the Crown ... 72 (of these) are mostly incorrigible ...', ibid., pp. 150–51.

44. Marsden, Observations on the Female Convicts ... , M.L. Ms. Note that Marsden told Bigge that if the women at the Factory 'were married & had an opportunity of quitting the Paths of Vice, they would be useful & decent', Marsden, evidence to Bigge, 1820, n.d.

45. Evidence of John Macarthur to Commissioner Bigge, n.d.

46. Bigge, *Report on the Colony* ... , p. 30. This Report was discussed by Sydney Smith in the *Edinburgh Review*, vol. 38, no. 15, pp. 96–7.

47. Robson, *The Convict Settlers* ... , p. 105.

48. See Court of Criminal Jurisdiction, Miscellaneous Criminal Papers, 5/1152; Return of Prisoners Tried, 1812–1813, 1815–24, 2/8237; Statistics of trials, 1819–24, capital charges, larceny, misdemeanours (specified) X726, pp. 33–42, A.O.N.S.W. See also Appendix 3, An Account of Fines, Penalties, etc.; ibid., Summary of Returns of Crimes, 1816–20.

49. Robson, *The Convict Settlers* ... , p. 9. Note that there is one major work on 'The Origins of the Women Convicts ...'; this is by Lloyd Robson, *H.S.*, vol. 11, November 1963.

50. Robson, *The Convict Settlers* ... , ch. 4, pp. 20–1, p. 74ff. See also Shaw, *Convicts*

and the Colonies ..., pp. 183ff. See also Manning Clark, *A History* ..., vol. 1, ch. 6, pp. 90ff.

51. Collins, *An Account* ..., Fletcher (ed.), vol. 1, pp. 380–1.
52. Observations on Drink ... Religion ... Female Convicts ..., attributed to Samuel Marsden, M.L. Ms.
53. For more detailed discussion of colonial women and crime, see Portia Robinson, 'The First Forty Years ...'
54. See Phillips, *Crime and Authority* ..., pp. 208–10 for similar cases.
55. Cited by Mr F. Buxton, M.P. , House of Commons Debates, 1, XXXIX, 816–9. 2 March 1819.
56. Phillips, *Crime and Authority* ... Investigating a later period, Phillips cites the Chief Constable of Wolverhampton: 'of thirty-eight such offences reported ... the offences were usually committed in brothels. Complainants were generally drunk—the following day decline to prosecute', pp. 208–10.
57. Robson, *The Convict Settlers* ..., pp. 76ff.
58. Shaw, *Convicts and the Colonies* ..., p. 363ff.
59. Colquhoun, *A Treatise on the Police* ..., p. 354. Note that a total of 404 persons were sentenced to death in 1811 but only 45 were actually hanged that year.
60. Phillips, *Crime and Authority* ..., pp. 208–10.
61. G.A.Wood, 'The Convicts', *J.R.A.H.S.*, vol. 8, part 4, 1922.
62. Henry Meister, cited in Parreaux, *Daily Life in England* ..., p. 123.
63. Letters of Elizabeth Macarthur, Piper Papers, M.L., vol. 4, p.109.
64. See Parreaux, *Daily Life in England* ..., pp. 129ff. For account of Fanny Temple, see ibid., p. 132.
65. Government and General Order, *Sydney Gazette*, 24 February 1810.
66. Select Committee on Criminal Commitments and Convictions, *P.P.* 1828, VI, p. 430, cited by Phillips, *Crime and Authority* ..., p. 42. Reference to Lord Eldon, ibid., p. 42.
67. Colquhoun, *A Treatise on the Police* ..., pp. 436ff.
68. Phillips, *Crime and Authority* ..., p. 237.
69. Robson, *The Convict Settlers* ..., p. 237.
70. Shaw, *Convicts and the Colonies* ..., pp. 363–65, 148ff.
71. *Nottingham Journal*, 1783–85, vol. XXXIX, no. 5031, 12 March 1784, cited in John Cobley, *Crimes of the First Fleet Convicts*, Sydney, 1970, p. 119.
72. Devon Record Office, Gaol Calendar, Epiphany Sessions, 1786, ibid., p. 36.
73. Select Committee on Criminal Commitments and Convictions, 1818, *P.P.*, 181, VI, pp. 430, 437.
74. *Debates*, 1, XX, 777/792, 2 March 1819, House of Commons.
75. *O.B.S.P.*, 1785–6, p. 680, trial no. 440, M.L. (Judith Jones/Ann Davis).
76. Colquhoun, *A Treatise on the Police* ..., p. 324: '... those individuals who are denominated as the Casual Poor ...'; also pp. 327–9.
77. See Manning Clark, *A History* ..., vol. 1, ch. 6, 'Convicts and the Faith of the Founders'; vol. 2, ch. 4, 'Darkness'.
78. See J.D.Marshall, *The Old Poor Law 1795–1834*, London, 1973, esp. 'Pauperism and Popular Pressure', pp. 38ff. See also ibid., pp. 26–32, 1, expenditure on poor relief in England and Wales, 1812–32, and adults on permanent relief out of the poor house.
79. *O.B.S.P.*, 1786–87, p. 183, trial no. 132, M.L. (Elizabeth Evans); ibid., 1783–4, p. 220, trial no. 192 (Elizabeth Beckford); ibid., 1784–5, p. 440, trial no. 353 (Mary Morton); ibid., 1784–5, p. 981, trial no. 748, (Elizabeth Dalton); P.R.O. Assizes 33/6, p. 207 (Elizabeth Powley), cited in Cobley, *Crimes* ..., p. 225; P.R.O. Assizes, 5/103, part 1, (Sarah Davies), cited in ibid., p. 70; *O.B.S.P.*,

1786–7, p. 131, trial no. 107 (Elizabeth Fitzgerald); ibid., 1786–7, p. 511, trial no. 379 (Jane Marriott).

80.   Court of Criminal Jurisdiction . . . , 17 November 1788; also Collins, *An Account* . . . , Fletcher (ed.), vol. 1, p. 205: warrant of emancipation for Thomas Restil.

81.   Court of Criminal Jurisdiction . . . , 31 January 1799, X905, pp. 67 & 88; 25 May 1800, X905, p. 469; 22 February 1805, 1149, p. 215, A.O.N.S.W.

82.   *O.B.S.P.*, 1784–5, p. 443, trial no. 359 (Elizabeth Lee); County Hall Bristol, Gaol Delivery Fiats, 1777–1820, Fiat 16 September 1786 (Ann Lynch), cited in Cobley, *Crimes* . . . , p. 173; Lancashire Record Office, Quarter Sessions Records, (Mary M'Cormack), cited in ibid., p. 173; P.R.O. Assizes, 24/26, Wiltshire Record Office, Quarter Sessions Papers (Mary Wickham), cited in ibid., p.288.

83.   Colquhoun, *A Treatise on the Police* . . . , pp. 436–38.

84.   Robson, *The Convict Settlers* . . . , p. 84.

85.   See, for example, 'Arrival and distribution of female convicts 1814–20', C.O. 210/118, microfilm 106. See also *Report of the Select Committee on Transportation*, House of Commons Papers, 1812, vol. ii, Paper no. 134.

86.   Based on an analysis of crimes in the colony: cases heard in the Court of Criminal Jurisdiction, 1788–1828, 4/1147A, 4/1147B, X905, 5/1149, 5/1150, 5/1119, 5/1120, 5/1121, 5/1143, 5/1144A, 5/1144B, T15; also Miscellaneous Criminal Papers, 5/1145, 5/1146. SZ776–81; T1–15. Return of 153 convicts who had been convicted in colonial courts after their sentences had expired, or after pardon, 12 March 1810–22 September 1823, 4/1638, A.O.N.S.W.

87,   *O.B.S.P.*, 1785–6, p. 194, trial no. 664, M.L. (Esther Abrams).

88.   Reported in the *Sydney Gazette*, 19 June 1804.

89.   *O.B.S.P.*, 1785, pp. 179, 232, 533. See also the *Sydney Gazette*, December 1805.

90.   The *Sydney Gazette*, 8 January 1805 (Elizabeth Leonard); ibid., 22 September 1805 (Bridget Horan); ibid., 29 September 1805 (Biddy Kean).

91.   King to Portland, 1 March 1802, *H.R.A.*, 1, III, p. 434.

92.   The *Sydney Gazette*, 17 March 1810, Notice by John Austin. See also Appendix 3, 'Absconding and Unfaithful Wives'.

93.   The *Sydney Gazette*, 29 September 1810 (Sarah Powell strangled herself); ibid., 22, 23 October 1809 (the house of Mary Ware, mother of native-born John Larkham, was destroyed by fire); ibid., 1 October 1809, (the house of William Bowman and his family was destroyed by fire).

94.   The *Sydney Gazette*, in 1810, for example, the following cases were among those reported: 'two year-old daughter of Matthew Timpson of Brickfields, 'fell into a fire . . . in the absence of her mother . . . died of burns' (31 March); 'eleven-year-old daughter of Katherine Baker was burnt so violently as to cause her death (12 May); at the Hawkesbury, Elvira Meurant, 6, 'died of burns . . . the result of her clothes taking fire'(18 August); J.Warby's daughter severely 'scalded . . . upsetting a large pot of boiling water left unguarded' (22 September); Thomas Allwright's daughter, an infant, 'stifled in a small pan of ley' (20 October); seven-year-old son of Samuel Thorley 'run over on the Racecourse, killed' (20 October); child attacked by dog, (20 October).

95.   The *Sydney Gazette*, 9 August 1807.

96.   See Appendix 3, 'Petitions for Maintenance in Bastardy, 1808–14', Bench of Magistrates, 5/1153, A.O.N.S.W.

CHAPTER FOUR

1.   Phillip to Sydney, 13 February 1790, *H.R.A.*, 1, I, p. 157. See also King's report,

'The State of His Majesty's Settlements in New South Wales', King to Portland, 31 December 1804, enclosure 1, *H.R.A.* 1, III, pp. 418–439.

2. Lachlan Macquarie, *Journals of His Tours in New South Wales and Van Diemen's Land*, Sydney, 1956. See also G. Mackaness (ed.), *Fourteen Journeys over the Blue Mountains, 1813–1841*, Sydney, 1965, ch. 1–10. For modern discussion of the hindrances to the spread of settlement, see B.H. Fletcher, *Landed Enterprise and Penal Society*, Sydney, 1976, ch. 8. For list of native-born settlers at Bathurst, see Appendix 4.

3. Macquarie's Diary, 2 February, 23 April 1818, M.L.

4. Discovery of Illawarra, Macquarie to Bathurst, 12 December 1817, *H.R.A.*, 1, IV, p. 713. Macquarie to Bathurst, 17 May 1818, ibid., 1, IX, p.795. Bigge, *Report on Agriculture and Trade* . . . , p. 6. Bigge, list of landholders in this district, B.T. 26, Vol. 123, p. 6005.

5. Macquarie to Bathurst, 28 April 1814, enclosure 10, 'General Statement of Inhabitants . . .', *H.R.A.*, 1, VIII, p. 187. Muster for Liverpool, Bunbary, Curran, Airds and Appin and Places Adjacent, 1814, M.L. See also Macquarie to Liverpool, 17 November 1812, 'List of Land and Town Grants and Leases, since the last Return, etc. . . .', *H.R.A.*, 1, VII, enclosure no. 2, pp. 653–4.

6. Muster for Liverpool . . . , 1814. References for persons and Memorials named in this chapter may be found in Indexes A and B.

7. Macquarie to Bathurst, 8 March 1819, *H.R.A.*, 1, V, p. 43. Macquarie to Bathurst, 30 November 1821, enclosure 3, ibid., 1, X, pp. 575–6. Bigge, *Report on the Colony* . . . , p. 164. For modern accounts, see W.A. Wood, *Dawn in the Valley*, Sydney, 1977; T.M. Perry, *Australia's First Frontier* London, 1965. ch. 5.

8. Bigge, B.T. Box 5427–8, General Order of 7 March 1818.

9. 'Return of Lands Cleared and other Improvements made by the Small Settlers . . . Hunter's River, 1823', M.L. See also Macquarie to Bathurst, 30 November 1821, enclosure 3, 'A General Statement of the Population . . .', *H.R.A.*, 1, X, p. 575. Macquarie to Bathurst, 28 April 1814, enclosure 10, 'General Statement of Inhabitants . . .', *H.R.A.*, I, VII, p. 187. For residence of native-born named in the 1814 Muster, see Appendix 6. For modern accounts, see Fletcher, *Landed Enterprise* . . . , pp. 158ff; S.H. Roberts, *History of Australian Land Settlement*, Melbourne, 1924. ch. 3.

10 Ibid., p. 15.

11. For discussion of the background to land grants in New South Wales, see B.H. Fletcher, 'The Development of Farming and Grazing in New South Wales, 1800–21', Ph.D. thesis, University of New South Wales, 1970, pp. 30ff. Note that in June 1797 Hunter found 150 settlers at the Hawkesbury who had not received land grants. Hunter to Portland, 10 June 1797, *H.R.A.*, 1, II, p. 17.

12. Instructions regarding the alienation of land were almost identical to Hunter, King, Bligh, Macquarie and, initially, Brisbane. These Instructions may be found in *H.R.A.*: Hunter, 1, I, pp. 520–7; King, 1. III, pp. 391–8; Bligh, 1, IV, pp. 8–15; Macquarie, 1, VII, pp. 190–7; Brisbane, 1, X, pp. 596–603. See secondary account in Perry, *Australia's First Frontier* . . . , p. 49.

13. Grenville to Phillip, 22 August 1789, *H.R.A.*, 1, I, pp. 124–29.

14. Instructions to Governor Hunter, *H.R.A.*, 1, I, p. 524.

15. See King, 'Report on the State of His Majesty's Settlements in New South Wales', 31 December 1803, *H.R.A.*, 1, I, pp. 418–439.

16. See Perry, *Australia's First Frontier* . . . , p. 23. See also H.A. McLeod Morgan, 'Notes on "An Account of a Journey towards Jugroy . . . 1805"', *J.R.A.H.S.*, vol. 25, part 6, 1939.

17. Macquarie to Bathurst, 12 December 1817, *H.R.A.*, 1, IX, p. 713.

18. Evidence of John Oxley to Bigge, November 1819. 'Surveyor-General Oxley to

Governor Macquarie', 1 November 1818, Macquarie to Bathurst, 1 March 1819, enclosure 2, *H.R.A.*, 1, X, pp. 26–31.

19. King to Hobart, 9 May 1803, *H.R.A.*, 1, IV, p. 74. King to Camden, 7 April 1806, ibid., 1, V, p. 74. Note that, although ease of access was initially linked with waterways, roads usually followed successful settlement: see Map 2. At the Hawkesbury, a road was constructed in 1794, Sydney being 'less than eight hours walk away': Grose to Dundas, 21 August 1794, ibid., 1, I, p. 483. See also Collins, *An Account* . . . , vol. 2, pp. 219ff.; Fletcher, thesis . . . , p. 131.

20. For a detailed account of the settlement and growth of the Hawkesbury district, see B.H. Fletcher, *Landed Enterprise and Penal Society* . . . See also Fletcher, thesis . . . ; Fletcher, 'Grose, Paterson and the Settlement of the Hawkesbury', *J.R.A.H.S.*, vol. 51, part 4, 1956.

21. For non-commissioned officers and men: Phillip's Instructions re land grants, *H.R.A.*, 1, I, p. 124. For ex-convicts: ibid., p. 14.

22. Fletcher, thesis . . . , p. 130: 'Regional Variations in Level and Progress, August 1799'. See also Hunter to Portland, 5 September 1799, enclosure 1, 'State of the Settlements . . .', *H.R.A.*, 1, II, pp. 385–6.

23. Grose to Dundas, 29 April 1794, *H.R.N.S.W.*, 2, p. 210, List of Settlers, 'A Plan of the First Farms on the Hawkesbury River', map by Surveyor-General Augustus Alt.

24. For map showing the location of these grants, see Campbell, 'Dawn of Rural Settlement . . .', p. 98.

25. Collins, *An Account* . . . , vol. 1, p. 225. For a secondary account see J.F. Campbell, 'Liberty Plains of the First Free Settlers, 1793', *J.R.A.H.S.*, vol. 22, part 5, 1936.

26. Collins, *An Account* . . . , vol. 1, p. 427. See also J.F. Campbell, 'Dawn of Rural Settlement . . .', p. 96.

27. 'List of settlers established at Mulgrave Place by Governor Hunter' may be found in ibid., pp. 107–8.

28. Hunter to Portland, 10 January 1798, *H.R.A.*, 1, II, p. 117.

29. 'Civil Condition of Landholders and Amounts Held in New South Wales from 22 February 1792–25 September 1800', 1802 Muster, B.T., Box 88, Series 1, Bigge Appendix.

30. Phillip to Sydney, 10 July 1788, *H.R.A.*, 1, I, pp. 54–6. Dundas to Phillip, 14 July 1792, *H.R.A.*, 1, I, p. 365.

31. See Fletcher, *Landed Enterprise* . . . , Appendix 4, p. 232, 'Area Granted by Various Governors 1788–1828'. See also Grose to Dundas, 16 February 1793, *H.R.A.*, 1, I, p. 416. For residential clause, see Dundas to Grose, 31 June 1793, enclosure 1, ibid., 1, I, p. 441.

32. Hunter to Portland, 12 November 1796, *H.R.A.*, 1, I, p. 667'. See also Note, ibid., p. 783.

33. Instructions to Governor Hunter, 23 June 1794, *H.R.A.*, 1, I, pp. 520ff.

34. Grenville to Phillip, 22 August 1799, enclosure, 'Phillip's Instructions re Land Grants', *H.R.A.* 1, I, pp. 124ff. Instructions to Governor Hunter, ibid., 1, I, pp. 523-4. Phillip to Grenville, 6 November 1791, 'Return of Lands Granted', *H.R.A.*, I, I, p. 279. Phillip to Nepean, 16 November 1792, enclosure 2, 'List of Marines who desired to be received as settlers . . .', *H.R.A.*, 1, I, p. 306.

35. See A.G.L. Shaw, 'Missing Land Grants in New South Wales', *H.S.*, vol. 5, no. 17, November 1951, no. 19, November 1982. See also Hunter to Portland, 10 June 1797, *H.R.A.*, 1, II, p. 19.

36. See Hunter to Portland, 6 February 1800, enclosure 1, 'An Account of Lands Granted . . .', *H.R.A.*, 1, II, pp. 456–464. See also Shaw, 'Missing Land Grants . . .'

37. Grenville to Phillip, 22 August 1789, enclosure, *H.R.A.*, 1, I, pp. 124–5.
38. See Bigge, B.T. 88, vol. 25, 'List of Free Settlers . . .' see also ibid., vol. 31, 'List of Grants, September 1800, to December 1803. See also 'An Account of Lands Granted or Leased, 1 August 1796 to 1 January 1800', Hunter to Portland, enclosure 1, *H.R.A.*, 1, II, pp. 454–65; Sullivan to King, 6 August 1802, and enclosure 1, ibid., 1, III, pp. 533–4.
39. *H.R.A.*, 1, III, pp. 533–4. See also Margot Badgery, 'Great-Grandfather's Farthing', *Descent*, vol. 6, part 4. Note that four of Badgery's sons became extensive landholders. For all references to the parents of the native-born landholders, see Appendix 7. For all references to the native-born landholders, See Appendix 7. For references to those native-born children whose parents held land in New South Wales prior to 1806, see analysis of the 1806 Muster in Appendix 2.
40. See M.J.E. Steven, 'Enterprise', *Economic Growth of Australia 1788–1821*, G.J.Abbott & N.B.Nairn (eds), Carlton, 1969, p. 126.
41. Suttor, *Journal* . . .
42. Macquarie to Bathurst, 7 October 1814, *H.R.A.*, 1, VIII, p. 126.
43. For detailed discussion of land alienation and the development of agriculture during this period, see B.H. Fletcher, 'Agriculture', *Economic Growth* . . . , Abbott & Nairn (eds), pp. 191–205.
44. 1806 Muster. The *Sydney Gazette*, 28 October 1806.
45. See Appendix 2 for analysis of the 1806 Muster.
46. For details of the total child population in 1806, see Appendix 1. It is estimated that 1444 of these children (approximately) had been born in the colony and 136 (approximately) had arrived with their parents. Note that 'children' are defined as listed as such in this Muster; 'family' is defined as parent/parents with resident children. Where there is no surviving record or confirmation of a marriage, the woman is listed as 'partner'. 'Rural children' denotes residency on a farm or property. For native-born children listed in their own right in the 1806 Muster, see Appendix 2.
47. See 1806 Muster, H.O. 10, Reel 72. Details of native-born sons resident with rural parents in 1806 and still resident in New South Wales in 1828 may be found in Appendix 7. For brief references, see Appendix 4.
48. This figure is erroneous. The total acreage was 1278.
49. For references to Memorials and Petitions listed in this Chapter, see Index A.
50. 'A Return of Land Granted to Individuals Born Within the Colony of New South Wales from the First January, 1810, to the First of January, 1827', Executive Council Minutes, 4115.6, Vol. 2, M.L.
51. The *Sydney Gazette*, 3 August 1806.
52. Government and General Order, 16 March 1806. The *Sydney Gazette*, 30 March 1806.
53. A. Harris, *Settlers and Convicts*, C.M.H. Clark (ed.), Melbourne, 1953, p. 67.
54. The *Sydney Gazette*, 17 February 1824.
55. James Tucker, *The Adventures of Ralph Rashleigh* . . . , p. 102.
56. Evidence of George Best to Bigge . . . , 4 September, 1820.
57. Phillip to Dundas, 19 March 1792, *H.R.A.*, 1, I, p. 339. For details of those parents of the native-born who had purchased their land, see Appendix 4.
58. Hunter to Portland, 20 August 1797, *H.R.A.*, 1, II, p. 23. King to Portland, 28 September 1806, *H.R.A.*, 1, II, p. 607.
59. See Fletcher, thesis . . . , pp. 59–60.
60. Grose to Dundas, 16 February 1793, *H.R.A.*, 1, I, p. 416.
61. Letters of Governor Hunter, 30 March 1797, p. 30, M.L. Note that Collins

reported grants forfeited by two settlers, May 1792, *An Account* . . . , vol. 1, p. 212.

62. See Dundas to Grose, 31 June 1793, *H.R.A.*, 1, I, p. 441.

63. For an attempt at cancellation, see King to John King, 21 August 1801, enclosure 1, Government and General Orders, 27 July 1801, *H.R.A.*, 1, III, p. 259. See also evidence of 'Settlers Memorial to Viscount Castlereagh', 17 February 1809, complaining of 'land jobbing by the officer . . . nearly whole districts were bought up by a few wealthy individuals', *H.R.N.S.W.*, 7, pp. 33–35.

64. Hunter to Portland, 2 June 1797 (for opinions on debt and bankruptcy), *H.R.A.*, 1, I, p. 23. See also 'Settlers Statement to Governor Hunter', 19 February 1798, Hunter to Portland, 2 March 1798, enclosure 1, ibid., 1, II, pp. 136–140.

65. J.D. Lang, *An Historical and Statistical Account of New South Wales*, London, 1840.

66. Grenville to Phillip, 22 August 1789, enclosure, *H.R.A.*, 1, I, pp. 124ff.

67. Phillip's Second Commission, *H.R.A.*, 1, I, p. 15.

68. Perry, *Australia's First Frontier* . . . , p. 24. Note that governors were prevented by their Instructions from giving large grants to emancipated or time-expired convicts.

69. For an indication of the size of individual holdings during this period see *An Accurate List* . . . , M.L.

70. These figures are based on an analysis of *An Accurate List* . . . ; they are approximate only.

71. Fletcher, thesis . . . , pp. 129, 205.

CHAPTER FIVE

1. The *Australian*, 19 January 1826.

2. E.S.Hall to Sir George Murray, January 1829, *H.R.A.*, 1, XIV, p. 578.

3. W.C.Wentworth, 'Address of Welcome to Governor Darling', Darling to Bathurst, enclosure 1, February 1826, *H.R.A.*, 1, XII, p. 145.

4. Edward Eagar to Bigge, 19 October 1819.

5. The *Australian*, 19 January 1826.

6. For the occupations of native-born males, 1828, see Appendix 7.

7. For occupations of came-free males, see ibid. For native-born apprentices, individual details, see Appendix 5. For came-free and convict apprentices, see ibid. For native-born tradesmen, see Appendix 8.

8. Col. Sec. In-Letters, 4/1756, p. 6, Male Orphan School, re apprenticeship.

9. In 1821 there were 60 boys in the Male Orphan School, of whom five became tailors and four shoemakers. Bigge Appendix, B.T., Box 25, p. 5521. Note the similarity of object with that of the Charity Schools of England: '. . . to preserve children from vagrancy and fit them for some sort of regular work', M.D. George, *London Life in the Eighteenth Century*, New York, 1961.

10. See, for example, W.O.15, reel 1302, piece no. 642, 1806–16, Description and Succession Books (Regimental), New South Wales Corps. For parentage of native-born apprentices, see Appendix 5. For parentage of non-landowning native-born, see Appendix 5.

11. For references to individual native-born apprentices mentioned in this chapter, see Appendix 5. For references to other individuals mentioned in this chapter, see Index B.

12. See *Report of the Commissioner of Inquiry into the Colony of New South Wales*, House of Commons, 3 vols., vol. 3, p. 71.

13. The *Sydney Gazette*, 22 September 1805.

14. The *Sydney Gazette*, 1 September 1805. Note that more extensive, but still limited, types of apprenticeship were available by 1811. As advertised in the *Sydney Gazette*: 2 April, '2 lads ... Mechanical Business'; 27 April, 'tanning and currying'; 17 August, 'Hatting Business'. In 1808 Rev. Hassall had written that he 'was at a great loss' to know what to do with the 'grown up boys' in his care 'there being no trades nor Masters fit to 'prentice boys to in his colony'. B.T. 49, Hassall Correspondence.

15. The *Sydney Gazette*, 18 August 1805.

16. Sir Josiah Child, 'A Discourse on Trade', cited by George, *London Life* ..., p. 212.

17. The *Sydney Gazette*, 1 November 1804. For native-born employed by Kable, see Appendix 5. For trades and tradesmen advertising in the *Sydney Gazette*, 1804–5, 1810, see ibid.

18. Note Governor Bligh's description, 'Lord, Kable and Underwood ... are of low character and came out as Convicts ...'. Bligh to Castlereagh, 30 June 1808, *H.R.A.*, 1, VI, p. 531.

19. The *Sydney Gazette*, 8 July and 26 August 1804. For the trades of the masters of the native-born apprentices, see Appendix 5. For the trades of masters of the came-free apprentices, see Appendix 5.

20. King to Hobart, 12 March 1804, enclosure 11, *H.R.A.*, 1, IV, p. 578.

21. The *Sydney Gazette*, 22 September 1805, 9 September 1809. Storer was unfortunate in the apprentice he selected, native-born Michael Nowland. Nowland ran away from his master in 1811 (the *Sydney Gazette*, 9 February 1811); in 1828 Nowland described himself as a blacksmith. Blaxcell: ibid., 25 June 1808; Campbell, ibid., 14 September 1806; Nichols: ibid., 1 September 1805; Kable and Underwood, ibid., 4 November 1804.

22. The *Sydney Gazette*, 10 April 1813.

23. The *Sydney Gazette*, Uther: 19 June 1813; Evening School: ibid. 25 September 1813.

24. George, *London Life* ..., Appendix V, p. 425, 'Disposal of Apprentices by the Parishes Within the Bills of Mortality'.

25. The most scholarly account of the children of the poor in contemporary London is by George, *London Life* ..., esp. ch. V, 'Parish Children and Poor Apprentices', and Appendix IV, 'Apprenticeship Cases from the Poor Sessions Record'. The most recent work is that of C.R. Dobson, *Masters and Journeymen, a Prehistory of Industrial Relations, 1717–1800*, London, 1980. For one view of the convict as labourer/worker in New South Wales, see Lelia Thomas, 'The Development of the Labour Movement in the Sydney District of N.S.W.', M.A.thesis, University of Sydney, 1919, ch. 1.

26. Buer, *Health, wealth and population* ..., p. 251.

27. See 'Child Labour and Apprenticeship', ch. VII, in M.D. George, *England in Transition*, London, 1931, p. 119.

28. Buer, *Health, wealth and population* ..., p. 251.

29. George, pp. 117, 118. See also Daniel Defoe, *A Tour Through the Whole Island of Great Britain*, London, 1962 p. 62: 'The very children after four or five years of age ... could every one earn their own bread'.

30. E.P.Thompson, *The Making of the English Working Class*, Penguin, 1968, pp. 366, 377.

31. George, *England in Transition*, p. 117.

32. *The Sydney Gazette*, 27 May, 3 June 1804, 18 August 1805.

33. *Report of the Select Committee of the House of Commons on Police in the Metropolis, P.P.*, 1828/v1/7.

34. Governor King to Lieutenant King, 23 May 1800, *H.R.N.S.W.*, 4, p. 87.

35. Collins, *An Account of the English Colony* . . . , p. 366.

36. George, *London Life* . . . , pp. 244ff.

37. Second report for the Society for Bettering the Conditions of the Poor, evidence from Porter, cited by George, *London Life* . . . , pp. 246, 386.

38. See, for example, Report on Parish Apprentices, 1815, ibid., p. 246.

39. Thompson, *The Making of the English Working Class* . . . , pp. 264ff.

40. Blackstone, *Commentaries on the Laws of England, 1765*, 1, pp. 423ff. See also George, *London Life* . . . , pp. 148–9, 361.

41. For discussion regarding the relationship between assigned convict labour and the institution of slavery, see W.D.Forsyth, *Governor Arthur's Convict System*, Sydney, 1970, ch. V, 'Slaves', pp. 85ff.

42. Governor Macquarie's Instructions, 9 May 1809, *H.R.N.S.W.*, 7, p. 139.

43. The *Sydney Gazette*, 25 May, 25 June 1806; 1 October 1809.

44. Bigge, *Report of the Commissioner of Inquiry* . . . , vol. III, p. 71.

45. Evidence of Thomas Bowden to Bigge, 27 January 1821, B.T., Box 8, pp. 3329–31, 3337–9. See also evidence of Rev. William Cowper, 23 January 1821, ibid., pp. 3347–54, 3368–71.

46. *An Act for the Preservation of the Health and Morals of Apprentices and Others, employed in the Cotton and other Mills, Cotton and other Factories*, 22 June 1802, 42 George III, C73.

47. Sir John Cam Hobhouse, M.P., *Parlt. Debates*, House of Commons, 2/xiii/p. 644–5, 16 May 1825.

48. For discussion of relations between parents and children of the poor, see Thompson, *The Making of the English Working Class* . . . , p. 295.

49. Hobhouse, *Parlt. Debates.*, House of Commons, 2/xiii/p. 6445.

50. George Crabbe, 'The Borough', 1810, cited by Thompson, *The Making of the English Working Class* . . . , p. 295.

51. Col. Sec In-Letters, Petition of George Clew, nailor, to T.D. Condamine, Esq., 31 May 1828, 4/2167, Memorial 114. References to Memorials referred to or cited in this chapter may be found in Appendix 5.

52. King to Hobart, 9 May 1803, *H.R.N.S.W.*, 5, p. 115.

53. The *Sydney Gazette*, 27 May 1804.

54. Bigge Appendix, evidence of Major Druitt to Commissioner Bigge.

55. Evidence of T. Messling to Bigge, 27 May 1821, Bigge Appendix, B.T., Box 1, p. 531. See also Bigge, *Report on the Colony* . . . , pp. 27, 33, 64–5.

56. W. Hepworth Dixon, *London Prisons*, London, 1850, pp. 178–81.

57. See Hunter to Portland, 29 May 1798, *H.R.A.*, 1, II, p. 153: '[I] make it an invariable rule to place [young male convicts] under the immediate direction of some artificer's gang, in order that they may be rendered useful mechanics in time and the country of course benefitted by their labour'. There are no reports remaining which would indicate the success or failure of the plan, or its adoption by Hunter's successors.

58. Extracts from the Committee of the Male Orphan Institution, 17 April 1822, re apprenticeship of some inmates, 4/1756. p. 6.

59. See George, *London Life* . . . , pp. 280, 392–3. For parish apprentices, see ibid., p. 224.

60. The *Australian*, 5 January 1826. Note that the father of another lad apprenticed to Bell also brought charges before the Court, claiming that Bell 'taught the boy very little and badly mistreated him. The master was enjoined to make good both deficiencies'. The *Australian*, 20 June 1828.

61. The *Australian*, 5 January 1826.

62. *The Times*, August 1795 (no exact date given), cited by George, *London Life* ... , p. 387.

63. F.K. Crowley, 'The Foundation Years', *Australia, A Social and Political History*, G.Greenwood (ed.), Sydney, 1955, p. 37.

64. George, *London Life* ... , pp. 280ff., 392–3.

65. The *Monitor*, 3 January 1826.

66. The *Monitor*, 8 November 1826.

67. Government and General Order, 22 September 1804, the *Sydney Gazette*, 23 September 1804.

68. The *Sydney Gazette*, 17 March 1805; 3 November, 10 November 1805; 9 March 1807; 21 September 1806.

69. The *Sydney Gazette*, 23 October 1808.

70. C.R. Pemberton, *Pel Verjuice*, (1806–12), cited by Henry Baynham, *From the Lower Deck. The Old Navy 1780–1840*, London, 1972, p. 129.

71. Bigge arrived at Hobart Town from Sydney on board Kelly's ship, *The Recovery* on 21 February 1820. On 23 March 1820, he 'despatched ... that skilfull seaman, James Kelly' on the *Governor Macquarie* to investigate possible sources of supply for timber. See Ritchie, *Punishment and Profit* ... , pp. 141, 146.

72. Thompson, *The Making of the English Working Class* ... , p. 266.

73. Evidence of Edward Eagar to Bigge, 19 October 1819.

74. Hunter to Portland, 19 May 1798, *H.R.A.*, 1, II, p. 153.

CHAPTER SIX

1. For the structure of female society, New South Wales, 1788–1828, see Appendix 3. For the ratio of men to women during the same period, see Appendix 6. For the structure of society in New South Wales, 1828, see ibid.

2. Marsden to Wilberforce, 6 February 1800, Hassall Correspondence, vol. II, p. 11, M.L.

3. Letters of Elizabeth Paterson, Mrs Paterson to Captain Johnson, 3 October 1800, M.L. Ms.; Ode by M. Massey Robinson, the *Sydney Gazette*, 9 June 1810.

4. Hassall to Burder, 8 August 1801, *H.R.N.S.W.*, 4, p. 447. Note also that King was familiar with the ideas and practices of the governors of the Canary Islands in relation to the poor, in particular the female orphans. See the Journal of Lieutenant King, June 1787, reprinted in *H.R.N.S.W.*, 2, pp. 517–8: 'In short, every female who is left an orphan, or who is distressed, has only to present themselves in order to partake of the benevolence of the founder'. Also note that in 1799 Marsden wrote to Wilberforce concerning the orphaned and abandoned children, adding that '... the young girls in particular are all likely to be ruined for want of some proper persons to superintend their education', Samuel Marsden, Some Private Correspondence, M.L.

5. Committee of the Orphanage to Governor King, 24 March 1803, *H.R.N.S.W.*, 5, p. 75.

6. Orphan School Report, 22 August 1820, B.T., Box 24, p. 4913.

7. Colonial Secretary In-Letters, Memorial of Thomas Hughes, 4/1780, p. 348. Note that references to all Memorials mentioned in this Chapter may be found in Index A.

8. Macquarie, Government and General Order, 27 January 1810, the *Sydney Gazette*, 27 January 1810.

9. Macquarie, Government and General Order, 24 January 1810, the *Sydney Gazette*, 24 February 1810. Note that on 1 March 1804 King wrote to Hobart that there were '... some very good schools ... for the education of the male and

female children who are not the objects of the Orphan Institution . . . conducted by the missionaries . . .', *H.R.N.S.W.*, 5, p. 324.

10.   Public Notice, Samuel Marsden, Treasurer of the Female Orphan School, published in the *Sydney Gazette*. Note that this school was called 'Yon blest Sanctuary' by Macquarie's poet, Michael Massey Robinson: see the *Sydney Gazette*, 9 June 1810.

11.   T. Brown to Viscount Castlereagh, 13 October 1809, *H.R.N.S.W.*, 7, pp. 216–7.

12.   Macquarie, Government and General Order, 24 February 1810, the *Sydney Gazette*, 24 February 1810.

13.   For further examples of Memorials from colonial women concerning their husbands and families, see Appendix 3.

14.   Letter of Elizabeth Paterson . . . , M.L. Ms., p. 3.

15.   The *Sydney Gazette*, 4 August 1810.

16.   Rev. Richard Johnson to the Society for the Propagation of the Gospel, 1 December 1796, *H.R.N.S.W.*, 3, p. 184.

17.   G.F.J. Bergman and J.S. Levi, *Australian Genesis: Jewish Convicts and Settlers, 1788–1850*, Sydney, 1974, p. 21. Note that on 6 February 1800 Marsden wrote to Wilberforce concerning the parentage of the colonial children: 'Some . . . are born on the passage to the Colony, others after the arrival of their parents. The others in general are either soldiers, sailors or prisoners. The former quit the country . . . the latter have . . . seldom the inclination or ability to care for their children'. Marsden, Some Private Letters, M.L.

18.   For composition of landowning families, 1806, see Appendix 4. For occupations of fathers/mothers of native-born daughters, resident with parent/parents, 1828, see Appendix 6. For civil condition of fathers/mothers, see Appendix 6.

19.   George, *London Life* . . . , pp. 141–2. See also Robson, *The Convict Settlers* . . . , pp. 75–6.

20.   See Appendix 3. See also Malcolmson, 'Infanticide in the Eighteenth Century', *Crime in England* . . . , Cockburn (ed.), pp. 187ff.

21.   Petition in Mitigation of Sentence, Petition of Mary Partridge, 4/1788, p. 11. Note that references for Petitions mentioned in this chapter may be found in Index A.

22.   For occupations of the native-born working women, see Appendix 6.

23.   See Hazel King, *Elizabeth Macarthur and Her World*, Sydney, 1980, p. 36.

24.   The *Sydney Gazette*, 1 June 1806, advertisement by Mrs Perfect; ibid., 10 August 1806, Mrs Williams; ibid., 6 August 1807, Mrs Merchant; ibid., 26 March 1809, Mrs Perfect; ibid., April 1809, Mrs Hodges.

25.   See King to Hobart, 1 March 1804, *H.R.N.S.W.*, 5, p. 324. For projected schools in Sydney, Parramatta and the Hawkesbury, see Castlereagh to Bligh, 31 December 1807, *H.R.N.S.W.*, 6, p. 393. For the charity schools established by Macquarie, see Government and General Order, 24 February 1810, *H.R.N.S.W.*, 7, p. 294: 'a public charity school . . . [to] be established at Sydney for the education of poor children'.

26.   Instructions to Governor Hunter, 23 June 1794, *H.R.A.*, 1, I, p. 265.

27.   Adam Smith, *An Inquiry into the Nature and Causes of the Wealth of Nations*, Edinburgh, 1859, pp. 353ff.

28.   Cited in F.A. Cavanagh, 'State Intervention in English Education', *History*, vol. 25, no. 98, September 1940, pp. 144ff.

29.   Instructions to Governor Bligh, 25 May 1805, *H.R.A.*, 1, VI, p. 18.

30.   Despatches of Governor King, *H.R.A.*, 1, III, IV; also *H.R.N.S.W.*, 2, pp. 517–8. See also Hassall to Burder, B.T. 49, p. 185.

31.   Hobart to King, 28 February 1802, Instructions, *H.R.A.*, 1, III, p. 394, article 8:

'. . . and that you do take particular care that all possible attention be paid to the due celebration of public worship . . .'. Note that it is also probable that Pitt was influenced by Wilberforce, to whom Samuel Marsden wrote frequently concerning the need to promote religion and education among the 'Rising Generation'. See Some Private Correspondence of Samuel Marsden, Letters to Wilberforce, M.L.

32. See Appendix 2. See also Macquarie to Castlereagh, 30 April 1810, *H.R.N.S.W.*, 7, p. 338: 'I have also established a Charity School at Sydney for the education of the poor of this place of both sexes'. Note also that in 1798 Richard Johnson drew up a set of 'Rules or Articles to be Observed Respecting the School at Sydney . . .'; see *Some Letters of the Rev. Richard Johnson*, G. Mackaness (ed.), *Australian Historical Monographs* . . . , vol. XIII, part 2, pp. 29–30. See also List of Children at Kissing Point School . . . , Hassall to L.M.S., Samuel Marsden, Private Letters. For a later period, see 'List of Children in attendance at Sydney Branch of Roman Catholic School', Andrew Higgins, Schoolmaster, 4/1749, pp. 80–82.

33. For references to persons mentioned in the text, see Index B. See also appropriate tables in appendices. For details of native-born 'working women' see Appendix 6.

34. For details of wives of native-born landholders, see Appendix 6.

35. For came-free working women, see Appendix 6. For ex-convict working women, see ibid.

36. See Appendix 6.

37. See ibid.

38. See Appendix 2.

39. See Appendix 7.

40. See Appendix 6.

41. See Appendix 6. For examples of native-born Catholic marriages, see Appendix 6.

42. Evidence of George Best to Commissioner Bigge, 4 September 1820.

43. Col. Sec. In-Letters, Memorial of Charlotte Currey, 4/1763, p. 155. For examples of native-born girls who married convicts or ticket-of-leave men, see Appendix 6.

44. Ships' Musters, reel 167, the *Francis Cope*, M.L.

45. Kerrison James Index, M.L., Coroner's verdict, 27 October 1825, M.L.

46. For an analysis of the civil condition of the wives of the native-born landholders, see Appendix 6.

47. This opinion was not shared by Fulton's former patron, the Bishop of Derry, who refused to give Fulton a character reference during the administration of Bligh. See Henry Fulton to Mrs Bligh, Banks Papers, M.L. Ms.

48. Memorial of Rev. Fulton, Chaplain, to Viscount Castlereagh, 14 February 1809, *H.R.N.S.W.*, 7, p. 31.

49. For landowning families, see Analysis of the 1806 Muster, Appendix 4. For parents of the native-born landholders, see Appendix 7. For wives of the native-born landowners, see Appendix 6. For parentage of wives of landowners, see Appendix 7.

50. For wives of tradesmen, see Appendix 8. For examples of native-born women who married tradesmen, see Appendix 6.

51. For marriages of the native-born, see Appendix 6.

52. For districts of residence, see Appendix 6, Appendix 7.

53. For comparative occupational tables, see Appendix 7.

54. The *Australian*, 20 January 1827. See also Clark, *A History* . . . , vol. 2, pp. 157ff.

55.   For residence of colonial women 1820, 1828 see Appendix 6.
56.   The numbers were: came-free, 861; native-born, 504; free by servitude, 486; pardoned, 27; convicts, 496. See Appendix 6.
57.   Ibid., the numbers were: came-free, 151; native-born, 277; ex-convict, 259; convict, 688.
58.   Ibid., the numbers were: came-free, 122; native-born, 382; ex-convict, 63; convict, 270.
59.   Ibid., the numbers were: came-free, 134; native-born, 42; ex-convict, 51; convict, 40.
60.   Ibid., the numbers were: came-free, 64; native-born, 132, ex-convict, 86; convict, 45.
61.   Ibid., the numbers were: came-free, 45; native-born, 37; ex-convict, 87; convict, 31.
62.   See Appendix 6.
63.   Waldersee, *Catholic Society* . . . , ch. 5, esp. pp. 123ff.
64.   For religion of husbands, see Appendix 6.
65.   The Ambrose Fitzpatrick Letters are held in St. Mary's Cathedral Archives, Sydney. See also *Freeman's Journal*, 25 November 1865, St. Mary's Archives.
66.   Ibid. Note that Fitzpatrick makes no mention of Kenny's school; this may have been because the family was at Parramatta, or because Kenny did not advertise his school as exclusively for Catholic children. See the *Sydney Gazette*, 6 October 1805.
67.   Robson, *The Convict Settlers* . . . , ch. 4, esp. pp. 206ff.
68.   Where one of these women was married by a clergyman of the Church of England, she usually signed the marriage certificate with a cross: few of these women were able to sign their own Memorials. See Appendix 3.
69.   Cited by Moran, *History of the Catholic Church* . . . , p. 409.
70.   Fitzpatrick in *Freeman's Journal*, 25 November 1865, St. Mary's Archives.
71.   See Macquarie to Fathers Conolly and Therry, 6 June 1820, Therry Papers, M.L. Note that Waldersee, *Catholic Society* . . . , discusses this point in detail and refers to E. O'Brien, *The Life of Archpriest Therry*, Sydney, 1922, p. 29, for the legality of these marriages, and to C.H. Currey, 'The Law of Marriage and Divorce in New South Wales (1788–1858)', *J.R.A.H.S.*, vol. XII, part 3, 1955, pp. 97–114. Walderseee, pp. 15ff.

CHAPTER SEVEN

1.   This is based on data from the Census of 1828. See Appendix 7 for a summary of the colonial landholders.
2.   Bigge, *Agriculture and Trade* . . . , p. 75.
3.   'Address of Welcome to Governor Darling', Darling to Bathurst, 1 February 1826, enclosure 1, *H.R.A.*, 1, XII, pp. 144ff. See also the *Australian*, 12 January 1826.
4.   Wentworth, Letters from William Charles to his father, D'arcy, 14 April 1816.
5.   The *Australian*, 19 January 1826.
6.   For identity of native-born landholders, see Appendix 7. For individuals mentioned in this chapter, see Appendix 7.
7.   Harris, *Settlers and Convicts* . . . , p. 71.
8,   Ibid., pp. 86–7.
9.   'A Return of Lands Granted to Individuals Born within the Colony of New South Wales from the First of January, 1810 to the First of January, 1827', henceforth referred to as 'Darling's List . . .'. See also Appendix 7 for native-born landholders; 1806 Muster for details of colonial landholdings; Appendix 4

for holdings of the parents of the native-born.

10. For comparative lists of occupations of native-born, came-free and ex-convict, see Appendix 7.

11. Age was not specifically stated in the Memorials of the native-born. The term most frequently used was 'arrived at full adult age'. John Pugh, for example, 'wished to enter the more mature and manly walks of life' (Col. Sec. In-Letters, 4/1825A, p. 433). It was Bigge who recommended that land should be granted to the native-born 'on their obtaining the age of twenty-four years'. Bigge, *Agriculture and Trade* . . . , p. 50. Bathurst suggested 'a minimum of 18 years . . . if not 21 years', Bathurst to Darling, 2 April 1827, *H.R.A.*, 1, XIII, p. 228.

12. Robson, *Convict Settlers* . . . , p. 9.

13. Note that all references for Memorials in this chapter may be found in Index A.

14. Bigge, *Agriculture and Trade* . . . , p. 75. For native-born resident with parent/parents, see Appendix 2. For parentage (where known) of all native-born landholders mentioned in the text, see Appendix 7.

15. Note the evidence given to Bigge by Reverend Samuel Marsden, 1820, undated: 'I have signed Petitions for Men who have been a number of years in the Colony agst [sic] whom I have never heard any misconduct, tho [sic] I cd [sic] not from my own knowledge say that they were sober Honest and Industrious. If they had been bad Characters, I must have known them to have been such'.

16. See also Castlereagh to Bligh, 31 December 1807, *H.R.A.*, 1, VI, pp. 202–3, for the suggestion that grants of land be made to 'those who marry' the apprenticed orphans of the colony. See also Macquarie to Bathurst, Despatch 22 of 1818, *H.R.A.*, 1, X, pp. 343–4, for Macquarie's refusal to make grants of land to 'the Young Unmarried Women, free by birth . . . merely on the Ground of their being Free'.

17. King to Hobart, 7 August 1803, *H.R.A.*, 1, IV, p. 310.

18. W.C. Wentworth, *A Statistical, Historical and Political Description* . . . , pp. 279ff.

19. Evidence of John Macarthur to Bigge, n.d.

20. Evidence of Edward Eagar to Bigge, 19 October 1819.

21. Bigge, *Agriculture and Trade* . . . , p. 50.

22. Minutes of the Executive Council, 4/1516 (No. 2) p. 209, Saturday 12 September 1829.

23. Oxley's Evidence to Bigge was that Petitions were presented at stated periods. In July 1826 Darling introduced a new standard 'Form of Memorial for Land by Settlers and others'. He noted that this could be adapted to 'the circumstances of Individuals born in the Colony'. Darling to Bathurst, 23 July 1826, sub-enclosure (C3) *H.R.A.*, 1, XII, p. 396. For Government Orders describing these new regulations, see ibid., sub-enclosure A, pp. 390–92.

24. See Bathurst to Darling, 14 July 1825, *H.R.A*, 1, XII, p. 21. Darling to Bathurst, 5 May 1826, ibid., pp. 266–7. For procedures, see 'Members of the Land Board to Governor Darling', 23 February 1826, ibid., p. 402ff.

25. Evidence of Edward Eagar to Bigge, 19 October 1819.

26. Darling to Murray, 1 March 1829, enclosure, 'Return of Lands Granted in the Colony of New South Wales in 1828', *H.R.A.*, 1, XIV, p. 671.

27. These percentages are based on Returns of the Colony, 1828, and the 1828 Census, A.O.N.S.W. For details of individual holdings, see Appendix 7.

28. Figures based on Returns of the Colony, 1828, and the Census of 1828, A.O.N.S.W.

29. Bigge, *Agriculture and Trade* . . . , p. 50.

30. Brisbane to Bathurst, 14 May 1825, *H.R.A.*, 1, II, p. 585.

31. For details, see Appendix 7. Note that figures must be regarded as approximate only: the nature of remaining records makes complete accuracy impossible.

32. Oxley to Bigge (before) 17 November 1819 . Note that Oxley also described the free settlers at Bathurst: 'There are a few native-born youths & the rest emancipated or pardoned convicts. They have fifty acres each granted to them'.

33. Based on an analysis of Darling's List. Note that this analysis does not include those named as native-born who were not actually born in the Colony. The figures must be regarded as approximate only, although checked against the Register of Grants held by the Registrar-General's Office, Registers 1–4, 7–8, 10–12, 19–21.

34. See Appendix 4.

35. See 1806 Muster, A.O.N.S.W.

36. *An Accurate List . . .* , pp. 6, 7, 10, 11, 28, 30, 31, 44.

37. For occupations, see Appendix 2. For native-born members of the New South Wales Corps, see ibid. See also 1806 Muster.

38. See, for example, Macquarie to Bathurst, 18 March 1816, *H.R.A.*, 1, IX, p. 65, Macquarie's opinion of Paterson: 'a Simple Good Natured Man, [who] was frequently so far Imposed upon that he gave Grants of Land Indiscriminately to all Persons that chose to ask for them'. Those 'Persons' appear to have been mainly of wealth, influence or social position. See also T.J. Robinson, 'A Quantitative Analysis of Conflict in New South Wales during the Administration of Governor William Bligh. 1806–1810', Vol. II, The Evidence, pp. 130–242, lists of persons to whom lands were granted. B.A. Hons. thesis, Macquarie University 1979.

39. See 'Regulation respecting Grants of Land and Allotments in the Towns', Bigge, *Agriculture and Trade . . .* , pp. 33–4. There is no mention of specific grants to the native-born, except 'the sons of persons who have been convicts', p. 50. Note that on Macquarie's departure, some 340,000 acres had been promised to those living in the colony, but these grants were unconfirmed. Brisbane to Bathurst, 10 April 1822, *H.R.A.*, 1, VII, pp. 318, 436ff., 825ff. ibid., vol. X, pp. 560ff. See also Note 136, ibid., p. 835. For Macquarie's own description of his method of making grants, see Macquarie to Bathurst 31 August 1820, ibid., pp. 343–4.

40. See Bigge, *Agriculture and Trade . . .* , pp. 33 ff. See also Darling to Bathurst, 26 January 1826, enclosure 4, Oxley to Darling, *H.R.A.*, 1, XII, pp. 379–80. For comment by Bathurst on the 'informality' of some of Macquarie's grants, see Bathurst to Brisbane, 30 May 1823, *H.R.A.*, 1, XI, p. 84.

41. Brisbane to Bathurst, 30 May 1823, *H.R.A.*, 1, XI, p. 84. For names of grantees, size, location and date of grant, see Macquarie to Goulburn, 24 November 1821, enclosure 1, 'List of Grants made in New South Wales from the 25th Day of August, 1812, up to the 25th Day of March, 1821', *H.R.A.*, 1, X, pp. 560ff. (Note that this List is for Grants of 100 acres and upwards only.)

42. *Darling's List . . .* , Nos 31 & 32, 22 September 1821 (Bowman); 87, 31 March 1821 (Fulton); 95, 31 March 1821 (Fitzgerald); 13, 16 January 1816 (Broughton); 35, 22 September 1821 (Bayly); 151, 1 October 1817, (Laycock); 171, 31 March 1821 (James Macarthur); 172, ibid., (William Macarthur); 250, 14 June 1821, 251, 16 January 1816, (William Charles Wentworth); 261, 31 March 1821 (Wills); 262, ibid., (Fulton).

43. Macquarie to Bathurst, 28 June 1813, *H.R.A.*, 1, VII, pp. 775–6. Macquarie to Bathurst, 22 October 1821, ibid., X, p. 459. Macquarie to Bathurst, 27 July 1822, ibid., p. 683.

44. Darling's List . . . , Nos 171, 172.

45. Bigge, *Agriculture and Trade . . .* p. 33. Note that approximately 228,000 acres had been granted within the Cumberland Plain from 1812 to 1821. See also

Macquarie to Liverpool, 17 November 1812, enclosure 4, *H.R.A.*, 1, VII, p. 639; Macquarie to Bathurst, 20 November 1821, enclosure 3, ibid., 1, X, p. 577.

46. Bigge, *Agriculture and Trade* . . . , p. 35. Note that 8585 acres were held by those who had received absolute pardons, 19,459 by the conditionally pardoned, and 765 by holders of tickets-of-leave. As Bigge noted, there is a discrepancy in these figures. That at least 60 per cent of the ex-convict settlers had purchased their land would suggest a degree of enterprise, industry and initative in amassing the necessary capital for purchase.

47. These figures are based on analysis of Macquarie's land grants. See Darling's List . . . ; Darling to Bathurst, 22 July 1826, enclosure 4, 'Surveyor-General Oxley to Governor Darling', *H.R.A.*, 1, XII, pp. 379ff. For discussion of the accuracy of the Musters, see Bigge, *Report on the Colony* . . .' pp. 95–9; Bigge, *Agriculture and Trade* . . . , p. 80. See also Appendix 6, Table 2, Population (adult) of New South Wales, 1828.

48. Bigge, *Agriculture and Trade* . . . , p. 48.

49. Bathurst to Brisbane, 9 September 1822, *H.R.A.*, 1, X, p. 790.

50. Bigge, *Agriculture and Trade* . . . , pp. 48–50, 91.

51. For Brisbane's reports and comments on his implementation of Bigge's recommendations (regarding land), see Brisbane to Bathurst, 28 April 1823, *H.R.A.*, 1, XI, : acknowledgement, pp. 74–5; clearing land, p. 79; advantages of new system, p. 324; regulations for land grants, p. 583.

52. Instructions to Governor Darling, 17 July 1825, *H.R.A.*, 1, XII, pp. 107–25. See also D. Jeans, 'Crown Land Sales and the Accommodation of the Small Settler in New South Wales, 1825–1842, *H.S.*, vol. XII.

53. Brisbane to Bathurst, 23 May 1825, enclosure, 'Observations on a Letter which appeared in the *Morning Chronicle* of 21 August 1824'. *H.R.A.*, 1, XI, enclosure p. 609.

54. See Ritchie, *Punishment and Profit* Melbourne, 1970, p. 250. Note references in footnote 54, ibid.

55. Bigge, *Agriculture and Trade* . . . , pp. 48–9. Brisbane to Bathurst, 23 May 1825, *H.R.A.*, 1, XI, pp. 331ff.

56. For free migration during the 1820s, see Clarke, *The Land of Contrarieties* . . . , ch. 5. See also Eddy, *Britain and the Australian Colonies* . . . , pp. 224–5; Eddy cites Darling to Hay: 'he [Darling] welcomed agriculturalists and mechanics . . .'. See also Peter Burroughs, *Britain and Australia*, pp. 120ff. Note that Burroughs emphasized that the Regulations of 1831 'reinforced restrictions which had already in the 1820s operated against the rapid and easy conversion of labourers into landowners', p. 120.

57. Cobbett's *Two-Penny Trash; or Politics for the Poor*, vol. 1, March 1831, cited by Clarke, *Land of Contrarieties* . . . , p.81.

58. Ibid., Clarke cites *Hansard*, 3rd series, vol. XIII, 28 June 1832, col. 1106. See also Macquarie's defence: 'From my own Personal local knowledge and long Experience in the Colony . . . disabilities and disqualifications . . . of the Emancipated Convicts . . . and their Descendants', Macquarie to Bathurst, 22 October 1821, *H.R.A.*, 1, X, p. 549

59. Darling, Letter to the land Board, Minute No. 118, 23 September 1829, M.L.

60. Bathurst to Brisbane, 31 May 1823, *H.R.A.*, 1, XI, p. 87. For form of Deed of Land Grant (Brisbane), see Brisbane to Bathurst, 10 April 1822, enclosure, ibid., 1, X, p. 631.

61. Bathurst to Brisbane . . . , 31 May 1823, *H.R.A.*, 1, XI, p. 87.

62. For contemporary accounts of the life of bush and agricultural workers, see Harris, *Settlers and Convicts* . . . , ch. V, 'A Glimpse of the Cedar-Brush'; VII,

'The Hawkesbury River and its Settlers'; XVI, 'Life Among the Shepherds'.

63. For contemporary accounts of conditions of labour and wages of agricultural workers, see *Report of the Select Committee of the House of Commons on the Depressed State of Agriculture*, *B.P.P.*, 1821, IX, 117–24. See also William Cobbett, *Rural Rides*, London, 1912, Vol. 2, pp. 1–7. For modern historical discussion, see E.P. Thompson, *The Making of the English Working Class*, Ringwood, 1968, esp. ch. 7, 'The Field Labourer'. For conditions of convict labour in New South Wales, see Bigge, *Agriculture and Trade . . .*, section VI, 'Nature of the Labour of Convicts in the service of Settlers', pp. 74ff.

64. Bathurst to Brisbane, 1 January 1825, *H.R.A.*, 1, XI, p. 440.

65. Minutes of the Executive Council, 4/1516 (No. 2), p. 209. Saturday 12 September 1829. See also Bathurst to Brisbane, 1 January 1825, enclosure no. 2, 'Summary of Rules for Emigrants Going to New South Wales', *H.R.A.*, 1, XI, p. 454ff.

66. Bathurst to Brisbane, 1 January 1825, ibid.

67. Ibid. For previous difficulties in the collection of quit rents, see Bigge, *Agriculture and Trade . . .*, p. 38. For discussion in the Macquarie period, see Fletcher, *Landed Enterprise . . .*, pp. 123–4. See also Burroughs, *Britain and Australia 1831–35 . . .*, p. 22, for the ineffectiveness of quit rents to restrict the size of free grants; ibid., p. 45, for the failure of quit rents to return substantial revenue to the Crown.

68. Bigge, *Report into the Colony of New South Wales . . .*, VIII, 'Nature of the Future Establishments for Convicts in New South Wales', pp. 155ff.

69. Brisbane to Bathurst, 14 May 1825, enclosure no. 1, 'Abstract', *H.R.A.*, 1, XI, p. 579.

70. Brisbane to Bathurst, 29 November 1823, *H.R.A.*, 1, X, pp. 181–2.

71. Brisbane to Bathurst, 10 April 1822, *H.R.A.*, 1, X, pp. 630–31. Bathurst to Brisbane, 30 May 1823, *H.R.A.*, 1, IX, pp. 83ff. Brisbane to Bathurst, 29 November 1823, *H.R.A.*, 1, XI, pp. 169ff.

72. *Darling's List . . .* References to name of grantee, date and size of grant may be found in Appendix 7.

73. Brisbane to Bathurst, 24 July 1824, *H.R.A.*, 1, XII, p. 331.

74. The *Sydney Gazette*, 20 May 1820.

75. Brisbane to Bathurst, 10 April 1822, *H.R.A.*, 1, X, p. 630. Enclosure is a copy of the Form of Deed for Land Grant, pp. 631–2. See also Roberts, *History of Australian Land Settlement . . .*, pp. 38ff., 41, note 22. For unpopularity of this regulation among the colonists, see Brisbane to Bathurst, 29 November 1823, *H.R.A.*, 1, XI, pp. 179ff. For attitude of the Colonial Office see Bathurst to Brisbane, 30 May 1823, ibid., 1, X, pp. 84–5. For Brisbane's defence of his regulation, see Brisbane to Bathurst, 23 April 1823, ibid., 1, XI, pp. 74ff.

76. Darling to Bathurst, 22 July 1826, enclosure no. 8, 'Surveyor-General Oxley to Governor Darling', *H.R.A.*, 1, XII, pp. 379ff.

77. Darling to Bathurst, 21 July 1826, enclosure 4, Oxley to Darling, 26 January 1826, *H.R.A.*, 1, XII, pp. 379–389. Minute no. 15, Darling, ibid., enclosure 3, pp. 378–9.

78. Darling to Murray, 1 March 1829, enclosure, *H.R.A.*, 1, XIV, pp. 671–2.

79. Note that it is outside the scope of the present work to investigate the results of these changes.

CHAPTER EIGHT

1. Phillip to Nepean, 28 September 1789, *H.R.A.*, 1, I, p. 87.

2. The *Sydney Gazette*, 27 May 1804. Note spelling: Bloodworth/Bloodsworth.

3. Evidence to Commissioner Bigge, B.T., Box 23: Robert Lowe, 10 July 1820; John Macarthur, n.d.; Major Druitt, 27 October 1819.
4. Thompson, *The Making of the English Working Class* . . . , pp. 575ff.
5. See Appendix 1.
6. For contemporary opinions in England, see 'An Address to the Public of strike-bound Manchester', *The Black Dwarf*, John Rylands Library, Manchester. See also the problems of the Spitafields silk-weavers in Henry Mayhew, *The Unknown Mayhew*, London, 1971, pp. 122–136.
7. Mayhew, ibid., p. 404. Thompson, *The Making of the English Working Class* . . . , pp. 274–5.
8. See Appendix 8.
9. Evidence of Major Druitt to Bigge, 2 November 1819.
10. See Appendix 7.
11. See Appendix 8.
12. For persons mentioned in this chapter, see Index B.
13. See Appendix 8.
14. The *Sydney Gazette*, 10 August 1806.
15. Ibid., 1 April, 14 July 1810. See also indexes to the *Sydney Gazette*, 1810 and Appendix 8.
16. For discussion on immigration from Britain in the 1820s, see Clarke, *The Land of Contrarieties* . . . , ch. V, 'Emigration, 1825–55'.
17. Thompson, *The Making of the English Working Class* . . . , pp. 259ff.
18. Mayhew, *The Unknown Mayhew* . . . , pp. 204ff.
19. 'Present Demand of Convict Labour', F. Goulburn, Col. Sec., 1828, New South Wales, enclosure 3, received 29 April 1825, 'Prices paid to good Mechanics and Tradesmen of the following Description in the Town of Sydney, New South Wales'.
20. Report of 'a highly respectable journeyman carpenter working for the best shops at the best prices', cited in Mayhew, *The Unknown Mayhew* . . . , pp. 412–416.
21. F. Goulburn, Col. Sec., 'Prices paid . . .'.
22. Ibid., enclosure 2, received 29 April 1825.
23. See Appendix 8.
24. The *Sydney Gazette*, 14 January 1810.
25. See Appendix 8. Note that references to native-born tradesmen and apprentices may be found in this table.
26. See ch. 7 for discussion of these changes and their effects.
27. See Appendix 6, for the native-born wives of tradesmen.
28. For details, see Appendix 8.
29. For one description of Sydney Town, see R. Therry, *Reminiscences of Thirty Years' Residence in New South Wales and Victoria*, Sydney, 1974, pp. 394ff.
30. The *Sydney Gazette*, 4 November 1804.
31. Ibid., 25 June 1809.
32. Ibid., 26 February 1809, 2 June 1810.
33. Col. Sec. In-Letters, Memorial of John Irving, 4/1811, pp. 132–3.
34. The *Currency Lad*, vol. 1, no. 1, September 1832; vol. 1, no. 7.
35. Note that in England 'the mill-wright [at least in London] was an aristocrat, who was protected both by his own organization . . . and by apprenticeship restrictions . . . and who maintained a wage of two or three guiness in the first years of the nineteenth century'. Thompson, *The Making of the English Working Class* . . . , p. 271.
36. The *Sydney Gazette*, 8 July 1804.
37. For ex-convict and immigrant tradesmen, see Appendix 8.
38. The *Sydney Gazette*, 23 September 1804.

39. For conditions of English workers, see Thompson, *The Making of the English Working Class* . . . , pp. 281ff., p. 259. For colonial wages, etc., see 'Prices paid to Good Mechanics and Tradesmen . . .', Col. Sec.'s Office, 6 October 1824, New South Wales, enclosure 3, received 29 April 1825.

40. Evidence of Thomas Bowden to Bigge, 22 January 1821, B.T. Box 8, pp. 3332, 3378–9.

41. T.J. Robinson, 'A Quantitative Analysis of Conflict...', pp. 132ff.

42. The *Sydney Gazette*, 5 November 1809.

43. Ibid., Burn, 6 November 1808; Hudson, 30 April 1808.

44. See G.P. Walsh, 'The Geography of Manufacturing in Sydney, 1788–1851', *Business Archives*, vol. 3, no.1, February 1963.

45. King to Banks, Sydney, 14 August 1804, Banks Papers, Braebourne Collection, vol. 7, King, 1788–1805, p. 224.

46. Evidence to Commissioner Bigge, B.T. Box 5, evidence of John Blaxland.

47. Walsh, 'The Geography of Manufacturing . . .', pp. 132ff.

48. An example may be found in the *Sydney Gazette*, 13 October 1805, regulations governing the size and price of bread. In 1811 bread prices were published several times per week; bakers were fined for selling short-weight; ibid., 3 August 1811.

49. The *Sydney Gazette*, 15 January 1809.

50. Ibid., 17 June, 26 August 1804, 3 August 1811.

51. See 'List of Bakers Licenced for one year, 1 October to 30 September 1821', B.T. Box 12, pp. 177–8, cited by Perrott, *A Tolerable Good Success* . . . , p. 118.

52. The *Sydney Gazette*, 9 June 1810; Bennett, 10 February 1804; Morgan, 2 September 1804; Kable, 11 August 1810; Rose, 8 September, 16 September; Murphy, 6 October, 27 October, 1 November 1810; Chapman, 18 August 1804.

53. See, for example, Government and General Orders, published in the *Sydney Gazette*: an account of the examination of candidates for licences, 28 October 1804; eleven names were submitted, six approved; unlicenced retailers were charged before the courts, 3 June 1804.

54. See Appendix 10.

55. The *Sydney Gazette*, 4 May 1806; 5, 12, 19 May 1810.

56. For the trades of the men of the New South Wales Corps, see W.O. 25, Returns, Registers, Various, reel 1302, piece nos. 642, 643.

57. The *Sydney Gazette*, 19 June 1809; 26 February 1808; 12 March 1809; 18, 25 June 1808; 9 July 1808; 24 September 1808; 12 November 1808; 17 December 1808; 17 February 1810; 14 July 1810. See also 'A Quantitative Analysis of Conflict', T.J. Robinson, pp. 132ff.

CHAPTER NINE

1. Peter Cunningham, *Two Years in New South Wales* . . . , p. 55.

2. Evidence of Edward Eagar to Commissioner Bigge, 19 October 1819.

3. The *Sydney Gazette*, 1803–1813. This was the period during which the native-born youth were of an age to seek employment or apprenticeships.

4. Cunningham, *Two Years in New South Wales* . . . , p. 55. J.T. Bigge, *Agriculture and Trade* . . . , p. 82: 'Many of the native-born youths have evinced a strong disposition for a sea-faring life, and are excellent sailors'. For civil condition of sailors and mariners resident in New South Wales in 1828, see Appendix 9.

5. 'To run' was to abscond or desert; to be 'cleared out' was to be discharged.

6. Ships' Musters, 1816–25, A.O.N.S.W., reels 561, 562. For an analysis of these Musters, see Appendix 9. Note that intention to leave the colony had to be published in the *Sydney Gazette*. Masters were specifically warned by the

Governor against 'harbouring convicts'. See Port Regulations, published in General Orders, the *Sydney Gazette*, 13 August 1809. For references to native-born seamen in this chapter, see Appendix 9. For references to apprentices, see Appendix 7. For references to Memorials referred to in this chapter, see Index A. For individuals, Index B.

7. For the possible link with American ships, see E.D. & A. Potts, *Young America and Australian Gold*, Queensland, 1974. See also T. Dunbabin, 'Whalers, Sealers and Buccaneers'. *J.R.A.H.S.*, vol. II, part 1, 1925.
8. The *Sydney Gazette*, 30 October, 6 November 1808. In 1810 seven cases of desertion were published in five months: 17 March, 31 March, 7 April, 28 April, 8 September, 15 September, 22 September 1810, also 13 October, 10 November 1810; 1 June 1806; 29 June 1806.
9. The *Sydney Gazette*, 29 June 1806.
10. Government and General Orders, 12 June 1806, the *Sydney Gazette*, 13 July 1806.
11. The *Sydney Gazette*, 13 July 1806.
12. Reported in the *Sydney Gazette*: the *Lucy*, 29 June 1806; the *Governor Hunter*, 13 July 1806; the *Venus*, 13 July 1806.
13. The *Sydney Gazette*, 20 July 1806.
14. The *Sydney Gazette*, 18 August 1805.
15. Evidence of Edward Eagar to Bigge, 19 October 1819.
16. Returns of the Colony . . . 1828, A.O.N.S.W.
17. Ibid.
18. Evidence of Edward Eagar to Bigge, 19 October 1819.
19. Note that the microfilm is difficult to decipher. It is not clear whether the vessel was the *Queen Caroline* or the *Queen Charlotte*; the former is more likely, the *Charlotte* being a colonial vessel and the *Caroline* registered at the port of London.
20. The *Sydney Gazette*, 13 May 1803.
21. Ibid.
22. Col. Sec. In-Letters, 4/1822A, p. 476.
23. Col. Sec. In-Letters, 4/1763, p.237.
24. The *Australian Almanac*, 1829, p. 134.
25. The *Sydney Gazette*, 13 October 1808, 15 October 1809.
26. See also Memorials from native-born seamen, Appendix 9.
27. For the attitudes of the colonial authorities towards convicts and ex-convicts 'escaping' as seamen, see, for example, Phillip to Nepean, 23 August 1790, *H.R.A.*, 1, I, p. 207.
28. See Baynham, *From the Lower Deck . . .*, esp. chs 4, 5.
29. List of crew members on the *Hillsborough* in *Voyage to Sydney in the Ship 'Hillsborough' 1798–99*, William Noah, North Sydney, 1978. Library of Australian History reprint of Noah's Journal, M.L. Ms.; crew list, pp. 9–10.

CHAPTER TEN

1. The *Australian*, 14 February 1827.
2. See Appendix 10 for details of land workers; ibid. for agricultural labourers; Appendix 7 for summary of occupations of all male native-born. Note that 'employed', in this instance, refers to those native-born who described an occupation in the Census Returns of 1828. It excludes those resident with parents for whom no occupation was listed.
3. Governor Darling to Sir George Murray, 21 January 1829, enclosure 1, Hall to Murray, 17 November 1828, *H.R.A.*, 1, XIV, p. 580. Note that Hall is describing 'the characteristics of the descendants of the convicts', i.e., the

native-born. See also Darling to Murray, 27 July 1820, sub-enclosure 8, Hall to Murray, 8 May 1830, ibid., 1, XV, p. 636.

4. 'Memorandum Relative to Mr Macarthur's Merino Sheep', Evidence of John Macarthur to Commissioner Bigge, 4 February 1820.

5. For male native-born resident with parents in 1828, see Appendix 2.

6. For individuals mentioned in the text, other than those included in parentage and occupational tables, see Index B.

7. For analysis of land-owning parents in 1806, see Appendix 4.

8. This is based on a detailed investigation of all Memorials for land grants from the native-born. The memorials are held in A.O.N.S.W.

9. For native-born seamen, see Appendix 9. For constables, clerks and schoolmasters, ibid.

10. The *Australian*, 14 February 1827.

11. James Atkinson, *An Account of the State of Agriculture and Grazing in New South Wales*, Introduction, B.H. Fletcher, Sydney, 1975, pp. 106, 109. Note that, on one or two occasions, there were advertisements in the *Sydney Gazette* which showed preference for a colonial-born. These positions were for employment in Sydney: 2 January 1828, 'Wanted, A Young Man, who is acquainted with the duties of the RETAIL BUSINESS, and writes a Fair Hand. None need apply who cannot be recommended for honesty. A COLONIAL YOUTH would be preferred . . .'.

12. For details of parentage: landholders, Appendix 7; tradesmen, Appendix 8; apprentices, Appendix 8; labourers, Appendix 10; agricultural workers, Appendix 10.

13. Evidence of William Howe to Commissioner Bigge, 22 January 1821.

14. Robson, *The Convict Settlers* . . . , Table 6(c), p. 194, Table 6(f), p. 197.

15. Wentworth, 'Address of Welcome to Governor Darling . . .', the *Australian*, 14 February 1827. Hall to Murray, 17 November 1828, *H.R.A.*, 1, XIV, pp. 58ff.

16. The exceptions were: James Hall, who had arrived as a single man at the age of thirty-three in 1823 and had become a shepherd for Mr Blaxland at Newington; J.B. Richards, who had arrived in 1824 at the age of twenty-four and was a sawyer at Bathurst; John Ritson, who had arrived in 1824 and was a stock-keeper for M. Balcombe at Argyle. Note John Macarthur's description of his own overseer: '. . . a respectable Young Man, who I hired in England from the King's Gardens at Kew. He is a Scotchman well skilled in Agriculture'. Macarthur's evidence to Bigge, n.d.

17. Comments by Brisbane on measures recommended by Bigge, *H.R.A.*, 1, XI, p. 577.

18. For comparative age groups of the three civil conditions, see Appendix 7.

19. For details of all native-born agricultural workers, see Appendix 10.

20. Note that this is a summary only; details of parentage, residence, etc., may be found in Appendix 10.

21. Comments by Brisbane on measures recommended by Bigge, *H.R.A.*, 1, XI, p. 577.

22. Evidence of the Rev. Robert Cartwright to Bigge, 26 November 1819.

23. Comments by Brisbane . . . , *H.R.A.*, 1, XI, p. 577.

24. Bigge, *Agriculture and Trade* . . . , p. 82.

25. Harris, *Settlers and Convicts* . . . , pp. 167, 182–5.

26. See 'The Myth of the Mariners', ch. 9. For Memorials from the native-born mariners and their parents, see Appendix 9.

27. Harris, *Settlers and Convicts* . . . , p. 88.

28. Phillip to Sydney, 15 May 1788, *H.R.A.*, 1, I, pp. 16ff. The sawyers were put ashore at Point Sutherland.

29. The *Sydney Gazette*, 15 July (Joseph Morley); 15 July (Simeon Lord); 22 July, 26 August, 2 September, 9 September (Simeon Lord); 23 September, 30 September (Bass and Bishop).

30. Note that references to Memorials mentioned in this chapter may be found in Index A.

31. Article reprinted in the *Australian*, 14 February 1827 (first published in England). The author is not named; from the working, style and sentiments, it is most probably based on 'A Letter from Sydney', attributed to E.G. Wakefield.

32. For parentage of native-born labourers, where this could be established, see Appendix 10.

33. Bigge, *Report on the Colony* . . . , pp. 19, 21–52.

34. Waldersee, *Catholic Society* . . . , p. 83.

35. Evidence of John Ellman, Jun., 'a substantial farmer', in *Report of the Select Committee on the Depressed State of Agriculture, P.P.*, 1821, IX, p. 121. Note that the flour, of which he would need four gallons a week, cost one shilling and three pence a gallon, that is, half of his weekly earnings; ibid., pp. 121–2.

36. William Cobbett, *Rural Rides*, London, 1912, vol. 2, pp. 1–2.

37. See Thompson, *The Making of the English Working Class* . . . , pp. 232–3: the difficulties of assessing standards in the period between 1790 and 1830.

38. Alexander Bell, Evidence to Commissioner Bigge, B.T., Box 21, p. 3646.

39. As with the landworkers, few of these native-born were baptized. Evidence as to parentage, where it exists, may be found in Appendix 10.

40. For districts in which the native-born labourers were employed, see Appendix 10.

41. Householders' Schedules, 1828 Census, Householders' Returns . . . , Box 47, pp. 283–41, M.L.

42. The term 'professional' has been chosen to denote a group with literate ability who were employed at 'white-collar' occupations. It consists of clerks, schoolmasters and a surgeon. For details of these native-born, see Appendix 10.

43. Col. Sec. Returns of the Colony, 1828, Police Establishments: Melville was approved from 5 March 1828.

44. *O.B.S.P.*, 1785–6, trial no. 224. See also Journal of Arthur Bowes, M.L. Ms., p. 6.

45. A detailed account of John Henderson may be found in the Miscellaneous Card drawer of M.L. It was compiled by T.D. Mutch. This account is based on those cards. Note that John Henderson, 'a surgeon', married Kezia Rose of Appin at St James' Church, 29 December 1828. It was noted that he was the son of Surgeon Balmain of the First Fleet. See also Ships' Musters . . . , M.L., *Minstrel* to London, 1820; the *Sydney Almanac*, 1828; the *Australian*, cited by Mutch.

46. Note that Wentworth attended Peterhouse at Cambridge, 'which had received copious benefactions from the Fitzwilliam family'. See Clark, *A History* . . . , vol. 2, pp. 48ff.

47. See comments by Brisbane on Bigge's Recommendations . . . , *H.R.A.*: 1. XI, p. 587.

48. *The Memoirs of James Hardy Vaux* . . . , McLachlan (ed.), pp. 99, 105, 110ff.

49. *Report of the Select Committee on Transportation*, House of Commons Papers, 1837–8, vol. XXII, Paper no. 669, p. 12.

50. Comments by Brisbane on Bigge's Recommendations . . . , *H.R.A.*, 1, XI, p. 587.

51. For native-born clerks, see Appendix 10. For native-born printers, dealers and publicans, ibid.

52. Harris, *Settlers and Convicts* . . . , p. 86.

53. Governors' Despatches, Brisbane, 1824, Despatch no. 13, A.O.N.S.W.

54. Ibid., vol. 3, no. 31, pp. 441–444.
55. Col. Sec., Returns of the Colony, Military Returns, Returns of the Local Corps, 1826, p. 61, A.O.N.S.W.
56. For the sons of fathers serving in the New South Wales Corps, see Appendix 2. For native-born who enlisted in the New South Wales Corps, see ibid. See also W.O. 25, Returns, Various.
57. For native-born constables, see Appendix 10. Note that there were no native-born in Bigge's list of colonial magistrates, *Report on the Colony...*, p. 80.
58. Bigge Appendix ... , B.T., Box 21, p. 35447, n.d., A.O.N.S.W.
59. Col. Sec. In-Letters, 4/1844B, p. 794, 4/1835, Memorial 31A. For the salaries paid and men employed, see Col. Sec., Returns of the Colony, 1828, Police Establishments, M.L. Chief Constable John Thorn received £130/-/- per year; Frederick Meredith £100/-/- a year; James Blackman, Chief Constable and Pound Keeper, £70/-/- a year; a district constable's salary averaged £51/17/-; an ordinary constable, £41/3/6; an ordinary constable and scourger, £36/12/- (there were no native-born scourgers). John Small, 'a constable of 12 years' received an annual pension of £9/3/-.
60. A search of the records of the Criminal Courts has not revealed any native-born who was capitally convicted during this period. Among the Memorials and Petitions in Mitigation of Sentence was a Memorial from native-born John Marman, sentenced to 'two years on board one of the colonial vessels'; Col. Sec. In-Letters, 4/1763, p. 237. Another Petition was from Joshua Peek senior, 'a prisoner of the Crown at Newcastle, together with his two sons, sent there from Van Diemen's Land two years ago', requesting permission to manufacture tobacco; ibid., 4/1867, p. 12.

BIBLIOGRAPHY (SELECT)

INDEX

1. Bibliographies, Indexes, Works of Reference
2. British Parliamentary Papers, Debates
3. Material copied by the Australian Joint Copying Project
4. Published Records, Collections of Documents
5. Newspapers, Periodicals, Contemporary and Modern
6. Official Records in the Possession of the State Archives Office of New South Wales and the Mitchell Library, Sydney
7. Private Papers in the Possession of the Dixson Library, Sydney; the Mitchell Library, Sydney; the National Library, Canberra; the State Library of Victoria; Sydney Catholic Archives, St. Mary's Cathedral, Sydney
8. Contemporary Printed Books, Reprints and Facsimile Editions
9. Modern Sources: A. Books
10. Modern Sources: B. Journal Articles
11. Modern Sources: C. Unpublished Theses
12. Modern Sources: D. Conference Papers, Circulated and/or Published

ABBREVIATIONS USED IN THE BIBLIOGRAPHY

Archives, libraries

The Archives Office of New South Wales	A.O.N.S.W.
The Sydney Archdiocesan Archives	St. Mary's Cathedral Archives
The Mitchell Library, Sydney	M.L.
The National Library of Australia, Canberra	N.L.A.
The State Library of Victoria	State Library, Victoria

Journals

The Australian Catholic Historical Society Journal	*J.A.C.H.S.*
Australian Economic History Review (formerly *Business Archives*)	*A.E.H.R. (Bus. Arch.)*
Australian Geographer	*A.G.*
Australian Jewish Historical Society Journal	*A.J.H.S.J.*
Australian Literary Studies	*Aust. Lit. Stud.*

Canadian Historical Review	*Can. Hist. Rev.*
Historical Studies, Australia and New Zealand	*H.S.*
Journal of the Royal Australian Historical Society	*J.R.A.H.S.*
Labour History	*L.H.*
Document collections	
Historical Records of Australia	*H.R.A.*
Historical Records of New South Wales	*H.R.N.S.W.*
Australian Dictionary of Biography	*A.D.B.*
Biographical Index, A.D.B., A.N.U.	Bio. Index, A.D.B.
London Missionary Society	L.M.S.
Society for the Propagation of the Gospel	S.P.G.
Parliamentary Papers	*P.P.*
British Parliamentary Papers	*B.P.P.*
Old Bailey Sessions Papers	*O.B.S.P.*
Australian Joint Copying Project	A.J.C.P.
Admiralty	Adm.
Board of Trade	B.T.
Colonial Office	C.O.
Foreign Office	F.O.
Home Office	H.O.
Public Record Office	P.R.O.
Treasury	T.
War Office	W.O.
Colonial Secretary	Col. Sec.
Memorials	M.
Petitions in Mitigation of Sentence	P.M.S.

1. BIBLIOGRAPHIES, INDEXES, WORKS OF REFERENCE

Adam, M.I., Ewing, J. & Munro, J., *Guide to the Principal Parliamentary Papers Relating to the Dominions, 1812–1911,* Edinburgh, 1913.

Australian Books, A Select List of New Publications and Standard Works in Print, National Library, Canberra, 1945 to date.

Australian Dictionary of Biography, Vols. 1, 2, D. Pike (gen. ed.), Melbourne, 1966, 1967.

Australiana Collection, H.H. Dutton, Catalogue, Adelaide, South Australia, 1966.

Australian Joint Copying Project Handbook, Parts 1-8, National Library, Canberra, and Library of New South Wales.

Australian National Bibliography, National Library, Canberra, 1961 to date.

Australian Public Affairs Information Service, a subject index to current literature, National Library, Canberra, 1945 to date. Relevant sections: Australian history, convicts.

Biographical Index and Family Papers, Australian Dictionary of Biography Office, A.N.U., Canberra.

Borchardt, Dietrich Hans, *Australian Bibliography, A Guide to Printed Sources of Information,* Rushcutters Bay, New South Wales, 1976.

Catalogue of Manuscripts, Letters, Documents in the Private Collection of the State Library of Victoria.

Dissertation Abstracts International, Ann Arbor, Michigan, University Microfilms, Vol. 30, no. 1, July 1969 to date.

Ferguson, Sir John Alexander, *Bibliography of Australia 1784–1900*, vols. I–VII, facsimile edition, 1975.

General Index to the Accounts and Papers, Reports of Commissioners, Estimates, 1801–1852, National Library, Canberra.

General Post Office Directory, New South Wales, October 1832, Mitchell Library, Sydney.

Gibbney, H.J., Biographical Register, Coombes Building, A.N.U., Canberra.

Guide to Convict Records in the Archives Office of New South Wales, The Archives Authority of New South Wales, Sydney, 1981.

Guide to Records Relating to Ships and Free Passengers, Archives Office, New South Wales.

Hendy-Pooley, G., *Index to the Sydney Gazette 1803–1825 inclusive*, Sydney, 1913, Typescript in National Library, Canberra.

Historical Abstracts, A Quarterly covering the Worlds Periodical Literature, 1775–1945, Vol. 1, no. 1 March to Vol. 16 no. 4, December 1970 becomes *Historical Abstracts, Part A, Modern History Abstracts, 1775–1914*, Santa Barbara, California, American Bibliographic Centre, Clio Press, vol. 17, no. 1, January 1971 to date. Sections: Australia: national character, settlement, economic history, penal settlements, social and cultural history, historical materials in Great Britain, manuscripts, historiography, crime, police and penal system, folklore, immigration, imperialism, local history, military history. Roman Catholic Church and social history.

Hogan, Terry, Yarwood, A.T. & Ward, Russel (comps.), *Index to Journal Articles on Australian History*.

How to Locate Australian Theses, A guide to theses in progress or completed at Australian Universities and the University of Papua New Guinea, The Library of the Australian National University, Canberra, 1977.

Index to Baptisms in New South Wales 1787–1800, transcribed by H.J. Rumsey, Mitchell Library, Sydney.

Index to Theses Accepted for Higher Degrees in the Universities of Great Britain and Ireland, London, Vol. I, 1950–51 to date.

Johnson, K. & Sainty, M. (eds), *Gravestone Inscriptions, N.S.W.*, Vol. I, Sydney, 1973.

Johnson, K. & Sainty, M. (eds), *The 1828 Census*, Sydney, 1980.

Johnson, K. & Sainty, M. (eds), *Land Grants, 1788–1809, New South Wales, Norfolk Island, Van Diemen's Land*, North Sydney, 1974.

Journal of the Statistical Society of London, General Index, London, 1854.

Lewin, Evans, *Subject Catalogue of the Library of the Royal Empire Society, Vol. 2, The Commonwealth of Australia, the Dominion of New Zealand, The South Pacific, General Voyages and Travels, and Arctic and Antarctic Regions*, The Royal Commonwealth Society, London, 1967.

Library of Congress of the United States of America: A Selected List of References on Australia, Library of Congress, Washington, 1942.

McKernan, M. & Collins, Diane, *Honours Theses in History, compiled for the Australian Historical Association*, Historical Association, Sydney, 1979.

Mander-Jones, Phyllis (ed.), *Manuscripts in the British Isles Relating to Australia, New Zealand and the Pacific*, Canberra, 1972.

Mutch, T.D., Register of Births, Deaths and Marriages, 1788–1814, 1815–1957, Mitchell Library, Sydney.

Mutch, T.D., Miscellaneous Indents 1790–1800, Mitchell Library, Sydney.

New South Wales Pocket Almanack 1806, 1808–1809.

Notebook of Quotations, Maxims and Phrases probably compiled by an Irishman, Ms. 1717, Mitchell Library, Sydney.

References to Australia in the *Times* newspaper between 1791 and 1829. Typescript in the National Library, Canberra.

Rumsey, H.J., Index to Baptisms, New South Wales, 1787–1800, B1182, B1186 Burials.

Subject Catalogue of the Royal Commonwealth Society, London, Vol. 6, *Australia, New Zealand, Pacific*, Boston, Massachusetts, 1971.

Union List of Higher Degree Theses in Australian Libraries, Hobart, University of Tasmania Library, cumulative to 1965 then annually to date.

The Macquarie Dictionary, Sydney, 1981.

Lexique historique de la France d'Ancien Regime, Guy Cabourdin and Georges Viard, Paris, 1878.

2. BRITISH PARLIAMENTARY PAPERS, DEBATES

Year	No. of Paper	Short Title, Volume, Page
1812	341	Select Committee on Transportation, 11, 573
1819	579	Select Committee on Gaols, VII, 1.
1822	448	Commissioner Bigge, on the State of the Colony of New South Wales, XX, 539.
1823	33	Commissioner Bigge, on Judicial Establishments of New South Wales and Van Diemen's Land, X, 515. Commissioner Bigge, on the State of Agriculture and Trade in New South Wales, X, 607.
1828	477	Governor Macquarie's Report to Bathurst, XXI, 538.
1837–8	518	Report from the Select Committee on Transportation, XIX, 186.

Great Britain: Parliamentary Papers relating to Australia, 1828.

Great Britain: Parliamentary Papers, Colonies - Australia, Vol. 3, 1816–1830.

Great Britain: Parliamentary Debates, 1770–1830.

Parliamentary History, Vols. 25–36, 1785–1803.

Cobbett's Parliamentary Debates, Vols. 1–21, 1803–4.

Hansard's Parliamentary Debates, Vols. 22–51, 1812–20.

Parliamentary Debates, Hansard, New Series, Vols. 1–16, 1820–27.

3. AUSTRALIAN JOINT COPYING PROJECT

Colonial Office

C.O. 324/66, 84–87, 105. Colonies, General. Entry Books. Series 1. 1801–1840, Reels 1201–1203.

C.O. 202/1–8 New South Wales. Entry Books 1798–1813. Reels 55–56.

C.O. 207/1–8 New South Wales. Entry Books relating to convicts 1788–1867. Reels 57–59.

C.O. 324/46, 61, 64–65, 103, 110–131, Colonies General. Entry Books, Series 1. 1793–1815. Reels 423–424.

C.O. 323/44–45, 91–95, 117–236, (IND.8300), Colonies, General. Original Correspondence. 1795–1831. Reels 934–938.

C.O. 325/3–36 (various). Colonies. General. Miscellanea. 1791–1858. Reels 996–997.

C.O. 206/61–62, New South Wales. Miscellanea. 1810–1845. Reels 997–998.

C.O. 714/6–15, 113–118, 130, 148–153, 162–163 (IND.18456–18629). Correspondence Indexes to 1812–1870. Reels 1043–1050.

C.O. 854/1–6. Colonies. General. Circular despatches 1808–1861. Reels 1053–1054.

C.O. 201/1–56. Original Correspondence. New South Wales, Despatches.

War Office

W.O. 4/845–846, Correspondence. Out-Letters. Secretary-at-war. 1789–1810. Reel 1073.

W.O. 40/16 Correspondence. Selected unnumbered papers 1802, Reel 1075.

W.O. 57/35 Commissariat Department. In-Letters. 1810–1815. Reels 1076–1077.

W.O. 25/642–643. Description and Succession Books (Regimental) New South Wales Corps. 1808–1816. Reel 1302

W.O. 4/845–846. Correspondence. New South Wales Corps 1789–1810. Reels 412, 1073.

W.O. 12/11230. Returns. Muster Books and Pay Lists. New South Wales Royal Veterans. 1826–1832. Reel 3917.

W.O. 17/2294–2313. Monthly Returns. New South Wales. 1791–1792, 1810–1829. Reels 418, 912–915.

Home Office

H.O. 10/1–18 Criminal, Convicts, New South Wales and Tasmania. 1788–1828, Reels 59–65.

H.O. 10/19–20 New South Wales General Muster 1825, Reel 66.

H.O. 10/21–28. New South Wales Census. 1828. Reels 67–69.

H.O. 10/36–37 New South Wales General Muster 1822, and 1806. Reel 72.

H.O. 11/6 Convict transportation Registers. Convicts transported 1787–1828. Reels 87–89.

H.O. 13/4–20. Criminal Papers. Entry Books. Correspondence and Warrants. 1786–1810. Reels 419–442.

H.O. 13/21–52 Criminal Papers. Entry Books. Correspondence and Warrants 1810–1828. Reels 3082–3094. 3097A–3098.

H.O. 16/1–2 Criminal Old Bailey Sessions. Returns of Convicted Prisoners 1815–1822. Reel 1542.

H.O. 26/1–24 Criminal Registers. Series 1. In Newgate Gaol etc. 1791–1828. Reels 2730–2741.

H.O. 27/1–33 Criminal Registers. Series II. In Gaols in all counties. 1805–1827. Reels 2752–2775.

H.O. 28/4–24 Various Correspondence and Papers, Departmental, Admiralty, Correspondence. 1784–1789. Reel 1163.

H.O. 28/25–50. Various. Correspondence and Papers, Departmental. Admiralty, Correspondence. 1799–1828. Reels 1055–1067.

H.O. 29/1–7. Various Correspondence and Papers, Departmental. Admiralty, entry books. 1779–1836. Reel 1164.

Blacker Manuscripts: relating to D'Arcy Wentworth and sons. Armagh County Museum. Reel M389.

Admiralty
Adm. 1/3824, Admiralty and Secretariat Papers. 1787–1792. Reel 412.

Board of Trade
B.T. 6/58, 88. General. Miscellanea, 1792–1807 Reel 288.

Privy Council Office
P.C. 1/37, 40, 61–62, 64. Papers, mainly unbound. 1786–1789. Reel 619.
P.C. 2/131–187 (various), Registers 1786–1810, Reel 619.

Treasury
T. 46/22 Registers. Victualling Lists. 1787. Reel 1106.
T. 62/120–121. Miscellanea. Maps and plans, Series 1, 1828. Reel 1106.
T. 64/83 Miscellanea. Various. 1813–1827. Reel 1107.

Records of cases from the County of Middlesex tried in the London Criminal Court 1774–1793. Greater London Record Office (Middlesex Records) Reel M581.

Quarter Sessions Records 1787–1789. Wiltshire Record Office. Reel M935.

Dr R.R. Madden's papers relating to the United Irishmen. University of Dublin. Trinity College Library. Reel M854.

Ipswich Borough Records 1789. Suffolk Record Office, Ipswich Branch. Reels M941–943.

Palmer, The Reverend Thomas Fyshe. Letters 1794–1796. Reel M391.

The Moore Papers 1793–1794: Memoirs and letters of Rev. Richard Johnson. Reel M.677.

Methodist Missionary Society, Records 1798–1916: Committee minutes 1804–1865. Reels M118–120.

Marsden Family papers 1793–1938. Reel M.382.

Macquarie Family Papers 1782–1839. Reel M460.

London Missionary Society: Records. Australia: Journals of W. Shelley, R. Hassall, L.E. Threlkeld and R.C. Morgan 1800–1842. Reel M.11. Letters 1798–1919. M11, M72–90, M638–640.

Grant, John, 1769–1810. Documents 1769–1803; Letters 1803–1810; Poems 1804–1805, Journal 1805–1810; Notebook 1809. Reel M462.

Dwyer, Michael, Papers 1798–1900.
   i)   Luke Cullen Papers. About the life of the Irish insurgent and New South Wales settler Michael Dwyer.
   ii) Notes, drafts and cuttings compiled by J. Cyril M. Weale c.1900. Reel M603.

Cunningham, Allan, Papers 1814–1839. Reel M692.

Scott Family Papers. Letters 1819–1852 from New South Wales to family in England. Cumbria Record Office. Reel M983.

Records of criminal cases from the City of London, tried at the Old Bailey 1756–1793.
   Index to persons indicted 1756–1792.
   Sessions Minute Books 1783–1793.
   Corporation of London Records Office. Reel M580.

Sir Joseph Banks, Correspondence 1773–1815. Reel M469.

Blackburn, David, Correspondence 1785–1796. Reel M971.

Papers of Lieutenant Richard Bastard and logbooks. Bedford County Record Office. Reel M591.

4. PUBLISHED RECORDS, COLLECTIONS OF DOCUMENTS

Clark, C.M.H. (ed.), *Select Documents in Australian History, 1788–1850*, Sydney, 1975.
Sources for Australian History, London, 1957.

Evans, L., & Pledger, P.P. (eds), *Contemporary Sources and Opinions in Modern British History*, Vol. 2, Melbourne, 1967.

Evans. L., & Nichols, P. (eds), *Convicts and Colonial Society, 1788–1853*, Sydney, 1976.

Hewison, A. (ed.), *The Macquarie Decade: Documents Illustrating the History of New South Wales, 1810–1821*, Melbourne, 1972.

Historical Records of Australia, Series 1, Vols. I–XVII; Series 4, Vol. I.

Historical Records of New South Wales, Vols. I–VII.

Historical Records of Newcastle, 1787–1887. 1 Vol., 1897.

Historical Records of New Zealand, 2 Vols.

Ingleton, G.C., *True Patriots All or News from Early Australia as told in a Collection of Broadsides garnered and decorated by Geoffrey C. Ingleton*, Sydney, 1952.

Old Bailey Sessions Papers, London, 1776–1833. 44 Vols.

Ritchie, J. (ed.), *The Evidence to the Bigge Reports, New South Wales under Governor Macquarie*, 2 Vols, Melbourne, 1971. Vol. 1: *The Oral Evidence*; Vol. 2: *The Written Evidence*.

Ward, R.B. (ed.), *Such was Life; Select Documents in Australian Social History, 1788–1850*, Sydney, 1969.

5. NEWSPAPERS, PERIODICALS

Contemporary
The *Australian*, 1824–1830.
The *Currency Lad*, 1832–1834.
The *Monitor*, 1826–1830.
The *Sydney Gazette and New South Wales Advertiser*, 1803–1830.
The *Edinburgh Review*.

Modern
The *Sydney Morning Herald*, December 1980, January 1981.

6. OFFICIAL RECORDS IN THE POSSESSION OF THE STATE ARCHIVES OFFICE OF NEW SOUTH WALES AND THE MITCHELL LIBRARY, SYDNEY

Note: There is occasional duplication with the records copied by the Australian Joint Copying Project.

'A List of Persons who have been Victualled from His Majesty's Stores commencing the 26th. day of February 1788, with the Births, Deaths and Discharges to 17th. November 1788., (M.L.).

Bench of Magistrates: Bench Books, 1788–1821, 1/296–1/304; County of Cumberland: Bench Book, 1815–21, 7/2691; Bench of Magistrates, 1815–21; Bench Book, 17 July 1815–15 July 1816, 7/2643; Bench of Magistrates, Sydney, Petitions for Maintenance in Bastardy, 1810–1814, 5/1153; Return of Proceedings taken at the Magistrates Court, Parramatta, 1 January–30 September 1822, X643, 1 July–31 December 1824, 4/6671; Return of Proceedings at the Court of General Sessions of the Peace, Parramatta, January–March 1826, 4/1917.2. (A.O.N.S.W.)

Colonial Secretary: Letters Received:
Petitions to the Governor from convicts for mitigation of sentences, 1810–1826, 4/1846–7;
Petitions from wives of convicts for their husbands to be assigned to them, 1826–7, 4/7084;
Copies of affidavits notifying loss of tickets-of-leave, certificates of freedom, etc., 4/1690;
Letters Received: 1789–1828
Letters Received: Bathurst, 4/1789; Newcastle, 6 Vols., 4/1894–4/1809; Oxley, 1810–1826, 4/1824, 4/1815; Wellington Valley, 1818–24, 4/1818.
Memorials re Land: 1810, 2 Vols., 1813–19, 1820–21, 5 Vols.

Colonial Secretary: Letters Sent:
Local and Overseas, 1809–1822, 4/3490–4/3504A.
Within the Colony, 1814–27, 4/3493–4/3520;
In-Letters (specific reference in text of thesis):

4/1094.2;   4/1732;   4/1733;   4/1752;   4/1756;

4/1760;	4/1762;	4/1763;	4/1765;	4/1770;
4/1771;	4/1779;	4/1775;	4/1780;	4/1782;
4/1786;	4/1787;	4/1788;	4/1821A;	4/1822A;
4/1823;	4/1824A;	4/1824B;	4/1825A;	4/1826B;
4/1826;	4/1828;	4/1829;	4/1830;	4/1831;
4/1832;	4/1833;	4/1834B;	4/1835B;	4/1836B;
4/1837;	4/1838B;	4/1839A;	4/1839B;	4/1840;
4/1841A;	4/1841B;	4/1842;	4/1843B;	4/1844C;
4/1846;	4/1848;	4/1848;	4/1849;	4/1858;
4/1860;	4/1866;	4/1873.		

Convict Indents: 1788–1810, 4/3996–7; first fleet, second fleet and ships arriving 1791–8, 4/3998; 1799–1801 (various ships), 4/3999–4/4003; 1801–1814, 4/4004; 1814–28, 4/4005–4/4013. (Note 4/4010 photocopy only).

Copies of Government and General Orders and Notices, 1789–96, Safe 1/88; General Orders of Lieutenant-Governor Paterson, September 1795–December 1797, Safe 1/86; General Order Book, 1809–1810; New South Wales Government and General Orders, Safe 1/86. Copies of Proclamations, Government and General Orders, etc., made and published by Governors-in-Chief of New South Wales from the establishment of the Colony to the end of 1821, 7/2655. Copies of Government and General Orders and Notices, 1810–1818, 7/2657–2658.

Court of Civil Jurisdiction: Precepts, 1797–1814, 1164; Rough Minutes of Proceedings and related case papers, 1788–1809, 1092; Minutes of Proceedings, 1799–1901, 1801–14, 17 Vols., 1095–1111.

Court of Criminal Jurisdiction: Reports of Proceedings, 1788–1825: Schedule of Prisoners Tried: 1147/A. 1147/B, X905, 1149, 1150, 1119, 1121; Miscellaneous Criminal Papers 1788–91, 1798–1800, 1152; Indictments, informations, depositions and related papers (Sydney), 1817–23, SB 576–83; Return, 153 convicts who after receiving remission, or after expiration of sentences, had been convicted of felony in the colonial courts, 12 March 1810–22 September 1823, 4/1638; Reports of prisoners tried in the Courts of Criminal Jurisdiction, June–November 1820, February 1822–January 1824, 4/7021; Judgement Book, 22 February 1822–11 February 1824, 4/1264.

Governors' Despatches: Vols. 1–3, A1192; Despatches to Secretary of State, and to Under-Secretary of State, 4/1364–5; Despatches Recommending Free Settlers, 4/1094; Transcripts of Missing Despatches from Governors of New South Wales, 1823–32, A 1267. (M.L.)

Lists, Various:
Lists of all Grants and Leases of Land Registered in the Colonial Secretary's Office between 26th. day of January 1788 and the 31st. day of December 1809, 7/2731;
Governor Darling's List of Land Grants to the Native-born 'A Return of Lands Granted to Individuals Born within the Colony from the First of January 1810 to the First of January, 1827'. (Copy: Q991 3, M.L.)

List of Free Settlers from England who have arrived and been Discharged from Different Ships, 1801., C.O.D., 201/202;
List of Persons holding land in the District of Baulkham Hills, A 767. (M.L.)

Morgues and Coroners Inquests: Reports of Inquests, 1796–1824, to June 1828, 2/8286–90, 5 Vols; Morgues and Coroners Inquests, 1809–1822, 4/1819.

Population Musters, Land and Stock:
New South Wales Mainland, 1800, 1 Vol., 1811, 1814, 1819, 3 Vols., 1820, Population of Richmond, Windsor, Castlereagh and Evan, 3 Vols.; 1820, Population of Wilberforce, 1 sheet; 1822, Population of Wilberforce and Liverpool, 2 Vols.; Muster for 1825, (M.L.); Col. Sec. Returns of the Colony, various; 1828 Census: Return of the Population of New South Wales according to a Census taken in November 1826, (based on Home Office Papers, 10/21–8), (A.O.N.S.W.); 1828 Census: Householders returns, Boxes, 47/1238–41; note that 1806 Muster is on P.R.O. reel 72. Land and Stock returns, New South Wales, 1818–22, 7 Vols. (A.O.N.S.W.)

Minutes of the Executive Council, New South Wales, 4/1516.

Register of Conditional Pardons: Royal Pardon Warrant, 1791–1873, C.O.D., 215; Absolute and Conditional Pardons, 1792–1809. SZ 75/47/76; Conditional Pardons, 1791–1825, C.O.D., 19.

Ships Musters, December 1816–June 1821, 4/4771; July 1821–December 1821. 4/4772; 1822. 4/4773, 1823, 4/4774, 1824–5, 4/4775. (Microfilm in A.O.N.S.W., reels 561/562.)

Supreme Court Documents: Bundle No. 1, Precepts 1788–1808; Bundle No. 5, Court of Criminal Judicature, 1788–1797; Bundle No. 9, Pardons, 1788–1803; Bundle No. 11, Magistrates Court, 1788–1800; Bundle No. 19, Miscellaneous, 1788–1803; Bundle No. 31, Probate, 1790–1814. Location: Bundle 9, Judge-Advocate's Office, 5/1151; Bundle 19, 5/1156; Bundle 1, 5/1143; Bundle 31, 5/1166.

7. PRIVATE PAPERS AND MANUSCRIPTS IN THE POSSESSION OF THE DIXSON LIBRARY, SYDNEY; THE MITCHELL LIBRARY, SYDNEY; THE NATIONAL LIBRARY, CANBERRA; THE STATE LIBRARY OF VICTORIA; SYDNEY CATHOLIC ARCHIVES, ST. MARY'S CATHEDRAL, SYDNEY

Arnold, Dr J.,   Journals, August 1810–December 1845; Letters, etc., 1810. (M.L.)
Atkins, R.,   Journal, 1792–1810. (M.L.)
Banks, Sir Joseph,   Papers. Braebourne Collection:
Vol. 3, Australia, 1786–1800;
Vol. 4, Australia, 1801–20;

Vol. 6, Miscellaneous Correspondence, 1766–1818;
Vol. 7, King, 1788–1805;
Vol. 8, Caley, 1795–1808;
Vol. 22, Captain Bligh and New South Wales, 1806–11;
Papers, 1766–1820, Ms. 743;
Correspondence, 1788–1820, Microfilm, FM4/1722. (M.L.)
Bastard, Lieutenant Richard, Papers and Logbooks:
1816–18, log of the *Sir William Bensley;*
1819, log of the *Lord Wellington.* (M591)
Bathurst, Henry, 3rd, Earl, Letters, 1825–7. (M.L.)
Baudin, Nicholas, Drawings, etc., Ms. 760. (M.L.)
Bauer, F.L., Drawings, etc., Ms. 840. (M.L.)
Black, J.H., Papers: John Henry Black, 1809–1812, Ms. 1188. (M.L.)
Blackburn, David, Letters:
to Richard Knight, Ms, (M.L.);
to his sister Margaret, and his mother. (A.J.C.P., Reel M971)
Bligh, Mrs. Elizabeth, Letters, 1781–1807. Ms. 4–92B. (M.L.)
Bligh, William, Miscellaneous, Letters, etc.:
Papers, 1808–10. (M.L.)
Blaxland, William, junior, Journal, Wallis Plains, 14 February 1821–
12 August 1821. (M.L.)
Blaxland Papers, 1793–1923. (M.L.)
Bonwick Transcripts: Bound volumes: Vol. 1, Biography Missionary;
New South Wales Returns, 1819–20;
Boxes: 1, 5, 9, 10, 11, 12, 13, 15, 16, 17, 19, 20, 21, 22, 23, 24, 25, 26, 28.
Brisbane Family, Papers 1715–1810:
Sir Thomas Brisbane, 1702–1859. Ms. 1191/1. (M.L.)
Brisbane, Sir Thomas, Letter Book. (M.L.)
Bowman Family, Papers (M.L.)
Brisbane, Sir Thomas, Papers, 1812–37, Microfilm, FM4/1626–7. (M.L.)
Broughton, William, Copy of marriage certificate, etc. Doc. 1063. (M.L.)
Caley, George, Papers, 1801–8, Microfilm FM4/2568. (M.L.)
Letters by, February 1809, 1816–18. Microfilm FM5/402–451. (M.L.)
Campbell, Captain James, Letter to his friend, Dr. Farr. Doc. 1174. (M.L.)
Catchpole, Margaret, Letters, etc., 1787–; 1807–8. Mss. 4/97, 4/80.
(M.L.)
Papers, contemporary accounts/newspapers, etc. (A.J.C.P., Reel M944).
Collins, David, Collins Family Papers, 1746–1867. Ms. 700. (M.L.)
Four Letters, 1793–1810. (Dixon Library)
Crook, William Pascoe, Letter to Revd. M. Wilkes, 16 November 1797, in
Letters Received by T. Haweis and others, Ms. 633. (M.L.)
Crook, Mrs. Hannah, Mrs. William Crook. Journal. September 1819–
August 1821. From Papetie. Ms. 5–194B. (M.L.)
Cunningham, Alan, Copy of exploration Journals, 1817–19; Letters; in
Notebooks and Correspondence, Ms. 75/1–19. (M.L.)
Papers, 1814–39. Microfilm FM4/3101. (M.L.). Letters by, 1817, in
Linnean Society of London Papers, 1790–1870: 1. Correspondence.
Microfilm FM4/2699. (M.L.)

Journal, May 1819–September 1822. Microfilm FM4/3104. (M.L.)

Darlot, James M., Reminiscences, 1834. Box 21/1. (State Library of Victoria).

Dredge, James, Diary, 24 May 1817–17 December 1833. (State Library)

Fitzpatrick, Ambrose, Letters of, dated 30 November 1884. (Sydney Archdiocesan Archives)

Forbes, Amelia Sophia, 'Sydney Society in Crown Colony Days', 1824–1839. Ms. 943. (M.L.)

Foveaux, J., Correspondence, etc., in New South Wales, Col. Sec. Papers, 1799–1830, Ms. 681/1–2. (M.L.)

Letter Book, Norfolk Island. A1444. (M.L.)

Godber, Josiah, Letters to Rebecca, his wife. Ms. 4199. (M.L.)

Godsell, Thomas, Journal on the voyage of the *Duff*, 1796. Ms. 21. (M.L.)

Gore, William, Land transactions, 1816–17. Microfilm FM3/659. (M.L.)

Greenway, Francis, Memoranda to from Lachlan Macquarie, 1817–22. Doc. 957. (M.L.)

Harris, Dr. John, Papers, 1791. A1597. (M.L.)

Hassall, Anne, Mrs. Thomas Hassall, nee Anne Marsden. Letters, Correspondence, etc., in Letters to Mrs. Stokes from the Marsden Family. Ms. 719. (M.L.)

Hassall, Anne, Correspondence. Vols. 1 and 2. (M.L.)

Hayes, M., Letters of Michael Hayes and Francois Girard, 1799–1833. (M.L.)

Henry, William, Papers re William Henry, 1774–1862. Ms. 1330. (M.L.)

Hume, Papers. (M.L.)

Hunter, John, Letter Book, 1795–1802. A1787. (M.L.)

Hunter, Captain John, Journal, 25 October 1786–22 May 1791. (Dixson Library)

Johnson, Rev. Richard, Letters to the Society for the Propagation of the Gospel, from Bain and Johnson on education in New South Wales, 1789–1799. (M.L.)

Johnston, George, Will, Documents, etc. Ms. 828. (M.L.)

Papers. (Dixon Library)

King, Anna Josepha, Journal. (M.L.)

Correspondence. Col. Sec. Papers 1799–1830. Ms. 681. (M.L.)

King, P.G., Letter Book, 1797–1808. Ms. 582. (M.L.)

Family Papers, including correspondence, journals, sketches by: Phillip Parker King and his wife, Harriet. Ms. 673. (M.L.)

Correspondence, in Col. Sec. Papers, 1799–1830. Ms. 681. (M.L.)

Lacey James, Letter to Mr. Macartney, 18 August 1792. Ms. (M.L.)

Lawson, William, Deeds to land grant at Kurrajong, etc. in Papers of Ellen Elizabeth Lamrock. A5429. (M.L.)

Correspondence, 19 December 1817–2 July 1824. (M.L.)

Levey, Solomon, Papers concerning estate, 1794–1846. A5441. (M.L.)

Linnean Society of London, Papers 1790–1870: 1. Correspondence, A. and B; III. Society for Promoting Natural History, 1789–97, Letter from W. Paterson re exploration of the Hawkesbury and discovery of the Grose River. Microfilm FM4/2699. (M.L.)

London Missionary Society, Records, 1797–1925. Journals and corre-spondence relating to Australia, 1798–1919. Microfilm FM4/328. (M.L.)

Lord Simeon, junior. Some letters from, to David Ramsay, c.1827. In Papers of David Ramsay. Ms. 564. (M.L.)

Macquarie family, Papers relating to Lachlan Macquarie, Governor of New South Wales and his immediate family. Microfilm FM4/1725. (M.L.)

Macquarie, Lachlan, Governor, Letters to his brother Charles, 1799–1824. Negative photoprints, 3 vols. Originals in the National Library of Scotland. Ms. 82. (M.L.)

Marsden, George, A.B.C. book of Maxims, 1720–1728, Ms. 1252. (M.L.)

Marsden family, Letters to Mrs Stokes, 1794–1824. 1 vol. Ms. 719. (M.L.)

Marsden, Rev. Samuel, Essays concerning New South Wales, 1807–18, with list of females in the colony 1806. Ms. 18. (M.L.)

Marsden, Rev. Samuel, Papers, 1794–1857. 2 boxes. A5412 (M.L.)

Miscellaneous Documents, 1770–1819. King, Phillip Parker, Admiral. Doc. 920. (M.L.)

Muir, Thomas, Papers relating to the Scottish Martyrs, mainly to the trials and transportation of Thomas Muir and Rev. Thomas Fysche Palmer, 1793–1814, 1 vol. Ms. 948 (M.L.)

New South Wales—Colonial Secretary, Papers 1799–1830+ 5 vols. Ms. 681. (M.L.)

Nichols, George Robert, Papers, 1822–1850, 1 folder. Ms. 375. (M.L.)

Oxley, John, Notebook, 1815–1823. Illus. with relates MS. 1 box. Ms. 589. (M.L.)

Prescriptions, Medical, Notebook IV. Microfilm FM/709. (M.L.)

Ramsay, David, Papers 1818–1845, 3 vols. Ms. 564. (M.L.)

Redfern Estate, Papers 1894–1938, 3 boxes, A5407. (M.L.)

Reibey, Mary, Mrs Thomas, Papers of the Reibey estate 1811–1909, 3 boxes. A5327. (M.L.)

Riley, Edward, Papers 1813–1907; with related documents 1793–1839, 6 boxes. A5326. (M.L.)

Rouse, Richard, Records probably of the Paramatta Lumber Yard presumably kept by or for Richard Rouse, 1805?–1821, with letters to Rouse, 1818–1841. Microfilm FM4/2119 (M.L.)

St John's Church, Wilberforce, N.S.W., Registers of baptisms, marriages and burials, 1826–1963, 1 reel. Microfilm FM4/1727. (M.L.)

Scott, Clara Eleanor, Mrs Richard, Papers relating to the Batman and Scott Families, 1726–1947, 1 box. Ms. 684. (M.L.)

Senior B.M., Lieut., 'Journal from the 10th of April 1810 to the 25th October 1810 during a Voyage from New South Wales to old England in the *Hindostan*', 1 folder. Ms. 820. (M.L.)

Siddens, Richard?, Capt., Pocket book; being an interleaved copy of the New South Wales pocket almanac for 1816 containing Ms memoranda and tallies. Ms. 653. (M.L.)

Smyth, Arthur Bowes, Papers connected with Arthur Bowes Smyth, 1962–1964, 1 box. Ms. 995. (M.L.)

The *Sydney Gazette and New South Wales Advertiser* Papers, 1824–1838, 37 vols. Ms. 26. (M.L.)

Underwood family,   Papers, 1793–1888, 2 boxes, A54444. (M.L.)

Walton, John, 'The History of John Smith (c.1762–1846) and his descendants and of Matthew Pearce (c.1762–1831) and his descendants'; with index 1964. Ms. 1071. (M.L.)

Wardell, Heirs of Dr,   Papers, 1793–1897, 2 boxes. A5330. (M.L.)

Wentworth family,   Papers 1674–1943, 4 boxes, 1 portfolio. Ms. 8. (M.L.)

Whalan family,   Papers 1791–1861, 1 vol., 1 folder. Ms. 6. (M.L.)

Wilshire, James, 'Journal .. kept on board the *Royal Admiral* ... from England to New South Wales', 5 May–July 1800. 1 volume. Ms. 1296. (M.L.)

Woodriff family,   Papers of Captain Daniel Woodriff, Captain Daniel James Woodriff and Daniel James Woodriff the younger 1803–1865, 1 box. Ms. 613. (M.L.)

8. CONTEMPORARY PRINTED BOOKS, REPRINTS AND FACSIMILE EDITIONS

Austen, Jane,   *Pride and Prejudice*, London, 1813.

Atkinson, J.,   *An Account of the State of Agriculture and Grazing in New South Wales*, London, 1826, facsmile edition, Sydney, 1975.

Bennet, H.G.,   *A Letter to Earl Bathurst, Secretary of State for the Colonial Department, on the Condition of the Colonies of New South Wales and Van Diemen's Land, as set forth in the evidence taken before the Prison Committee in 1819*, London, 1820.

Bennett, George,   *Wanderings in New South Wales*, London, 1834.

Bigge, J.T.,   *Report of Commissioner of Inquiry, on the State of Agriculture and Trade in New South Wales*, House of Commons, 13 March 1823, facsimile edition, 1966.

Blaxland, G.,   *A Journal of a Tour of Discovery Across the Blue Mountains*, London, 1823.

Bradley, W.,   *A Voyage to New South Wales, The Journal of William Bradley, R.N., of H.M.S. Sirius, 1786–1792*, North Sydney, Trustees of the Public Library of New South Wales in association with Ure Smith, 1969.

Burr and Company,   *An Accurate List of the Names of the Land Holders in the Colony of New South Wales Pointing out the number of Acres in Each District as Granted from the Crown* (corrected to 1813), London, 1814.

Burton, W., 'State of society and crime in New South Wales during Six Years' Residence in that Colony', *The Colonial Magazine and Commercial Maritime Journal*, R.M. Martin (ed.), Vol. I, 1840.

Cobbett, William,   *Rural Rides*, Vol. 2, London, 1912.

Collins, David, *An Account of the English Colony in New South Wales*, 2 Vols., London, 1798; reprinted by the Libraries Board of South Australia, Adelaide, 1971.

Colquhoun, Patrick, *A Treatise on the Police of the Metropolis*, London, 1838.

Croker, T.C. (ed.),   *Memoirs of Joseph Holt*, 2 Vols., London, 1838.

Cunningham, P., R.N.,   *Two Years in New South Wales. A Series of Letters comprising sketches of the Actual State of Society in that Colony ...* , 2 Vols.,

London, 1827, reprinted by the Libraries Board of South Australia, Adelaide, 1966.

Defoe, Daniel, *A Tour Through the Whole Island of Great Britain*, London, 1962.

Description and View of the Town of Sydney, New South Wales, The Harbour of Port Jackson and Surrounding Country, now exhibiting in the Panorama, Leicester Square, first published in London, 1829, reprinted by the Library of Australian History, North Sydney, 1978.

Dictionary of the Vulgar Tongue, 1811, reprint, foreword Robert Crome, Illinois, 1971.

Dixon, W. Hepworth, *London Prisons*, London, 1850.

Harris, A., *Settlers and Convicts, Recollections of Sixteen Years Labour in the Australian Backwoods*, London, 1847, C.M.H. Clark (ed.), Melbourne University Press, 1953.

Henderson, John, *Observations on the Colonies of New South Wales and Van Diemen's Land*, Calcutta, 1832; reprinted by the Libraries Board of South Australia, 1965.

Holt, Joseph, *Memoirs of Joseph Holt, General of the Irish Rebels in 1798*, 2 vols, London 1838.

Hood, John, *Australia and the East*, London, 1843.

Howard, John, *The State of the Prisons*, 1777, London, 1929.

Hunter, Captain John, *An Historical Journal of Events at Sydney and at Sea 1787–1792*. Facsimile edition, Sydney, 1968.

Johnson, Rev. Richard, *Some Letters of the Rev. Richard Johnson, B.A.*, George Mackaness (ed.), Dubbo, 1954.

Johnston, George, *Proceedings of a General Court Martial . . . for the Trial of Lieut.-Col. George Johnston . . . on a charge of Mutiny . . . taken in shorthand by Mr Bartrum at Clement's Inn*, London, 1811.

Lang, J.D., *An Historical and Statistical Account of New South Wales, both as a Penal Settlement and as a British Colony*, 2 vols., London, 1840.
Reminiscences of My Life and Times both in Church and State in Australia for upwards of Fifty Years, D.W.A. Baker (ed.), Heinemann, Melbourne, 1972.

Macarthur, James, *New South Wales; Its Present State and Future Prospects*, London, 1837.

Macarthur-Onslow, S., *Some Early Records of the Macarthurs of Camden*, Sydney 1914, reissued 1973.

Mann, D.D., *The Present Picture of New South Wales, 1811*, first published by John Booth, London, reprinted by John Ferguson, Sydney, in association with the Royal Australian Historical Society, 1979.

Lachlan Macquarie, Governor of New South Wales, Journals of his Tours in New South Wales and Van Diemen's Land 1810–1822, Sydney, Trustees of the Public Library of New South Wales, 1956.

Marsden, S., *Some Private Correspondence of the Rev. Samuel Marsden and his Family, 1794–1824*, G. Mackaness, (ed.), Sydney, 1942.

Mayhew, Henry, *The Unknown Mayhew*, London, 1971.

Myers, Captain John, *The Life, Voyages and Travels of Captain John Myers*, London, 1817.

Nicol, John, *The Life and Adventures of John Nicol, Mariner*, London, 1822.

Peron, M.F., *A Voyage of Discovery to the Southern Hemisphere*, trans. from the French, London, 1809.

Scott, James, *Remarks on a Passage to Botany Bay, 1787–1792, a First Fleet Journal*, Sydney, Trustees of the Public Library of New South Wales in association with Angus and Robertson, 1963.

Smith, Adam, *An Inquiry into the Nature and Causes of the Wealth of Nations*, Edinburgh, 1859.

Suttor, W.H., *The Memoirs of W.H. Suttor, Australian Historical Monographs*, George Mackaness (ed.), reprinted, Dubbo, 1976.

The Sydney Gazette and New South Wales Advertiser, facsimile edition vols. 4 and 5, Sydney, State Library of New South Wales with Angus and Robertson, 1968, Vols 6 & 7, 1969; Vol. 8, 1970; Vol. 9, Canberra, 1973.

Tench, Watkin, *Sydney's First Four Years, being a reprint of the Expedition to Botany Bay and a Complete Account of the Settlement at Port Jackson*, London, 1793; L.F. Fitzhardinge (ed.), Angus and Robertson, Sydney, 1961.

Therry, R., *Reminiscences of the Thirty Years Residence in New South Wales and Victoria*, facsimile edition, Sydney, 1974.

The Voyage of Governor Phillip to Botany Bay, with contributions by other officers of the First Fleet, and Observations on Affairs of the time by Lord Aukland, originally published 1789; reprinted with Introduction and Annotations by James J. Auchmuty, by the Royal Australian Historical Society in association with Angus and Robertson, Sydney, 1970.

Trollope, Anthony, *Australia and New Zealand*, Vol. I, London, 1968.

The Spanish at Port Jackson, the visits of the Corvettes Descubierta and Afrevida, 1793, facsimile edition, Sydney, 1967.

Turnball, John, *Voyage Around the World in the Years 1800, 1801, 1802, 1803, and 1804*, 3 Vols., London, 1805.

The Voyage of Captain Bellinghausen to the Antarctic Seas, 1819–1820, F. Debenham (ed.), Hakluyt Society, London, 1945.

Wakefield, Edward Gibbon, *A Letter from Sydney, The Principal Town of Australasia: and Other Writings on Colonization*, London, 1929, first published in the *Morning Chronicle*, 1829.

Outline of a Plan for a Proposed Colony of South Australia, London, 1834.

Wentworth, W.C., *Statistical, Historical and Political Description of the Colony of New South Wales*, London, 1819, facsimile edition, Adelaide, 1978.

White, J., *Journal of a Voyage to New South Wales*, (ed.), A.H. Chisholm, Sydney, 1962.

Wilkes, Charles, *Narrative of the O.S. Exploratory Expedition during the Years 1838, 39, 40, 41, 42*, Vol. II, Philadephia, 1845.

Worgan, George B., *Journal of a First Fleet Surgeon*, North Sydney, Library Council of New South Wales in association with the Library of Australian History, 1978.

9. MODERN SOURCES

A. BOOKS

Abbott, G.J. & Nairn, N.B. (ed.), *Economic Growth of Australia, 1788–1821*, Melbourne, 1969.

Adams, J.T., *Provincial Society, 1690–1793*, New York, 1927.

Adamson, J.W., *English Education, 1789–1902*, London, 1930.

Alden, John R., *Pioneer America*, London, 1966.

Austin, A.G., *Australian Education 1788–1900*, Melbourne, 1972.

Auchmuty, J.J., *John Hunter*, Melbourne, 1968.

Barnard, M., *Macquarie's World*, Melbourne, 1947; Sydney, 1961.

Bassett, Marnie, *The Hentys*, London, 1965.

Bassett, M., *The Governor's Lady, Mrs Philip Gidley King: An Australian Historical Narrative*, London, 1962.

Bateson, Charles, *The Convict Ships*, 1788–1868, Sydney, 1974.

Baynham, Henry, *From the Lower Deck, The Old Navy 1780–1840*, London, 1972.

Bergman, G.F.J. & Levi, J.S., *Australian Genesis: Jewish Convicts and Settlers, 1788–1850*, Sydney, 1974.

Blainey, G., *The Tyranny of Distance*, Melbourne, 1966.

Bowd, D.G., *Macquarie Country: A History of the Hawkesbury*, Melbourne, 1969.

Bowden, K.M., *Captain James Kelly of Hobart Town*, Melbourne, 1964.

Buer, M.C., *Health, Wealth and Population in the Early Days of the Industrial Revolution*, London, 1968.

Burroughs, Peter, *Britain and Australia 1831–1855*, Oxford, 1967.

Butlin, S.J., *Foundation of the Australian Monetary System 1788–1851*, Sydney, 1968.

Cannon, Michael, *Who's Master? Who's Man?*, Melbourne, 1971.

Clark, C.M.H., *A History of Australia*, Vols. I–III, Melbourne, 1961, 1968, 1973.

Clark, C.M.H., *A Short History of Australia*, London, 1969.

Clark, C.M.H., *The Convicts 1788–1792; A Study of a One in Twenty Sample*, Sydney, 1965.

Clark, Manning, *Occasional Writings and Speeches*, Melbourne, 1980.

Clarke, F.G., *The Land of Contrarieties*, Melbourne, 1977.

Cleverly, John, *The First Generation School and Society in Early New South Wales*, Sydney, 1971.

Cobley, John (ed.), *The Crimes of the First Fleet Convicts*, Sydney, 1970.

Cobley, John, *Sydney Cove 1788*, Sydney, 1962; *Sydney Cove, 1789–1790*, Sydney, 1963; *Sydney Cove 1791–1792*, Sydney, 1965.

Cockburn, J.S. (ed.), *Crime in England 1550–1800*, London, 1977.

Coghlan, T.A., *General Report on the Eleventh Census of New South Wales*, Sydney, 1894.

Coghlan, T.A., *Labour and Industry in Australia*, Vol. 1, Melbourne, 1969.

Collison, Robert, *The Story of Street Literature*, London, 1973.

Cramp, K.R., *A Story of the Australian People*, Sydney, 1939.

Crowley, F. (ed.), *A New History of Australia*, Melbourne, 1974.

Currey, C.H., *The Brothers Bent*, Sydney, 1968.

Currey, C.H., *Sir Frances Forbes*, Sydney, 1968.

Currey, C.H., *The Transportation, Escape and Pardoning of Mary Bryant*, Sydney, 1963.

Dallas, K.M., *Trading Posts or Penal Colonies*, Hobart, 1969.

Dixson, Miriam, *The Real Matilda, Women and Identity in Australia 1788–1975*, Victoria, 1976.

Dobson, C.R., *Masters and Journeymen: A pre-history of industrial relations*, London, 1980.

Donaldson, G., *The Scots Overseas*, London, 1966.

Dow, G.M., *Samuel Terry, The Botany Bay Rothschild*, Sydney, 1974.

Eddy, J.J., *Britain and the Australian Colonies*, Oxford, 1969.

Eldershaw, M. Barnard, *An Historical Narrative on the Life and Times of Captain John Piper*, Sydney, 1973.

Ellis, M.H., *Francis Greenway, His Life and Times*, Sydney, 1953.

Ellis, M.H., *John Macarthur*, Sydney, 1967.

Ellis, M.H., *Lachlan Macquarie, His Adventures and Times*, Sydney, 1958.

Evatt, H.V., *Rum Rebellion*, Sydney, 1955.

Fitzpatrick, Brian, *British Imperialism and Australia, 1783–1833, An Economic History of Australia*, Sydney, 1971.

Fitzpatrick, Brian, *The Australian People 1788–1945*, Carlton, 1946.

Fletcher, Brian H., *Landed Enterprise and Penal Society, a History of Farming and Grazing in New South Wales before 1821*, Sydney, 1976.

Forsyth, W.D., *Governor Arthur's Convict System, Van Diemen's Land 1824–36*, Sydney, 1970.

Frost, Alan, *Convicts and Empire: a Naval Question 1776–1811*, Melbourne, 1980.

George, M.D., *England in Transition*, London, 1931.

George, M.D., *London Life in the Eighteenth Century*, New York, 1961.

Greenwood, G. (ed.), *Australia: A Social and Political History*, Sydney, 1951.

Hainsworth, D.R., *Builders and Adventurers: Traders and the Emergence of the Colony 1788–1821*, Melbourne, 1968.

Hainsworth, D.R., *The Sydney Traders, Simeon Lord and his Contemporaries, 1788–1850*, Melbourne, 1972.

Hancock, W.K., *Australia*, Brisbane, 1964.

Harris, Grant Carr (ed.), *The Secrets of Alexander Harris*, Sydney, 1961.

Hay, D. et al. (eds), *Albion's Fatal Tree*, London, 1977.

Heney, Helen, *Australia's Founding Mothers*, Melbourne, 1978.

Hobsbawm, E.J., *Industry and Empire: an Economic History of Britain Since 1770*, London, 1969.

Hooper, T.C., *Prison Boys of Port Arthur*, Melbourne, 1967.

Inglis, K.S., *The Australian Colonists: An Exploration of Social History 1788–1870*, Melbourne, 1974.

Kiernan, T.J., *The Irish Exiles in Australia*, Melbourne 1954.

King, Hazel, *Elizabeth Macarthur and Her World*, Sydney, 1980.

King, Hazel, *Richard Bourke*, Melbourne, 1971.

Knaplund, Paul, *James Stephen and the British Colonial System, 1813–1847*, Madison, 1953.

Knight, Ruth, *Illiberal Liberal: Robert Low in New South Wales 1842–1850*, Melbourne, 1966.

Knorr, K.E., *British Colonial Theories 1570–1850*, Toronto, 1944.

Kunz, E. & E., *A Continent Takes Shape*, Hong Kong, 1961.

Lacour-Gayet, Robert, *A Concise History of Australia*, Harmondsworth, 1976.

Lansbury, Carol, *Arcady in Australia: the Evocation of Australia in Nineteenth Century English Literature*, Melbourne, 1970.

Lazarev, A.P., *Zapiski o Plavangi voennogo shlypa blagon amernogo namebnage v*

Beringoe prolyv y vokrus sveta dlya otkrgtia v 1819, 1820, 1821, 1822. Governing Body of Archival material within the Ministry of Internal Affairs of U.S.S.R.

Levi, J.S., & Bergman, G.F.C., *Australian Genesis, Jewish Convicts and Settlers 1788–1850*, Melbourne, 1974.

McCaffrey, F., *History of Illawarra and its Pioneers*, Sydney, 1922.

Mac Giolla choille, B., *Transportation Ireland–Australia 1798–1848*, Kilkenny, 1983.

McIntyre, K.G., *The Secret Discovery of Australia*, London, 1977.

Mackaness, G., *Blue Bloods of Botany Bay*, London, 1953.

Mackaness, George (ed.), *Fourteen Journeys over the Blue Mountains, 1813–1841*, Sydney, 1965.

Mackaness, G., *The Life of Vice-Admiral William Bligh*, Sydney, 1931.

Mackintosh, Neil K., *Richard Johnson Chaplain to the Colony of New South Wales, 1755–1827*, North Sydney, 1978.

McLeod, A.L. (ed.), *The Pattern of Australian Culture*, New York, 1963.

McMinn, W.G., *A Constitutional History of Australia*, Sydney, 1979.

McQueen, Humphrey, *A New Britannia*, 1970.

Madgwick, R.B., *Immigration into Eastern Australia, 1788–1851*, Sydney, 1937.

Mansfield, R., *An Analytical View of the Census of New South Wales, for the Year 1846*, Sydney, 1941.

Marshall, Dorothy, *Industrial England, 1776–1851*, Bristol, 1973.

Marshall, J.D., *The Old Poor Law 1795–1834*, London, 1973.

Martin, G. (ed.), *The Founding of Australia*, Sydney, 1973.

Marwick, Arthur, *The Nature of History*, London, 1970.

Melbourne, A.C.V., *Early Constitutional Development*, Oxford, 1934.

Moran, P.F., *History of the Catholic Church in Australasia*, Sydney, n.d.

O'Brien, Eris, *Foundation of Australia*, Sydney, 1950.

O'Brien, Eris, *The Life and Letters of Arch-priest J.J. Therry*, Sydney, 1922.

O'Farrell, Patrick, *The Catholic Church in Australia, a Short History, 1788–1867*, Sydney, 1966.

O'Farrell, P., *The Catholic Church and Community in Australia, A History*, Melbourne, 1977.

Onslow, S.M. (ed.), *Some Early Records of the Macarthurs of Camden*, Sydney, 1973.

Parreaux, A., *Daily Life in England in the Reign of George III*, Carola Congreve (trans.), London, 1969.

Perrott, Monica, *A Tolerable Good Success: Economic opportunities for women in New South Wales 1788–1830*, vol. I. Macquarie Colonial Papers, Portia Robinson (ed.), Sydney, 1983.

Perry, T.M., *Australia's First Frontier*, London, 1965.

Phillips, David, *Crime and Authority in Victorian England*, London, 1977.

Phillips, Marion, *A Colonial Autocracy: New South Wales under Governor Macquarie, 1810–1821*, Sydney 1971.

Pike, D., *Australia: The Quiet Continent*, Cambridge, 1966.

Potts, E.D. & A., *Young America and Australian Gold*, Queensland, 1974.

Radzinowicz, Sir Leon, *A History of the English Criminal Law and its Administration from 1750*, London, 1946–68, 4 Vols.

Redford, A., *Labour Migration in England 1800–1825*, London, 1965.

Ritchie, John, *Punishment and Profit: The Reports of John Bigge on the Colonies of New South Wales and Van Diemen's Land 1822–1823: their origins, nature and significance*, Melbourne, 1970.

Roberts, S.H., *History of Australian Land Settlement*, Melbourne, 1924.

Robson, L.L., *The Convict Settlers of Australia: An Enquiry into the Origins and Character of the Convicts transported to New South Wales and Van Diemen's Land, 1789–1852*, Melbourne, 1965.

Roe, M., *Quest for Authority in Eastern Australia, 1835–1851*, Melbourne, 1965.

Rowley, C.D., *The Destruction of Aboriginal Society*, Victoria, 1970.

Rudé, G., *Protest and Punishment*, Oxford, 1978.

Rusden, W.H., *History of Australia*, 3 Vols, London, 1883.

Salt Annette, '*These Outcast Women*', Sydney, 1974, Vol. 2, *Macquarie Colonial Papers*, Portia Robinson (ed.).

Shaw, A.G.L., *Convicts and the Colonies; A Study of Penal Transportation from Great Britain and Ireland to Australia and other parts of the British Empire*, London, 1966.

Shaw, A.G.L. (ed.), *Great Britain and the Colonies, 1815–1865*, Suffolk, 1970.

Shaw, A.G.L., *The Story of Australia*, London 1955.

Shyrock, R.H., *Medicine and Society in America 1660–1860*, New York, 1960.

Smith, F.B., *The People's Health 1830–1910*, Canberra, 1979.

Stacey, A.W. (ed.), *A Basic History of Ryde*, 1792–1964, Ryde, 1965.

Summers, Anne, *Damned Whores and God's Police*, Victoria, 1975.

Sweeney, C., *Transported: In Place of Death. Convicts in Australia*, Adelaide, 1981.

Sweetman, E.V., *Australian Constitutional Development*, Melbourne, 1925.

Thompson, E.P., *The Making of the English Working Class*, Ringwood, 1968.

Tobias, J.J., *Crime and Industrial Society in the Nineteenth Century*, London, 1967.

Turney, C. (ed.), *Pioneers of Australian Education*, Vol. I, Sydney, 1969.

Waldersee, J., *Catholic Society and New South Wales 1788–1860*, Sydney, 1974.

Walker, R.B., *The Newspaper Press in New South Wales, 1803–1920*, Sydney, 1976.

Wannan, B., *Early Colonial Scandals: The Turbulent Times of Samuel Marsden*, Melbourne, 1972.

Ward, J.M., *Earl Grey and the Australian Colonies 1846–1857: A Study of Self-Government and Self-Interest*, Melbourne, 1958.

Ward, J.M., *Empire in the Antipodes*, London, 1966.

Ward, J.M., *James Macarthur, Colonial Conservative*, Sydney, 1981.

Ward, Russel, *Australia, A Short History*, Sydney, 1975.

Ward, Russel, *The Australian Legend*, Melbourne, 1958.

Willard, Myra, *History of the White Australia Policy to 1920*, Melbourne, 1923.

Wood, F.L., *A Concise History of Australia*, Sydney, 1935.

Wood, W.A., *Dawn in the Valley*, Sydney, 1977.

B. JOURNAL ARTICLES

Abbott, G.J.,   'Staple Theory and Economic Growth, 1788–1820', *Bus.*

Arch., Vol. 5, No. 2, August 1965.

Allars, K.G., 'George Crossley—An Unusual Attorney', *J.R.A.H.S.*, Vol. 44, Part 5, 1958.

'Barron Field: His Association with New South Wales', *J.R.A.H.S.*, Vol. 53, Part 3, 1967.

Anderson, M., 'The Story of Hunter's Hill', *J.R.A.H.S.*, Vol. 12, Part 2, 1926.

'The Story of Pittwater', *J.R.A.H.S.*, Vol. 6, Part 3, 1920.

Atchison, J.F., 'Early Explorations of Liverpool Plains and New England', *A.D.H.S.*, No. 13, 1970.

Auchmuty, J.J., 'Governor Phillip', *J.R.A.H.S.*, Vol. 56, Part 2, 1970.

'The Background to the Early Australian Governors', *H.S.*, Vol. 6, No. 23, 1954.

'The Biographical Approach to History', *J.R.A.H.S.*, Vol. 41, Part 5, 1955.

Austin, M., 'Paint My Picture Truly', *J.R.A.H.S.*, Vol. 51, Part 4, 1965.

'William Minchin of the New South Wales Corps', *J.R.A.H.S.*, Vol. 50, Part 6, 1964.

'Bayonet and Baton', 2 Parts: *Defence Force Journal*, March/April, 1980. No. 20; No. 21.

Badgery, Margot, 'Great Grandfather's Farthing', *Descent*, Vol. 6, Part 4.

Baker, T., 'The Crossing of the Blue Mountains and the Founding of Bathurst', *J.R.A.H.S.*, Vol. 47, Part 12, 1908.

Barton, G.B., 'The Life and Times of W.C. Wentworth', the *Australian Star*, 19 November 1898.

Bax, A.E., 'Australian Merchant Shipping, 1788–1849', *J.R.A.H.S.*, Vol. 38, Part 6, 1952.

Beaglehole, J.C., 'The Colonial Office, 1782–1854', *H.S.*, Vol. 1, No. 3, April 1941.

Beever, E.A., 'The Origins of the Wool Industry in New South Wales', *Bus. Arch.*, Vol. 5, No. 2, 1965.

Bell, J. 'A History of Picton', *J.R.A.H.S.*, Vol. 8, 1923.

Bell, R., 'Samuel Marsden—Pioneer Pastoralist', *J.R.A.H.S.*, Vol. 56, Part 1, 1970.

Binns, K., 'Three Early Views of Sydney', *J.R.A.H.S.*, Vol. 6, Part 6, 1920.

Blackburn, D., 'Letters of David Blackburn', *J.R.A.H.S.*, Vol. 20, Part 5, 1934.

Bladen F.M., 'Notes on the Life of John Hunter, Admiral, Governor of New South Wales', *J.R.A.H.S.*, Vol. 1, Part 3, 1906.

Benjamin, D.J., 'Ellis Bent—Australia's First Lawyer', *J.R.A.H.S.*, Vol. 38, Part 2, 1952.

Bennett, J.M., 'Richard Atkins—An Amateur Judge Jeffreys', *J.R.A.H.S.*, Vol. 52, Part 4, 1966.

Bergman, G.F.J., 'James Larra, the Commercial Nabob of Parramatta', *A.J.H.S.J.*, Vol. 5, No. 3, n.d.

'John Harris, the First Australian Policeman', *A.J.H.S.J.*, Vol. 5, No. 2, n.d.

'Solomon Levey—from Convict to Merchant Prince', *J.R.A.H.S.*, Vol. 54, Part 1, 1968.

'Two Jewish Convicts, Joseph Samuel and Isac Simmons', *A.J.H.S.J.*, Vol. 5, No. 8.

Bertie, C.H., 'Governor Macquarie', *J.R.A.H.S.*, Vol. 16, Part 1, 1930.
'Old Castlereagh Street', *J.R.A.H.S.*, Vol. 22, Part 1, 1936.
'Old Pitt Street', *J.R.A.H.S.*, Vol. 6, Part 2, 1920.
'Street Names of Early Sydney and Some Street History', *J.R.A.H.S.*, Vol. 36, Part 1, 1950.

Binns, K., 'The Publication of Historical Records of Australia', *H.S.*, Vol. 1, No. 2, October 1940.

Bolton, G.C.B., 'The Idea of a Colonial Gentry', *H.S.*, Vol. 13, No. 51, 1958.

Brody, E.H., 'William Lee of Larras Lake', *J.R.A.H.S.*, Vol. 25, 1939.

Burley, T.M., 'The Evolution of the Agricultural Pattern in the Hunter Valley of New South Wales', *Australian Geographer*, Vol. 8, No. 5, September 1962.

Byrnes, J.V., 'Andrew Thompson 1773–1810', *J.R.A.H.S.*, Part 1: Vol. 48, Part 2, 1962; Part 2: Vol. 48, Part 3, 1962.

Cable, K.J., 'Saint James Church, King Street Sydney 1819–1894', *J.R.A.H.S.*, Vol. 50, Part 4, 1964; continued: Vol. 50, Part 5, Vol. 50, Part 6, 1964.

Cameron, N.L., 'The Convict in the Australian Novel', *A.D.H.S.*, No. 14, 1971.

Campbell, E., 'Prerogative Rule in New South Wales 1788–1823', *J.R.A.H.S.*, Vol. 50, Part 3, 1964.

Campbell, J.F., 'Discovery and Settlement of New England', *J.R.A.H.S.*, Vol. 8, Part 5, 1972.
'Early Settlement on the Lower Nepean River—Penrith to the Hawkesbury River', *J.R.A.H.S.*, Vol. 22, Part 4, 1936.
'John Howe's Exploratory Journey from Windsor to the Hunter River in 1819', *J.R.A.H.S.*, Vol. 14, Part 4, 1928.
'Liberty Plains of the First Free Settlers, 1793', *J.R.A.H.S.*, Vol. 22, Part 5, 1936.
'Notes on Exploration Under Governor Phillip', *J.R.A.H.S.*, Vol. 12, Part 1, 1926.
'Rose Hill Government Farm to the Founding of Parramatta', *J.R.A.H.S.*, Vol. 12, Part 6, 1927.
'Rural Settlement about Brush Farm, 1791–1800', *J.R.A.H.S.*, Vol. 13, Part 6, 1927.
'The Dawn of Rural Settlement in Australia', J.R.A.H.S. *J.R.A.H.S.*, Vol. 11, Part 2, 1925.
'The First Decade of the Australian Agricultural Companies, 1824–1834', *J.R.A.H.S.*, Vol. 9, Part 4, 1923.
'The Genesis of Rural Settlement on the Hunter', *J.R.A.H.S.*, Vol. 12, Part 2, 1926.

Cabourdin, G., 'Le remariage', *Annales de Demographie Historique*, October, 1978.

Cavanagh, F.A., 'State Intervention in English Education', *History*, Vol. 25, No. 98, September 1940.
'The Old Woman from Botany Bay', *J.R.A.H.S.*, Vol. 43, Part 3, 1957.

Churchward, L.G., 'Australian-American Trade Relations, 1791–1939', *E.R.*, Vol. 2, No. 5, April 1942.

Clark, C.M.H., 'Hancock's "Australia" and Australian Historiography: A Note', *H.S.*, Vol. 13, No. 51, October 1968.

'Some Influences of European Civilization in Australia', *T.H.R.A.*, Vol. 7, No. 2, 1958.

'The Choice of Botany Bay', *H.S.*, Vol. 19, No. 35, November 1960.

'The Origins of the Convicts Transported to Eastern Australia, 1787–1852', Part 1: *H.S.*, Vol. 7, No. 26, May 1956; Part 2: *H.S.*, Vol. 7, No. 27, November 1956.

'The Writing of History', *C.D.H.J.*, March 1967.

Conlon. A., 'Mine is a Sad Yet True Story: Convict Narratives, 1818–1850', *J.R.A.H.S.*, Vol. 55, Part 1, 1969.

Connell, R.W., 'The Convict Rebellion of 1804', *M.H.J.*, Vol. 5, 1965.

Cramp, K.R., 'William Charles Wentworth—Explorer, Scholar, Statesman', *J.R.A.H.S.*, Vol. 4, Part 8, 1918.

Cubis, D.E.M., 'Australian Character in the Making, New South Wales, 1788–1901', *J.R.A.H.S.*, Vol. 24, Part 3, 1938.

Curlewis, H.H., 'Mrs. Hawkins Journey to Bathurst', *J.R.A.H.S.*, Vol. 23, Part 5, 1937.

Currey, C.H., 'The First Crossing of the Blue Mountains by Governor and Mrs. MacQuarrie and the Foundation of Bathurst on May 7, 1815', *J.R.A.H.S.*, Vol. 41, Part 3, 1955.

'The Foundation of the Benevolent Society of New South Wales on May 6, 1818', *J.R.A.H.S.*, Vol. 48, Part 1, 1962.

Currey, C.H., 'The Law of Marriage and Divorce in New South Wales (1788–1858), *J.R.A.H.S.*, Vol. 41, Part 3, 1955.

Dallas, K.M., 'The First Settlement in Australia considered in relation to Sea-Power in World Politics', *T.H.A.P.*, No. 3, 1952.

Davey, L. et al, 'The Hungry Years, 1788–1792, *H.S.*, Vol. 3, No. 11, November 1947.

Dowd, B.T., 'Augustus Alt, First Surveyor-General of New South Wales', *J.R.A.H.S.*, Vol. 68, Part 5, 1962.

'Charles Grimes: Second Surveyor-General of New South Wales', *J.R.A.H.S.*, Vol. 22, Part 4, 1936.

Dowling, Edward, 'Early Colonial Printers', *J.R.A.H.S.*, Vol 1, Part 2, June 1906.

'An Account of Norfolk Island, the first Criminal Court held there, with a further sketch of the Island and its occupants', *J.R.A.H.S.*, Vol. 1, Part 11, September 1908.

Driscoll, F., 'Macquarie's Administration of the Convict System', *J.R.A.H.S.*, Vol. 27, Part 6, 1941.

Dunbabin, T., 'Whalers, Sealers and Buccaneers', *J.R.A.H.S.*, Vol. 11, Part 1, 1925.

Dunlop, N.J., 'William Redfern, the First Australian Medical Graduate and his Times', *J.R.A.H.S.*, Vol. 14, Part 2, 1928.

Earnshaw, B., 'The Colonial Children', in *The Push from the Bush*, No. 9, July 1981.

Eldershaw, F., 'Captain John Piper', *J.R.A.H.S.*, Vol. 26, Part 6, 1940.

Eddy, J.,   'John Joseph Therry, Pioneer Priest,' *J.C.H.A.*, Vol. 1, Part 3, 1964.

Ellis, M.H.,   'Some Aspects of the Bigge Commission of Inquiry into the Affairs of New South Wales, 1819–1821', *J.R.A.H.S.*, Vol. 27, Part 2, 1941.

Elford, K.,   'A Prophet Without Honour: The Political Ideas of John Dunmore Lang', *J.R.A.H.S.*, Vol. 54, Part 2, 1968.

Ferguson, J.A.,   'Edward Smith Hall and the *Monitor*', *J.R.A.H.S.*, Vol. 17, Part 3, 1931.

'George Peat and his Ferry', *J.R.A.H.S.*, Vol. 11, Part 4, 1925.

'The Howes and their Press', *J.R.A.H.S.*, Vol. 13, Part 6, 1937.

Fink, Averil,   'James Hardy Vaux, Convict and Fatalist', *J.R.A.H.S.*, Vol. 48, Part 5, December 1962.

Fitzhardinge, L.F.,   'A Convict's Letter from N.S.W., 1792', *H.S.*, Vol. I, No. I, April 1970.

'The Origin of Watkin Tench', *J.R.A.H.S.*, Vol. 50, Part I, 1964.

Fitzhardinge, V.,   'Russian Ships in Australian Waters, 1807–1835', *J.R.A.H.S.*, Vol. 51, Part 2, 1965.

Fletcher, B.H.,   'Administrative Reform in New South Wales under Governor Darling', *Australian Journal of Business Administration*, Vol. XXXVIII, September, 1979.

'Grose, Paterson and the settlement of the Hawkesbury', *J.R.A.H.S.*, Vol. 51, Part 4, 1965.

'New South Wales 1788–1821: An Appraisal of Recent Historical Writing', *Teaching History*, July, 1973.

'The Development of Small Scale Farming in New South Wales under Governor Hunter', *J.R.A.H.S.*, Vol. 50, Part 1, 1964.

'The Hawkesbury Settlers and the Rum Rebellion', *J.R.A.H.S.*, Vol. 54, Part 3, 1968.

Fogarty, J.P.,   'New South Wales Wool Prices in the 1820s: Note', *A.E.H.R.*, Vol. 9, No. 1, March 1969.

Foster, A.C.,   'George Howe and the "*Gazette*" Office', *J.R.A.H.S.*, Vol. 10, Part 2, 1924.

'Odd Bits of Old Sydney', *J.R.A.H.S.*, Vol. 7, Part 3, 1965.

Foster, W.,   'Francis Grose and the Officers', *J.R.A.H.S.*, Vol. 51, Part 3, 1965.

Frost, Alan,   'As it were another America', *Eighteenth Century Studies*, Vol. 7, Part 3.

Fry, H.T.,   'Cathay and the Way Thither: The Background to Botany Bay', *H.S.*, Vol. 14, No. 56, April 1971.

Gandevia, B.,   'Mortality at Sydney Cove', *Australian and New Zealand Journal of Medicine*, April 1974.

'Socio-Medical Factors in the Evolution of the First Settlement at Sydney Cove 1788–1803', *J.R.A.H.S.*, Vol. 61, Part 1, March 1975.

Gilbert, L.A.,   'Strange Characters They Were: The Cedar Cutters of Early New South Wales', *A.D.H.S.*, No. 16, 1973.

Gill, J.C.H.,   'Genesis of the Australian Whaling Industry, and its development to 1850', *R.H.S.Q.*, Vol. 8, No. 1, 1965–66.

'Macquarie Towns in the Hawkesbury Valley', *R.H.S.Q.*, Vol. 7, No. 3,

1964–65.

'The Hawkesbury River Floods of 1801, 1806 and 1809 and their effect on the Economy of the Colony of New South Wales', *R.H.S.Q.*, Vol. 8, No. 4, 1968–69.

Gray, A.J., 'Ann Smith of the *Lady Penrhyn*', *J.R.A.H.S.*, Vol. 43, Part 5, 1957.

'John Bennett of the *Friendship*', *J.R.A.H.S.*, Vol. 44, Part 6, 1958.

'John Irving, the First Australian Emancipist', *J.R.A.H.S.*, Vol. 40, Part 6, 1954.

'Peter Burn', *J.R.A.H.S.*, Vol. 45, Part 2, 1956.

'Social Life at Sydney Cove, 1788–1789', *J.R.A.H.S.*, Vol. 44, Part 6, 1958.

Greenwood, G., 'The Contact of American Whalers, Sealers and Adventurers with the New South Wales Settlement', *J.R.A.H.S.*, Vol. 29, Part 3, 1943.

Grimshaw, P., 'Women and the family in Australian history - a reply to *The Real Matilda*', *H.S.*, Vol. 18, No. 72, April 1979.

Hainsworth, D.R., 'In Search of a Staple: The Sydney Sandalwood trade 1804–09', *Bus. Arch.*, Vol. 5, No. 1, Feb. 1965.

'Iron Men in Wooden Ships, the Sydney Sealers', *Labour History*, XIII, 1967.

'The New South Wales Shipping Interest 1800–1821: A Study in Colonial Entrepreneurship', *A.E.H.R.*, Vol. 8, No. 1, March 1968.

Hartwell, R.M., 'Australia's First Trade Cycle', *J.R.A.H.S.*, Vol. 42, Part 2, 1956.

'The Australian Depression of the Eighteen-Twenties', *H.S.*, Vol. 3, No. 11, November 1947.

Havard, W.L., 'First Divine Service West of the Blue Mountains', *J.R.A.H.S.*, Vol. 21, Part 1, 1935.

'Francis Howard Greenway, Macquarie's Architect', *J.R.A.H.S.*, Vol. 22, Part 3, 1936.

'Gregory Blaxland's Narrative and Journal Relating to the first Expedition over the Blue Mountains, New South Wales', *J.R.A.H.S.*, Vol. 23, Part 1, 1937.

'Hamilton Hume and the Road to Bathurst', *J.R.A.H.S.*, Vol. 21, Part 2, 1935.

Havard, W.L., 'Pierce Collits and his Inns', *J.R.A.H.S.*, Vol. 23, Part 5, 1937.

Havard, W.L. & O., 'A Frenchman Sees Sydney in 1819', *J.R.A.H.S.*, Vol. 24, Part 1, 1938.

'Some Early French Visitors to the Blue Mountains and Bathurst', *J.R.A.H.S.*, Vol. 24, Part 4, 1938.

Hawkins, E., 'Journey from Sydney to Bathurst in 1822', *J.R.A.H.S.*, Vol. 9, Part 4, 1923.

Hill G.S., 'Discovery and Early Settlement of New England', *J.R.A.H.S.*, Vol. 9, Part 3, 1923.

Housion, Andrew, 'Archdeacon Cowper', *J.R.A.H.S.*, 1916.

'Old Bits in the History of Parramatta', *J.R.A.H.S.*, Vol. 2, Part VII, 1903.

Hume, L.J., 'Working Class Movements in Sydney and Melbourne before the Gold Rushes', *H.S.*, Vol. 9, No. 35, 1960.

Inglis, K.S.,   'Catholic Historiography in Australia', *H.S.*, Vol. 8, No. 31, November 1958.

Irvin, E.,   'Australia's "First" Dramatists', *Aust. Lit. Stud.*, Vol. 4, No. 1, May 1969.

Jeans, D.,   'Crown Land Sales and the Accommodation of the Small Settler in New South Wales, 1825–1842', *H.S.*, Vol. XII.

Jervis, J.,   'Early Exploration and Settlement of Shoalhaven', *J.R.A.H.S.*, Vol. 27, Part 1, 1941.

'Brisbane Water District', *J.R.A.H.S.*, Vol. 34, Part 6, 1948.

'Camden and Cowpastures', *J.R.A.H.S.*, Vol. 21, Part 4, 1935.

'Exploration and Settlement of the North-Western Plains', *J.R.A.H.S.*, Vol. 26, Part 2, 1940.

'Wallis Plains and Maitland', *J.R.A.H.S.*, Vol. 26, Part 2, 1940.

'Wellington Valley', *J.R.A.H.S.*, Vol. 20, Part 4, 1934.

'Jervis Bay: Its Discovery and Settlement', *J.R.A.H.S.*, Vol. 22, Part 2, 1936.

'Illawarra, A Century of History, 1788–1888', *J.R.A.H.S.*, Vol. 28, Parts 2-6, 1942.

'The Clarence River', *J.R.A.H.S.*, Vol. 25, Part 3, 1939.

Jervis, J.,   'The Western Plains', *J.R.A.H.S.*, Vol. 42, Part 1, 1956.

'The Hunter Valley', *J.R.A.H.S.*, Vol. 39, Part 3, 1952, and Part 4, 1953.

'Solomon Wiseman and his Ferry', *J.R.A.H.S.*, Vol. 27, Part 5, 1941.

'The Birthplace of John Batman', *J.R.A.H.S.*, Vol. 24, Part 6, 1938.

'The Journals of William Edward Riley', *J.R.A.H.S.*, Vol. 32, Part 4, 1946.

Jose, A.,   'Nicholas Bauden', *J.R.A.H.S.*, Vol. 20, Part 6, 1939.

'Sydney and District in 1824 as Described by a French Visitor', *J.R.A.H.S.*, Vol. 10, Part 4, 1924.

Joseph, A.P.,   'On Tracing Australian Jewish Genealogy', *A.J.H.S.J.*, Vol. 5, No. 3 (no date).

Kemp, M.C. and T.B.,   'Captain Anthony Fenn Kemp', *J.R.A.H.S.*, Vol. 51, Part 1, 1965.

Kemp, R.E.,   'Commercial Life in Australia a Century Ago', *J.R.A.H.S.*, Vol. IV, Part 3, 1917.

Kerr, J.,   'Merchants and Merinos', *J.R.A.H.S.*, Vol. 46, Part 4, 1960.

'The Macarthur Family and the Pastoral Industry', *J.R.A.H.S.*, Vol. 47, Part 3, 1961.

'The Wool Industry in New South Wales 1803–1830', *Business Archives*, Vol. 1, and Vol. 2, Part 1.

Kerneck, S.,   'Presson versus Turner: A Commentary on the Frontier Controversy', *H.S.*, Vol. 14, No. 53, 1969, pp. 3–18.

King H.,   'Problems of Police Administration in New South Wales, 1825–1851', *J.R.A.H.S.*, Vol. 44, Part 2, 1958.

'Some Aspects of Police Administration in New South Wales, 1825–1851', *J.R.A.H.S.*, Vol. 42, Part 5, 1956.

'The Struggle for the Freedom of the Press in N.S.W., 1825–31', *T.H.*, No. 13, May 1965.

King, H.W.A. & Woolmington, E.R.,   'The Role of the River in the

Development and Settlement in the Lower Hunter Valley', *A.G.*, Vol. 8, No. 1, September 1966.

Kramp, K.R., 'William Charles Wentworth—Explorer, Scholar, Statesman', *J.R.A.H.S.*, Vol. 4, Part 8, 1918.

Lea-Scarlett, E.J., 'The Discovery of Lake George', *C.D.H.J.*, December 1970.

'The Genesis of Sutton', *C.D.H.J.*, June 1971.

Lee W.G., 'A Monument to William Lee', *J.R.A.H.S.*, Vol. 25, 1938.

Leroy, P.E., 'Samuel Terry', *J.R.A.H.S.*, Vol. 47, Part 5, 1961.

'The Emancipists, Edward Eager and the Struggle for Civil Liberties', *J.R.A.H.S.*, Vol. 48, Part 4, 1962.

Lesson, Pierre, 'Sydney and District in 1824 as described by a French visitor', *J.R.A.H.S.*, Vol. 10, Part 4.

Liston, C.A., 'William Charles Wentworth—the Formative Years 1810–1824', *J.R.A.H.S.*, Vol. 62, Part 1, 1976.

McDonald, D.I., 'Child and Female Labour in Sydney, 1876–1898', *A.N.U.H.J.*, Nos. 10 and 11, 1973–4.

McGuarre, J.P., 'A Hundred Years Ago', *J.R.A.H.S.*, Vol. 5, Part 2, 1919.

'Early Schools of New South Wales', *J.R.A.H.S.*, Vol. 2, Part 3, 4, 1909.

'Lachlan Macquarie and his Time up to 1810', *J.R.A.H.S.*, Vol. 4, Part 2, 1917.

'The Humour and Pastimes of Early Sydney', *J.R.A.H.S.*, Vol. 1, Part 3, 1906.

Mackaness, G., 'Some Private Correspondences of the Mardsen Family (1794–1824)', *J.R.A.H.S.*, Vol. 23, Part 6, 1937.

'The Discovery of the Hunter River', *J.R.A.H.S.*, Vol. 16, Part 3, 1930.

Mackay, E.A., 'Medical Men as Pastoral Pioneers', *Medical Journal of Australia*, 13 October, 1974.

McLachlan, N.D., 'Edward Eager (1787–1866): A Colonial Spokesman in Sydney and London', *H.S.*, Vol. 10, No. 46, May 1963.

MacLauren, E.C.B., 'The Ancient Family of Rouse', *J.R.A.H.S.*, Vol. 43, Part 6, 1957.

McMartin, A., 'The Payment of Officials in Early Australia, 1786–1826', *P.A.*, Vol. 17, No. 1, March 1958.

'Aspects of Patronage in Australia, 1786–1836', *P.A.*, Vol. 18, No. 4, December 1959.

Macmillan, D.S., 'The Beginnings of Scottish Enterprise in Australia: The Contribution of the Commercial Whigs', *Bus. Arch.* Vol. 2, No. 2, August 1962.

Macnab, K. & Ward, R., 'The Nature and Nurture of the First Generation of Native-Born Australians', *Historical Studies of Australia and New Zealand*, Vol. 10, No. 39, Nov. 1962, pp. 298–308.

McNally, N., 'The Men of '98', *J.R.A.H.S.*, Vol. 3, Part 1, 1969.

McQueen, H., 'Convicts and Rebels', *L.H.*, No. 15, November 1968.

'Reply to Russel Ward', *Overland*, o. 48, Winter 1971.

Margarey, Susan, 'The Invention of Juvenile Delinquency in Early Nineteenth Century England', *Labour History*, Number 34, May 1978.

Meaney, F.I., 'Governor Brisbane and the Freedom of the Press in New

South Wales, 1824–25', *A.D.H.S.*, No. 12, 1969.

Mitchell, R. Else,   'George Caley: His Life and Work', *J.R.A.H.S.*, Vol. 25, Part 6, 1939.

'The Foundation of New South Wales and the Inheritance of the Common Law', *J.R.A.H.S.*, Vol. 49, Part 1, June 1963.

Morgan, H.A. MacLeod,   'Notes on "An Account of a Journey towards Jugroy . . . .1805" by George Caley', *J.R.A.H.S.*, XI, 1955.

'The Bulga or Coal River', *J.R.A.H.S.*, XLIV, Part IV, November 1958.

Moreton, P.H.,   'The Vaucluse Estate from 1793 to 1829 and Those connected with it', *J.R.A.H.S.*, Vol. 15, Part 6, 1930.

Napier, S.E.,   'Balmain: The Man and the Suburb', *J.R.A.H.S.*, Vol. 14, Part 5, 1928.

'One Hundred and Fifty Years of Australian Drama', *J.R.A.H.S.*, Vol. 24, Part 6, 1936.

Norris, J.,   'Proposals for Promoting Religion and Literature in Canada, Nova Scotia and New Brunswick', *The Canadian Historical Review*, XXXVI, 1955.

O'Callaghan, T.,   'Police Establishment in New South Wales', *J.R.A.H.S.*, Vol. 9, Part 6, 1923.

O'Grady, E.,   'Hamilton Hume', *J.R.A.H.S.*, Vol. 49, Part 5, 1964.

Parsons, T.G.,   'Does the Bigge Report follow from the Evidence', *H.S.*, Vol. 15, No. 58, April 1972.

'Governor Macquarie and the Assignment of Skilled Convicts in New South Wales', *J.R.A.H.S.*, Vol. 58, Part 2, 1972.

'New South Wales Corps—A Rejoinder', *J.R.A.H.S.*, Vol. 52, Part 5, 1966.

'Courts Martial, the Savoy Military Prison and the New South Wales Corps', *J.R.A.H.S.*, Vol. 63, Part 4, 1978.

'The Social Composition of the Men of the New South Wales Corps' *J.R.A.H.S.*, Vol. 50, Part 4, 1964.

Perkins, H.,   'Father Harold: The Story of a Convict Priest', *J.A.C.H.S.*, Vol. 3, Part 3, 1971.

Perry, T.M.,   'The Spread of Rural Settlement in New South Wales 1788–1826', *H.S.*, Vol. 6, No. 24, May 1955.

Phillipp, F.A.,   'Notes on the Study of Australian Colonial Architecture', *H.S.*, Vol. 8, No. 32, May 1959.

Phillips, A.A.,   'The Cross-Eyed Clio: Humphrey McQueen and the Australian Tradition', *Meanjin*, Vol. 30, No. 1, March 1971.

Pooley, G.H.,   'Early History of Bathurst and Surroundings', *J.R.A.H.S.*, Vol. 1, Part 11, 1908, Part 12, 1908.

'Windsor and Richmond', *J.R.A.H.S.*, Vol. 2, Part 1, March 1909.

Price, C.A.,   'Jewish Settlers in Australia', A.J.H.S.J., Vol. 5, No. 8.

Ramson, W.S.,   'Early Australian English', *Australian Quarterly*, Vol. 35, No. 3, Sept. 1963.

'Primary Sources for the Study of the Vocabulary of Nineteenth Century Australian English', *Aust. Lit. Stud.*, Vol. 1, No. 4, December 1964.

Raudzens, G., 'Upper Canada and New South Wales to 1855: the feasibility of comparative colonial history', *J.R.A.H.S.*, Vol. 67, Part 3, 1981.

Reese, T.R., 'Colonial America and Early New South Wales: Introductory Notes to a Comparative Study of British Administrative Policies', *H.S.*, Vol. 9, No. 33, November 1959.

Ritchie, J.D., 'The Colonial Office, New South Wales and the Bigge Report, 1815–1820' New Zealand Geographer, IX, 1953.

Robinson, Portia, 'The First Forty Years: Women and the Law', *In Pursuit of Justice*, J. Mackinolty & H. Radi (ed), Sydney, 1979.
'Figuring the Nature of a Times Deceas'd; the Convict Records', *Conference Papers, Society of Australian Archivists*, Melbourne, 1981.

Robson, Lloyd, 'The Origins of the Women Convicts transported to New South Wales and Van Diemen's Land 1787–1852', *H.S.*, Vol. II, November 1963–April 1965.
'The Historical Basis of "For the Term of His Natural Life"', *Aust. Lit. Stud.*, Vol. 7, No. 2, December 1963.

Roe, M., 'Australia's Place in the "Swing to the East" 1788–1810', *H.S.*, Vol. 8, No. 30, May 1958.
'Colonial Society in Embryo', *H.S.*, Vol. 7, No. 26, May 1956.
'Philip Gidley King', *A. Quart.*, Vol. 30, No. 3, September 1958.

Rogers, D., 'A Saga of Two Hundred Years: The Families of Governor King and Captain John MacArthur', *V.H.M.*, Vol. 33, No. 41, May 1963.

Rose, L.N., 'The Administration of Governor Darling', *J.R.A.H.S.*, Vol. 8, Parts 2 and 3, 1922.

Rowland, E.C.V., 'Early Schools in New South Wales', *J.R.A.H.S.*, Vol. 33, Part 5, 1947.
'Further Notes on Simeon Lord', *J.R.A.H.S.*, Vol. 37, Part 6, 1951.
'Simeon Lord—A Merchant Prince of Botany Bay', *J.R.A.H.S.*, Vol. 30, Part 3, 1944.

Rudé, G., '"Captain Swing" in New South Wales', *H.S.*, Vol. 11, No. 44, April 1965.

Rumsey, H.J., 'Jews in the (N.S.W.) Census of 1828', *A.J.H.S.J.*, Vol. I, No. 4, n.d.

Saclier, M., 'Sam Marsden's Colony: Notes on a Manuscript in the Mitchell Library, Sydney', *J.R.A.H.S.*, Vol. 52, Part 2, 1966.

Shaw, A.G.L., 'Missing Land Grants in New South Wales', *H.S.*, Vol. 5, No. 19, November 1952.
'Rum Corps and Rum Rebellion', *M.H.J.*, Vol. 10 1971.
'The New South Wales Corps', *J.R.A.H.S.*, Vol. 47, Part 2, 1961.
Review of 'Against the Wind', *H.S.*, Vol. 18, No. 72, April 1979.

Smith S.H., 'William T. Cape and other pioneers of secondary education in Australia', *J.R.A.H.S.*, Vol. V, Part V, 1919.

Steele, W.A., 'The First Land Grant Beyond the Blue Mountains', *D.R.A.H.S.*, Vol. 24, Part 4, 1938.

Sturma, M., 'Eye of the Beholder: The Stereotype of Women Convicts, 1788–1852', *Labour History*, Number 34, May 1978.

Steven, J.E., 'Robert Campbell and the Bligh Rebellion, 1808', *J.R.A.H.S.*, Vol. 48, Part 5, 1963.

Steven, M.J.E., 'The Changing Pattern of Commerce in New South Wales, 1810–1821', *Bus. Arch.* Vol. 3, No. 2, Aug. 1963.

Torr, H.,   'The Singletons', *C.D.H.J.*, December 1971.

Waldersee, J.,   'Emancipist in a Hurry: François Girard', *J.R.A.H.S.*, Vol. 54, Part 3, 1968.

'Old St. Mary's—Sydney's Debt to Father Therry', *J.A.C.H.S.*, Vol. 2, Part 3, 1968.

Walker, R.B.,   'Tobacco Smoking in Australia, 1788–1914', *H.S.*, Vol. 19, No. 75, October 1980.

Walsh, G.P.,   'Factories and Factory Workers in New South Wales, 1788–1900', *L.H.*, No. 21, November 1971.

'The Geography of Manufacturing in Sydney, 1788–1851', *Bus. Arch.*, Vol. 3, No. 1, February 1963.

Ward, J.M.,   'James MacArthur, Colonial Conservative, 1798–1897', *J.R.A.H.S.*, Vol. 66, Part 3, December 1980.

Ward, Russel,   'An Australian Legend', *J.R.A.H.S.*, Vol. 47, Part 6, 1961.

'The Australian Legend Re-visited', *H.S.*, Vol. 18, No. 71, October 1978.

'Convicts and Rebels: A Reply', *L.H.*, No. 16, May 1969.

'Felons and Folksongs', *Meanjin*, Vol. 15, Spring 1956.

Watson, J.H.,   'Early Shipbuilding in Australia', *J.R.A.H.S.*, Vol. 6, Part 2, 1920.

Weatherburn, K.A.,   'Exploration of the Jervis Bay, Shoalhaven and Illawarra Districts, 1797–1812', *J.R.A.H.S.*, Vol. 46, Part 2, 1960.

Wood, G.A.,   'Explorations Under Governor Phillip', *J.R.A.H.S.*, Vol. 7, Part 1, 1926.

'The Convicts', *J.R.A.H.S.*, Vol. 8, Part 4, 1922.

C. UNPUBLISHED THESES

Macnab, K.,   'The Currency Lads', B.A. Hons. thesis in the possession of Dr K. Macnab, History Department, University of Sydney.

Proctor, Simon K.,   'Aspects of the Sydney Press, 1803–1827', M.A. thesis, A.N.U., May 1967.

Robinson, T.J.,   'A Quantitative Analysis of Conflict in New South Wales during the administration of Governor William Bligh, 1806–1810', 2 Vols., B.A. Hons. thesis, Macquarie University, 1979.

Thomas, Lelia,   'The Development of the Labor Movement in the Sydney District of N.S.W.', M.A. thesis, University of Sydney, 1919.

Tilley, A.G.,   'Opposition to Governor Darling in New South Wales', Sydney, B.A. Hons. thesis, 1971.

Walsh, G.B.,   'A History of Manufacturing in Sydney 1788–1850', M.A. thesis, A.N.U., 1969.

D. CONFERENCE PAPERS: CIRCULATED AND/OR PUBLISHED.

ANZAAS Jubilee Congress, Adelaide, May 1980:

Frost, A., 'Lighting the Dark Backward of Australian Time: the Historiography of the Decision to Colonize New South Wales.

Robinson, Portia, 'The Unhappy Objects': Colonial Women in Eastern Australia.

ANZAAS Congress, Auckland, 1979:

Robinson, Portia, 'The Hatch and Brood of Time', the first generation of white Australians, Eastern Australia, 1787–1828.

Women and the Law Conference, University of Sydney, August, 1978:

Robinson, Portia, 'Women and the Law, the first forty years'.

Society of Australian Archivists Conference, Trinity College, University of Melbourne, 1981:

Robinson, Portia, 'Figuring the Nature of a Times Deceas'd: the Convict Records'. (Published, *Conference Papers, Society of Australian Archivists, Melbourne 1981*.)

Robinson, Portia, 'From Colleen to Matilda: Irish convict women', Kilkenny, Ireland 1983.

Robinson, Portia, 'The Colonial Women of Botany Bay', paper given to Australian Studies Centre, London, 1984.

INDEXES

INDEX A

SELECT LIST OF MEMORIALS AND PETITIONS

Note:
1 Memorials cited are from original bound volumes in the Mitchell Library, or from the microfilm copies in Archives Authority of New South Wales. Page reference is usually given for the originals; usual reference for microfilm is by number.
2 Contemporary spellings of proper names varies in originals.

Bay, Mary   CSIL 4/1761, p. 178

Bell, Archibald jnr   CSIL 4/1848, M 21

Best, Thomas   CSIL 4/1836, M 64

Biggers, Thomas and Andrew   CSIL 4/1823, M 52

Blaxland, John   CSIL 4/1752, p. 94: request that his servant Mary King be not removed from his service to join her husband at the Derwent as 'I have four daughters whom she is now instructing in music ...'

Bloodworth/Bloodsworth, James   CSIL 4/1836, p. 327; 4/1836, M 56

Blue, William   CSIL 4/1765, p. 215; CSIL 4/1782, p. 86

Board William   CSIL 4/1722, p. 22

Bolgar, Edward   CSIL 4/1836, M 73A, reel 1073

Boxley, Francis   CSIL 4/1760, p. 19: wrote that he had served his apprenticeship in HM Dockyard and 'was doing comfortably for himself until January last when repairing a mill at Richmond the works got hold of his right arm and crushed the bone in such a manner as renders him entirely incapable of earning a subsistance for himself ... has no friend to look to only the sympathising Government'. Piper recommended him as 'a very industrious lad ... an object worthy of pity'

Bradley, Ann   CSIL 4/1779, p. 32

Bradley, Jonas   CSIL 4/1779, p. 32

Bray, John   CSIL 4/1839, M 32: requested a ticket of occupation for two square miles on which to run his 400 sheep

Bryan, Catherine, re her character: V. Jacobs   CSIL 4/1761, pp. 45–8

Burke, James   CSIL 4/1823, M 99; CSIL 4/1828B, M 36

Butcher, William   CSIL, PMS 4/1976, p. 31

Byrne, Hugh   CSIL 4/1835B, M 1823

Chapman, Ann and William   CSIL 4/1760, M 58; CSIL 4/1770, p. 168

Chapman, William   CSIL 4/1760, p. 52

Chaseling, Ann   CSIL 4/1836B, M 181: father, Thomas Chaseling, 'for more than twenty-one years has been settled on a grant of 30 acres on the Banks of the Hawkesbury ... He has endured many losses from floods ...'

Cheers, Richard   CSIL 4/1832, M 130; CSIL 4/1829, M 51

Clarke, Joseph   CSIL 4/1826B, M188

Clee, Richard   CSIL 4/1863B, M 835

Clew, George, P. to T.D. Condamine Esq.   CSIL 4/2167, M 114

Coffee, Joseph   CSIL 4/1849, p. 41. Affidavit X1824, 4/1690, p. 89

Cole, Hannah   CSIL 4/1759, p. 115

Colletts, James and Joseph   CSIL 4/1836, Ms 207–8

Collis, James   CSIL 4/1863B, p. 920

Connelly, Margaret   CSIL 4/1848, p. 6

Connor, Michael   CSIL 4/1846, M 27, reel 1069; CSIL 4/1836, M 216, reel 1073

Cozier, William   CSIL 4/1836B, M 229, p. 1001: 'by trade a smith, a native of Parramatta', ... 'brought up as a smith ...'

Cubitt, Daniel snr   CSIL 4/1756, p. 123: Daniel snr appointed Master of the Row Guard Boat and his son Daniel appointed Coxswain.   CSIL 4/1760, reel 2190, p. 47: Daniel snr stated he had held position of Master of the Row Guard Boat from 26.4.1822, the date of its establishment. CSIL 4/1829, No. 47, reel 1069: Daniel snr stated he had been 30 years in the service of Government and requested a government residence for his wife and large family

Currey, Charlotte (née Cubitt)   CSIL 4/1763, p. 155: Petition for clemency for her husband, Thomas Currey

Dalton, Richard snr   CSIL 4/1786, p. 143

Dargon/Dargan, James, convicted with Timothy Lacey. His parents wrote to the Governor asking for clemency for their 'unfortunate son' for they feared that should he be transported to Van Diemen's Land 'with convicts and their slothful and hardened habits' it would cause 'future misfortune' to their boy; the mother was an ex-convict. CSIL, PMS 1825, 4/1873, p. 59; Memorial of Mary Dargon

Dargon, Mary   CSIL 4/1873, p. 59; CSIL 4/1831, M 31, PMS 4/1866, p. 41

Davis, James   CSIL 4/1841, M 196, reel 1078

Davis, Nancy   CSIL 4/1779, p. 10

Day, Thomas jnr, 'a boatbuilder and shipwright by trade ... served his time under Thomas Moore Esq.'. 24.10.1825   CSIL 4/1841A, Memorial 206 of Thomas Day snr. Thomas Day was described as 'a very sober and industrious young man, and has property sufficient I believe to enable him to cultivate a Farm ... He is deserving of encouragement' (William Cowper) CSIL 4/1841, M 20

Day, Thomas   CSIL 4/1826, M 34: 'Thomas Day, Invalid from H.M.'s 73rd Regiment'

Dell, John   CSIL 4/1823, M 184

Douglas, Henry, re Elizabeth Sidebottom CSIL 4/1756, p. 53, reel 2170

Douglas, William   CSIL 4/1823, M 199, reel 1067; CSIL 4/1837, M 287, reel 1074

Douglass, William   CSIL 4/1826, M 27; CSIL 4/1781, p. 353; CSIL 4/1837, M 287

Duggan, Mary   CSIL 4/1848, p. 128, reel 1227

Edney, John Pte   CSIL 4/1781, p. 326: Edney took his wife and son, first to Ceylon with the Regiment, then to England; Edney and his son returned to NSW to settle in 1818. John Edney snr   CSIL 4/1823, M 221; John Edney jnr   CSIL 4/1823, M 221A

Egan, Daniel   CSIL 4/1841B, M 256; CSIL 4/1788, p. 145

Eggleton, William   CSIL 4/1823, M 223: 'arrived 36 years ago ... has been a free man nearly 20 years ... during which period his conduct has been uniformly good nor has he ever had his name brought into question ...'

Ezzey/Ezzoy, John   CSIL 4/1827, M 325

Fieldhouse, George   CSIL 4/1825, M 237

Fishburne, William   CSIL 4/1838, M 549

Fletcher, Edward   CSIL 4/1837, M 341

Flood, Joseph   CSIL 4/1841, M 282

Foley, David, arrived convict on the *Guildford* CSIL 4/1763, p. 187

Foulcher, David   CSIL 4/1824, M 255

Frances, Thomas jnr   CSIL 4/1824, M 256

Frazier, John   CSIL 4/1771, p. 299

Fry, Margaret and Richard   CSIL 4/1781, p. 402; CSIL 4/1755, p. 180

Fulton, Henry   14 Feb. 1809, *H.R.N.S.W.*, 7, p. 31; letter to Mrs Bligh, Banks Papers, MSS ML

Gosport, John and Joseph   CSIL 4/1824, M 289

Griffiths, John   CSIL 4/1837, M 404, reel 1074; CSIL 4/1710 or 4/1780, M 124, p. 181: describes himself as a settler at Port Dalrymple; it would appear that he had returned to NSW to marry Elizabeth Thorley of Richmond, 12.8.1822

Gulley, Thomas   CSIL 4/1858; PMS No. 145

Hacking, Edward   CSIL 4/1837, M 408

Hanks, Joseph   CSIL 4/1842, M 346, reel 1079

Hannibus, John   CSIL 4/1824, M 308

Hansey, Thomas   CSIL 4/1824, M 310

Henry, James   CSIL 4/1824, M 338, reel 1068; CSIL 4/1830, M 16, reel 1070

Herne, Abraham   CSIL 4/1824, M 341

Higgins, Andrew, schoolmaster   CSIL 4/1794, pp. 80–2: list of children in attendance at Sydney Branch of R.C. School

Holland, Charlotte, *Glatton*, housekeeper CSIL 4/1846, p. 132

Holmes, William   CSIL 4/1832, M 470

Hughes, Thomas   CSIL 4/1780, p. 348

Hughes, William   CSIL 4/1094, p. 2

Hume, Hamilton   CSIL 4/1848, M 413, Testimonial

Humm, Daniel   CSIL 4/1837, M 483, reel 1275

Hyland, Lawrence   CSIL 4/1837, M 461

Irving, John   CSIL 4/1838, M 755; CSIL 4/1760, p. 17; CSIL 4/1811, p. 132–3

Jacklin, Joseph   CSIL 4/1822A, M 23; CSIL 4/1822A, p. 919

Jacobs, V.   CSIL 4/1761, pp. 45–8

Jenkins, James   CSIL 4/1836, M 689: in Oct. 1823 Jenkins' father wrote to the Governor and stated he had purchased 410 acres and 'there being 700 acres, chiefly rocks and swamps adjoining my farm' he requested a ticket of occupation, adding that the 'deceased McDonnell's grant [had been] willed to my children'.   CSIL 4/1835, M 160; CSIL 4/1835, M 509

Jones, Mary, midwife   CSIL 4/1759, p. 94, reel 2171

Keighran, John   CSIL 4/1848, M 413
Kelly, Judith, arrived *Sydney Cove*   CSIL 4/1846, p. 124
Kennedy, Ann   CSIL 4/1848, p. 19
Kennedy, 'Daniel'   CSIL 1810, 4/1821, M 171A: claims to be 'an old marine'
Kennedy, Donald jnr   CSIL 4/1838, M 535
Kenny: Edward   CSIL 4/1830, M 205; Francis, 27, B.C. 1801, Catholic, farmer, Lake George   CSIL 4/1771, p. 299

Mobbs, John   CSIL 4/1825A M 505: father had arrived unconvicted and married an ex-convict woman, owned 907 acres in 1828
Moore, Peter   CSIL 4/1825A, p. 31
Morgan, William   CSIL 4/1825A, p. 47
Morley, Hannah, publican   CSIL 4/1759, p. 144
Mortimer, George   CSIL 4/1825A, p. 53
Morris, Martha   CSIL 4/1848, p. 240
Mosley, James   CSIL 4/1825A, p. 55; CSIL 4/1821A, p. 55
Murphy, Stephen   CSIL 4/1822, M 236: evidence at Inquest, 1816: 4/1819, p. 556
Morris, John   CSIL 4/1825A, p. 237

Nowland: Michael, Henry, William and Edward   CSIL 4/1838, M 721

O'Hara, John   CSIL 4/1836B, M 735
Onslow, George   CSIL 4/1763, pp. 245–7
Orr, James: father of William, Spencer, Ebenezer & James   CSIL 4/1843B, pp. 921–33, M 644
Osborn, Catherine   CSIL 4/1846, p. 172
Osburn, William   CSIL 4/1835, M 238; CSIL 4/1825, M 582: apprenticed his son to boatbuilder Thomas Day
Owens, James and Thomas, father of   CSIL 4/1825A, M 584

Partridge, Mary   PMS, CSIL 4/1788, p. 11
Payten, Nathaniel   CSIL 4/1825A, p. 367
Packer, James   CSIL 4/1826B, M 1243
Peacock, John Jenkins   CSIL 4/1839A, M 751
Peat, George   CSIL 4/1839, M 755; 4/1771, p. 216: he worked in partnership with

James Webb and John James Peacock
Peek/Peck, Joshua snr and sons Joshua and Thomas   CSIL 4/1867, p. 12: Peck snr 'a prisoner of the Crown at Newcastle sent there from V.D.L. two years ago; requests permission to 'manufacture tobacco'
Peiseley, Francis   CSIL 4/1825A, M 351
Pennell, Martha   CSIL 4/1732, 4/1733, p. 163
Pithers/Pitches, William   CSIL 4/1825, M 618
Podmore, Sarah, B.C. daughter Richard Podmore   CSIL: 4/1839B, M 83 permission to marry Joseph Spencer
Police Establishments, salaries paid; men employed: CSIL 4/1844B, p. 794; CSIL 4/1835, M 318A. Col. Sec. Returns of the colony, 1828, Police Establishments: Thorn, John, Chief Constable £130 p.a.; Meredith, Frederick, £100 p.a.; Blackman, James, Chief Constable and Poundkeeper £70 p.a.; District Constable's salary averaged £51.17.0; Ordinary Constable £41.3.6; Ordinary Constable and scourger £36.12.0
Powell, Edward snr   CSIL 4/1822, M 1066: 'arrived as a settler ... after the prime of his life had been devoted to King and Country in the times of warfare ... eight children'
Powell, Edward   CSIL 4/1839A, M 781; CSIL 4/1844, M 660
Power/Poer/Poor, Timothy, brother-in-law of Morgan Poer/Poor   CSIL 4/2167, M 95
Pugh, John   CSIL 4/1825A, p. 433: Pugh 'wished to enter the more mature and manly walks of life'
Pugh, Samuel   CSIL 4/1839, M 1824: requested a town allotment to carry out the business of cable and rope making

Quinland, Judith   CSIL 4/1846, p. 186

Regan, William   CSIL 4/1822, M 275; CSIL 4/1831, M 316
Roberts, James and John   CSIL 4/1825, M 650, reel 1068
Rolf/Rolph, Ann, cambric weaver, *William Pitt*   CSIL, PMS, 4/1846, p. 191
Rope, William   CSIL 4/1839, M 842

Sanders, Thomas jnr   CSIL 4/1839, M 866
Scott, Hugh   CSIL 4/1825, M 732, reel 1068
Scott, Thomas   CSIL 4/1839A, p. 619
   Joseph Scott was a publican at Upper Minto with 110 acres
Shoals, Joseph   CSIL 4/1839A, p. 621
Sidebottom, Elizabeth, *Speke* 1808   CSIL 4/1846, p. 198; CSIL 4/1848, pp. 314–316: assists butcher husband

Sidgwick, Ann   CSIL 4/1846, p. 142
Smith, Ann, nursemaid, *Aeolus*   CSIL, PMS 4/1846, reel 1227, p. 201: nursemaid to Lewis family on voyage to Australia; pardon requested so she could serve family on voyage to England
Smith, Captain David   CSIL 4/1822A, p. 476
Smith, Mary, mantua maker, *Broxbornbury* CSIL, PMS 4/1849, p. 33: requested TL; granted 7/8/1815
Spears, James   CSIL 4/1828, M 921; CSIL 4/1839, M 921: land grants to the three sons listed in Darling's List of Land Grants to the Native-Born: James, no. 414, 24.8.1824, 60 acres; George, no. 415, 13.8.1824, 60 acres; John, no. 412, 27.11.1825, 60 acres

Thompson, Ann   CSIL 4/1761, p. 64
Townson, Sarah   CSIL 4/1846, p. 223
Tucker, John   CSIL 4/1833; CSIL 4/1835
Tuckerman, Stephen   CSIL 4/1825, M 751
Tuckwell, George   CSIL 4/1825, M 752: 'I recommend him to the notice of Your Excellency being a free born subject of this colony'
Tuckwell, William   CSIL 4/1756, p. 176–7
Turnbull/Turnball, John   CSIL 4/1840, M 1004

Webb, Hannah, nee Mocklan, wife of Richard Webb formerly assigned to John Blaxland CSIL 1819, PMS 4/1860, p. 79: recommended as honest and industrious
Wells, Sarah   CSIL 4/1761, p. 96
Wilson, Caleb   CSIL 4/1761, p. 51
Wilson, George   CSIL 4/1840, M 1066; CSIL 4/1786, p. 103, no. 194
Wood George   CSIL 4/1824, M 801: apprenticed to James Smith of Sydney; CSIL 4/1825, M 801: received 200 acres
Wood, John   CSIL 4/1825, M 802
Wright, Charles, John and Robert   CSIL 4/1825B, M 811, reel 1068: 'Robert a cooper in govt. employ';   CSIL 4/1844C, M 81: John served an apprenticeship with John Harrison of Van Diemen's Land, Charles at Govt. Lumber Yard; all 3 received 60 acres each
Wyatt, Rachael   CSIL 4/1732, 4/1733, p. 153: 'That Memorialist came out to this colony with the hope of bettering the situation of an unfortunate Husband'
Wynn, Elizabeth, *Aeolus*   CSIL PMS, 1810–1816, 4/1846, reel 1227, p. 245: placed as Assistant Matron of the Orphan School

INDEX B

PERSONS MENTIONED IN THE TEXT

Note:
This is a selective index to contemporary persons mentioned in the text. It refers to name/family only and is not descriptive, except in the case of governors and major officials. Where a contemporary is cited in the text, the subject matter is included in this index. Where two or more persons have the same first and second names, they are identified by occupation or civil condition.

Abbott, Lieut. Edward   107
Abrams, Esther   69, 77, 90, 150
Acres, Joseph   102; son Thomas   99, m. Lucy Day   160–1
Adams, Pte William   117
Allcorn/Alcorn: Edward   110, 113; Elizabeth   174; John   110, 260; Richard jnr and wife Charlotte (née Gulledge)   110
Ambrose, Thomas and family   245–6, 254
Anderson, George, and parents Pte Robert Anderson and Mary Franklin   123
Anderson, Gerald, and parents   218
Arndell, Surgeon   69; m. Elizabeth Dalton   166

Atkinson, James, on colonial labour   261
Avery, Thomas   163

Badgery: James snr   108, 110, 111–12; Andrew, Henry, James, William   112
Badgery, John and family   110
Bain, Chaplain   76
Baker, Ann   81
Balmain, Surgeon William: and Margaret Dawson   89; and population statistics 24; and son John Henderson   89, 105
Banks, Sir Joseph   108, 228; patron of James Badgery   110

Barnet/Barnett, Daniel   102; son Barney 269
Barrisford, John   107
Bates, James, marriage of   164
Bates: Lydia   174; Thomas   104, 107, 111
Bathurst, Henry 3rd Earl   41, 101, 108; attitudes to BC   41, 191, 199; Instructions to Brisbane   197; and land   198, 199, 200; letters from Macquarie   41, 101, 108
Batman, William, and family   260
Baxter, William   132
Bay, Mary   93
Baylis/Bayliss/Bayless: Joseph and Ann (née Croft)   28, 232; son John   231, 232; Edward   223; William and Ann (née Price)   271; William and Louisa (née Ezzy)   104
Bayly, Lieut. Nicholas, and family   117, 194
Beal/Beales, Charles, and family   157, 210
Bean, James   113
Becket/Beckett, James   167; daughter Mary   189
Beckford, Elizabeth   87
Bell, Archibald: evidence to Bigge   50, 269; son Archibald jnr   114
Bell, Mr, ill-usage of apprentice   136
Bellamy, Sarah   77; legal dispute with sons   230
Benn, John, m. Eliza Lydia Griffith   106
Bennett, Mrs   229
Bent, J.H., evidence to Select Committee on Gaols (1819)   41
Best, George   167, 174; evidence to Bigge 114, 164; son George   191; son Thomas m. Mary Beckett   189; wife Hannah Mullens   77
Bicknell, James   141
Bigge, J.T.: attitudes to BC   14, 42, 179, 191, 250, 252, 259–60; attitude to convicts/ex-convicts   196–7, 265, 266; attitude to free settlers   197; as commentator   44; on Female Factory   79; influence on society 200, 204; on land grants   186–7; and Male Orphan School   131; and rural workers   266
Biggers, Thomas   117; m. Elizabeth Fitzgerald   88; son Andrew   256, employed by Reibey   251; son Thomas   245
Bird, Elizabeth   77
Bishop, Mary: m. Samuel Day   160; and son   161
Black, John Henry, m. Louisa Skinner   166, 174
Blackman, James, and family   111
Blackman, William, and wife Sarah (née Cobcroft)   105
Blackstone, –, on rights of apprentices/slaves   130
Bland, Mrs, and Captain Brake   83

Blaxcel, Garnham   113, 125
Blaxland, Gregory   53, 108, 113; advertisement for apprentice   130; evidence to Bigge   47
Blaxland, John: and cloth production   228; and education of daughters   151; Brisbane and grants to son   202; land grants to, with Gregory   108; re Mary King   94
Blakefield, Charles   224
Bligh, Governor William: concern for Rising Generation   66; Instructions re BC education   153; lack of Instructions re BC land   186; letter to, re women convicts 65; opinion, on absconders and mutineers 138, 240, on convicts   48; and John Palmer   78
Bloodsworth, James   167, 230; and Sarah Bellamy   77; daughter Ann m. Thomas Bray   167; son George   253, and Eliza Chipp   173, m. Maria Cox   244; son James   230
Blower, Martha   155
Blue, William: and family   260; son Robert   228
Board, George William
Bogg, R.   137
Bogg, Thomas   228
Bolgar, Edward   249, 251, 253
Bolton, Thomas   117
Boswell, James   234
Bosworth, Mary   93
Boulton, Thomas, and son Isaac   271
Bourne, John   239
Bowman, John   104, 196; sons George and William   111, 113
Bowden, Thomas, evidence to Bigge   59, 131
Brackenreg, Charles James: and father James   123; m. Mary Ann Stubbs   173
Braddock, John, and son John   271
Bradley, Jonas   189
Bradley, John   141
Bradley, Jonathan   238; and parents Abraham Moor and Mary (née Dairs)   249
Bradley, Thomas and William   189
Braund, Mary, m. William Bryant   85
Bray, John: and family   167; son Thomas and family   194; son William and family   249
Brennen, Peter   224
Brisbane, Governor Sir Thomas: and apprentices   135, 201–2; and land alienation   147–8, and BC   186, 193, 201; land grants   186, 188, 195, 196–7, 199, 200, 201, 202–3, 267, 270, 275; land purchase regulations   198, 263; land sales   197; opinion on workforce, inhabitants   197; Petitions to   142, 151; proposes Colonial Cavalry   276; Report to Bathurst, on Bigge and BC   191, on

Bigge's recommendations   196–7; John
   Ritchie's opinion of   197
Brogan, John and Eliza   162
Broughton, Eliza   260; and son William
   194
Brown, Henry   232
Brown, Pte John   232
Brown, William   188
Brozill/Brazell, William   238, 244
Bryan, Catherine, Petition of V. Jacobs
   re   95
Bryant, William   85
Buckle, Richard, m. Hannah Dark   173
Burgin, William snr: and Sarah Tandy and
   Mary West   110; son Henry and
   family   110, 223; son William and
   family   110
Burrel, Anne   155
Burton, Chief Justice W., on BC   44
Burke, James, and father   189
Butcher, William, and mother Ann Butcher,
   foster-mother Hannah Hobson (alias Mary
   Hobbs)   248
Butler, Joseph, and family   102, 123; son
   Lawrence   138, 275; son Walter   123
Byfield, Sarah and family   157
Byrne, Thomas and John   274
Byrnes, William and son David   123

Calcutt, Ann, and James Becket/Beckett
   189
Caley, George   101
Campbell, John   53; as character witness
   189
Campbell, Robert: and brig *Venus*   240; and
   land   113; as merchant   125, 238
Cann, James, employed by John Herring
   264
Carrol, Mary, and de facto husband   91
Carter, James   59
Cartwright, Robert, evidence to Bigge   265
Carver, William, employed by George
   Howell   271
Castlereagh, Viscount (2nd Marquess of Lon-
   donderry): letter from Rev. Henry Fulton
   166; letter to King   108; letter to Wilber-
   force   75
Catchpole, Margaret   77
Cavanagh, Owen   260; described by King
   112; m. Margaret Dowling   112
Chaceling family   167
Chaffey/Chafey, Elizabeth, and William Free-
   man and sons George, John, James   224
Chamberlain, Martha, m. George Best   164
Champley, John   141
Chandler, John   138
Chandler, William, daughter Sarah and
   family   154

Chapman, William snr: and son
   George   238, 245; son James   143; son
   William   134–5, 221
Charlton, James, employed by John Piper
   270
Cheers, Richard: and wife Esther (née
   Weaver) and family   108; sons John and
   Richard   244
Child, Sir Josiah, on children of the poor   124
Chipp, Eliza, and father and George
   Bloodsworth   173
Clark, Lieut. Ralph: on governors' powers
   51; on *Lady Juliana*   73
Clark, Zachariah   88
Clarkson, Catherine   138
Clee, Richard   188
Clarke, Joseph   270
Clew, George   132–3
Cluer, William   211
Cobbett, William   269
Cobcroft, John: described by King   112; and
   sons John and Richard and families   105,
   112
Coffee, Joseph   238
Cole, Elizabeth   84
Cole, Hannah   93
Colebrook, Thomas, and wife Betty (née
   Wade) and son Thomas jnr   144
Colletts/Collett, Pierce   111, 189, 264; and
   sons James and John family   264; son
   Joseph   189
Collins, Judge-Advocate David: on Irish
   women convicts   80; on *Lady Juliana*
   32–3; on Eliner Magee   24
Collis, George, and wife Mary   110; son
   James   113
Colquohoun, Patrick   87; on London
   harlots   82
Condon, Thomas   269
Connelly, James, m. Sarah Maloney   76
Connolly, Pte Andrew, and son James and
   family   105
Connolly, Margaret, m. Thomas O'Brien   92
Conolly, James, and parents James Harris
   and Elizabeth Phillips   123
Conolly, Father   171
Connor, James, and parents James Harris and
   Elizabeth Phillips   123
Connor, Michael, and father   248, 254
Cook, Maria, and Daniel Cubbitt   26
Cook, Thomas, and son Thomas jnr   123,
   143
Cooper, Elizabeth, wife of John Ryan jnr   105
Cornwall, Isaac   110
Cosier/Cozier, Thomas, and sons Thomas jnr
   and William   123
Cottrell, Pte Thomas, and Ann Lynch   89
Cowen, Andrew, and wife Agnes   157

Cowper, William: evidence to Bigge   59; testimonial for Elizabeth Sidebottom   93

Cox, Edward, and father   191–2

Cox, William of Clarendon, employed James Powell and Richard Podmore's sons   163

Cozier, Dorinda, m. Thomas Street   174

Crane, Sarah   157

Creamer, Elizabeth, and John   157

Croft, Joseph   59

Croft, Ann, m. Joseph Baylis   28

Crook, W.P.   23; and evening school   126

Crowder, Thomas, employed by Richard Hall   266

Crowder, Thomas Restill, m. Sarah Davis   88

Cruise, Edward   266

Cubbitt/Cubitt, Daniel: and family   26, 174; daughter Charlotte m. Thomas Currey   164–5; son John/Jonathan   210, 239, 249, 275

Cunningham, James, and son John and family   105

Cunningham, Surgeon Peter   45; on BC   14, 237; on ex-convicts   56

Cummings, David   239

Curtis, Peter   231

Dalton, Ann, m. William Fielder   220

Dalton, Elizabeth Burleigh: British crime   87; m. Surgeon Arndell   69, 166

Dalton, Richard, and son William, daughter-in-law Rebecca (née Scrivenson)   217, 218

Dargen, James, and wife Sophia (née Ezzy)   104

Dargin, Thomas (1), ex-convict, and wife Mary (née Loveridge) and son   113

Dargin, Thomas (2), ex-soldier, and wife Mary (née Warren)   150

Dargon, James   174

Dargon, Joseph   168

Dark, Hannah, m. Richard Buckle   173

Darling, Eliza   72

Darling, Governor Ralph: and Address of Welcome   42, 56, 179; and apprenticeships   132, 137; and forms of land tenure   203; and land grants   186, 187, 197, 204, to BC   113, 192, 193, 203, cancellation of   116, small   200

Davidson, James John   113

Davies, Sarah   87, 88

Davis, Eliza, m. George Onslow   165

Davis, James, and father Pte Evan Davies   246

Davis, Joseph   211

Davis, Nancy   148–9

Davis, William   181

Dawson, Margaret   89, 105; de facto wife of Balmain   173; son John Henderson   105

Day, Samuel: and wife Mary (née Bishop) and family   160–1; daughter Lucy   151, m. Thomas Acres   160; son Thomas   161, 173, 190, 218

Day, Sgt   107

Deacy, James   141

Deane, William   226; and father William snr   230

Dell, John: and wife Elizabeth (née Robinson), son John jnr and family   123; daughter Elizabeth   26

Despraedo, Manuel and Ellen   162

Dick, Alexander, m. Charlotte Hutchinson   174

Dickson, John   157

Dight, John snr, and wife Hannah   112; son John and daughter Hannah   54, 222

Dixson, Father Harold   169; and population records   25, 26

Donnelly, Garrett and George, sons of Pte Simon Garrett   123, 226

Dowling, Margaret, m. Owen Cavanagh   112

Dring, Elizabeth   151

Driver, John: advertisement for apprentice   130; son John m. Elizabeth Powell   166; wife of   72

Druitt, Major George, evidence to Bigge   133, 208, 209

Duggan, William   94

Duggen, Mary, m. John Tarlton   94

Dundas, Henry   23; and land grants   116; report from Grose   101

Dundas, Jane   90

Dunston/Dansam family   112

Dykes, Alexander, m. Sophia Bishop   174

Eagar, Edward: and apprentices   144; and BC   14, 237; evidence to Bigge   121–2, 242; on governors' powers   188; and land   186

Eather/Ether/Euther, Thomas snr   110; son Charles and family   105; son James   143; son Thomas jnr   264

Eaton, William (1), m. Mary Haydon   85

Eaton, William (2), and wife Jane and family   158

Edney, John/William: Memorial to Brisbane   273–4; and parents John Edney and Hannah Jones   273

Eagan, Daniel   218

Eggleston, William   264

Eldon, Lord, on crime   84

Ellam, Deborah, m. John Herbert   111

Elliott, Mary   174

Evans, Elizabeth   80

Evans, James: son Charles   271; and son James   123

Evans, William (1): and wife Mary and
   family   123, 260; son John   228
Evans, William (2), and mutiny   240
Everingham, Matthew, and family   167, 174;
   daughter Maria m. Thomas Cotton   164;
   son William   202
Ezzy/Ezzey/Ezzoy, Jane, and family   104

Fitzwilliam, Earl, and William Charles
   Wentworth   273
Fletcher, Eliza, and family   158–9
Fletcher, Edward, and family   58
Flood, Joseph: and Ann Germaine   249; son
   John   123, 228; sons Joseph and Thomas
   228
Flynn, Father, deported from New South
   Wales   170
Foley, David, and family   165
Foster, James (1), apprentice   143
Foster, James (2), ship's boy   251
Foulcher, James   189
Frances, Thomas, and father   190
Franklin, Mary, and family   123
Farmer, Thomas, and parents John Farmer
   and Ann Johnston   244
Ferrier, Catherine   93
Field, Edward: and family   122; daughter
   Maria m. son of Anthony Rope   167; son
   George   202
Fielder, William: and father   220; m. Ann
   Dalton   220
Fieldhouse, George   232, 270
Fish, Elizabeth, m. Edward Powell   112
Fitzgerald, Elizabeth, m. Thomas Biggers
   88
Fitzgerald, Jane, m. William Mitchell   107
Fitzgerald, Richard   196
Fitzpatrick, Ambrose   170–1
Fitzpatrick, Phillip   143
Frazier, Eleanor   103
Frazier, John, Memorial to Brisbane   275–6
Freebody, Simon   112
Freeman, William, and wife Elizabeth (née
   Chaffrey) and sons George, James,
   Thomas   224, 226–7
Fry, George, and sons John, Richard,
   Samuel   226
Fry, John, and parents Richard and
   Margaret   143
Fulton, Anne, wife of Rev. Henry Fulton   70
Fulton, Rev. Henry   196, 271; and discrimi-
   nation against children of convicts   165–6;
   employed Alexander McDonald   271; wife
   Anne   70
Furner, John, employed by Richard Siddons
   264
Fry, Richard   254

Fryer, Catherine, de facto wife of Matthew
   Prior   85

Galvin, Susan, and family   154
Garrett, Pte Simon, and son George
   Donnelly   123
Garside/Gearside, Samuel   110
Gascoigne, Olive/Olivia, wife of Nathaniel
   Lucas   222
Geddes, Henry   239
George, Ann   77, 81–2
Gerrald, Joseph, letter from Samuel Parr   41
Goodin/Goodwin, Edward: and family   111;
   son James   234
Going, John   226
Gorman, Elizabeth, and sister
   Catherine   154
Goulburn, Colonial Secretary Frederick:
   issues list of labour costs   214; Memorial re
   Police Corps from Francis Kenny   276
Gout, Sarah   77
Graham, George   232
Green, Caroline, m. Everitt Summons   174
Green, George, and family   141
Green, James, and Elizabeth Sims   173
Greenwood, James   156
Gregory, Edward, and family   138
Gregory, George, and family   137–8
Grenville, W.H.: Instructions to Shapcote re
   women   33; Instructions to Phillip re
   convicts   117, re land grants   107
Grey, Sir George, receives evidence re BC
   54
Griffiths, Elizabeth   156
Griffiths, Eliza Lydia, m. (1) John Benn (2)
   John MacDonald   106
Griffiths, John/Jonathan   246–7; and brother
   William   250
Griffiths/Griffen, Pte Michael, and family
   106
Grinus, George   251
Grono, William, and family   167
Grose, Lieut.-Governor Francis: Instruc-
   tions from Dundas re population statistics
   23–4; and land grants   103, 107, 116;
   report to Dundas re land grants   101–2
Gulledge, Thomas, and sons Thomas jnr and
   Isaac   110
Gulley, Henry   242

Hale, Henry   156
Hall, Edward Smith: on BC   121; on
   discrimination   259; on purchase
   regulations   263
Hallam, John, and Valetta   162
Hamilton, Alexander   163
Hancey, Thomas, and brother Richard   230

Hand, William   254
Hanks, William   249; and father   249; and sisters Phoebe and Louisa   242
Hannibus, John   190
Harrex, Sarah, and family   157
Harris, Alexander: describes rural family 114, Tom Small   275; on innkeepers 181; on public houses   182; on sawyers 266; opinions on colonial society   45
Harris, Ann, accused of seducing Thomas Jones   94
Harris, Pte James, and wife Elizabeth (née Phillips) and son James jnr   123, 226
Harris, John: assaulted   82; land grant to   117; letter against   166
Harrison, Mary   85
Hassall, James, employed by Samuel Fry   226
Hassall, Rev. Rowland   112; comments on Marsden and Male Orphan School   43; and sons James and Thomas   113
Hatwood, William   226
Haydon, Mary, m. William Eaton   88
Hayes, Mary   76
Hayes, Michael, advertises in *Sydney Gazette*   227
Hazleen, William, and parents   217
Hector, Catherine, and brothers   154
Henderson, John: advertises   273; parents of   89, 105; as surgeon   272–3
Herbert, John: and wife Deborah (née Ellam) and family   111; son Thomas   266
Herring, Mary   155
Hibbs, Peter   260
Higgins, Mary, m. Thomas Seymour.   173–4
Hill, David, and father   224
Hobart, Lord, letter from King   133, 186
Hobbs, Elizabeth   76
Hobby, Thomas   191
Hobhouse, Sir John, on child labour   131
Hobson, Hannah (alias Mary Hobbs), and foster son   248
Holland, Charlotte   91
Holmes, Margaret, m. Patrick Shannon   251; m. John Millet   252; son James   251
Hoppy, James   228
Horan, Bridget   91
Horsley, Mr   108
Hough, Henry, and family   123, 222, 223
Howe, Ann   173
Howe, George snr, and sons Robert and George   123, 275
Howe, William (1), advice to Bigge   262
Howe, William (2), mariner   173
Howe, William (3), BC   254
Howell, George   222; employed by William Carver   271; and parents   223

Howell, John, employed by James Hassall 264
Howell, Pte John, and son Henry and family 105
Howell, Peter   157
Howick, Viscount, on colonial civil liberties 198
Hudson, Sgt Thomas, m. Eleanor Lennard 92
Hughes, Henry   223
Hughes, Matthew, and daughters Susannah and Margaret and family   159
Hughes, Thomas, and 'orphan' daughter 147
Hughes, William, and brother Jonathan   243
Hume, Andrew Hamilton   99; daughter Isabella m. George Barber   166; son Hamilton   191, m. Elizabeth Dight   222
Humm, William, and parents William Humm and Mary (née Hook)   245
Humphries, William   220
Hunter, Governor John: concern for Rising Generation   66; and juvenile convicts   61; lack of Instructions re BC land   186; and land grants   103, 116; sale   111; little encouragement for ex-convicts   57; opinion of women convicts   65; and population 24; receives Instructions re church and school 152, re land grants   101
Huon, Elizabeth, m. William Mitchell   174

Inch, Joseph, and family   161
Innett, Ann: and Lieut. King   74; m. William Robinson   77
Irving, John, parentage and career, m. daughter of Lieut. Ball and Sarah Partridge 220–1

Jacklin, Joseph and John, and family   190
Jacobs, V., Petition re Catherine Bryan   95
James, Henry: son of William Henry   245, 247; as ship's apprentice   253
Jamison, Sir John: letter to Bathurst re Macquarie   108; son Thomas   193
Jennings, John   231
Jenkins, James   193
Johnson, James, and family   141
Johnson, Mary   84
Johnson, Sarah, and son James   141
Johnson, Rev. Richard: letter from King 43; letter to S.P.G. re convicts   41, re convicts and children   149; receives land grant   118; wife Mary   70, 72
Johnson, Major George   150; m. Esther Abrams   69, 77; son George jnr   194; letter re, from Rev. Henry Fulton to Viscount Castlereagh   166

Johnstone, Elizabeth, and family 157
Jones, John 220
Jones, Judith (alias Ann Davis) 86
Jones, Mary 156
Jones, Thomas (1) 114
Jones, Thomas (2), seduced by Ann
  Harris 94

Kable/Cable, Henry 72, 174, 230; and
  apprentices 124, 125, 138; daughter
  Diana 151; son Edgar 264; son
  George 275; and Underwood 219–20,
  238
Kean, Bridget 91
Keighran, Patrick 269
Kiernon, William 254
Kellick, Richard 217
Kelly, Captain James 237, 250, 253
Kelly, Judith 92
Kennedy, Ann, de facto wife of Thomas
  O'Neale 92
Kennedy, Donald: and family 172; daughter
  Catherine 171–2
Kennedy, Elizabeth More, m. Andrew Hamil-
  ton Hume 166; daughter Isabella m.
  George Barber 166
Kennedy, Jane 77
Kennedy, Lawrence, m. Ann Shannon 173
Kennedy, Mr, employs George
  Donnelly 226
Kenny, Edward 193; brother Francis 170,
  193, Memorial to Goulburn 276
Kent, Lieut., letter from Governor King 43
Keppard, Richard 228
King, Anna Josepha 72; and BC children
  45, 149; and Female Orphan School
  147; recommends housekeeper
  91
King, Governor Philip Gidley: on absconders
  and deserters 138; concern for Rising
  Generation 43, 153; and flax production
  228; lack of Instructions re BC
  education 152, 153, re BC land 186; and
  choice of Norfolk Island settlers 89; and
  land, alienation 101, 186, grants 106,
  107, 108, limited arable 101, sale of 116;
  on population 24; on Roman Catholics
  24, toleration 76ff.: sees need for protecting BC girls 149; on women, and 1860
  Muster 74, 78, and Female Muster 69,
  Irish 80, as labour 37
King, Philip Parker 237, 242, 250
King, Under-Secretary: letter from Governor
  King 53, from Margarot 69
Kinsall, Thomas 143
Kirk, Patrick, and son 143
Knight, Daniel 232

Lacey, James 32
Lacey, Timothy 174, 188; letter from
  Brisbane 275; and William Baldwin and
  John Brown 278
Lamb, James 156
Lamb, Rebecca, wife of John Ezzy 104
Lambe, William, employed by Richard
  Pritchard 274
Lane, Henry, Petition re Charlotte Holland
  91
Lane, James, and son 143
Lane, M. 211
Lane, William, and father George Lane 123
Landers/L'Andre, William, and parents
  Antoine L'Andre and Ann (née Cook) 246
Lang, J.D., on Macquarie's land grants
  116–17
Langford, John, m. Susannah Wilkinson 76
Larra, James 194, m. Susannah Langford
  (née Wilkinson) 76
Laycock, Joshua 194
Lavello, James (1), wheelwright 224
Lavello, James (2), blacksmith 223
Lawson, William (1), seaman 240
Lawson, William (2), and sons 193
Leadon, Peter 244
Lee, Elizabeth 88–9
Lee (or Pantony), Maria, m. James Bloods-
  worth jnr 230
Leeson, Thomas, and convict servants 114
Leighton, George, Petitition for daughter
  Mary 151
Lennard, Eleanor, m. Sgt Thomas Hudson
  91–2
Leonard, Elizabeth, m. Kellyhorn 90–1
Limeburner, John 156
Loder, George 110, 190
Longford, William, and father 274
Lord, Simeon 125, 174, 204; and accountant
  Henry Black 166; and apprentices 126;
  employment of sawyers 267; hat and cloth
  manufacturer 228; land, owned 113,
  purchased 116; sons Francis and George
  57; wife of 72
Loveridge, Mary, wife of Thomas Dargin/
  Dargon 113
Lowe, Robert, evidence to Bigge 207
Lucas, Captain, re absconding
  apprentice 138
Lucas, Nathanial and wife Olive/Olivia (née
  Gascoigne) 222; son George 217; son
  John 222
Lucas, Penelope, governess to Elizabeth
  Macarthur 151
Lynch, Ann 88; de facto wife of Pte Thomas
  Cottrell and son Thomas 89
Lyons, Jane, m. Edward Robinson 154

MacAlpine, Peter, employed by John Nevill 270

McCabe, Edward, and family   141

McCabe, Eleanor   82

McCann, Patrick, and family   172

Macarthur, Mrs Elizabeth   72, 83: children   46; on convict women   45; education of daughter Elizabeth   151; letter to mother   55; and nursemaid   55; as wife   76

Macarthur, Hannibal: in Fitzpatrick's letters   170–1; and land   113

Macarthur, James   191; evidence to Select Committee (1837–8)   54; land grants to   193, 196, 203; and Wentworth   208

Macarthur, John   53; evidence to Bigge 47, 54, 76, 78, 207; land grants to sons 196, 202; opinion of Parramatta   78; receives proposal for Colonial Youths 186, 259–60

Macarthur, William   191, 193, 196

McCarthy, James, and children Elizabeth, James and Owen   76, 154

McCormack, Mary, m. William Parr   89

McDonald, Alexander   271

MacDonald, Edward, and family   76

MacDonald, Marie   170

McDougal, William   245

McGlin, Ann, and family   159

McGowan, Clara, and family   155

McGuigan, Alexander   188

McKay, Daniel   144

McKeever, Thomas   266

McKin, David   92

Mackintosh, Sir James, on crime   86

McKone, Maria   93

McLaughlin, John   245

Macleay, Alexander   72

McLeod, Alexander   232

McManus, James, and family   104

McNulty, John, and father   226

Macquarie, Elizabeth   72

Macquarie, Governor Lachlan   277; and assignment   130; and BC   148, 158, 188; and Brisbane   197; and D'arcy Wentworth 179; and ex-convicts   57; and General Order (1810)   26, 83–4; and land, grants 51, 118, 194, conditions for grants 195, Bigge's attitude to   187, Memorials for   187, 188, 193, 245, 246, no Instructions for BC land   186, promised but not granted   202; letters from W. Plummer 67, 75, from J.A. Wylde   277; letters to Bathurst   41, 101, 108; and marriages by Father Therry   171; Memorials from women   92; pardon for Ann Kennedy 92; Petition from Capt. Smith   249;

testimonials from   203; on wives and children of New South Wales Corps   31

Madgwick, R.B.   29

Magee, Eliner, death and burial with son   24

Maloney, Sarah, m. James Connelly   76

Mansfield, Hannah, m. James Wallbourn 173

Mansfield, Michael   138

Margarot, Mrs, letter re   69

Martin, Mary, daughter of Edward Merrick and Mary Russel   106

Maskey, Edward   243

May, Christopher   224

Mayhew, Henry   208–9, 212, 215

Mazzegara, John, wife Mary and family   141

Melville, Robert   277

Meredith, Frederick, and brother William 277

Merrick, Edward, ex-convict and sons   104; land grants   106

Messling, Thomas   133

Mitchell, William (1), Marine, m. Jane Fizgerald   107

Mitchell, William (2), landowner, m. Elizabeth Huon   174

Mitchell, William (3), seaman deserter   239

Mobbs, John   189

Mocklan, Hannah   183

Moran, Dr   157

Morgan, Eleanor, and son Edward   260

Morgan, William (1), baker   229

Morgan, William (2), BC   190

Morgan, William (3), ex-convict overseer 174

Morley, Hannah   93

Morris, Charles, and brother John   218

Morris, George   232; and family   226

Morris, James, and son James jnr   232

Morris, John   232; and brothers   226

Morris, Martha   93

Morris, Mary, and family   157

Morris, Thomas   232; and brothers   226

Morris, William   232

Morton, Mary   88

Mosley, James   189

Moss, Isaac   174

Mowbray, George   138

Mudie, James: employs George Podmore 271; opinion on Botany Bay   45

Mullens, Hannah, wife of George Best   77

Mullins, Ann, wife of George Peat   222

Munday, John (1), Marine settler   107

Munday, John (2), BC seaman   238

Murphy, Hugh   229

Murphy, Stephen and family   143

Murphy, Thomas   174

Murray, Andrew   217

Murray, Sir George, letter from E.S. Hall 121

O'Hara, Edward   231
O'Neale, Thomas   92
Oliver, Andrew   227
Onslow, George, and wife Mary (née McEvoy)   165
Osburn, Catherine   92
Osburn, George   144
Osburn, William, and family   143–4
Oxley, Surveyor-General John: evidence to Bigge   47, 101, 193; land grants   195; report to Darling   203
Owens, James, parents and brother Thomas 189

Palmer, John: evidence to Select Committee (1812) 77–8; opinion of colonial society 177–8
Park, Esther, and husband   156
Parnell, Tom, described by Alexander Harris   181
Parr, William, m. Mary McCormack   89
Parreaux, André, on British morals   82, 83
Parrott, William, m. Mary Tyrrell   174
Parsons, Edward   230
Parsons, Sarah   161
Partridge, Mary, and daughter Ellen   151
Paterson, Mrs Elizabeth: and Female Orphan School   147; opinion of colonial society 45–6; and protection of BC girls 149
Paterson, William   92; and land grants 107, 116; population statistics   24
Pawley, John   232
Pawley, Sarah, and family   154
Pawley, Thomas, and father   249
Pawley, William, and father   232
Payten, Nathanial, and father Isaac   142
Peacock, John James   193; partner of Peat and Webb   222
Pearce, Elizabeth   151; m. James Best   164
Pearce, Matthew, and family   164
Pearson, Thomas   174
Peat, Charles   220
Peat, George, m. Frances Ternan   173; career and parentage   222
Pemberton, C.R., on seaman   139
Pendray, William   143
Pennell, Martha, and husband John   70
Perkins, W.M., and wife Louisa   278
Peyton, Thomas   35
Phelps, George, and father Richard Phelps 230
Phillip, Governor Arthur: and education of children   152; and land grants   100, at Norfolk Island for orphans   86, Instruc-

tions from Grenville   107, 117, mountain barrier to   99, no Instructions re BC 186, segregation by civil condition 102; landing at Botany Bay   267; letter to Under-Secretary Nepean   207; opinion of women convicts   65, of settlers   115; Petition of Marie MacDonald re religion   170
Phillips, Elizabeth, and family   123
Piper, Captain John   53; married   166; son John jnr   193
Pithers, James, and family   143
Plummer, T.W., on women convicts   66, 75
Podmore, George   271
Poer/Poor, Morgan   157–8; and family   278
Portland, Duke of, letter from Governor King 43
Powell, Edward snr   247, 252; m. Elizabeth Fish   112; sells land   116; son Edward jnr   167, 247, 251, 252, land grant   253; son James   224 (Note: difficulty in distinguishing between two sons of Edward Powell)
Powley/Pullen, Elizabeth   87, 88, 110, 118, 161
Prentice, Charles snr   232, 233; son Charles and John   232
Prentice, John, and sister Mary   231
Prentice, Jonathan, and father   249
Prior, Matthew, and de facto Catherine Fryer/Prior   85
Prosser, Sgt   107
Pugh, Samuel   231; and wife Ann, son Samuel   154

Quinland, Judith, de facto wife of David McKin   92

Radford, Sgt   107
Ralph, Thomas, and parents Luke and Mary   245
Ramsay, John, and parents John and Mary   224
Redfern, Surgeon William   273
Redmond, Edward   266
Regan, William, and son John and family   142, 194, 216–7, 233
Reibey, Mary   69, 72, 84; son George   250, and W.C. Wentworth   251; son Thomas   194
Reid, Henry   141
Reynolds, Pte Edward, and son Edwin and family   105
Reynolds, Mary, and son Francis, daughter Elizabeth   136, 137, 144
Reynolds, William: and daughter Elizabeth   229; sons James and Richard   228

Richards, Lawrence   107

Ricketts, James, and parents Samuel and Mary   245

Rixon, James   271

Roberts, James   231

Roberts, John, and brothers George and James   247

Roberts, Sarah, m. Thomas Silk   172

Robinson, Elizabeth, wife of John Dell   123

Robinson, Michael Massey   274

Robinson, William, m. Ann Innett   77

Rolph, Ann   92

Rope, Anthony: and wife Elizabeth (née Pullen/Powley)   88, 110, 161, 174; daughter Mary   167; sons John and William   161

Rose, Joshua, Richard and John   194

Rose, Thomas   250

Rouse, Walter   102–3

Rowley, Capt.   116

Ruse, James   174, 207

Russel, Mary, wife of Edward Merrick   106

Ryan, John (1), convict, m. Mary Rope   172

Ryan, John (2), ex-convict, and son John Ryan jnr   105

Ryan, Pte John (3)   107

Saunders, Thomas (1), and family   102

Saunders, Thomas (2)   189, 190

Schofield, Alice, wife of Stephen Murphy   143

Scott, Hugh, and brother Walter   247

Scott, Thomas, Memorial of   189

Scrivenson, Rebecca   217

Sewell, John   223

Seymour, Thomas   174; m. Mary Higgins   173

Shannon, Ann, m. Lawrence Kennedy   173

Shannon, James, and parents Patrick Shannon and Margaret Holmes   251–2

Sharp, William   231

Sherwin, William   272; and brother John   274

Shillito, Mary Ann, and husband   156

Shuker, George, m. Elizabeth Williams   173

Sidaway/Sideway, Robert, and de facto wife Mary Marshall   77

Sidebottom, Elizabeth   93

Sidgwick, Ann, Petition of   92

Silk, William, and family   172

Silverthorn, John, m. Mary Wickham   89

Sims, Elizabeth, m. James Green   173

Skinner, Louisa, m. John Henry Black   166, 174

Skinner, Samuel   210; advertises for apprentices   125

Small, John: m. Mary Parker   111; and family   110

Small, John and William, brothers-in-law of Robert Merville   277

Small, Thomas, described by Alexander Harris   181, 275

Small, William, and father   224

Smallwood, Esther, m. John Grono   167; and family   112

Smallwood, James   174

Smart, Thomas snr, and son Thomas   227

Smith, Andrew   271

Smith, Ann, wife of William Smith   57–8

Smith, Capt. David, Petition   249; to Van Diemen's Land   250, 253

Smith, Mr James   142

Smith, Mary   155

Smith, Sir Sydney, on Botany Bay society   3, 52; on 'Currency'   42

Smith, William (1), m. Ann   57–8

Smith, William (2), ex-convict landholder   183

Soar/Soars, Catherine, m. John Bootle   164

Spearing, J.H.   226

Spears, William, and sons   202; son James   267

Spencer, Joseph   163; m. (1) Hannah Gromes (2) Sarah Podmore   28

Spolin, Mary, and husband   156–7

Sprigmore, Charlotte   85

Squire, James   113

Stanfield, Daniel   107

Storer, Thomas   125; advertises for apprentices   223

Street, Thomas, m. Dorinda Crozier   174

Stubbs, Mary Ann, m. Charles Brackenbreg   172–3

Summers, Everitt, m. Caroline Green   174

Suttor, George   73; and land grants   108, 202; and New South Wales Corps   35; opinion of women convicts   65; wife of   72

Sydney, Ann, and husband Thomas Cosier and son William   223

Talbot, Mary   32, 96

Tandy, Sarah, and William Burgin   110

Tralton, John, m. Mary Duggan   94

Ternan, Frances, m. George Peat   173

Therry, Father, and Catholic marriages   171, 173, 174

Thompson, Andrew   113

Thompson, Ann   93

Thompson, George   181

Thorley, Philip   168

Thorn, Humphrey   231

Thorn John   231, 277

Tillery, Sarah, m. Edward Macdonald   76

Tindall, James, and brother Daniel   141

Tirley, Mary   90

Town, John, and family   210, 260
Townson, Sarah, de facto wife of William
    Neal   92
Trimbley, Joseph snr, and sons James and
    Joseph jnr   260
Tucker, James (1), and *Ralph Rashleigh*   114
Tucker, James (2), and family   99
Tuckwell, George, and mother   218
Tuckwell, Richard   110
Turnball, George, m. Louisa Everingham
    167
Turnball, John, and family   97, 99
Turnbull, Captain George   46
Tutnbull, Mary, and family   154
Tyrrell, George, wife Ann and parents
    William and Ann (née Wade)   215–6
Tyrell, Mary, m. William Parrott   174
Tyrell, William   174

Underwood, James snr: and
    apprentices   125, 138; son James jnr   250;
    wife of   72
Underwood, Joseph   174
Uther, Reuben   126

Vardy, John, and son Thomas   271
Vaux, James Hardy: as clerk   274; on
    convicts   42
Voltaire, on work   204

Wade, Betty, and family   144
Wakefield, Edward Gibbon   30, 45
Walker, Ann, and daughter Sarah   156
Walker, John   224
Walker, William   156
Wall, George   231
Wall, Mary Ann   231
Wallbourn/Wallbourne, James, m. Hannah
    Mansfield   173, 174
Warby, John, and infant daughter   35
Warren, Mary, m. Thomas Dargin   150
Warrington, Thomas   217
Waterhouse, Thomas   253
Watson, James: and family   222–3; brother
    John   252; sister Elizabeth   123
Weaver, Esther, wife of Richard Cheers   108
Weavers, Enoch   26
Webb, James   222
Webb, Joseph, and brother Thomas   116

Webb, Richard, m. Hannah Mocklan   183
Wells, Sarah   93
Wentworth, D'arcy: on liquor licences   93;
    and Macquarie   179; at Sydney Hospital
    273
Wentworth, William Charles   208, 251,
    272–3; Address of Welcome to Governor
    Darling   42, 56, 179; and Australia   19;
    and the *Australian*   46, 145, 179, 180; on
    'inherited taint'   44; and land alienation
    180, 263; land grants   193, 194,
    discrimination against BC   179–81; on
    social barriers   50; suggests colonial
    plantations   186
West, Mary, m. William Burgin   110
West, Sgt   107
Westbrook, Richard   239
White, Thomas Douglas, and family   277
Wickham, Mary, m. John Silverthorn   89
Wilberforce, William, letter from
    Castlereagh   75
Wilkinson, Capt.   138
Wilkinson, Susannah, m. (1) John Langford
    (2) James Larra   79
Williams, Elizabeth, m. George Shuker   173
Williams, George   230
Williams, Mr   108
Williams, Thomas, employed Richard
    Fry   226
Wilson, Caleb   93
Wilson, George (1)   58–9
Wilson, George (2)   173
Windsor, Richard   271
Wood, George Pitt   17, 142
Wood, John, and parents   190
Wood, Mary Ann, m. Thomas Avery   163;
    parents Benjamin Crew and Sarah Wood
    163
Wright, Charles   28
Wright, Joseph: and wife Eleanor   225; son
    Jonathan   225, 245; sons Thomas and
    Robert   223, 275

Yeates, John, and master John Champley
    159
Yeoman, John, and family   159
Yoel, J.   211
Young, Ann   157

INDEX C

OCCUPATIONS IN NEW SOUTH WALES

Note:
This is a select listing only. Occupations are listed as described by contemporaries; see Census of New South Wales, 1828, occupations listed. Where the same occupation is described variously, it is cross-referenced in this index.

accountant   166
agricultural labourer/worker   59, 259, 260, 261, 263, 265, 266, 267, 269; *see also* agricultural pursuits; land worker
agricultural pursuits   186, 246–7
agriculturalist   183, *see also* farmer; land-holder
apothecary and druggist   273
apprentices   27, 61, 121–44, 194, 204, 208–10, 216–19, 220, 222–8, 230–4, 237–9, 242, 244–5, 247, 248, 250–3, 259–68, 279
artificer   207, 260; *see also* mechanic
assigned servants   79, 90, 91, 95, 114, 125, 130, 135, 136, 137, 139, 150, 151, 155, 163, 164, 173, 209, 261, 263, 268, 269, 270

baker   211, 212, 229–30, 231
barber   211
barrister   272
blacksmiths   61, 93, 122, 123, 124, 139, 210, 211, 213, 214, 218, 219, 223, 231, 232
boatman   249
boat-builder   56, 111, 133, 141, 144, 161, 213, 218, 233; master   117
boatswain   218
bookbinder   211
boot-closer   211
bootmaker   137, 214, 225, 228
brass-founder   211
brewer   211, 232
bricklayer   134, 139, 211, 214
brick-maker   103, 138, 214
brush-maker   211
builder   27, 142, 215; master   218, 221
bullock-driver   262, 265
bushranger   276
bush-worker   199, 266, 279; *see also* agricultural worker; land worker
butcher   163, 210, 211, 214, 288, 230, 231, 233, 269; master   231
butler   156

cabinet-maker   141, 161, 211, 214, 215, 217, 218, 224, 230, 231, 242, 245
calico-printer   211

cambric worker   92
carpenter   59, 61, 102, 122, 123, 125, 133, 136, 141, 142, 143, 144, 174, 208, 210, 211, 214, 215, 216, 217, 218, 220, 222, 225, 228, 230, 232, 237, 244, 245, 246, 250, 251, 253; and joiner   173; ship's   37
carter   111, 123, 128, 217, 220, 242, 249
carver   142
chaplain   23, 24, 26, 44, 58, 66, 67, 70, 72, 73, 74, 76, 78, 84, 93, 94, 117, 162, 171; *see also* clergyman
charwoman   156
chimney sweep   129
clergyman   25, 26, 70, 76, 93, 127, 160, 162, 172; *see also* chaplain
clerk   58, 143, 174, 181, 261, 273, 274, 275; attorney's   274
coach-maker   214, 215, 218, 249
comb-maker   165
Commandant   274
Commissary   77, 88, 90, 274
Commissioner   44, 47, 78
constable   58, 90, 104, 110, 111, 144, 174, 181, 217, 222, 231, 247, 248, 249, 275, 276, 277, 278, 279; *see also* District Constable
cook   88, 89, 155, 156, 158
cooper   213, 214, 215, 218, 219, 224, 245, 246, 250, 253, 277; ship's   37, 173
cordwainer   231, 232
Coroner   112, 160, 165, 222
craftsman   54, 126, 139, 233; *see also* mechanic
cutler   211

dairymaid/dairywoman   80, 155, 156, 157, 158
dairyman   5, 56, 58, 70, 72, 111, 156, 262
dealer   56, 58, 70, 72, 111, 141, 157, 160, 275, 279; *see also* agent
distiller   160, 211
District Constable   58, 104; *see also* constable
draper   227
dressmaker   157, 158, 242; *see also* seamstress
drummer   103, 104, 107, 111
dyer   126

engineer   133
engraver   211

farmer   54, 56, 57, 58, 72, 99, 100, 101, 102,
   104, 105, 106, 108, 109, 110, 111, 112, 113,
   114, 116, 122, 138, 142, 143, 150, 154, 155,
   156, 157, 158, 159, 160, 164, 167, 171, 172,
   173, 179, 180–6, 189, 191–9, 200, 202, 204,
   207, 210, 216, 223, 224, 230, 232, 246, 247,
   252, 253, 256, 259, 260, 261, 263, 267, 269,
   271, 275, 278; *see also* landholder; landowner
farm manager   189, 260, 264
farrier   214
fencer   232, 262, 265
file-cutter   211
fisherman   81
flax-dresser   211
framework-maker   211

gaoler   58, 81, 92
gardiner [*sic*]   160, 164, 211, 213, 220, 265
glazier   220
goldsmith   211
governess   57, 72, 94, 151, 155, 158
government servant   150, 151, 157, 159, 163,
   164, 250, 269
grazier   54, 100, 161, 179, 180, 182, 259, 261,
   263; *see also* landholder; landowner
gunsmith   211
gun-filer   211

hairdresser   211; *see also* barber
harness-maker   213, 216, 225, 226, 228
hat-maker   135
hat manufacturer   126, 228
housekeeper   66, 71, 90, 91, 155–8

indentured servant   162, 169, 174
innkeeper   58, 105, 111, 155, 158, 181, 275;
   see also publican
instrument maker, mathematical   160
iron founder   213
ironmonger   211

jeweller   142, 210, 211
Judge-Advocate   24

Keeper of the Pound   254

labourer   1, 52, 53, 55, 58, 59, 72, 100, 102,
   118, 123, 135, 139, 149, 150, 154, 162, 163,
   173, 174, 179, 181, 199, 226, 228, 245, 254,
   262, 267, 268, 269, 270, 272, 278, 279;
   skilled   139, 230, 233
landholder   109, 118, 122, 157, 158, 160, 165,
   168, 171, 172, 179, 180, 181–3, 190, 191,
   192, 194–6, 201, 270, 272; *see also* landowner

landowner   56, 72, 115, 118, 141, 150, 157,
   173, 181, 182, 183, 193, 200, 204, 210, 217,
   218, 223, 230, 259, 260, 261, 264, 274, 275;
   see also landholder
land worker   253, 259, 260, 261, 262, 263,
   264, 265, 269, 270, 272; skilled   259, 263;
   see also agricultural worker
laundress   89, 149, 155, 156, 157, 158, 248
locksmith   211, 213

magistrate   93, 94, 117, 136, 239, 240
mantua maker   155, 156, 158
Marine, Royal   29, 31, 51, 52, 55, 69, 70, 72,
   77, 85, 89, 101, 102, 103, 104, 106, 107, 110,
   112, 113, 117, 170, 173, 175, 202, 224, 230,
   238, 268, 271
mariner   139, 173, 237, 240, 241, 247, 252,
   253, 255; master   166; *see also* sailor; seafarer; seaman
mason   214

Master of the Benevolent Society   217
Master of the Guard of the Row Boat   164,
   165, 249
mechanic   *see* tradesman
merchant   54, 56, 125, 126, 160, 174, 274
midshipman   253
midwife   24
miller   155, 160, 210, 211, 214, 222, 233
milliner   155
millwright   112, 123, 174, 213, 214, 219, 222,
   223
missionary   44, 110, 134, 162

nailor   132, 133
needlewoman   156; *see also* dressmaker;
   seamstress
Night Watch   222; *see also* constable
New South Wales Corps   163, 167; officers
   of   56, 65; non-commissioned officers
   of   100, 103, 107; privates   93, 105, 106,
   107, 123, 173, 189, 218, 225, 230, 238, 246,
   271
nurse   156
nursemaid   55, 60, 61, 89, 155, 156, 158;
   child's   39

office-keeper   155
official   29, 51, 53, 65, 77, 101, 113, 150, 183,
   193, 194; civil   34, 51, 52, 53, 67, 72, 101,
   106, 108; military   34, 51, 52, 53, 67, 72,
   101, 106; *see also* individual entries
overseer   105, 179, 181, 260, 262, 263, 265,
   266, 267; *see also* agricultural labourer; land
   worker

painter   213, 214, 231

pastrycook   156, 211, 229, 230
pipe-maker   155, 210
plaisterer [*sic*]   213, 214, 231
plumber   213, 220
potter   125, 126, 210, 211
priest   25, 76, 170; *see also* clergyman
printer   123, 138, 212, 275
prostitute   39, 59, 68, 69, 74, 75, 78, 79, 81,
    82, 84, 89, 90, 95, 248; *see also* whore
publican   58, 72, 110, 111, 138, 150, 154, 159,
    160, 162, 174, 181, 188, 232, 244, 269, 271,
    275, 278, 279; *see also* innkeeper
pump-borer   213

rope-maker   143, 231, 245

saddler   123, 163, 214, 231, 232
sailor   112, 138, 202, 238, 240, 241, 246, 252,
    253, 254, 255, 268; *see also* mariner; seafarer;
    seaman
sawyer   28, 226, 230, 262, 265, 266, 267
schoolmaster   58, 152, 158, 164, 181, 261,
    273
school mistress   155, 170, 261
scourger   160
seafarer   138, 252, 253, 254, 255; *see also*
    mariner; seaman
sealer   237, 241, 244, 245, 247, 251, 253
seaman   125, 138, 139, 150, 173, 237–50,
    252, 253, 255; with fisheries   241; *see also*
    mariner; sailor; seafarer
seamstress   55, 149, 155, 156, 157, 158; *see*
    also dressmaker; needlewoman
'Seminary instructor'   151
servant   51, 52, 53, 55, 58, 59, 66, 71, 72, 77,
    78, 82, 83, 88, 89, 94, 108, 141, 149, 150,
    154, 155, 157, 158, 163, 181, 199, 203, 209,
    212, 254, 263, 271, 272, 273, 278, 279;
    domestic   36, 60, 73, 80, 87, 89, 151, 152,
    153, 166, 167, 168; farm   89; rural   90,
    261
settler   24, 28, 30, 34, 35, 48, 51, 52, 53, 55,
    66, 67, 69, 72, 74, 94, 99, 101, 102, 103, 106,
    107, 108, 109, 110, 111, 112, 113, 115, 116,
    117, 121, 130, 143, 150, 151–3, 155, 157,
    166–8, 172, 174, 175, 180, 182, 183, 186,
    187, 193, 195–200, 202, 203, 209, 216, 218,
    224, 226, 230, 232, 244, 246, 247, 249, 250,
    251, 264, 265, 267, 271; *see also* farmer; land-
    holder; landowner
shepherd   156, 232, 265, 266, 269
shingler   231, 232
ship-builder   125, 141, 215, 252, 253
ship's company/crew   37, 250, 251, 252, 253,
    254; boy   240, 242, 246, 248, 250, 251, 253,
    254, 255; captain/master   239, 242, 243,

249, 250, 251, 252, 253; carpenter   37;
    chandler   160, 231; mate   250, 251, 252,
    253; officer   247, 250, 251, 252, 253;
    owner   125, 174; steward   245, 250
shipwright   134, 135, 143, 147, 218, 219, 220,
    221, 230, 233, 238, 245, 249, 252, 253
shoe-binder   156
shoemaker   28, 59, 122, 123, 125, 131, 138,
    141, 156, 157, 159, 163, 174, 211, 212, 214,
    218, 224, 225, 226, 227, 228, 232, 233
shopkeeper   58, 72, 106, 136, 150, 155, 156,
    160, 183, 232, 279
silversmith   142, 174, 211
soldier   31, 38, 51, 52, 69, 70, 72, 92, 93, 101,
    102, 103, 107, 112, 113, 117, 123, 143, 150,
    175, 189, 200, 202, 203, 230, 268, 273, 277,
    279; *see also* New South Wales Corps
stock-holder   142, 189, 191, 193, 263, 264,
    266; keeper   155, 158
stockman   259, 265, 266
stone-cutter   123, 214, 225
stonemason   32, 123, 154, 213, 218, 219, 225
street walker   *see* prostitute; whore
Superintendent   217, 227, 234, 246, 262, 274
surgeon   24, 42, 56, 57, 69, 89, 105, 221, 272,
    273, 274; ship's   33
surveyor   174

tailor   59, 83, 122, 123, 125, 131, 143, 211,
    213, 214, 225, 226, 227, 228, 232, 233, 249
tanner   103, 214, 231, 232
tenant   180
timberman   265
tin-man   213, 214
tinsmith   211
trader   125, 126, 250; river   222, 241, 243,
    252, 254
tradesman   30, 55, 57, 58, 72, 100, 118, 121,
    122, 123, 124, 125, 126, 127, 131, 132, 140,
    144, 150, 158, 172, 173, 174, 181, 194, 204,
    214–5, 221, 222, 223, 225, 227, 228, 229,
    231, 232, 233, 234, 242, 245, 252, 253, 259,
    262, 263, 268, 269, 271, 275; master   54,
    250; *see also* specific trades
turner   211, 214, 226, 231, 232
tutor   57, 72

upholsterer   136, 143, 211, 214

washerwoman   55, 89, 156, 157, 158
watch-maker   211, 214, 215
watchman   247
weaver   123, 126, 205, 208, 226, 228
wheelwright   93, 104, 111, 143, 154, 165, 167,
    211, 213, 214, 218, 219, 232
whore   66, 68, 73, 80, 82; *see also* prostitute

INDEX D

GENERAL SUBJECT

Note:
References to districts and places are not exhaustive. Contemporary records seldom distinguish between Patrick's Plains and Paterson's Plains, hence the contemporary abbreviation Pat's Plains is included here.

Aborigines   35
agricultural workers: BC as   259, 260, 261, 262, 263, 264, 269–70, 278–9; CF as   262, 263–4; civil condition of   261, 264, 265; 'class' hierarchy   262, 264, 265–8; classified   259, 261; convicts and ex-convicts as   262, 264, 268–9; diversity of occupations   262–3, 265; *see also* labourers; Index C
Airds, Appin   99, 161, 193, 220, 226, 271
An Accurate List of Landholders   118, 194
apprentices   12–14; absconders   137–8; advertisements for   123–4, 125, 126, 130, 131, 138, 219, 220, 223, 289; assumptions re parentage   124; BC as   122, 142–3, 194; CF as   122, 140–1; education of   126, 138–9; English apprentice system   14, 121, 129–31, 137; indentures   135–7; juvenile convicts as   61, 132, 134; land grants   142–3, 194; masters   125, 134, 136, 141–2, 144; Memorials   134; named 134–5, 136, 141, 142, 143, 144; opportunities prior to 1810   125; parentage 122–3, 143–4; ships'   15, 139; statistics (1828)   122; trades of   125, 142, 143, 144; treatment of   136–7; *see also* child labour; seamen; Index C
Argyle   136–8

bakers, Government regulations   229; *see also* Index C
Bankstown   107
baptisms   24–5, 76
Bathurst   216, 231, 264
Baulkham Hills   27, 43
Bringelly   238
Britain: assumptions, re Botany Bay   3–5, 8, 42, 153, re BC   5, 41, 198–9; attitudes towards BC and land   200, child labour   13; convicts and Botany Bay   3, 7, 42–3; land ownership   101, 117, 197ff; crime and prostitution   82; common law marriages   17; migration to New South Wales   29–30; morality of women   8
Bulnaming   117
bushworkers, described by Alexander Harris   182, 199, 266–7

butchers: lack of training   231; licensed by Government   230; *see also* Index C

Cabramatta   217
came free (CF): as labourers   269–70; as land workers   261–5; *see also* children; migrants
Castle Hill   167
Catholics   10; attitudes towards   80; BC, as labourers   270, as stonemasons   225; colonial parents   169–70; marriage 76ff, 162ff, 171–2; residential concentration   169; sense of identity   169–70; toleration   25, 76, 170–1; *see also* Irish
cavalry, colonial, proposal for   226–7
Census of New South Wales (1828): as evidence for parentage of BC   51; as source of 'new' evidence   26–9, 51, 57, 60, 91, 153, 179, 180, 208, 209, 241, 259, 260, 262, 263, 267; possible inaccuracies in   28; tables based on   102, 104–5, 141, 142, 158, 159, 160, 162, 163, 171, 180, 182, 183, 191, 211, 215, 219, 226, 229, 267–8, 272
child labour   12–13; colonial patterns   124, 127, 129–30, 200; conditions in Britain 129, 131–2; NSW, 'rural'   113–14, 115, 'town'   127–8; *see also* apprentices
children: accidents to   94; BC and colonial society   38, 100, 102–6, 240; causes of death   34–6; childhood   12–13; civil condition   23, 32ff, analysis of (1806)   106ff; of 'convicts'   32ff; contemporary assumptions   5, 23, 42–3, 124; departure from NSW   37–9; described by officials   23, 43, 55; destitute and abandoned   43, 45–6; of first fleet   23; illegitimacy   37, 75–6; immigrant, parentage of   29, 34, 55; infanticide   36–7; military and official   31 ff, 35; morality 33, 34–6; 'National'   75; parentage 23, 29, 31, 53, 54; parental concern 12–13, 94; 'rural'   108–9; social origins, NSW   55–7, Britain   124, 131; *see also* apprentices; child labour; native-born
churches: named   24, 28, 164, 174, 225, 274; provision for   4, 25, 76; *see also* Catholics; parish registers

Church of England, monopoly of 25, 76, 80
Clarendon 224
Clarke, F.G. 198
cloth production 228
CSIL see Memorials/Petitions; Index A
colonial society: British opinions 3, 8, 38, 42, 44, 46, 51–2; 'class' structure 72, 139–40, 174–5; 'convict' society 50–1; described by Macquarie 41; influence of convict women 65, of skilled convict labour 233–4, of social mobility 150; nature of 11, 51–62, 72, 150, 233–4; role of women 16–17, 67, 174–5; 'rural' 204
Concord 103, 106, 112, 167
concubines 95; Marsden's opinions 17, 74–7; see also Female Register; prostitution; women
convicts/ex-convicts/emancipists: accompanied by wives/children 32–4, 70; accounts in novels 45; as agricultural workers 263; assigned 159ff, 209, 266, 268–9, contact with BC 114; and colonial society 4, 55, 61; contemporary attitudes and opinions 3, 7, 41–3, 47–8, 166; departure from NSW 37; dependence on labour of 214–15, 233–4; enlistment in Indian Army 37–8; immunity to infectious diseases 35; inherited 'taint' 5, 41, 43, 44, 45, 198–9; juvenile 61, 116–18, 134; as labour force 199–200, 261; land grants to (1820) 203; marriage patterns of 162; married to BC 162; occupational mobility 56; as parents 42; 'rural' families 108–13; as settlers 116ff; skilled 139, 140, 214, 215, 220, advantages for 208, 209–10, 268; statistics 34, 61, 132–3; 'trade' families 123, 142–3; wages for labourers 269; see also women
Cooke 157, 226
Cornwallis 168, 192, 270
County of Westmoreland 99
crime: and BC 150–1, 157–8, 188, 190, 275, 277–8; in Britain, 'casual' 87–8, 'professional' 88–9, receivers 88–9; and Female Factory 79ff; and immorality 73–9; link with economic opportunities 90; of serving girls 85–90; statistics, England/Wales 81, 82; violent 84–6, lack in NSW 86–7; and women 80–92
criminal 'class', definitions 52
criminality 48–9; contemporary assumptions 84
Cumberland Plain 100, 101, 108, 117, 124, 141, 166, 168, 191
Currency Lad see newspapers
'Currency' Lads and Lasses: article in Australian 259; and Botany Bay 168; defined

by Cunningham 42, 168; lasses 147, 149, 169, 172

Darling's List 113ff, 192–3, 203
deaths: accidental 35; of children 32–3, 34ff, 165; of individuals 24, 35, 165, 216, 251; see also infanticide
Derwent 94
Dock Yards, apprenticeships at 122, 143, 194, for juvenile convicts 61

Eastern Farms 102, 108
Edinburgh Review, and Sydney Smith on NSW 42, 52
education: of apprentices 138–9; attitudes of British government 152–3; of BC children 57, 151, 153–4; of Catholic children 170; of daughters of wealthy 72, 151; Instructions, to Bligh 152–3, to Hunter, lack of 152, to King 153; land set aside for schools 4, 152; opinion of Bishop of London 172; parents to pay for 154; Public Charity School 148; religion 153; seminaries 69, 151; see also Female Orphan School; Male Orphan School; apprentices
emancipists, opinions on 49, 56, 57, 78; see also convicts/ex-convicts/emancipists
Evan 110, 156, 161, 168, 172, 191, 212, 223, 246, 271

families: apprentices and 'trade' children 123–4, 130, 143, 144, 208–9; BC children 52–6, 'Australian' 7–8, 166–7; BC girls 147, 149ff, 160–1, 172, Australian cited on 166–7, morality, tainted women, marriage 2, 30, 55, 177ff; colonial 94, 109ff; colonial society 52–62; of ex-convicts 93, 161, 174–5, 189, 190; of Marines 31; official and military 31–2; opinion of Palmer 77; 'rural' 154; of seamen 266–7; of settlers 103, 290; 'trade' 123, 142–4; wealthy 55–6; of widows/widowers 154; of working women 156–7; see also native-born; women
Female Factory (Parramatta): and BC servants 154; and Bigge 79; contractor to build 143; and Macarthur 78; and Marsden 78; numbers in 79, 169; roles of 79; see also crime; women
Female Orphan School: and education 153; establishment of 147–8; Instructions re 153; case of Cruise 266, of Hughes 147; King's opinion of 50–1; Macquarie and impropriety 148; marriage from 174; Marsden and inmates 43; serving girls 59–91, 154–5

Female Register   74–6; *see also* concubine
ferrying   224, 241
Field of Mars   102
first fleet: chaplain's wife   70; children on
   23, 29; Marines' wives on   70; women
   convicts   81–2, 86; for individuals   *see*
   Index B
Fletcher, B.H.   118
fisheries   241, 253
free settlers/migrants (CF): and British
   government   29–31; CF agricultural
   workers   263; CF children   29ff, with
   parents (1828)   160, of convicts   31–40,
   of military and officials   31ff; influence and
   patronage   108; land grants   100, 108,
   198; marriage patterns of   161–2; married
   to BC   106; 'rural' families   111;
   women   70, 71, 72, 76

George's River   103, 232
Glebe   227
Goulburn Plains   168, 216
Government and General Orders: (1804)
   deserters and apprentices   138; (1810)
   registration of marriages, etc.   26; (1804)
   registration of bakers   229; (1810) regulations for bakers   229; (1810) de-facto wives
   and inheritance   148; (1810) orphans and
   Public Charity School   148; (1818) land
   grants and conditions   90–1; (1820) land
   regulations   203; (1822) amendments to
   regulations   203
governors' powers   51, 188

Hawkesbury District   101–2, 107, 110, 192,
   222, 264
Hawkesbury farmers   102 (Table)
Hunter River   99, 100, 168
Hunter Valley   100, 168, 202
Hunter's Hill   247, 267

infanticide: in Britain and NSW   36–7; and
   serving girls   73
Illawarra/Jervis Bay District   99, 168, 270
Irish: attitudes of British government   25–6;
   case of Mary Talbot   32; Castle Hill
   uprising   25; Church of England
   services   25; convicts and pardons   92;
   districts of residence (1828)   169;
   education   170; in Ireland, crime   80,
   marriage   76, 1798 Rebellion and
   transportation   225; land grants to
   rebels   189; landowners   111, 193; in
   Liverpool and Manchester   80; lower
   orders   55; Loyal Association   124;
   marriage   17, 76, 171ff; murder of Biddy
   Horan   91; opinions of, Collins   80,
   King   24, 80, 174, Marsden   26, 86;

parents of BC   170; rebels and
   offspring   193, 225; recollections of
   settler   170–1; as stonemasons,
   stonecutters   225; toleration   25, 76;
   women   80–1; *see also* Catholics; families;
   women; for individuals   *see* Index B

Jewish convicts, and marriage   76
juvenile convicts   61, 132, 133, 134

Kangaroo Island   248
King George's Sound   79
Kissing Point   111, 181, 216, 224, 230, 277

labourers: apprentices as   209; BC as   270;
   BC as agricultural   259–60; comparative
   civil conditions (1828)   210, 268; conditions in Britain   214–15, 268, in
   NSW   13, 139, 209, 268, 269; convicts
   as   209; definitions   268; nature of labour
   in NSW   199–200, 209–10, 233–4, 254–5;
   opinions of, Atkinson   261, Bathurst
   199–200, Waldersee   269; preference
   for free overseers   265; seamen as   139,
   254; skilled, scarcity of   207–8, 209;
   wages for   214, 269, *see also* apprentices;
   child labour; convicts; trades; women;
   Index C
Land Board   187–8, 198
land grants: aims of British government   117;
   and assigned servants   114; attitudes of
   British workers   198; and BC   100, 118,
   185–9, 192, 194–5, 200; Bigge's recommendations   197; Brisbane's purchase
   regulations   196–200; conditions of
   195; discrimination re   76, 121–2,
   179–80, 197–9, 259; from Brisbane   201,
   Darling   113ff, 203–4, pre-1813   194,
   Hunter   101, Macquarie   195, Phillip
   100; grantees, civil condition of (1828)
   182–3; Instructions to governors   100–2;
   lack of segregation   102–3; location
   101–3, 104–5, 106, 107, 108, 111, 112,
   202, choice of   101, 102, 115; and
   marriage   76; Memorials   184–5, 186,
   188–90; opinions of Bathurst, Eagar/
   Wentworth   121–2; patronage   108; procedure for   187; regulations for   194; sale
   of   116; size, in Canada   117, in NSW
   106–13, 117, 192–3; to BC   118, 192–6,
   201, 203–4, parents of   100; to convicts
   and ex-marines   107; to free settlers
   108–12, 197–8; to former seamen   246–
   7; to military   100; to officials   117; *see
   also* convicts/ex-convicts; native-born; free
   settlers; women
land ownership: analysis (1806)   109–13;
   attitudes of *Australian*   121, wealthy   54;

and BC   115, 179–80, 186–7, 190–1, 199, 260; BC women   157; CF children   141; and civil condition (1828)   106, 182–3; colonial attitudes   180; and Darling   203–4; effects of purchase regulations   262–3; free settlers advantaged   194–5; land alienated by 1813   118; purchase, and BC   182, and parents of BC   115; statistics   118
Liberty Plains   102, 103, 112
Liverpool   99, 163, 175, 217, 222, 228, 269
Liverpool Plains   202
Lower Minto   58, 163, 154, 223, 232
Lumber Yards: and apprentices   122, 194; and juvenile convicts   61

Male Orphan School: and apprentices   122, 123; and Bigge   59; Committee report   135; conditions in   131; and juvenile convicts   133; and King   133; trades taught   226, 227; *see also* apprentices, child labour, orphans, trades
manufactories 126; *see also* Index C
Marines: children of   13, 29, 31; de facto wives of   89, 185; encouraged to settle   101; landowners (1806)   110; settlers at Norfolk Island (1792)   107; size of land grants   107; wives of   77; *see also* NSW Corps
marriage: in Britain   17; and land grants   105, 106; legal, religious, common law   17, 76, 171, 172; Marsden on   74–7; in NSW   76–7, 161, 166, 162–3, 167–8; registers   27–8; and 'rural' families   166–7; statistics   171, 181; *see also* convicts; families; native-born; women
Memorials/Petitions: as evidence   8–9, 27, 58, 60, 91–4, 188–90; from BC   113ff, 188; convict/ex-convict women   91–4; parents   12, 15, 189ff, 146–7, 248, 249, 250; *see also* Index A
Monitor   see newspapers
Mulgrave Place   103, 104–5, 107, 108, 112, 224
Musters: (1806) analysis of land ownership   110–13, as evidence for women   74, BC and orphans listed   60, BC girls   151, description of   10, King's observations   74, 78, purchase of land   115–16, 'rural' children   108, 109ff, tradesmen and apprentices   194, wealth of families   151; (1814) population   99; (1821) population   196; *see also* Ships' Musters

native-born (BC): and agricultural occupations   259–60, 262, 263, 264, 267, 270; and baptism   24; in building trades   215–18; character of   42–3; char-

acteristics of   61; children and colonial society   50–1, 188; civil condition of parents   53–8, 163; close family links   10–13, 16, 38, 58, 216–7, 218, 220, 222, 225, 226–7, 228, 232, 252; colonial sentences   250, 278; contemporary assumptions   5, 6–7, 13–14, 38, 42–3, 50, 54, 188; convict parents   58; death of children   24; defined by Bent   41; described by Cunningham   42; diversity of experiences   108; education   18, 152–4; effect of land grant system   118; evidence of native birth   23, 270–9; family background   266, 270–1, 273, 275; family women   18, as 'homogeneous class'   52; influences on   38, 41, 42, 50, 188; immunity to diseases   35; inherited 'taint'   44, 148–9, 188–9; intermarriage   166–7; labourers 168, 169–71; as labour force   121; land expectations   193; land grants to   225, 245, 246, 247, 297, size of   192–6; landowners   188, 259; as law enforcers 15, 275, 277–8; marriage   28, 162–3; Memorials   189; numbers   34, 99, 109, or mariners   29, 241, 243, 252, of 'rural' children   100–2, 113–18, of tradesmen (1828)   209, 211, 238; opinions of Macarthur   54; proportion in colonial society   34; role of   103; widows   17, 28; *see also* apprentices; children; education; families; women
Nepean   100, 101, 108
Newcastle   154, 264
newspapers: *Australian*, on BC as settlers   122, on Botany Bay   3, on 'Currency'   168, 259–61, on land grants to BC   179–80, opinion of BC   121, 122, 261; *Currency Lad*   221; *Dublin Chronicle*, on Mary Talbot   32; *Monitor*, on BC   121, 259; *Sydney Gazette*, advertisements   123–4, 126, 130, 137–9, 151, 211, 219, 220, 223, 224, 227, 237, 262, on bakery regulations   229, on colonial children   13, 124–5, describes absconding seamen   243, on Fanny Flirt   168, and Howe family   123, 275, on Macquarie's General Order   148, obituary for Bloodsworth   207, on orphans   148, 194, on parents of BC   128, 133, on punishment of seamen   240, Public Notices   94, reports demand for rope   231, reports lightning damage   216, reports mutiny   240, reports on women   91, on 'rural' children   114, as source   46
New South Wales Corps: Catholics in   170; children of   13, 15, 31, 35, 167; convict agents and dealers for   56; enlistment   107, of sons   277; fathers of BC   106, 123, 161, 163, 164, 271; land grants to

103, 107, 117; landowners (1806)   110,
111, 112; recalled   31, 35, 53, 218; tradesmen and sons   123; wives of   31, 92, 93,
170
Norfolk Island   80, 107, 112

occupations   *see* Index C
officials: children of   31–2; as 'middle
class'   51; wives of   72
orphans: advertisement for   130; case of
Mary Herring   155; definition of   59;
employment   233; in England   14; in
Male Orphan School   59; marriage   174;
see also apprentices; child labour; Female
Orphan School; Male Orphan School

Parramatta   47, 78–9, 93, 100, 111, 122, 223,
224, 228, 231, 232, 242, 251, 267, 274, 277
Pat's Plains   99, 168, 192, 222, 246, 264
parish registers, as sources   23, 25, 28
pensioners   143, 144, 150
Petersham   117, 156, 163, 271
Pitt Town   100, 156, 163, 164, 167, 168, 175,
192, 207, 223, 224, 225
'poet laureate'   274
Police Corps: proposal for   276–7;
Mounted   272
population: and parish registers   24;
Catholics   25; children   23, 29; civil condition (1821)   196; 'convict' proportions
199; effects of transportation   52; Instructions to governors re   24; residence of
women (1828)   169; sources of   23;
statistics   24–5; structure of   53; *see also*
children; native-born; women
Portland Head   138, 164, 168, 192, 216;
Lower   156, 157, 167, 218
Prospect   58, 94, 111, 155, 270
prostitution: case of Hannah Hobbs   248; in
England/Ireland   81–2; estimated numbers, London   82, NSW   84; evidence to
Bigge   78–9; maintenance for bastards
NSW   94; 'vicious prostitutes'   95; *see also*
women; Index C

religion   *see* Catholics; churches; Irish;
native-born; marriage; parish registers;
women
respectability: BC and land discrimination
179–80; and criminals   49–50; description
of BC innkeeper   131; expectations of
landowners   186; opinions of, Bigge   179,
Wentworth (*Australian*)   179–81; and
parents   188–9; *see also* colonial society,
convicts, native-born, women
Richmond/North Richmond   100, 106, 110,
141, 154, 158, 159, 169, 192, 222, 246, 269,
270

'Rising Generation': and apprenticeships
126; concern for, by King   43, by Marsden
147; duty of parents   128; future
prospects   6; *see also* 'Currency', native-
born
river trade   218, 222, 241, 243
Rocks, the   60, 72
Royal Veteran Company   144

Sackville Reach   164, 167
schools: 'Catholic'   170; for apprentices
125; provision for   4, 152; seminaries
151; *see also* education
seamen: apprentices   238, 253; BC, employed as   238–9, as officers   250–52, on
British ships   244, on colonial ships
245ff; British   139, 253; deserters   138,
239–40; discipline of   139, 240; land grants
to   112, 246, 249; marriages of   166, 172;
parentage   252–5; proportion BC in
Fisheries   241; Spanish   46; *see also* native-
born; Ships' Musters
Select Committees: on Transportation (1812)
evidence of John Palmer to   77, and ex-
convict women   38, and families   33–34,
38, 40, 41, and morality   34; on Police
(1819)   52; on Gaols (1819) evidence of
Bent   41; on Criminal Commitments and
Convictions (1828)   85–6; on Police in the
Metropolis (1828)   128–9; on Transportation (1837–8)   54
servants: BC   59, 154, 271–2; CF   55;
'criminal class'   73; female, British
crimes of   87–90, lack of crime in NSW
90–1; and infanticide   36–7; male, NSW
271–2; and marriage   155; as unskilled
labour   271; *see also* labour; women;
Index C
settlers: and apprentices   127; and assigned
labour   130; attitude of Bathurst   199–
200; districts settled   99–101; education of
children   153; 1806 Muster   109–16;
Instructions to Brisbane re grants   199;
opinions of BC as   122; opinions of
governors   115–16; *see also* convicts/ex-
convicts; free settlers; land grants; land
ownership; native-born
Seven Hills   155, 164
sheep owners, BC   292
ships' apprentices/ships' boys   14–15, 124,
138–9, 238, 239, 240; *see also* apprentices;
child labour; Index C
ships: destinations of   243, 244, 245–6, 251,
252; named, *Active*   244, 245, 252;
Alfred   244; *Alligator*   248; *Ann*   251;
Asia   245; *Auroa*   239; *Bathurst*, HMS
42; *Bellona*   247; *Buffalo*, HMS   231;
Campbell Macquarie   242, 247, 251, 253;

Caroline 243, 244; *Daphne* 244;
Elizabeth 139, 244, 249; *Elizabeth Henrietta* 249; *Elizabeth Mary* 247, 251;
Emerald 244; *Experiment* 92; *Fame* 243, 244; *Glory* 244, 246, 247, 250; *Governor Bligh* 244, 247; *Hillsborough* 255;
Hope 251; *Jane* 252; *John Bull* 244, 245, 251; *John Shore* 244; *Jupiter* 238;
Kangaroo 252; *King George* 240, 244; *Lady Juliana* 32, 73, 112; *Little Mary* 243, 245;
Lynx 244, 251, 252; *Mary Anne* 278;
Marquis Cornwallis 80; *Midas* 247;
Minstrel 273; *Neptune* 33, 110, 156, 275;
Newcastle 243; *Pitt* 33; *Perseverance* 244;
Phoenix 252; *Porpoise* 166; *Prince of Wales* 103; *Queen* 33; *Queen Charlotte* 249;
Regalia 244; *Rosella* 248; *Samuel* 245;
Scarborough 247; *Sirius* 112; *St Michael* 246; *Venus* 240
Ships' Musters 15, 29, 165, 237–8, 241–3, 252
South Australia 31
stockholders 193
Sutton Forest 216, 223, 264
Sydney 60, 61, 72, 107, 122, 138, 147, 153, 154, 173, 175, 210, 216, 222, 223, 224, 226, 228, 231, 232, 234, 251, 267, 274, 277
Sydney Almanac 273
Sydney Gazette see newspapers

ticket-of-leave: and marriage 28, 157, 165; petition of Mary McKone 93; settlers 172; women 156
trades: in NSW 210–11, 215–34; 'trade' families 123; *see also* labour; native-born; Index C
tradesmen: BC 210–12, 215–34; colonial, advantages for 208–9, 210, 213–14, 225–6, civil condition of (1828) 213, trades of 210ff, wages of 214–15, 226; petition to accompany first fleet 31; *see also* apprentices; convicts/ex-convicts; native-born; labour; Index C
trade unions, lack in NSW 208

Van Diemen's Land 37, 238, 243, 244, 246, 249–50, 278; emigration from NSW 37; women transported from NSW 79, 151
Victualling List (1788) 23

Wallis Plains 99, 157, 216

Western Australia 31
whaling 237, 244
Wilberforce 35, 100, 154, 159, 168, 192, 223, 228, 246, 270
Windsor 100, 110, 135, 163, 167, 175, 188, 192, 248, 269, 270, 271
women, BC: assumptions 149–58; background 149; class origins 150; and crime 150–1; education 151–2; employment, attitudes towards 157ff, compared with Britain 150, 154, 'rural' 154; husbands 163–4; influence, of occupations 172ff, of religion 162; landholders 157; occupations (1828) 155, 158; occupations of fathers 158–9; opinions of 147; proportions married (1828) 161–2; role of 147–8, 174–5; statistics 158; structure of female society 150ff; *see also* children; Currency; families; native-born; 'Rising Generation'; women, colonial
women, colonial: accompanying husbands to NSW 31–4; assumptions re morality 16–17, 65–7, 73–80, 81–4; British crimes 80–90; CF 70, 71; childbirth 24; convicts, assigned 68–9, characteristics of 73, 79–83, children of, in Britain 32–3, civil condition of 55, 58–9, 70–3, 163–4, class origins of 73, 80–1, 150–51, number transported 84, occupations of 92–3; 'damned whore' stereotype 66–7, 73, 80, 81; departure from NSW 38, 92; employment 150–4, 155–7, 158; evidence, traditional 67, 'new' 68–9; General Order (1810) 83–4; infanticide 36–7, 73; lack of criminality in NSW 86–7, 89; land grants to 103, 104; lifestyles, Britain and NSW compared 94–6; liquor licences 93; Marsden and Female register 75ff; Marsden's attitudes 76–8, 95–6; as mothers of BC 31, 65, 69; Musters 69; nature and structure of female society 55, 70–2; opinions, of historians 66–7, of contemporaries 46, 65, 66–7, 69, 73; Petitions 91–4; and pregnancy 37; and prostitution in Britain 81–2; punishment 136; 'unhappy objects' 78; wives of convicts, CF 33, of Marines/NSW Corps 31, 35; working women 155–6, 157; *see also* families; native-born